Design and Construction of Ports and Marine Structures

McGRAW-HILL SERIES IN TRANSPORTATION

Harmer E. Davis, *Consulting Editor*

Horonjeff – The Planning and Design of Airports
Quinn – Design and Construction of Ports and Marine Structures

Design and Construction of Ports and Marine Structures

ALONZO DeF. QUINN

Vice-president and Chief Engineer, Frederick Snare Corporation Contracting Engineers, New York City

McGRAW-HILL BOOK COMPANY

New York Toronto London

DESIGN AND CONSTRUCTION OF PORTS
AND MARINE STRUCTURES

 Library of Congress Catalog Card Number: 60–15003

v
51062

PREFACE

The scope of engineering for ports and marine structures includes the design and construction of many types of structures and civil works which come within the field of civil engineering. However, mechanical and electrical engineering also play an important part. The subject is a very broad and challenging one to designers and construction engineers, and it is encouraging to see the progress which has been made in recent years in the development of modern ports all over the world. Much of the "rule of thumb" design of harbors and protective works has been replaced by more rigorous engineering analyses brought about through model studies, wave research, soil mechanics technique, and new methods and materials of construction.

The problem in writing a book on ports is not a lack of subject matter, but rather the reduction of the great abundance of descriptive and technical information to that which will be of most value to the engineer and student in gaining a broad understanding of the subject and the problems involved. This is an age of specialization, and while the port engineer may be involved with soil mechanics, foundations, hydraulics, wave phenomena, prestressed concrete, etc., he is not expected to be an expert on all or any one of these subjects. There are many specialists in these fields, and their services should be retained whenever the problem warrants.

Because of lack of space, it has not been possible to cover completely the subject of port engineering and construction, and the author has elected to omit such material as graving drydocks, floating drydocks, marine railways, shipbuilding ways, ferry slips, and dredging. These are specialized subjects which have been covered quite extensively in the past.

Writing a book is something which can be done rather conveniently and leisurely when one retires, but to gather all the material, make the illustrations, and write a manuscript for a technical book is a monumental task for one who is actively engaged in his professional work. It has been possible for the writer to accomplish this in the short period of a year only through being able to draw upon the wealth of information in the files of the Frederick Snare Corporation, which was obtained during its 60 years of engineering and construction experience in the United States, Latin America, and other parts of the world. To the Frederick Snare Corporation the writer is deeply indebted; he is also very grateful to the following persons in the engineering department of the Frederick Snare Corporation: to Robert R. Zeigler for complete review of the manuscript and for supervising the preparation of the illustrations; and to George E. Somma, Franklin D. Robinson, William W. Rodgers, Peter Jolowicz, William Stepner, David Opoznauer, Robert G. McDowell, and Joseph L. Waldvogel for their valuable contributions.

It is impossible for any one person to originate from personal knowledge and experience all the information which comprises the subject matter of a technical book of this kind. So, in addition to the valuable assistance received from those already acknowledged, the author wishes to thank all the publishers and authors from whom material for this book has been drawn. The author has given credit, where due, directly in the text or with the illustrations, and if any acknowledgment has been overlooked, it is deeply regretted.

Alonzo DeF. Quinn

CONTENTS

Preface v

Chapter 1. Growth and Regulation of Ports 1

1.1 History of Port Growth; 1.2 Factors Affecting the Growth of Ports; 1.3 Port Authorities; 1.4 Regulatory Bodies; 1.5 Financing.

Chapter 2. Wind, Tides, and Waves 26

2.1 Wind; 2.2 Tides; 2.3 Waves.

Chapter 3. Harbor Planning and Construction 71

3.1 Introduction; 3.2 Ship Characteristics as They Relate to Port Planning; 3.3 Harbor and Channel Lines; 3.4 Planning a Port; 3.5 Site Investigation; 3.6 Hydraulic Model Investigations; 3.7 Description of Various Selected Ports.

Chapter 4. Breakwaters 147

4.1 Types of Breakwaters and Factors Determining Their Selection; 4.2 Rock-mound Breakwaters; 4.3 Examples of Rock-mound Breakwaters; 4.4 Concrete Block and Rock-mound Breakwaters; 4.5 Examples of Concrete Block on Rock-mound Breakwaters; 4.6 Tetrapod and Tribar Armored Breakwaters; 4.7 Examples of Tetrapod and Tribar Construction; 4.8 Experimental Design Studies of Mound Breakwaters; 4.9 Examples of Breakwater Models; 4.10 Vertical-wall Breakwaters; 4.11 Examples of Vertical-wall-type Breakwaters; 4.12 Pneumatic and Hydraulic Breakwaters; 4.13 Floating Breakwaters.

Chapter 5. Wharves, Piers, Bulkheads, Dolphins, and Moorings 226

5.1 Introduction; 5.2 Factors Controlling Selection of Type of Dock; 5.3 Types and Materials of Construction; 5.4 Design Considerations; 5.5 Design of Piles and Cylinders for the Support of Docks; 5.6 Dock Fenders; 5.7 Typical Examples of the Design of Docks; 5.8 Unusual Dock Construction; 5.9 Dolphins; 5.10 Moles, Trestles, and Catwalks; 5.11 Offshore Moorings; 5.12 Mooring Accessories; 5.13 Shipping Terminal Utilities; 5.14 Cathodic Protection.

Chapter 6. Port Buildings 388

6.1 Introduction; 6.2 Transit Sheds and Warehouses; 6.3 Examples of Modern Transit-shed Construction; 6.4 Cold-storage Buildings; 6.5 Port Administration Buildings.

Chapter 7. General Cargo-handling Equipment 423

7.1 Introduction; 7.2 Loading and Unloading the Ship; 7.3 Handling on Land; 7.4 Handling in the Hold; 7.5 Pallets; 7.6 Containers; 7.7 Roll-on, Roll-off Service.

Chapter 8. Bulk Cargo Shipping Terminals 438

8.1 Introduction; 8.2 Storage Facilities; 8.3 Material-handling Equipment; 8.4 Self-unloading Ships; 8.5 Terminal Facilities; 8.6 Oil Terminals; 8.7 Some Modern Bulk Cargo Terminals.

Chapter 9. Offshore Marine Structures 465

9.1 Introduction; 9.2 Mobile Wharves; 9.3 Radar Platforms; 9.4 Lighthouse Platforms; 9.5 Permanent Drilling Islands; 9.6 Fixed Drilling and Production Platforms; 9.7 Mobile Drilling Units; 9.8 Self-contained Platforms.

Chapter 10. Navigation Aids 507

10.1 Introduction; 10.2 Purpose; 10.3 Buoys; 10.4 Fixed-structure Channel Markers; 10.5 Navigation Lights on Piers, Wharves, Dolphins, etc.; 10.6 Fixed-structure Beacon Lights on Breakwaters, Shore, etc.; 10.7 Lighthouses; 10.8 Lightships; 10.9 Range-light Installations; 10.10 Radar Reflectors; 10.11 Marine Beacon-light Lanterns; 10.12 Moorings.

Index 523

Chapter 1 GROWTH AND REGULATION OF PORTS

1.1 History of Port Growth

The history of the growth of ports is a fascinating and interesting subject. It reaches back to the time of the ancients, as early as, and perhaps before, the year 3500 B.C. Up to the time of the fall of the Roman Empire, harbors, most of which were located in the Mediterranean, the Red Sea, and the Persian Gulf, were built on a scale of grandeur and solidity. Because of the availability of cheap and unlimited manual labor (mostly slave labor) in ancient times, docks and other harbor works received as much attention as their monumental contemporaries, pyramids and temples. Harbor structures were so well constructed in those days that it is only because of the lack of world leadership and the consequent neglect, which followed the fall of the Roman Empire, that they disappeared, either being buried by earthquakes or through decadence; and they were never restored. In recent years, some of the construction in these old harbors has been revealed by the findings of archaeologists through surveys, excavations, and old documents. Among these findings, many interesting and valuable features of harbor engineering, which have been lost for centuries, have shown up and are now reappearing in modern port design. A particular feature common to most ancient ports was the well-planned and effectively positioned seawall or breakwater, a feature frequently employed in modern ports. For a brief but very interesting historical account of harbor engineering development, the reader is referred to that excellent treatise, "The Design, Construction and Maintenance of Docks, Wharves and Piers" by F. M. Du-Plat-Taylor.

It was not until the nineteenth century that a revival of interest in port works reappeared. The advent of steam power, the eagerness of navigators and explorers in their search for new lands and trade routes, the expansion of the British Empire through her colonies, and other influences, all contributed to a reevaluation of the importance of sea trade, which subsequently grew by leaps and bounds. As the volume of shipping grew, the demand for more vessels became apparent. As the new vessels took on larger proportions, the demand for increased port facilities became necessary. Thus, for the first time in world history, the ports of the world experienced their first real "growing pains," and, except for the interruption brought about by two major world wars, they have grown continuously.

Perhaps one of the greatest influences on the growth of world sea trade and the consequent demand for more and larger port facilities is the strategic location of the United States. With its three coast lines, the Atlantic, the Pacific and the Gulf Coasts, and the Saint Lawrence Seaway to the Great Lakes, sea trade to and from ports all over the world tends to make this country the focal point for the water-borne traffic of the world.

1.2 Factors Affecting the Growth of Ports

There are many factors affecting the growth of ports, such as the increase in world population and the development of overseas raw material sources. These and others of a more general nature will be discussed in the following paragraphs.

General Factors. Ships of early times sailed out of river ports with small shipments of goods for other nearby river ports in the same country. With few exceptions it took centuries before enough advanced navigational skill was developed by the shipmasters to venture any great distance. But, with the bold examples set by such navigators as Columbus, Drake, Raleigh, Cook, Magellan, and others, the superstitions and fears of unknown waters and lands soon disappeared. Thus, larger ships with larger crews soon were sailing the high seas transporting goods from continent to continent instead of between river ports on their own coasts. As this sea-borne traffic increased, the entrances to the rivers, on which were located the ports of call, became so crowded with shipping that building piers or quays along the banks of the river was necessary in order to permit the vessels to berth and at the same time keep clear of the channel. Here we see the beginnings of the modern port as we know it.

The people of the world need clothing, food, and the conveniences that make living comfortable, but the countries of the world are not all endowed with the same degree of fertility, natural wealth, and resources to produce all these needs without importing goods from other lands. By the same token, the uneven distribution of the population of the world creates in many countries a demand for essential goods which is much greater than what can be produced within the country. Consequently, the remainder must be met by imports. To pay for these goods, however, it is necessary to export either raw materials from the natural resources of the country or goods of which there is a greater supply than demand. This interchange of goods and raw materials between countries which are reached by sea-borne traffic brings about the demand for shipping and the port facilities to serve it. Better feeling between the countries and people of the world, the lowering of trade barriers, the awakening of the many backward peoples of the world to the better things of life are bringing about a greater interchange of goods and raw materials, thereby stimulating the growth of ports.

Table 1.1 **Total Merchant Fleets of the World and Total World Population**

Year	Number of ships *	Gross tons †	Dead-weight capacity, long tons	World population, ‡ millions
1946	12,297	69,806,000	98,026,000	2,360
1947	12,377	70,430,000	98,676,000	2,390
1948	12,643	71,549,000	100,703,000	2,430
1949	12,868	73,640,000	103,461,000	2,460
1950	13,282	75,718,000	107,215,000	2,500
1951	13,646	78,821,000	110,655,000	2,530
1952	14,019	81,924,000	114,946,000	2,570
1953	14,370	85,102,000	119,427,000	2,610
1954	14,793	89,258,000	124,754,000	2,650
1955	15,148	92,944,000	129,975,000	2,690
1956	15,615	97,655,000	136,880,000	2,740
1957	16,293	104,770,000	147,316,000	2,800
1958	16,966	112,314,000	158,047,000	2,852
1959	17,250 §	117,700,000 §	166,000,000 §	2,950 §

* SOURCE: Maritime Administration, U.S. Department of Commerce.
† Cubic measurement: 1 gross ton = 100 cu ft.
‡ SOURCE: Statistical Office of the United Nations.
§ Estimated.
NOTE: Fleet totals are for ocean-going ships of 1,000 gross tons and over and do not include inland waterway vessels.

Increase in World Population. World shipping and the consequent demand for port facilities, whether they are new or the expansions of existing facilities, can be considered a function of the world population and its willingness and ability to exchange goods. As the population increases so does the potential demand for goods, and, as a result, the number of ships to transport the goods must increase. Moreover, as the ships grow in number and size to handle the growing volume of trade, so must accommodations be provided to dock the vessels quickly and safely in the ports of call, to unload and reload them rapidly, and to provide them with all services, such as fuel, water, and food supplies, for quick turnaround.

A look at the statistics on the growth of maritime vessels carrying

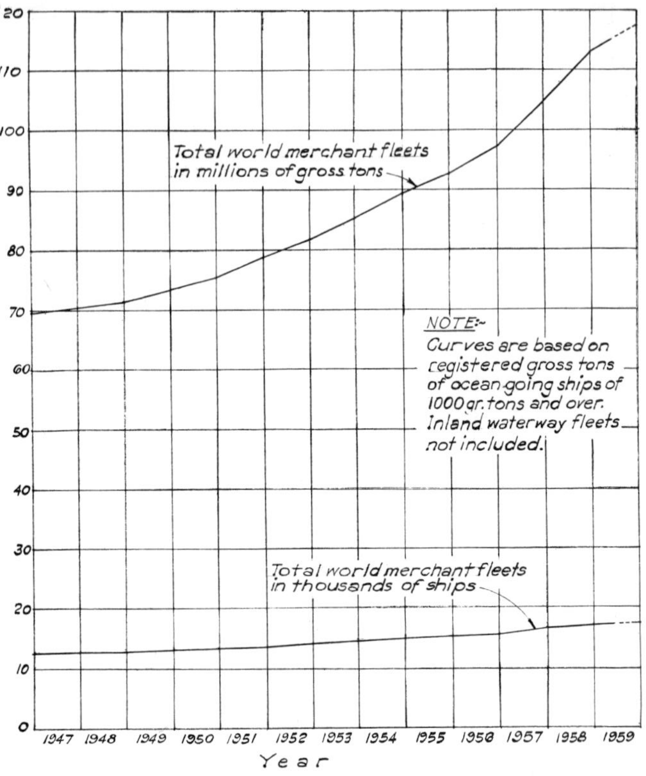

FIG. 1.1 Growth curves for total merchant fleets of the world after World War II.

ocean-going goods will confirm what has been stated above (see Table 1.1). The values from Table 1.1 have been plotted as curves in Figs. 1.1 and 1.2, and from the curves we are able to observe the remarkable growth of ocean-going vessels for the years after World War II. More especially in the last decade has the rate of growth increased greatly. For a closer relationship between world population growth and the ocean-going world merchant fleets, curves 1 and 4 of Fig. 1.2 have been made to show the growth for the total world merchant fleets in thousands of gross tons per million of world population, and the number of vessels per million of world population, respectively. These curves are interesting in that they not only depict a steady growth in both population and the number of vessels, but also indicate that the total gross tonnage of merchant fleets is growing more rapidly than the total number of vessels. For example, from curves 1 and 4 of Fig. 1.2 it is seen that at the end of 1946 there were five vessels, each of them approximately 30,000

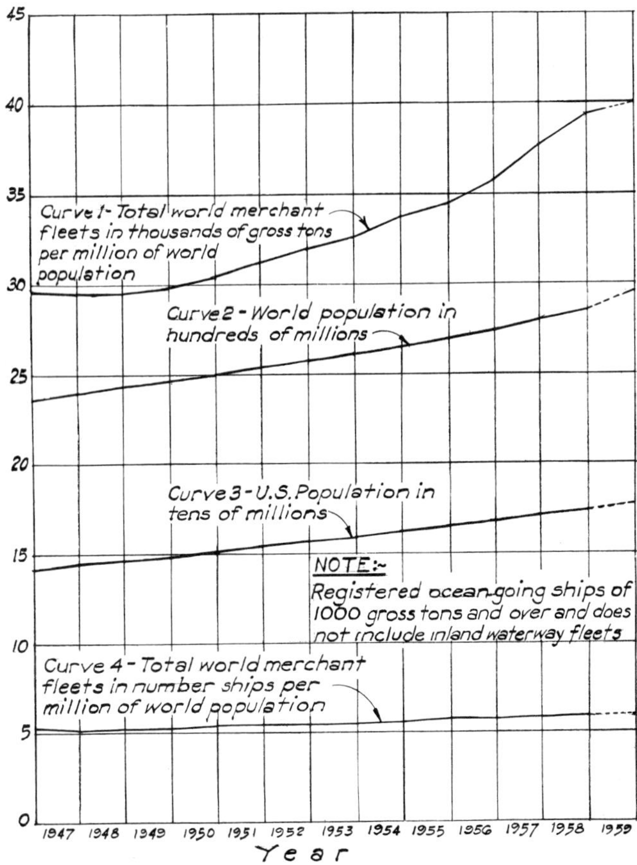

FIG. 1.2 Growth curves showing gross tonnage of ships and total number of ships as functions of total world population.

gross tons, per million of population. At the end of the year 1959, however, it is estimated that there were six vessels of about 41,000 gross tons per million of population, or about 6,800 gross tons per vessel per million of population. This indicates that, while world population is increasing, not only are world fleets increasing in number, but their gross tonnage rate per million of population is increasing also. In other words, if the gross tonnage rate per million of population is increasing, it is obvious that the net tonnage or cargo-carrying capacity of the ships is increasing at an even faster rate, since the ratio of net to gross tonnage has increased also. We can conclude therefore that

1. More and more peoples of the world are getting goods today which were not available to them, say, ten years ago or more.
2. More types of goods are in demand and are reaching the consumers through the medium of world trade.

A further illustration of the growth of sea-borne traffic can be made without directly involving the world population. Let us consider the total quantity of goods loaded on ocean-going vessels in international trade during the last decade. The values are listed in Table 1.2 and are

***Table* 1.2 Total Goods Loaded on Water-borne Vessels in International Trade**

Year	*Millions of metric tons*	*Year*	*Millions of metric tons*
1948	490	1954	730
1949	500	1955	830
1950	550	1956	910
1951	640	1957	960
1952	660	1958	950
1953	680		

SOURCE: United Nations Statistical Office. (Does not include coastal or inland waterway shipping.)

also plotted in Fig. 1.3, as illustrated by curve 2. If we now take the tons of goods loaded in international trade (Table 1.2) and divide these amounts by the annual gross tonnage of world merchant fleets of Table 1.1 for the corresponding years, we arrive at results which represent the theoretical number of trips per year of all vessels of the world merchant fleets loaded to capacity. These results have been plotted to give curve 1 of Fig. 1.3. Since Table 1.1 gives the gross tonnage of the world merchant fleets, these have been used for convenience instead of net tonnage. Therefore, the numerical values of the number of trips are approximate, but, since there is a fairly constant relationship between gross tonnage and net tonnage, the results illustrate and substantiate the progress in maritime trade. A study of curve 1 shows that, theoretically, all the ships of the world merchant fleets loaded to capacity made an average of 6.8 trips each to transport the goods loaded in international trade in the year ending 1948. In the year ending 1958, the ships made an average of over 8.5 trips each or an increase of about 25 per cent in the movement of vessels to and from world ports. From the figures given in Table 1.1, for the years 1946 to 1959, the number of ships of the world merchant fleets increased from 12,297 to an estimated 17,250, or about 40 per cent. Also, in the same period, the gross tonnage went from 69,806,000 to an estimated 117,700,000, an increase of 68 per cent. With these increases as evidence, plus the fact that the loaded vessels made 25 per cent more trips per year in 1958 than in 1948, it is no wonder that there has been a tremendous demand for increases in port construction and expansion. It takes but little imagination to see that, as a result of the increase in ships and shipping, the growth of port facilities is a continual process based on the growing demands of the rapidly growing world population.

General Industrial Growth. The industrial organizations today, with their vast resources and research facilities, are producing enormous quan-

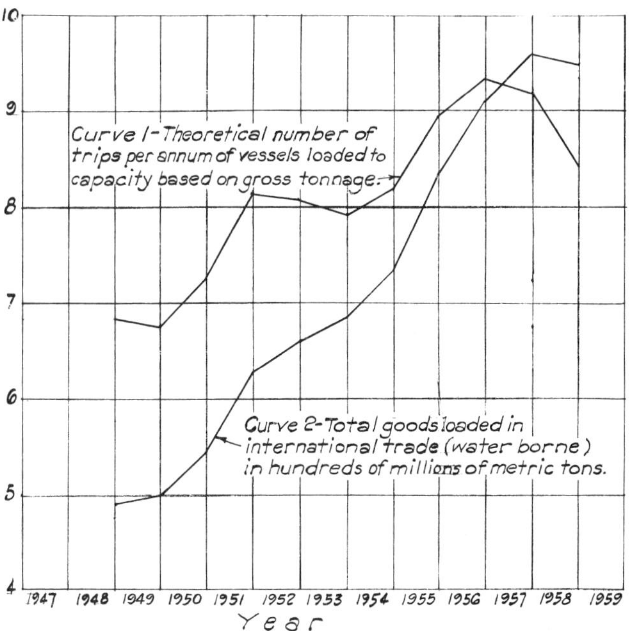

FIG. 1.3 Growth curves showing total goods loaded in international trade and theoretical number of trips per year of all vessels loaded to capacity.

tities of a variety of goods for consumption. Many of the products being marketed today were not even conceived at the beginning of the century. Other goods have been available to peoples of almost all income levels in the last decade or two, only because of their low cost effected by mass production. Competition among manufacturers and producers gives the world markets large quantities of a variety of goods at prices within the range of the average consumer. And to reach the average consumer the manufacturer must maintain a sales promotion to keep his product in use and to obtain new users, which he does through the newspaper, radio, television, educational programs, offices and sales forces abroad, and other mediums.

Through the work of some of the special agencies set up by the United

Nations, combined with the widespread influence of the missionaries and their work in far-off countries, and through the contacts made by people in foreign travels and the exchange of students and educators, many of the backward peoples of the world have, for the first time, not only enough of the basic needs for living, but many other conveniences as

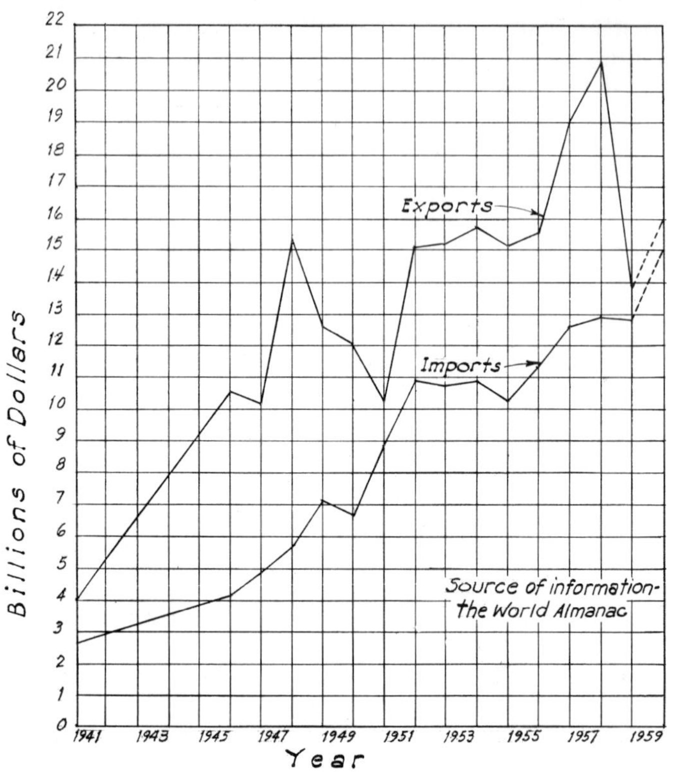

FIG. 1.4 Values of United States merchandise exports and imports.

well. As an example of growth in value of exports and imports for any one country, the growth of the value of merchandise handled by United States ports since the year 1940 shows an almost incredible rise. Amounts of exports and imports for the various years have been plotted separately in Fig. 1.4. From 1940 to 1959, inclusive, the growth of exports in dollar value was approximately 300 per cent. For the same period, the growth of imports in dollar value was 475 per cent. Even after making allowances for the higher cost of goods today than 15 to 20 years ago, the growth represents phenomenal progress, and it is almost needless to comment on the obvious effect such an increase has had on the demand for shipping and port facilities.

Growth of the Petroleum Industry. Perhaps no single commodity has influenced the growth of world shipping and port facilities more than that of the petroleum industry. Expansion in this industry has been the cause of major changes in the design of port works and has resulted in a tremendous growth in new construction.

The growth of the petroleum industry, since the first commercial oil well was dug in Titusville, Pennsylvania, on August 27, 1859, not only has affected the economy of the United States, but also has affected the whole world industrially, economically, and politically. For example, the

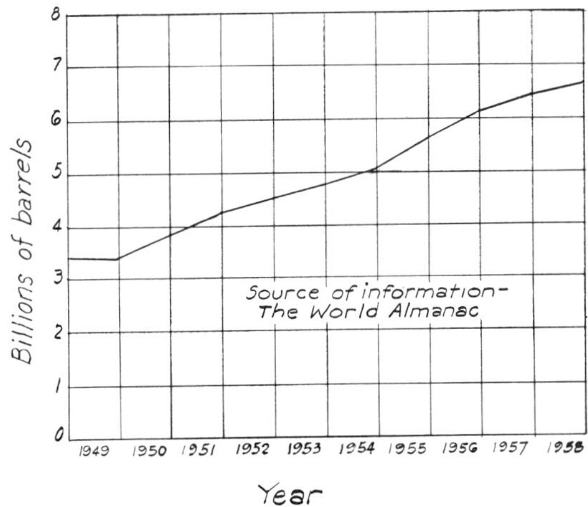

FIG. 1.5 World production of crude petroleum.

first commercial oil well in the United States produced 20 bbl a day. That was a little more than one hundred years ago. Figure 1.5 shows the world production of crude petroleum in recent years. In 1959, the United States produced approximately 7.5 million bbl and consumed over 9 million bbl of oil each day. This means that some 1.5 million bbl of oil had to be imported from overseas in vessels which had to be accommodated at United States ports having adequate facilities for unloading and distribution.

The various uses of petroleum and petroleum products have increased over the years. Petroleum is now consumed in vast quantities for lubricants, for fuel for heating and for powering vehicles on land and sea and in the air, and for the ever-increasing variety of items being derived from the petrochemicals, such as synthetic fibers, plastics, synthetic rubber, and paints. All these products, as they are marketed, create additional demands on shipping. Today, the tonnage of crude oil and its products is nearly equal to the combined tonnage of all other commodities in ocean trade.

Nearly 80 per cent of all the oil produced in the free world comes from three places: the United States, the Middle East, and Venezuela. Of the three, only the United States is required to import oil above that which she produces in order to meet her demands. Table 1.3 shows a comparison of the quantities of production of crude oil for the various countries, together with the quantities which each consumes. The production and consumption rates are given in barrels per day, a barrel being the equivalent of 42 United States gallons. It is seen from the table

***Table* 1.3 World Distribution of Crude Oil for 1958**

Country	Production, barrels per day	Consumption, barrels per day
United States	7,500,000	9,000,000
Mideast	4,300,000	500,000
Latin America	3,300,000	1,600,000
Communist Bloc	2,500,000	2,500,000
Far East and Oceania	500,000	1,400,000
Canada	500,000	800,000
Europe	200,000	2,300,000
Africa	100,000	500,000
Totals	18,900,000	18,600,000

SOURCE: A Century of Oil, *New York Times*, May 31, 1959.

that the United States, although she is the largest producer, must import some one and one half million barrels of oil daily to meet consumer demands. At the same time, the European countries combined must import more than two million barrels daily, while the Far East imports approximately one million barrels per day. Conversely, the Mideast produces almost nine times more than she consumes, while the Latin American countries produce more than twice their needs for consumption. The surplus quantities of production over consumption, naturally, make up the quantities of oil exported to those countries which have deficiencies. For instance, according to statistics compiled by the Statistical Office of the United Nations for the year 1958, there were loaded in ocean-going tankers of the world fleets 290 million metric tons of crude oil and approximately 155 million metric tons of refined products. This means that, if we assume a crude oil having an average specific gravity of 0.88, the ocean-going tanker fleets carried 2.1 billion bbl of crude oil in 1958 or 5,650,000 bbl a day, exclusive of some additional 3 million bbl of refined products a day.

To transport these enormous quantities of oil and oil products to all parts of the globe presents a great demand for vessels. In order to achieve this, it required over 34 million gross tons of tanker vessels of 100 gross tons and over, or almost 30 per cent of the world merchant fleets. As a matter of comparison, just before the outbreak of World War II, there were less than 12 million gross tons of tankers in existence, or less than 17 per cent of the world merchant fleets.

All the foregoing references to shipping and the resultant demand for port facilities are confined to ocean-going vessels for the reason that such vessels are larger and carry more cargo and therefore providing for them presents the major port problems. Also, enormous quantities of shipping must be handled within the individual countries through coastal and inland waterway routes. For example, in 1958, tankers and barges of all sizes transported over 375 million bbl of crude oil between points in the United States and more than double that amount in refined products.

The Development of Specialized Ports. The specialized port is generally one that can efficiently handle commodities, such as liquids that are carried in tankers, and bulk materials, such as sugar, grain, fertilizer, cement, coal, and crushed ores. All of these require specialized equipment and facilities for handling and storage. They also require large land areas for storage and are usually located on the periphery of ports away from the general cargo and passenger terminals. In some areas, where a single commodity is the only material to be shipped, the port facilities are designed especially to handle it. Examples of this are the oil, bauxite, and iron-ore shipping terminals scattered throughout the world at locations where oil and mineral ores are found and then shipped to other ports. The predominant bulk liquid cargo shipped in tankers is petroleum or products of petroleum. Some other liquids shipped in tankers are molasses, latex, vegetable oils, liquid sugar, and, more recently, wine and orange juice. The amount of these liquids is small compared with the quantities of petroleum and petroleum products being transported by the vast fleet of tankers now in operation. Tanker vessels have grown not only in numbers in the last 10 to 15 years, but their sizes have increased enormously; so much so, that few ports at present are able to provide for the berthing of the largest tankers, which have a dead-weight capacity of 106,000 long tons, a loaded draft of 49 ft 4 in., a length of 940 and a breadth of 132 ft. In contrast, the largest tanker at the close of World War II was the T-2 tanker having a dead-weight capacity of 16,350 long tons, a loaded draft of 30 ft 2 in., a length of 523 ft 6 in., and a breadth of 68 ft. The reasoning behind the development of these supertankers for use in shipping petroleum is that the oil industry has found that it costs very little more to operate the larger tankers than it does to operate the smaller ones.

The use of these very large tankers has created a problem in port design because of their draft, which exceeds the depth of most navigable channels and harbors. It would be difficult and costly for many existing ports to modify their facilities in order to receive the larger vessels. Therefore, new oil terminals have been built which will accommodate these vessels, and others are in the planning stage or under construction. At the present time, where large tankers must use ports with inadequate channel depths, it is necessary for them to anchor in deep water and then transfer part of their cargo to smaller tankers, such as the T-2 type, until they reduce the draft to that which will permit the use of the existing channel; or they may anchor offshore in deep water and transfer their cargo by submarine pipeline.

Bulk cargo terminals which include facilities for handling grain, coal, ore, bauxite, phosphates, and other bulk materials are becoming more important, since large volumes of materials can be loaded and unloaded in very short intervals of time, resulting in lower costs. The need for developing new raw material sources, such as iron ore, copper, and bauxite, has resulted in an increase in the number of shipping terminals financed and managed by private enterprise. Many of these terminals have been constructed in remote regions of the world, where it has been necessary to bring in all construction equipment, skilled labor, and supervision, and most, if not all, of the permanent materials and equipment required for the work. The building of many of these terminals has required the construction of complete town sites with schools, hospital, stores, etc., and the installation of all utilities, such as power and light, water supply, and sewage disposal. Projects of this type, including mining and processing equipment, railroad or highway transportation, and port facilities, have required the expenditure of as much as $300 million and as long as four years to build.

Port Modernization and Rehabilitation. Prior to World War II there were few startling achievements in port works expansion. Growth had been more or less a gradual advance over the years; but after the end of the war, and as a result of the severe usage of port facilities during the war years in addition to deterioration, obsolescence, and war damage, it was evident that a major program was necessary for the development of port works in the form of new construction, modernization, and rehabilitation. Many ports outside the United States suffered severe damage by bombing, and the work of rebuilding these ports was extensive and costly.

In the United States an accelerated construction program for port development was begun after World War II, which, by the end of the year 1955, amounted to over three-quarters of a billion dollars in expenditures. The Port of New York Authority made an exhaustive survey of the programs of the various port interests in the 10-year period subsequent to the end of World War II, and later, upon further study, revised its findings to cover the 12-year period ending December 31, 1957. The total expenditures for port development for the 12 years, according to the studies, were found to exceed one billion dollars. A summary of the expenditures by regions is given in Table 1.4 which is taken from an article

***Table* 1.4 Port Development Expenditures by Regions of the United States and Canada, January 1, 1946, to December 31, 1957**

Figures in thousands of dollars

Region	General cargo facilities		Specialized facilities		Totals
	New	Modernized and rehabilitated	New	Modernized and rehabilitated	
North Atlantic	141,417	75,721	117,822	40,938	375,898
South Atlantic	20,110	7,580	5,849	4,035	37,574
Gulf Coast	75,125	12,760	53,420	11,433	152,738
Pacific Coast	73,215	40,460	48,133	5,178	166,986
Great Lakes	24,214	2,100	105,349	15,373	147,036
Alaska, Hawaii, Puerto Rico	29,198	3,314	5,425	240	38,177
Canada	22,383	36,355	26,985	8,480	94,203
Totals	385,662	178,290	362,983	85,677	1,012,612

From a survey conducted by the Port of New York Authority, and published in the August, 1958, issue of *World Ports and The Mariner*.

published in the August, 1958, issue of *World Ports and The Mariner* by Roger Gilman, Director of Port Development for the Port of New York Authority. The amounts given reflect all known funds that were actually spent or were definitely committed up to the end of 1957 and include construction that was underway, contracts that were awarded, and financing that had been definitely arranged. Only funds that had been spent to construct or improve marine terminals used primarily by ocean-going vessels are included. Furthermore, the amounts do not include expenditures for land, acquisition of existing facilities, dry dock or ship repair pier construction costs, pleasure boat facilities, and barge or harbor craft terminal expenditures. Table 1.5 shows a comparison of port development expenditures for various United States ports from 1946 to 1957.

At no time in the history of world maritime trade has the growth of ports been so extensive or received the world-wide interest given it after World War II. Some countries like Germany, France, and the United Kingdom were forced into vast programs for rehabilitating their many ports and harbors as a result of the destruction brought about by war damage. New construction was begun in accordance with designs

***Table* 1.5 Comparison of Port Development Expenditures by United States Ports, January 1, 1946, to December 31, 1957**

Figures in thousands of dollars

Port	General cargo facilities		Specialized facilities	Total	New general cargo berths
	New	Modernized and rehabilitated			
New York	100,022	48,807	22,281	171,109	50
Los Angeles	18,500	22,100	6,100	46,700	12
Philadelphia	6,500	3,905	34,630	45,035	4
Chicago	9,470	......	35,360	44,830	7
Baltimore	7,250	3,780	29,815	40,845	2
New Orleans	21,713	5,053	12,205	38,971	14
Long Beach	25,000	3,000	9,420	37,420	23
Boston	14,625	14,640	7,350	36,615	10
Toledo	2,500	......	29,900	32,400	2
Newport News	1,370	80	30,465	31,915	10
Houston	15,162	1,902	6,123	23,187	9
Portland, Ore.	7,485	4,465	9,705	21,655	6
Norfolk	7,100	250	10,854	18,204	8
Mobile	8,000	160	8,010	16,170	6

From survey conducted by the Port of New York Authority, published in November, 1958, issue of *Via Port of New York.*

conforming to the modern-day demands of larger ships, new methods of cargo handling, and the trend toward land transportation by motor truck. This progress and growth are far from being concluded. Most port authorities plan to provide for the modernization of their ports to be carried out in stages during the years ahead. The Port of New York, for example, has plans calling for more than $400 million to be spent in the next decade or more, doubling that spent during the 12-year interval since the close of the war. The City of New York, through its Department of Marine and Aviation, is in the midst of a five-year (1957–1962) program of rebuilding along New York's waterfront at an estimated cost of $200 million.

Engineering Advancement in Port Design. Recent years have seen much of the "rule of thumb" design eliminated in the engineering of ports and harbors. This is being done through laboratory research where large-scale models of harbors and structures are subjected to forces simulating actual conditions. Coincident with this research, we have in the last 25 years experienced great advances in engineering. Today the port engineer is better equipped to design confidently and to predict the behavior of many types of structures which formerly did not permit a rational analysis, and the results of such progress in engineering are noticeable in the expansion of port and harbor systems to meet the increasing demands of shipping. Following is a list of some of the more important features contributing to the advancement in port construction and growth.

Soil mechanics. Over the past 30 years, this branch of engineering has grown until it now plays a major role in the design of foundations and other structures in contact with earth. Its useful application permits not only economy but also the elimination of much assumption in foundation analysis.

Wind, tides, and waves. Much has been and is being done in research on this subject in order to obtain a better understanding of the behavior and the impact of wind, tides, and waves on marine structures. Most of the research is being conducted in well-equipped laboratories, where large-scale models of harbors and various types of marine structures are subjected to forces simulating those occurring under actual conditions.

Breakwaters. New types of protective armor, such as concrete tetrapods and tribars, have been introduced after having been tested and found stable under wave action on steeper slopes than can be used for conventional concrete blocks and rock.

Prestressed and precast concrete. Prestressed concrete has already attained prominence and is widely used for piles, columns, slabs, and girders. Precast sections, which are not prestressed, have been used also to advantage, to save formwork and speed up construction over water.

Fendering systems. Many new systems of fendering have been developed to protect docks, and ships as well, when berthing. These include rubber fenders of various shapes, Raykin buffers, steel springs, and gravity fenders of several different types.

Corrosion protection. Improved protective coatings for both steel and concrete have enabled much lighter and more economical types of construction to replace the heavy masonry type of quay walls, where permanency is a requirement. Steel below water level can now be made reasonably permanent by the use of cathodic protection.

New methods of cargo handling and distribution. In recent years, major changes have come about in the methods of cargo handling and transportation. Specialized equipment is now essential in certain ports where bulk materials and liquids are to be loaded and unloaded in record time. Many ports, in the course of rehabilitation, are being modernized with such equipment as belt conveyors, bucket elevators, pumping devices, and pneumatic systems, the latter being used for handling liquids and loose granular materials such as grain, granular coal, and sugar. Fork-lift trucks and mobile cranes are now commonplace at modern cargo docks because of their maneuverability and timesaving features. The growth of motor truck transportation has added considerably to the flexibility of cargo movement and has influenced the layout of piers and sheds.

Construction Progress. The construction industry has met the challenges that engineering design has presented. In equipment and skills, it has advanced far in the last 25 years.

In the field of concrete work, the design and control of concrete mixes are given special attention to attain workability, durability, density, and strength. Special admixtures are available today to advance or retard the set-in concrete and minimize shrinkage. Aggregates are carefully selected and tested before being used, and the water-cement ratio is controlled by using the maximum permissible for the strength required. High-strength concrete of 5,000 lb per sq in. or greater can now be produced with reliability. The use of vibrators is now almost universal for concrete work.

Pile-driving equipment has kept pace with construction progress. Heavy and more efficient equipment is in use today, which can handle and drive the long and heavy prestressed-concrete piles.

1.3 Port Authorities

The planning, building, and operation of a port is a complex undertaking, especially for the larger ports, and to control all the factors which are necessary to make a port function smoothly is a great responsibility. Adding to the complexity is the fact that ownership of ports sometimes involves many different agencies. For instance, part of a particular port may be owned or operated by private interests, another part by railroads, and still other parts by the municipality; also, it may be under the ownership or jurisdiction of the state or Federal government. Private interests may include those companies dealing in grain, coal, ores, cements, fertilizers, fruit, etc. These companies may have their holdings exclusively, or jointly with railroads and/or the municipality. Where municipal ownership is concerned, the pier may be leased on a long-term basis to a steamship company, to an industrial concern, or to a stevedoring company. However, such divided ownership complicates the development and operation of the port, especially when one considers the many methods of transportation and the heavy industrial concentration in the vicinity of large ports. For instance, New York Harbor with its 650 miles of usable waterfront, has a number of governing bodies. In the year 1917, a commission was assigned by the Governors of New York and New Jersey to study the conditions related to commerce and trade in the metropolitan area and to make recommendations for improvements. In 1921, after much study, the recommendations of the commission led to the joint authorization, by the legislatures of the two states, of a Port Compact, whereby there was created the Port of New York Authority, the first port authority in the United States. The Port Compact was approved by Congress and signed by the President of the United States.

The Port of New York Authority is a self-supporting corporate agency of the two states of New York and New Jersey and, under the Port Compact, it is responsible for two basic jobs, the development and operation of transportation and terminal facilities in the Port District, and the promotion and protection of the commerce of the port. The Authority is governed by 12 commissioners, 6 of whom are appointed by the Governor of New York and 6 by the Governor of New Jersey. The 12 commissioners, who are headed by an executive director, serve without pay for a term of six years.

As of 1960 the Port of New York Authority owns about 25 per cent of the steamship piers in the Port of New York. New York City, under the supervision of its Department of Marine and Aviation, owns about 45 per cent while about 15 per cent is owned by private terminal operators, 10 per cent by railroads, and 5 per cent by the United States government.

Following the example of New York, many other ports in the United States have established port authorities for the administration and promotion of their own maritime interests, and, in doing so, they have accomplished much toward putting the planning of future improvements and the operation of the facilities on a sound basis. This is possible because of the very nature of a port authority which is essentially a bridge between government and private enterprise. Although created by the government, it is not subject to political controls, and, because of the duties it is charged with and obligated to fulfill, the port authority functions as an integral part of the economic system. The men chosen to head these organizations are usually leaders in business, industry, banking, shipping, law, and engineering, and they are well versed in the planning, execution, and administration of the large-scale projects involved in port works and commerce. Furthermore, they are backed up and supported by the prestige and authority of the government, and, therefore, they can exercise much more authority than private enterprise. This is especially notable in the condemnation of waterfront property, the development of land transportation facilities, and waterfront planning, all of which are vital problems for the development of ports. Then, there is the problem of capital investment, which may run into hundreds of millions of dollars for a given program. (New York expended over $171 million for a 12-year period, 1946–1957, inclusive.) Private interests might have a difficult time financing port works requiring a large amount of capital, because of uncertainty as to the future growth of the port, and because of the small financial return usually forthcoming during the development period between the opening of the new facility and the attainment of a sufficient amount of shipping to place the port on a profitable basis. The port authority, because of its public interest and over-all control of planning and operation, is very often in a better position to raise the required capital.

The creation of publicly controlled port authorities in United States ports has been a major step forward in port progress, and it is interesting to note that the functions performed by the various authorities have much in common with one another. Some of the major functions performed by port authorities are listed as follows:

Development planning
Traffic promotion
Raise capital
Own and develop independent terminals
Exercise the right of eminent domain
Lease wharf facilities
Operate harbor craft
Operate facilities for air, rail, or highway transportation

Concerning the foregoing list, it is appropriate to remark that the majority of the leading port authorities of the United States have the power to exercise the right of eminent domain. Some or all of the above functions are commonly executed by most port authorities, with the possible exception of the last item. At the present time, few port authorities operate terminal facilities for air, rail, and highway transportation even though they may have the power to do so. However, this is one of the purposes for which the Port of New York Authority was created, and in this field it operates, as of 1960, five air terminals, two motor truck terminals, a railroad freight terminal, a bus terminal, a grain terminal, five marine terminals, two tunnels, and four bridge crossings. This list continues to grow because of the prestige which the Authority has attained as a result of its successful handling of these facilities.

Relatively speaking, when one considers the length of time it has taken for the major ports to grow to their present size and capacity under a multiplicity of ownership and the exceedingly short time since the creation of port authorities, it is understandable that port authorities generally have not achieved a state of full ownership or control of all facilities in a given port. The process of transferring ownership of port facilities is, of necessity, an unhurried procedure. There is a tremendous amount of work involved in making waterfront improvements, which requires long-range planning, expert design, and availability of large amounts of capital.

A port authority may be of considerable importance to a port, whether its role in the operation of the piers is small or large. Once a public authority has established itself in a port as a thoroughly capable organization in pier operation, it will attract other owners to offer their piers (usually on a lease basis) for modernization and operation. As of 1960 the Port of New York Authority operates about 25 per cent of the piers in the New York–New Jersey area. This figure represents an increase of approximately 150 per cent over the last 12 years, during which time an extensive modernization program was embarked upon. This progress can well be attributed to the expert manner in which the Authority has carried out its duties, plus its additional responsibility—that of promoting and conducting the commerce of the New York–New Jersey port. This latter additional responsibility is administered through the Authority's Port Commerce Division which is international in scope and which is divided into four sections: trade development, port promotion, traffic management, and traffic research.

The trade development section has eight regional offices in areas where existing and prospective shippers using the New York–New Jersey ports can best be reached. These strategic locations are New York, Chicago, Cleveland, Washington, D.C., Rio De Janeiro, London, Zurich, and San Juan, Puerto Rico. Each of these locations is the hub of an area generating or receiving a large volume of cargo, which is shipped or could be shipped via New York Harbor. It is in these areas that the representatives of the Authority's trade development body contact traffic managers and others dealing with the movement of water-borne commerce, rendering such information as to enable shippers to expedite the movement of their cargo via New York Harbor. New facilities, cargo-handling techniques, lists of foreign freight forwarders and truckmen, government import and export regulations, and much other valuable information, including special shipping literature, are readily transmitted to shippers to aid them in facilitating their work.

The port promotion section is concerned with producing and distributing port literature, newsletters, advertising exhibits, motion pictures, and a monthly magazine. Its job is to bring to the attention of shippers the value of the port in the interest of saving time and money.

The traffic management section functions as a protective agency in that it protects users of the port from discriminatory transportation rates and practices. This section, through the traffic manager and his staff, often initiates action to improve port transportation services, fosters more favorable rates, and supplies rate information to shippers when requested. The traffic management section, in close cooperation with the Authority's law department, represents the port in proceedings before the Interstate Commerce Commission and other regulatory agencies.

The fourth branch of the Port Commerce Division is the trade research section, which interprets and evaluates trends in foreign trade. Its findings are valuable guides in charting future action since it makes possible the pin-pointing of areas in which increased trade development activities or a more favorable transportation rate structure would result in more trade in the port.

A stimulus for all port authorities is the common bond derived from their membership in the American Association of Port Authorities. That organization, whose origin traces back almost half a century, combines a technical society and a trade association aimed at promoting the port industry, not only for the United States, but also for Canada and Latin America. With committees in its make-up such as port development and construction, maintenance, hazardous cargoes, fire prevention, port practices, operation rules and terminal rates, law legislation, and other highly useful subdivisions, it imparts to its members much valuable information, which would require large expenditures of monies annually in research if acted upon independently by the individual port. Members in the American Association of Port Authorities include authorities from all the major ports of the United States and Canada, and from many of those in Latin America. Its major objectives may be summarized as follows:

1. To encourage water-borne transportation by the promotion of national and international publicity.
2. To exchange technical information relative to port construction, maintenance, operation, construction and management.
3. To promote the importance of port authorities in their relationship to the communities.
4. To cooperate with the Federal government in assuring that channels and waterways connecting with United States ports are properly maintained and expanded as necessary to meet the needs of commerce.
5. To strive for uniform practices in ports as opposed to the variations created in the past by private enterprise. This means emphasis on methods of management, construction and financing, establishment of rate structures, a standard technical port language, and other similar problems.
6. To work toward a common objective.

The economic importance of the port industry has long been recognized by the United States government, and the voice of the American

Association of Port Authorities is of importance in the national affairs of the United States.

1.4 Regulatory Bodies

Aside from the owners or agencies who build and operate a port, there are certain functions having to do with the regulation of navigation and maintenance of the navigable waters of the United States, which are performed by agencies of the Federal government and are under the control of various departments of the government, as follows:

Corps of Engineers. Under the Department of the Army, the Corps of Engineers performs the following functions with respect to the maintenance and regulation of navigable waters. It establishes and controls the harbor lines, which in turn set the location and limits of waterfront structures when they are adjacent to navigable waters. It is responsible for the maintenance and improvement of channels in all navigable waters, and in this respect it controls most of the dredging performed in the United States. It is also responsible for the removal of any and all obstructions to navigation, such as shipwrecks, landslides, debris, or stray objects which might foul the channels, and for the control of pollution in the harbors. It reviews any proposal for new or rehabilitated waterfront structures and issues permits for their construction, and exercises supervisory powers over harbors by the patrol of the main entrances to prevent any possible blocking by small craft. The Corps of Engineers is also responsible for the development and operation of the inland waterway systems. It collects port commerce statistics which are published by both the Corps of Engineers and the United States Maritime Administration of the Department of Commerce.

United States Coast Guard. This group, under the jurisdiction of the U.S. Treasury Department, primarily exists to prevent loss of life and property due to unsafe and illegal practices upon the high seas and in navigable waters subject to the jurisdiction of the United States; but it also performs many important jobs for the benefit of the mariner and shipper. It provides and maintains some 39,000 or more aids to navigation, such as lighthouses, buoys, bells, fog signals, and radio beacons, which are located at various places along 40,000 miles of navigable waters. It is responsible for the removal of derelicts and other menaces to navigation, and for icebreaking to keep the channels open during freezing weather. It maintains the International Ice Patrol to report amounts of iceberg drift for the benefit of vessels crossing the North Atlantic, and also maintains ocean weather stations. During times of floods and hurricanes, it furnishes aid to those in distress and provides medical aid to seamen when required, and is engaged at all times in lifesaving activities. It patrols the North Pacific Ocean and Bering Sea to regulate the taking of fur-bearing sea mammals and fish. It controls marine inspection and enforces maritime laws on the high seas and navigable waters of the United States in order to prevent the smuggling of taxable goods or goods which may be banned for import. It regulates and enforces laws governing dangerous cargoes and maintains an educational program in marine safety for ship operators and boatmen.

U.S. Bureau of Customs. For the protection of shippers, domestic trade, and the public in general, as well as for the purpose of collecting tariffs due the government in accordance with the Tariff Act, the U.S. Treasury Department operates and controls the Bureau of Customs. Its purpose is to prevent the smuggling of illegal and undeclared goods, to investigate violations of customs and navigation laws, and to supervise the export and import of controlled and restricted materials. At all ocean ports used by vessels handling foreign trade, the Customs Service has an established office through which every vessel of foreign registry must be cleared upon arrival and departure. Here, also, American vessels engaged in trade between the United States and foreign ports must be cleared. In close cooperation with the Bureau of Narcotics, also a division of the U.S. Treasury Department, the Bureau of Customs enforces the prohibitive features of the Narcotics Drug Import and Export Act.

Immigration and Naturalization Service. This is a branch of the U.S. Department of Justice which controls the entry of foreign citizens into the country. Aliens wishing to enter the country for permanent or temporary residence must present to the immigration officials documents of identity and nationality, along with their visas, to determine their fitness and admissibility under American laws.

The United States Maritime Administration. This branch of the U.S. Department of Commerce functions as the administrator of regulations for the control of rates, services, routes, practices, agreements, charges, classifications, and tariffs of common water-borne carriers engaged in foreign commerce.

The Bureau of Foreign Commerce. This is also a branch of the U.S. Department of Commerce. It gathers and distributes marketing information for the manufacturers and exporters of the United States and controls the issuing of licenses to exporters. Since foreign trade is an important part of industry, the Department of Commerce maintains a staff of specialists who supply information on new trade leads, foreign economic developments, trade statistics, export market possibilities, United States export controls and import regulations, foreign laws affecting United States exports, and many other important facts.

Food and Drug Administration. This is an important arm of the U.S. Department of Health, Education, and Welfare. Under it, the enforcement of the Federal Food, Drug, and Cosmetic Act is exercised, as it affects imports and exports.

Interstate Commerce Commission. This is a regulatory body which controls rates and services for coastwise and inland water carriers engaged in transportation in interstate commerce. It also regulates trucks and railroads in the same manner.

U.S. Department of Agriculture. The control of perishable foods and the administration and enforcement of the laws of the Perishable Commodities Act, the Export Apple and Pear Act, and other related statutes are handled through the Fruit and Vegetable Division of the U.S. Department of Agriculture. The inspection of meat and meat products, as well as animals, for both import and export is the responsibility of the Agricultural Research Service.

Quarantine. Vessels arriving from foreign ports are required to undergo quarantine inspection of ships and passengers by the United States Public Health Service, a division of the U.S. Department of Health, Education, and Welfare. Incoming vessels are anchored in the proximity of the designated quarantine station, whereupon medical officers of the Public Health Service board the incoming vessel for inspection. The vessels are not moved until they are cleared, unless otherwise officially authorized to proceed to some other designated location by the health officials. If fumigation of the vessel is required, as a result of contamination or infestation which may be harmful to health, the ship remains at the anchorage until fumigation, usually done by private companies, is complete and the vessel is officially cleared.

Security Associations. Theft or pilferage is a serious problem on most waterfronts. Much of this is petty, but its widespread practice makes it costly, since a good deal of it is carried out by well-organized groups. Annual losses in foodstuffs and merchandise are heavy and require much vigilance on the part of the police and private protective agencies in detection and prevention. Protective systems and police details are indispensable requisites on docks, and they entail large annual expenditures to maintain them. Security organizations exist whose membership comprises the maritime industry. Their function is to suppress theft and pilferage and to cooperate with the Federal, state, and city governments in the gathering of legal evidence to aid in prosecution. They also assist in court proceedings, inspect cargo-handling methods on piers for greater security, and train guards and watchmen in pier security measures.

Waterfront Commissions. Malpractice in hiring waterfront labor has proved to be somewhat of a plague in many ports. In the past it has been serious enough to result in the diversion of shipping to other ports. To counteract these conditions in New York, the Waterfront Commission of

New York Harbor was established in 1953 by a compact between New York and New Jersey, to cope with unjust practices in the hiring of waterfront labor and the methods of public loading on piers. The commission consists of four members, who serve for a term of three years, two appointed by the governor of each state. The commission is empowered to control hiring by requiring pier superintendents and hiring agents to be licensed and longshoremen to be registered. Persons with disqualifying criminal records and others whose presence on the piers would jeopardize public peace and safety are excluded from waterfront employment.

Pilotage. Any ship bound to or from a foreign part is required to take on a pilot, when entering or leaving an American port. Upon entering the harbor a pilot boat pulls up alongside the vessel and the pilot boards the ship to supervise the remainder of the ship's passage. Rates for this service are usually charged in accordance with the amount of maximum draft of the vessel. In New York, for instance, the rate is $7 per foot of maximum draft (June, 1959) to berth in the Port of New York. Other charges are assessed when additional special services are rendered. Rates also increase as the distance of travel increases. For instance, ocean-going vessels plying the Hudson River north of Yonkers, New York, and south of Troy, New York, are required to pay pilotage fees varying from $5 to $12.25 per foot of maximum draft, depending upon the distance covered.

1.5 Financing

When the port structure is a municipal project, it may be financed by the municipality out of reserve funds appropriated for the purpose. In cases where funds are not available and the project is considered essential, funds may be obtained from a bond issue sponsored by the city. Interest on such bonds is paid from the monies received from pier rentals. Rental of the structure is usually on a long-lease basis, 20 years or more, with options of renewal at possible progressive increases in annual rent for the ensuing years. Provisions in the agreement usually require that the lessee carry fire and other necessary insurance to protect the city's investment, and maintain the structure in first-class condition. Other provisions may be included in the agreement, such as the retention by the city of part of the receipts of certain services offered to the public by the lessee. An example of this is at pier 40 in New York where the Holland-America Line, the lessee, turns over to the city part of its receipts for roof-top parking when the annual return exceeds a fixed amount.

Autonomous port authorities obtain their capital for new construction or for the modernization of old structures from bond issues and from reserve funds. Reserve funds are accumulated from net income derived from revenues and investments. Port authorities which operate similarly to the Port of New York Authority and which are authorized by the state, or states, to function as autonomous organizations in the interest of the public, have no stockholders or equity holders. Their revenues and reserves must be disbursed for specific purposes in accordance with provisions of various statutes and agreements with holders of the bonds. The debt service, created by the bond issue and paid annually from the revenues and reserves, includes interest and the amortization of the principal, and, after its payment, any remaining revenues are transferred to the various reserve funds of the authority. The amount of the balance of these reserve funds usually must meet established requirements of the statutes of the authority and certain stipulations set up in the bond issue.

Chapter 2 WIND, TIDES, AND WAVES

2.1 Wind

The circulation of masses of air more or less parallel to the earth's surface is known as *wind*. This motion of the air is brought about by changes in the temperature of the atmosphere. When air is warmed its density becomes less, and as a result it ascends and is replaced by colder air which flows in and under it. The changes in temperature in the atmosphere brought about by the different surface absorption of heat by land as compared with water and by mountains as compared with valleys, and the changes brought about by night and day result in local

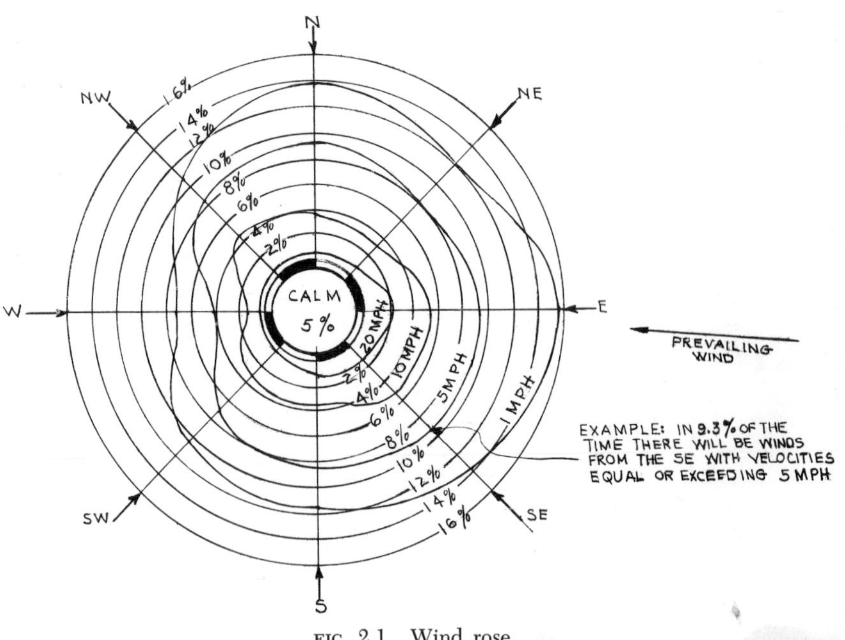

FIG. 2.1 Wind rose.

winds and breezes. The cooling breezes at the seashore during the daytime or those from the mountains to replace the warm air in the valleys at night are examples of this phenomenon. Aside from local winds and breezes, there is a general flow of air brought about by the warmer air at the equator being replaced by colder air flowing in from the north and south and being deflected by the rotation of the earth.

Nearly every location is subject to what is termed the *prevailing wind*, or a wind blowing from one general direction of the compass for a major portion of the year. *Monsoons* are prevailing winds which are seasonal, blowing in one direction over part of the year and in the opposite direction the remainder of the year. Monsoon winds are prevalent in the western Pacific. Prevailing winds are not necessarily the strongest winds. Very often winds of greater intensity, but which occur less frequently, come from other directions. The direction of the wind is given by the point of the compass from which it comes toward the observer. The side of a structure facing the direction from which the wind comes is the *windward* side and the opposite side is the *leeward* side.

The direction, frequency, and intensity of winds at a particular location over a period of time are represented graphically by a *wind rose* which is illustrated in Fig. 2.1.

The force of winds is classified in accordance with a scale established by Admiral Beaufort, known as Beaufort's scale, in which the range of intensity is given 13 numbers, 0 to 12, each number representing an approximate velocity and general description of intensity. Table 2.1 gives the Beaufort scale.

***Table* 2.1 Beaufort Wind Scale**

Beaufort number	Description	Velocity, miles per hour
0	Calm	0–1
1	Light air	1–3
2	Slight breeze	4–7
3	Gentle breeze	8–12
4	Moderate breeze	13–18
5	Fresh breeze	19–24
6	Strong breeze	25–31
7	Moderate gale	32–38
8	Fresh gale	39–46
9	Strong gale	47–54
10	Whole gale	55–63
11	Storm	64–75
12	Hurricane	Above 75

The pressure of the wind varies with the square of the velocity and is given by the formula $p = cv^2$, where c is a constant usually taken as 0.00256 when v is in miles per hour and p is in pounds per square foot. The total wind pressure on a structure varies with its shape, and, therefore, the pressure p is multiplied by a factor varying between 1.3 and 1.6, the smaller value usually being adequate for the low, flat surface of a ship or dock. In designing docks for the force of wind against the ship and for wind loads from operating equipment on the dock, such as moveable loading towers or cranes, a considerable amount of judgment must be exercised in selecting the wind velocity to be used in the design. It is customary to assume that equipment such as loading towers will not operate when the wind is stronger than 15 miles per hour and, therefore, a wind pressure of 5 lb per sq ft under operating conditions is considered adequate. Likewise a ship is not expected to remain alongside a dock during severe storm and hurricane conditions and a design force exceeding 20 lb per sq ft is seldom warranted.

2.2 Tides

The tide is the periodic rise and fall of the ocean waters produced by the attraction of the moon and sun. The movement is most noticeable on shores which shelve gradually and expose a wide expanse of beach between high- and low-water tide levels. Generally, the average interval between successive high tides is 12 hours 25 minutes, half the time between successive passages of the moon across a given meridian. The moon exerts a greater influence on the tides than the sun. This influence varies directly as the mass and inversely as the cube of the distance, and therefore the ratio is about 7:3.

The highest tides which occur at intervals of half a lunar month are called *spring tides*. They occur at or near the time when the moon is new or full, i.e., when the sun, moon, and earth fall in line, and the tide-generating forces of the moon and sun are additive. When the lines connecting the earth with the sun and the moon form a right angle, i.e., when the moon is in her quarters, then the actions of the moon and sun are subtractive, and the lowest tides of the month occur, called the *neap tides*.

Owing to the retardation of the tidal wave in the ocean by frictional forces, as the earth revolves daily around its axis, and as the tide tends to follow the direction of the moon, the highest tide for each location is not coincident with conjunction and opposition, but occurs at some constant time after new and full moon. This interval is known as the *age* of the tide, which may amount to as much as two and one-half days.

Large differences in tidal range occur at different locations along the ocean coast because of secondary tidal waves set up by the primary tidal wave or mass of water moving around the earth; these are also influenced by the depth of shoaling water and configuration of the coast. The highest tides in the world occur in the Bay of Fundy where a rise of 100 ft has been recorded. Inland and land-locked seas, such as the Mediterranean and the Baltic, have less than 1 ft of tide, and the Great Lakes are not noticeably influenced.

Tides which occur twice each lunar day are called *semidiurnal tides,* and since the lunar day, or time it takes the moon to make a complete revolution around the earth, is about 50 minutes longer than the solar day, the corresponding high tide on successive days is about 50 minutes later. In some places, such as Pensacola, Florida, only one high tide a day occurs, and the tides are then called *diurnal tides.* If one of the two daily high tides is incomplete, i.e., if it does not reach the height of the previous tide, as at San Francisco, California, then the tides are referred to as *mixed diurnal tides.* There are other exceptional tidal phenomena. For instance at Southampton, England, there are four daily high waters, occurring in pairs, separated by a short interval. At Portsmouth, there are two sets of three tidal peaks per day.

Tide tables have been published for most parts of the world. Admiralty Tide Tables cover major ports in the United Kingdom and elsewhere, while the United States Coast and Geodetic Survey lists the tides for the major harbors in the United States and other parts of the world. Table 2.2 gives the spring and mean tidal ranges for some of the major ports in the United States and foreign countries.

In using the tide tables of the United States Coast and Geodetic Survey it must be kept in mind that they give the times and heights of high and low waters and not the times of the flood or slack water. For stations on the ocean coast there is usually but little difference between the time of high or low water and the beginning of ebb or flood current, but for places in narrow channels, landlocked harbors, or along tidal rivers, the time of slack water may differ by several hours from the time of high or low water. The predicted times of slack water and tidal current velocities are given in tidal current tables published by the United States Coast and Geodetic Survey, one for the Atlantic Coast of North America and the other for the Pacific Coast of North America and Asia.

The rise of the tide is referred to some established datum of the charts, which varies in different parts of the world. The British Admiralty charts use the level of mean low-water springs; in the United States it is mean low water; in France and Spain it is the lowest low water. *Mean high water* is the average of the high water over a 19-year period, and *mean low water* is the average of the low water over a 19-year period. *Higher high water* is the higher of the two high waters of any diurnal tidal day, and *lower low water* is the lower of the two low waters of any diurnal tidal day. *Mean higher high water* is the average height of

Table **2.2 Mean and Spring Tidal Ranges for Some of the Major Ports of the World**

	Mean range	Spring range
Anchorage, Alaska	26.7	29.6 *
Antwerp, Belgium	15.7	17.8
Bilbao, Spain	9.0	11.8
Bombay, India	8.7	11.8
Boston, Mass.	9.5	11.0
Buenos Aires, Argentina	2.2	2.4
Callao, Peru	1.8	2.4
Canal Zone, Atlantic side	0.7	1.1 *
Canal Zone, Pacific side	12.6	16.4
Capetown, Union of South Africa	3.8	5.2
Cherbourg, France	13.0	18.0
Dakar, Africa	3.3	4.4
Galveston, Tex.	1.0	1.4 *
Genoa, Italy	0.6	0.8
Hamburg, Germany	7.6	8.1
Havana, Cuba	1.0	1.2
Hong Kong, China	3.1	5.3 *
Honolulu, Hawaii	1.2	1.9 *
La Guaira, Venezuela	...	1.0 *
Lisbon, Portugal	8.4	10.8
Liverpool, England	21.2	27.1
Manila, Philippines	...	3.3 *
Murmansk, U.S.S.R.	7.9	9.9
New York, N.Y.	4.4	5.3
Oslo, Norway	1.0	1.1
Quebec, Canada	13.7	15.5
Rio de Janeiro, Brazil	2.5	3.5
Rotterdam, Netherlands	5.0	5.4
San Francisco, Calif.	4.0	5.7 *
San Juan, Puerto Rico	1.1	1.3
Seattle, Wash.	7.6	11.3 *
Southampton, England	10.0	13.6
Sydney, Australia	3.6	4.5
Valparaiso, Chile	3.0	3.9
Vladivostok, U.S.S.R.	0.6	0.7
Yokohama, Japan	3.5	4.7

* Diurnal range.

SOURCE: Tide Tables, U.S. Coast and Geodetic Survey.

the higher high water over a 19-year period, and *mean lower low water* is the average height of the lower low waters over a 19-year period. *Highest high water* and *lowest low water* are the highest and lowest, respectively, of the spring tides of record. *Mean range* is the height of mean high water above mean low water. The mean of this height is generally referred to as *mean sea level. Diurnal range* is the difference in height between the mean higher high water and the mean lower low water.

2.3 Waves

The behavior of water waves is one of the most intriguing and probably one of the least understood of nature's phenomena. Water waves may be caused by certain artificial disturbances such as moving vessels or explosions; or they may be caused by earthquakes, tides, or winds. It is the last which produce the waves in which engineers are most interested and which have the most influence on the design of marine structures. Generally, the tides, because of their slow rise and fall, have little effect on the formation of waves, except in the case of *tidal bores.* Tidal bores are a regular occurrence at certain locations and are a high crested single or solitary type of wave caused by the rush of flood tide up a river, as in the Amazon, or by the meeting of tides as in the Bay of Fundy.

Wave Form and Generation. Waves manifest themselves by curved undulations of the surface of the water occurring at periodic intervals, except for (1) waves of translation and (2) solitary waves or single waves of translation without any depression below still-water level.

Wave disturbance is felt to a considerable depth, and, therefore, the depth of water has an effect on the character of the wave. Deep-water waves are those which occur in water having a depth greater than one-half the wave length ($d > L/2$), at which depth the bottom does not have any significant influence on the motion of the water particles. Shallow-water waves are those which occur in water having a depth less than one-half the wave length ($d < L/2$), and the influence of the bottom changes the form of orbital motion from circular to elliptical or near-elliptical. Waves break when the forward velocity of the crest particles exceeds the velocity of propagation of the wave itself. In deep water this normally occurs when the wave height exceeds one-seventh of the wave length. When the wave reaches shallow water where the depth is equal to about one and one-quarter of its height it will usually break, although it may break in somewhat deeper water, depending upon the strength of the wind and the condition of the bottom. Figure 2.2 gives the maximum height of wave as a function of the water depth.

An unbroken wave is a wave of oscillation, and even after breaking in deep water the wave will usually re-form into an oscillatory wave of

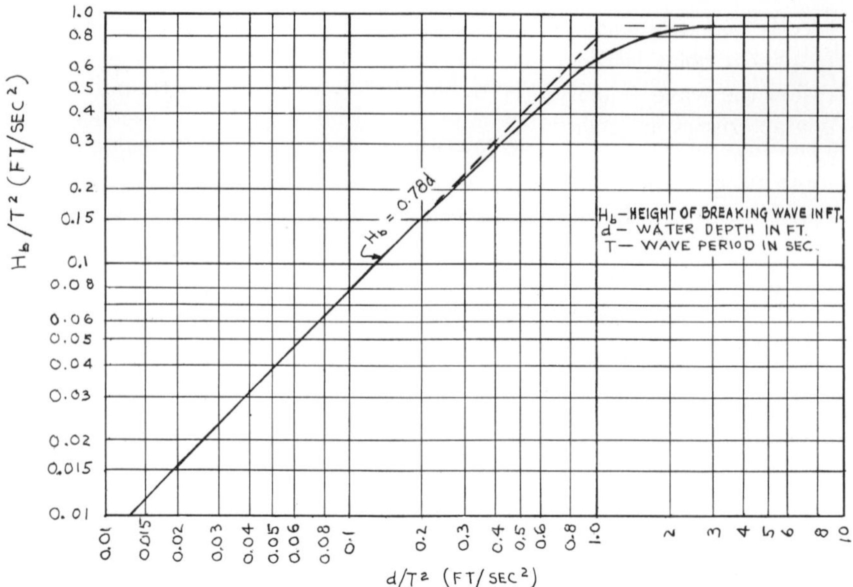

FIG. 2.2 Breaking index curve. (*From paper entitled Selection of Design Wave for Offshore Structures, by C. L. Bretschneider, Proceedings of the ASCE, March,* 1958.)

reduced height. It is only when it reaches shallow water and breaks without being able to re-form that it becomes a wave of translation, a familiar sight in the form of breakers along the shore. The only pure wave of translation is the solitary wave, which is a single crest of water above the still-water level, traveling without change of form at a constant speed, with a net displacement of water in the direction of wave travel. It is further characterized by its independence from wave length.

Figure 2.3 shows the oscillatory wave form and its characteristics. In deep water, each particle of water on the wave surface describes a circle, the radius of which is one-half the wave height about its normal center, midway between the crest and trough of the wave. The center line of rotation is elevated above the still-water level by the height h_0 because the crest is at a greater distance above still water than is the trough below it. The difference depends upon the wave steepness; for a very steep wave the proportion is about two-thirds above and one-third below the still-water level. At any instant the small arrows on the circular paths indicated by dotted circles in Fig. 2.3 show the relative position of the particles and their direction of motion in the formation of the wave. The heavy line connecting the arrows is the wave form at the surface of the water at that particular instant, the length between two consecutive crests is the wave length L, and the height between the trough and the crest is the wave height or amplitude H. The wave form travels over the water surface, and the time for two consecutive crests to pass a point is the wave period T. The speed of the wave form is called the wave velocity or velocity of wave propagation. These various characteristics are related by the following equations:

$$v = \frac{L}{T} = \sqrt{\frac{gL}{2\pi}} = \frac{gT}{2\pi} \qquad L = \frac{2\pi v^2}{g} = \frac{gT^2}{2\pi} \qquad T = \sqrt{\frac{2\pi L}{g}} = \frac{2\pi v}{g}$$

where v = velocity of propagation of wave, ft per sec
L = wave length (distance between consecutive wave crests), ft
T = wave period (time for wave to travel L ft), sec

If one characteristic is known, the others can be computed, and by substituting numerical values for the constants π and g, the acceleration of gravity, the following is obtained:

$$v = 2.26\sqrt{L} = 5.12T$$

$$L = 0.195\, v^2 = 5.12T^2$$

$$T = 0.442\sqrt{L} = 0.195v$$

The above relationship will be better understood by referring to Fig. 2.3, which shows the surface configuration of the ideal deep-water oscillatory wave as a trochoid formed by the particles of water in their circular orbits. This trochoid moves in the path of point A on the perimeter of a circle with a diameter equal to the wave height, which circle is concentric with a larger rolling circle whose circumference is equal to the wave length. Originally it was thought that the wave form was cycloidal; i.e., the particles of water in their circular orbits moved in the path of

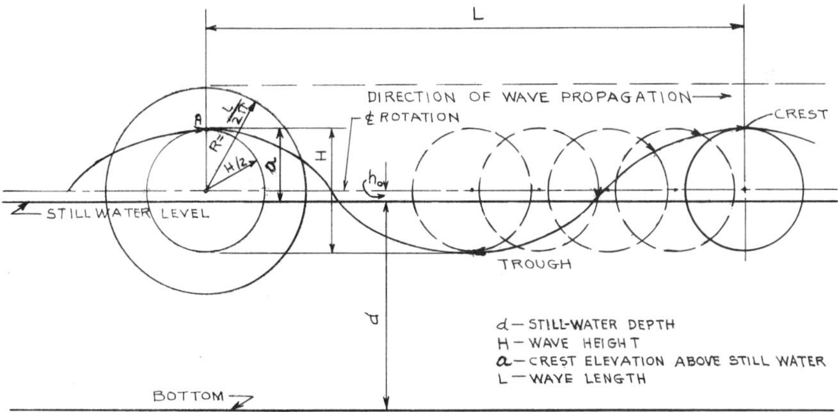

FIG. 2.3 Deep-water wave characteristics and form.

a given point on the perimeter of a circle with a diameter equal to the wave height. However, since waves have lengths varying from 12 to 40 or more times the wave height, it is obvious that, since the perimeter of the orbital motion of the surface particle is only a fraction of this length, the wave form must be created by a circle of orbital motion rolling in a larger circle whose perimeter is equal to the wave length. This results in the fixed point on the inner circle tracing a curve known as a trochoid. Since v, the forward velocity of the large rolling circle of radius R, equals $\sqrt{gR}$, by substituting $L/2\pi$ for R, it follows that $v = \sqrt{gL/2\pi} = 2.26\sqrt{L}$.

To the observer it may appear that the propagation or travel of the wave form, and particularly the crest, is due to a net displacement of the

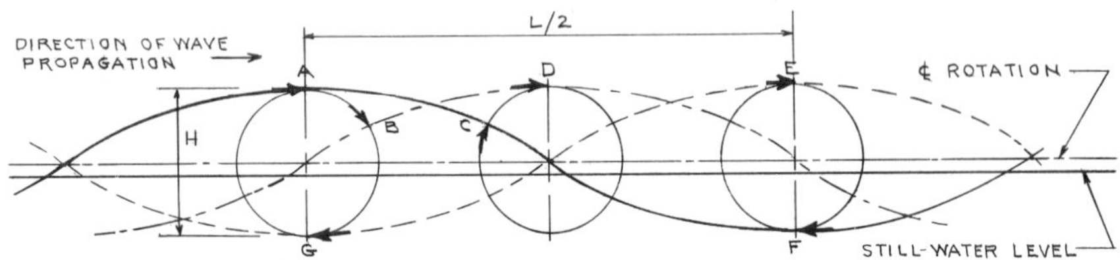

FIG. 2.4 Orbital motion related to wave propagation.

water in the direction of the wave travel. That this is not true is borne out by the fact that a floating object in deep water will rise and fall with the undulations of the waves but will not move horizontally unless it is moved by wind or current, except for a small back and forth motion caused by the orbital motion of the water particles.

It is the wave form and not the water which moves over the surface as a result of the orbital motion of the surface water particles, which oscillate back and forth, but do not advance. This is illustrated in Fig. 2.4. When the crest is at A and the trough is one-half wave length ahead at F, the surface water particle at A is moving clockwise in the direction of the propagation of the wave form and has reached its highest position; that at F is also moving clockwise but has reached its lowest position and is moving in a direction opposite to the wave travel. Further along on the wave surface at C, a water particle is moving upward, and, as the wave crest advances to D, an instant later, the particle at C has moved upward to D and that at A has moved downward to B on the advanced wave surface. When the crest reaches E, the particle at F has traveled around its orbital path to E and the particle at B has reached its lowest position in the trough at G. This means that behind the advancing crest the water is falling, as shown by the direction of the arrow at B, and ahead of the crest the water is rising, as indicated by the arrow at C.

At the crest and trough the orbital motion is horizontal and in opposite directions, and at one-quarter wave length each side of the crest the motion is vertical, its direction being downward behind the crest and upward in front of the crest.

So far we have discussed only the wave surface. The amplitude of waves in deep water decreases rapidly with the depth but the wave length remains the same, as shown in Fig. 2.5. The radii of the generat-

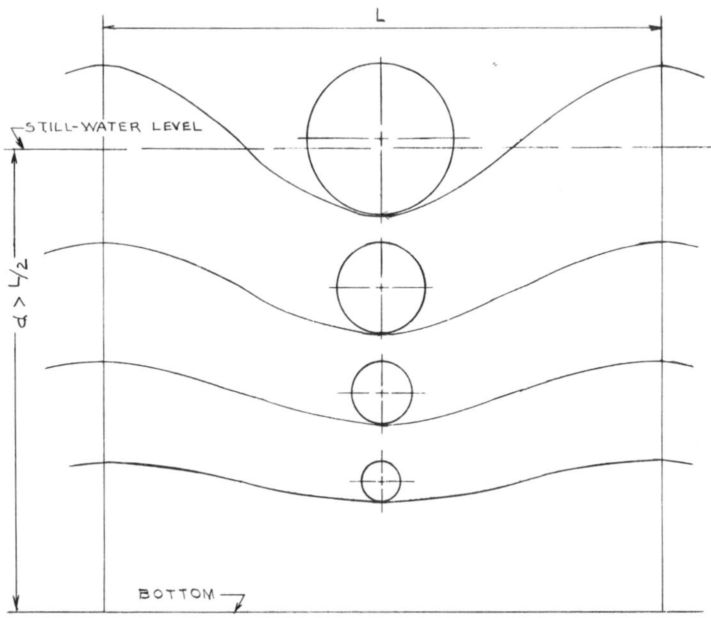

FIG. 2.5 Decrease in wave amplitude and orbital radii with increased depth.

ing circles, according to theory, decrease with the depth below the surface in a geometrical progression of which the common ratio is $1/\sqrt{e}$, where e is the base of Naperian logarithms. For a wave having a length equal to $15H$, the orbital radius at the deep-water limiting depth of $L/2$ or $7.5H$ would be only one twenty-third of the orbital radius at the surface. From this it is apparent that the bottom at this depth would have little effect on the form of the wave. Since the orbital velocities are proportioned to the orbital radii, they are largest at the surface and decrease rapidly with depth, becoming negligible at a depth of either $L/2$ or $2T^2$.

Wave motion in shallow water ($d < L/2$) is affected by the sea bottom, and the circular motion of the water particles becomes nearly elliptical, the major axis being horizontal. The ratio of the major to the minor axis becomes greater with increased depth, until near the bottom the orbital motion is almost entirely horizontal. Unlike the circular orbital motion in deep water, in which the horizontal and vertical velocities are equal, the orbital velocity in shallow water is greater in a horizontal than in a vertical direction. The velocity of wave propagation v in shallow water is obtained by multiplying the velocity in deep water ($v = 2.26\sqrt{L}$) by c, where $c = \sqrt{b/a}$, and b/a is the ratio of the vertical to the horizontal axis of the elliptical orbital motion, as given in Table 2.3. It should be noted that, when the depth is equal to $L/2$, the ratio is close to unity and the velocity is substantially that of a deep-water wave.

Whereas the motion of deep- and shallow-water waves maintains a

***Table* 2.3 Coefficients c for Velocity of Wave Propagation and μ for Orbital Velocity in Shallow Water**

d/L	c	μ	d/L	c	μ
0.05	0.552	1.814	0.30	0.977	1.023
0.10	0.746	1.340	0.35	0.988	1.013
0.15	0.858	1.165	0.40	0.994	1.007
0.20	0.922	1.085	0.45	0.997	1.004
0.25	0.958	1.044	0.50	0.998	1.002

certain degree of symmetry throughout the depth, as shown in Fig. 2.5, breaking waves lose this characteristic and are known by the rapid forward motion of the crest, while the lower part of the wave is slowly moving seaward in the opposite direction, there being a long, flat trough of relatively quiet water in back of the breaking crest. Unlike the wave travel, in form only, of a deep- or shallow-water wave, the breaking wave near shore causes a net forward displacement of a mass of water, since the orbital velocity at the surface has exceeded the velocity of wave travel.

The preceding description of wave form and generation has been written to give the reader a general understanding of this phenomenon in an easily comprehensible form. It is not intended to do more than touch on the various wave theories, and, without attempting to mention all of them, the following are some of the more important ones:

F. V. Gerstner, in 1802, laid the foundation for the modern wave theories. His formulas for geometrical relationships gave the first theoretical equations of wave motion. He assumed circular orbits with decreasing diameters at increasing depths, which is true only for deep-water waves. All particles have a constant angular velocity, and the surface of the water and all other streamlines with constant pressure are trochoids or curves described by a point on the spoke of a wheel while the wheel is rolling along a straight line.

G. B. Airy, in 1845, took a very similar approach but went beyond the pure geometrical treatment. He used elliptical orbits where necessary, but assumed that the crest is as high above still-water level as the trough is below it. This is true only for very small waves, which means that the Airy theory is correct only for very small waves, although it is valid for any depth.

G. G. Stokes, in 1880, pointed out some discrepancies in Gerstner's reasoning and, by eliminating them, developed formulas which take into account the fact that the crest rises higher above still-water level than the trough falls below it. The Airy theory is a special form of the Stokes theory for the case of very small waves.

In 1888 Saint-Venant and Flamant adapted the Gerstner theory to shallow-water waves by assuming the orbital motion to be elliptical.

All the preceding theories treat with oscillatory waves. J. Scott Russell, in 1838, first reported the existence of single waves of translation without any depression below the still-water level. He studied their characteristics, but in his time no significant application existed for this type of wave. The solitary wave theory grew in importance when later investigators found that oscillatory waves close to or at the maximum steepness, tidal bores, seismic waves, etc., could best be described by formulas developed for the solitary wave. All these applications occur in relatively shallow water and are, or can be considered as, single disturbances. The particular importance of the solitary wave theory lies in the fact that the engineer is interested mainly in maximum waves, which often can be treated as solitary waves with sufficient accuracy.

The engineer in the design of ports and marine structures will be confronted, in general, with the following problems involving wave action, which, except where noted, will be covered in subsequent sections in this chapter.

Forecasting wave height and length
Wave action on mound breakwaters (see Chap. 4)
Wave run-up on slopes (see Chap. 4)
Wave action on vertical walls, particularly breakwaters
Wave action on piles, cylinders, and caissons

Forecasting Wave Height and Length. The size of a wave for a particular location will depend upon the velocity of the wind, the duration of the wind, the direction of the wind, the greatest distance over which the wind can act, and the depth of the water.

In determining the wave to be used in the design of a structure at a particular location, only in exceptional cases will the designer be able to rely on a complete set of observations stretching over a sufficiently long period of time. General observations have been made, and the order of maximum significant wave height is generally known for such bodies of water as the Atlantic Ocean (45 ft), the Pacific Ocean (60 ft), the Mediterranean Sea (20 ft), the Black Sea (30 ft), the Great Lakes (25 ft), the Gulf of Mexico (40 ft), and Lake Maracaibo (10 ft). It is interesting to note that great expanses of water like the oceans do not necessarily produce waves of proportionally greater height than much smaller bodies such as the Gulf of Mexico or the Great Lakes. Ocean storms are generally more or less local, and the very long distance is not a controlling factor.

Thomas Stevenson, in 1864, established the first formulas for the relationship of fetch (F, nautical miles) and wave height (H, ft):

$$H = 1.5\sqrt{F} \qquad \text{for long fetches } (F > 30 \text{ nautical miles})$$

and

$$H = 1.5\sqrt{F} + 2.5 - \sqrt[4]{F} \qquad \text{for short fetches } (F < 30 \text{ nautical miles})$$

They were developed from observations on lakes but checked with waves on the coast of the North Sea. They give the wave height only for maximum wind velocity in the observation area, since they do not include wind velocity as a variable.

Captain D. D. Gaillard, Corps of Engineers, United States Army, in 1904, reported an extensive collection of observations on the height of ocean waves. D. A. Molitor, in his paper, Wave Pressure on Sea-walls and Breakwaters, published in the *Proceedings* of the American Society of Civil Engineers (May, 1934), gives the following formulas for determining wave height for inland lakes based on the formulas of Thomas Stevenson with the introduction of wind velocity as a variable and the use of statute miles instead of nautical miles:

$$H = 0.17\sqrt{UF} \qquad \text{for values of } F \text{ greater than 20 miles}$$

$$H = 0.17\sqrt{UF} + 2.5 - \sqrt[4]{F} \qquad \text{for values of } F \text{ less than 20 miles}$$

where U = wind velocity, statute miles per hour
F = fetch, statute miles
H = wave height, ft

The ratio of wave length to height depends on the wind velocity, the duration of the storm, the depth of water, and the character of the bottom. According to observations made by Captain Gaillard, the ratio L/H for inland lakes, in relatively shallow depth, is between 9 and 15, and for ocean waves L/H is between 17 and 33. The ratios are more or less inversely proportional to the wind intensity, with the smaller ratio for the stronger wind intensity.

Since World War II considerable work has been done on the forecasting of tide and wave conditions from meteorological, oceanographic, and geographic data. The forerunner of this came during the war, when the need for predicting the wave conditions at invasion landing beaches

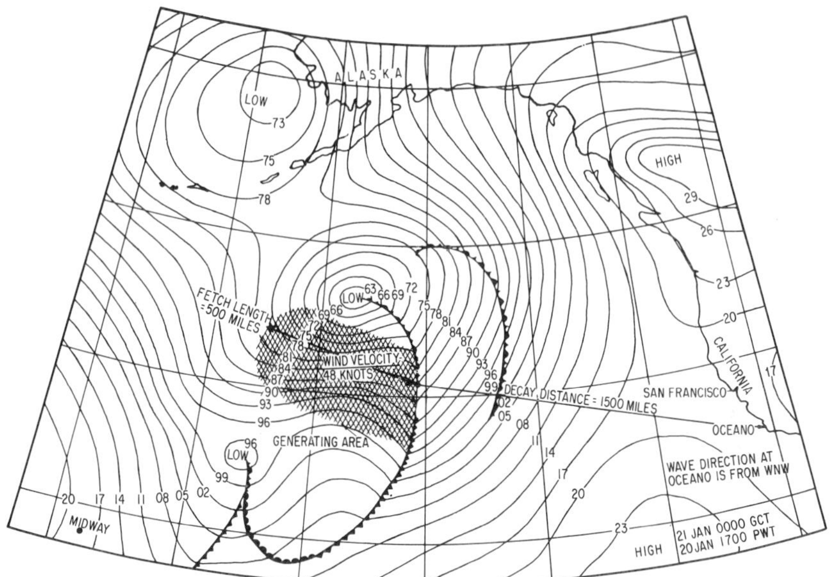

FIG. 2.6 Synoptic weather map, showing generating area, fetch, and decay distance. (*From Waves, Tides, Currents and Beaches: Glossary of Terms and List of Standard Symbols, by R. L. Wiegel, Council on Wave Research.*)

spurred forecasting research. After the war, the advent of offshore structures for oil wells and radar stations kept research work going. In making observations on the height of wave for design purposes it is necessary to keep in mind that in a train of waves the height of individual waves will vary greatly. Anyone who has watched the waves or has been on the water during a storm knows that every so often a wave much higher than any of the others will come along. The average height of the highest one-third of the waves for a stated interval has been termed the significant height, and it has been found that the highest or maximum wave has a height of about 1.87 times the significant height.

The following factors have their influence on the generation and decay of waves, and data about these factors are needed to forecast the design wave.

Fetch. Storms are limited in area, and waves are generated only within this area. The horizontal extension of the generating area in the direction of the wind is called the fetch. Synoptic weather maps (Fig. 2.6) help in determining generating area and fetch for a given location. At coastal points the fetch is limited by geographical barriers such as islands and promontories, and the fetch has to be determined for each direction.

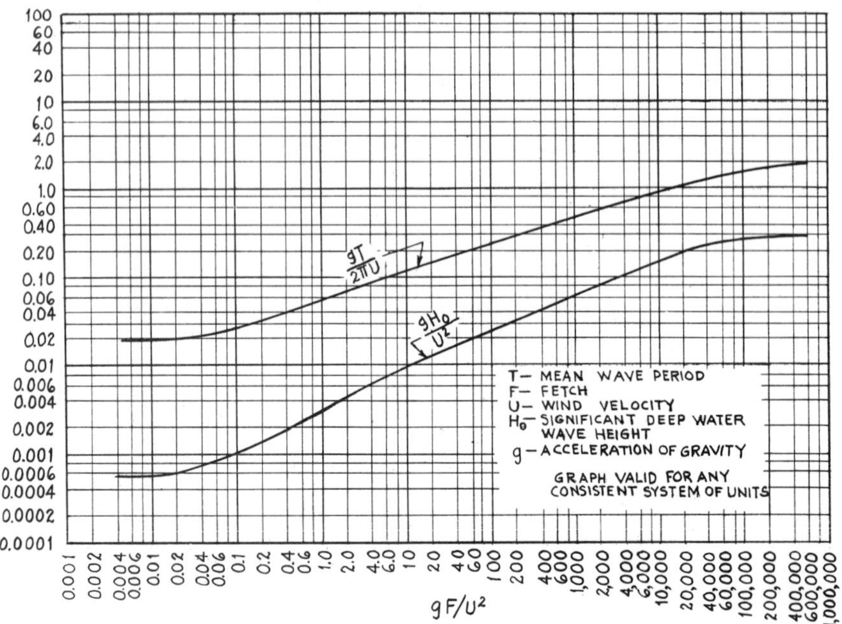

FIG. 2.7 Significant wave height and period as functions of fetch and wind velocity, for deep water and unlimited wind duration. (*From paper entitled Revisions in Wave Forecasting: Deep and Shallow Water, by C. L. Bretschneider, Proceedings of Sixth Conference on Coastal Engineering, published by Council on Wave Research.*)

Wind velocity and direction. Waves are generated by the transfer of energy from air moving over the water surface. The transfer is effected in two ways. (1) The water surface reacts to small differences in pressure of the moving air, which creates the first variations in the water level. These are increased by the difference in pressure exerted by the moving wind on the back and on the front of the wave. (2) Tangential stress occurs between the two fluids, air and water, which are in contact and moving at different speeds relative to each other. Since both normal pressure and tangential stress are functions of the wind velocity, it follows that wave characteristics also are functions of wind velocity.

H. U. Sverdrup and W. H. Munk in their paper, Wind, Sea and Swell: Theory of Relations for Forecasting, published by the Hydrographic

Office, United States Navy, in 1947, developed a theory for the growth of waves based on the energy budget of significant waves. They established graphs for the relationships among fetch, wind velocity, wave height, and wave period. Figure 2.7 shows similar graphs as published by C. L. Bretschneider in his paper, Revisions in Wave Forecasting: Deep and Shallow Water, published in the *Proceedings* of the Sixth Conference

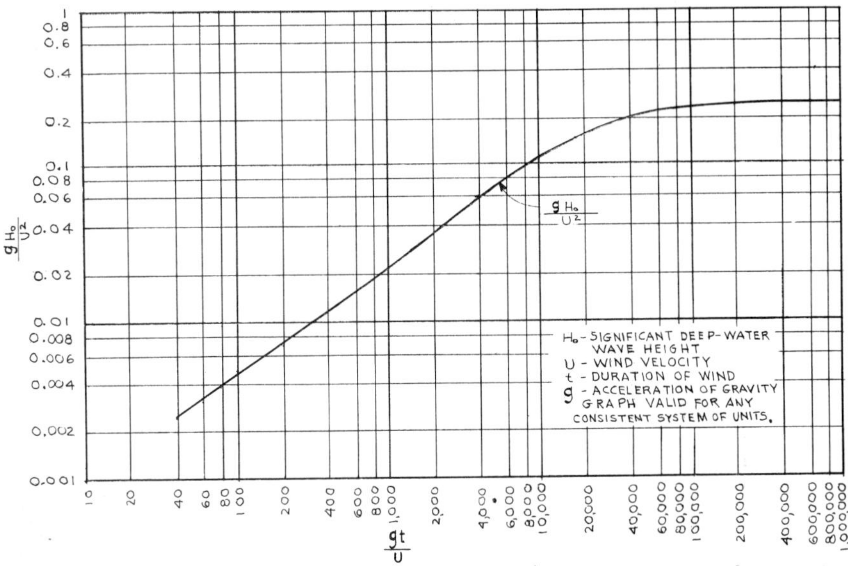

FIG. 2.8 Wave height as a function of wind duration for constant wind velocity and unlimited fetch. (*From Wind, Sea and Swell: Theory of Relations for Forecasting, by H. U. Sverdrup and W. H. Munk, United States Hydrographic Office.*)

on Coastal Engineering (1958). The straight portion of the graph corresponds closely to the formulas

$$H_0 = 0.0555UF^{0.5}$$

and

$$T = 0.5U^{0.5}F^{0.25}$$

where U, the wind velocity, is in knots and F is in nautical miles. The wave height H_0 thus determined corresponds to the significant wave height in deep water. Structures should be designed for the maximum height which is about 1.87 times the significant height.

Wind duration. Only after a wind of a certain velocity has blown for a certain time will the wave generated by it have attained the characteristics typical for this wind velocity. The wave increases rapidly at first, but grows at an ever-slower rate the longer the wind lasts. According to Sverdrup and Munk, the relationship between wave height and wind duration follows the curve given in Fig. 2.8. However, it is normally assumed that the wind blows long enough for the maximum wave to develop for that particular wind velocity, unless observed wind data contradict this assumption.

Water depth. Waves generated in shallow waters are limited in height by two factors: bottom friction and breaking. Bottom friction increases with growing waves, and eventually a steady state is reached where the energy transmitted by the wind is spent by bottom friction and no energy is left for wave growth. The wave characteristics of the steady state are thus related to the water depth and, of course, to the wind velocity. They also depend on the friction factor which can be taken as $f = 0.01$ for most cases. Figure 2.9 gives this relationship in graph form. The wave height in shallow water has a further limitation. Before the wave reaches the steady state it may break. This occurs when the wave reaches a height approximately 0.8 times the still-water depth (Fig. 2.2). Once a wave has started breaking, the additional energy transmitted to it by the wind is spent in its breaking crest, and no more growth can be achieved.

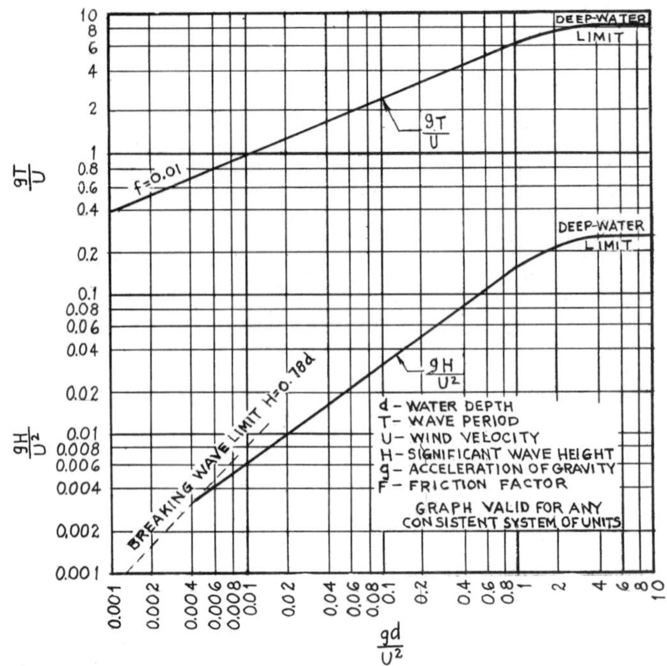

FIG. 2.9 Significant wave height and period as functions of water depth and wind velocity, for shallow water of constant depth and unlimited fetch and wind duration. (*From paper entitled Revisions in Wave Forecasting: Deep and Shallow Water, by C. L. Bretschneider, Proceedings of Sixth Conference on Coastal Engineering, published by Council on Wave Research.*)

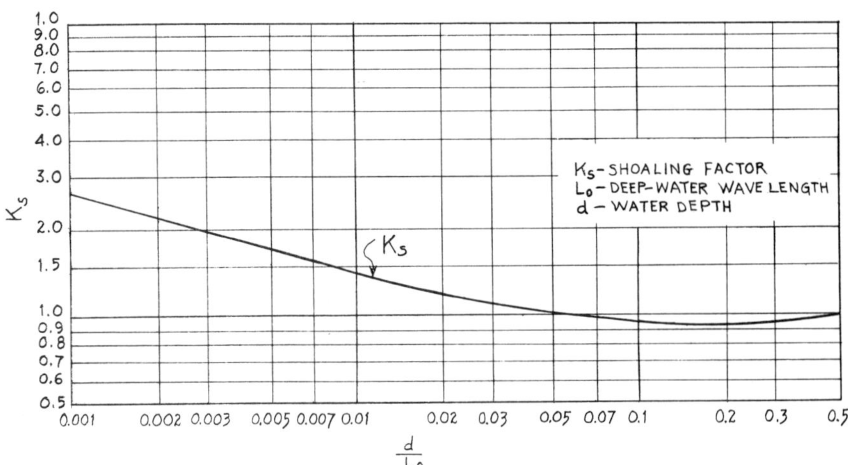

FIG. 2.10 Swell moving into shoaling water; shoaling factor. (*From Breakers and Surf, United States Hydrographic Office.*)

Another important consideration is the behavior of waves generated in deep water, which move into shallow waters without any further wind acting on them. In this case the bottom normally has a bottom slope m, and two counteracting influences take place on the wave height. One is the bottom friction which tends to reduce the wave height, and the other is the shoaling effect which tends to increase the wave height. As waves move into shoaling waters, the wave energy becomes confined in ever-decreasing depths of water. The amount of water on which the energy is acting becomes smaller, the energy per water particle increases, and the wave height increases. This can be shown to occur at a rate indicated by the shoaling factor K_s given by the graph in Fig. 2.10. On the other hand, the bottom friction increases as the water depth decreases. The combined effect has been investigated by C. L. Bretschneider and R. O. Reid and is given in Bretschneider's report, Generation of Wind Waves over a Shallow Bottom, published by the Beach Erosion Board (1954). They propose the following formula:

$$H = H_0 K_s \left[\frac{fH_0}{mT^2} \int_{\infty}^{d/T^2} \phi_f \, \delta \left(\frac{d}{T^2} \right) + 1 \right]^{-1}$$

where H = wave height at depth d
H_0 = wave height in deep water
K_s = the shoaling factor (Fig. 2.10)
f = friction factor (assumed $f = 0.01$)
m = bottom slope
ϕ_f = a function of K_s and d/L

The integral

$$\frac{d}{T^2}\int_{\infty}^{d/T^2} \phi_f \, \delta\left(\frac{d}{T^2}\right)$$

is given in terms of d/T^2 in Fig. 2.11, which facilitates the numerical solution of actual problems.

A wave generated in deep water, when reaching shoaling waters, changes not only its height but also its length. The period, however, remains constant. Airy already has established the relationship between the deep-water wave length L_0 and the shallow-water wave length L_A:

$$\frac{L_A}{L_0} = \tanh \frac{2\pi d}{L_A}$$

As stated before, the Airy theory is applicable only for very small waves. Reid and Bretschneider developed a correction factor L/L_A for wave steepness, which is a function of water depth, wave height, and period. Graphs for both ratios are published in Bretschneider's paper, Selection of Design Wave for Offshore Structures, in the August, 1958, *Proceedings* of the American Society of Civil Engineers. From them the combined graph of Fig. 2.12 for L/L_0 was developed, which allows the

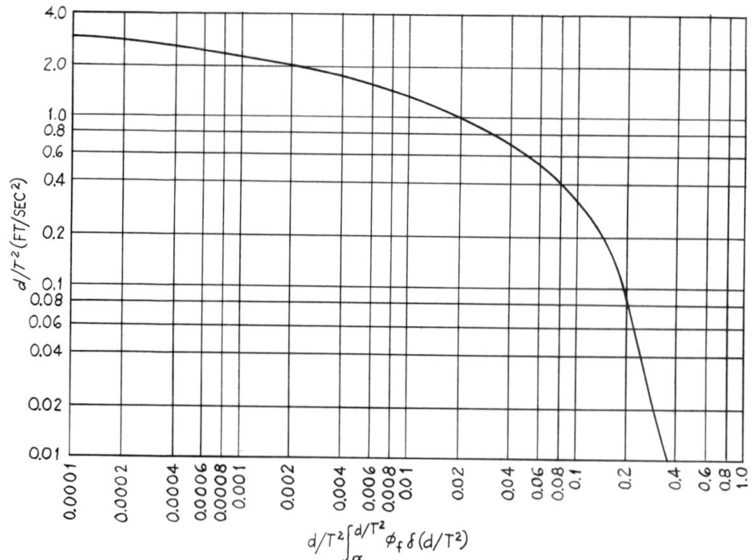

FIG. 2.11 Swell moving into shoaling water; values of integral in formula for bottom friction. (*From Modification of Wave Height Due to Bottom Friction, Percolation, and Refraction, by C. L. Bretschneider and R. O. Reid, United States Beach Erosion Board.*)

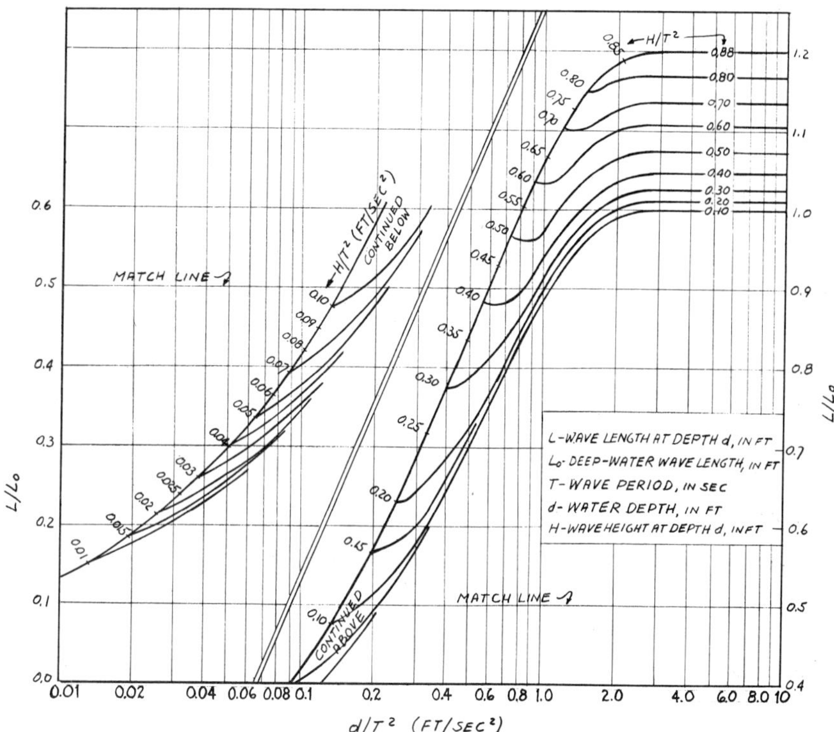

FIG. 2.12 Swell moving into shoaling water; wave length as function of water depth, wave height, and period.

computation of the wave length at any depth from the deep-water wave length L_0.

Finally the ratio $a:H$ of the crest height above still-water level to wave height also changes as a wave moves into shoaling waters. Figure 2.13 is the reproduction of a graph given by Bretschneider in the paper mentioned, which enables one to find the crest elevation above still-water level if water depth, wave height, and wave period are known.

Wave decay. As waves travel away from their generating area, they continuously lose energy and their height decreases, but their length, period, and velocity of progress increase (see Fig. 2.14). It is mainly the air resistance which brings about the decay of the waves, while the influence of the molecular viscosity or internal friction is negligible.

There are a number of other factors which influence the characteristics of waves, especially in harbors or coastal areas:

Diffraction. A typical example of wave diffraction occurs in a harbor completely protected by breakwaters (see Fig. 2.15). The gap in the breakwater which serves as a shipping channel admits a certain amount

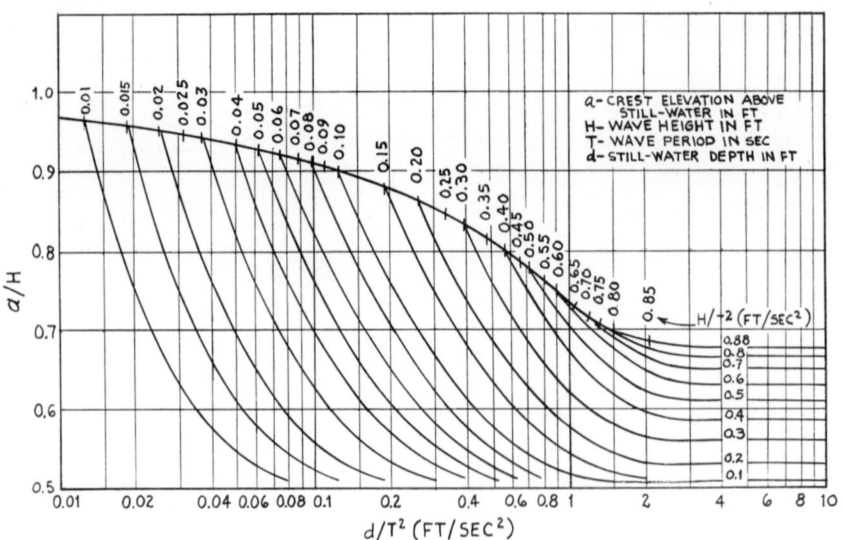

FIG. 2.13 Crest elevation in shoaling water as function of water depth, wave height, and period. (*From paper entitled Selection of Design Wave for Offshore Structures, by C. L. Bretschneider, Proceedings of the ASCE, March,* 1958.)

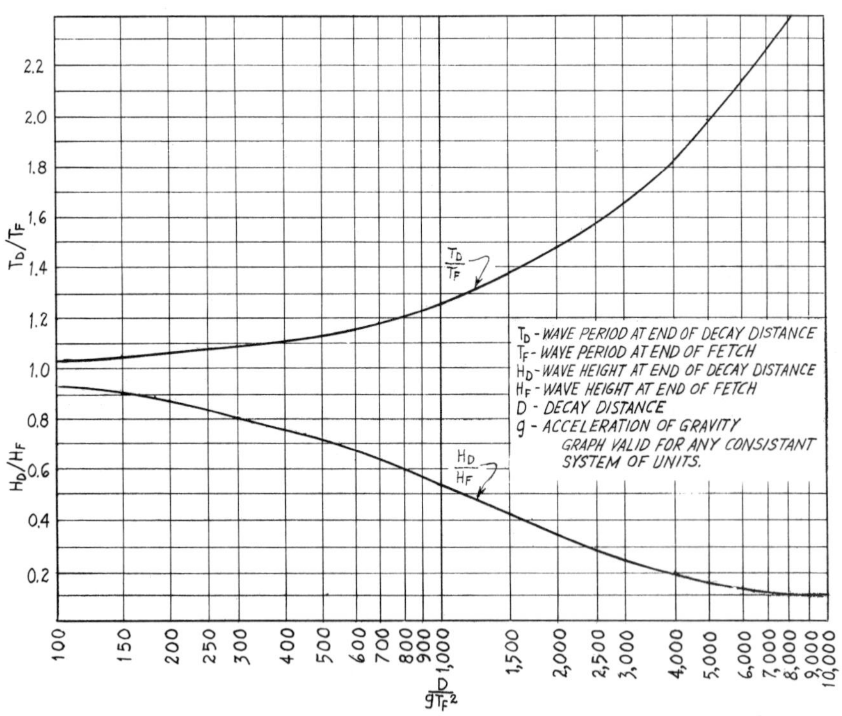

FIG. 2.14 Wave decay, wave height, and period as functions of decay distance. (*From Wind, Sea and Swell: Theory of Relations for Forecasting, by H. U. Sverdrup and W. H. Munk, United States Hydrographic Office.*)

of waves into the otherwise still waters of the harbor. These waves expand over the whole harbor area in wave fronts which have their center at the gap. Since the wave fronts become ever more extensive as they travel away from the gap, their energy decreases. Therefore, the farther away a structure is from the gap, the smaller are the waves acting upon it (see page 93).

Refraction. If a wave group travels in shallow water at an angle to the contour lines of the bottom, the waves in shallower water become

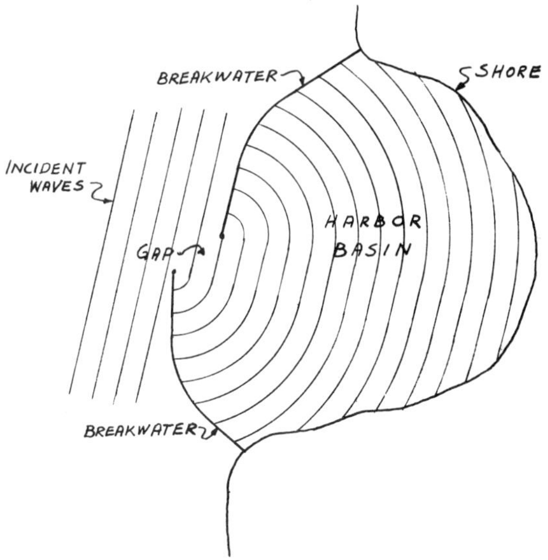

FIG. 2.15 Schematic diffraction pattern.

shorter and their velocity decreases. This means that as the portion of a wave in deeper water advances more rapidly than the portion in shallow water, the wave front turns and tends to become parallel to the bottom contours. At a gently sloping beach the wave crests are always nearly parallel to the coast line for any angle they may form out at sea. The wave height is governed by the refraction coefficient (equal to the square root of the ratio of the spacing between adjacent orthogonals at two different points) in addition to the shoaling coefficient discussed above. Figure 2.16 shows a typical refraction diagram and its construction. It is taken from the manual "Breakers and Surf" of the Hydrographic Office, United States Navy (November, 1944). Assume that a refraction diagram is to be constructed for waves from a given direction and with given deep-water characteristics H_0, L_0, and T. First, parallel deep-water wave crests are drawn on a hydrographic chart at convenient distances nL_0 where n is the crest interval. In most cases, drawing every crest would bring the lines too close to one another. Curve *A* represents the values of nL for each depth as computed from L_0 with the help of Fig. 2.12, and is drawn on transparent paper at the same scale as the chart. The example of Fig. 2.16, where $n = 2$, shows how points on crest line 10 can be constructed from crest line 8. Place curve *A* on the chart so that the 10-fathom line and the broken center line on graph *A* and the 10-fathom contour line on the chart intersect in one point, marked *a*. By moving

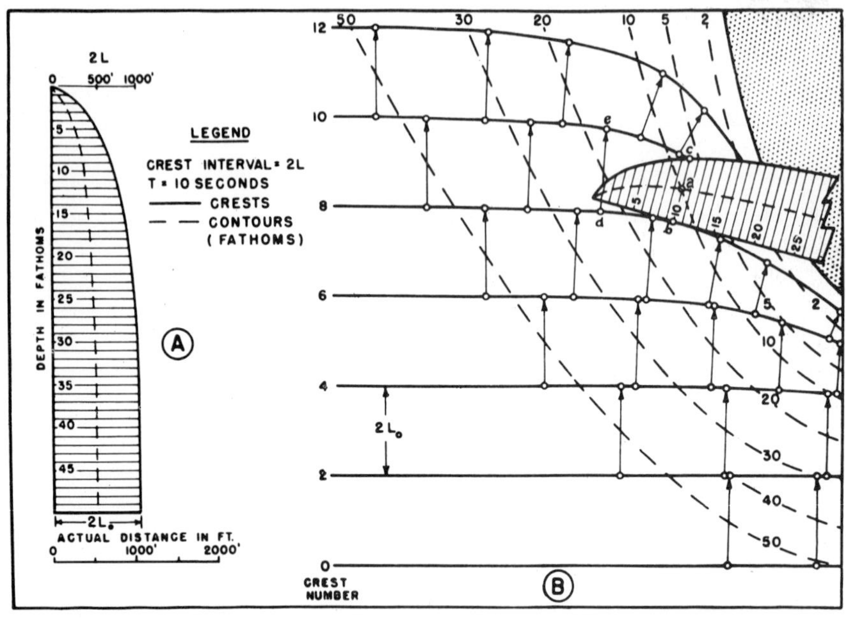

FIG. 2.16 Construction of refraction diagram. (*From Breakers and Surf, United States Hydrographic Office.*)

point *a* along the contour line and turning the graph, the straight side of graph *A* can be made tangent to crest 8. Point *c* marks then a point of crest 10. This procedure is repeated for each contour line, until crest 10 is completed. Construction of crest 12 can then be started in similar manner.

Reflection. Nonbreaking waves acting on a vertical wall, cliff, or steep beach do not lose their energy by the impact but are reflected. They may form a standing wave or clapotis. As a matter of principle, it is desirable to destroy the wave energy inside a harbor as soon as possible, and not to allow it to be reflected back and forth. There are many methods to minimize wave reflection in harbors. Breakwaters must be aligned in such a way that the waves reflected from them are not directed toward piers and other harbor installations. Their interior slope can be designed for the waves to break, which spends the wave energy. Special spending beaches can be planned at points of maximum wave action in a harbor.

Tidal bores. When waves travel in a channel with converging sides, their total energy acts on a decreasing width with the result that they grow higher and higher. In exceptional cases a tidal wave may form a steep wall of water, which rushes up such a channel or river estuary, forming what is known as a tidal bore.

A *seiche* is a very long standing wave on a large but limited body of water, generally occurring when a storm dies down after producing a wind tide.

Swells are waves generated by storms which occur outside the area of observation.

Wave Action on Vertical Walls. Vertical walls may be mainly classified in two groups, breakwaters and seawalls. Breakwaters are normally built in water deep enough to keep attacking waves from breaking. Seawalls, on the other hand, are generally built at the top of a beach and are subjected to the action of breaking waves. There is a considerable difference in wave pressure between the two types, breaking waves exerting a much greater pressure. The energy of the breaking wave is destroyed at the wall and, therefore, transmits a much greater energy to the wall than the nonbreaking wave, whose energy is mostly reflected by the wall.

If the wall is not built high enough, part of the wave will overtop the wall and cause disturbance on its lee side. Overtopping also may not be desirable for reasons of structural safety of the wall. Therefore, it will be assumed that the wall is high enough to obstruct totally the attacking waves.

A considerable amount of full-scale and model test data has been collected since the first full-scale tests by Thomas Stevenson in the middle of the last century. A number of formulas were developed based on theoretical considerations and on experimental data. The complexity of actual wave patterns, the large number of variable factors, and the difficulty in reproducing models which give data significant for the prototype have all contributed to the fact that even now the design of a vertical breakwater or seawall cannot be achieved with the same degree of safety and economy possible for many other structures.

The wave pressure against vertical walls consists of (1) the hydrostatic pressure which varies as the wave rises and falls along the wall, and (2) the dynamic pressure exerted by the moving water particles. A number of theories and formulas have been developed over the years for the determination of the pressure of waves on vertical walls. Solutions produced by d'Auria (1890), Lira (1926), and Iribarren (1938) have been called the static-dynamic methods. These assume that the presence of the wall does not affect the wave movement, which is contrary to actual conditions, and, therefore, they have not obtained general acceptance. Victor Benezit, in 1923, was the first to consider the effect of the clapotis, or standing waves reflected by the wall, on the pressure against the vertical wall. In 1928 George Sainflou derived equations for pressures on vertical walls, based on certain approximations of the motion of standing, elliptically trochoidal waves in front of the wall. M. Gourret, in 1935, analyzed the methods of Benezit and Sainflou and developed another group of formulas which give results very similar to the Sainflou formulas.

From the Saint-Venant and Flamant theory a water particle at the surface of a deep-water wave oscillates about a point whose height above still-water level is given as

$$h_0 = \frac{\pi H^2}{4L} \coth \frac{2\pi d}{L}$$

Therefore, the crest height above still-water level, $a = h_0 + H/2$. When this wave is reflected from a vertical wall a clapotis is created. The surface of this clapotis at its highest position is also a trochoid according to Saint-Venant and Flamant. The height of the center of oscillation above still-water level is raised to

$$h_{0c} = \frac{\pi H^2}{L} \coth \frac{2\pi d}{L}$$

or four times the height in the case of the unreflected wave. The wave height of the clapotis is $2H$, twice the wave height of the unreflected wave. The crest height above still-water level, $a = H + 4h_0$ or slightly more than twice the crest height for the unreflected wave.

Sainflou computed a general formula for the pressure on a vertical wall, from which the pressure diagram shown in Fig. 2.17 can be constructed, and the pressure at the bottom is

$$\gamma d \pm p_2 = \gamma d \pm \frac{\gamma H}{\cosh 2\pi d/L}$$

where γ = specific weight of water.

The plus sign applies for the wave at crest position and the minus sign for the wave at trough position. Straight lines may be substituted for the actual pressure curves without affecting the results appreciably, which simplifies the calculation of pressure on a vertical wall. For the wave at crest position the wave pressure at the still-water level, by simple proportion, is

$$p_1 = (\gamma d + p_2) \frac{H + h_{0c}}{H + h_{0c} + d}$$

Where still-water hydrostatic pressure acts on the opposite side of the wall the resulting net pressure on the wall is shown in the lower portion of Fig. 2.17, where the diagram on the left gives the pressure for the

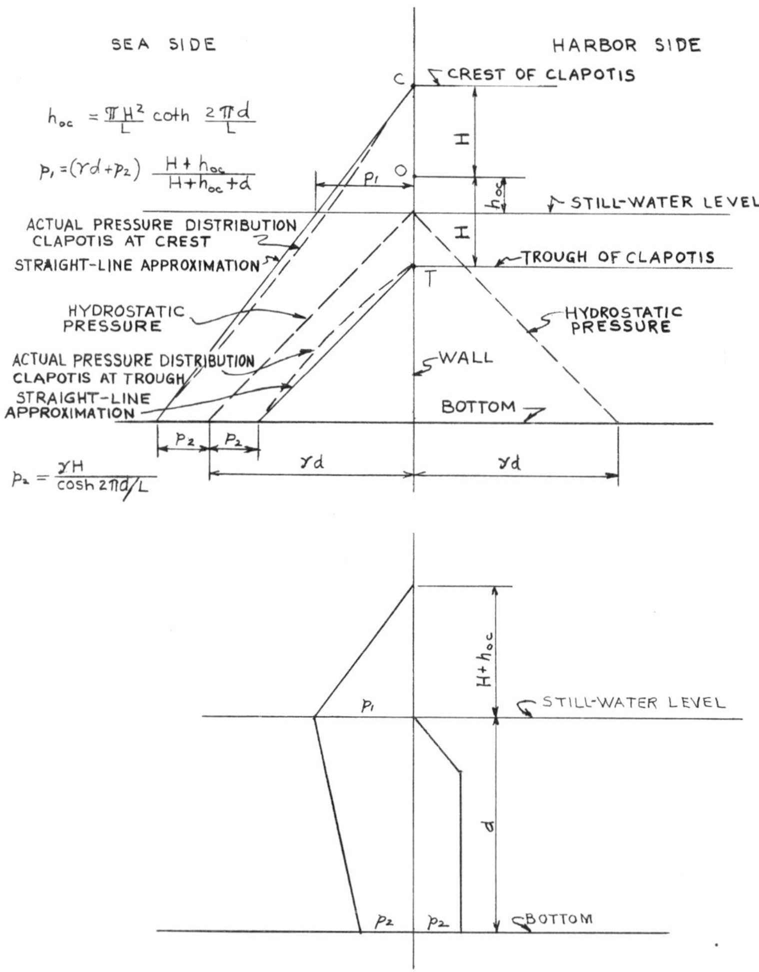

FIG. 2.17 Wave pressure on vertical walls, according to Sainflou.

clapotis at crest position, and the diagram on the right gives the pressure for the clapotis at trough position.

In 1934 D. A. Molitor developed an empirical method of computing wave pressures on a vertical breakwater, using test data gathered in the Great Lakes at the beginning of the century by Captain D. D. Gaillard. The pressure diagram proposed by Molitor is shown in Fig. 2.18 and is constructed as follows. The maximum wave pressure is

$$p_1 = \frac{k\gamma}{2g}(v + v_o)^2$$

where k = a coefficient, between 1.3 and 1.7 for winds 30 to 70 miles per hour on the Great Lakes and 1.8 for ocean storm waves

γ = specific weight of water (64.4 lb per cu ft for salt water)

g = acceleration of gravity (32.2 ft per sec per sec)

v = velocity of wave propagation, ft per sec ($v = 2.26c\sqrt{L}$; for values of c see Table 2.3)

v_o = maximum orbital velocity, ft per sec ($v_o = 7.11\mu H/\sqrt{L}$; for values of μ see Table 2.3)

H = wave height, ft

L = wave length, ft

The maximum wave pressure occurs at a height h_1 above still-water level:

$$h_1 = 0.12H$$

If the wave is fully obstructed by the wall, it will reach a height of $2a$ above still-water. At that height the pressure is zero. The crest height of the unobstructed wave, according to Captain Gaillard, is

$$a = \frac{H}{2} + \frac{H^2}{L} \qquad \text{for } d > 1.84H$$

and

$$a = \frac{H}{2} + \frac{2H^2}{L} \qquad \text{for } d < 1.84H$$

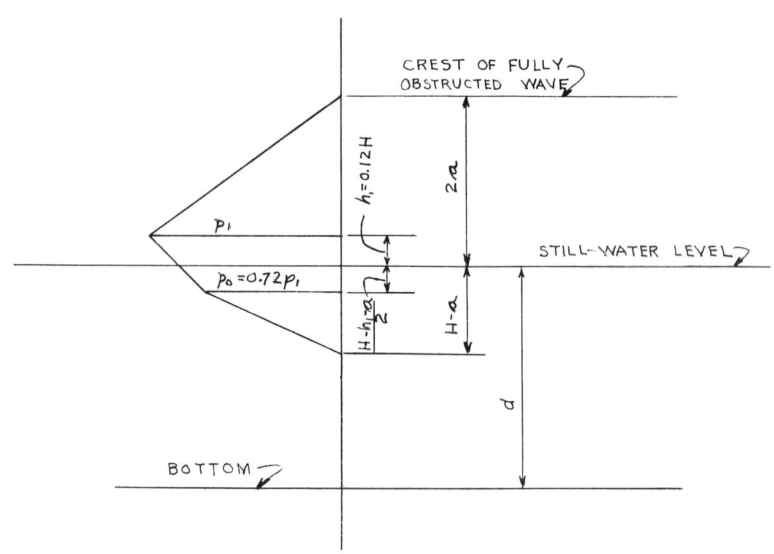

FIG. 2.18 Wave pressure on vertical walls, according to Molitor.

The pressure diagram is a straight line between the crest of the fully obstructed wave and the point of maximum pressure h_1 above still-water level. Molitor assumes that at and below the trough elevation ($H - a$ below still-water level) the wave pressure is zero. Halfway between the trough elevation and the point of maximum pressure, the wave pressure is $0.72p$. Molitor's pressure diagram gives the maximum pressure at each elevation. It is therefore not a diagram for one particular wave position and gives values of total pressure which are too high. It also ignores the pressure below the wave trough.

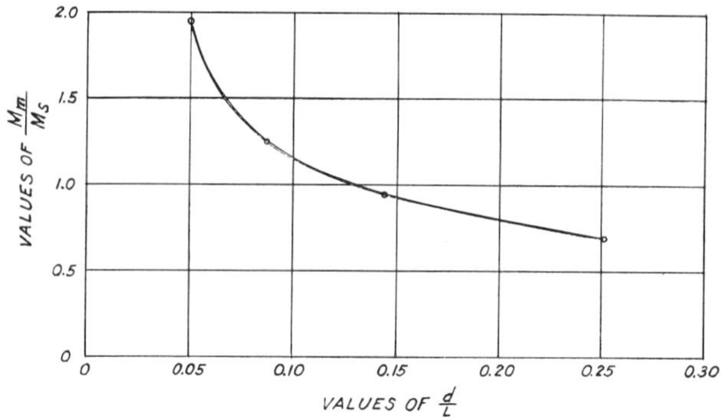

FIG. 2.19 Comparison of test results of overturning moment on vertical breakwater with moment obtained from Sainflou theory. (*From paper entitled Wave Forces on Breakwaters, by R. Y. Hudson, Transactions of the ASCE,* 1953.)

Robert Y. Hudson, hydraulic engineer, chief of Wave Action Section, United States Army Engineer Waterways Experiment Station, Vicksburg, Mississippi, in a paper published in the *Transactions* of the American Society of Civil Engineers, volume 118, 1953, reviewed the theories already mentioned. In addition this paper gives a comparison between the results of tests at the United States Waterways Experiment Station and overturning moments about the base calculated from the Sainflou theory. This comparison is shown in Fig. 2.19. It is interesting to note that for ratios of d/L in the range of 0.1 to 0.2, which are quite commonly found in actual installations of breakwaters, the moments obtained from the Sainflou theory agree quite closely with the model test moments. It is only when the value of d/L approaches 0.05 that a wide divergence exists and for this ratio the depth of water is so shallow that the wave approaches the breaking condition. For example, if the depth of water is 20 ft, the height of wave 20 ft, and the length 400 ft, d/L will equal 0.05; but the wave will break when it approaches a depth equal to or a little greater than its height, and, therefore, the Sainflou theory should not be used. If the breakwater is properly designed so that the depth of water is at least $2H$ or 40 ft, d/L becomes 0.10 and the ratio of

M_m/M_s becomes about 1.15, or a reasonably close agreement between the test results and the Sainflou theory.

The author believes that for the purely oscillatory wave condition which occurs in front of a vertical breakwater, where the water is too deep for the wave to break, the theory of Sainflou gives the closest approximation to the actual wave force which occurs against the vertical face of the breakwater.

Figure 2.20 shows a typical vertical-wall breakwater in 70-ft depth of water resting on a rubble base at a depth of 50 ft, and subjected to the

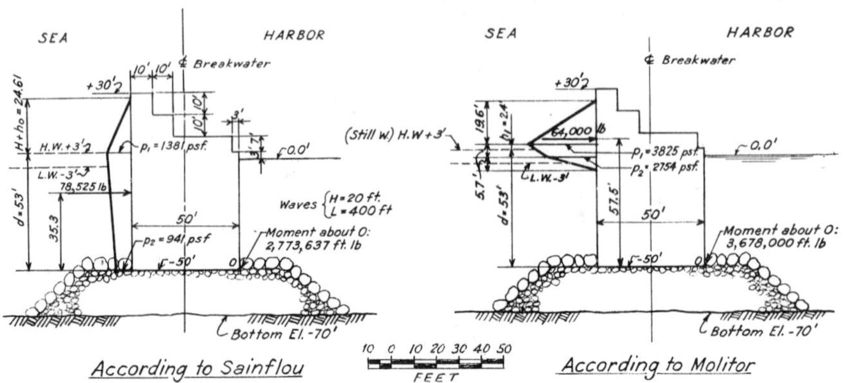

FIG. 2.20 Comparison of wave forces on vertical-wall breakwaters, derived by Sainflou and Molitor theories.

force of a 20-ft nonbreaking wave with a length of 400 ft. Therefore, $H/L = 0.05$ and $d/L = 0.125$. The wave-pressure diagram, total horizontal force, and overturning moment about the base are indicated for the methods of wave-force determination of Sainflou and Molitor.

The derivation of the wave force in each case is as follows, assuming still water at the high-water stage of $+3$ ft.

Sainflou. The net wave pressure at the toe of the breakwater is given as

$$p_2 = \frac{\gamma H}{\cosh\,(2\pi d/L)}$$

Using the value of $\gamma = 64.4$ lb per cu ft for the specific weight of sea water, we obtain

$$p_2 = 941 \text{ lb per sq ft}$$

The maximum wave pressure is given as

$$p_1 = (p_2 + \gamma d)\,\frac{H + h_{0c}}{d + H + h_{0c}} = 1{,}381 \text{ lb per sq ft}$$

which occurs at the still-water level.

The height above the still-water level of the wave crest at the wall is given as $H + h_{0c}$

where $$h_{0c} = \frac{\pi H^2}{L} \coth \frac{2\pi d}{L} = 4.61$$

By computing the total area of the wave-pressure diagram, the total wave force per linear foot of breakwater can be determined as

$$P = (H + h_{0c})\frac{p_1}{2} + \frac{p_1 d}{2} + \frac{p_2 d}{2} = 16{,}993 + 36{,}596 + 24{,}936 = 78{,}525 \text{ lb}$$

and its overturning moment about point O as

$$M = 16{,}993\left(d + \frac{H + h_{0c}}{3}\right) + 36{,}596\frac{2d}{3} + 24{,}936\frac{d}{3} = 2{,}773{,}637 \text{ ft-lb}$$

Molitor. According to Molitor the maximum wave pressure is

$$p_1 = \frac{k\gamma}{2g}(v + v_o)^2$$

$$v = 2.26 \times 0.830 \times \sqrt{400} = 37.5 \text{ ft per sec}$$

$$v_o = 7.11 \times 1.209 \times \frac{20}{\sqrt{400}} = 8.6 \text{ ft per sec}$$

Coefficients $c = 0.830$ and $\mu = 1.209$ are obtained from Table 2.3.

$$p_1 = \frac{1.8 \times 64.4}{2 \times 32.2}(37.5 + 8.6)^2$$

$$p_1 = 3{,}825 \text{ lb per sq ft}$$

The maximum wave pressure occurs at $h_1 = 0.12H = 2.4$ ft above still-water level.

The height of the wave crest above the still-water level, assuming that the breakwater obstructs the wave completely, is given as

$$2a = 2\left(\frac{H}{2} + \frac{H^2}{L}\right) = 22.0 \text{ ft}$$

The wave pressure becomes zero at the depth of the unobstructed wave trough, or $H - a = 9.0$ ft below still-water level. Midway between this point and the point of maximum pressure the wave pressure is given as

$$p_2 = 0.72p_1 = 2{,}754 \text{ lb per sq ft}$$

As in the Sainflou method the total horizontal wave force and the overturning moment can be found as

$$P = 64{,}000 \text{ lb} \qquad \text{and} \qquad M = 3{,}678{,}000 \text{ ft-lb}$$

Wave Action on Single Piles. The advent since World War II of the offshore oil-drilling platforms, radar stations, and other marine structures of a similar nature has resulted in extensive experimental research and study of wave forces on piles. Leaders in this work have included, among others, J. R. Morison, M. P. O'Brien, J. W. Johnson, and S. A. Schaaf of the department of engineering, University of California, who published a paper, The Force Exerted by Surface Waves on Piles, in the *Journal of Petroleum Technology* (1950); R. O. Reid (department of oceanography and meteorology, A & M College of Texas) and C. L. Bretschneider (Beach Erosion Board) in their report, Surface Waves and Offshore Structures: The Design Wave in Deep or Shallow Water, Storm Tide, and Forces on Vertical Piles and Large Submerged Objects (Report of the Texas A & M Research Foundation, unpublished); R. L. Wiegel and K. E. Beebe (Institute of Engineering Research, University of California) and J. Moon (Signal Oil and Gas Company) in their paper, Ocean Wave Forces on Circular Cylindrical Piles (*Proceedings* of the American Society of Civil Engineers, April, 1957).

Waves acting on piles exert pressures which are the result of drag and inertial forces and are evaluated in the following paragraphs.

Drag forces. The flow with constant velocity (steady flow) of a fluid around an obstacle and the resultant forces (drag) exerted on the obstacle have been studied extensively. Normal and tangential stresses exist between the obstacle and the fluid. At low velocities the fluid flows smoothly around the obstacle, the normal stresses around it are practically constant and the stresses are mainly tangential or shear stresses, and the force is called "surface drag." At higher velocities the smooth flow separates from the sides of the obstacle, creating areas of lower pressure behind and along the sides of the obstacle where eddies and turbulence appear. The difference in pressure along the surface of the obstacle causes a different type of force, the "form drag." The unit drag force, which comprises both the surface and form drag on a circular pile, can be expressed by the formula

$$f_D = C_D \frac{\gamma}{2g} D u^2$$

where f_D = drag force, lb per lin ft of pile
C_D = drag coefficient
γ = unit weight of fluid (64.4 lb per cu ft for sea water)
D = diameter of pile, ft
u = velocity of fluid, ft per sec

For steady flow the drag coefficient is dependent upon the shape, dimension, and roughness of the pile and on the Reynolds number $R = uD/\nu$, where ν is the kinematic viscosity of the fluid. For water of about 70°F, $\nu = 10^{-5}$ ft² per sec and $R = 10^5 uD$.

Morison et al., in their paper mentioned above, presented experimental proof that the same formula may be used even when the flow is not steady but constantly changing its velocity, as is the case in a wave passing a pile. The horizontal component u of the orbital velocity is substituted for the fluid velocity, and the total drag force on the pile at any moment can be determined by integrating the above formula over the whole height of the pile:

$$F_D = C_D \frac{\gamma}{2g} DH^2 K_D$$

where

$$K_D = \frac{1}{H^2} \int_{-d}^{\eta} \pm\, u^2\, dz$$

and z = a vertical coordinate
d = depth of water below still-water level
η = distance of a surface particle above ($+\eta$) or below ($-\eta$) still-water level

The maximum value of the drag force in the direction of the wave travel occurs when the crest passes the pile ($\eta = a$), and the maximum value in the opposite direction occurs when the trough passes the pile ($\eta = a - H$).

Inertial force. In addition to the forces acting normally and tangentially on the surface of the pile, which are combined in the term "drag force," the constantly accelerating or decelerating masses of water exert also a mass force, i.e., a kind of impact force, on the pile, which is termed "inertial force" and which can be computed numerically from the formula

$$f_i = C_M \frac{\gamma\pi}{4g} D^2 \frac{du}{dt}$$

where f_i = inertial force, lb per lin ft of pile
C_M = coefficient of mass
du/dt = horizontal fluid acceleration, ft per sec per sec

The total inertial force on the pile at any moment can be found as

$$F_i = C_M \frac{\gamma}{2g} D^2 H K_i$$

where

$$K_i = \frac{\pi}{2H} \int_{-d}^{\eta} \frac{du}{dt}\, dz$$

This force is zero at crest and trough positions with the maximum values occurring between these two positions. Therefore, the total maximum force is not the summation of the maximum values of F_D and F_i, since they occur at different times within the wave cycle. For high waves in shallow water the drag force is predominant, and the maximum force against the pile occurs at or near the crest of the waves. For low waves

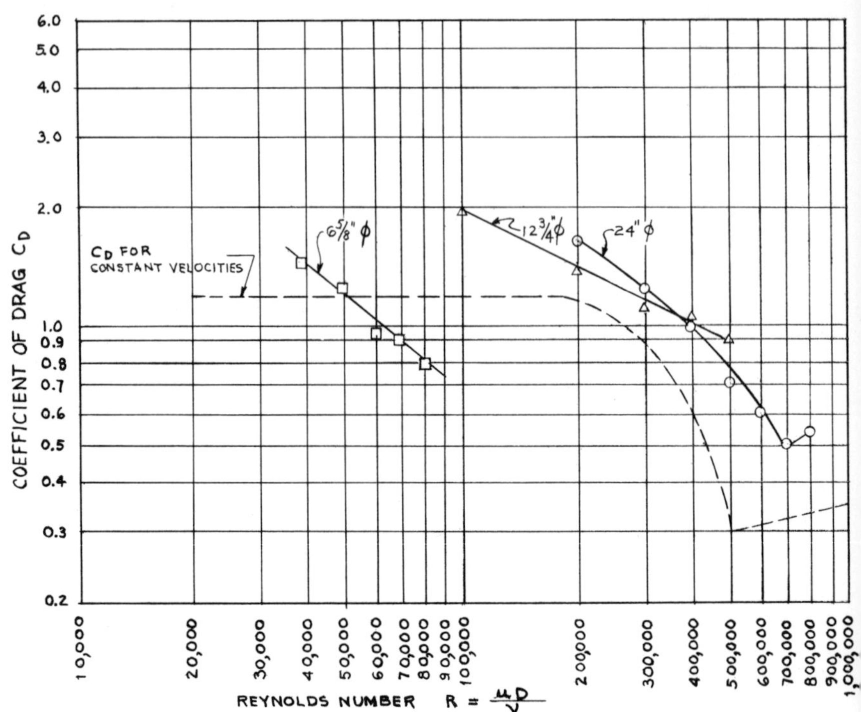

FIG. 2.21 Coefficient of drag as function of Reynolds number and pile diameter. (*From paper entitled Ocean Wave Forces on Circular Cylindrical Piles, by R. L. Wiegel, K. E. Beebe, and J. Moon, Proceedings of the ASCE, April,* 1957.)

in deep water the inertial force is predominant, and the maximum force occurs at a phase angle of about 90° (one-quarter wave length) or when the water surface at the pile is close to the still-water level.

Relatively little is known about numerical values of drag or mass coefficients in wave action on piles of large diameter. The University of California ran full-scale tests on piles up to 24 in. in diameter. Results were reported by R. L. Wiegel, in a paper, Ocean Wave Forces on Circular Cylindrical Piles, in the 1957 *Proceedings* of the American Society of Civil Engineers. According to this report, three factors caused a considerable scatter of test results: (1) the wave flow around a pile is not steady; (2) individual waves vary considerably within a wave train; and (3) turbulences and eddies produced by the forward-moving phase of the wave influence the pressure on the return phase of the wave. However, the average values for the coefficient of drag show a dependency on the Reynolds number and the pile diameter as shown in Fig. 2.21. For the larger diameters the curves for C_D approach the curve of C_D for constant velocities. The Texas A & M Research Foundation made a

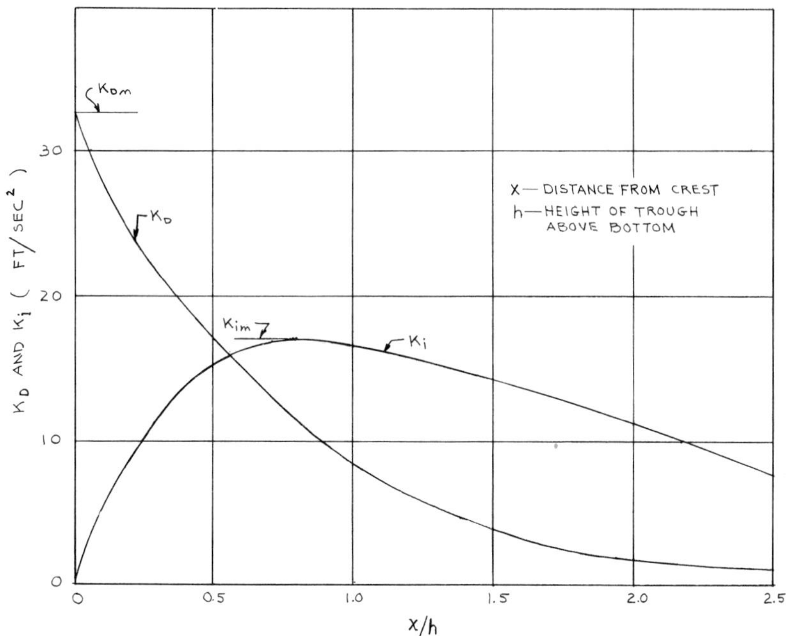

FIG. 2.22 Coefficients K_D and K_i as functions of x/h for maximum solitary wave in shallow water. (*From Surface Waves and Offshore Structures: The Design Wave in Deep or Shallow Water, Storm Tide, and Forces on Vertical Piles and Large Submerged Objects, by R. O. Reid and C. L. Bretschneider, report of the Texas A & M Research Foundation, unpublished.*)

series of tests on 16- and 30-in. diameter piles, the results of which are given in their final Technical Report 55-7, dated July, 1957. For the 30-in. test pile the optimum values for C_D and C_M are given as 1.00 and 1.45, respectively.

The coefficients K_D and K_i vary with the phase angle θ, K_D obtaining its maximum value K_{Dm} at the crest $(\theta = 0)$ and trough $(\theta = 180°)$ positions, while the maximum value K_{im} occurs at phase angles which depend on the type of wave. For waves near the breaking height the solitary wave theory gives values for K_D and K_i in terms of x/h, which are shown in Fig. 2.22, where x is the horizontal distance from the crest and h is the depth of water below the trough. The values of $K_{Dm} = 32.4$

and $K_{im} = 16$ for the solitary wave are the maximum values of this graph. For very small deep-water waves the following relationship applies:

$$K_D = K_{Dm}|\cos\theta|\cos\theta \qquad \text{in which } |\cos\theta| \text{ is always positive}$$

and $\quad K_i = K_{im}\sin\theta$

Although these formulas are correct only for very small deep-water waves, they can be used as a rough approximation for other conditions,

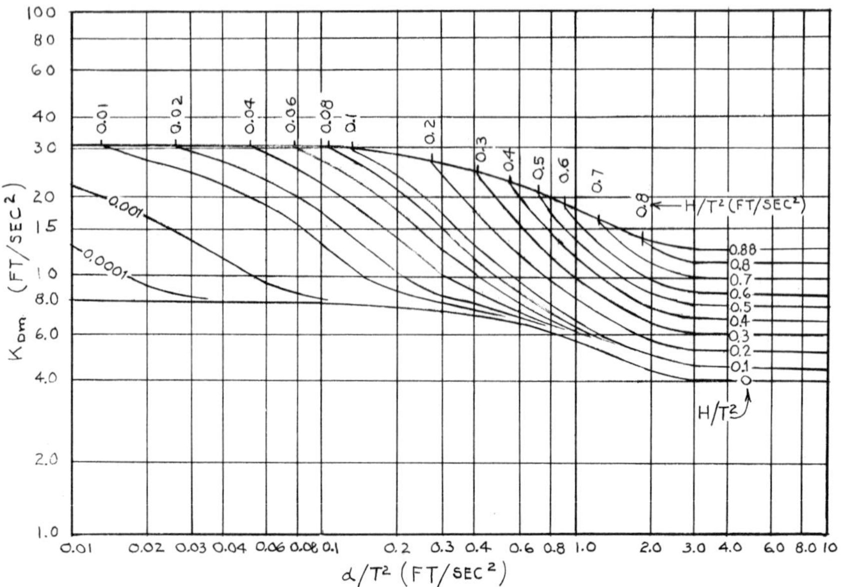

FIG. 2.23 Coefficient K_{Dm} as function of water depth and wave height. (*From Surface Waves and Offshore Structures: The Design Wave in Deep or Shallow Water, Storm Tide, and Forces on Vertical Piles and Large Submerged Objects, by R. O. Reid and C. L. Bretschneider, report of the Texas A & M Research Foundation, unpublished.*)

provided that $d/T^2 > 0.1$. To determine K_{Dm}, Reid and Bretschneider propose Fig. 2.23, where K_{Dm} is given in terms of d/T^2 and H/T^2. The graph shows in full lines the values which can be computed from the different wave theories. Figure 2.24 gives the values of K_{im} in terms of d/T^2 and H/T^2 for the different wave theories.

After K_D and K_i have been determined or estimated for different values of θ, it is necessary to obtain them in terms of the horizontal distance x from the crest. The relationship between θ and x is

$$\theta = 2\pi x/L$$

where θ is given in radians (1 radian = 57.296°). The wave length L can be determined from the graph of Fig. 2.12. Having determined the values of the drag force F_D and of the inertial force F_i and in order to be able to design the pile or pile group, it is necessary to find the location of the forces. It would be desirable to know the location for each phase angle or position in the wave. Normally, however, the result is not greatly affected, if the locations of the maximum forces F_{Dm} and F_{im} are used in each case. Figures 2.25 and 2.26 give the heights S_D and S_i

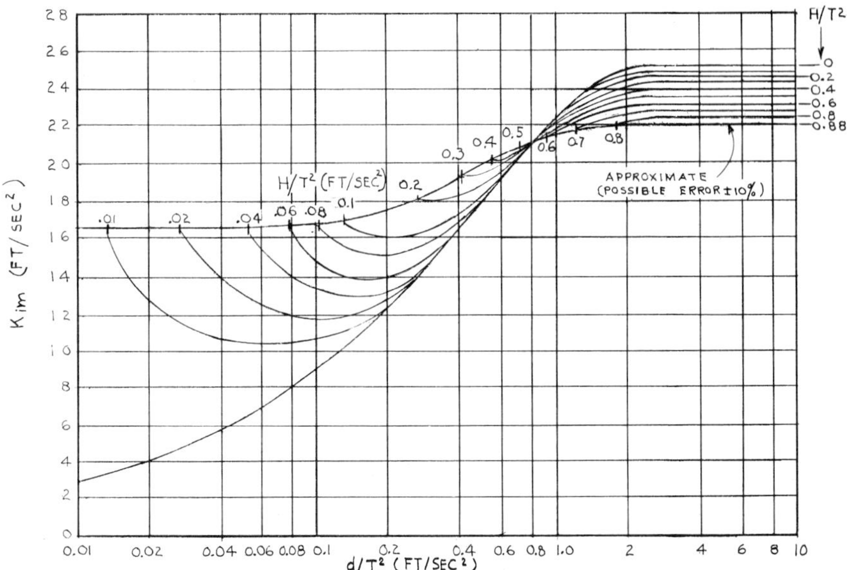

FIG. 2.24 Coefficient K_{im} as function of water depth and wave height. (*From Surface Waves and Offshore Structures: The Design Wave in Deep or Shallow Water, Storm Tide, and Forces on Vertical Piles and Large Submerged Objects, by R. O. Reid and C. L. Bretschneider, report of the Texas A & M Research Foundation, unpublished.*)

of F_{Dm} and F_{im}, respectively, above the bottom, in terms of water depth and wave height.

The wave forces are smallest for piles of cylindrical cross section. For piles with flat or irregular surfaces, such as concrete and H piles, respectively, very little is known of the effect of the shape on drag and inertial forces. In 1954 a paper by J. R. Morison, J. W. Johnson, and M. P. O'Brien, Experimental Studies of Forces on Piles, was published in the *Proceedings* of the Fourth Conference on Coastal Engineering, which gives results of tests made in 1950 on 1-in.-wide sections of cylinders, H piles, and flat plates in a wave tank, subjecting them to three different types of waves. In this case, no attempt was made to find the influence of drag and inertial forces separately.

The tests indicated that the wave forces are smallest for a cylindrical section, increasing about 25 per cent for a flat plate of the same projected width, between 42 and 158 per cent for H sections perpendicular to the wave, and between 122 and 258 per cent when oriented at 45°. The wide range in results for the H pile was apparently due not only to its orientation but also to the different types of waves to which it was subjected.

Wave Action on a Group of Piles. When a structure is supported on piles, it is necessary to find the maximum wave pressure on the whole

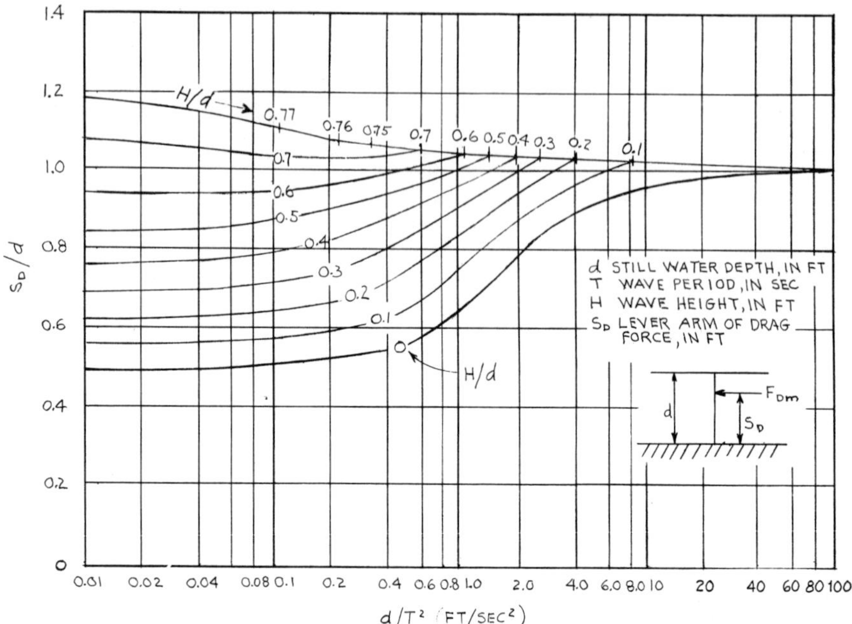

FIG. 2.25 Elevation above bottom of total drag force F_{Dm} as function of water depth and wave height. (*From Surface Waves and Offshore Structures: The Design Wave in Deep or Shallow Water, Storm Tide, and Forces on Vertical Piles and Large Submerged Objects, by R. O. Reid and C. L. Bretschneider, report of the Texas A & M Research Foundation, unpublished.*)

group of piles. The influence of the presence of one pile on the wave action on a neighboring pile may be ignored unless the piles are spaced very close together.

Tests with piles arranged in rows show that the center pile in a row of three piles parallel to the wave crest receives a moment about the bottom of the pile which is up to 2.4 times greater than the moment for a single pile, if the gap is only one-half the pile diameter. This increase diminishes rapidly when the gap is widened and can be considered negligible when the gap reaches 1.5 times the pile diameter.

When three piles are arranged in rows perpendicular to the wave crest, a sheltering effect takes place at the center pile, the moment being reduced an average of 30 per cent for a gap of 1.5 times the diameter. Data for greater gaps are not yet available, and it is advisable not to count on any sheltering effect in actual design.

When the total pressure on one pile is at its maximum, this will also be the case for all piles located on a line parallel to the crest of the wave, but piles located ahead or in back of this line will not be subjected to the maximum pressure. The graphs given previously for forces on single

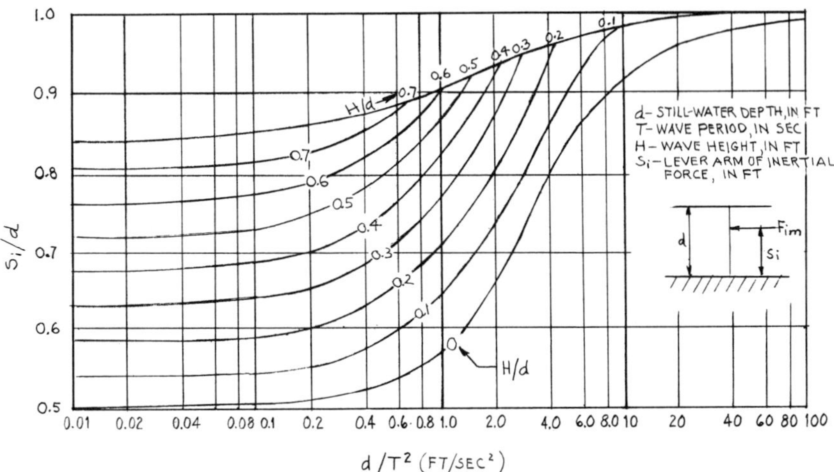

FIG. 2.26 Elevation above bottom of total inertial force F_{im} as function of water depth and wave height. (*From Surface Waves and Offshore Structures: The Design Wave in Deep or Shallow Water, Storm Tide, and Forces on Vertical Piles and Large Submerged Objects, by R. O. Reid and C. L. Bretschneider, report of the Texas A & M Research Foundation, unpublished.*)

piles permit the construction of a curve showing the total pressure on a pile at various positions of the wave. Once this curve is known the position of the wave with respect to the pile group can be found which will give the maximum total force on the group.

The following is an example illustrating the previously described method of computing the wave force on a group of piles or cylinders.

Example. Figure 2.27 shows a drilling platform type of structure used in the Gulf of Mexico, which is supported by six 8-ft-diameter steel cylinders, three in each of two rows. The platform is to be used in various locations, with water depths varying from 60 to 120 ft. It is desired to determine the required height of the platform above still-water level so that it will be above the crest of the highest wave, and the maximum wave pressure and overturning moment about the point of support of the cylinders assumed to be 10 ft below the sand bottom. Structures in the Gulf may be subjected to waves generated by hurricane winds of

125 miles per hour (U = 108 knots). The maximum fetch F for any proposed location is assumed to be 44 nautical miles. Charts of the area indicate that the bottom slope m is 1:500. The coefficient f for the bottom friction is assumed to be 0.01. From the fetch and wind velocity, the period and significant deep-water wave height can be determined.

$$H_0 = 0.0555UF^{0.5} = 39.8 \text{ ft}$$

$$T = 0.5U^{0.5}F^{0.25} = 13.4 \text{ seconds}$$

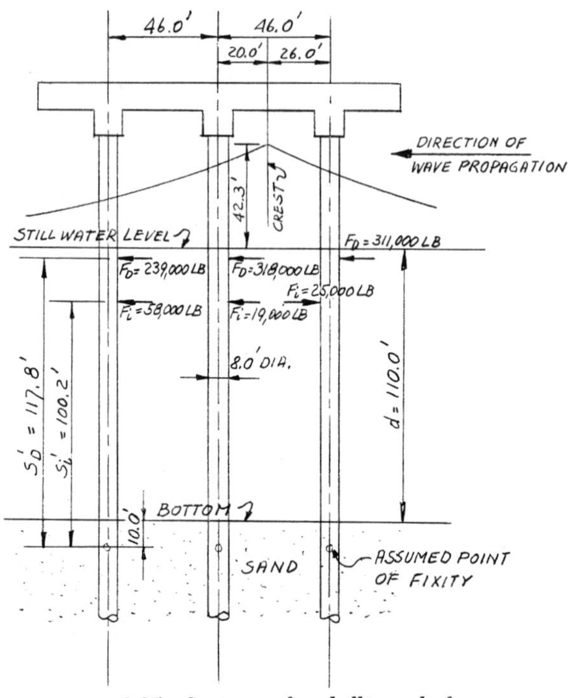

FIG. 2.27 Structure for drilling platform.

The highest wave is estimated to be $H_{max} = 1.87H_0 = 74.5$ ft. The deep-water wave length is $L_0 = 5.12T^2 = 918$ ft.

From this deep-water data the wave height and crest elevation above still-water level are computed and tabulated in Fig. 2.28 and Table 2.4 for the various depths between 60 and 120 ft, in 10 ft increments, as follows: the shoaling coefficient K_s, as given in column 4, may be taken from the graph (Fig. 2.10), but for greater accuracy it has been taken from tables by R. L. Wiegel, Gravity Waves—Tables of Functions, published by the Council on Wave Research. The wave height at depth d is given by the formula

$$H = H_{\max}K_s\left[\frac{fH_{\max}}{mT^2}\int_{\infty}^{d/T^2}\phi_f\,\delta\left(\frac{d}{T^2}\right)+1\right]^{-1}$$

The value of $fH_{\max}/mT^2$ is constant and equal to 2.075 for all depths. Values for

$$\frac{d}{T^2}\int_{\infty}^{d/T^2}\phi_f\,\delta\left(\frac{d}{T^2}\right)$$

are taken from the graph of Fig. 2.11 and are entered in column 5. By dividing these figures by d/T^2, the values of the integral are obtained

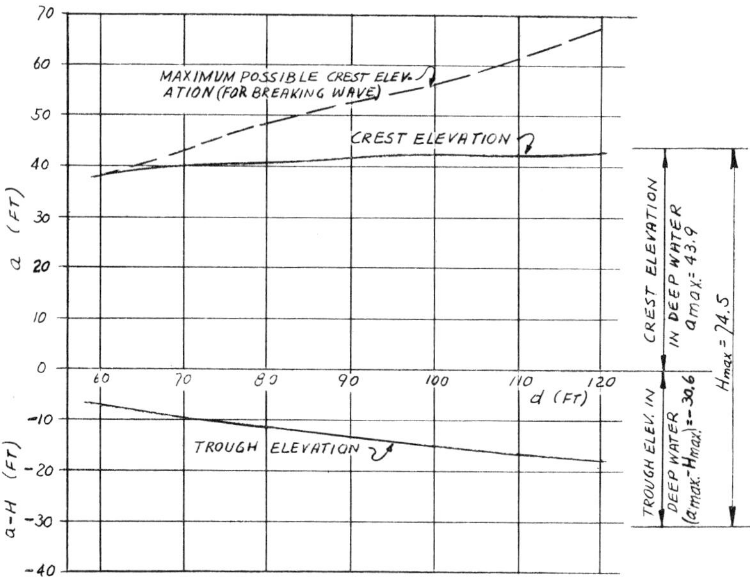

FIG. 2.28 Structure for drilling platform; wave height and crest elevation as functions of water depth.

(column 6). The values for H are then computed and listed in column 10. Now H/T^2 can be computed for each depth, which enables the crest elevation a above still-water level (column 13) to be obtained from the graph of Fig. 2.13. Column 14 gives the trough elevation $(a - H)$ below still-water level. Table 2.4 shows the values of a and $(a - H)$ as a function of the depth d. The crest and trough elevations for the maximum deep-water wave are also shown, where for $H_{\max}/T^2 = 0.42$, Fig. 2.13 gives $a_{\max} = 0.59$, $H_{\max} = 43.9$ ft, and $a_{\max} - H_{\max} = -30.6$ ft.

The next step is to find the critical depth, or the depth for which the moment of the wave forces is at its maximum. This is computed and tabulated in Table 2.5. The first five columns of this table are self-

Table 2.4 Structure for Drilling Platform; Wave Height and Crest Elevation as Functions of Water Depth

d, ft (1)	d/T^2, ft/sec² (2)	d/L_0 (3)	K_s (4)	$\frac{d}{T^2}\int$ (5)	$\int$ (6)	$2.075\int$ (7)	$1+2.075\int$ (8)	$H_{\max}K_s$, ft (9)	H, ft (10)	H/T^2, ft/sec² (11)	a/H (12)	a, ft (13)	$a-H$, ft (14)	H_b/T^2, ft/sec² (15)	H_b, ft (16)	a_b/H_b (17)	a_b, ft (18)
120	0.669	0.131	0.9166	0.044	0.066	0.137	1.137	68.2	60.0	0.334	0.71	42.6	−17.4	0.48	86.1	0.78	67.2
110	0.614	0.120	0.9204	0.048	0.079	0.164	1.164	68.5	58.8	0.327	0.72	42.3	−16.5	0.43	77.2	0.79	61.0
100	0.557	0.109	0.9263	0.055	0.098	0.204	1.204	68.9	57.2	0.319	0.74	42.3	−14.9	0.39	70.0	0.80	56.0
90	0.501	0.098	0.9344	0.064	0.128	0.266	1.266	69.5	54.9	0.306	0.76	41.7	−13.2	0.36	64.7	0.81	52.4
80	0.445	0.087	0.9457	0.074	0.165	0.342	1.342	70.5	52.4	0.292	0.78	40.8	−11.6	0.33	59.2	0.82	48.6
70	0.390	0.076	0.9607	0.085	0.218	0.452	1.452	71.5	49.3	0.275	0.81	40.0	−9.3	0.29	52.0	0.83	43.1
60	0.334	0.065	0.9815	0.100	0.300	0.622	1.622	73.1	45.0	0.250	0.84	37.8	−7.2	0.25	45.0	0.84	37.8

Table 2.5 Structure for Drilling Platform; Critical Depth for Maximum Overturning Moment

d, ft (1)	H, ft (2)	d/T^2, ft/sec² (3)	H/T^2, ft/sec² (4)	H/d (5)	h, ft (6)	L/L_0 (7)	L, ft (8)	K_{Dm}, ft/sec² (9)	K_{im}, ft/sec² (10)	F_{Dm}, 1,000 lb (11)	F_{im}, 1,000 lb (12)	S_D/d (13)	S_i/d (14)	S'_D, ft (15)	S'_i, ft (16)	M_D, 1,000 ft-lb (17)	M_i, 1,000 ft-lb (18)
120	60.0	0.669	0.334	0.500	102.6	0.85	780	15.0	20	302	115	0.96	0.82	125.0	108.4	37,800	12,500
110	58.8	0.614	0.327	0.535	93.5	0.84	770	16.8	20	325	113	0.98	0.82	117.8	100.2	38,300	11,300
100	57.2	0.557	0.319	0.572	85.1	0.82	752	18.0	20	330	110	0.99	0.83	109.0	93.0	36,000	10,200
90	54.9	0.501	0.306	0.610	76.8	0.80	734	20.0	19	337	100	1.01	0.84	100.9	85.6	34,000	8,600
80	52.4	0.445	0.292	0.655	68.4	0.77	707	21.5	19	330	95	1.02	0.85	91.6	78.0	30,200	7,400
70	49.3	0.390	0.275	0.705	60.7	0.75	688	23.8	19	324	90	1.04	0.86	82.8	70.2	26,800	6,300
60	45.0	0.334	0.250	0.750	52.8	0.72	660	26.3	19	298	82	1.06	0.87	73.6	62.2	22,000	5,100

$L_0 = 918$ ft; $T^2 = 179.6$; $F_{Dm} = C_D \frac{\gamma}{2g} DH^2K_{Dm} = 5.6H^2K_{Dm}$; $F_{im} = C_M \frac{\gamma}{2g} D^2HK_{im} = 96HK_{im}$; $S'_D = \frac{S_D}{d} \times d + 10$; $S'_i = \frac{S_i}{d} \times d + 10$; $M_D = F_{Dm} \times S'_D$; $M_i = F_{im} \times S'_i$.

Table **2.6** **Structure for Drilling Platform; Tabulation of Wave Force and Moment Computations**

x, ft (1)	θ, deg (2)	$\sin\theta$ (3)	$\cos\theta$ (4)	$\lvert\cos\theta\rvert\cos\theta$ (5)	K_D, ft/sec² (6)	K_i, ft/sec² (7)	F_D, 1,000 lb (8)	F_i, 1,000 lb (9)	F_T, 1,000 lb (10)	$M_D = F_D S'_D$, 1,000 ft-lb (11)	$M_i = F_i S'_i$, 1,000 ft-lb (12)	M_T, 1,000 ft-lb (13)
0	0.0	0.0000	+1.0000	+1.0000	+16.8	0.0	+325	0	+325	+38,300	0	+38,300
10	4.7	+0.0819	+0.9966	+0.9932	+16.7	+ 1.6	+323	+ 9	+332	+38,100	+ 900	+39,000
20	9.4	+0.1633	+0.9866	+0.9734	+16.4	+ 3.3	+318	+ 19	+337	+37,500	+ 1,900	+39,400
30	14.0	+0.2419	+0.9703	+0.9415	+15.8	+ 4.8	+306	+ 27	+333	+36,100	+ 2,700	+38,800
40	18.7	+0.3206	+0.9472	+0.8972	+15.1	+ 6.4	+292	+ 36	+328	+34,400	+ 3,600	+38,000
50	23.4	+0.3971	+0.9178	+0.8424	+14.2	+ 7.9	+275	+ 45	+320	+32,400	+ 4,500	+36,900
60	28.0	+0.4695	+0.8829	+0.7795	+13.1	+ 9.4	+254	+ 53	+307	+29,900	+ 5,300	+35,200
80	37.4	+0.6074	+0.7944	+0.6311	+10.6	+12.1	+205	+ 68	+273	+24,200	+ 6,800	+31,000
100	46.7	+0.7278	+0.6858	+0.4703	+ 7.9	+14.6	+153	+ 82	+235	+18,000	+ 8,200	+26,200
150	70.1	+0.9403	+0.3404	+0.1159	+ 1.9	+18.8	+ 37	+106	+143	+ 4,400	+10,600	+15,000
200	93.5	+0.9981	−0.0610	−0.0036	− 0.1	+20.0	− 2	+113	+111	− 200	+11,300	+11,100
250	116.9	+0.8918	−0.4524	−0.2047	− 3.4	+17.8	− 66	+101	+ 35	− 7,800	+10,100	+ 2,300
300	140.3	+0.6388	−0.7694	−0.5920	− 9.9	+12.8	−192	+ 72	−120	−22,600	+ 7,200	−15,400
350	163.6	+0.2823	−0.9593	−0.9203	−15.5	+ 5.6	−300	+ 32	−268	−35,300	+ 3,200	−32,100
400	187.0	−0.1219	−0.9925	−0.9851	−16.6	− 2.4	−321	− 14	−335	−37,800	− 1,400	−39,200
450	210.4	−0.5060	−0.8625	−0.7439	−12.5	−10.1	−242	− 57	−299	−28,500	− 5,700	−34,200
500	233.8	−0.8070	−0.5906	−0.3488	− 5.9	−16.1	−114	− 91	−205	−13,400	− 9,100	−22,500
550	257.1	−0.9748	−0.2233	−0.0499	− 0.8	−19.5	− 16	−110	−126	− 1,900	−11,000	−12,900
600	280.5	−0.9833	+0.1822	+0.0332	+ 0.6	−19.7	+ 12	−111	− 99	+ 1,400	−11,100	− 9,700
650	303.9	−0.8300	+0.5577	+0.3110	+ 5.2	−16.6	+101	− 94	+ 7	+11,900	− 9,400	+ 2,500
700	327.2	−0.5417	+0.8406	+0.7066	+11.9	−10.8	+230	− 61	+169	+27,100	− 6,100	+21,000
750	350.6	−0.1633	+0.9866	+0.9734	+16.4	− 3.3	+317	− 19	+298	+37,400	− 1,900	+35,500
770	360.0	0.0000	+1.0000	+1.0000	+16.8	0.0	+325	0	+325	+38,300	0	+38,300

$\theta = 360x/L = 0.467x$ for $L = 770$ ft; $K_D = K_{Dm}\lvert\cos\theta\rvert\cos\theta$; $K_{Dm} = 16.8$; $K_i = K_{im}\sin\theta$; $K_{im} = 20$; $F_D = C_D \dfrac{\gamma}{2g} DH^2K_D = 19{,}360\,K_D$ for $C_D = 0.7$, $\gamma = 64.4$, $g = 32.2$, $D = 8$, $H = 58.8$; $S'_D = S_D + 10 = 117.8$; $F_i = C_M \dfrac{\gamma}{2g} D^2HK_i = 5{,}645K_i$ for $C_M = 1.5$; $S'_i = S_i + 10 = 100.2$.

explanatory. Column 6 gives the height of the trough above the bottom, $h = d + a - H$. The next two columns give the wave lengths L at depths d as computed from the deep-water wave length L_0 by means of the graph of Fig. 2.12. Next, the coefficients K_{Dm} and K_{im} are found from Figs. 2.23 and 2.24, respectively. Selecting a drag coefficient $C_D = 0.7$ and a mass coefficient $C_m = 1.5$, the wave forces F_{Dm} and F_{im} can now be computed and entered in columns 11 and 12. Their lever arm above the bottom is then found by multiplying the values of S_D/d and S_i/d, from Figs. 2.25 and 2.26, by d. To figure the moments about the point of support, 10 ft is added to the lever arms, which values, S'_D and S'_i, are entered in columns 15 and 16. Then the maximum moments of the

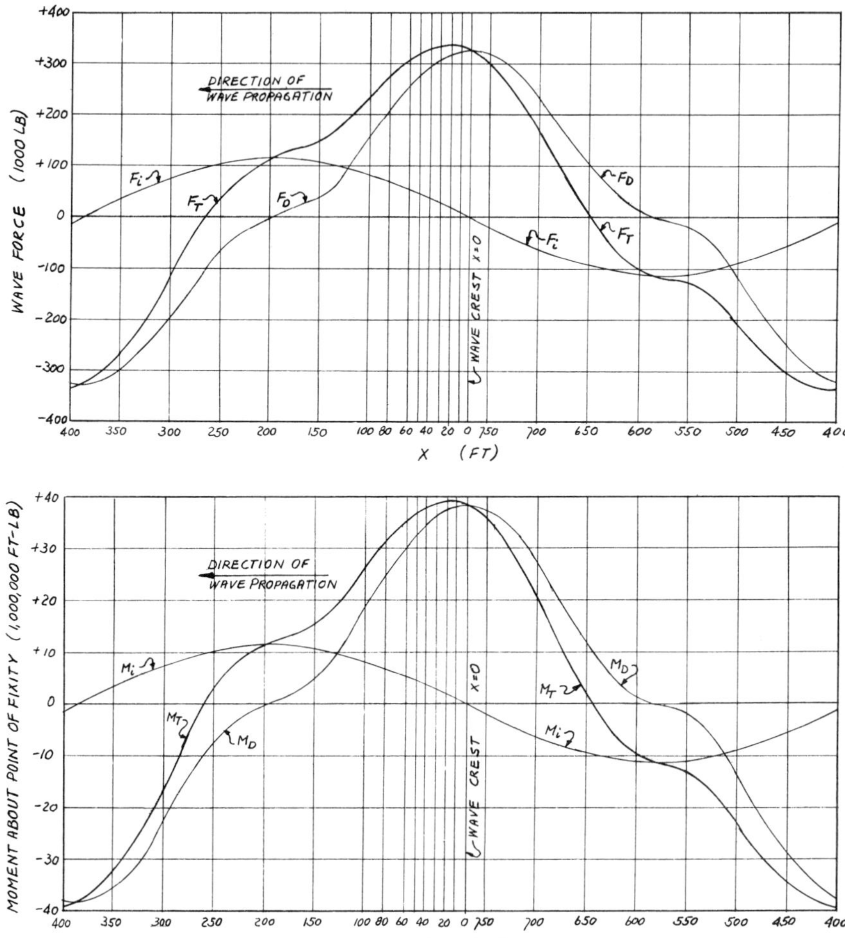

FIG. 2.29 (*a*) Structure for drilling platform; wave force diagrams. (*b*) Structure for drilling platform; wave moment diagrams.

drag force $M_D = F_{Dm}S'_D$ and of the inertial force $M_i = F_{im}S'_i$ are computed and tabulated in columns 17 and 18. The maximum moments for each do not occur at the same time, and, since the drag force moment is always greater than the inertial force moment, the depth of 110 ft, where the maximum drag force moment occurs, is the critical depth.

To determine the forces at each of the three piles in a row, the variation of the forces along the wave must be determined. This is computed and tabulated in Table 2.6. The characteristics of the wave in 110 ft of water are $H = 58.8$ ft, $L = 770$, $K_{Dm} = 16.8$, $K_{im} = 20.0$, $S'_D = 117.8$ ft, $S'_i = 100.2$ ft, as previously determined. The forces are computed at varying distances x from one crest to the next. The values of x are given in terms of the phase angle θ (column 2), where $\theta = 2\pi x/L = 0.008x$ in radians or $\theta = 0.46x$ in degrees. K_D and K_i are then found from $K_D = K_{Dm}|\cos\theta|\cos\theta$ and $K_i = K_{im}$, from which F_D and F_i are determined in the same manner as before. These values of F_D and F_i occur at the same time and can be added to find the total wave force F_T for each phase angle. Each of the three piles in the row will contribute to the overturning moment. Columns 11 to 13 give the moments $M_D = F_DS'_D$, $M_i = F_iS'_i$ and $M_T = M_D + M_i$ for each value of x. Figure 2.29*a* shows forces F_D, F_i, and F_T in terms of x, and Fig. 2.29*b* shows moments M_D, M_i, and M_T in terms of x. The position of the three piles along the wave can now be found where the sum of the three moments on the three piles is a maximum. This is the moment to be used for the design of the platform. The position of the three piles for maximum moment, as indicated on the graph, is found to be where the center line of the platform is 20 ft forward of the wave crest. In this position the total overturning moment is equal to 33,900,000 + 39,400,000 + 34,700,000 = 108,000,000 ft-lb.

Chapter 3 HARBOR PLANNING AND CONSTRUCTION

3.1 Introduction

A *harbor* is a water area partially enclosed and so protected from storms as to provide safe and suitable accommodation for vessels seeking refuge, supplies, refueling, repairs, or the transfer of cargo.

Harbors may be classified (1) as natural, seminatural, or artificial, and (2) as harbors of refuge, military harbors, or commercial harbors. Commercial harbors may be either (*a*) municipal or (*b*) privately owned.

A *natural harbor* is an inlet or water area protected from the storms and waves by the natural configuration of the land. Its entrance is so formed and located as to facilitate navigation while ensuring comparative quiet within the harbor. Natural harbors are located in bays, tidal estuaries, and river mouths. Well-known natural harbors are New York, San Francisco, and Rio de Janeiro, which is one of the finest in the world.

A *seminatural harbor* may be an inlet or a river sheltered on two sides by headlands and requiring artificial protection only at the entrance. Next to a purely natural harbor, it forms the most desirable harbor site, other things being equal. Plymouth and Cherbourg take advantage of their natural location, to become well-protected harbors by the addition of detached breakwaters at the entrances.

An *artificial harbor* is one which is protected from the effect of waves by means of breakwaters or one which may be created by dredging. Buffalo, New York; Matarani, Peru; Hamburg, Germany; and Le Havre, France are examples of artificial harbors; but these also date back to ancient times when such harbors as Tyre, Sidon, and Carthage were formed.

A *harbor of refuge* may be used solely as a haven for ships in a storm, or it may be part of a commercial harbor. Sometimes an outer harbor is constructed which serves as an anchorage, while the basin within the inner breakwater constitutes a commercial harbor. The essential features are good anchorage and safe and easy access from the sea during any condition of weather and state of tide. Well-known harbors of refuge are the one at Sandy Bay, near Cape Ann, on the coast of Massachusetts and that at the mouth of Delaware Bay. A fine example of a combined harbor of refuge and commercial harbor exists at Dover, England.

A *military harbor* or naval base is one existing for the purpose of accommodating naval vessels and serving as a supply depot. Guantanamo, Cuba, Hampton Roads, Virginia, and Pearl Harbor, Hawaii are only a few of the well-known naval bases.

A *commercial harbor* is one in which docks are provided with the necessary facilities for loading and discharging cargo. Dry docks are sometimes provided. Many commercial harbors are privately owned and operated by companies representing the steel, aluminum, copper, oil, coal, timber, fertilizer, sugar, fruit, chemical, and other industries. Municipal- or government-controlled harbors, oftentimes operated by port authorities, exist in many cities and countries and are usually a part of a rather extensive port works, such as the harbors at New York, Los Angeles, London, and La Guaira, Venezuela.

A *port* is a sheltered harbor where marine terminal facilities are provided, consisting of piers or wharves at which ships berth while loading or unloading cargo, transit sheds and other storage areas where ships may discharge incoming cargo, and warehouses where goods may be stored for longer periods while awaiting distribution or sailing. Thus the terminal must be served by railroad, highway, or inland-waterway connections, and in this respect the area of influence of the port reaches out for a considerable distance beyond the harbor. The *tributary area* of a port consists of that portion of the adjacent area for which freight transportation costs are lower than they are to competing ports. The opening of the Saint Lawrence River Seaway has resulted in completely new tributary areas for many of the Great Lakes ports for certain commodities. The harbor then is a very important part of a comprehensive system of works and services which comprise a port.

A *port of entry* is a designated location where foreign goods and foreign citizens may be cleared through the custom house.

Ocean ports are usually located in natural harbors in bays, tidal estuaries, and river mouths, or they may be formed on an unprotected shore line by the construction of breakwaters. In a broader sense and from the standpoint of commerce and foreign trade, they are any ports of call which can be reached directly by large ocean-going vessels. In this respect they may be located several hundreds of miles up rivers or on lakes, although from a harbor engineering viewpoint such are usually considered to be river or lake ports. The opening of the Saint Lawrence Seaway, for instance, has in effect created ocean ports out of such lake ports as Buffalo, Cleveland, and Chicago. Philadelphia and New Orleans are many miles from the ocean on large rivers with maintained deep-water channels, yet they are thought of in terms of ocean rather than river ports. The port of Houston, Texas, located some 50 miles inland, is a striking example of the artificial creation of an ocean port by means of dredging a deep-draft ship canal to the ocean.

Some ocean ports, even though located in natural or seminatural harbors, require extensive protective works to reduce the wave heights and currents alongside the docks to a point where they will not endanger the vessel at its mooring or interfere with the transfer of cargo.

Inland-waterway ports are found on navigable rivers, canals, and lakes. They are generally served by river or lake boats and barges, which may also tranship goods to and from ocean ports.

A *free port or zone* is an isolated, enclosed, and policed area in or adjacent to a port of entry, without a resident population. Furnished with the necessary facilities for loading and unloading, for supplying fuel and ship's stores, for storing goods and reshipping them by land and water, it is an area within which goods may be landed, stored, mixed, blended, repacked, manufactured, and reshipped without payment of duties and without the intervention of customs officials. The purpose of the free zone is to encourage and expedite that part of a nation's foreign trade which its government wishes to free from the restrictions necessitated by customs duties. The most important free port in Europe is Hamburg, which was originated about 1883 and has grown ever since.

A *marine terminal* is that part of a port or harbor which provides docking, cargo-handling, and storage facilities. When only passengers embark and disembark along with their baggage and miscellaneous small cargo generally from ships devoted mainly to the carrying of passengers, it is called a *passenger terminal*. When the traffic is mainly cargo carried by freighters, although many of these ships may carry also a few passengers, the terminal is commonly referred to as a *freight or cargo terminal*. In many cases it will be known as a *bulk cargo terminal*, where such products as petroleum, cement, and grain are stored and handled. For instance, a refinery will usually have a storage-tank farm, pipelines for transporting the crude oil and refined products, and docking facilities for mooring the tankers while they are being loaded and unloaded; all these comprise the marine terminal of the refinery. This type of marine terminal is covered in further detail in Chap. 8.

An *offshore mooring* is provided usually where it is not feasible or economical to construct a dock or provide a protected harbor. Such an anchorage will consist of a number of anchorage units, each consisting of one or more anchors, chains, sinkers, and buoys to which the ship will attach its mooring lines. These will be supplemented in most cases by the ship's bow anchors. Bulk cargo is usually transported to or from the ship by pipeline or trestle conveyor, while other cargo may be transferred by lighter.

An *anchorage area* is a place where ships may be held for quarantine inspection, await docking space while sometimes removing ballast in preparation for taking on cargo, or await favorable weather conditions. Special anchorages are sometimes provided for ships carrying explosives or dangerous cargo and are usually so designated on harbor maps by name and depth of water. Anchorages are usually located away from the marine terminal and adjacent to main channels so as to be near deep water but out of the path of the main traffic. They may be in naturally protected areas or protected from wind and waves by breakwaters.

A *turning basin* is a water area inside a harbor or an enlargement of a channel to permit the turning of a ship. When space is available the area should be at least twice the length of the ship to permit either free turning or turning with the aid of tugs, if wind and water conditions require. When space is limited the ship may be turned by either warping around the end of a pier or turning dolphin, either with or without the use of its lines, and the turning basin will be much smaller and of a more triangular or rectangular shape.

3.2 Ship Characteristics as They Relate to Port Planning

The length, beam, and draft of the ships that will use the port will have a direct bearing on the design of the approach channel, the harbor, and the marine terminal facilities, and the last will be affected also by the type of vessel and its capacity or tonnage. These characteristics for representative ships of principal types and their growth trend are given in Tables 3.1 to 3.5, inclusive. The wind areas for selected ships are given in Table 3.6.

Displacement tonnage is the actual weight of the vessel, or the weight of water she displaces when afloat, and may be either "loaded" or "light." *Displacement loaded* is the weight, in long tons, of the ship and its contents, when fully loaded with cargo, to the Plimsoll mark, or load line, painted on the hull of the ship. The *Plimsoll mark* is the designation used on British ships, but the term "load line" is more commonly referred to on American vessels and designates the depth under the maritime laws to which the ship may be loaded in different bodies of water during various seasons of the year. *Displacement light* is the weight, in long tons, of the ship without cargo, fuel, and stores.

Dead-weight tonnage is the carrying capacity of a ship in long tons and the difference between displacement light and the displacement when loaded to the Plimsoll mark or load line. It is the weight of cargo, fuel, and stores which a ship carries when fully loaded down to the load line as distinguished from loaded to her space capacity. This tonnage varies with latitude and season, as well as the salinity of the water, because of the effect of temperature and salinity on the specific gravity and buoyancy of the water in which the vessel is operating. A vessel with a tropical dead weight of 8,800 tons has a summer dead weight of 8,600 tons and a winter dead weight of 8,300 tons. Unless otherwise indicated dead-weight tonnage is a mean of all three. Dead-weight tonnage is one of weight, and gross tonnage one of measurement; both indicate carrying capacity.

Ships are registered as gross or net tonnage expressed in units of 100 cu ft. Thus *gross tonnage* is the entire internal cubic capacity of a ship, and *net tonnage* is the gross tonnage less the space provided for the crew, machinery, engine room, and fuel.

Cargo or freight tonnage is a commercial expression and is the basis of the freight charge. It may be either a tonnage of weight or of measurement. When 40 cu ft weighs 1 ton or less, the freight ton (2,240 lb) is 40 cu ft. If, however, the cargo weighs more than 1 ton per 40 cu ft, the freight tonnage is the actual weight of the cargo. Most ocean freight is accepted on a weight or measurement basis at the shipping company's option, and usually whichever gives the greatest revenue controls. For instance, if the rate is $0.45 per cubic foot or $0.80 per 100 lb, 1 ton of freight by weight would cost $17.92 and 1 ton by measurement (40 cu ft) would cost $18. However, if the package measured 40 cu ft and weighed only ½ ton, the charge would still be $18, although by weight measurement it would amount to only $8.96.

An ordinary sea-going vessel which can carry a nominal dead weight of 8,000 tons of cargo, fuel, and stores will have a displacement of about 11,500 tons, a gross of about 5,200 tons, and a net of about 3,200 tons.

The *draft* of a ship, expressed in relation to the displacement as being loaded or light draft, is the depth of the keel of the ship below water level for the particular condition of loading.

Ballast is the weight added in the hold or ballast compartments of a ship to increase its draft after it has discharged its cargo and to improve its stability. It usually consists of water and is expressed in long tons. In an ocean-going tanker salt-water ballast replaces a certain amount of petroleum when the ship is unloaded, whereas a dry cargo or passenger vessel has separate compartments for ballast.

3.3 Harbor and Channel Lines

For a great many years the navigable waters of the United States have been under the control of the Corps of Engineers, Department of the Army. It has done an outstanding job both in the development and in the maintenance of these waterways for navigation. Much credit is due

Table 3.1 **Characteristics of Tankers**

Year built	Name or class	Length		Breadth	Depth	Draft loaded (summer)	Tonnage, long tons	
		Over-all	Bet. perp.				Dead-weight	Displacement
1901	*Cowassee*	302′6″	287′0″	42′2″	23′2″	21′5″	3,960	5,000
1906	*W. S. Porter*	399′2″	385′0″	49′8″	28′11″	24′0″	6,500	
1908	*Texas*	413′3″	409′2″	52′8″	27′1″	24′0″	9,232	
1914	*John D. Archbold*	474′6″	458′3″	60′0″		26′1″	9,546	
1916	*Charles Pratt*	516′6″	500′0″	68′0″	38′4″	27′3″	14,990	
1921	*T. J. Williams*		465′0″	60′0″	36′3″	27′8″	11,990	17,875
1921	*Cacalilao*	435′0″	420′0″	56′0″	33′6″	27′2″	9,975	13,300
1930	*Brilliant*		481′4″	65′9″	37′0″	28′11″	14,565	20,200
1931	*Bridgewater*	467′0″	450′0″	62′0″	34′0″	27′8″	12,585	16,000
1941	T-2 class tankers	523′6″	503′0″	68′0″	39′3″	30′2″	16,350	21,880
1943	*Atlantic Sun*	547′3″	521′0″	70′0″	40′0″	30′5″	17,575	24,110
1948	Esso *Zurich*	628′0″	601′1″	82′6″	42′6″	32′5″	26,550	34,690
1950	*Atlantic Seaman*	659′6″	626′8″	85′0″	45′0″	34′3″	30,155	39,664
1953	*Tina Onassis*	775′7″	723′3″	95′2″	51′6″	37′10″	45,230	58,420
1953	*Petroking*	673′0″	645′0″	92′0″	46′0″	34′8″	38,045	48,010
1954	*W. Alton Jones*	707′0″	677′0″	93′0″	48′6″	36′8″	38,911	49,660
1954	*World Glory*	736′4″	705′0″	102′0″	50′0″	37′9″	45,509	58,625
1955	Sinclair *Petrolore*	789′0″	756′0″	106′0″	54′2″	40′7″	56,089	75,630
1956	Cities Service *Baltimore*	661′0″	630′0″	90′0″	45′3″	34′2″	32,710	42,751
1956	*Universe Leader*	854′9″	815′0″	125′0″	61′3″	46′2″	85,515	109,630
1957	Esso *Gettysburg*	715′0″	685′0″	93′0″	48′7″	36′9″	37,689	50,176
1957	*Tidewater*	785′10″	749′8″	102′0″	53′0″	39′3″	53,069	69,186
1958	*Sansinena*		810′0″	104′0″		41′9″	60,000	
1961	(Under Construction)	940′0″	895′0″	132′0″	67′2″	49′4″	106,000	137,000

Table **3.2 Characteristics of Bulk Carriers (Ore, Coal, etc.)**

Year built	Name	Length		Breadth	Depth	Draft loaded (summer)	Tonnage, long tons	
		Over-all	Bet. perp.				Dead-weight	Displacement
1902	*Ben E. Tate*		363′8″	50′0″	28′0″	20′9″		
1907	*B. F. Jones*		527′10″	54′0″	31′2″	26′2″ *		
1917	*Homer D. Williams*		580′0″	60′0″	32′0″			
1922	*Marore*	571′6″	550′1″	72′0″	44′0″	34′1″	22,980	31,000
1938	*John Hulst*		594′3″	60′0″	32′6″	22′3″ *		19,000
1942	*Leon Fraser*		623′3″	67′0″	35′0″	24′0″ *	18,100	23,900
1945	*Venore*	582′11″	560′0″	78′0″	43′9″	34′4″	24,251	32,449
1954	*Ore Chief*	794′0″	756′0″	116′0″	56′0″	38′9″	60,000	80,000
1955	*Leader*	680′0″	651′1″	88′0″	48′0″	34′7″	34,200	44,981
1957	*Cosmic*	744′1″	708′8″	100′5″	50′6″	37′3″	46,673	61,245
1958	*Consolidation Coal*	635′0″	610′0″	75′0″	47′3″	32′5″		

* Fresh-water draft—Great Lakes.

Table 3.3 Characteristics of General Cargo Ships

Year built	Name or class	Length		Breadth	Depth	Draft loaded (summer)	Tonnage, long	
		Over-all	Bet. perp.				Dead-weight	Displacement
1899	*El Sud*	405′9″	390′11″	48′3″		22′0″	3,417	
1903	*Virginian*		490′0″	58′0″	35′6″	29′0″	11,200	18,425
1909	*Jean*	382′2″	311′0″	46′1″	24′2″	21′0″	4,600	
1910	*El Sol*	430′0″	405′7″	53′1″	33′8″	26′0″	6,850	
1912	*Dakotan*		416′2″	53′6″	31′6″	27′4″	8,950	13,250
1913	*Columbian*		404′0″	53′9″	28′10″	25′9″	7,900	12,000
1916	*Edgar F. Luckenbach*	442′0″	425′0″	57′3″	42′0″	29′5″	13,000	
1918	*Lagos Erie*		400′0″	52′0″	31′0″	25′2″	8,069	11,616
1918	*Invincible*		440′2″	56′0″	38′0″	28′9″	11,721	15,940
1919	*Mc. Keesport*		395′6″	55′0″	34′11″	27′2″	9,808	13,150
1920	*Abercos*		402′0″	53′0″	34′6″	26′7″	9,414	12,760
1932	*Seatrain Havana*		460′0″	63′6″	38′3″	26′2″	10,900	16,460
1934	*Angelina*	410′11″	390′0″	55′0″	30′6″	25′0″	7,600	10,800
1939	C-2 class C2-S-AJ1	459′1″	435′0″	63′0″	31′6″	27′8″	10,775	13,869
1940	C-3 class C3-S-A2	492′0″	465′0″	69′6″	33′6″	28′7″	12,300	18,215
1942	Liberty ships EC2-S-C1	441′6″	417′9″	56′11″	37′4″	27′8″	10,800	14,100
1945	Victory ships VC2-S-AP2	455′3″	436′6″	62′0″	38′0″	28′7″	10,800	15,199
1946	C-4 class C4-S-B5	520′0″	496′8″	71′6″	43′6″	32′10″	15,036	22,094
1950	*Schuyler Otis Bland*	475′0″	450′11″	66′0″	41′6″	30′0″	10,516	15,910
1952–59	*Mariner* class	563′8″	528′6″	76′0″	35′6″	29′11″	12,910	21,093
1957	*Azalea City* (C-2 containership)	468′0″	442′2″	72′0″	40′2″	24′2″	7,891	13,125
	Seafarer C4-S-RM19a (none yet built)	529′0″		74′6″		29′10″	13,480	

Table **3.4 Characteristics of Passenger Ships**

Year built	Name	Length		Breadth	Depth	Draft loaded (summer)	Tonnage, long tons	
		Over-all	Bet. perp.				Dead-weight	Displacement
1900	*Ivernia*	582′0″		64′11″	37′10″	31′6″		
1907	*Lusitania*	762′2″		87′10″	56′7″	35′6″		
1914	*Aquitania*	868′8″		97′0″	49′8″	35′0″		
1926	*Mohawk*		387′6″	54′0″	23′6″	18′2″	2,900	7,180
1928	*Liberté*	936′10″	893′5″	102′0″	48′0″	34′4″	10,420	
1929	*Bremen*	898′8″		101′11″	48′2″			
1929	*Irpinia*		509′6″	66′9″	35′0″	23′1″	5,597	13,985
1930	*Excalibur*		450′0″	61′6″	42′6″	28′0″	9,495	15,395
1931	*Homeric*		605′0″	79′0″	44′6″	27′3″	8,000	25,000
1932	*Lurline*		605′0″	79′0″	44′6″	28′3″	11,300	26,141
1932	*Manhattan*		666′0″	86′0″	47′0″	30′9″	13,249	33,500
1933	*Peten*		415′0″	60′0″	34′9″	24′4″	4,270	10,950
1933	*Queen of Bermuda*	579′6″	553′5″	76′8″	39′0″	27′1″	6,175	
1935	*Normandie*	1,029′0″		117′11″	57′7″	36′6″		
1936	*Queen Mary*	1,019′6″	975′2″	118′7″	68′6″	39′5″	17,000	
1938	*Nieu Amsterdam*	758′6″	713′8″	88′4″	50′0″	31′6″	8,735	
1940	*Queen Elizabeth*	1,031′0″	987′5″	118′7″	68′5″	39′7″	16,881	
1940	*America*	723′0″	662′8″	93′3″	55′8″	32′9″	14,331	35,440
1950	*Independence*	682′6″	633′0″	89′0″	52′11″	30′2″	11,790	30,090
1952	*United States*	990′0″	916′10″	101′7″		32′0″		
1958	*Argentina*	617′10″	570′0″	84′0″	45′3″	27′0″	10,170	22,700
1958	*Santa Rosa*	584′0″	535′2″	84′0″	43′1″	27′2″	8,713	20,298
1960	*Savannah* (nuclear-powered)	595′6″	545′0″	78′0″	41′0″		10,190	21,800

***Table* 3.5 Characteristics of Large Ships of United States Navy**

Year built	Type of ship: Name or class	Length		Breadth	Draft		Displacement, long tons	
		Over-all	Water line		Std.	Full load	Standard	Full load
	Battleships							
1912	*Arkansas* class	562′0″	555′6″	106′0″	26′0″	32′0″	26,100	31,000
1914	*Texas* class	573′0″	566′0″	106′0″	26′0″	31′6″	27,000	32,000
1916	*Nevada* class	583′0″	575′0″	107′11″	27′6″	32′6″	29,000	
1916	*Pennsylvania* class	608′0″	600′0″	106′3″	28′0″	33′6″	33,100	
1918	*New Mexico* class	624′0″	600′0″	106′3″	29′6″	34′0″	33,400	
1921	*Colorado* class	624′0″	600′0″	97′6″	30′6″	35′0″	32,500	
1941	*North Carolina* class	729′0″	704′0″	108′0″	26′8″	35′0″	35,000	45,500
1942	*South Dakota* and *Indiana* classes	680′0″		108′2″	26′9″	37′0″	35,000	44,500
1943–44	*Iowa* class	887′3″	861′3″	108′0″		38′0″	45,000	57,600
	Cruisers							
1934	*New Orleans* class	588′0″	574′0″	61′9″	19′5″	23′6″	9,950	
1938	*Brooklyn* class		600′0″	61′6″	19′9″		9,700	
1939	*Wichita* class	614′0″	600′0″	61′9″	19′10″		9,324	13,400
1942–45	*Cleveland* and *Fargo* classes	610′0″	600′0″	66′0″	20′0″	25′0″	10,500	13,750
1942–46	*San Diego*, *Juneau*, and *Oakland* classes	541′0″		52′10″	14′9″	25′0″	6,000	8,000
1943–46	*Baltimore* and *Oregon City* classes	673′6″		71′0″		26′0″	13,600	17,200
1944	*Alaska* class	808′6″		91′0″		31′6″	27,500	32,500
1948–49	*Des Moines* class	716′6″		75′4″		26′0″	17,000	21,500
1948–49	*Worcester* class	679′6″		70′8″		26′0″	14,700	18,500
1953	*Northampton*	676′0″		71′0″		29′0″	13,000	17,200

	Aircraft Carriers							
1927	*Lexington* and *Saratoga*	888′0″	830′0″	105′6″	24′2″	32′0″	33,000	40,000
1934	*Ranger*	769′0″	728′0″	80′1″	19′8″		14,500	
1938	*Enterprise*	809′6″	761′0″	83′3″	21′8″		19,800	
1942	*Essex* class	885′10″	874′0″	93′0″	29′0″		27,100	33,000
1942	*Bogue* class	494′0″	465′0″	69′6″	23′3″		7,800	
1943	*Casablanca* class	498′10″	487′0″	80′0″		19′9″	6,730	10,200
1943	*Independence* class	618′0″	600′0″	71′6″	20′0″		11,000	13,000
1943	*Anzio* class	512′0″		108′0″		19′8″	7,800	10,200
1944–46	*Commencement Bay* class	553′0″		75′0″		30′6″	12,000	23,875
1945–47	*Midway* class	968′0″		136′0″	32′9″		45,000	55,000
1946–47	*Saipan* class	683′7″		76′9″			14,500	20,000
1955	*Forrestal*	1,039′0″		252′0″		37′0″	54,600	76,000
1956–61	*Saratoga* and *Kitty Hawk* classes	1,046′0″		252′0″		37′0″	56,000	78,700
1961	*Enterprise* (nuclear-powered)	1,100′0″		252′0″			74,700	85,350
	Rebuilt Aircraft Carriers							
1950–59	*Hancock* and *Oriskany* classes	899′0″		192′0″		31′0″	33,100	42,600
1952	*Oriskany* class (axial)	899′0″		152′0″		31′0″	33,100	40,800
1952	*Antietam*	899′0″		154′0″		31′0″	30,000	38,000
1956–60	*Midway* class	974′0″		210′0″		36′0″	51,000	62,000

Table 3.6 Wind Areas for Selected Ships

Name	Type	Tonnage, long tons		Light draft wind area, sq ft
		Dead-weight	Loaded displace-ment	
Cowassee	Tanker	3,960	5,000	5,400
Cacalilao	Tanker	9,975	13,300	13,700
Bridgewater	Tanker	12,585	16,000	14,400
T-2 tankers	Tanker	16,350	21,880	19,000
Atlantic Seaman	Tanker	30,155	39,664	29,000
W. Alton Jones	Tanker	38,911	49,660	36,500
World Glory	Tanker	45,509	58,625	36,500
Universe Leader	Tanker	85,515	109,630	38,910
Liberty ships	Cargo	10,800	14,100	15,300
Victory ships	Cargo	10,800	15,199	15,400
Mariner class	Cargo	12,910	21,093	24,000
Midway class	Aircraft carrier	.....	55,000	66,000
Colorado class	Battleship	......	......	25,500
North Carolina class	Battleship	......	45,500	32,700
South Dakota and *Indiana* classes	Battleship	......	44,500	31,500
Iowa class	Battleship	......	57,600	43,000
New Orleans class	Cruiser	......	......	22,000
Brooklyn class	Cruiser	......	......	23,000
Cleveland and *Fargo* classes	Cruiser	......	13,750	26,000
San Diego, *Juneau*, and *Oakland* classes	Cruiser	......	8,000	20,000
Alaska class	Cruiser	......	32,500	38,000
Des Moines class	Cruiser	......	21,500	32,300
Worcester class	Cruiser	......	18,500	28,000

this organization for the noteworthy advances it has made in developing the rivers and harbors to meet the demands of a growing commerce in which the vessels over the years have increased in tonnage and in their principal measurements of length, beam, and draft.

To define certain limits for channels and harbors the following terms have become well established. A *bulkhead line* is the farthest line offshore to which a fill or solid structure may be constructed. Open pier construction may extend outward from the bulkhead line to the *pierhead line*, beyond which no construction of any kind is allowed, except by special permit. This line is established to prevent piers from being constructed too far out into the water, since such construction might cause interference with navigation. The pierhead lines may or may not coincide with *channel lines,* which define the limits of navigable channels that are dredged and maintained at established depths by the Federal government. These depths are usually referred to low water. Open water of navigable depth is called a *fairway.*

3.4 Planning a Port

The decision to build a port, and its location, generally will be determined by factors having to do with (1) its need and economic justification, (2) prospective volume of seaborne commerce, and (3) availability of inland communications by both land and water. These considerations must precede the technical studies and planning of the port and are briefly as follows:

1. The need for a port may arise in a number of ways:

a. A naval base or a military terminal may be needed to supply inland army or air bases, such as the recently constructed Port of Rota, Spain.

b. A seaport may be needed to serve a nearby inland city which has grown to the extent of requiring an outlet for its foreign commerce. The development of a port is usually, but not always, associated with the growth of the city of which it is a part, as, for instance, La Guaira, the principal port of Venezuela, whose growth has been minor compared with Caracas, which is located about 20 miles inland and served by an excellent highway to the port.

c. The need for a privately owned commercial port will arise when it is required as a shipping terminal for the commodity or product which is being developed and for which shipping facilities are either not available or not economical to use. In recent years the development of sources of raw materials such as iron ore, bauxite, oil, and copper, in places such as Canada, South America, Africa, and the Far East, has resulted in the construction of new commercial ports in many parts of the world.

d. Generally, the building of a municipal port requires the expenditure of a large sum of money which in many cases will have to be raised by bond issues or by borrowing from banks, unless it is government-subsidized. Therefore, the project to be economically feasible will have to show an income above its operating costs, sufficient to cover the fixed charges. A privately owned commercial port does not require the same economic justification because it is usually secondary to the main project. For instance, once it has been decided to develop iron ore in a certain location where transportation by ore carrier is required, a shipping terminal is a necessity, and the only question that arises would be its most desirable and economical location within a relatively limited area.

2. Before embarking upon the construction of a municipal port, extensive surveys and studies will have to be made to determine the initial and future commerce anticipated from the tributary area where the freight

rates will be less than to competing ports. Privately owned commercial ports, on the other hand, generally have their tonnages fairly well established over the life of the project, and the port can be designed to meet these requirements.

3. The availability of inland communications has an important bearing on the location of a port. Unless the tributary area is served with good highways, railroads, and waterways leading to inland cities, or the terrain and conditions are favorable for the development or enlargement of these arteries of communication, a port will not flourish. There are many excellent natural harbor locations which from an engineering standpoint would be ideal for the construction of a port, but which are poorly situated with respect to inland communications. A glance at the great harbors of the world will show that these are served by extensive arteries of communication.

Assuming that the above studies have been made and the general location of the harbor has been established, as well as its principal use and the type and tonnage of traffic to be handled, the next step, which in some cases will have been initiated during the above studies, will be to make preliminary studies and layouts of the port in preparation for making a complete site investigation to gather all the information which will be needed in making the final design of the port.

Information for this preliminary planning can usually be obtained from the following sources: the U.S. Department of Commerce through the United States Coast and Geodetic Survey, the Navy Department through the Hydrographic Office, and the United States Corps of Engineers, who have surveyed a great many of our navigable waters. Charts or information can be obtained from the U.S. Government Printing Office, Washington 25, D.C., or from the nearest U.S. District Engineer's Office. These charts are very valuable in the initial planning of the harbor as they give information on the depth of water, the general character of the bottom, and the range of tides. Meteorological data covering winds, temperature, and rainfall are published by the U.S. Weather Bureau, Washington 25, D.C. If there is no U.S. Weather Bureau near the site, this information may possibly be obtained from the nearest airport. The tremendous increase in air traffic in all parts of the world during recent years has opened up a new source of information on weather conditions. Tide and current tables are published by the U.S. Department of Commerce, Coast and Geodetic Survey, and can be obtained from the U.S. Government Printing Office, Washington 25, D.C.

If the port is to be located in some part of the country or world where none of the above information is available, it will be necessary to make a preliminary site reconnaissance. For the preliminary survey, aerial contour mapping may be a quick and convenient way of obtaining topography. Aerial photographs will be useful, especially in examining the coast and adjacent shore for suitable locations of the port, if this has not been already fixed by other strategic reasons. Aerial photography will often show up shoals, reefs, mouths of rivers, and other important details along the shore. Soundings can be taken quite quickly with a fathometer, giving a general picture of the depths of water, even though they may not be accurately located and referenced to fixed monuments and base lines. The depth and presence of rock, as well as the depth of over-burden, can be determined, as described in Soil Investigations (page 104), by means of a Marine Sonoprobe (trademark of Magnolia Petroleum Company).

With the general requirements of the port having been established and preliminary site information obtained, the next step will be to make preliminary studies of harbor and port layouts, which will usually be supplemented with approximate cost estimates based on certain assumptions which will have to be verified when making the site investigation. This preliminary planning will include the following:

Determining Best Location of Harbor. Unless the site is fixed by specific requirements of the port, several locations of the harbor will have to be studied, to determine the most protected location involving the least amount of dredging and with the most favorable bottom conditions as well as a shore area suitable for the development of the terminal facilities.

It may be impossible to fulfill all of the above conditions, as one or more may predominate to the exclusion of others. For instance, the shore terrain, both as to condition of ground and elevation or because of the location of a river, may make it mandatory to locate the harbor at a specific location. Also, existing communication facilities or their future construction may control the location, as it may be impossible because of impassable terrain to bring in a railroad or highway connection at a point where the water conditions may be most favorable for the location of the harbor. Since all ports, unless they are only marine transfer stations, must be fed by land or inland waterway communications, it follows that their terminus will have a major bearing on the location of the port. The adjacent shore may be low and swampy, requiring expensive foundations for terminal facilities. However, if the harbor or channel requires dredging, and the material is sand, it may be spoiled in the port area to make land at little additional cost. On the other hand the adjacent shore may be precipitous and high above the water, making it virtually impossible to find sufficient area for the onshore facilities, except for bulk material terminals, which utilize conveyors and pipelines for loading and unloading the ships, and where the terminal storage and other facilities may be located some distance inland from the harbor. Also, rocky cliffs along the shore may be excavated to provide rock for the construction of breakwaters and the area on shore thus formed may be used for the terminal facilities. Such a port is that at Matarani, Peru, which is shown in Fig. 3.26 and described on page 130. Generally, the level of the port area onshore should be at or a little above the level of the docks. In a great many areas, where the range of tide is only 2 to 3 ft, the ideal level for the adjacent land would be 15 to 20 ft above low water. In areas where higher tides or tidal waves may occur, the adjacent land should be well above these levels. Rivers with large variations in river stage—some places as much as 50 ft—will need to have high ground above maximum flood stage for the location of the terminal facilities.

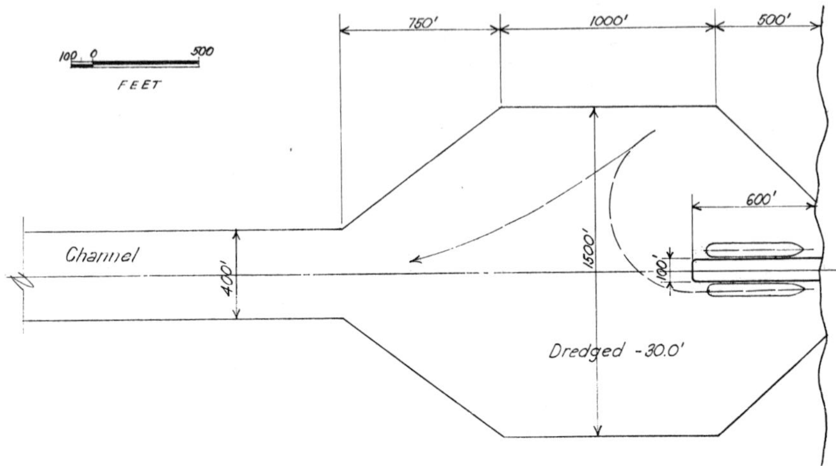

FIG. 3.1 A typical layout for a very small artificial harbor.

The depth of water, other things being equal, will be a major factor in the location of the port. A deep-water bay is, of course, ideal, but where the port must be located along the exposed coast, a study of the hydrographic charts will generally indicate areas where the water is deep close to shore and other areas where the required harbor depth would not be reached for several thousand feet offshore. The latter might require a prohibitive amount of dredging. However, the deep-water location may find the water a short distance offshore so deep that the construction of protective breakwaters may be of prohibitive cost. In cases where bulk materials are to be shipped, the only solution may be an offshore anchorage with submarine pipeline, if liquids are to be handled, or a lightly constructed trestle or ropeway may be used to transport bulk solids such as bauxite, iron ore, and salt.

Bottom conditions are of utmost importance. The underwater excavation of rock is very expensive, and this should be avoided if at all possible, except in special cases where it may be combined with the construction of the dock. Such a port is Taconite Harbor, on the north shore of Lake Superior, which is described on page 123 and shown in cross section in Fig. 3.22. However, the bottom may consist of a very deep bed of soft material, such as mud, silt, or clay, which, although it can be removed easily with suction dredges, would make the construction of breakwaters and docks very expensive, if not prohibitive, because of poor foundation conditions.

Size and Shape of Harbor and Turning Basin. The number and size of ships using a harbor will determine its size to a large extent, but existing site conditions will also have an important influence. Generally speaking,

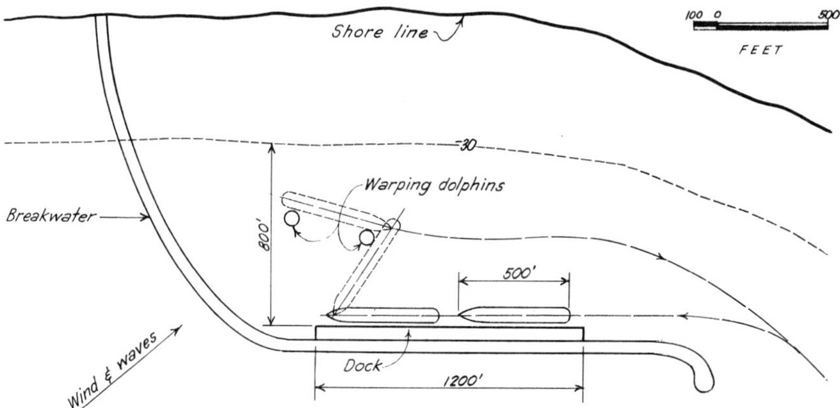

FIG. 3.2 An artificial harbor restricted in area because of deep water.

unless the harbor is a natural one, its size will be kept as small as will permit safe and reasonably comfortable operations to take place. The use of tugs to assist the maneuvering of the ships in docking may also influence the size of the harbor. The minimum harbor area is the space required for the docks plus the turning basin in front of them, and in some layouts, where the ship is turned by warping it around the end of the pier or turning dolphin, the harbor may be further restricted in area. For instance, a harbor with a single pier and turning basin and a long approach channel from the open sea, as shown in Fig. 3.1, requires the minimum amount of space and can accommodate two 500-ft ships. This artificial harbor is formed by dredging a channel through shallow water, protected by offshore reefs and islands, and enlarging the inshore end to provide the minimum area of harbor which will accommodate the shipping requirements specified for the project. In leaving its berth the ship must warp itself around the end of the pier so as not to have to back out through the long approach channel.

Figure 3.2 shows a second type of restricted harbor area. Here, the

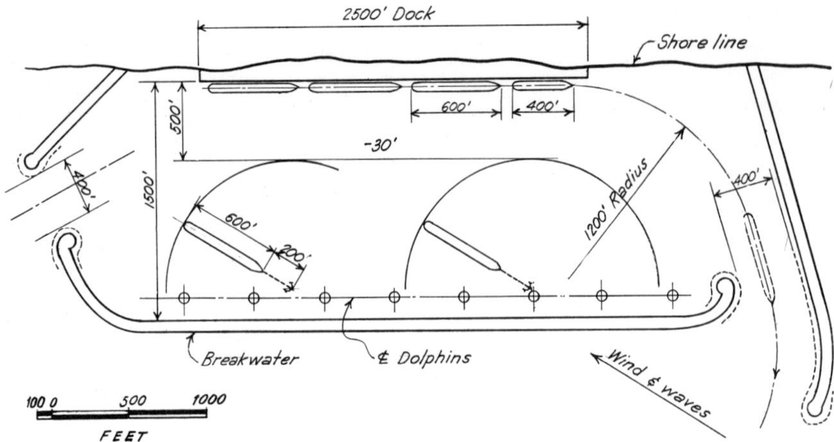

FIG. 3.3 An artificial harbor of medium size with separate openings for entering and leaving.

prevailing wind and waves are in one direction, and quiet water is obtained in the harbor by a curved breakwater parallel and connecting to the shore at one end. Because of the rapid increase in depth of water offshore, it is necessary to restrict the width of the harbor and to use a breakwater pier or quay type of construction accommodating two 600-ft vessels with turning dolphins.

One type of the less restricted harbor is long and narrow with an entrance at one end and an opening for leaving at the opposite end, as shown in Fig. 3.3. Berthing accommodations are for three 600-ft and one 400-ft ship along a 2,500-ft wharf. The 1,500-ft width of harbor is adequate for anchoring two vessels awaiting their turn to dock.

Another less restricted harbor is the more or less square type of harbor, protected with two breakwater arms, with one opening, several docks, and a large turning basin having an area sufficient to inscribe a turning circle with a radius equal to twice the length of the largest ship. This is the smallest radius a ship can comfortably turn on, under continuous headway, without the help of a tug. Figure 3.4 shows such a harbor. However, there is still little space to anchor vessels awaiting their turn to dock or to take refuge from storms, without interfering with traffic to and from the docks. The minimum size turning basin is one with a radius equal to the length of the ship, but this requires careful maneuvering of the ship to make the turn.

Figure 3.5 is one of the finest natural harbor locations in the Western Hemisphere, where ocean-going vessels can seek refuge in time of storm. Only recently has it been developed as a shipping terminal, and there is ample room for additional docks, their locations being more or less controlled by the condition of the bay bottom and the terrain on shore. The bay is approximately 6 miles in width and 6 miles long, and it is protected at its entrance by several islands, which are far enough apart to provide deep-water channel approaches, yet geographically so situated as to provide almost complete protection to the bay. The waves within the bay seldom exceed 3 ft in height, and these are generated by the wind blowing across the exposed surface of the water. It must be kept in mind that if a natural harbor is too large, it may permit the generation of local waves within the harbor, which will make berthing difficult, if not impossible, without breakwater protection or the formation of an inner harbor to protect the docks. For comfortable berthing the wave height should not exceed 2 ft, and winds should not exceed 10 to 15 miles per hour, although wave heights up to 4 ft have been allowed

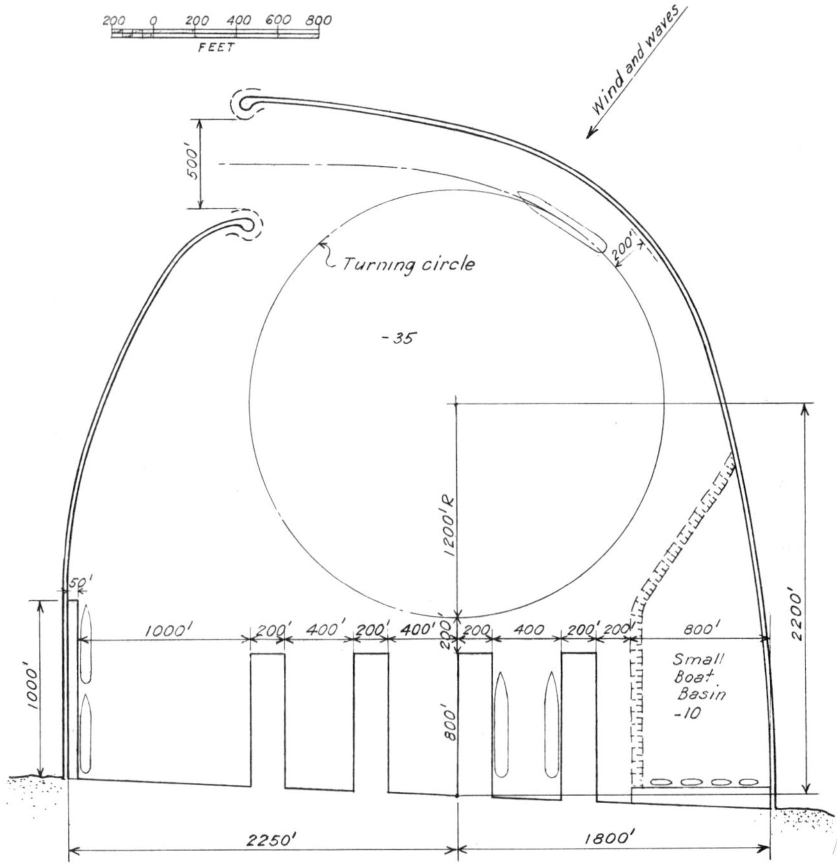

FIG. 3.4 A typical layout for a medium-size artificial harbor with full-size turning basin.

where bulk cargo is being handled and where the wind direction is such as to hold the ship off the dock. In general, winds and current are more bothersome in docking a vessel, when light, than are the relatively small harbor waves, and may necessitate the use of a tug.

Figure 3.6 shows an artificial harbor large enough to provide berthing space for 14 ocean-going vessels and a number of smaller coastal vessels,

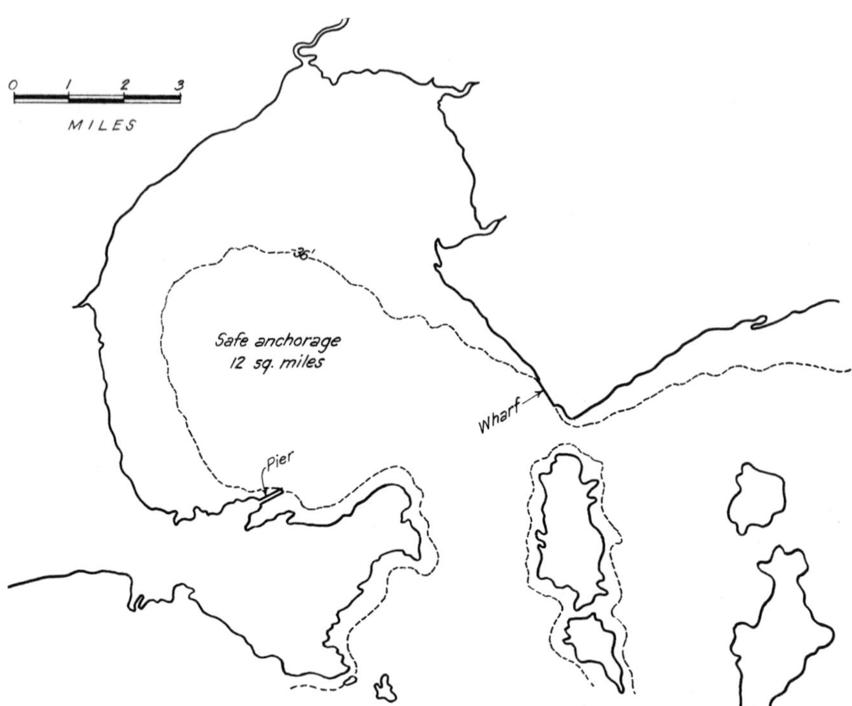

FIG. 3.5 A natural harbor with a very large anchorage area.

a turning basin, and additional space for the shallower draft vessels to anchor for protection from storms or to await their turn in docking. The area of the harbor covers about 1½ square miles. The relatively shallow water permits the construction of breakwater protection, which provides an area for anchoring coastal vessels and, supplemented by dredging a limited area within the harbor, enables the port to be used by ocean-going vessels as well. It is important to keep in mind that these large ships can usually ride out a storm which would normally require the smaller coastal vessels to seek shelter, and, therefore, it is not so important to provide a deep-water anchorage for them within the harbor, as for the smaller vessels.

The above are typical examples of harbor layouts, but each harbor must be studied in light of existing conditions and specific requirements for that particular project.

Type, Location, and Height of Breakwaters. Breakwaters are required for the protection of artificial and semi-natural harbors. Their location and extent will depend upon the direction of the maximum waves, the configuration of the shore line, and the minimum size of harbor required for the anticipated traffic in the port. They may consist of two "arms" out

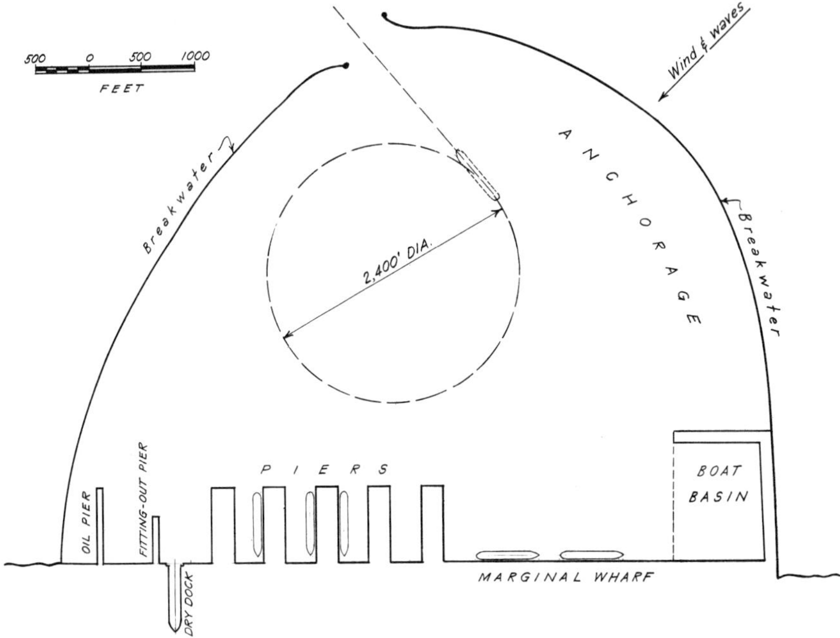

FIG. 3.6 A typical layout for a very large artificial harbor with anchorage area.

from the shore, plus a single breakwater, more or less parallel to the shore, thereby providing two openings to the harbor, as shown in Fig. 3.3, or one opening when connected to one of the arms, usually resulting in a curved alignment, as indicated in Fig. 3.2; or the harbor may be protected with a single arm out from shore; or it may be protected by two arms converging near their outshore ends and overlapping to form a protected entrance to the harbor, such as shown in Fig. 3.4. The selection of the most suitable arrangement will depend principally upon the direction of the maximum waves, and its effectiveness in quieting the harbor may be checked by model tests as described in Sec. 3.6.

Rarely will a location be found where the waves are from one direction only, and generally it will be better in a harbor having two openings for the ships to enter from the direction of the minimum wind and waves and to leave toward the direction of the maximum wind and waves. This is because upon leaving the harbor the ship usually has the freedom of open water in which to maneuver, whereas upon entering the harbor it is immediately in a restricted area and must approach the docks at reduced speed and at a certain inclination to its face.

A single breakwater arm may be used where the waves predominate from one direction only, or where the configuration of the shore line may reduce the fetch in the opposite direction to an extent that the wave-generating area is not sufficient to permit the formation of bothersome waves within the harbor.

The design of breakwaters, including the selection of the type, is covered in Chap. 4.

Location and Width of Entrance to Harbor. In order to reduce the wave height within the harbor, entrances should be no wider than necessary to provide safe navigation and to prevent dangerous currents when the tide is coming in and going out. The entrance width should be in proportion to the size of the harbor and the ships using it. In general the following widths will be found satisfactory: small harbors, 300 ft; medium harbors, 400 to 500 ft; and large harbors, 500 to 800 ft. When the entrance is between breakwaters with sloping faces, the width is measured at the required harbor or channel depth below low water, the entrances being appreciably wider than the above figures when measured at low-water level. For instance, if the required width of entrance is 500 ft and the entrance is between two breakwaters having slopes of 1 on 3, then for a harbor depth of 30 ft the width at low-water level would be 680 ft. In such cases it is advisable to mark the full harbor depth of the entrance by means of buoys, one or more being placed on each side of the entrance channel.

The entrance should be on the lee side of the harbor, where possible; if it must be located at the windward end of the harbor the breakwaters should overlap so that the vessel will have passed through the restricted entrance and be free to turn with the wind before it is hit broadside by the waves. In this manner the interior of the harbor will be protected from the waves. It is usually impossible, however, except at too great a sacrifice of ship maneuverability, to completely prevent the harbor from feeling the effect of the waves to some extent.

When the entrance to a harbor is unobstructed, storm waves from the sea will pass through the opening into the harbor, and unless they are reflected by a vertical surface they will gradually decrease in height as they progress away from the entrance and as the harbor widens with respect to the entrance width. The following equation by Stevenson may be used to approximate the wave height within the harbor, although model tests will give a more accurate picture of wave conditions and are considered essential when studying various arrangements of breakwaters for important harbors.

$$h_p = H\left[\sqrt{\frac{b}{B}} - 0.02\sqrt[4]{D}\left(1 + \sqrt{\frac{b}{B}}\right)\right]$$

where h_p = height of reduced wave at any point p in harbor
H = height of wave at entrance
b = breadth of entrance
B = breadth of harbor at p, being length of arc with center at midway of entrance and radius D
D = distance from entrance to point of observation

All dimensions are in feet. The equation has several limitations. It does not apply to points less than 50 ft from the entrance. The length of the arc is measured between its points of intersection with the two diverging side walls of the harbor. In cases when one of the breakwaters meets the shore at a shorter distance, its line of direction must be extended landward to intersect the arc.

In tidal harbors where there are strong currents, the width of the entrance should be sufficient to prevent the velocity of the current running through the opening at ebb tide from exceeding 4 ft per sec; otherwise it may affect the navigation of ships and possibly create scour at the base of the adjacent breakwaters.

If the waves pass through the entrance and strike a vertical face on the opposite side of the harbor they will reflect, which will increase the wave height within the harbor. This can be corrected by building wave-absorbing beaches, which are flat slopes of rock or granular material placed in front of the vertical surface. However, when this vertical surface is a wharf or bulkhead used for the berthing of ships, it is impossible to use a beach. Other means must be resorted to, such as the installation of short-wave-deflecting spur walls or wave traps along the approach channel to the dock.

When the entrance is formed or deepened by dredging, and where the bottom is fine sand or silt, the effect of the projecting breakwaters on the littoral currents will need to be carefully checked, as the projecting breakwater may act as a groin, tending to cause the deposition of sand at the entrance to the harbor, unless the tidal currents are sufficient to disperse the material as it is deposited. If such is not the case, continual maintenance dredging may be required to keep the entrance and harbor at required depth for navigation. Sometimes the entrance and outer part of the harbor or channel are dredged several feet deeper than required, in order to provide space for the deposition of material so as to limit the maintenance dredging to once every two to three years or more.

Depth of Harbor and Approach Channel. For ideal operating conditions the water in the approach channel, in the entrance, and in the harbor should be of sufficient depth to permit navigation at lowest low water when the ship is fully loaded. This depth must include an allowance for the surge of the ship, which is about one-half the wave height, the out of trim or squat when in motion, and from 2- to 4-ft clearance under the keel, the larger figure being used when the bottom is of hard material such as rock. In a very soft mud bottom the keel may at times touch bottom due to surge and squat, without doing any damage to the ship, but it would be disastrous to have its fully loaded weight bump a hard rock bottom. Therefore, a greater allowance must be made in the depth when the bottom is hard and the harbor and approach channel or approach sea lanes must be carefully swept to make sure that there are no obstructions, such as reefs or rocky pinnacles, boulders, or sunken ships, above the required depth for safe navigation. Since a good design is predicated upon a maximum wave height in the harbor of not over 2 ft, allowing 1 ft for out of trim of the ship, the minimum harbor depth below lowest low water then becomes the loaded draft plus 4 ft, when the bottom is soft, or up to 6 ft when the bottom is rock. These are average figures and the depth in any harbor should be based upon a study of all the conditions, including wave heights, as determined from model tests. Since the excavation of rock is a very costly item, if this is present above the required harbor depth, it is important for the designer to examine carefully the need for the full depth in the harbor. In some commercial harbors the ships come in light and depart loaded, as, for instance, an iron-ore shipping terminal. If there are separate channels for entering and leaving the harbor, the depth at the entrance may be reduced somewhat. Moreover it may be satisfactory to excavate to the full depth only along the docks and to wait for high tide for the loaded ships to depart, thereby permitting a reduced depth in the remainder of the harbor.

Until recent years a harbor depth of 35 to 40 ft would take care of most ships. The Liberty and Victory cargo ships can operate in 32 ft of water. The Panama Canal has a maintained dredged depth of 40 ft; the Delaware River, 40 ft; New York Harbor, 40 ft. The harbor of refuge at the entrance to Delaware Bay affords a safe anchorage area of 552 acres with a minimum low-water depth of 30 ft and an additional area of 237 acres with a minimum low-water depth of 24 ft. The ports of Baltimore and Montreal have a maintained channel depth of 35 ft; that of Boston has been increased from 35 to 40 ft. In general, while ships increased in tonnage, the loaded draft was limited to not over 40 ft so as not to exceed the principal harbor and channel depths in the world. Ships like the *Queen Elizabeth*, which draws 39.5 ft loaded, schedules its departure from New York Harbor on the rising tide. The advent of the supertanker with a dead-weight tonnage of 84,000 to 100,000 tons and a draft of 47 ft presents a new problem in harbor design. The approach to this problem to date has been one of the following:

1. The use of submarine lines and an offshore anchorage in water 55 to 60 ft in depth
2. The transfer of part of the load to smaller tankers in deep water, so as to reduce the draft to under 40 ft which will permit it to proceed to its port of call
3. The construction of a special deep-water unloading terminal

Tides have a very important influence on the depth of the harbor. Table 2.2, in Chap. 2, gives the tidal ranges in feet at principal ports throughout the world. It will be noted that the tidal range along the coasts of the United States seldom exceeds 10 ft, and, therefore, the harbors are dredged to provide the required depth for navigation at lowest low water. The condition is entirely different in the British Isles and on the western coast of Europe, where the Port of Liverpool, England, has a spring tidal range of 27 ft; London, England, 20 ft; Calais, France, 20 ft; and others have even greater variations. In the majority of cases this fluctuation in sea level has resulted in the use of wet docks for the accommodation of shipping, so that the vessels can remain afloat at all stages of the tide. These dock systems require entrance locks with massive gates, heavy swing or bascule bridges and the machinery for working them, pumping equipment, and other accessories. Since all this results in great cost, as well as continuing operational and maintenance expense, the question arises as to the limiting range for the natural tidal working of ports without recourse to enclosed docks. Generally, about 10 to 15 ft is considered to be the dividing point. This, of course, depends upon the cost of dredging and the area available for the marine terminal facilities. While the wet dock has certain advantages in that it eliminates the tidal current and the necessity of shifting the ship's mooring lines, it has the disadvantage of restricting the departure of the vessel, sometimes for several hours, until high tide.

Number, Location, and Type of Docks. Docking facilities vary widely from port to port. They may consist of a single pier or as many as a thousand piers in the Port of New York. The number of berths will depend upon the anticipated number of ships to use the port and the time it will take to discharge and take on cargo or passengers. This will vary for different kinds of cargo, but on an average a vessel will not be in port more than 48 hours, and many bulk cargo ships are loaded in 24 hours or less.

The design of docks, piers, wharves, and bulkheads is covered in Chap.

5. The selection of the type of dock and the material used for its construction will depend upon a number of factors, such as:

Special requirements or local customs and practice: Such is the case in comparing European and American construction, the former with its predominance of massive quays of masonry and concrete, and the latter with its relatively light, open structures of piling and framed decks.

Site conditions: especially foundation conditions and corrosiveness of water.

Availability of materials: timber, steel, concrete, rock, etc.

Permanency of construction: While municipal ports are usually considered to be permanent installations, many commercial ports are constructed to be used only for a limited period of time.

Economy of construction: Several alternate types of docks, using different kinds of materials, may need to be studied to determine the most economical construction.

Size and weight of ships using the port: The larger and heavier ships of today limit, in many instances, the use of timber construction. Moreover their greater draft, requiring a depth of water alongside the dock of as much as 50 ft, may rule out the use of sheet-pile bulkheads or wharves.

Method of construction: This may exert an important influence on the type of construction finally selected. Massive quay walls require huge, floating derricks to lift the heavy masonry or concrete blocks. Water conditions may be so rough that floating marine equipment cannot be used at the site, necessitating the construction to be carried out by overhead methods.

The dredging may not be done until after the docks are built. As a general rule, this will preclude the use of piles and open-pier type of construction, as it may be difficult to remove the material in under the dock to a safe slope after the dredging is completed.

The time schedule may control, as some types of construction are much faster than others. Mobilization time for certain types of equipment and long delivery dates on some materials will have their influence on the type of construction adopted.

Wharves and piers should be located in the most sheltered part of the harbor or along the lee side of the breakwaters. Where possible the pier should be so oriented as to have the ship alongside headed as nearly into the wind and waves as possible. This is particularly important if the harbor is not well protected.

Shore Facilities for Marine Terminals. Onshore marine terminal facilities may consist of one or more of the following depending upon the size of the port and the service it renders.

Transit sheds. These are located immediately in back of the apron on the pier or wharf. Their function is to store for a short period of time cargo awaiting loading or distribution after being unloaded from ships.

Warehouses. These may replace transit sheds at some marine terminals, but when used to supplement the latter they are usually located inland and not on the pier structure. A preferred layout along wharves or bulkheads is for the warehouses to be located a short distance in back of the transit sheds, the two structures being separated a sufficient distance to accommodate trucks or railroad cars at loading platforms. Warehouses provide both short- and long-term storage, and their use may be for general storage, bonded dutiable goods, or cold storage.

Bulk storage may be in open piles over conveyor tunnels, which may be covered with sheds when protection from the elements is required; in bins and silos or elevators as commonly referred to when grain is stored; or in storage tanks, if liquid. These will be located as near to the waterfront as possible, and sometimes directly alongside the wharf or pier, to enable direct loading into the hold of the ship. However, where the terrain adjacent to the harbor is not suitable or the area is inadequate, the bulk-storage facilities may be located some distance away, and the material transported from the ships by conveyor or pipeline, as described in Chap. 8.

Terminal building. This will house the port administration personnel and the custom officials if a separate custom house is not provided. It should be located in a prominent and convenient position with respect to the docks.

Guard houses are located at strategic points in the port area, at the entrance gates of highways and railways, the entrances to piers or terminal areas, bonded storage, etc.

Stevedores warehouses will house the cargo-handling gear, wash and locker rooms, and other facilities for the stevedores.

Miscellaneous buildings and structures may consist of a fire house and fire-fighting equipment, power plant, garages, repair shops, dry docks, marine railways, fishing piers, or yacht basins.

The area comprising a port or falling within its jurisdiction will vary with the nature and tonnage of the cargo to be handled and the services to be provided at the port. The area may vary from less than 1 to over 1,400 square miles for the Port of New York.

3.5 Site Investigation

After the preliminary layouts of the port have been completed and before starting the final design, it will be necessary, in most instances, to obtain additional site information. Not only is this necessary to arrive at a sound and economical layout for the port, including a reasonably accurate estimate of the cost, but the contractors who will be called upon to submit bids for the construction will want to know about the subsoil and other conditions affecting their work.

The site investigation will generally consist of the following items of work: (1) a hydrographic survey of the harbor and channel area, including the sweeping of the bottom, if required, (2) a topographic survey of the marine terminal area on shore, (3) soil investigation by making borings and/or probings on water, and borings and/or test pits on land, supplemented by soil testing and analyses, if required, (4) tide and current observations, (5) obtaining information on wind, waves, and earthquakes if in an area of seismographic disturbance, availability and cost of materials and labor, availability of housing, and local ordinances and building codes.

Hydrographic Survey. This is made to determine the elevations of the bottom of the body of water and should extend over an area somewhat larger than the proposed channel and harbor. In addition, it should locate the shore line at low and high water and all structures or obstructions in the water and along the shore, such as sunken ships, reefs, or large rocks. Sometimes it will be desirable to have a diver survey the condition of the bottom, determining the size of the boulders or rocks, sunken ships, etc., which will require removal if they are lying on the bottom where it is above or a short distance below the required depth of the harbor. In addition, all borings and soundings should be located.

Since both hydrographic and topographic surveys are usually required, a single-control base line, which consists of a series of connecting lines whose lengths and bearings are determined, is located on shore to serve for both soundings and shore details. The intersections of the lines should be monumented so that they will not be lost and can be used later on when the port is constructed. For vertical control, one or more bench marks should be established near the shore line, so that a tide gauge may be set nearby.

The determination of the relief of the bottom of the body of water is made by soundings or by the use of a fathometer designed for hydrographic surveys. The latter method is being used by the Coast and Geodetic Survey and has superseded lead-line soundings to a large extent. The locations of the soundings are determined by one of the following methods:

1. By taking soundings on a known range line and reading one angle from a fixed point on shore
2. By taking soundings from a boat and reading two angles simultaneously from two fixed points on shore
3. By reading two angles from a boat to three fixed points on shore, by means of a sextant

4. By reading a direction and a vertical angle simultaneously from an elevated point on shore
5. By taking soundings at known distances along a calibrated cable stretched between a station on shore and a fixed station in the water on an established range line

A fathometer or depth-recording instrument is usually mounted in a motorboat which is kept on course on established range lines, as the recording chart produces a horizontal, natural profile of the bottom. The fathometer, designed for hydrographic surveying, when operated by experienced personnel and properly adjusted and calibrated daily, is now considered superior to lead-line soundings, both as to accuracy and the speed with which the survey can be made. The accuracy is definitely improved where currents are high enough to affect the lead line by appreciably deviating it from the vertical; personal errors in reading the depths are eliminated; and where the bottom is very soft the fathometer gives a more accurate depth indication, as the lead weight may penetrate the bottom an unknown amount without being detected by the observer.

The depth of the sounding is referred to water level at the time it is made, and later is corrected to the datum water level by means of tide gauges or tide tables. Therefore, it is important to keep a record of the time and day the soundings are made. When the tide gauge does not have a self-recording device, frequent readings will have to be taken throughout the survey. Soundings, where plotted on the drawing, are usually referred to low-water datum.

Soundings should be made at approximately 25-ft intervals along lines spaced from 50 to 100 ft on centers, depending upon the irregularity of the bottom. Closer spacing may be needed where greater detail is required to determine sharp changes in the profile of the bottom or to outline obstructions.

Soundings are plotted on a drawing generally referred to as a hydrographic map which should show the datum, high- and low-water lines, contour lines of equal depth interpolated from the soundings, and principal land and water features. Contour depths may be either in feet, meters, or fathoms, although the last is not used generally for making harbor and marine terminal studies and layouts. In the South American countries, where the metric system is used, the depth of water is customarily referred to in meters. Since the sea bottom is usually less precipitous and the slopes are more gentle and uniform than are those on land, the scale of the hydrographic map may be somewhat smaller than would normally be used for plotting the land topography. Unless the harbor area is very large a scale of 1 in. = 200 ft or 1:2,000 in a proportional scale will be satisfactory. It is desirable to have all of the hydrography on one sheet, if possible, as this gives a better over-all picture of the harbor. However, this may not be possible if the harbor is very large, or if there is a long approach channel. In general the scale should be large enough so that not more than ten contour lines, in 2-ft intervals, occur within 1 in.

If dredging of the harbor or channel is required, the material is usually measured in place to determine the quantity for payment. To determine this quantity, soundings on fixed sections are taken before and after dredging, and the change in cross sections is determined by computation or by planimeter. Payment is usually specified to be made for material removed down to a maximum of 2 ft below the required dredge bottom, but all material must be removed to at least the minimum depth specified.

Topographic Survey. Land topography of the marine terminal area should be obtained so as to plot contours of the ground at 2- to 5-ft intervals, the latter figure being used where the country is rough and in areas where there is to be little or no construction of importance. In building areas, elevations on 25-ft centers in both directions, with additional elevations taken at abrupt changes in ground, will provide satisfactory information. Where there is a dense ground cover the cross-profile method will be found most suitable. These profiles may be made with level and tape or stadia, on about 100-ft centers, by clearing paths to permit an unobstructed line of sight. The ground between the 100-ft profiles should be examined, as far as possible, and any prominent irregularities in ground level estimated and noted, so that contours, which are interpolated from elevations along the profiles, can be estimated for the areas in between.

Topographic maps, in addition to showing the contours of the ground, should locate all borings and test pits, buildings, utilities, and any prominent landmarks. Contours generally are referred to high-water datum. The map scale should be such that the contour lines are not spaced closer than 30 to the inch. Where considerable detail is involved the scale should be 1 in. = 100 ft or 1:1,000 or less, but for small-scale maps 1 in. = 1,000 ft or 1:10,000 or more may be used.

Soil Investigations. For the harbor and channel areas, borings or probings should be made at strategic points to determine information on the subsoil conditions at the locations of breakwaters, piers, wharves, bulkheads, and other marine structures.

When dredging is involved borings or probings should be taken on approximately 250- to 500-ft centers over the area to be dredged.

Borings which are made at the location of marine structures should be located along definite lines, such as the center line of a pier or breakwater, and on close enough centers to enable a reasonably accurate profile of the soil strata to be plotted. Usually 100-ft centers will suffice for this purpose. If the structure is of considerable width two or more lines of borings should be made so that transverse sections of the soil strata can be plotted.

The depth of the borings will depend upon the soil encountered and the depth to bedrock. In most locations a penetration of 150 ft below low-water level will encounter either rock or soil of suitable bearing value to support pile or caisson foundations. Generally speaking, a penetration of 40 ft into firm material will insure an adequate support for the marine structures. For determining information on the soil to be dredged, borings or probings need to be carried only to a depth of 2 ft below dredged bottom, but if rock is encountered above this level one or more of the borings should be drilled to a depth of 5 ft below dredged bottom and as much of the core recovered as possible to determine the character of the rock, as this will have an influence on the cost of its removal. For determining the elevations of the top of rock, jet probings may be used in place of borings, as these are quicker and cheaper to perform.

Except for soil under breakwaters, the additional load imposed by open piers and other similar marine structures on the underlying soil is not large. Therefore, dry sample wash borings made with 2½-in. casing will usually provide adequate information. However, in some locations where the soil is plastic, it will be desirable to make undisturbed-soil sample borings and soil tests to determine the depths to which piles or cylinders should be driven. Likewise, where there is an appreciable load added to the underlying plastic soil, such as under breakwaters or gravity quay and dock walls, or where sheet-pile bulkheads or dock walls must be designed to support the lateral pressures of the fill and surcharge in back of them, it will be desirable to make soil tests on undisturbed samples, so as to determine the shearing strength and consolidation coefficient of the soil.

To make the borings and probings over water it will be necessary to have a small, flat deck barge or pontoon on which to support the boring equipment. The latter is sometimes constructed of empty oil drums and wood framing as shown in Fig. 3.7. Where the water is very rough it will be necessary to lower spuds onto the bottom and raise the barge above the reach of the waves. A drill barge or pontoon, equipped with spuds, is shown in Fig. 3.8.

The amount and type of equipment will depend upon the information to be obtained. For jet probings, a gasoline-engine-driven pump, which will deliver 250 gal per min at 100 lb per sq in. pressure, a small A frame, with pulley, mounted at the end of the barge, and a sufficient number of lengths of 1¼-in. pipe will suffice. The addition of a gasoline engine, drive hammers, drill pipe, casing, and split-barrel sampler, plus mis-

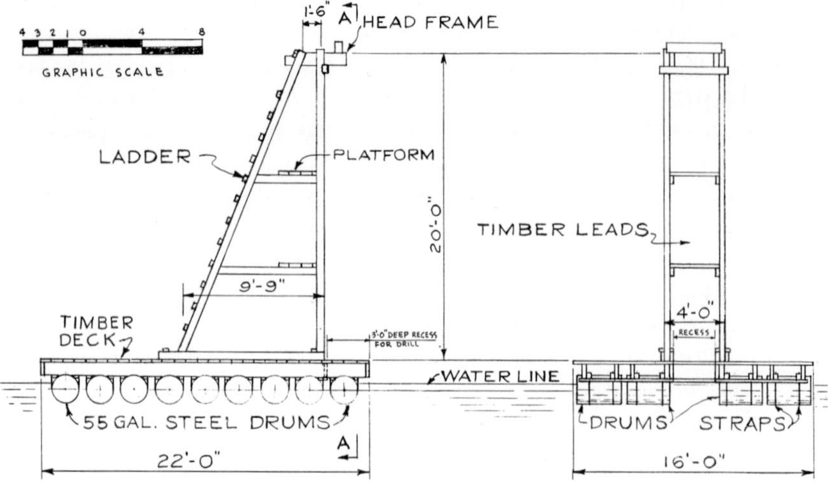

FIG. 3.7 Drill barge which can be constructed in remote locations for making borings over water.

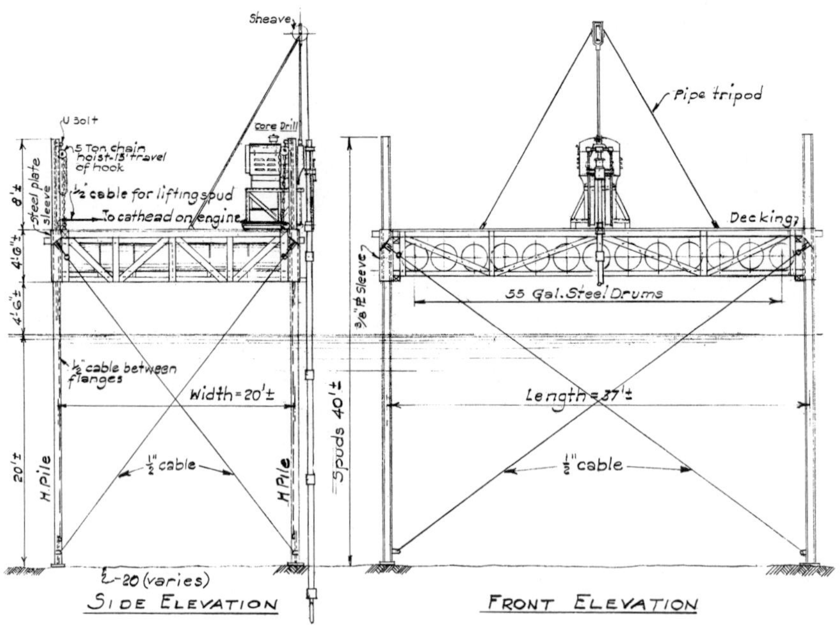

FIG. 3.8 Drill barge, equipped with spuds, for making borings over rough water.

cellaneous accessories, will enable dry sample wash borings to be made. The casing should be 2½-in. extra-heavy, wrought-iron pipe, generally in 5-ft lengths with threaded ends and couplings, although in deep water the size is sometimes increased to 4 in. or larger. Steel pipe is not satisfactory as it will not stand up under hard driving and will usually break at the threads. Drill rods are generally in 10-ft lengths, with flush-type couplings. They vary in size and are commonly referred to by letters, such as E, A, B, and N rods, which have external diameters of 1$\frac{5}{16}$, 1⅝, 1$\frac{29}{32}$, and 2⅜ in., respectively. Drive or drop hammers are cast-iron weights, generally of two sizes: 140 lb for driving the sampler and 300 lb for driving the casing. For obtaining dry samples a split-barrel sampler is commonly used. The barrel is split lengthwise so that it can be taken apart and the sample removed in the exact state in which it was recovered from the ground. The sampler is available in several sizes, but, for use with 2½-in. casing, a 2-in. external diameter, giving a 1½-in. diameter sample, is most commonly used. It has a ball valve in the head to prevent the pressure of the head of water in the connecting drill rod from forcing the material out of the sampler when it is raised out of the hole. When the soil is loose and granular, making it difficult to retain it in the sampler, the sampler should be equipped with a flap valve located just above the cutting edge. This can be removed, if not needed.

When undisturbed samples are to be taken in silts and clays, the casing should be preferably not less than 3½ or 4 in. in diameter which will permit the use of a 3-in. thin-wall Shelby tube sampler. This sampling device consists of a thin-wall metal tube (steel or brass), the upper end of which is attached to a head, with ball check valve, by means of flat-head machine screws. Standard tubes are 2⅛, 3, and 3½ in. in external diameter and are 26½ in. long. The tube is jacked or forced (not driven) into the soil the required depth, after which it is removed from the hole and the thin-wall tube detached from the head. Both ends are then filled or sealed with paraffin, capped, taped, and dipped in paraffin.

The Shelby tube thin-wall type of sampler has been found to be one of the better types of samplers for removing plastic soil in as undisturbed condition as possible. The thin cutting edge and its small area relative to the gross area of the tube result in keeping the distortion of the sample to a minimum.

When rock is to be drilled, the wash boring equipment will need to be supplemented by a core-drilling machine, core barrels, and diamond bits, together with some additional miscellaneous tools.

Borings at harbors and marine terminals should be made with the same care and, generally, in the same manner as those for more monumental structures on land. For dry-sample wash borings and undisturbed-soil sampling an acceptable procedure follows.

1. The barge or pontoon is anchored or spudded on the bottom at the specified location and the casing lowered through the water until it reaches bottom where it is either pushed or driven if necessary, until it penetrates to a depth of 5 ft.

2. The casing is washed out to the bottom, taking care not to wash below the bottom, and a sample is taken of the soil using the split sampler or a bailer if the material is very soft, as is often the case when the bottom is silt or mud.

3. The casing is then driven an additional 5 ft, and the process of washing out and taking the sample is repeated.

4. The procedure of driving the casing, washing it out, and taking the sample is continued until the required depth is reached.

5. If plastic soils are encountered and soil analyses are required, samples should be recovered using the Shelby tube sampler. In this case the casing should be washed out only to about 1 ft from the bottom and the remainder of the material removed with a clean-out auger. The sampler is then pushed into the bottom to the required depth and withdrawn.

6. A record should be kept of the blows per foot in driving the casing and the blows for the first and second 6 in. in driving the sampler. Figure 3.9 illustrates a suitable form for recording the boring information. In drilling rock a record should be kept of the speed of drilling, the depth drilled, and the amount of core recovered.

7. Samples removed from the split-barrel sampler should be placed immediately in 8-oz glass jars, with screwed on covers, which should be dipped in paraffin. Although these are not treated as undisturbed samples, it is a good policy to prevent them from drying out so that, upon later examination, they will represent a reasonably accurate condition of the soil as removed. Each glass jar should be labeled, giving the boring number, sample number, and depth at which the sample was taken.

Rock cores should be placed in wood boxes with wood dividing strips, the pieces of core being placed in the order in which they are removed from the hole. The number of the boring and the top and bottom of the core should be marked along the divider strip, opposite the core from each hole.

When the bottom is to be explored over an extensive area, considerable time may be saved by supplementing the borings by the use of the Marine Sonoprobe, which will indicate the top of rock and the amount of overburden, the character of the latter being distinguishable as between mud, clay, and sand. Although the Sonoprobe is not intended to replace borings, it is a valuable tool in determining the locations where they will be of most value. Likewise the borings are an important guide to the correct interpretation and correlation of the Sonoprobe information in the areas between the borings; thus one supplements the other.

The instrument functions like a small reflecting seismograph. Sound pulses are generated at rates of three to twelve per second, and have a frequency of about 3,800 cycles per second as compared to around 13,000 or more for a fathometer. The sound waves are propagated through the water and into the bottom where part of the energy is reflected back by the interface between each pair of sedimentary beds that have the necessary contrast in acoustic impedance. The reflected sound waves are then picked up by the receiving transducer, converted into electrical signals, and recorded on continuously moving electrosensitive paper.

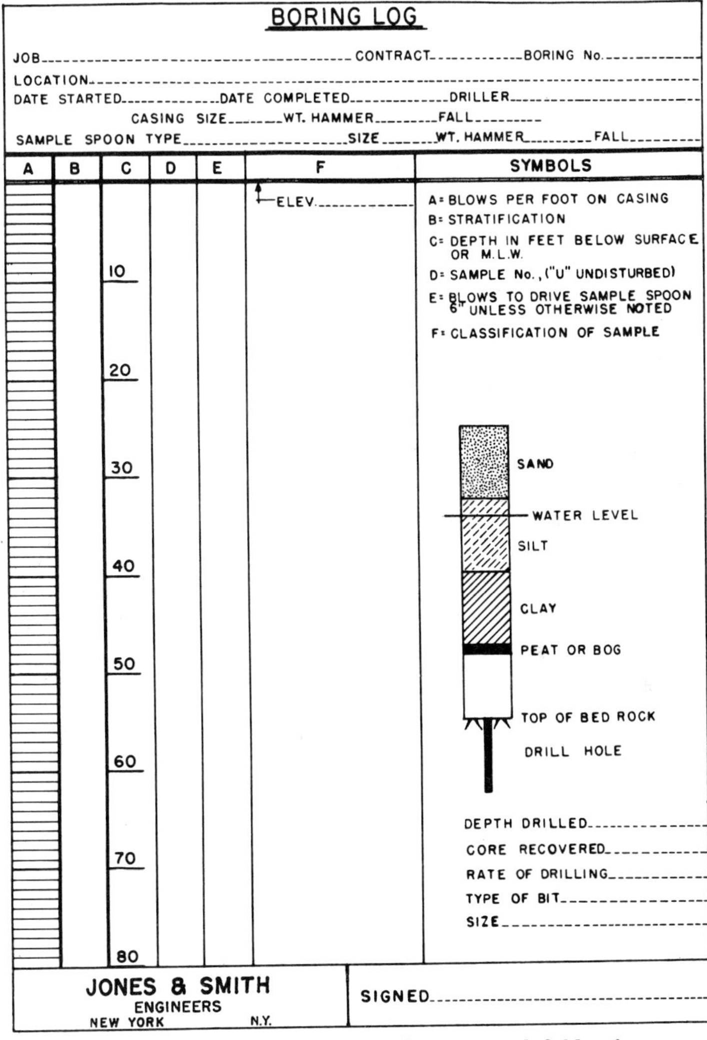

BORING LOG

JOB .... CONTRACT .... BORING No. ....

LOCATION ....

DATE STARTED .... DATE COMPLETED .... DRILLER ....

CASING SIZE .... WT. HAMMER .... FALL ....

SAMPLE SPOON TYPE .... SIZE .... WT. HAMMER .... FALL ....

A	B	C	D	E	F	SYMBOLS
					ELEV.	A = BLOWS PER FOOT ON CASING B = STRATIFICATION C = DEPTH IN FEET BELOW SURFACE OR M.L.W. D = SAMPLE No., ("U" UNDISTURBED) E = BLOWS TO DRIVE SAMPLE SPOON 6" UNLESS OTHERWISE NOTED F = CLASSIFICATION OF SAMPLE
		10				
		20				
		30				SAND
						WATER LEVEL
		40				SILT
						CLAY
		50				PEAT OR BOG
						TOP OF BED ROCK
		60				DRILL HOLE
						DEPTH DRILLED ....
		70				CORE RECOVERED ....
						RATE OF DRILLING ....
						TYPE OF BIT ....
		80				SIZE ....

JONES & SMITH
ENGINEERS
NEW YORK N.Y.

SIGNED ....

FIG. 3.9 Boring report form for recording essential field information.

Borings on land are made in a similar manner.

Soil Analyses. Soil samples should be carefully classified. Since most soils are mixtures of sands, silts, or clays, sieve and sedimentation analyses will need to be made in the laboratory. The size of particles larger than 0.074 mm, which corresponds to the U.S. Standard sieve no. 200, is usually determined by sieving; smaller sizes require sedimentation tests. From the results of these tests plotted in the form of gradation curves, the various fractions of sand, silt, and clay may be determined in accordance with the ASTM or the Unified Soil Classification System, as shown in Fig. 3.10,

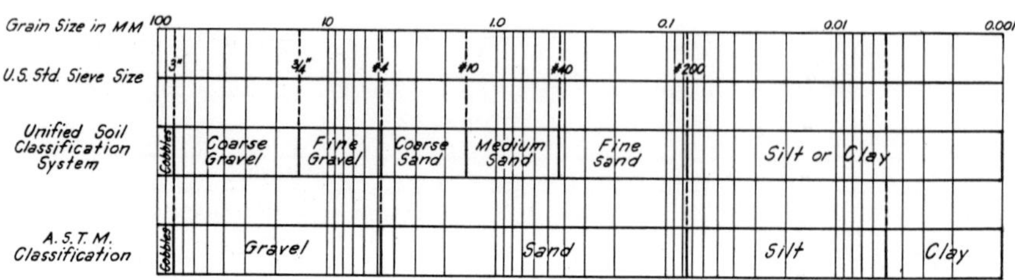

FIG. 3.10 Graph showing relation of grain size to soil classification.

which gives the corresponding U.S. Standard sieve sizes and the diameter of the grains in millimeters. The Unified Soil Classification System was adopted by the Corps of Engineers and the U.S. Bureau of Reclamation in January, 1952, and table 1, from Technical Memorandum 3-357 of the Waterways Experiment Station is shown in Fig. 3.11. This system employs not only the grain size determination but also the plasticity and compressibility characteristics as the basis of soil identification. Figure 3.12 shows the triangular soil classification chart of the Mississippi River Commission used by the Corps of Engineers before the adoption of the Unified System. The author considers this chart to be very useful in the field of foundations for port and marine structures. From this information engineering classifications of the soils may be made and soil profiles drawn showing the soil stratification. These are usually drawn to a distorted scale of one horizontal to ten vertical.

Other routine tests are usually performed for the determination of the water content, the specific gravity, and the voids ratio.

The water or moisture content is the ratio of the weight of water to the weight of solids.

$$w = \frac{W_w}{W_s} 100$$

where w = water content, per cent of weight of solids
W_w = weight of water
W_s = weight of solids

When all the voids are filled with water the voids ratio e, which is the ratio of the volume of voids to the volume of solids, is equal to

$$e = \frac{w}{100} G$$

where G = specific gravity of the solid material.

The bulk specific gravity γ of the soil above the water level is the ratio of the total weight of the soil in air to the total volume of the soil and voids. If no moisture is present, the bulk specific gravity γ_d is

$$\gamma_d = \frac{G}{1 + e}$$

which, when multiplied by the weight of a cubic foot of water, 62.4 lb, will give the weight of a cubic foot of dry soil. If all voids are filled with water,

$$\gamma_s = \frac{G + e}{1 + e}$$

and the unit weight of a cubic foot fully saturated is $\gamma_s \times 62.4$. If the voids are only partially filled with capillary water,

$$\gamma_w = \frac{G(1 + w/100)}{1 + e}$$

and the unit weight of a cubic foot is $\gamma_w \times 62.4$. If the soil is entirely submerged or buoyant,

$$\gamma_b = \frac{G - 1}{1 + e}$$

and the unit weight of a cubic foot submerged is $\gamma_b \times 62.4$.

Unconfined compression tests, which are similar to standard tests on concrete cylinders, are relatively simple to make if the soil is cohesive, and they will give the cohesive or shearing strength of the soil, which is one-half the unconfined compressive strength when ϕ, the angle of internal friction, is equal to zero

$$c = \frac{q_u}{2}$$

where c = cohesion, lb per sq ft
q_u = compressive strength at failure, lb per sq ft

UNIFIED SOIL CLASSIFICATION
(Including Identification and Description)

Major Divisions			Group Symbols	Typical Names	Field Identification Procedures (Excluding particles larger than 3 in. and basing fractions on estimated weights)		
1	2		3	4	5		
Coarse-grained Soils More than half of material is larger than No. 200 sieve size.	Gravels More than half of coarse fraction is larger than No. 4 sieve size.	Clean Gravels (Little or no fines)	GW	Well-graded gravels, gravel-sand mixtures, little or no fines.	Wide range in grain sizes and substantial amounts of all intermediate particle sizes.		
			GP	Poorly graded gravels or gravel-sand mixtures, little or no fines.	Predominantly one size or a range of sizes with some intermediate sizes missing.		
		Gravels with Fines (Appreciable amount of fines)	GM	Silty gravels, gravel-sand-silt mixture.	Nonplastic fines or fines with low plasticity (for identification procedures see ML below).		
			GC	Clayey gravels, gravel-sand-clay mixtures.	Plastic fines (for identification procedures see CL below).		
	Sands More than half of coarse fraction is smaller than No. 4 sieve size.	Clean Sands (Little or no fines)	SW	Well-graded sands, gravelly sands, little or no fines.	Wide range in grain size and substantial amounts of all intermediate particle sizes.		
			SP	Poorly graded sands or gravelly sands, little or no fines.	Predominantly one size or a range of sizes with some intermediate sizes missing.		
		Sands with Fines (Appreciable amount of fines)	SM	Silty sands, sand-silt mixtures.	Nonplastic fines or fines with low plasticity (for identification procedures see ML below).		
	(For visual classification, the 1/4-in. size may be used as equivalent to the No. 4 sieve size)		SC	Clayey sands, sand-clay mixtures.	Plastic fines (for identification procedures see CL below).		
The No. 200 sieve size is about the smallest particle visible to the naked eye.					Identification Procedures on Fraction Smaller than No. 40 Sieve Size		
Fine-grained Soils More than half of material is smaller than No. 200 sieve size.					Dry Strength (Crushing characteristics)	Dilatancy (Reaction to shaking)	Toughness (Consistency near PL)
	Silts and Clays Liquid limit is less than 50		ML	Inorganic silts and very fine sands, rock flour, silty or clayey fine sands or clayey silts with slight plasticity.	None to slight	Quick to slow	None
			CL	Inorganic clays of low to medium plasticity, gravelly clays, sandy clays, silty clays, lean clays.	Medium to high	None to very slow	Medium
			OL	Organic silts and organic silty clays of low plasticity.	Slight to medium	Slow	Slight
	Silts and Clays Liquid limit is greater than 50		MH	Inorganic silts, micaceous or diatomaceous fine sandy or silty soils, elastic silts.	Slight to medium	Slow to none	Slight to medium
			CH	Inorganic clays of high plasticity, fat clays.	High to very high	None	High
			OH	Organic clays of medium to high plasticity, organic silts.	Medium to high	None to very slow	Slight to medium
Highly Organic Soils			Pt	Peat and other highly organic soils.	Readily identified by color, odor, spongy feel and frequently by fibrous texture.		

(1) Boundary classifications: Soils possessing characteristics of two groups are designated by combinations of group symbols. For example GW-GC, well-graded gravel-sand mixture with clay binder.

(2) All sieve sizes on this chart are U. S. standard.

FIELD IDENTIFICATION PROCEDURES FOR FINE-GRAINED SOILS OR FRACTIONS

These procedures are to be performed on the minus No. 40 sieve size particles, approximately 1/64 in. For field classification purposes, screening is not intended, simply remove by hand the coarse particles that interfere with the tests.

Dilatancy (reaction to shaking)

After removing particles larger than No. 40 sieve size, prepare a pat of moist soil with a volume of about one-half cubic inch. Add enough water if necessary to make the soil soft but not sticky.

Place the pat in the open palm of one hand and shake horizontally, striking vigorously against the other hand several times. A positive reaction consists of the appearance of water on the surface of the pat which changes to a livery consistency and becomes glossy. When the sample is squeezed between the fingers, the water and gloss disappear from the surface, the pat stiffens, and finally it cracks or crumbles. The rapidity of appearance of water during shaking and of its disappearance during squeezing assist in identifying the character of the fines in a soil.

Very fine clean sands give the quickest and most distinct reaction whereas a plastic clay has no reaction. Inorganic silts, such as a typical rock flour, show a moderately quick reaction.

Dry Strength (crushing characteristics)

FIG. 3.11 Unified Soil Classification Table. (*Courtesy of United*

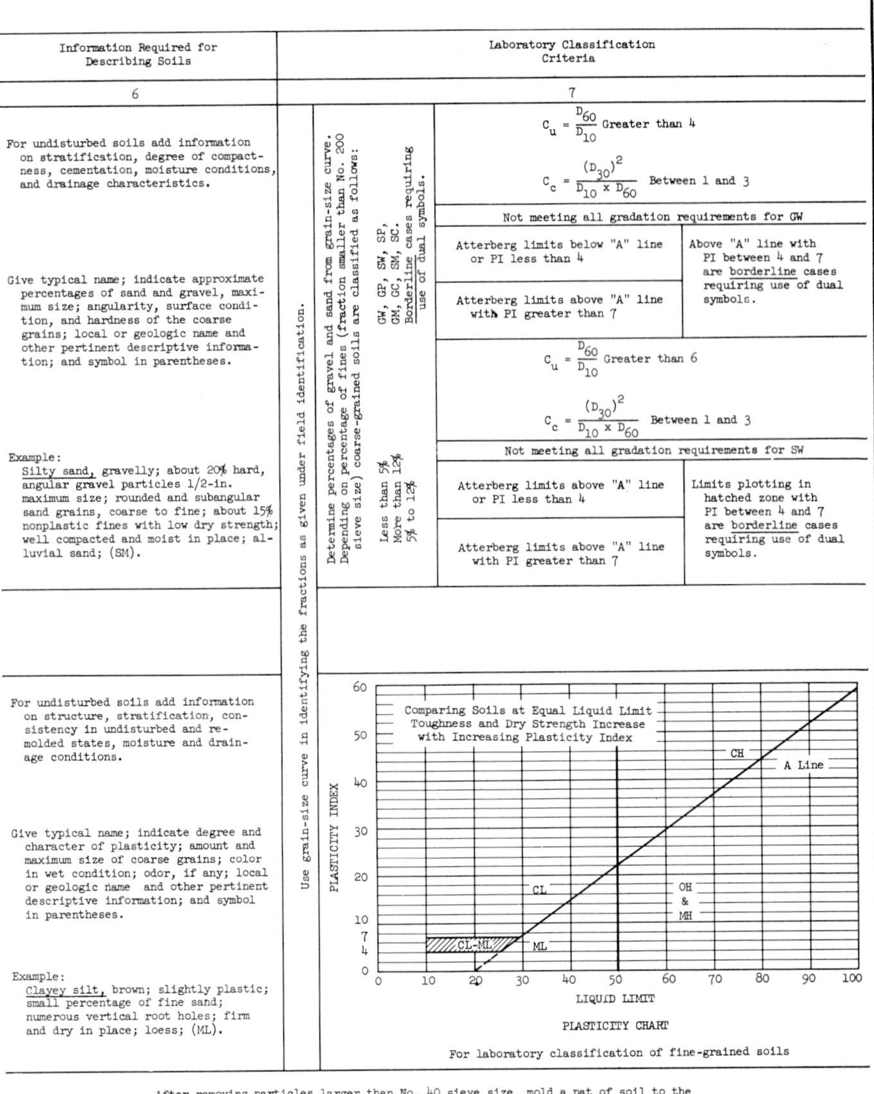

Information Required for Describing Soils	Laboratory Classification Criteria			
6	7			
For undisturbed soils add information on stratification, degree of compactness, cementation, moisture conditions, and drainage characteristics.	Use grain-size curve in identifying the fractions as given under field identification.	Determine percentages of gravel and sand from grain-size curve. Depending on percentage of fines (fraction smaller than No. 200 sieve size) coarse-grained soils are classified as follows: Less than 5% GW, GP, SW, SP; More than 12% GM, GC, SM, SC; 5% to 12% Borderline cases requiring use of dual symbols.	$C_u = \frac{D_{60}}{D_{10}}$ Greater than 4 $C_c = \frac{(D_{30})^2}{D_{10} \times D_{60}}$ Between 1 and 3	
			Not meeting all gradation requirements for GW	
Give typical name; indicate approximate percentages of sand and gravel, maximum size; angularity, surface condition, and hardness of the coarse grains; local or geologic name and other pertinent descriptive information; and symbol in parentheses.			Atterberg limits below "A" line or PI less than 4	Above "A" line with PI between 4 and 7 are borderline cases requiring use of dual symbols.
			Atterberg limits above "A" line with PI greater than 7	
			$C_u = \frac{D_{60}}{D_{10}}$ Greater than 6 $C_c = \frac{(D_{30})^2}{D_{10} \times D_{60}}$ Between 1 and 3	
			Not meeting all gradation requirements for SW	
Example: Silty sand, gravelly; about 20% hard, angular gravel particles 1/2-in. maximum size; rounded and subangular sand grains, coarse to fine; about 15% nonplastic fines with low dry strength; well compacted and moist in place; alluvial sand; (SM).			Atterberg limits above "A" line or PI less than 4	Limits plotting in hatched zone with PI between 4 and 7 are borderline cases requiring use of dual symbols.
			Atterberg limits above "A" line with PI greater than 7	
For undisturbed soils add information on structure, stratification, consistency in undisturbed and remolded states, moisture and drainage conditions.		PLASTICITY CHART (see below)		
Give typical name; indicate degree and character of plasticity; amount and maximum size of coarse grains; color in wet condition; odor, if any; local or geologic name and other pertinent descriptive information; and symbol in parentheses.				
Example: Clayey silt, brown; slightly plastic; small percentage of fine sand; numerous vertical root holes; firm and dry in place; loess; (ML).				

PLASTICITY CHART

For laboratory classification of fine-grained soils

After removing particles larger than No. 40 sieve size, mold a pat of soil to the consistency of putty, adding water if necessary. Allow the pat to dry completely by oven, sun, or air-drying, and then test its strength by breaking and crumbling between the fingers. This strength is a measure of the character and quantity of the colloidal fraction contained in the soil. The dry strength increases with increasing plasticity.

High dry strength is characteristic for clays of the CH group. A typical inorganic silt possesses only very slight dry strength. Silty fine sands and silts have about the same slight dry strength, but can be distinguished by the feel when powdering the dried specimen. Fine sand feels gritty whereas a typical silt has the smooth feel of flour.

Toughness (consistency near plastic limit)

After particles larger than the No. 40 sieve size are removed, a specimen of soil about one-half inch cube in size, is molded to the consistency of putty. If too dry, water must be added and if sticky, the specimen should be spread out in a thin layer and allowed to lose some moisture by evaporation. Then the specimen is rolled out by hand on a smooth surface or between the palms into a thread about one-eighth inch in diameter. The thread is then folded and rerolled repeatedly. During this manipulation the moisture content is gradually reduced and the specimen stiffens, finally loses its plasticity, and crumbles when the plastic limit is reached.

After the thread crumbles, the pieces should be lumped together and a slight kneading action continued until the lump crumbles.

The tougher the thread near the plastic limit and the stiffer the lump when it finally crumbles, the more potent is the colloidal clay fraction in the soil. Weakness of the thread at the plastic limit and quick loss of coherence of the lump below the plastic limit indicate either inorganic clay of low plasticity, or materials such as kaolin-type clays and organic clays which occur below the A-line.

Highly organic clays have a very weak and spongy feel at the plastic limit.

States Army Engineer Waterways Experiment Station.)

If the shearing resistance of the soil is dependent upon both friction and cohesion, the triaxial shear test, in which the test cylinder is confined under a constant pressure while the vertical pressure is gradually increased until failure takes place, should be performed. The results are shown graphically by means of the Mohr circle diagram, in which the slope of the tangent line is the tangent of the angle of internal friction and the intercept on the vertical axis is the cohesion. If the intercept is zero the soil is granular and noncohesive.

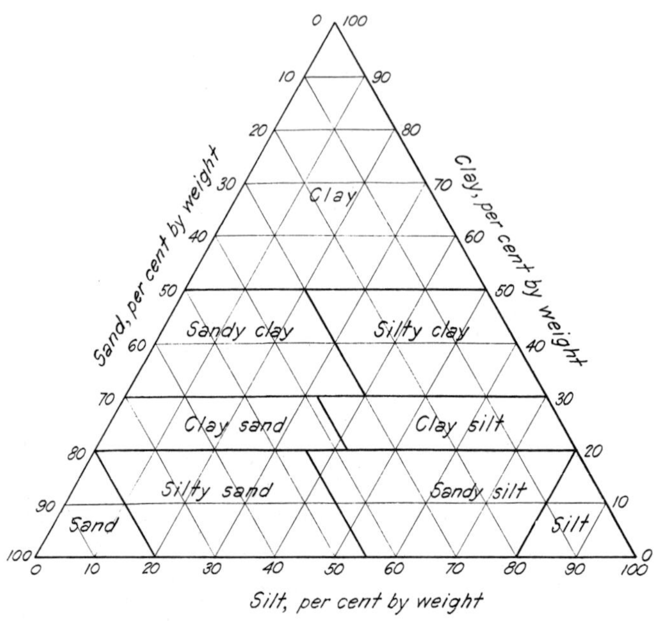

FIG. 3.12 Triangular soil classification chart of the Mississippi River Commission. (*No longer used by the Corps of Engineers.*)

When settlement of the cohesive soils is an important factor, as under breakwaters or solid quay walls or where fill is to be added to raise the ground level, consolidation tests should be performed which will enable the determination of the probable amount of settlement under the additional load on the soil and the time required for it to take place. Also, it will be possible from the consolidation curve to estimate the greatest pressure under which the clay sample had been consolidated during its past geological history. This will give an indication as to whether the ground on which the shore facilities of the marine terminal are to be constructed is fully consolidated under its own weight or is still undergoing settlement.

Assuming that laboratory tests have been performed and that pressure-void ratio curves have been plotted, the settlement can then be computed quite simply from the following expression

$$S = \frac{e_1 - e_2}{1 + e_1} H$$

where S = settlement, in.

e_1 = voids ratio for pressure, tons per sq ft, at elevation where sample was taken

e_2 = voids ratio for increased pressure, tons per sq ft, resulting from surcharge load

H = thickness of compressible layer, in.

Also, assuming that the coefficient of consolidation c_v has been determined and that the time factor T, a dimensionless number, has been plotted for various percentages of consolidation U, then the time t for a certain percentage of consolidation U can be determined from

$$t = \frac{1}{c_v} H^2 T$$

where H = one-half the thickness of the compressible layer if it is between two pervious sand layers, or the full thickness if it is underlain with an impervious layer, such as rock. Since c_v is usually in square centimeters per minute, H will need to be in centimeters.

Current Observations. When investigating the site of a proposed port or harbor, it is usually desirable to obtain information concerning the general direction and velocity of currents in the area. One type of device used in taking current observations is shown in Fig. 3.13. As can be seen from the figure, this device or target consists of a surface float with a pole and flag, a submerged float that is moved by the current, and a counterweight consisting of a wire basket to which is added scrap metal in sufficient quantity so that the surface float rides evenly on the water surface. In taking the current observations, it is customary to lay out a base line or lines on shore with a transit set up at each end. The float is then dropped in the water beyond the area of the breakers and permitted to move along in the direction of the current. The transitmen take sights on the flagpole at predetermined time intervals, and the course and speed of the float are determined by plotting the results of the observations. Usually a dozen or more of these tests are performed during the ebb and flow of the tide. These tests, of course, should be performed during periods of relative calm. If the observations are carefully taken, the results will give a very good idea as to the general direction and velocity of the currents in the area being investigated.

Tidal Observations. In some locations the United States Coast and Geodetic Survey may have established tide-gauge stations, and tide tables may be available. For those locations where this information is not available it will be necessary to install a tide gauge in order to determine the

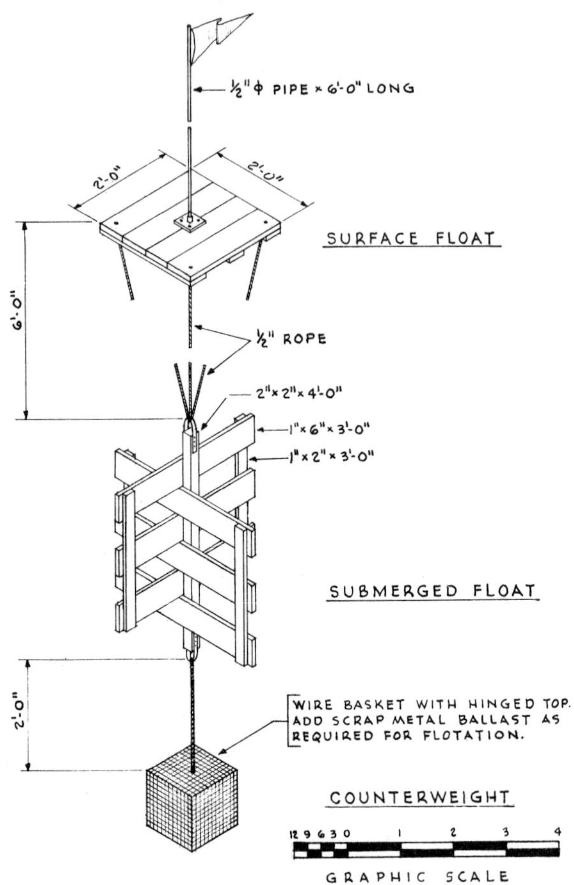

FIG. 3.13 Device for making current observations.

mean high- and mean low-water levels and to establish a datum for referencing the water level at the time of making the soundings.

The tide gauge, in its simplest form, consists of a vertical post, driven into the bank below lowest low-water level, and graduated in feet or meters. Where there is an extreme range of tide, more than one such indicator may be required, located across the bank at ascending levels, in order to cover the complete range of the tide.

In locations where there is a swell, the gauge may consist of a rod, with a float at its lower end and a pointer on its upper end, enclosed in a pipe to protect it from the waves. Above the pipe there is a graduated scale along which the pointer travels as the water level rises and falls. The bottom of the pipe should have a small hole to permit the water to seek its true level inside the pipe. Such a device for measuring the tide is usually mounted alongside a pier or wharf.

In important locations where it is desirable to have a continuous recording of the tide level over a long period of time, a self-recording apparatus should be installed. This may consist of a float hung in a stilling well with a small opening below the lowest wave trough. The float is connected to a self-recording instrument by a small cable or chain with a counterweight. The recording instrument may be set on a stand or table inside a building, or it may have a weatherproof housing, with a glass face, for outdoor mounting. The recording mechanism may be actuated by an electric or spring-wound clock, the recording pencil tracing a curve of the water level with respect to time on graph paper. All parts of the apparatus should be constructed of rust-proof materials, such as a hard-rubber float, stainless-steel cable, and an aluminum case to house the recording instrument.

3.6 Hydraulic Model Investigations

Probably no single factor has contributed so much to placing the design of harbors on a sound engineering basis as has the testing of hydraulic models. In this respect the hydraulic laboratory of the Waterways Experiment Station at Vicksburg, Mississippi, and the NEYRPIC Hydraulic Laboratory at Grenoble, France, have performed a number of model investigations on outstanding harbors. The following will present one such test by each of these laboratories.

Model Investigation of Taconite Harbor. In 1954 the Waterways Experiment Station made a hydraulic model study of Taconite Harbor, which is located on the north shore of Lake Superior. A description of the construction of this harbor appears on page 123 and a plan of the harbor is shown in Fig. 3.22.

The hydraulic model was constructed of concrete in an existing wave basin, using a linear scale of 1:150, model to prototype. The model was designed and operated in accordance with Froude's model laws, which resulted in the model-prototype relationships being derived from the linear scale L_r of 1:150 and a specific weight scale γ_r of 1:1, as shown in Table 3.7.

The model covered an area of about 6,000 sq ft equivalent to 4.8 square miles in the prototype. The model breakwaters were constructed of crushed stone. The waves were reproduced to scale by a movable, plunger-type wave machine, 40 ft in length. Wave heights were measured with

Table 3.7 **Model-prototype Relationships**

Characteristics	Dimensions	Model-prototype scales
Length	L	$L_r = 1:150$
Area	L^2	$A_r = L_r^2 = 1:22{,}500$
Volume	L^3	$\overline{V}_r = L_r^3 = 1:3{,}375{,}000$
Time	T	$T_r = L_r^{1/2} = 1:12.25$
Velocity	L/T	$V_r = L_r^{1/2} = 1:12.25$
Unit pressure	F/L^2	$P_r = L_r\gamma_r = 1:150$
Force	F	$F_r = L_r^3\gamma_r = 1:3{,}375{,}000$
Weight	F	$W_r = L_r^3\gamma_r = 1:3{,}375{,}000$

an electrical wave-height gauge designed and constructed at the Waterways Experiment Station.

The purpose of the investigation was to determine whether the proposed harbor plan would adequately protect the docking area from wave action, and, if it would not, to devise a plan that would provide sufficient protection at a minimum cost. The original plan of the harbor construction and 23 modifications of the original plan were tested.

Although the east breakwater had been designed for a maximum wave height of 20 ft from the northeast (Sec. 4.3), the frequency of this height of wave was so low that its importance with respect to the design of the harbor was not considered to be a controlling factor. A 10-ft wave from the northeast was estimated to occur once every 13 months. Figure 3.14 is a photograph of the model of the original harbor being subjected to such a wave, and Fig. 3.15 gives the resulting wave heights inside and outside the harbor. It should be noted that the maximum wave height inside the harbor is 2.0 ft, except for a short distance near the end of the dock where the height increases to 3.0 ft.

As reported by the Waterways Experiment Station, it was concluded from the model study that:

1. The original plan of the harbor would provide excellent protection for vessels moored along the harbor docks from all storms, except extremely high waves from directions between N 75° E and east and average severe storm waves from the south to the southwest directions.

2. The east breakwater of the original plan could be shortened 355 ft without a significant increase in wave action in the docking area.

3. None of the plans tested would provide adequate protection from severe storms from directions between south and southwest.

4. Rubble wave absorbers placed at selected positions in and adjacent to the harbor would improve wave conditions at the west navigation opening and in the eastern portion of the harbcr.

5. The west side of the outer end of the east breakwater should be constructed in such a way that a large portion of the incident wave energy would be absorbed.

Since the outer end of the east breakwater is in relatively deep water (about 100 ft), the reduction in length of 355 ft resulted in a large saving in cost of construction, several times the cost of making the model test of the harbor.

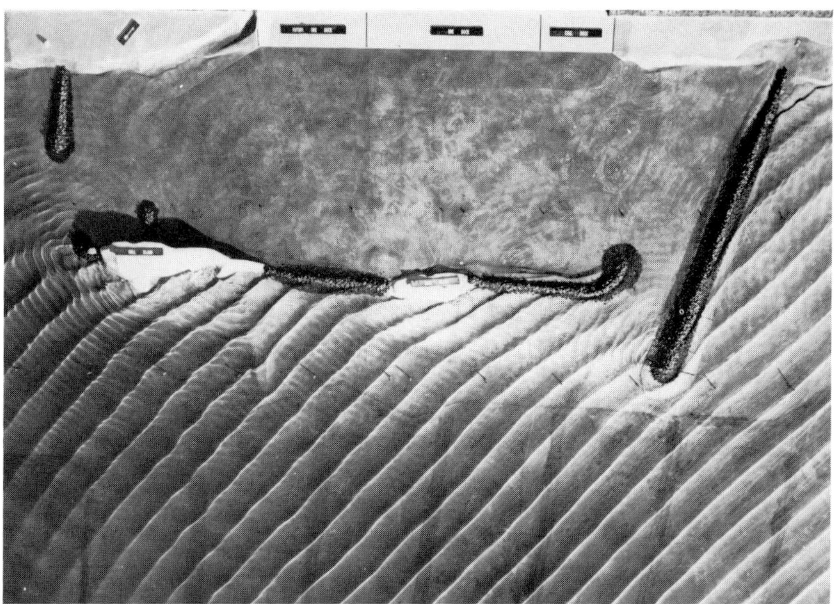

FIG. 3.14 Model of Taconite Harbor being subjected to 10-ft wave (prototype) from the northeast. (*From Technical Memorandum* 2-405 *of the United States Army Engineer Waterways Experiment Station.*)

Model Investigation of Zonguldak Harbor. In 1950 the NEYRPIC Hydraulic Laboratory at Grenoble, France, carried out experimental investigations on a model of Zonguldak Harbor, constructed according to the design which had been prepared for the enlargement of the existing harbor. The construction of this harbor is described on page 129, and a plan of the harbor is shown in Fig. 3.24.

The main function of this investigation was to study the effect on the quietness of the harbor of certain wave heights from different directions and to measure the amplitude of the agitation in the harbor; another function was to make certain changes in the design, if necessary, to improve the quietness of the harbor.

The characteristics of the waves specified for the investigation are as shown in Table 3.8.

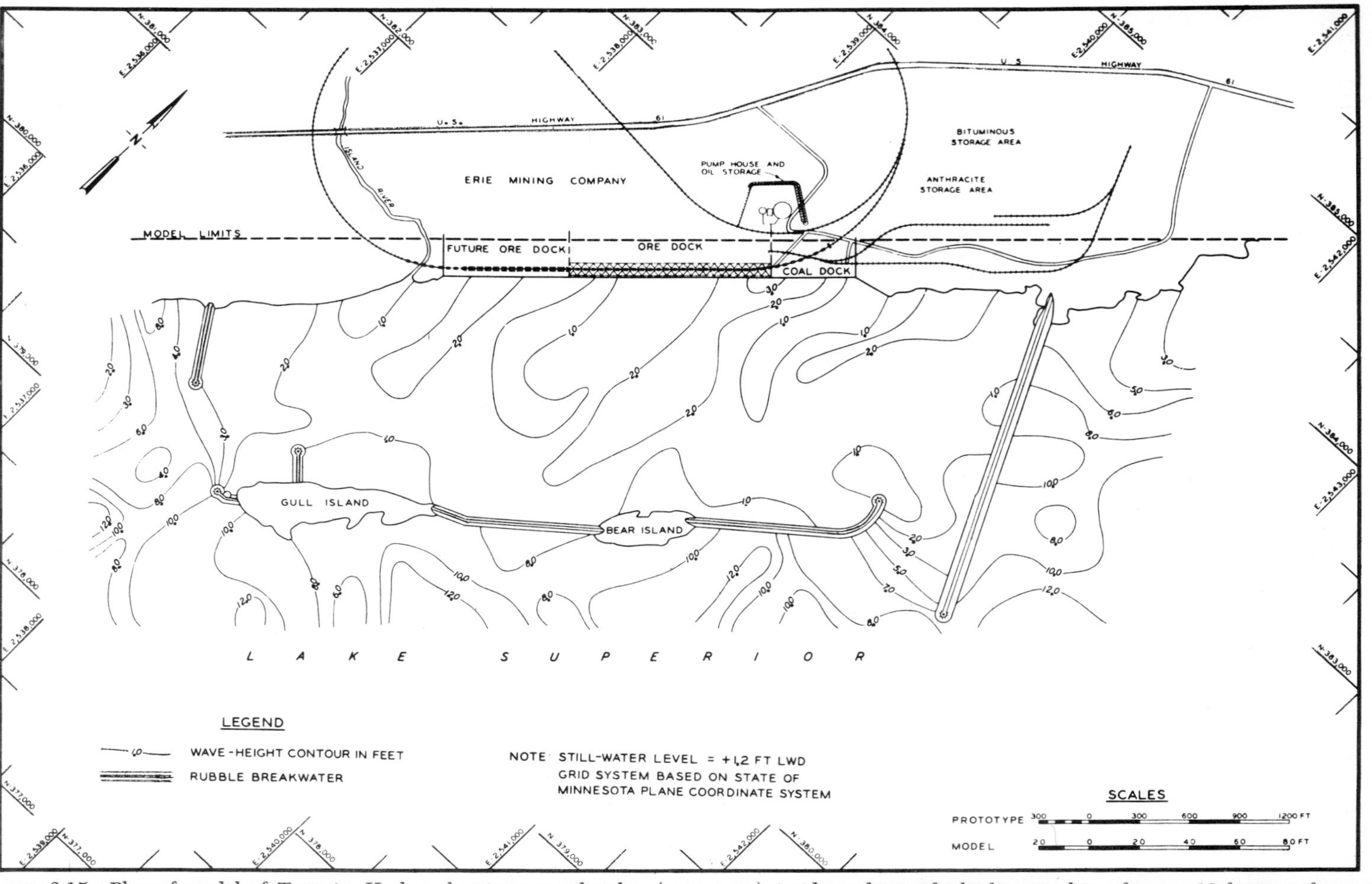

FIG. 3.15 Plan of model of Taconite Harbor showing wave heights (prototype) inside and outside harbor resulting from a 10-ft wave from

Table 3.8 **Characteristics of Waves for Model Test of Harbor**

Direction	Period, sec	Height of waves
N 70° W	6	3 meters (10 ft)
N 33° W	8	5 meters (16½ ft)
N 50° W	8	7 meters (23 ft)
N 30° E	9	9 meters (29½ ft)

The model, as constructed, is geometrically similar to the prototype, on a linear scale of 1:100, as shown in Fig. 3.17. It was constructed in a closed shelter to protect it from the wind and rain. The sea bed and the coast line were modeled in accordance with the hydrographic and topographic surveys which had been made of the site, and the breakwaters were made out of concrete in accordance with the original designs prepared for the protection of the harbor.

The principal wave-generating equipment consisted of eight independent blades of variable orientation which could oscillate about a horizontal axis and also pivot about a vertical axis, in order to be orientated as required to produce the waves in the three different directions specified. The waves from the direction of N 30° E were produced by means of separate equipment consisting of one single-wave blade. In front of the wave blades were placed wave filters of a design patented by the NEYRPIC Laboratory. These filters have the same function as absorbing beaches located in front of vertical walls, and their purpose is to diminish, as far as possible, the magnitude of reflected waves.

The measurement of the reduction of wave height within the harbor area was determined by the variations of resistance at the terminals of an electric circuit consisting of a metal rod immersed a certain distance into the water of the model, so that the end of the rod would be below the trough of the maximum wave. Water forms a conducting medium between the rod and a metallic earth connection immersed in a corner of the model. The rod-water circuit is one of variable resistance and is included as the fourth arm of an unbalanced Wheatstone bridge. An external source of current is supplied to the Wheatstone bridge. Since the resistance of the rod-water circuit is a function of the relative immersion of the rod in the water, which varies with the passage of crests and troughs, it follows that the variation in the electrical resistance of the circuit is linearly in proportion to the height of the wave. The results are projected on to a continuously unwinding film by a cathode-ray oscillograph which forms a diagonal in the Wheatstone bridge, giving a record of the variations in amplitude from which the wave heights may be obtained by using a curve of the calibration of the measuring point. This electrical apparatus was checked by another electrical device and was found to be accurate to within 4 to 6 in. of the true amplitude of the wave.

In order to carry out a continuous recording of amplitudes along

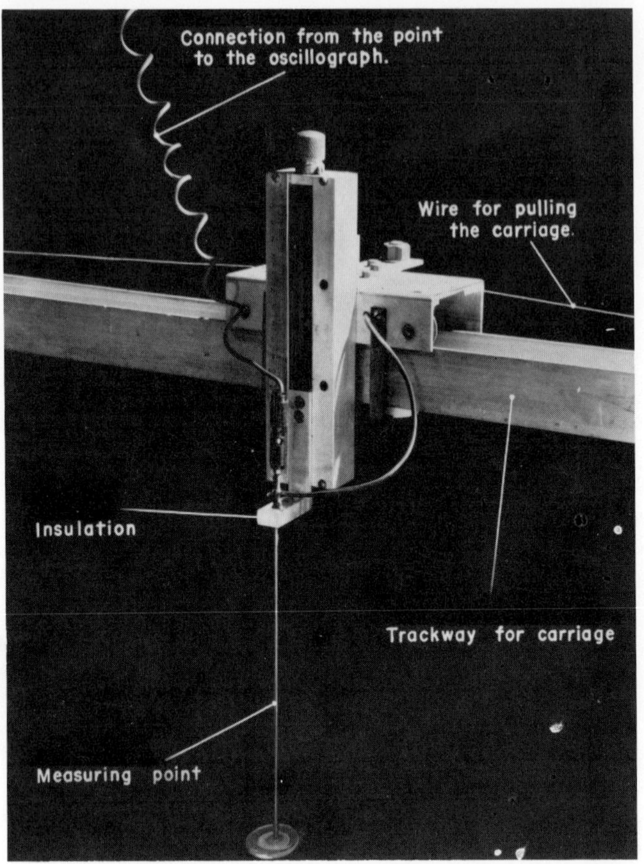

FIG. 3.16 Wave-measuring device for harbor model investigations. (*From report on Zonguldak Harbor model by the NEYRPIC Hydraulic Laboratory, Grenoble, France.*)

specified base lines, the resistance-measuring point was mounted on a small rule graduated in millimeters which itself could be moved in the fixed guide so as to adjust the depth of the immersion of the point. The guide was fitted to a carriage which rolled along level rails, the speed of the movement being slow enough to avoid creating a disturbance in the water. The carriage with measuring point is shown in Fig. 3.16, and provides a very convenient method of determining the wave amplitudes along established lines in the model of the harbor. Readings were taken along four different base lines within the harbor, as shown in Fig. 3.17,

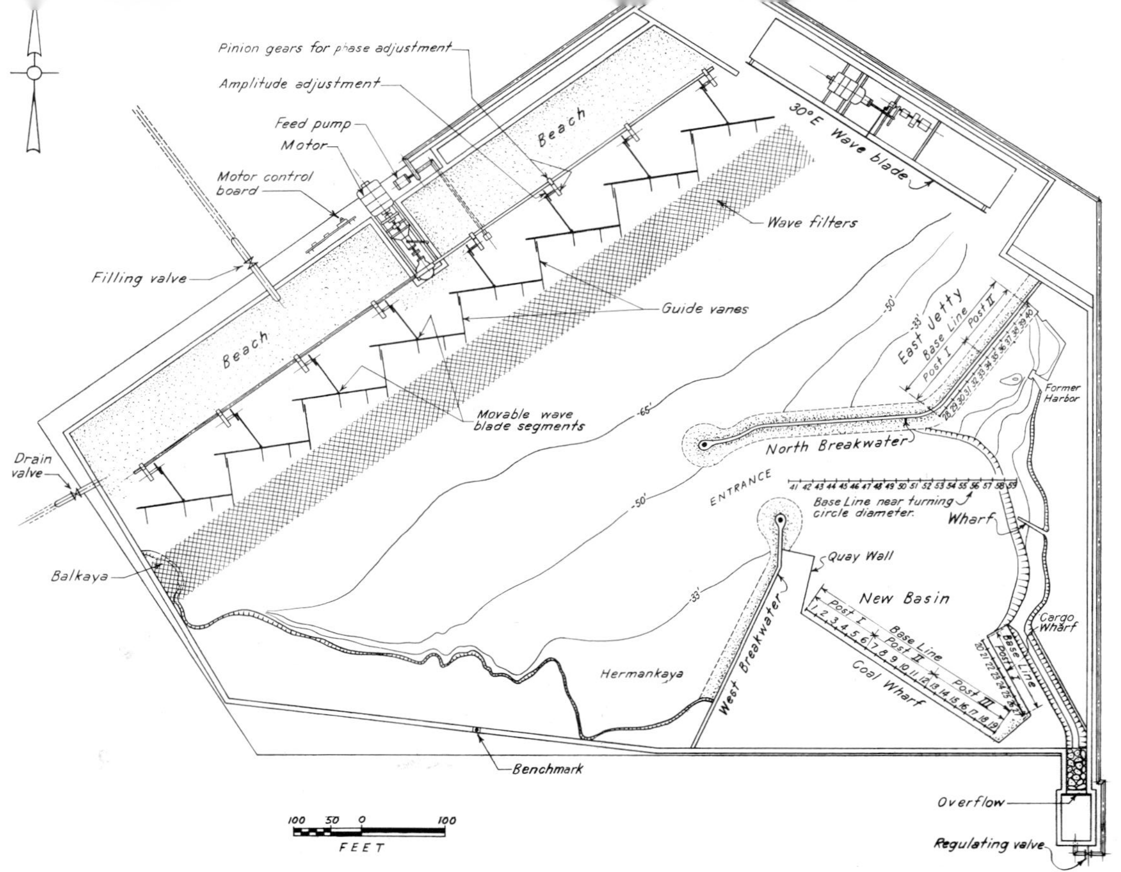

FIG. 3.17 Plan of model of Zonguldak Harbor showing base lines for making readings on wave amplitudes. (*From report on Zonguldak Harbor model by the NEYRPIC Hydraulic Laboratory, Grenoble, France.*)

and the wave heights were established at 59 different points. These readings, which indicate the amplitude of the waves within the harbor of the original design for the four different wave heights specified, are shown in Table 3.9.

In addition to testing the model of the harbor based on the original design, a number of tests were run on modifications of the harbor, which were designated as types *A* to *J*, inclusive, involving such changes as the addition of wave-absorbing beaches, groin and wave traps, and an under-

Table 3.9 **Height of Waves in Feet within the Harbor of Zonguldak for Different Wave Heights outside the Harbor**

Wave characteristics at sea	Direction of oncoming waves			290°				327°				355°					30°									
	Time period and wave length			6 sec 180′				8 sec 328′				8 sec 328′					9 sec 410′									
	Wave height			10′				16′				23′					30′									
Wave characteristics within the harbor	Type of harbor studied			A	B	C	D	A	B	C	D	A	B	C	D	E	A	B	C	D	E	F	G	H	I	J
	New Basin	Coal Wharf Base Line	Post I	1.9	1.4	2.5	0.9	2.1	2.3	1.6	1.0	1.9	1.5	2.1	1.1	0.9	2.0	1.9	1.6	1.0	1.2	1.6	—	1.1	1.0	—
			Post II	2.6	2.0	1.9	1.6	2.4	2.4	1.9	1.1	1.7	1.4	1.9	1.3	0.8	2.5	2.0	2.2	1.5	1.4	1.6	1.2	1.0	1.1	—
			Post III	2.8	2.6	2.7	1.6	3.2	2.7	2.5	1.5	3.4	2.4	2.2	2.0	1.2	2.8	2.4	2.4	2.0	1.3	2.0	1.1	1.3	1.5	—
		Cargo Wharf Base Line	Post I	2.6	2.1	2.6	2.0	2.5	2.4	2.3	1.7	3.0	2.8	2.5	1.8	1.4	3.0	2.5	2.2	1.9	1.5	2.2	0.7	1.5	1.2	0.4
	Former Harbor	East Jetty Base Line	Post I	2.7	2.7	3.0	3.0	3.2	3.2	2.8	2.8	2.9	2.9	2.8	2.8	3.6	3.4	3.4	2.9	2.9	2.7	1.9	1.0	2.0	0.8	0.8
			Post II	2.7	2.7	1.7	1.7	3.5	3.5	2.8	2.8	1.9	1.9	2.7	2.7	3.8	2.4	2.4	2.0	2.0	2.3	2.2	0.8	1.8	1.0	0.3
	Base Line near Turning circle diameter			3.1	3.1	3.2	3.2	4.1	4.1	3.1	3.1	5.1	5.1	4.0	4.0	3.7	4.1	4.1	2.9	2.9	3.4	3.6	1.3	2.6	2.2	1.3

sea jetty located outside the entrance to the harbor. The influence of these modifications on the amplitude of the waves within the harbor is apparent from the readings of wave heights listed in Table 3.9. In general, it can be said that the original design of the harbor, supplemented by the addition of a wave-absorbing beach in the southeast corner, where the coal and cargo wharves converged to form a pocket, is well protected from the waves and provides reasonably quiet water along the docks, the maximum amplitude of wave being not over 3 ft at any location.

3.7 Description of Various Selected Ports

There are many well-known ports throughout the world. Probably no two authors would pick out the same group for discussion. The following ports have been chosen, not necessarily as the most prominent, the largest, or the oldest in the world, but because they represent a fairly good cross section with respect to type, age, use, location, etc. These ports are located on oceans, rivers, and lakes. Most of those selected have artificial harbors, as these illustrate to a greater extent the planning of the port; about one-third are of relatively recent construction; most of them are municipal ports but one is a privately owned commercial port. In all, 12 ports are reviewed.

La Guaira, Venezuela. This port for Caracas, capital of Venezuela, originally consisted of a small breakwater pier for accommodating coastal

FIG. 3.18 View of the completed port of La Guaira, Venezuela. (*Courtesy of the Frederick Snare Corp.*)

vessels. In 1945 a cargo pier with warehouse was added, but it was not until 1948 that a major program of port construction was initiated, which by 1951 saw La Guaira become a major port with a well-protected harbor dredged to a minimum depth of 34½ ft below mean sea level. Figure 3.18 is a view of the completed port and Fig. 3.19 shows the plan as finally constructed.

Venezuela's continually increasing trade by 1948 was evidenced by the necessity of having as many as 20 ships anchor outside the harbor, waiting for a chance to dock. However, with the completion of the port construction there had been added a cargo wharf extending along the shore for 3,030 ft, enabling six large freighters to be berthed at one time with warehouses behind the berths; a 164-ft-wide by 1,135-ft-long pier and passenger warehouse, providing four berths for cargo and passenger

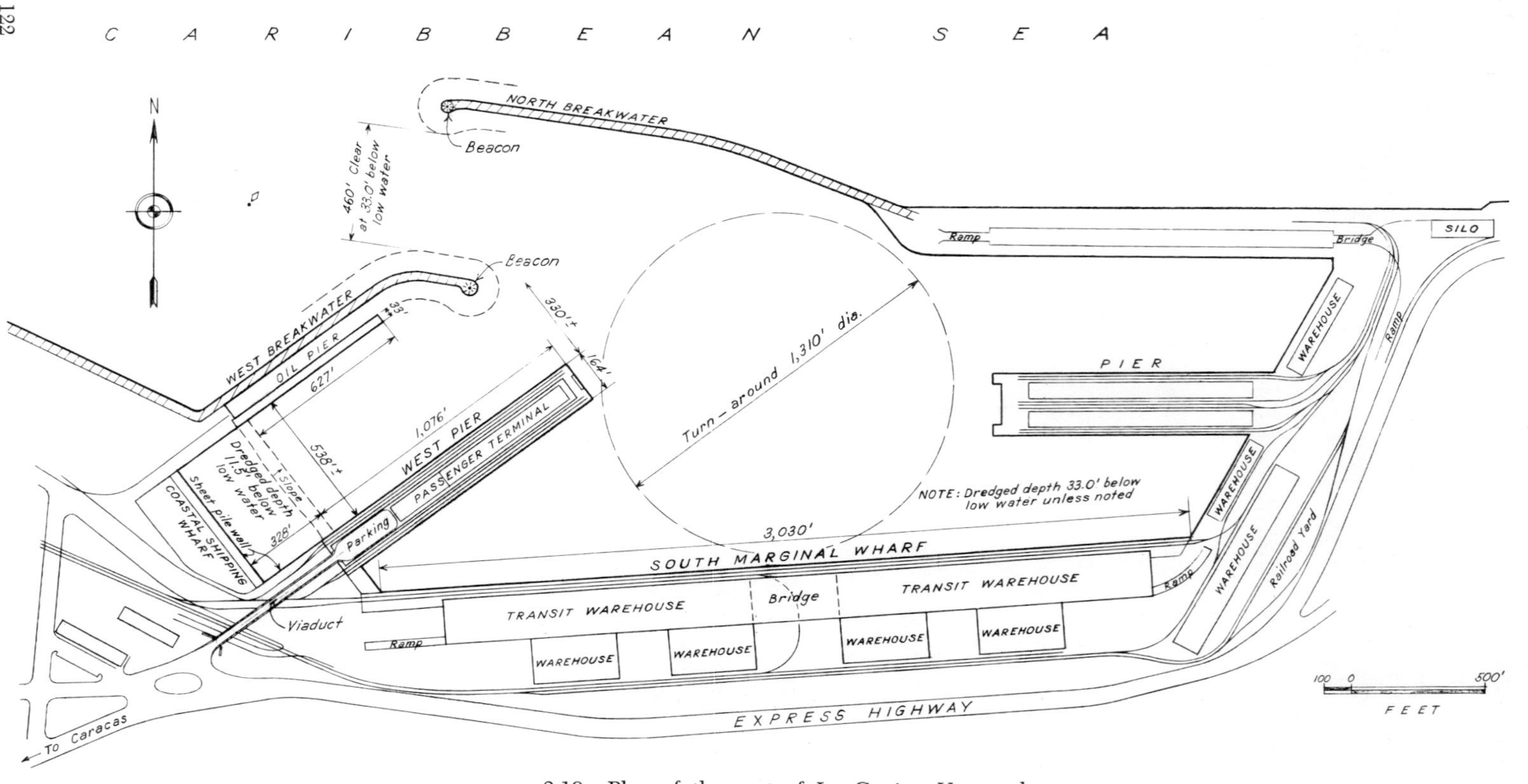

FIG. 3.19 Plan of the port of La Guaira, Venezuela.

ships (described on page 398); a 680-ft oil-unloading pier; and 1,100 ft of sheet-pile bulkhead for docking small ships used in coastal trade. The harbor is protected by two breakwaters projecting out more than 2,000 ft from shore into 40 ft of water and providing a protected turning basin.

The spoil from the dredging, together with waste from a quarry developed for construction of the breakwaters, was used to create more than 20 acres of new land in back of the wharf, pier, and bulkheads. On this fill, an administration building, warehouses, roads, and railroad sidings were built.

As previously pointed out a port must have good arteries of communication. Until the time of the enlargement of the Port of La Guaira its only highway connection with Caracas was a two-lane winding road through the mountains, rising nearly 3,000 ft in a distance of 15 miles and requiring an hour by automobile to make the trip to Caracas. The enlargement of the port saw the construction of a four-lane express highway between the port and the capital, and by means of a tunnel and bridges the time to make the trip was reduced to only one-third of what it was by way of the old highway. A viaduct from the express highway provides direct access to the embarkation floor of the passenger terminal. Thus traffic does not have to cross railroad tracks and other roads at the dock level.

Taconite Harbor. This port, completed in 1956 on the north shore of Lake Superior, 80 miles from Duluth, provides a shipping terminal for iron ore mined and beneficiated at a plant costing over $300 million at Hoyt Lakes, Minnesota, about 75 miles inland from the port. This project was privately financed by a group of steel companies and is managed by a private corporation representing these companies.

The harbor is named after the iron ore "taconite"—an extremely hard rock containing 25 to 30 per cent iron, which is found in massive strata in this area of Minnesota. In order to make this low-grade ore suitable for blast furnaces and more economical to transport it was necessary to enrich it by processing it into the form of pellets about the size of walnuts. This enriched iron ore is transported by railroad to the harbor where it is loaded into ore carriers (see page 453) which take it to various lake ports for use by steel mills.

When it was finally decided to proceed with the construction of this tremendous project it was necessary to find a suitable site for a shipping terminal along the north shore of Lake Superior, within the shortest possible distance of the mine and beneficiating plant at Hoyt Lakes.

The shore is for the most part quite rocky and precipitous, exposed to severe storms from the northeast where the unimpeded reach or fetch of wind and wave is some 250 miles. Waves on the order of 20 ft from trough to crest have been known to occur, and those of 5 to 10 ft occur quite frequently, making it impracticable to ship out of an unprotected harbor. Natural harbors along the lake shore are few and far between.

Fortunately, at a place almost directly east of the plant site there were two islands lying about 1,500 ft offshore and so situated as to form the nucleus of a good harbor if supplemented by some additional breakwater construction. Figure 3.20 is a view during the construction of the harbor, showing the two islands offshore.

FIG. 3.20 View during the construction of Taconite Harbor, Lake Superior. (*Courtesy of the Erie Mining Co.*)

In planning the harbor, consideration had to be given to protection against the severe storms from the northeast, as well as storms of lesser intensity from other directions. Since from a westerly direction the maximum waves are not expected to exceed 5 ft, the entrance to the harbor was placed at this end which could be left more open to permit vessels to approach the dock directly on a reasonably flat angle for easy mooring.

As shown in Fig. 3.21 and Fig. 3.22, protection from storms from the south is provided by filling in between the two islands and by extending a breakwater arm from the easterly island, a distance of about 1,100 ft. Fortunately, the water is relatively shallow here as a rock shelf extends out from this island to within about 300 ft of the end of the breakwater. The opposite condition existed at the end of the east breakwater where the water is over 100 ft deep. This breakwater arm extends out from shore a distance of about 1,700 ft. At the extreme end of the arm the width of the base is close to 400 ft.

Because of the availability of rock from the harbor excavation, except for the heavy armor stone, all-rock breakwaters were adopted, which are described in Sec. 4.3.

As to the design of the dock, with its storage and loading facilities, the long and comparatively narrow shape of the harbor pointed to a

FIG. 3.21 View of Taconite Harbor after completion of construction of breakwaters. (*Courtesy of the Erie Mining Co.*)

bulkhead type of dock. This, together with the necessity of supporting a very considerable tonnage of pellets stored as closely as possible to the boats alongside, in order to expedite and simplify loading operations, suggested cutting back the comparatively straight rocky shore line in such a way as to widen the harbor and at the same time provide suitable foundations for storage bins.

In order to make it possible for boats to dock along the wall it was necessary to excavate rock and overlying sand and gravel to a depth of 30 ft below lake level. This meant the removal of nearly 1 million cu yd of material, either by underwater blasting and dredging or in the dry behind a cellular cofferdam, to shut out the lake, as shown in Fig. 3.20. The latter method was adopted by the contractor and proved to be most economical as well as simplifying the excavation for the dock wall and its construction.

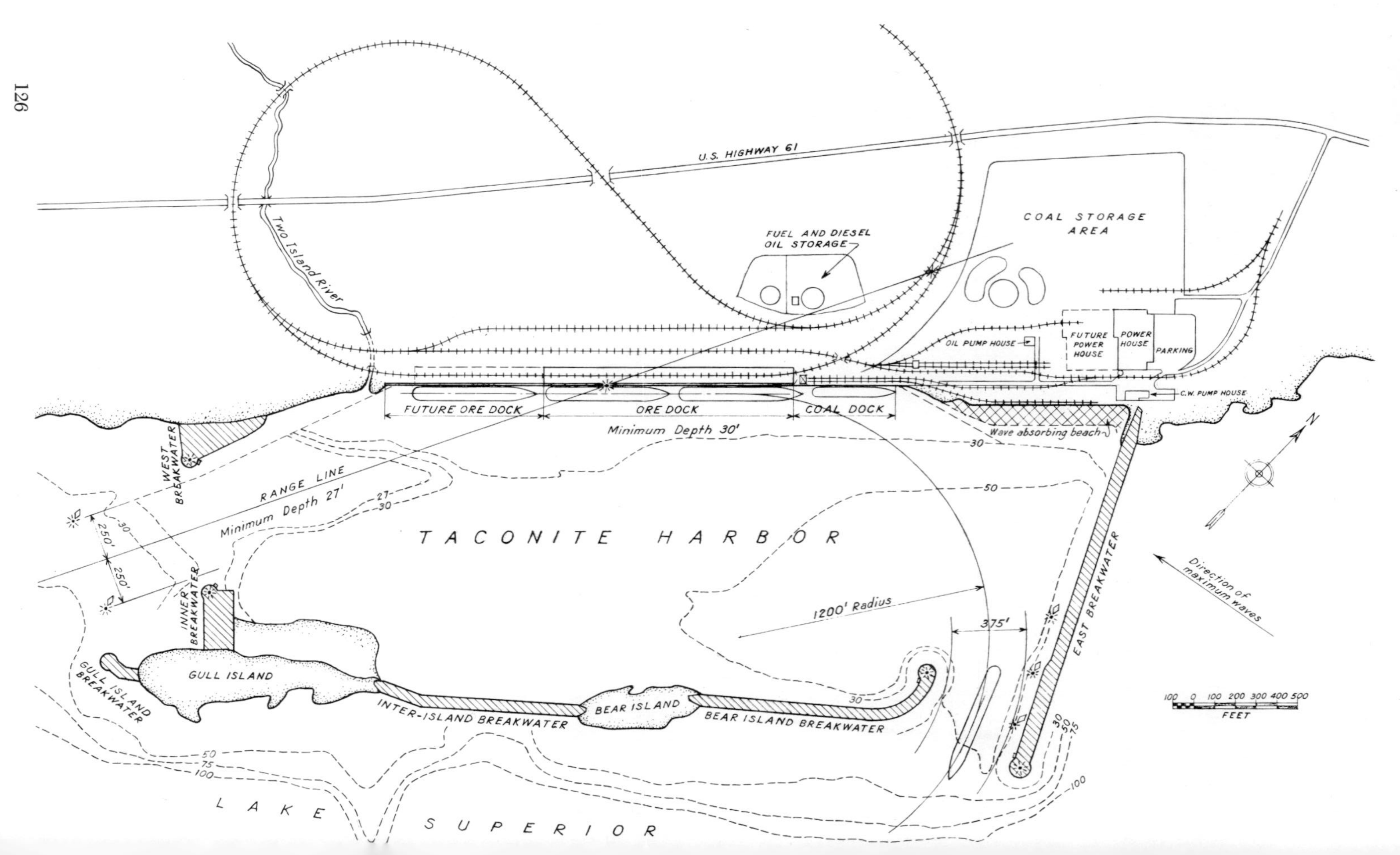

U.S. HIGHWAY 61
Two Island River
FUEL AND DIESEL OIL STORAGE
COAL STORAGE AREA
OIL PUMP HOUSE
FUTURE POWER HOUSE
POWER HOUSE
PARKING
C.W. PUMP HOUSE
FUTURE ORE DOCK
ORE DOCK
COAL DOCK
Minimum Depth 30'
Wave absorbing beach
WEST BREAKWATER
RANGE LINE
Minimum Depth 27'
250'
250'
TACONITE HARBOR
INNER BREAKWATER
1200' Radius
375'
EAST BREAKWATER
N
Direction of maximum waves
GULL ISLAND
GULL ISLAND BREAKWATER
INTER-ISLAND BREAKWATER
BEAR ISLAND
BEAR ISLAND BREAKWATER
100 0 100 200 300 400 500
FEET
LAKE SUPERIOR

The cellular cofferdam, which was installed in about 35 ft of water to hold back the lake for a distance of well over 2,000 ft along the shore, ranks among the few of its kind in size and boldness of operation. The cells are 50 ft in diameter and the top of the sheet piles was set 12 ft above low-water level to prevent overtopping by storm waves. The cofferdam was constructed in two parts, the first taking in the entire dock wall and the second and much smaller one, the area of rock excavation beyond the westerly end of the dock.

The first cofferdam was later subdivided into two sections by a cellular wall installed about midway along the dock. This made possible the flooding of the easterly end and removal of a sufficient number of sheet-pile cells to permit boats to tie up and unload at the coal dock prior to the completion of the entire dock wall. The contract called for this early completion to permit rail and accessories for the railroad and other construction materials and equipment to be shipped by boat and unloaded at the harbor. In all, about 7,500 tons of sheet piling were used for the cofferdam construction.

The Port of Rota. This is the principal port of entry for the U.S. bases in Spain and was substantially completed in 1958, except for a finger pier which was started in 1959 and completed in 1960. Here an unused part of the coast on Cadiz Bay in southwestern Spain was made into a harbor to accommodate the largest carriers and tankers, as well as to receive planes brought in by ships for an adjacent naval air station.

This harbor location was selected for the port because it is partly sheltered and has a natural deep-water approach. The shore is relatively flat and was sparsely populated.

Requirements for the port at Rota were a protected harbor with a 2,500-ft turning basin of 35-ft depth for the largest aircraft carriers, a 1,000-ft wharf which could be extended in the future to triple its size, and provisions for oil tanker loading and unloading. A 1,100- by 150-ft finger pier was added in 1960.

The harbor layout, as shown in Fig. 3.23, was influenced by the necessity of having the breakwater perpendicular to the southwest ocean swells and orienting the piers parallel to the prevailing southeast winds. It was further influenced by the necessity of separating the aircraft unloading facilities at the main wharf from the tanker pier and the desirability of balancing, as well as possible, the dredge and fill quantities.

The breakwater protects both the marginal wharf and the tanker pier from ocean storms. The inner 2,000-ft section of the breakwater, which is approximately perpendicular to the shore, is backed up with a hydraulic fill to provide access from the low-level area on shore to the wharf. The outer 5,000-ft section, which extends in a southeast direction, is perpendicular to the southwest ocean storms and is slightly skewed to reflect waves in toward shore rather than out toward the breakwater head and

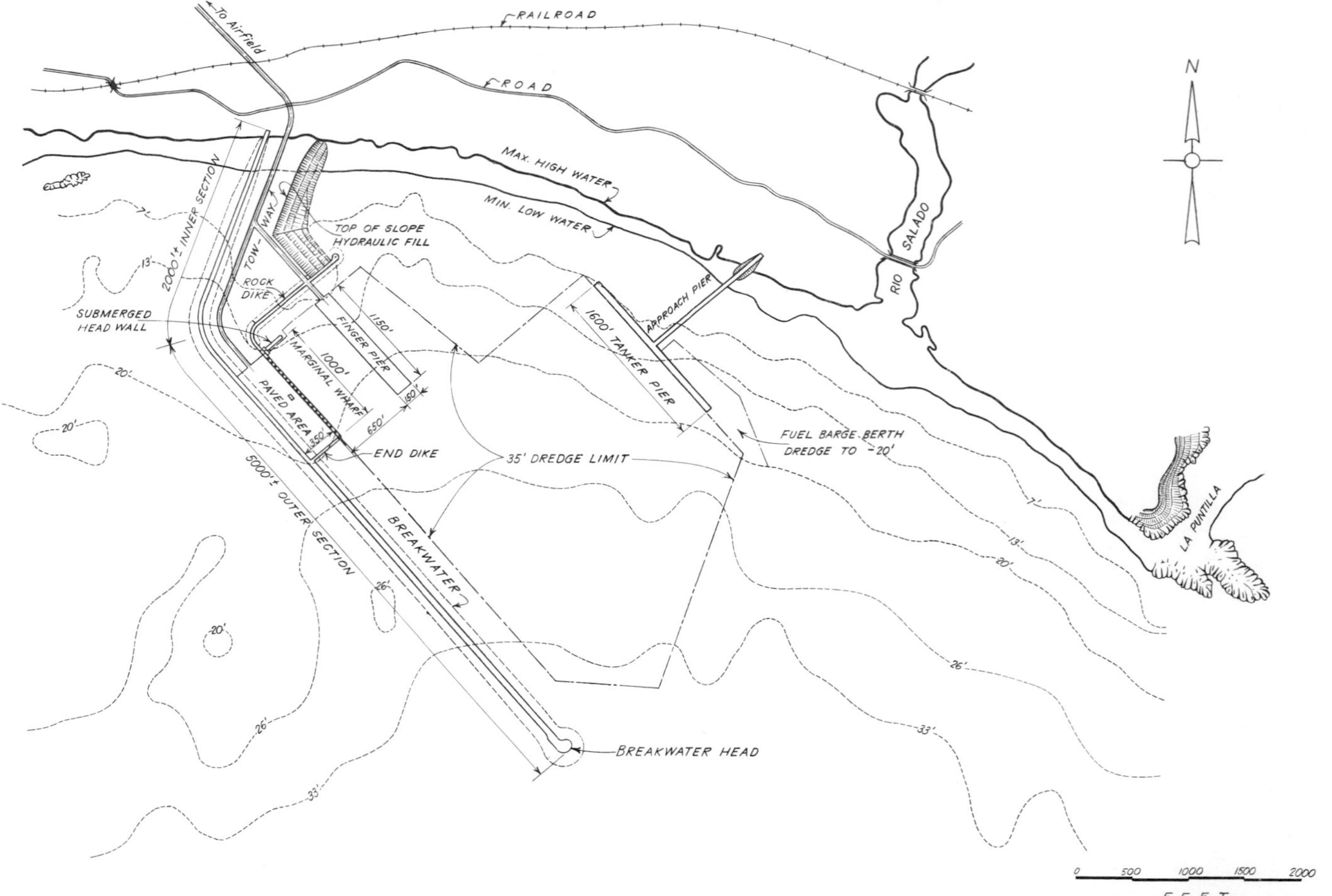
To Airfield
RAILROAD
ROAD
N
MAX. HIGH WATER
MIN. LOW WATER
RIO SALADO
LA PUNTILLA
TOW-WAY
TOP OF SLOPE
HYDRAULIC FILL
ROCK
DIKE
2000'± INNER SECTION
SUBMERGED
HEAD WALL
1150'
FINGER PIER
1000'
MARGINAL WHARF
150'
650'
PAVED AREA
350'
END DIKE
APPROACH PIER
1600' TANKER PIER
FUEL BARGE BERTH
DREDGE TO -20'
35' DREDGE LIMIT
5000'± OUTER SECTION
BREAKWATER
BREAKWATER HEAD
7'
13'
20'
26'
33'
0
500
1000
1500
2000
FEET

into the path of approaching vessels. Near the inshore end of the southeast arm of the breakwater and parallel to it is located a marginal wharf of concrete block, 1,000 ft long, which is connected with the breakwater by an apron 350 ft wide, consisting of hydraulic fill topped with asphalt pavement.

The construction of the breakwater is described in Sec. 4.7 and is one of the most important breakwaters recently constructed with an armor course of tetrapods.

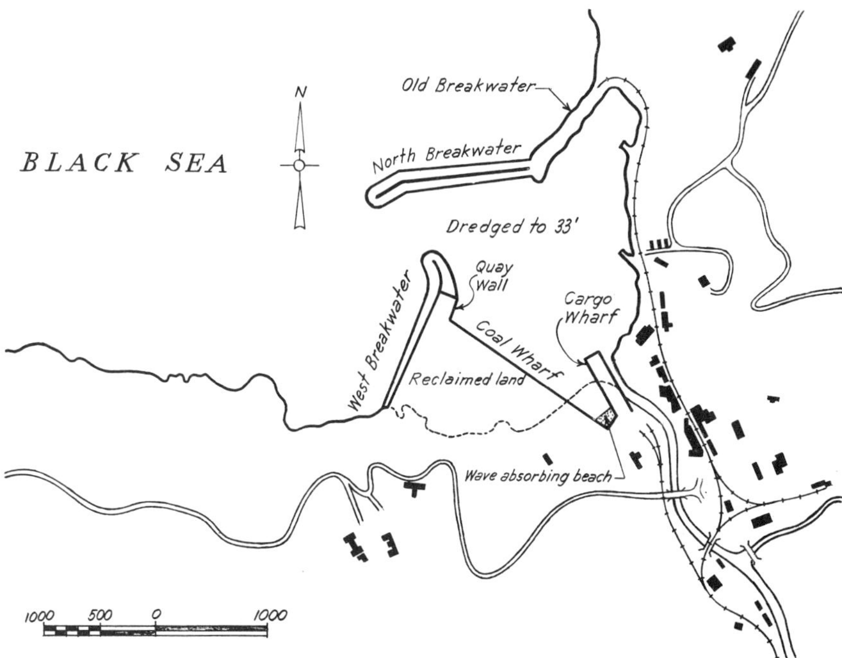

FIG. 3.24 Plan of Zonguldak Harbor, Turkey.

Port of Zonguldak. In 1949 the Turkish government decided to make use of a small existing harbor at Zonguldak, located on the north shore on the Black Sea, approximately 150 miles east of Istanbul, by enlarging it into an important harbor for exporting the coal coming from this region. The existing harbor at that time consisted of a small breakwater extending out from land in a southwest direction for approximately 1,000 ft and the water area which it protected was too small to serve the needs of the proposed harbor. Therefore, a plan was laid out in which the existing breakwater would be extended about 1,500 ft in a more or less westerly direction and a new breakwater would be constructed out from the shore, at the west end of the harbor, for a distance of about 1,400 ft. This arrangement provided a protected harbor with a turning basin 1,230 ft in diameter and space for 1,673 lin ft of coal wharf and 656 ft of cargo wharf, as shown in Fig. 3.24. Between the coal wharf and the west breakwater an area of approximately 20 acres was reclaimed by depositing 635,000 cu yd of dredged material from the harbor. The harbor was dredged to a depth of −32.8 ft below mean sea level, which required the removal of 1,560,000 cu yd of material.

As described on page 115, a model of the harbor was tested to determine the effect of the waves on the quietness of the water along the docks and within the turning basin of the harbor.

The docks are of the typical European type of construction using heavy precast-concrete blocks laid on a foundation course of rubble and backed up with a rock fill to reduce the lateral earth pressure. The construction of the breakwaters is described in Sec. 4.5.

FIG. 3.25 Matarani (Peru) Cove before construction of the port. (*Courtesy of the Frederick Snare Corp.*)

The Port of Matarani. Located on the Peruvian coast about 7 miles northeast of the roadstead of Mollendo, this port was built during the years 1938–1941. It was intended to replace Mollendo, a port of entry for the southern part of Peru, where it is necessary to anchor ships in the open sea and rehandle their cargo by means of lighters, with a port having a protected harbor.

The site selected was known as Matarani Cove, near the ruins of the town of Islay which dates from the times of the Incas. The photograph in Fig. 3.25 shows the site of this port prior to construction.

The cliff shown in Fig. 3.25 was opened up as a quarry to provide rock for the breakwaters and the quarry floor thus obtained became the open area in back of the port buildings that were constructed later. A description of the breakwaters is given in Sec. 4.3, but it can be mentioned that the south breakwater is one of the deepest in the world (about 140 ft) and was considered economically feasible only because of the unlimited supply of rock of all sizes.

The port has a cellular-type bulkhead wharf approximately 1,500 ft long which was constructed of sheet-pile cells filled with rock resting on a previously prepared rubble base, the top of which was leveled off

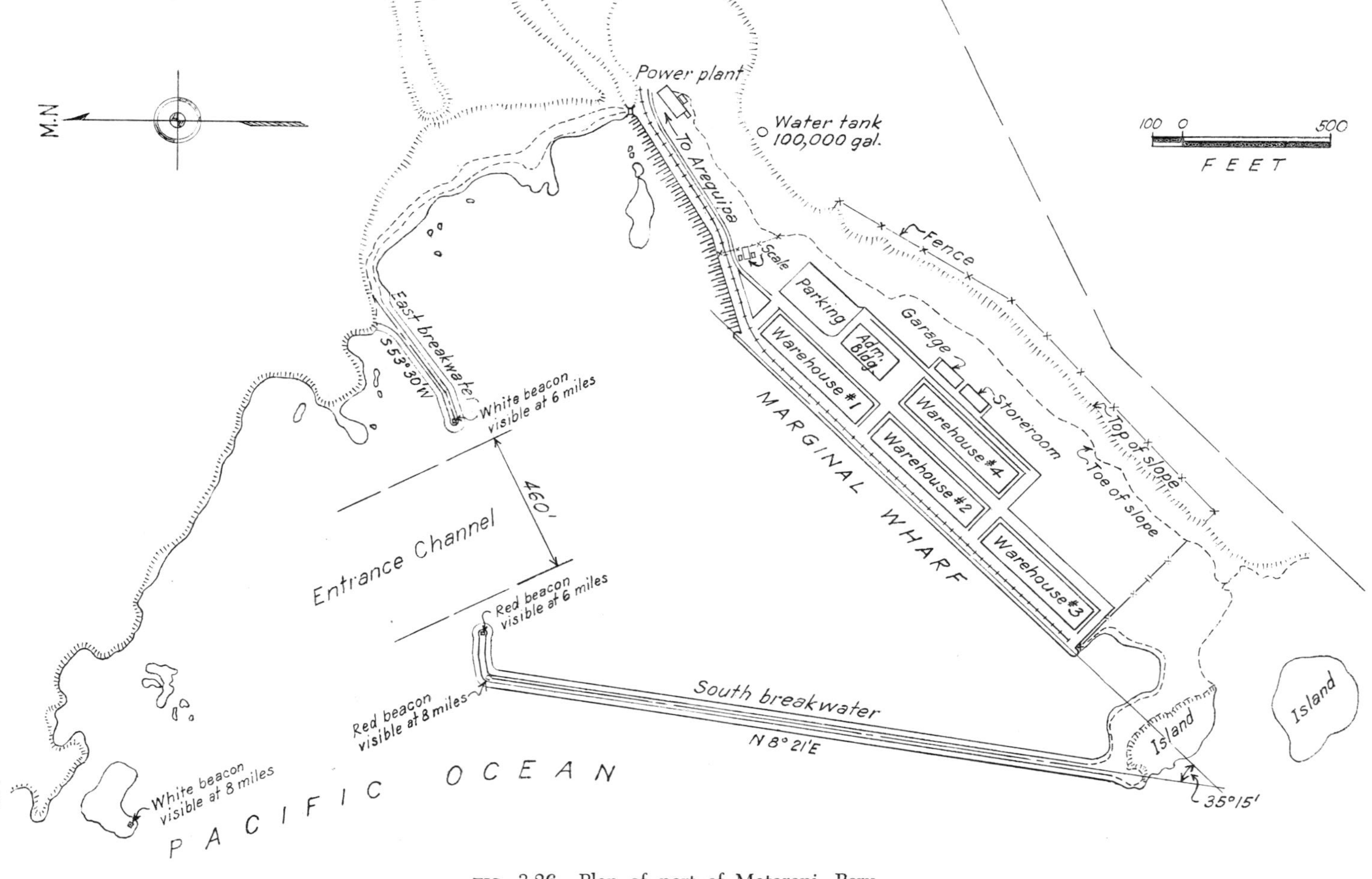

FIG. 3.26 Plan of port of Matarani, Peru.

at elevation −36. The cells are surmounted by a concrete cantilever-type wall with counterforts to which is fastened the timber- and wood-pile springing-type fender system. The finished grade in the port area is +12.5.

The port buildings consist of four warehouses each 90 by 420 ft, making a total storage area of 150,000 sq ft, a two-story administration and customs building 90 by 180 ft, a power plant, garage, etc.

FIG. 3.27 Aerial view of completed port of Matarani, Peru. (*Courtesy of the Frederick Snare Corp.*)

The port is connected to the city of Arequipa and the interior of southern Peru by rail and highway. Figure 3.26 shows the plan of the port, and an aerial view is shown in Fig. 3.27.

The Port of Callao. This Peruvian port handles about 60 per cent of that country's exports and imports in addition to a considerable volume of coastwise shipping. The harbor, which is about one square mile in area, is protected by two rock breakwaters, the north one being about 7,100 ft long and the south one about 3,500 ft long. A plan of this port is shown in Fig. 3.28.

The original port, built in 1870, consisted of a "Darsena," or boat basin, which handled craft up to 20 ft draft. This basin is now within the area protected by the breakwaters and is used principally for coastwise shipping and by ships requiring repairs.

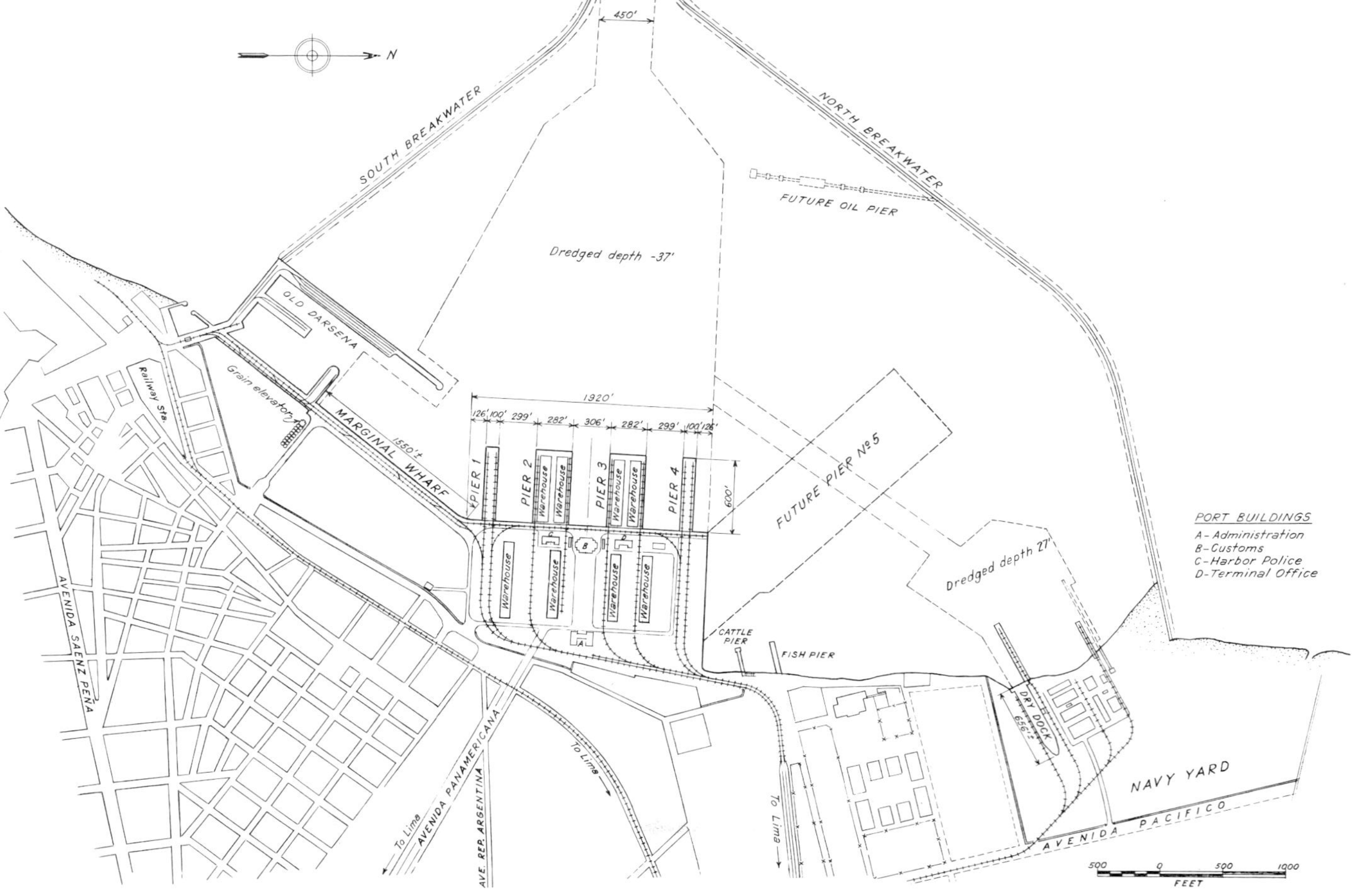

FIG. 3.28 Plan of port of Callao, Peru.

The present berthing facilities, in addition to the Darsena, consist of a bulkhead wharf some 3,600 ft long and four finger piers. The north and south piers are 600 ft long by 100 ft wide, and are of open-pile construction. The two center piers are 600 ft long by 282 ft wide and were constructed in the form of a U with the center part containing hydraulic fill retained by a wall around the inner periphery. A view taken during the construction of these piers is shown in Fig. 3.29.

FIG. 3.29 View taken during construction of piers at port of Callao. (*Courtesy of the Frederick Snare Corp.*)

The two center piers each have two warehouses 540 by 90 ft and there are four warehouses back of the bulkhead. In addition, the port has a grain elevator with a capacity of 23,000 tons of wheat and two discharge towers with a total capacity of 300 tons per hour.

At the northerly end of the harbor there is located the Naval Arsenal and dry dock. The port has ample open storage space and the facilities for handling cargo are quite modern. All service railroad tracks are standard gauge, and the railroad runs from the port area to Lima, the capital, and then continues on up into the Andes where it taps many of Peru's mineral resources, particularly copper and vanadium.

It can be seen that there are ample anchorage facilities for all types of ships in the outer portion of the harbor. In general, the areas used by ocean-going vessels are dredged to −37 ft.

Two air views of this notable port are shown in Figs. 3.30 and 3.31.

FIG. 3.30 Aerial view of port of Callao, taken in 1939, showing old Darsena, new bulkhead, piers, warehouses, and port buildings. (*Courtesy of the Frederick Snare Corp.*)

FIG. 3.31 Aerial view of Callao port works, taken in 1939. (*Courtesy of the Frederick Snare Corp.*)

The Port of Southampton, England. This may well be classed as one of the outstanding ports of the world. It ranks as the premier passenger terminal not only of England, but of all Europe. It is located about ten miles from the English Channel, where the rivers Test and Itchen meet with Southampton waters.

The port has a normal tide range of 13 ft and is unique in that two high tides, about 2 hours apart, occur daily.

FIG. 3.32 View of the port of Southampton, England. (*Courtesy of the Institution of Civil Engineers, London.*)

The development of the port is of particular interest from an engineering standpoint because of the distinct change which took place in 1933 in the type of dock construction. Prior to that time, as shown in Fig. 3.32, the docks were located, generally, in the basins at the intersection of the rivers Test and Itchen.

In 1933 the port was materially expanded by constructing a quay wall about 7,500 ft long on the river Test, as shown in Fig. 3.32, west of the Royal Pier, and filling the lowland in back to reclaim about 400 acres of land for the construction of warehouses, factories, and other port facilities. The channel was extended up the river by dredging in front of the docks and turning basins were formed at each end, with a depth of 35 ft below low water. The water depth was increased to 45 ft immediately in front of the quay wall at the east end and 40 ft at the west end. The quay wall consisted of 146 concrete monoliths, 45 ft square in plan, 14 of which were sunk to 30 ft and the remaining ones to 7 ft below dredged bottom. The dock provides berthing accommodations for eight of the largest ships at one time, including the *Queen Mary* and the *Queen Elizabeth.*

In 1933 the King George V graving dock, the largest in the world, was completed and put into use. Built primarily for the liner *Queen Mary,* the dock measures 1,200 ft long by 135 ft wide.

FIG. 3.33 View of the port of Hamburg, West Germany. (*Courtesy of Hamburger Hafen-und Lagerhaus-Aktiengesellschaft.*)

The Port of Southampton is a notable example of growth by expansion through the employment of its natural endowments.

The Port of Hamburg. Located at the junction of the northern and southern Elbe River, approximately 76 miles from the North Sea, a view of this harbor is shown in Fig. 3.33.

From a historical standpoint, the Port of Hamburg occupies a unique position in Western Europe. Its first quays with cranes and transit sheds were put into service in 1866, and in 1888 a free port was created which has grown ever since. By the beginning of World War I the volume of traffic had grown to 28 million tons. The 1914–1918 war only caused an interruption in the growth of the port, since all port facilities were left intact, and by 1929 the traffic had reached a new peak of 29 million tons. World War II was of more serious consequence, as the coming of peace in 1945 saw the city largely destroyed and the port a heap of debris, destroyed warehouses, and sunken ships.

The rebuilding of the port, since the end of World War II, has been a long and difficult task but, although it has not fully regained its normal prewar traffic volume, it has again become the greatest German seaport, handling about 27 million tons of cargo to and from all parts of the world.

It was just before World War II that the first major change in dock design was initiated, in which the heavy block masonry wall type of dock construction gave way to light reinforced-concrete relieving-type platforms supported on piles. The reconstruction after World War II saw a continuation of this trend in which new docks were constructed in front of or in combination with the old quay walls, and the faces of the new transit sheds and warehouses were located somewhat inland from their former locations, so as to provide wider aprons to accommodate railroad traffic and wharf cranes. Along with the reconstruction went the deepening of the harbor basins and approaches to 30 to 32 ft below low water. Fifty-eight dredged basins are available for handling up to 250 seagoing vessels at one time. Mooring dolphins which had always been an important part of the docking facilities were renewed, and in some locations steel-box-pile sections replaced the old Hamburg-type dolphins consisting of either 8 or 16 wood piles, on a 1-to-8 batter, braced near the high- and low-water levels. Many dolphins were constructed for berthing on both sides.

The layout of the port is characterized by the absence of piers, the almost universal use of basins off the main river channels so as not to interfere with river traffic, and the wide use of dolphins in the open basins for transhipment of cargo from one vessel to another.

The port has handling and storage facilities for all commodities of the world market and for all types of cargo, and liner sailings are made to most world ports.

The Port of Sydney. Situated on the fertile eastern coast of Australia, this port serves the New South Wales capital and its environs, the nation's largest center of population, and a hinterland comprising almost all the state's area of some 309,000 square miles.

An aerial view of Sydney, looking south across the harbor bridge and wharves, is shown in Fig. 3.34.

Assisted by its geographic position and natural advantages, Sydney Harbor has developed into a major world port and is regarded by mariners as one of the most spacious and protected natural harbors in the world. The largest vessels may enter or leave in complete safety at any state of tide, and during World War II, when Sydney was the base of the British Pacific Fleet as well as a major supply base for American operations, the *Queen Mary* and *Queen Elizabeth* were frequent visitors. Four vessels of the "Queen" type, in addition to many other craft, could be accommodated comfortably in the harbor at one time. The largest number of seagoing ships actually recorded as being in the port at one time is 194, this figure including a considerable proportion of vessels of the larger types.

The full area of the port extends over 13,600 acres, approximately 21 square miles, and about half this area carries a depth of water not less

FIG. 3.34 View of Sydney, Australia, looking south across the harbor bridge and wharves. (*Courtesy of the Australian News and Information Bureau.*)

than 30 ft at low tide. The average width of the harbor is slightly less than one mile, but, although it extends only about 13 miles inland, there are approximately 152 miles of foreshore bordering the various arms and the many sheltered bays.

Because it is almost landlocked, Sydney Harbor provides excellent shelter for shipping but, although endowed with great natural advantages, it has not been developed to its present position as a major port without the outlay of considerable capital expenditure and much careful work and planning by the harbor authority. The steep nature of much of the foreshore and the great depth of water and underlying silt have added to the cost of providing wharves and approaches. At Walsh Bay, for instance, many of the piles in the jetties were spliced to make lengths up to 145 ft, as the water at the outer end is about 50 ft deep and the depth of silt over the solid strata made it necessary for the piles to be driven 70 or 80 ft to secure a firm foundation. To provide good access to the wharves, particularly in the Walsh Bay and Darling Harbor areas, much of the port roadway system had to be cut out of the solid rock, sometimes to a depth of 60 ft, at heavy expense.

The principal wharfage at the Port of Sydney is most conveniently and centrally located from the point of view of both commerce and shipping, as it is situated within four or five miles of the sea and within one mile of the heart of the city. The length of commercial wharfage, not including berths for harbor craft, is more than 70,000 ft or 13 miles, of which about 55,000 ft are owned by the board. This wharfage comprises more than 80 general-cargo berths for oversea and interstate vessels, over 40 berths for intrastate ships, and a number of special berths for handling cargoes such as bulk oil, timber, or coal. Wharves and jetties for ferries and other harbor craft provide a total berthing length of about 6,000 ft. There are also six dolphin berths at Snails Bay which have been provided specially for use by vessels discharging timber to lighters, and sixteen tie-up berths for vessels undergoing repairs or out of commission.

The majority of the wharves are of timber-pile construction, although the "solid-fill" method of construction has been adopted for most recent work. All of the wharfage built in recent years has concrete decking and the timber decking of older wharves and jetties is being replaced with concrete as renewal of the deck becomes necessary.

Most of the commercial berths in the port are equipped with roomy cargo sheds which have a total area of well over 3 million sq ft, or approximately 73 acres, and this accommodation is being increased steadily by new construction. Rail facilities connected with the main railway system of the state are provided at many of the wharves in the Pyrmont, Glebe Island, Rozelle Bay, and Balmain areas and rail tracks are laid on the wharf apron at many of these berths, although at present less than 5 per cent of the total imports are handled direct to rail from vessels and only about 10 per cent of exports (excluding grain and flour, which are handled at specially equipped berths) are delivered to the wharves direct from rail.

The port has facilities for docking the largest vessel afloat and is a major repair base for both naval and commercial ships. The Captain Cook Graving Dock, on the east of the approach to Woolloomooloo Bay, ranks among the largest graving docks in the world, its dimensions being 1,133 ft by 147 ft 7½ in. with a depth of 45 ft 2 in. over the sill at high water.

The Port of Quebec. This port is located on the north shore of the Saint Lawrence River at its confluence with the Saint Charles River, about 160 statute miles downstream from Montreal.

Quebec Harbor serves a large pulp- and paper-producing area and is the principal port serving the asbestos mines of the southeastern part of the province, the world's greatest asbestos mining region. It is also the nearest large port to the new iron-ore developments in northeastern Quebec and Labrador.

This harbor is a tidal port with a mean tidal range of about 16 ft. It has channels of sufficient depth and width to accommodate with safety all but the largest vessels. About two-thirds of the 41 berths at Quebec Harbor have minimum depths alongside of 35 ft or more. Most of the remainder have limiting depths of 25 to 30 ft. From this, it is apparent that most of the berths have sufficient depth of water to accommodate most ocean ships.

The Harbor is divided into two principal sections known as Princess Louise Docks and Wolfe's Cove Terminals, as shown in Fig. 3.35.

The first major harbor development took place in 1877 with the construction of Princess Louise embankment and the inner and outer basins. Additional berthing facilities were built as the need arose and a grain elevator of 1 million bu capacity was built in 1914. Additions were made to the elevator in 1917, 1929, and 1958 to bring it to its present capacity of 6 million bu.

Construction of Wolfe's Cove Terminals was carried out from 1925 to 1931. This freight and passenger terminal provides facilities which are among the best in the world. They consist of a wharf with a berthing length of over 4,900 ft, a two-story shed, 1,380 by 100 ft, six rail lines at the rear of the shed, ample open-storage space, and first-class accommodations for passengers.

Practically all main shipping facilities at Quebec Harbor are administered by the National Harbours Board.

An unusual feature of Quebec Harbor is Princess Louise Basin consisting of a wet dock, 34 acres in extent, known as the Inner Basin, where a constant depth of water is maintained, and a tidal harbor, 19 acres in area, known as the Outer Basin. The two basins are separated by a cross wall 960 ft long and 153 ft wide. Access to the Inner Basin is provided by lock gates of sufficient width to permit passage of the largest freighter.

The port has unexcelled repair facilities consisting of a dry dock, 1,150 ft long by 120 ft wide at the entrance, which can dock the largest ship afloat; a second dry dock, 624 ft long by 61.5 ft wide; and a marine railway with lifting capacity of 2,000 tons.

The Port of Cleveland. Ideally located on Lake Erie and close to the Welland Canal, the gateway to the Saint Lawrence Waterway, the Port of Cleveland at the present time ranks fourth among the leading Great Lakes ports in tonnage handled.

The port comprises two distinct developments, the Inner Harbor, or

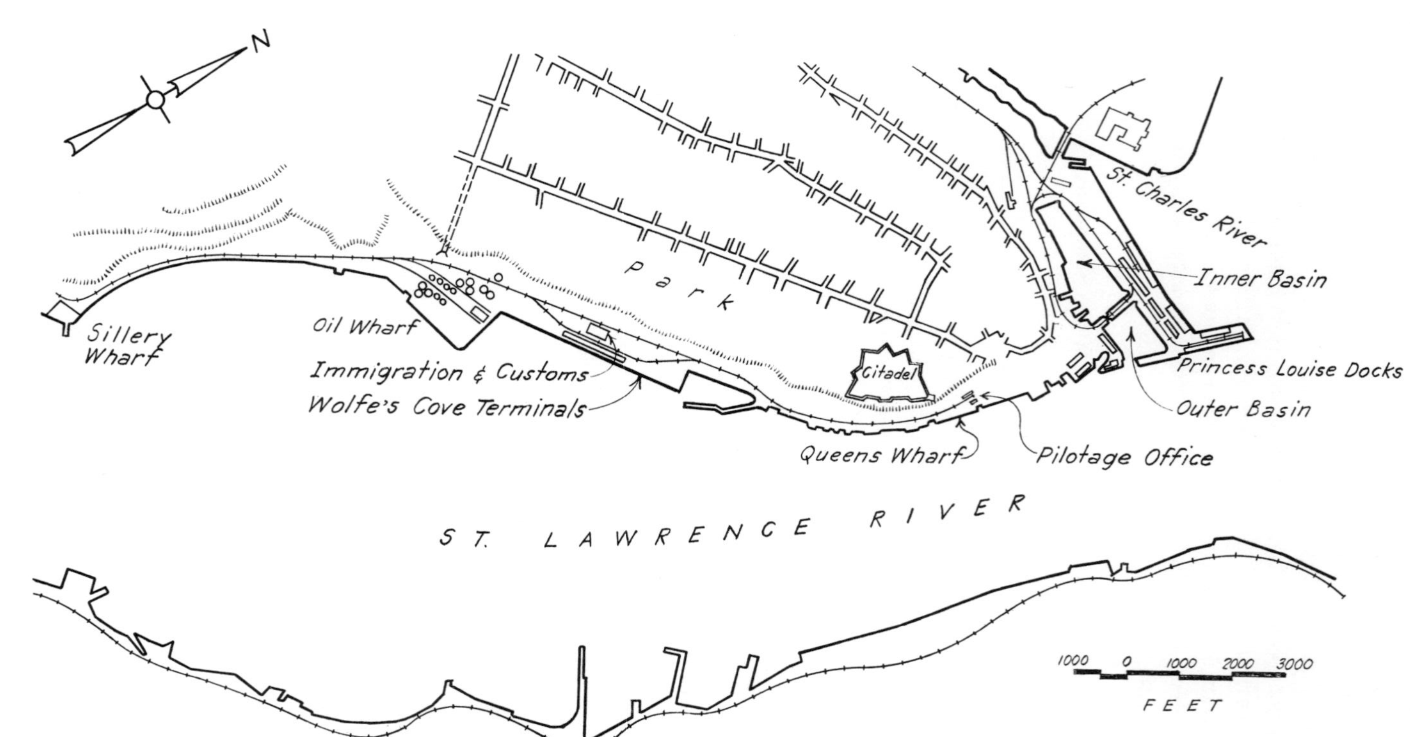

FIG. 3.35 Plan of port of Quebec, Canada. (*Courtesy of National Harbours Board.*)

the Cuyahoga River section, and the Outer Harbor or lake front area. The Inner Harbor, which extends far inland, has been serving a large proportion of Cleveland's huge industrial production for over 100 years. The area is served by 8 railroads, 12 air lines, 8 bus lines and 150 motor highway carriers, the latter utilizing new modern roads, turnpikes, and other arteries built in recent years. Between the years 1937 and 1962, $75 million will have been spent on a very well-planned river-improvement program.

The Outer Harbor is protected by a breakwater, parallel to the lake front, which extends for a length of over 5 miles. The basin between the breakwater and the pierhead line varies between 1,700 and 2,400 ft in width. This breakwater, although started in the year 1884, was not completed until 1915. Conditions of improvement of the Outer Harbor, as of June 30, 1958, are shown in Fig. 3.36. Recently completed were the new West 3d Street Dock, adding roughly 8 acres to the dock capacity, and the West 6th Street Dock, which added roughly another 6 acres. These new docks added berthing facilities for four ships up to 600 ft in length. When the Outer Harbor is completed, it will provide berthing space for ships up to 27 ft draft and over-all lengths of up to 650 ft, and will then accommodate all sizes of vessels using the Seaway.

The Port of Rio de Janeiro. This port is located inside Guanabara Bay, Brazil, a natural harbor about 15 nautical miles long and up to 10 miles wide. A series of peninsulas and islands with relatively high elevations protect the entrance to the bay and have made it unnecessary to build any kind of artificial protection for the port. Only a short 1,000-ft-wide channel had to be dredged to give ocean-going vessels access to the port with a minimum depth of 30 ft. The tidal range is about 8 ft.

The port serves not only the city of Rio de Janeiro itself but the potentially rich state of Minas Gerais, which is being rapidly developed, and portions of several other Brazilian states. It handles about 6 million tons of general cargo, with over 3.5 million tons of overseas cargo.

Traffic in the port was very heavy as early as the end of the last century, when more than 100 ships anchored at one time in the harbor. However, there were practically no piers or wharves, all cargo being handled by lighters. In the early part of this century, the first marginal wharf, known as the Gamboa Wharf, with a length of almost 11,000 ft and with 26 to 33 ft of water depth, was built along the south shore of a cove north of the city. It consisted of a continuous trapezoidal concrete wall with stone facing on both sides, constructed by means of steel caissons and cofferdams. In 1924 a second section of marginal wharf, known as the Sao Cristovao Wharf, was built along the west shore of the cove, with a length of 4,700 ft. This wharf is made of reinforced-concrete arches on piers which were founded directly on a firm soil stratum, and backed up

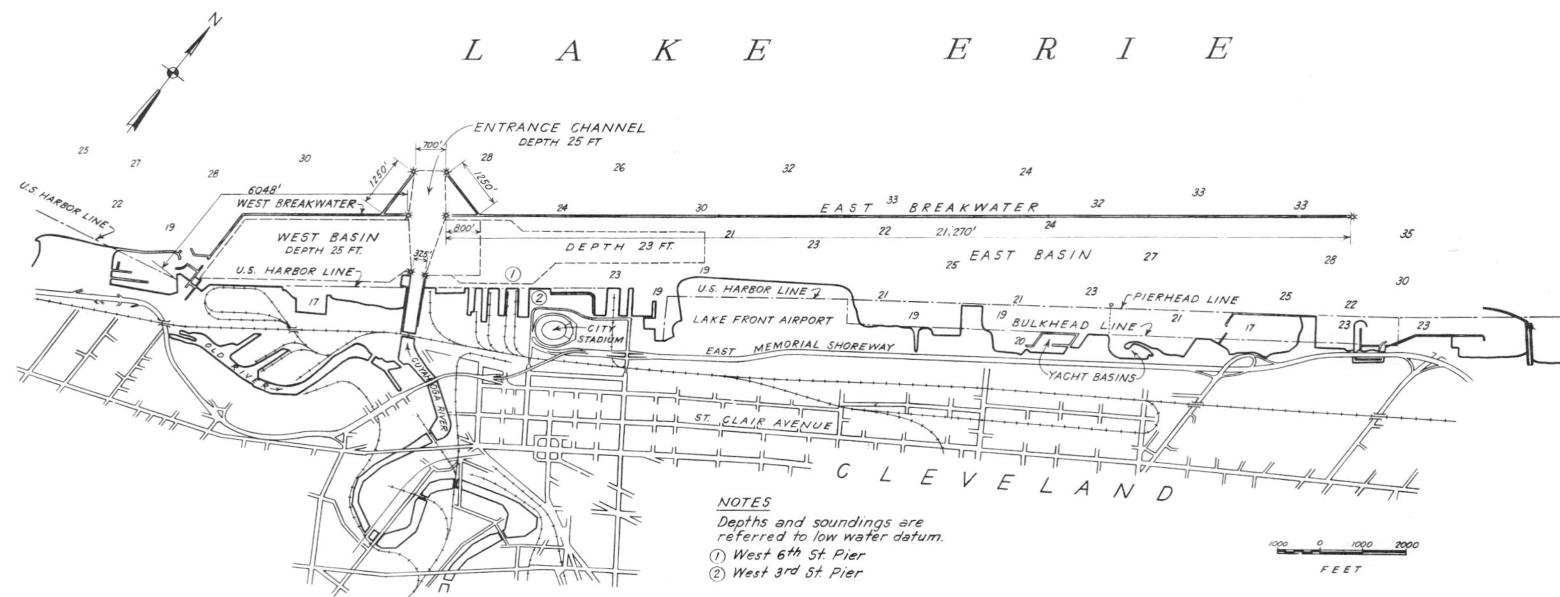

FIG. 3.36 Plan of outer harbor of port of Cleveland. (*Courtesy of Department of Port Control, City of Cleveland.*)

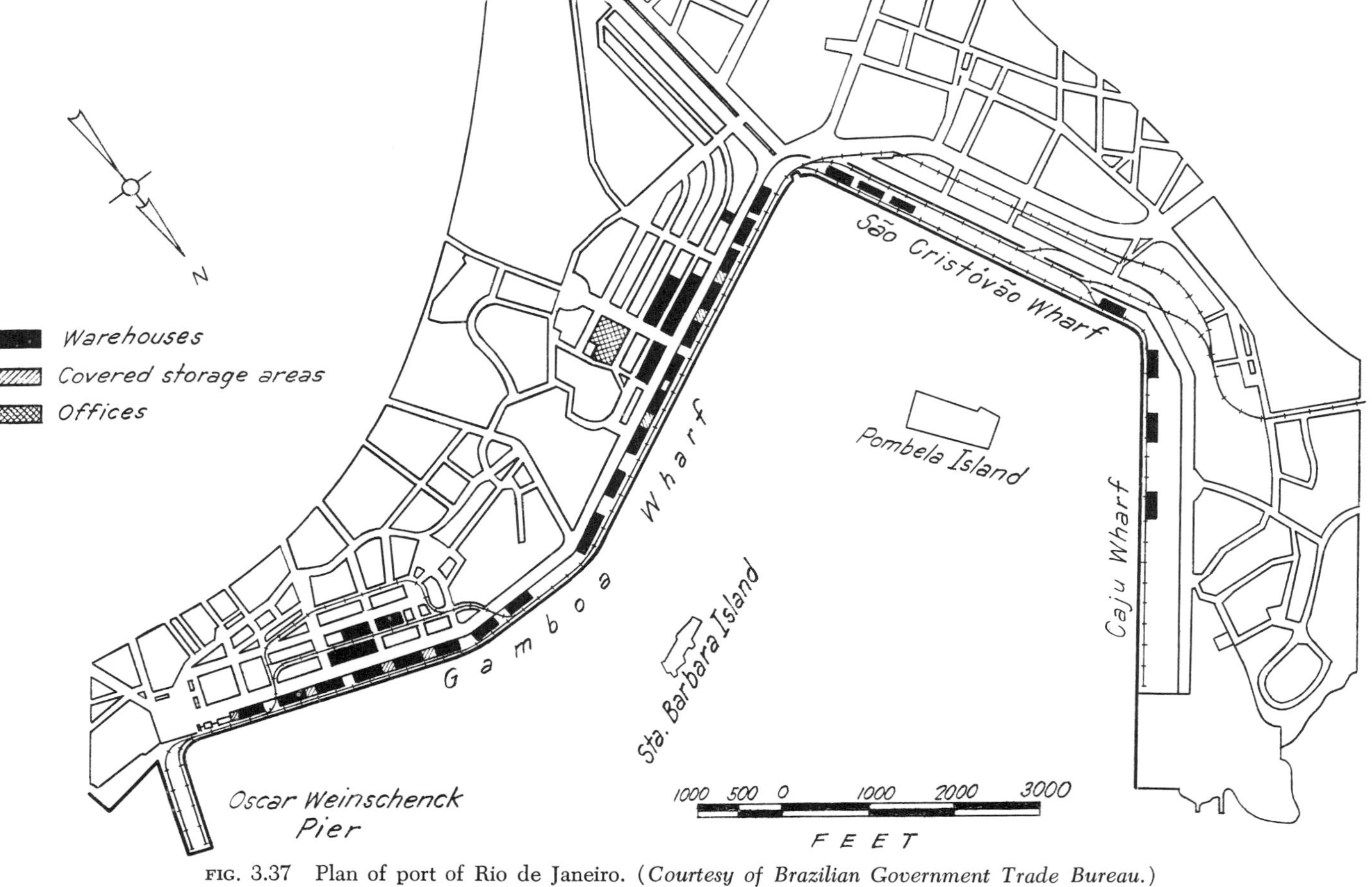

FIG. 3.37 Plan of port of Rio de Janeiro. (*Courtesy of Brazilian Government Trade Bureau.*)

by a rubble dike which retains the backfill. It is mostly used for coal and ore handling. In 1949 a third section of marginal wharf, known as the Caju Wharf, was built on the north shore of the cove, with a length of 4,300 ft. It consists of steel sheet piling tied back to concrete anchors and capped by a concrete wall. This section is used for lumber, chemicals, and oil products.

In 1949, the only finger pier of the port was built for overseas passenger service. It has a length of 1,300 and a width of 270 ft. The pier consists of fill, retained by concrete sheet-piling walls tied to 50-ft-wide concrete relieving platforms which rest on batter piles. The pier eventually will contain a complete passenger terminal. Figure 3.37 shows a general plan of the port.

Chapter 4 BREAKWATERS

4.1 Types of Breakwaters and Factors Determining Their Selection

A breakwater is a structure constructed for the purpose of forming an artificial harbor with a water area so protected from the effect of sea waves as to provide safe accommodation for shipping. There are two classes of breakwaters: those giving protection to commercial harbors or their entrances and those sheltering an anchorage or roadstead, being used by vessels to escape the violence of storms or while awaiting orders and their turn to dock. Such an anchorage may be an outer harbor where there are no docks.

There are many different types of breakwaters which have been constructed in all parts of the world. Natural rock and concrete or a combination of both are the materials which form 95 per cent or more of all breakwaters constructed. Steel, timber, and even compressed air have served to a lesser extent to break the force of the sea waves.

Most breakwaters function only to provide protection, but occasionally they serve a dual purpose by becoming part of a pier or supporting a roadway. The former is termed a breakwater pier or quay and the latter a mole.

The general arrangement of breakwaters for the protection of harbors has been described in Chap. 3, Harbor Planning and Construction. Chapter 4 will treat mainly of the different types of breakwaters, their design and construction.

There are two main types of breakwaters, the mound type and the wall type. Falling under the first classification and identified more commonly by the materials out of which they are constructed are the following: (1) natural rock, (2) concrete block, (3) a combination of rock and concrete block, and (4) concrete tetrapods and tribars. These types of breakwaters may be supplemented in each case by concrete monoliths or seawalls to break the force of the waves and to prevent splash and spray from passing over the top. In the second main classification of breakwaters there are such types as: (1) concrete-block gravity walls, (2) concrete caissons, (3) rock-filled sheet-pile cells, (4) rock-filled timber cribs, and (5) concrete or steel sheet-pile walls.

The type of breakwater to be used is usually determined by the availability of materials at or near the site, the depth of water, the condition of the sea bottom, its function in the harbor, and, last but not least, the equipment suitable and available for its construction.

Since the main purpose of the breakwater is to provide protection

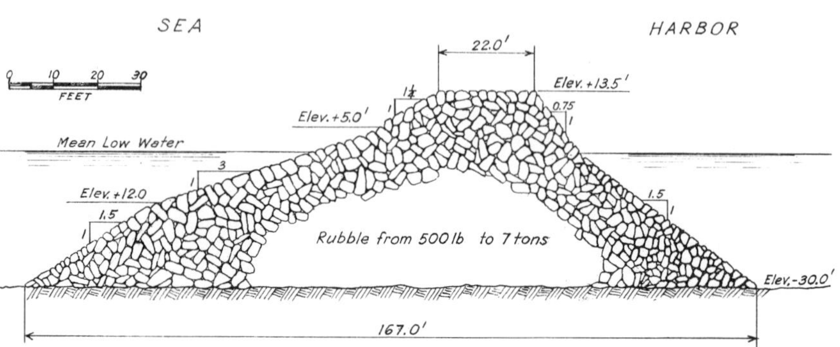

FIG. 4.1 First rock-mound breakwater constructed in the United States: the Delaware Breakwater. (*From report by Joseph F. Hasskarl,* XIIth *International Congress of Navigation, Philadelphia,* 1912.)

from the waves, it follows that an understanding of wave action and its forces is one of the more important elements in its design. For this the reader should study Chap. 2 carefully. Another important element is the character of the sea bottom which must take the final reaction from the force of the waves against the structure which has been placed to dissipate the energy of the waves. In this respect, since most breakwaters are gravity structures, they depend upon their weight for stability. Therefore, the depth of water and the character of the bottom are important factors in their design. Practical considerations usually limit the height of vertical-type breakwaters to a water depth of not over 60 ft below mean sea level, and where used in deeper water they are generally founded on a rock fill below this level; otherwise the width of the structure becomes unwieldy. The character of the bottom may well be the determining factor in the type of breakwater selected, as it is usually difficult, if not impossible, and expensive to prepare a solid foundation on soft material for the support of a wall-type gravity structure.

Since rock is one of the main materials used in the construction of breakwaters, its availability will have to be investigated. In this respect not only will it be necessary to determine that it is economically feasible to produce and deliver to the site a sufficient quantity of rock, but its density, soundness, and ability to break into large pieces when quarried will be important factors in determining its use.

The abundance of durable rock and familiarity with quarrying methods to produce large quantities of rock at economical costs have led to the adoption of rock-mound breakwaters to a greater extent than any other type for the protection of harbors along the North America and South America seacoasts. The first breakwater ever constructed in the United States, as shown in Fig. 4.1, is the Delaware Breakwater near Cape Henlopen, Delaware, a rock mound which was commenced in 1828, but not completed until 1869. It is 5,267 ft long and has served as a prototype for other mound breakwaters.

On the Great Lakes the early practice was to use large amounts of timber because of its availability and cheapness, but in recent years rock and concrete have been used more extensively.

Continental practice, particularly in Italy, has greatly favored the vertical-wall type, supplemented in very deep water by a rubble base. Extreme depths of water, often over 100 ft, and great wave heights have in many cases brought about this general practice. Experience over many years in using this type of construction for docks and other marine structures, resulting in confidence and familiarity in the casting and placing of large concrete blocks and monoliths, either hollow or solid, and the more common use of a combination breakwater and dock, or quay, have contributed to the use of this type of design in European practice.

4.2 Rock-mound Breakwaters

Although there are many variations in the classes of fill and the locations and proportions of these materials within a mound breakwater, the following two distinct types of construction appear to stand out above others and to be worthy of comment: (1) a rock mound in which the core material extends above water level and is covered with an envelope of armor rock sometimes separated from the core material by one or more intermediate layers, and (2) that in which the core fill is stopped a considerable depth below water level and covered with a medium-weight rock, which forms the base for the heavy armor capping. Figure 4.2 illustrates the former type of construction and Fig. 4.3 the latter type.

The first type of construction, which will hereafter be referred to as type 1, consists of a core of small rock, customarily referred to as "run-of-quarry" material, placed as fill on the sea bottom and extending to above water level. This material is protected with a surface course, or envelope, of large rock, selected as to size and shape and laid to well-defined slopes. One or more intermediate layers of rock of smaller sizes usually termed the "secondary armor," or the "filter course," and in the lower regions the "bedding course," may separate the inner core and the outside envelope of large armor rock. Briefly then, such a breakwater consists of three distinct parts: the core, the secondary armor, and the armor course. While there may be some modifications in the use of all three components, such as the elimination of the filter course or the omission of the core material by using an all-armor rock mound, generally speaking the larger and more extensive breakwaters embody all three components.

In this type of construction the core is customarily extended out from

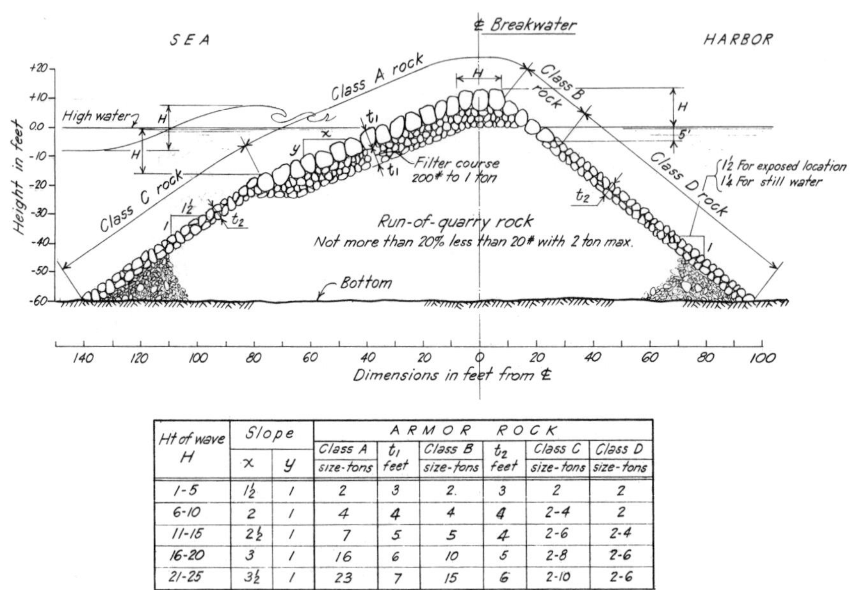

Ht of wave H	Slope x	Slope y	ARMOR ROCK Class A size-tons	t_1 feet	Class B size-tons	t_2 feet	Class C size-tons	Class D size-tons
1-5	1½	1	2	3	2	3	2	2
6-10	2	1	4	4	4	4	2-4	2
11-15	2½	1	7	5	5	4	2-6	2-4
16-20	3	1	16	6	10	5	2-8	2-6
21-25	3½	1	23	7	15	6	2-10	2-6

FIG. 4.2 Design section, rock-mound breakwater: type 1.

shore by end- or side-dumping from trucks which operate on top of the core as it is brought up above water level. This requires the top of the core to be above the highest water level and the material out of which it is constructed to be broken rock of sufficient size and with a minimum amount of fines, so that it will not be washed away by the waves during the period of construction. There are disadvantages in this method: (1) The top may have to be made somewhat wider than otherwise required by the breakwater design, in order to provide space for the trucks to operate. (2) The upper surface of the core, to form a roadway, will contain a considerable amount of fines, which will become compacted from the travel of the trucks. Before placing the capping armor rock, the top surface of the core will have to be removed, or the fines washed out, so as to make a more pervious bed directly under the armor rock. In lieu of this, a filter layer, several feet in thickness, consisting of coarse, clean material, will have to be placed on top of the roadway. This may increase the height of the breakwater somewhat more than is required by the design. (3) Unless placing the armor rock follows immediately that of the core, a considerable amount of storm damage may occur and the top of the recently placed core material may be washed away to several feet below water level. However, the advantages in economy of construction and the smaller percentage of heavy rock required usually outweigh the above disadvantages.

In the above respect, nature may dictate the design, because, in quarry-

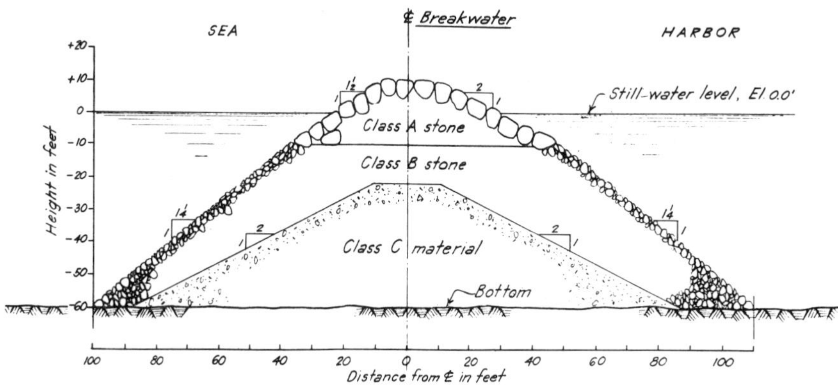

FIG. 4.3 Design section, rock-mound breakwater: type 2. *Class A stone* is selected from quarry. No pieces less than 1 ton and at least 95 per cent by weight weighing 10 ton or more each. *Class B stone* is quarry run. Not more than 25 per cent by weight in pieces less than 20 lb and not less than 40 per cent in pieces of 1 ton or more. *Class C material* is a residuum from quarry operations or a dredged material.

ing the rock for the construction of a breakwater, unless special drilling and blasting are used to control the breaking of the rock, there will usually result a large percentage of fine material, which is suitable for the core of the breakwater, if protected with rock of sufficient size to withstand being dislodged under the force of the waves.

It is the exceptional case when the blasting will result in an excess of large rock beyond what is required to provide a protective envelope for the core material. Usually, the drilling and blasting technique will have to be carefully laid out and controlled to obtain sufficient amounts of large rock, and this may have to be supplemented by the addition of concrete blocks. A rock-mound breakwater of the type shown in Fig. 4.14, constructed in 60 ft of water, to withstand a 20 ft wave, requires the following approximate percentages of different sizes of rock: core material of less than 5-ton size, 83.5 per cent; armor rock of 2- to 8-ton size, 8.0 per cent; of 8- to 15-ton size, 2.5 per cent; of 12- to 20-ton size, 6.0 per cent.

However, unless the armor rock is laid carefully and fitted together so that there are practically no voids—a job which is very difficult to perform because of the irregularity of the large pieces of rock, and which is not considered the best practice because of its low permeability—some of the finer material of the core may be washed away, destroying the support under the armor rock and ultimately causing it to be dislodged, resulting in the eventual disintegration of the breakwater. Therefore, it is important to protect the core, unless it is built of coarse, clean rock, with an intermediate layer or filter course of selected rock, which will prevent the loss of the finer core material through the larger voids between the pieces of armor rock, and which will permit good drainage of the water left behind by the backwash of the waves. Unless this water can readily escape it may build up a high hydrostatic head which may displace the armor rock.

The armor rock may consist of one or more layers, with the heavier stone in the outside layer. Likewise the weight of stone should vary along the periphery of the envelope enclosing the core and should be heavier for a distance below water level usually equal to the maximum height of wave to and over the top of the breakwater, where the wave action is most severe. This is generally referred to as capping. The heavier rock should be carried down the lee side of the breakwater to a short distance below the water level, where it will then be reduced in size along the remainder of the slope to sea bottom.

The second type of construction, as shown in Fig. 4.3, which is similar to that proposed by the Bureau of Yards and Docks for the Roosevelt Roads breakwater, is based on the core being placed as dredged material or being dumped from scows or from a trestle. The top of the core is a considerable distance below water level and the core is covered with a medium-weight rock to a level about equal to the height of the wave below mean sea level, where it forms a base on which to place the heavier armor rock extending to the top of the breakwater.

A model following the dimensions of the prototype breakwater indicated in Fig. 4.3 was tested by the United States Waterways Experiment Station for the Bureau of Yards and Docks, United States Navy, for the purpose of establishing guides for safe slopes and rock sizes. The conclusions, as given in the 1953 report, are, generally, as follows.

1. The class C material can be placed without any protection with its top elevation not exceeding the following values:

Wave height, ft	*Top elevation below still-water level, ft*
7–8	20
10–11	30
15–16	40
20–21	50

2. If during construction higher waves are expected than would correspond to the above table, the class B material should be placed on both harbor-side and sea-side slopes, simultaneously with the construction of the class C core. Placing of the class B material on either the harbor-side or sea-side slope only is not considered advisable, as during a heavy storm class C material might be deposited at places where the design calls for placing of class B material.

3. For 21.0-ft waves the top elevation of the class B material should not be raised above about -15 ft below still-water level. In this case a blanket of class B material about 8 ft thick would be sufficient. The depth of the top of the class B material blanket is more critical than its thickness.

4. Class A cap rock should be placed as soon as possible, otherwise a heavy storm may erode the class B cover layer. Tests indicated that the class A cap rock of the prototype size was not stable on a 1-on-2 slope but was stable on a 1-on-4½ slope.

This type of construction enables the use of more fine material in the quarry waste than would be desirable for the run-of-quarry material required for the previously described type of construction, and permits the use of materials other than quarried rock, such as sand, coral, and dredgings, providing they can be placed under water without exceeding a slope of about 1 on 3, after which the width of the breakwater may become unwieldy. However, the amount of class B or medium-size rock is considerably increased over that required for the previously described type of construction, but this may not be a problem unless the quarry is deficient in this size of rock. Another disadvantage is that the top armor rock will have to be placed from a trestle or by the use of floating derricks. This makes it less susceptible to storm damage during construction, but installation with floating equipment often results in considerable loss of time because work cannot be done on the water during stormy periods.

The design of a rock-mound breakwater must be based to a large extent on experience, supplemented in some cases by information obtained from model tests. There is no exact analytical analysis which can be made, but there are certain approximate formulas and design criteria which can be used by the designer to arrive at a safe design.

When information is not available on the wave characteristics at the location of the breakwater, the maximum height and length of wave will need to be approximated, based on hypothetical formulas given in Chap. 2, which take into consideration the wind, fetch, and depth of water. To determine the height of the top of the breakwater, the maximum wave height so derived must be superimposed on the maximum elevation of the tide, and then an allowance made for the change in height in crest level caused by the obstruction to the wave. For a vertical wall obstructing the wave, this increase in height will be about twice the height of the wave above the still-water level. However, a mound breakwater, because of its sloping surface, which may cause the wave to break, will not need to be as high as a vertical-wall breakwater. Also, the irregularity and roughness of the sloping surface of the armor rock will break up the waves and result in a considerable dissipation in wave energy and formation of spray, which is a familiar sight at many breakwaters. Therefore, unlike the vertical-wall breakwater, it is generally safe to assume that a rock-mound breakwater will provide adequate protection if its top is placed at the maximum height of the wave (trough to crest) before breaking and above highest tide. For very flat slopes, this height may be reduced somewhat. Figure 4.7 shows the relationship between slope and height of crest to prevent wave overtopping.

Usually the passage of spray over the top of the breakwater will not be objectionable, but in the case of a breakwater pier or mole, provision will have to be made to fully obstruct the wave. This can be accomplished by placing a seawall on top of the rock mound. This will usually have its base on the top of the core material, so that it is firmly anchored below the armor rock and its foundation support will not be undermined by wave action. This wall may have a curved face on the seaward side in order that the waves and spray will be deflected upward and seaward.

The minimum width of the top of the breakwater should be approximately equal to the height of the maximum wave, although the size of the capping rock and the minimum width of the top of the core to accommodate construction equipment, such as trucks and cranes, may be controlling factors.

The stability of a rock breakwater is dependent mainly upon the weight and shape of the individual pieces of armor rock and the slope on which they are laid, providing they are properly placed on the slope and with respect to each other so as to form a stable and reasonably close-fitting envelope around the core. It can be proved analytically and by model tests that the weight of the individual pieces of armor rock will vary with the degree of the slope on which they are laid, i.e., steeper slopes requiring heavier rock and flatter slopes lighter rock. The following equation by Iribarren has been used to determine this relationship between weight and slope for different wave heights.

$$W = \frac{KH^3S_r}{(\cos\alpha - \sin\alpha)^3(S_r - 1)^3}$$

where W = weight of individual cap rock, kg
K = a coefficient, 15 for rubble stone and 19 for artificial blocks
H = height of wave from trough to crest, meters
α = angle of slope with horizontal
S_r = specific weight of cap rock or block, metric tons per cubic meter

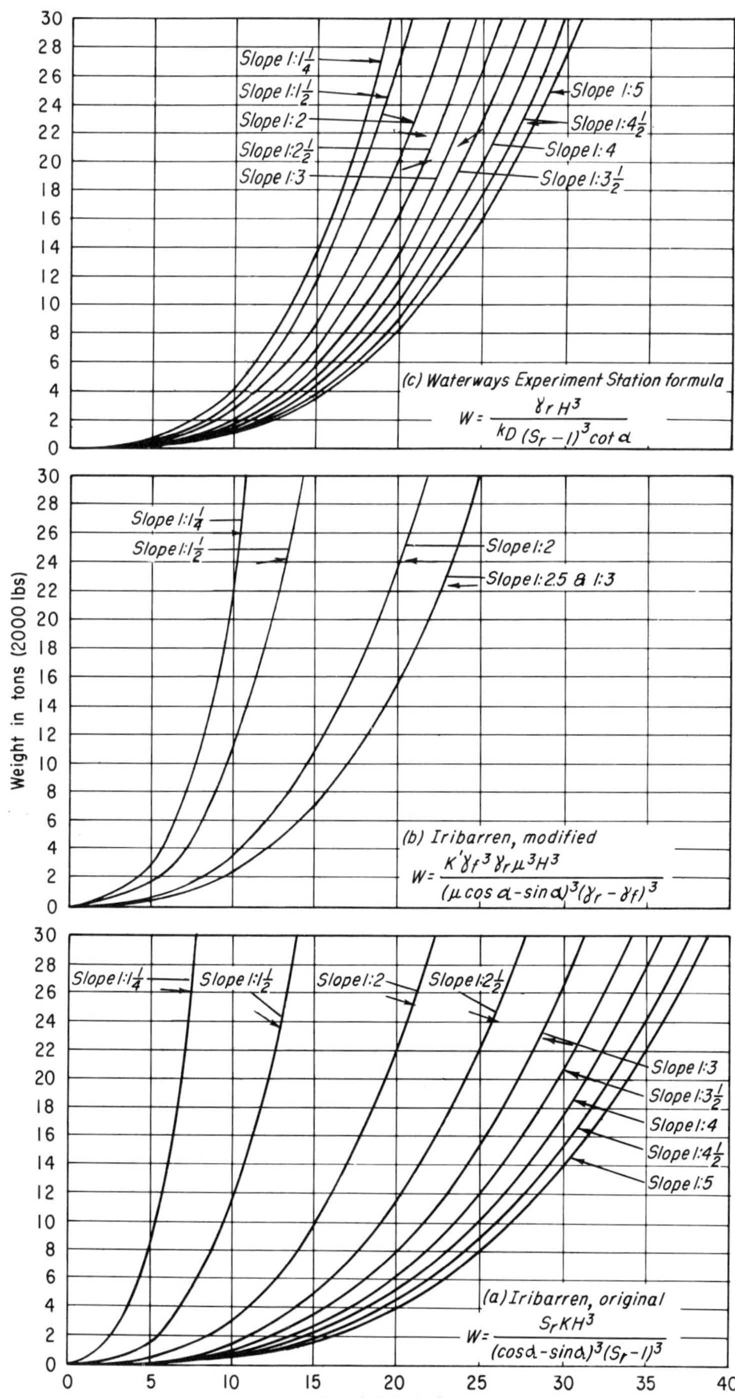

FIG. 4.4 Relationship among weight of rock, slope of armor course, and wave height. (*a*) Original Iribarren. (*b*) Modified Iribarren. (*c*) Waterways Experiment Station formula.

By changing the weight to tons, the height of wave to feet, and assuming the coefficient of friction equal to 1, the coefficient K equal to 15, and the specific gravity of the rock as 2.73, the curves in Fig. 4.4 have been plotted showing the relationship between weight of rock, slope of armor course, and height of wave.

A more general form of the above equation, as proposed by Hudson of the United States Army Engineer Waterways Experiment Station, is

$$W = \frac{K'\gamma_f{}^3\gamma_r\mu^3H^3}{(\mu \cos \alpha - \sin \alpha)^3(\gamma_r - \gamma_f)^3}$$

where W = weight of individual cap rock
H = height of wave
K' = undetermined dimensionless coefficient
γ_f = specific weight of liquid in which cap rock is submerged
γ_r = specific weight of cap rock
α = angle of sea-side slope
μ = coefficient of friction

This equation is dimensionally homogeneous and any constant system of units can be used. In the English system of units, when $\gamma_f = 62.4$, $\gamma_r = 170$, and $\mu = 1$, the coefficient 15 for K becomes .015 for K'.

The report of June, 1953, by the United States Army Engineer Waterways Experiment Station, Vicksburg, Mississippi, on the stability of rock-mound breakwaters (hydraulic model investigation), which was initiated by the Bureau of Yards and Docks in 1942 for the purpose of determining whether the breakwater proposed for construction of Roosevelt Roads, Puerto Rico, would be adequate to withstand the largest waves occurring at the breakwater site and revised from time to time to include tests to determine the accuracy of the Iribarren and Epstein-Tyrrell formulas for the design of rubble breakwaters, sets forth the conclusion that the Iribarren formula for the design of rubble breakwaters can be made sufficiently accurate by using the formula in conjunction with curves of dimensionless coefficients, such as those developed during the investigation. Figures 4.5 and 4.6 show the curves, as reproduced from the 1953 report, for values of K' for variations in depth of water d, wave height H, and wave length L.

Therefore, by using the variable K' for an average condition where d equals 60 ft and L equals 300 ft, curves have been added to Fig. 4.4*b*, showing the relationships among the weight, slope, and height of wave.

According to the model tests performed by the Waterways Experiment Station, and as illustrated in Fig. 4.4*a* and *b*, the Iribarren formula gives answers which (1) are conservative for breakwater slopes of 1 on 1¼,

(2) are in agreement with the test results for breakwater slopes of 1 on 1½ and 1 on 2, and (3) result in unsafe designs for breakwaters with slopes above 1 on 2. From an over-all point of view the results of the tests were encouraging. However, it was proved conclusively that the

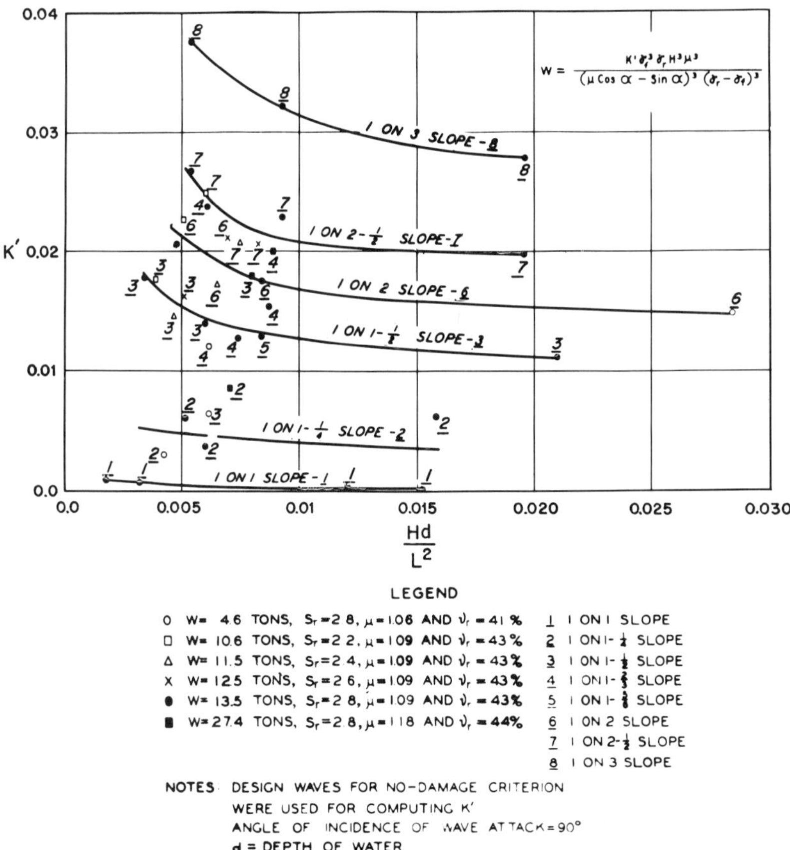

FIG. 4.5 Variations of K' with α and Hd/L^2. (*From United States Army Engineer Waterways Experiment Station,* 1953 *Report.*)

formula cannot be considered adequate unless used in conjunction with curves of corrective coefficients K', and conclusions reached later from investigations started in 1951, as described in the following paragraph, were that the experimental coefficient K' varies appreciably with the coefficient of friction μ and accurate values for the coefficient μ for variable armor units are very difficult to determine. The tests indicated that the Epstein-Tyrrell formula, similar in form to the Iribarren formula, should not be used for the design of rock-mound breakwaters. Only limited tests were made on concrete blocks and results of one test only would indicate that Iribarren's formula cannot be used for designing masonry-type breakwaters.

In 1951 the United States Army Engineer Waterways Experiment Sta-

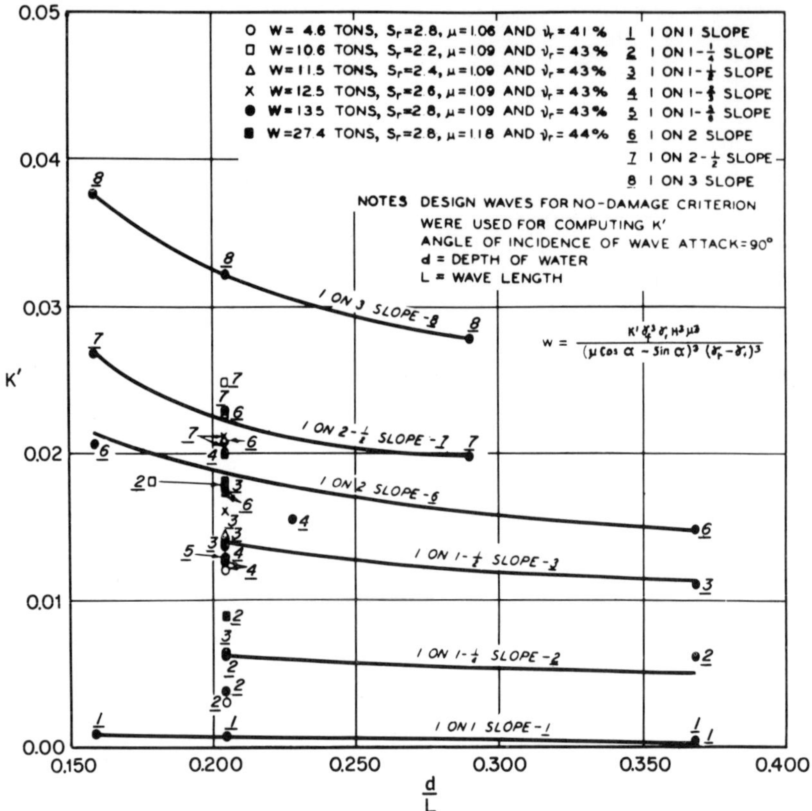

FIG. 4.6 Variations of K' with α and d/L. (*From United States Army Engineer Waterways Experiment Station,* 1953 *Report.*)

tion started tests for the Office, Chief of Engineers, concerning the stability of rubble-mound breakwaters with quarry-stone armor units as cover-layer material, and tests concerned with wave action on a pile of quarry-stone armor units placed pell-mell were reported on in Research Report 2-2, July, 1958. These tests were performed on a breakwater section in which the quarry-stone layer cover comprised the whole of the breakwater section above a horizontal plane at a depth below still-water level equal to the wave height H. Based on theory and the results of the tests, the following formula, similar to Iribarren's formula, was adopted:

$$W_r = \frac{\gamma_r H^3}{k_D(S_r - 1)^3 \cot \alpha}$$

where W_r = weight of individual armor rock, lb
H = height of wave, ft
k_D = damage coefficient = 3.2 for no damage and no overtopping criteria
α = angle of armor-rock slope with horizontal
S_r = specific gravity of armor rock
γ_r = specific weight of rock, lb per cu ft

For the conditions tested, the stability of rubble-mound breakwaters was found to be not appreciably influenced by variations in the ratio of relative depth of water (depth divided by wave length) and wave steepness (height of wave divided by wave length), and for a given shape of armor unit the coefficient k_D is a function primarily of the amount of damage done to the mound of armor units for a given wave height. The tests were made on armor units which were fairly smooth and rounded. Preliminary tests of special-shaped armor units showed that k_D varies appreciably with the shape of the unit. Additional tests will be needed to determine whether k_D varies appreciably within the range of shapes that can be expected to be obtained from different quarries. For a very irregular shape, such as a tetrapod, which natural rock would never approach in irregularity, a value of 8.3 was found for k_D, as described in Sec. 4.6.

By changing W_r to tons and assuming a specific gravity of 2.73 for the armor stone, curves have been added to Fig. 4.4*c*, giving the relationship among weight, slope, and height of wave.

In comparing the curves based on (1) the Iribarren formula, (2) the more general form as originally proposed by Hudson for the Bureau of Yards and Docks, but later superseded by formula 3, taking into account the variable factor K', and (3) the formula derived for the tests for the Office, Chief of Engineers, by the United States Army Engineer Waterways Experiment Station report in 1958, it is apparent that a reasonably good agreement has been reached for a slope of 1 on 2 but that there is a considerable divergence for steeper and flatter slopes than this. From a practical consideration this does not appear to be too serious because most breakwater slopes on the exposed seaward side will not be steeper than 1 on 1½ owing to flattening of the core rock by wave action during construction; and slopes above 1 on 3 will generally result in prohibitive quantities of rock. In cases where either steeper or flatter slopes than 1 on 2 are required, the author prefers to use the values given in the table in Fig. 4.2, which are on the conservative side.

Since the primary function of a breakwater is to provide adequate protection to the harbor from wave action, it is important to have the crest at an elevation which will prevent serious overtopping of the breakwater. Most waves will break on or just before they reach the armor slope and will run up the sloping surface.

Research Report 2-2, July, 1958, of the United States Army Engineer Waterways Experiment Station, provides information, based on results of tests, on wave run-up on rubble-mound breakwaters. The report concludes that breakwater slope and wave steepness are the primary variables affecting wave run-up in water of depths corresponding to relatively large values of relative height H/d, and that wave run-up decreases with increasing values of wave steepness and flatness of slope. The run-up factor R/H for smooth, impervious slopes obtained in model tests of Lake Okeechobee levees is about twice that obtained for the comparatively rough and porous slopes used in the stability tests of rubble-mound breakwaters. Figure 4.7 gives the run-up height on rubble-mound breakwaters and smooth impervious slopes. It is interesting to note that for an average condition (where the ratio of wave height to length H/λ equals 0.07) and for a slope of 1 on 2, the ratio R/H of the run-up (measured vertically above the still-water level) to the height of the wave is about 0.9. Therefore, if the crest is placed at a height equal to H above the highest tide level, the breakwater should be reasonably free of being overtopped.

The designer must use a considerable amount of judgment in specifying the weight of rock and slope on which it is to be laid, as this should be coordinated with the method of constructing the breakwater and the anticipated percentages of various sizes of rock expected to be produced in the quarry. There is little point in specifying 20-ton armor stone on a 1-on-2 slope, if the available rock is the type which will produce only a small percentage of this class of rock, whereas a 1-on-3 slope would permit the use of 12-ton rock available in sufficient quantity. While it is usually impossible to determine accurately the percentages of various different classes of rock which will be produced by a given quarry before the operation of the quarry, a knowledge of the kind of rock and information from exploratory drilling at the quarry site should enable a realistic design to be made. The slopes can be modified to a certain extent, if necessary, after actual experience has been obtained in operating the quarry. However, it must be kept in mind that while flat slopes are desirable from the standpoint of stability one must not lose sight of the fact that the volume of core and bedding material increases considerably and the placing of this may be restricted to more difficult and expensive methods. For instance, it is well known that one of the cheapest methods of placing core material is by direct dumping from trucks which use the core material as a base on which to operate. This results in side slopes under water, which are not flatter than 1 vertical to 1¼ horizontal, although they may be flattened over a period of time by wave action to 1 vertical to 1½ horizontal or flatter. This means that additional rock, usually of larger size than the core material, must be placed to flatten the slope to that specified for setting the armor rock. If this slope is very

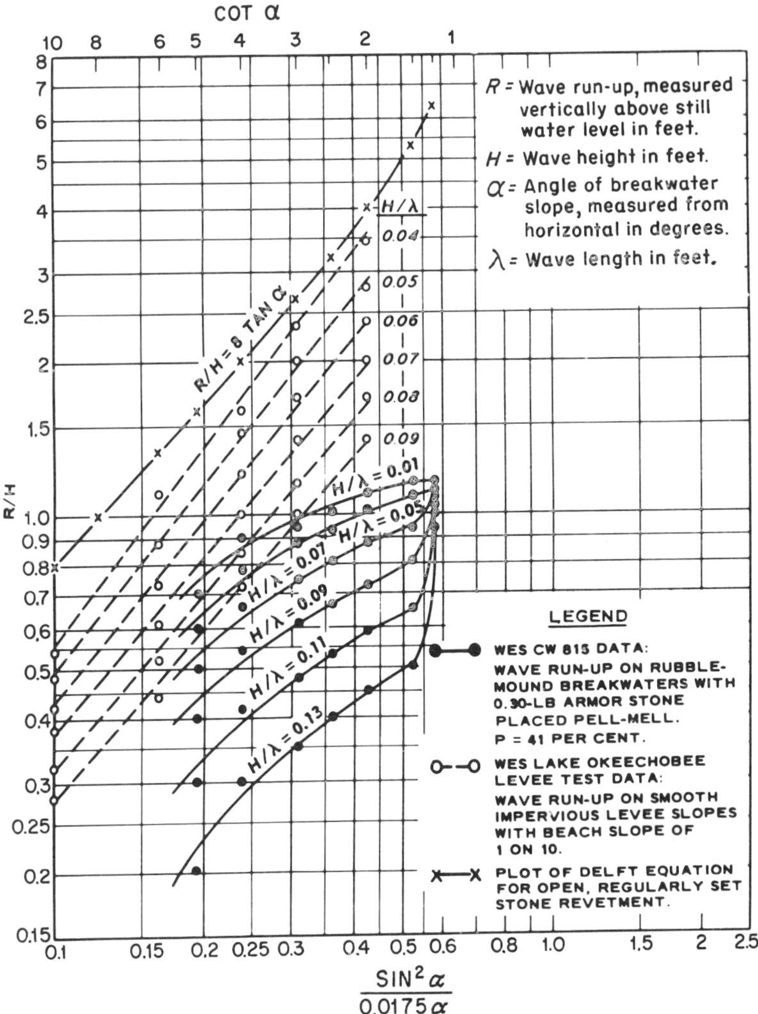

FIG. 4.7 Wave run-up height for rock-mound breakwaters and smooth impervious slopes. (*From United States Army Engineer Waterways Experiment Station, Research Report* 2-2, *July*, 1958.)

R = wave run-up, measured vertically above still-water level, ft
H = wave height, ft
α = angle of breakwater slope, measured from horizontal degrees
λ = wave length, ft

flat and the water is deep, this material cannot be placed while one is operating from the top of the core material, as the reach will be excessive. Therefore, it will be necessary to dump this rock from scows or place it with marine equipment. Likewise, the reach required of a crane operating on top of the core will become excessive to handle and place the heavier armor rock. Generally, it will be found desirable from an economic standpoint to use the steepest slopes possible with the rock available for the job and it may be cheaper to supplement this with concrete blocks, if sufficient large rock is not available, rather than to flatten the slope to such an extent that the size of the breakwater becomes unwieldy. Rock-mound breakwaters have been constructed in depths of water up to 140 ft, with base widths approaching 400 ft. Figure 4.18 is an example of such a breakwater.

It is evident from an examination of the graph in Fig. 4.4*c* that there is a practical limit of wave height where the weight of rock will exceed that which can be economically produced in a quarry, and which can be transported and handled by equipment customarily used in this type of operation. Twenty-ton rock is about the largest size which can be economically produced and handled. Where heavier armor rock is required, concrete blocks should be substituted, as these can be cast on shore close to the location of the breakwater and handled with special equipment. Typical examples of rock-mound breakwaters and methods of construction are given in Sec. 4.3.

Foundation conditions are an important factor in the selection of the type of breakwater to be used. Where the sea-bottom soil conditions are unfavorable, the rock-mound type breakwater should be used, unless the bottom is so soft and of such great depth that an excessive amount of rock would be required to reach a satisfactory supporting medium; otherwise the mound would be unstable and would fail. In such cases, where wave height is not large, a bulkhead type of breakwater, as described in Sec. 4.11, with its support carried to firm material, should be used. In no case should a gravity-wall type breakwater be used where the strength of the bottom is not sufficient to support the load without excessive settlement, as this will result eventually in the failure of the breakwater due to uneven settlement. However, it may be possible to consolidate the soft material by dumping rock until a stabilized base has been built and allowed to settle for a period of time prior to constructing the upper part of the breakwater. In lieu of this, a trench may be excavated to firm material and filled with rock or other good foundation material.

A rock-mound breakwater will withstand a considerable amount of settlement as the nature of its construction permits internal adjustment to take place without affecting its over-all strength. The amount of settlement should be estimated and allowed for in determining the height to which the breakwater is to be constructed; otherwise the top may eventually have to be raised. It is difficult and expensive to increase the height of a breakwater at a later date, as this may mean the addition of a complete new envelope of armor rock in order to provide the necessary stability for the new pieces of rock to be added, as from Fig. 4.14 it is readily

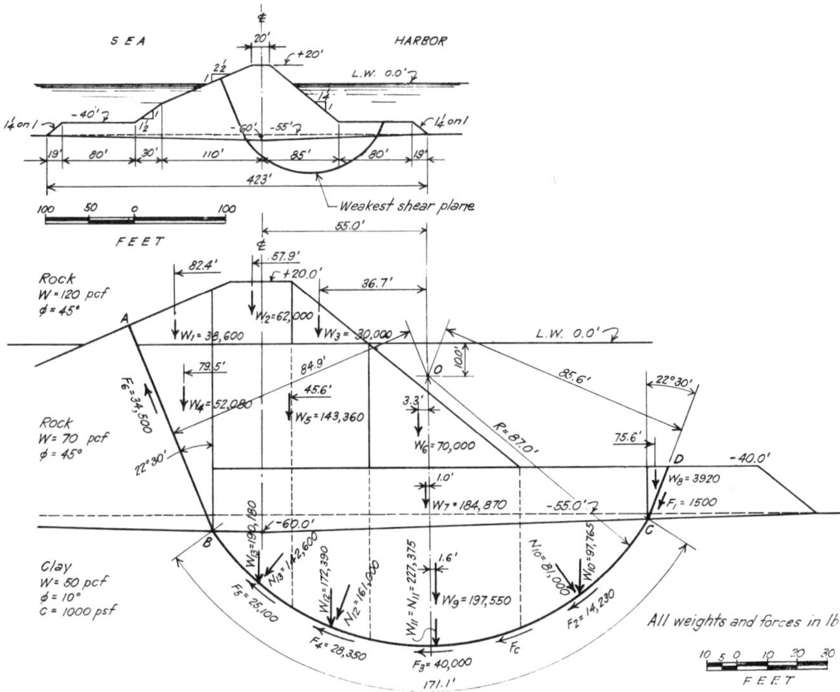

FIG. 4.8 Typical example of analysis of foundation base for support of rock-mound breakwater on soft bottom.

apparent that the lower part of the breakwater must be built out to provide a shoulder on which to set the lower pieces of armor rock.

Whenever a rock-mound breakwater is to be constructed on a soft bottom it is important first to place a layer of rock over the bottom for a width considerably wider than the base of the breakwater. The purpose of this is not only to distribute the load over a wider base but also to prevent shear failure and erosion of the underlying soil at the toe of the rock mound. It is a well-known fact that when the load placed on the soil exceeds its bearing value, the soil will fail by shearing along a curved plane, cutting the bottom at some distance beyond the toe of the superimposed load and upheaving the soil in that area. Therefore, a base of a stronger material, extending beyond the toe and the plane of failure,

Driving Moment

W_1:	38,600 ×	82.4 =	3,180,640 ft-lb
W_2:	62,000 ×	57.9 =	3,589,800 ft-lb
W_3:	30,000 ×	36.7 =	1,101,000 ft-lb
W_4:	52,080 ×	79.5 =	4,140,360 ft-lb
W_5:	143,360 ×	45.6 =	6,537,216 ft-lb
W_6:	70,000 ×	3.3 =	231,000 ft-lb
W_7:	184,870 ×	1.0 =	184,870 ft-lb
			18,964,886 ft-lb

Resisting Moment

W_8:	3,920 ×	75.6 =	296,352 ft-lb
W_9:	197,550 ×	1.6 =	316,080 ft-lb

Friction forces:

Rock: $\phi = 45°$, $\tan \phi = 1$

F_1:	1,500 ×	85.6 =	128,400 ft-lb
F_6:	34,500 ×	84.9 =	2,929,050 ft-lb

Clay: $\phi = 10°$, $\tan \phi = 0.17633$

F_2:	14,230		
F_3:	40,000		
F_4:	28,350		
F_5:	25,100		
	107,680 ×	87.0 =	9,368,160 ft-lb

Cohesion force:

F_c:	171.1 × 1000	=	171,100
	171,100 ×	87.0 =	14,885,700 ft-lb
			27,923,742 ft-lb

Factor of safety:

$$\frac{27,923,742}{18,964,886} = 1.47$$

will reduce the possibility of failure. This is because of its weight, which is most effective in resisting the upheaval of the underlying soil beyond the toe, and its increased shearing value. The base should have a thickness and shearing strength which will provide a factor of safety of not less than 1.5 against a shear failure at the toe, and it should extend out sufficiently far so that the critical plane of failure will have to pass through its base. Figure 4.8 and the following example illustrate this principle.

Example. Assume that a mound breakwater is to be constructed in 55 ft of water on a clay bottom having a shearing strength equal to $c + n \tan \phi$, where c, the cohesion, has a value of 1,000 lb per sq ft, and ϕ, the angle of internal friction, is 10°. The dimensions of the breakwater are shown to resist a 20-ft wave. It is desired to find the thickness and width of base to safely support the mound breakwater, assuming run-of-quarry rock is available for this purpose.

From comparative trial computations, it has been found that line *ABCD* defines the weakest surface for a slide. The rotation center for this slide is 0. By finding the driving and resisting moments around point 0, the safety factor against a shear failure can be established (see page 164).

4.3 Examples of Rock-mound Breakwaters

There are many important breakwaters of this type in the world, particularly in the Western Hemisphere. The following have been selected as typical examples illustrating different types of design and methods of construction, and their selection does not infer that those omitted are necessarily less important.

Figure 4.9 shows a typical cross section through the west breakwater of the Port of La Guaira, Venezuela, constructed in 1950. It is an excellent example of type 1 construction, being built entirely with equipment operating on the top of the core. The breakwater is designed to withstand waves up to 20 ft in height and has armor rock up to 20 tons in weight. The core material, which was placed on a firm bottom, is run-of-quarry rock varying in weight from 100 lb to 4 tons. In order to provide adequate width at the top of the core for the operation of the 20-ton Euclid trucks, which transported the rock from the quarry to the breakwater, without increasing the design width of the finished top of the breakwater, the corner of the core material on the harbor side was removed at the time of setting the armor rock to the required slope of the underside of this rock. Figure 4.10 shows a 20-ton piece of armor rock being lifted from a truck by a crane and Fig. 4.11 shows the armor rock set in place on the core. Note that the rock is quite uniform in size and shape and is being set with great care, using wire-rope slings, to reduce the void spaces between the individual rocks to a minimum.

The rock, which is a basalt, was obtained from a quarry located about

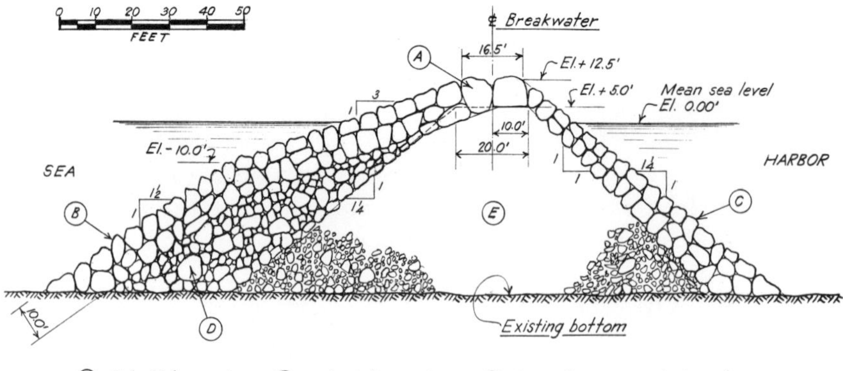

FIG. 4.9 Cross section through the west breakwater, La Guaira, Venezuela.

FIG. 4.10 20-ton armor rock being lifted from truck. (*Courtesy of Frederick Snare Corp.*)

FIG. 4.11 Armor rock set in place on core of breakwater. (*Courtesy of Frederick Snare Corp.*)

5 miles from the breakwater. The quarry blasting was done by the tunnel and coyote hole method, as shown in Fig. 4.12, and the entire rock face, which exceeded 100 ft in height, was blasted at one time, resulting in as much as 120,000 cu yd of rock being broken up in a single blast. This method produced the desired amount of large armor rock. Figure 4.13 shows the quarry face. An average of 0.542 lb of powder was used to break up 1 cu yd of rock in place.

A similar type of breakwater was constructed on the north shore of Lake Superior in 1956, differing mainly in the omission of the filter course or secondary armor and the method of setting the armor rock. Figure 4.14 shows a typical cross section. The breakwater is approximately normal to the shore line and extends out into the lake a distance of about 1,400 ft. The bottom varies in depth up to 100 ft below lake level at its outer end and is of firm material. The fill for the core, which was placed by truck, was obtained from the harbor excavation. The rock is a fine-grained basalt and breaks into relatively small pieces, only about 6 per cent being heavier than 8 tons.

The breakwater is exposed to storm waves up to 20 ft in height. Lake level is controlled but offshore winds tend to raise the lake level some 2 to 3 ft at times. During the construction the exposed core material was badly washed and eroded to below water level during stormy periods, which were quite frequent during the fall and winter months, with the

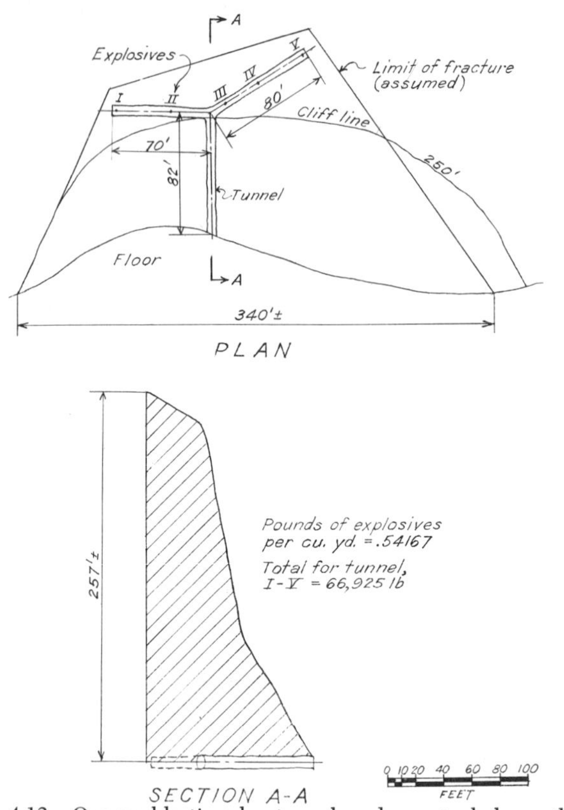

FIG. 4.12 Quarry blasting by tunnel and coyote hole method.

result that most of the fine material was washed away, and when the upper part of the core was reshaped, there resulted a good pervious bed on which to set the armor stone. Model tests had indicated the desirability of having a good pervious layer or filter course of rock under the heavy armor capping on the top and exposed side of the breakwater. With this knowledge in mind and with the help of nature, this condition was readily achieved, without the use of a separate filter course.

The armor rock was obtained from a quarry, opened especially for this purpose, located approximately 5 miles from the harbor site, the

FIG. 4.13 Quarry face. (*Courtesy of Frederick Snare Corp.*)

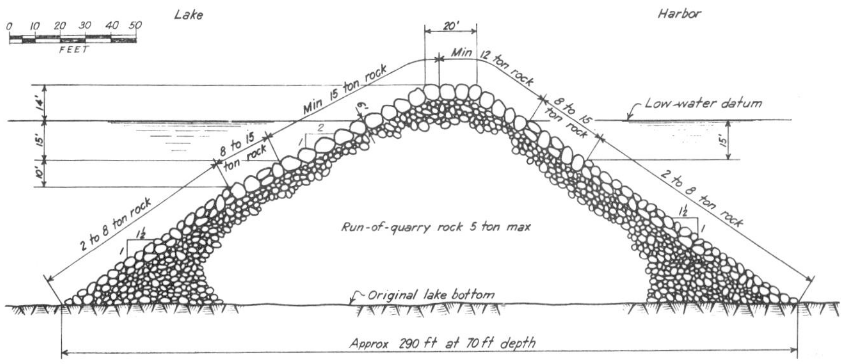

FIG. 4.14 Section through northeast breakwater at Taconite Harbor, Lake Superior.

rock being a hard anorthosite. This type of rock is ideal for breakwater armor as it is coarse-grained and breaks well into large pieces with few, if any, cleavage planes. This is important in an area where severe freezing takes place, as the heavy pieces of rock placed on the breakwater must not be broken into smaller pieces by the effects of freezing and thawing; otherwise the effectiveness of the armor is lost. The basalt which

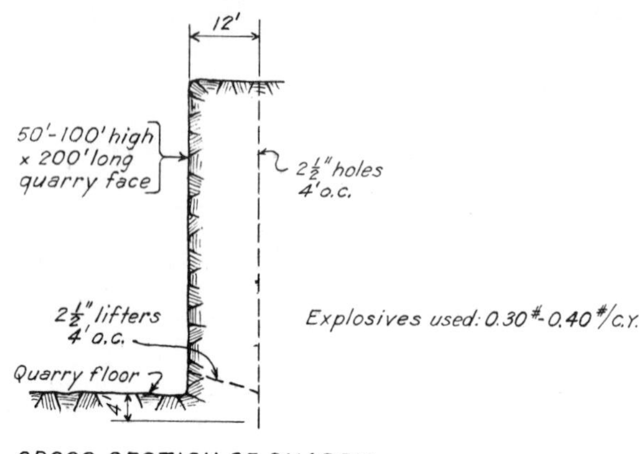

FIG. 4.15 Drilling pattern for blasting quarry face for large armor stone for breakwater at Taconite Harbor.

Analysis of Breakage

Class	A	B	C	D
	<3*T*	3–8*T*	8–15*T*	>15*T*
Total tons	640,500	96,000	123,000	153,000
Percentage	63.3	9.5	12.1	15.1

predominates in this area was found to have numerous planes of weakness, which opened up still further once the rock had been removed from its natural formation. This permitted water to enter with the result that, following freezing, some large pieces of rock, 10 to 15 tons in weight, which originally looked like good armor rock, broke into several 2- to 3-ton pieces when handled.

Since it was desired to produce only armor rock from the quarry, all of the core material being supplied from the harbor excavation, the drilling and blasting technique was carefully studied and experimented with until the most satisfactory method had been developed. This is illustrated in Fig. 4.15, the 2½-in. drill holes being located on 4-ft centers on a line 12 ft in back of the face, which was as much as 100 ft in height and 200 ft in length. The massive formation was blasted to a sharp, clean face as shown in Fig. 4.16. Large blocks, 50 to 60 tons in weight, were readily broken into usable sizes by drilling jackhammer holes on 12-in. centers and using light charges to split the rock on the drill line. From 0.30 to 0.40 lb of explosive was used per cu yd of rock blasted.

Approximately 1 million tons of rock was blasted, resulting in the

FIG. 4.16 Quarry face after blasting. (*Courtesy of Erie Mining Co.*)

following proportions of different weights of rock: less than 3 tons, 63.3 per cent; 3 to 8 tons, 9.5 per cent; 8 to 15 tons, 12.1 per cent; and greater than 15 tons, 15.1 per cent.

The armor rock was transported from the quarry to the breakwater on flat-bed trailer trucks, where it was unloaded and placed on the core by a floating derrick, as shown in Fig. 4.17. This figure also shows how each piece of rock was lifted and lowered into position by a grapple of 25-ton capacity.

The harbor at the Port of Matarani, Peru, which was completed in 1941, is well protected by two breakwaters and a spit of land which permit entrance from the north. The south breakwater is about 2,000 ft long and the east breakwater about 500 ft long. A description of this interesting port may be found in Chap. 3.

FIG. 4.17 Placing armor rock by floating derrick. (*Courtesy of Erie Mining Co.*)

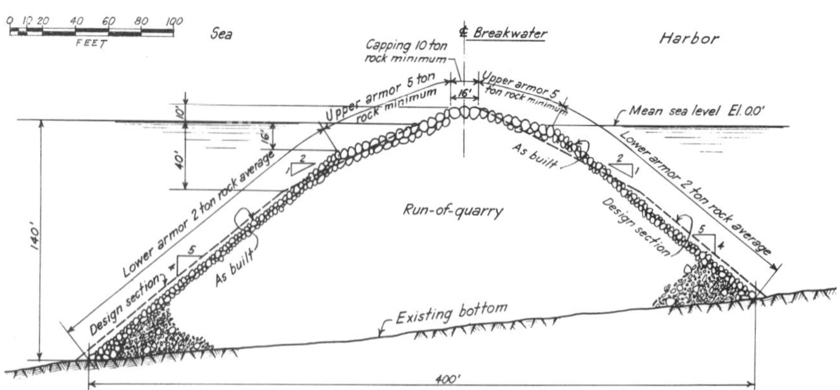

FIG. 4.18 Cross section through south breakwater at Matarani, Peru.

The south breakwater is considered one of the deepest in the world, and contains a total of about 1.9 million cu yd of rock, including armor rock. At its deepest portion the breakwater is 400 ft wide at the bottom and 140 ft from crest to bottom. A cross section of this breakwater is shown in Fig. 4.18.

The design section of the breakwater is shown in this figure by a dashed line, and it can be noted that the point where the 1-on-1¼ slope intersects the 1-on-2 slope of the upper armor rock is higher in the actual construction than originally contemplated. In other words, the 1-on-1¼ slope was brought up as far as possible while still remaining stable under the action of "bravezas," which occur during severe storms at sea when a series of high waves are thrust against the shore with short intermittent periods of relatively calm water.

Unlimited rock was available for construction of the Matarani breakwaters, since the port itself is, in effect, carved out of the cliffs which border the Peruvian coast at this point. The suitable rock obtained from quarry operations was used in the construction of the breakwaters, and quarry waste and other rock were used in making land between the existing shore line and the bulkhead line. Thus, all materials obtained were put to good economic use.

The core and lower and upper armor rock were placed by means of dump trucks and side-dump trailers, and at the same time the heavier capping rock was stored on the seaward side (see Fig. 4.19). The capping rock was later placed and fitted by a crane which proceeded from the outer end shoreward. A view of this operation is shown in Fig. 4.20.

FIG. 4.19 View of south breakwater, Matarani, Peru, showing roadway on top of core, prior to placing capping armor. (*Courtesy of Frederick Snare Corp.*)

FIG. 4.20 View of east breakwater, Matarani, Peru, showing capping rock. (*Courtesy of Frederick Snare Corp.*)

4.4 Concrete Block and Rock-mound Breakwaters

This type of construction may consist of (1) concrete blocks, cubic or rectangular in shape, or (2) a combination of concrete blocks and rock, the latter usually serving as a foundation or base to support the blocks.

This type of construction is used where natural rock is not available, or where it cannot be produced economically or in large enough size required for armoring the breakwater. The latter condition is quite often encountered, especially when the breakwater must be designed for large wave heights.

As previously pointed out, a 20-ton rock is about the largest size which can be economically produced in sufficient quantity for armor rock, under the most favorable quarry conditions. Since a 1-on-3 slope is about the practical limit on which to place this armor, it is apparent from Fig. 4.4 that some form of artificial block will have to be used when the wave height exceeds about 20 ft.

The weight of artificial blocks of concrete is limited only by the equipment capable of handling them. Except for this limitation it is possible to design breakwaters for waves of any size, which, as we know them to exist, do not exceed 45 ft in height at any location where a breakwater would need to be constructed. Concrete blocks of 50 to 60 tons are quite commonly used, and on rare occasions blocks weighing as much as 400 tons have been used.

Artificial blocks are laid either pell-mell, as shown in Fig. 4.21, or fitted to a certain designed pattern, as illustrated in Fig. 4.22. When laid in a pell-mell fashion, they possess good hydraulic roughness and permeability, two of the desirable characteristics in a breakwater armor. However, to cover and protect the rock core of a breakwater adequately requires a greater volume of these blocks than of natural rock; this can usually be laid in one layer, which still gives a good degree of roughness and permeability because of its natural, irregular shape. It is, therefore, important to have a good secondary armor or filter course of natural rock to protect the core and to support the concrete blocks when laid in a pell-mell fashion. For this reason a mound breakwater of type 2 construction, where the class *A* stone is replaced with pell-mell blocks, as previously shown in Fig. 4.3, is preferred over type 1 construction, which in effect is an all-concrete block mound in the upper region where the wave effect is most severe. In shallow depths of water, not exceeding 20 ft, the concrete blocks would rest directly on the sea bottom, unless it is too soft to support the blocks, and the construction is termed a concrete block-mound breakwater.

Probably the greatest uncertainty in concrete block armor laid in pell-mell fashion is the sliding and consolidation which takes place while the breakwater is going through its period of adjustment. Unlike rock which is of irregular shape and of varying sizes, thereby affording good interlocking and keying without much movement of the individual pieces which make up the armor course, the concrete blocks with their flat sides and limited number of shapes may undergo considerable sliding before they reach a stable condition. In so doing they may open up a gap in the armor, leaving the core exposed to erosion, unless it is covered with

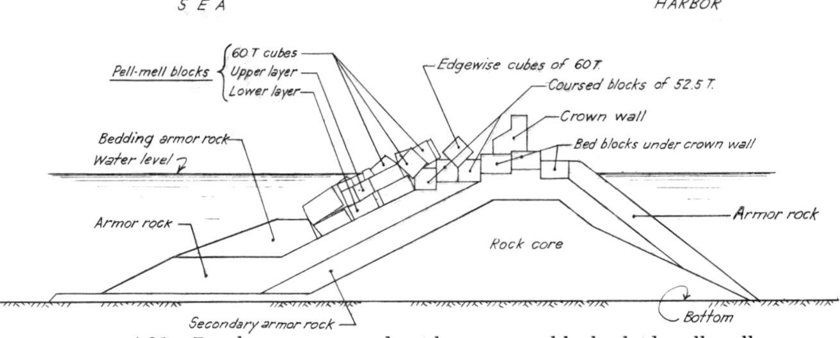

FIG. 4.21 Breakwater armored with concrete blocks laid pell-mell.

at least two layers of blocks, even though they are laid in a pell-mell or irregular fashion. However, the use of concrete blocks laid pell-mell is a generally accepted solution because of the ease in which the structure can be repaired as compared to concrete blocks which are fitted or laid to pattern.

Armor made with fitted blocks results in a structure which acts differently than that made with pell-mell blocks, which more nearly approaches the behavior of the natural rock-mound breakwater. If the blocks are laid on a relatively flat slope, the main part of the energy of the waves is dissipated in breaking and running up the surface of the

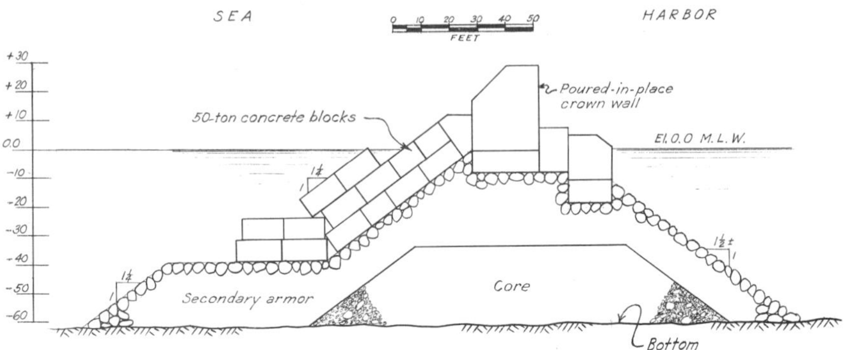

FIG. 4.22 Breakwater armored with concrete blocks laid to designed pattern.

embankment. This results in a somewhat higher crest than for pell-mell-type formations and necessitates the construction of a seawall or monolith on top of the breakwater. Such a condition is indicated in Fig. 4.22.

If the slope is more vertical, requiring the use of heavier blocks which are usually laid in stepped courses, the effect is more like that of a vertical-wall-type breakwater. Roughness is lacking, and the permeability is low due to the blocks being fitted relatively tight to each other. Therefore, underpressures may be high, particularly at the toe of the slope, and displacement of the blocks may occur, unless precautions are taken to see that they are bedded on a course and pervious layer of rock. Repair of this type of breakwater is expensive and difficult. Because the fitted blocks are liable to uplift at the toe, owing to lack of permeability between the blocks, an alternative and preferred type of construction is to use pell-mell blocks in the lower part of the slope and overtopping the first course of fitted blocks, and to use the larger fitted blocks in the upper region where the direct impact of the waves is the greatest. Here the foundation bed can be more carefully prepared and leveled to receive the blocks, which can then be more accurately fitted together so as to form a stable structure.

The design of concrete block-mound breakwaters, like rock-mound breakwaters, must be based to a large extent on experience and information obtained from model tests. The Iribarren formula, which has been found to be reasonably accurate for the design of rock-mound breakwaters, provided experimental values for K' are used, is not considered reliable for the design of concrete block breakwaters, and no experimental values are available for the coefficient K'. Breakwaters which are to utilize concrete blocks should preferably have their design based on the results of model tests.

Various sizes of cubes and rectangular parallelepipeds, as well as intermixtures of these shapes, have been experimented with in model tests. These are described more fully in Sec. 4.9.

Edges of blocks, as a rule, are chamfered, and when laid in a fitted manner the top face is sometimes serrated, as, for example, in the breakwater shown in Fig. 4.20.

4.5 Examples of Concrete Block on Rock-mound Breakwaters

Generally speaking, this type of construction has met with greater favor in European countries than it has in the Western Hemisphere where rock-mound breakwaters predominate.

However, in the latter sphere one noteworthy example of a concrete block on rock-mound type of breakwater, with the blocks laid to a fitted pattern, is the breakwater at the Naval Air Station at Coco Solo, Canal Zone. This breakwater, built under wartime conditions, is of a rather unusual type, in that it was constructed of three distinct classes of material. It consists of a coral base, a coral core, a secondary armor of quarry rock, and an outer armor and capping course of rock and concrete blocks. A cross section of this breakwater is shown in Fig. 4.23.

The breakwater is approximately 3,300 ft long and connects the existing east breakwater at the northerly entrance to the Panama Canal with the −12 contour off Margarita Island. The average depth of water along the center line of the breakwater is about 34 ft below mean low water. Borings at the site indicated that between elevations −38 and −42 there existed a layer of coral about 2 ft thick, and that below this layer there existed a stratum of mud varying in thickness from 46 to 74 ft. In order to distribute the weight of the breakwater and at the same time prevent the lateral flow of the mud underlying the coral crust, the designers elected to use the coral base scheme, allowing for a settlement during construction of about 4 ft. The continuity of the coral crust and the character of the underlying mud were further investigated during the building of the construction trestle in order to adjust the width and thickness of the base, if necessary.

The coral base, consisting of clean coral sand, finger coral, head coral, and other approved similar materials, was deposited in uniform layers up to elevation −25 by means of a hydraulic dredge. The dredged material was taken from areas, as directed, in the vicinity of Margarita Island.

The coral core, consisting of the same materials as specified for the base, was deposited by the same process, with natural side slopes, to approximately elevation 0.0.

At this stage of construction, the contractor began building his construction trestle by means of a traveler which drove the wood piles,

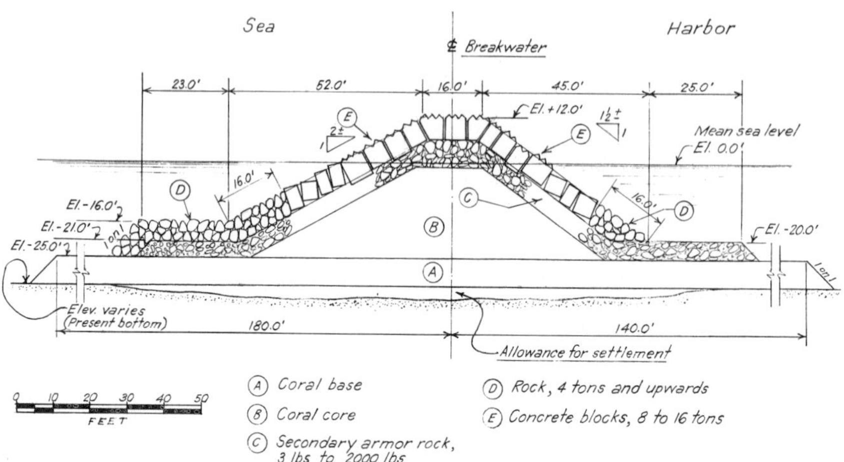

FIG. 4.23 Cross section through breakwater at Naval Air Station, Coco Solo, Panama Canal.

capped them, and laid the trestle deck and rails for the traveler and railroad dump cars. A typical cross section of this trestle and the traveler is shown in Fig. 4.24.

At the same time a suitable quarry site was opened for supplying the secondary armor. The rock obtained was a basalt. Views of this quarry are shown in Figs. 4.25 and 4.26, during and after a blast. This particular blast was made by drilling 13 well holes and using 6,500 lb of black powder and 2,850 lb of 30 per cent gelatin. The in-place measurement before blasting was 20,000 cu yd, and the bulk rock obtained was 35,000 cu yd. As can be seen from the foregoing, 0.4675 lb of explosive was required per cu yd in place.

As the erection of the construction trestle proceeded, at the rate of three bents per 24-hour day, or 1 bent per 8-hour shift, the placing of the secondary armor was begun. This secondary armor consists of a well-graded mixture of quarry-run stone ranging in weight up to 2,000 lb, with not more than 10 per cent in fragments smaller than 3 lb each, and was dumped from railroad cars loaded at the quarry by power shovel.

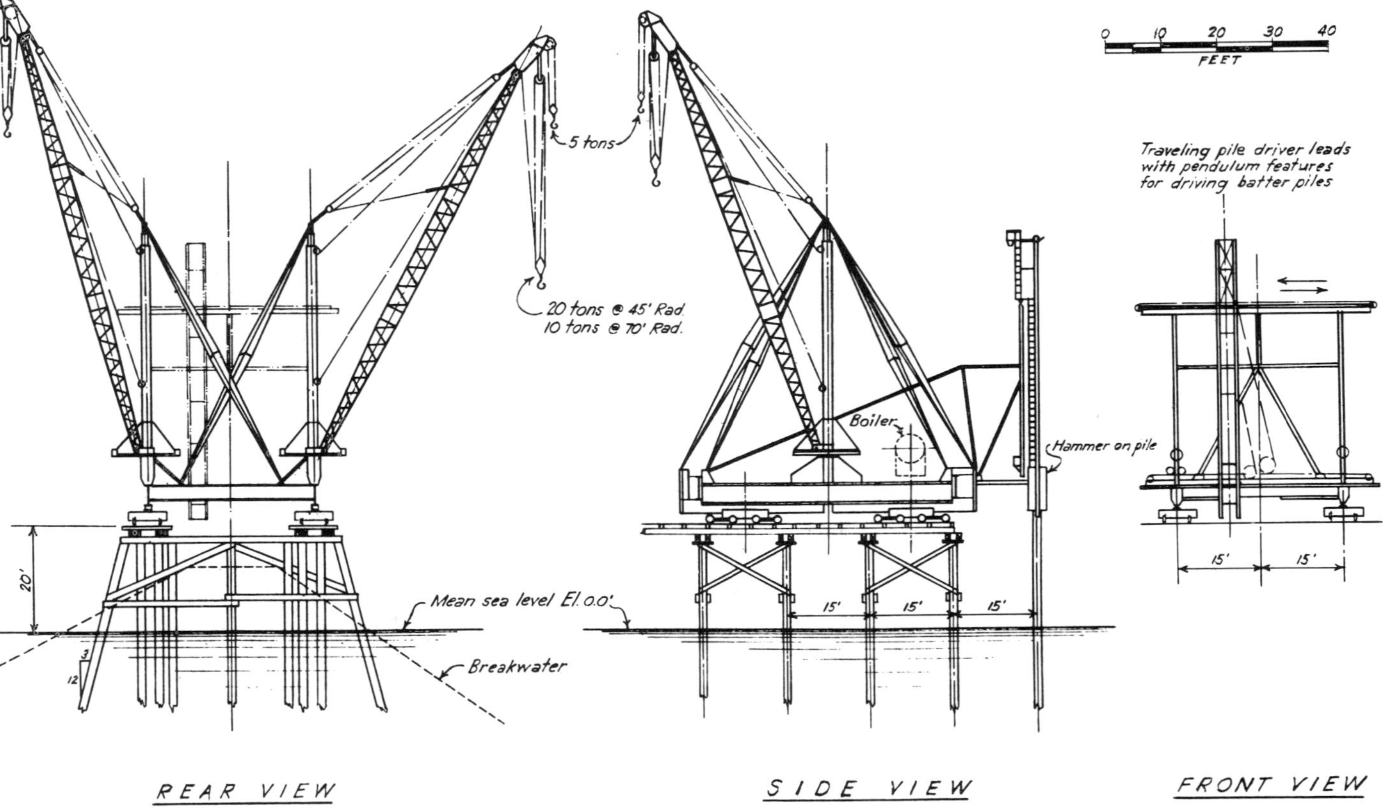

FIG. 4.24 Typical cross section of trestle and traveler used for construction of Coco Solo breakwater.

FIG. 4.25 Face of quarry for obtaining rock for Coco Solo breakwater at instant of blast. (*Courtesy of Frederick Snare Corp.*)

FIG. 4.26 Face of quarry after blast—Coco Solo breakwater. (*Courtesy of Frederick Snare Corp.*)

Since large rock for armor of the specified weight was not economically available in pieces weighing 8 tons or more, the contractor elected to use precast-concrete blocks for the upper armor and capping. This meant the construction of a sizeable casting yard, the plan and cross section of which are shown in Fig. 4.27. The blocks were cast in special steel

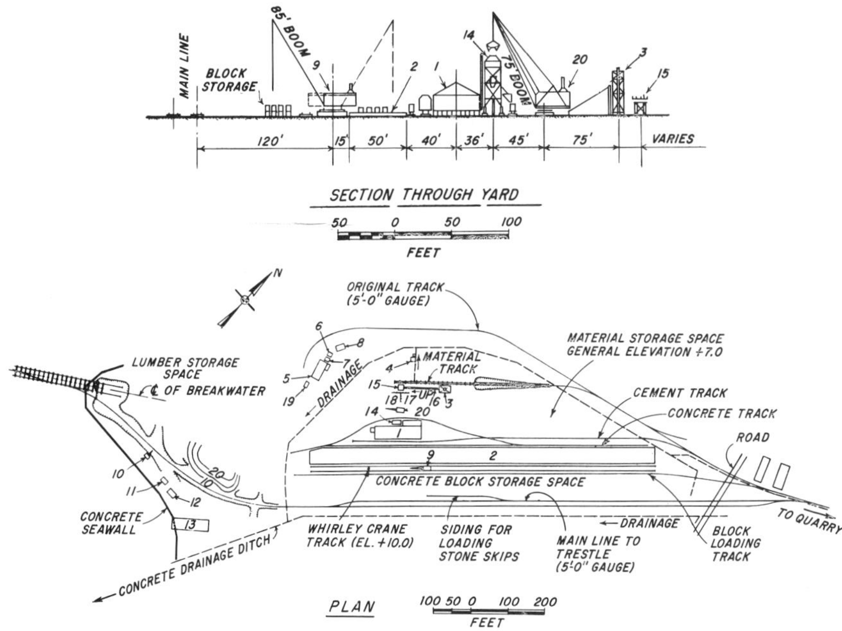

FIG. 4.27 Casting yard for making concrete blocks–Coco Solo breakwater. (1) Cement storage shed; (2) concrete block casting platform (50 by 1,120 ft); (3) aggregate hopper; (4) settling tank; (5) storehouse; (6) saw shed; (7) carpentry shed; (8) concrete building; (9) whirley crane; (10) water tank; (11) oil storage; (12) concrete building; (13) office and quarters; (14) concrete plant; (15) screening plant; (16) aggregate conveyor; (17) sand stock pile; (18) gravel stock pile; (19) shed; (20) whirley crane.

forms, using concrete with a 28-day strength of 3,000 lb per sq in. The blocks to be used above the water line had one serrated face as can be seen in Fig. 4.23. All blocks had 6- by 6-in. chamfered corners and were cured with curing compound for not less than 14 days.

In general, laying of the armor and capping were performed in a "reverse direction," that is, the traveler placed the lower 4-ton rock armor from railroad cars with an orange-peel bucket and handled and placed the 8- to 16-ton concrete blocks for the upper armor and capping, starting at the outshore end of the breakwater, where it connected to the existing east breakwater and proceeded inshore toward Margarita Island, removing all exposed portions of the construction trestle during this process. Below the water line, the block armor was set as nearly as practicable to line and grade, beginning at the toe and working toward the center line, lowering the blocks into place without sliding or rolling, and interlocking the pieces so as to receive the maximum practicable amount of support from adjacent pieces. Above the water line the blocks were set to line and grade with a tolerance of plus or minus 9 in. measured perpendicular to the breakwater. The specifications required that joints parallel to the center line of the breakwater be staggered, except at the two lines of intersection of slope with cap. A developed plan is shown in Fig. 4.28.

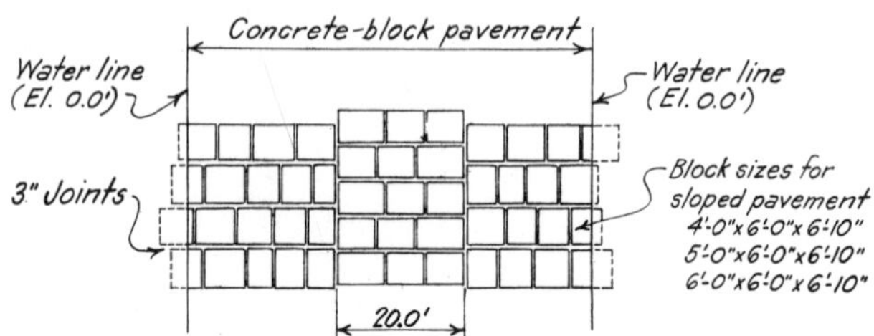

FIG. 4.28 Pattern for setting concrete blocks for Coco Solo breakwater.

The Port of Safi, in Morocco, is fully exposed to the sea and is not protected by the coast in any way. The harbor is formed and protected by a breakwater that runs approximately parallel to the shore and connected to it at one end, which prior to extension in 1955 was about 4,000 ft long. The breakwater, shown in Fig. 4.29, is designed for a maximum wave height of 25 ft. At this location the tide varies between −16 and +13 ft from low-water level of 0.00. The breakwater consists of a rock mound protected on the seaward side by rectangular concrete blocks, weighing approximately 45 metric tons each, laid in a semifitted and pell-mell manner. A concrete superstructure, which is supported on two courses of concrete blocks, extends from about the high-water level to elevation +31.2 ft. The base is 242 ft wide in a 46-ft depth of water.

Figure 4.30 shows a cross section through the north breakwater for the harbor of Zonguldak, Turkey. Its final cross section and the arrangement of the concrete block armor were arrived at after very extensive model testing in the NEYRPIC Laboratory at Grenoble, France, which is described in Sec. 4.9.

The north breakwater is designed for 8.5-meter waves. The maximum depth of water is 17 meters at the extreme end of the breakwater. A photograph of the completed breakwater is shown in Fig. 4.31.

Since the condition of the bottom indicated the probability of some settlement, a rock-mound type of breakwater, armored with concrete

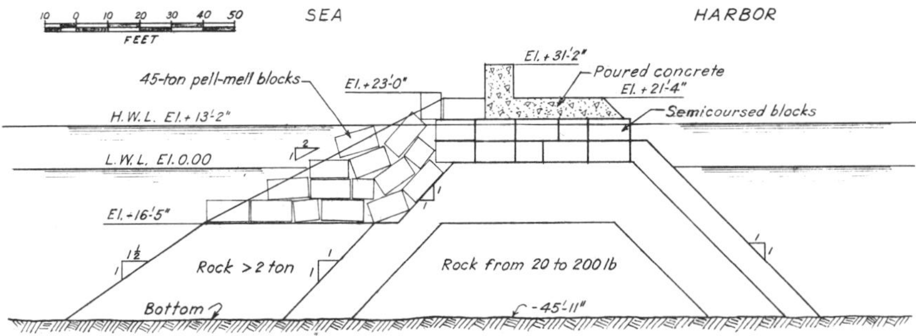

FIG. 4.29 Section through breakwater at Safi, Morocco.

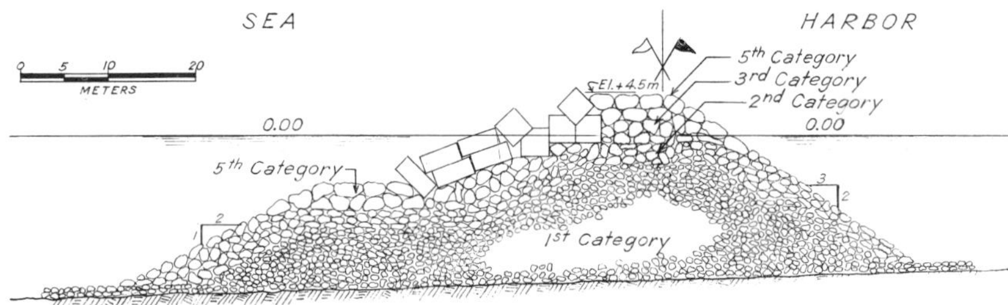

FIG. 4.30 Section through north breakwater at Zonguldak, Turkey.

FIG. 4.31 View of completed north breakwater, Zonguldak, Turkey. (*Courtesy of Netherlands Harbor Works, Amsterdam, Holland.*)

blocks on the sea side, was selected in lieu of a vertical-wall-type breakwater. The availability of suitable rock for its construction was also an important factor in the selection of this type of breakwater. The rock was side-dumped from scows, except for the heavy armor placed in back of the crown blocks.

The model tests generally indicated that the 60-ton concrete blocks would provide the best and most stable construction if laid in a pell-mell

FIG. 4.32 Showing uplift pressure on blocks. (*From Construction Progress Report of Netherlands Harbor Works, Amsterdam, Holland.*)

fashion, except for the three rows of blocks forming the crown of the breakwater, which were laid in a fitted manner.

The concrete blocks were constructed with 6-in. beveled edges which increased the porosity of the armor layer and helped to reduce the uplift pressure on the underside of the blocks when the wave receded. Figure 4.32, which is a photograph taken during a storm while the breakwater was being constructed, shows that this uplift pressure is a real factor to be considered in the stability of the armor course.

The concrete blocks were manufactured in a casting yard on shore, serviced with a railroad track and traveling bridge gantry, which lifted the blocks on to flat-bed railroad cars. These were then transported to the loading-out dock where a portal crane transferred the blocks from the railroad cars to barges. Figure 4.33 shows the special-shaped quay wall or crown blocks in the casting yard, and Fig. 4.34 shows one of these

FIG. 4.33 Casting yard for making concrete blocks, Zonguldak, Turkey. (*From Construction Progress Report of Netherlands Harbor Works, Amsterdam, Holland.*)

FIG. 4.34 Sixty-ton concrete block being lifted from flatcar to barge. (*From Construction Progress Report of Netherlands Harbor Works, Amsterdam, Holland.*)

blocks being lifted from the flatcar to the barge. The blocks were placed on the breakwater by floating cranes. This work was interrupted at times by rough weather and considerable damage was done to the partially completed breakwater.

4.6 Tetrapod and Tribar Armored Breakwaters

Tetrapods are four-legged, truncated-cone-shaped, precast-concrete units, as shown in Fig. 4.35, developed by the NEYRPIC Hydraulic

FIG. 4.35 Tetrapod armor unit. (*Courtesy of NEYRPIC, Grenoble, France.*)

Laboratory in Grenoble, France, and licensed by the Société d'exploitation de brevets pour travaux à la mer, under the name Sotramer. Systematic trials made it possible to determine the best proportions between the different dimensions of the block to obtain the best hydraulic and structural properties.

Tribar is the name of a special-shaped armor unit for which a patent has been obtained by Robert Q. Palmer, chief of the Planning and Reports Branch, United States Army Engineering District, Honolulu, Hawaii. The shape of this unit is shown in Fig. 4.36.

Tetrapod and tribar designs have the advantage over standard concrete blocks in permitting steeper slopes and units of lighter weight. This is due to their better "shape factor" and superior absorption of wave energy. The latter is effected by the high degree of irregularity and permeability of the surface, which results in the division of the mass of water into paths of turbulent flow which oppose each other in the interstices of the facing.

FIG. 4.36 Tribar armor unit. (*Courtesy of Robert Q. Palmer, chief of the Planning and Reports Branch, United States Army Engineer District, Honolulu, Hawaii.*)

The truncated-cone shape of the legs of the tetrapods and the almost complete absence of plane surfaces provide a good keying effect and prevent sliding, thereby enabling the blocks to be placed on a slope approaching 1 on 1.

As a result of all these properties it has been possible to reduce the unit weight as compared to standard concrete blocks for the same degree of stability. This coupled with the high voids ratio, being slightly higher than 50 per cent when laid in two layers, results in a reduction of the amount of concrete required. In addition the steeper slope and lower run-up value of the waves, because of the high degree of irregularity of the surface, enable a reduction in the volume of the remainder of the supporting structure. This latter factor may be of considerable importance at the entrance to the harbor, where the armor protection must be carried

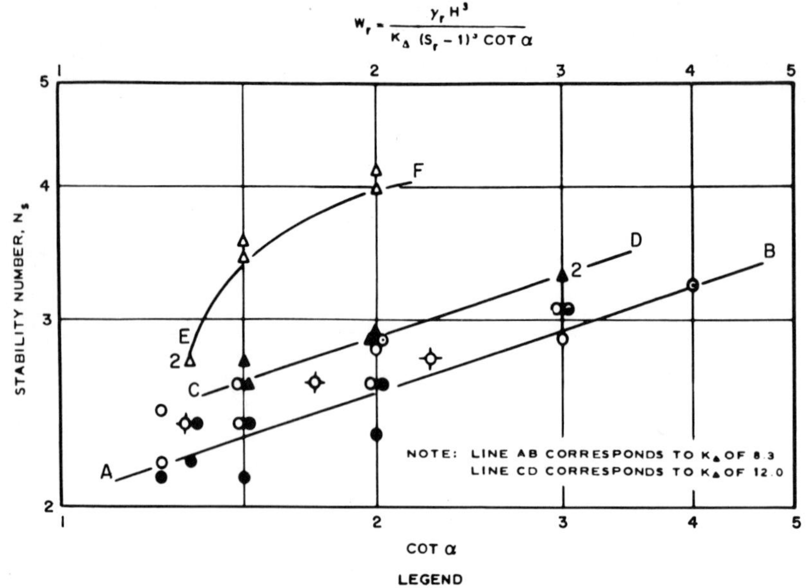

LEGEND

SYMBOL	TYPE OF ARMOR UNIT	METHOD OF PLACING ARMOR UNITS	NUMBER OF LAYERS OF ARMOR UNITS	TYPE OF SECTION
○	CONCRETE TETRAPODS	PELL-MELL	2	1
●	CONCRETE TETRAPODS	UNIFORM	2	2
◉	CONCRETE TETRAPODS	PELL-MELL	2	3
⌖	LEADITE TETRAPODS	UNIFORM	2	4
△	LEADITE TRIBARS	UNIFORM	1	5
▲	LEADITE TRIBARS	PELL-MELL	2	6

W_r = WEIGHT OF INDIVIDUAL ARMOR UNITS, LB

γ_r = SPECIFIC WEIGHT OF ARMOR UNIT, LB PER CU FT

H = HEIGHT OF DESIGN WAVE, FT

K_Δ = EXPERIMENTAL COEFFICIENT

S_r = SPECIFIC GRAVITY OF ARMOR UNIT, RELATIVE TO WATER IN WHICH PLACED (γ_r/γ_w)

α = ANGLE OF BREAKWATER SLOPE, MEASURED FROM HORIZONTAL, DEG

N_s = STABILITY NUMBER = $\dfrac{\gamma_r^{1/3} H}{W_r^{1/3} (S_r - 1)}$

FIG. 4.37 Tribar and tetrapod cover layers: stability number as a function of breakwater slope, shape of armor unit, and method of placing armor units for the no-damage and no-overtopping criteria. (*From United States Army Engineer Waterways Experiment Station Miscellaneous Paper* 2-296, *January,* 1959.)

around the head end of the breakwater. The steeper slope of the armor permits a narrower entrance and thereby affords greater protection to the interior of the harbor.

The United States Army Engineer Waterways Experiment Station at Vicksburg, Mississippi, has been carrying on a testing program and

FIG. 4.38 Special sling for lifting tetrapods. (*Courtesy of NEYRPIC, Grenoble, France.*)

studies on the stability of tribar and tetrapod armor units. The results of these tests through August, 1958, have been reported in Miscellaneous Paper 2-296, January, 1959, entitled Design of Tribar and Tetrapod Cover Layers for Rubble-Mound Breakwaters. The results of the stability tests are given in graphical form in Fig. 4.37. A value of 8.3 for K_Δ is recommended for tetrapods placed pell-mell in two layers, and a value of 12.0 for K_Δ for tribars placed pell-mell in two layers. Curve *EF* is the lower-limit curve for one layer of tribars placed uniformly. Until more data are available, it is not recommended that one-layer construction be attempted.

Tetrapods have been used in sizes up to 40 tons a unit, although 25 tons has been the more common size for large breakwaters. The units are molded in metal forms which come apart in four sections. The tetrapods used on the first structures were equipped with lifting eyes for ease of handling on the site and in placing on the breakwater. This imposes a tension on the comparatively weak concrete, and, since some of the units are not reinforced, a more economical and reliable method of handling

FIG. 4.39 Placing the first layer of tetrapods on rock embankment. (*Courtesy of NEYRPIC, Grenoble, France.*)

on the site has been developed and patented. This consists of a specially designed sling or linkage, as shown in Fig. 4.38, which grips the tetrapod by its three bottom legs, ensuring that all concrete is in compression, and thereby eliminating cracking of the concrete.

Once the tetrapod is on the ground and the bottom mold removed, a simple sling can be placed around it, which will permit it to be placed in the breakwater with either one leg up or one leg down. Figure 4.39 shows the method of placing the first layer with the three legs resting on the rock embankment and one leg up at right angles to the embankment. Figure 4.40 shows the placing of the second layer, with one leg down at right angles to the embankment.

Sotramer, the licensee of tetrapods, recommends certain specifications for building up the tetrapod armor layer, from which are quoted some of the more important items, as follows:

The tetrapods should be laid in two layers, each consisting of an equal number of blocks.

The surface density for each class of tetrapod must be adhered to.

Surface density is defined as the total number of tetrapods required for a complete two-layer revetment on a given area.

Example. For an area of 100 m^2:

10.0 m^3 tetrapods: 22 tetrapods required altogether (11 per layer)
6.3 m^3 tetrapods: 30 tetrapods required altogether (15 per layer)
4.0 m^3 tetrapods: 40 tetrapods required altogether (20 per layer)
3.2 m^3 tetrapods: 47 tetrapods required altogether (23 per layer)

FIG. 4.40 Placing the second layer of tetrapods. (*Courtesy of NEYRPIC, Grenoble, France.*)

A laying plan should be drawn up, fixing the positions of the crane hook in advance; these should be made to correspond to the intersections of a regular squared grid.

The hook positions for a second layer should be situated at the intersections of a grid that, although identical to the first, is offset by half a space in each direction with respect to it. The grid spacing is as follows:

3 m for 10.0 m^3 tetrapods
2.60 m for 6.3 m^3 tetrapods
2.20 m for 4.0 m^3 tetrapods
2.05 m for 3.2 m^3 tetrapods

The above values give the spacing of the block in the plane of the embankment. The horizontal spacing must allow for the slope of the embankment.

Table **4.1 Physical Characteristics of Tribars**

Diameter of vertical leg, ft	Height, ft	Volume		Weight, tons				No. of tribars per 100 sq ft	
		Cu ft	Cu yd	Conc. 145 pcf	Conc. 150 pcf	Conc. 155 pcf	Conc. 160 pcf	Single layer	Double layer
1.5	3.0	22.1	.82	1.61	1.66	1.72	1.77	7.52	12.03
2.0	4.0	52.5	1.95	3.81	3.94	4.07	4.20	4.23	6.77
2.25	4.5	74.8	2.77	5.42	5.62	5.80	5.99	3.34	5.34
2.50	5.0	102.6	3.80	7.44	7.70	7.95	8.21	2.70	4.32
2.75	5.5	136.6	5.06	9.90	10.24	10.58	10.93	2.24	3.58
3.0	6.0	177.4	6.57	12.85	13.30	13.75	14.19	1.88	3.01
3.16	6.33	207.3	7.68	15.03	15.54	16.06	16.58	1.69	2.70
3.25	6.5	225.4	8.35	16.34	16.91	17.47	18.04	1.60	2.56
3.33	6.67	242.5	8.98	17.58	18.19	18.80	19.40	1.53	2.45
3.5	7.0	281.6	10.43	20.41	21.12	21.83	22.52	1.38	2.21
3.58	7.16	301.3	11.16	21.84	22.59	23.35	24.10	1.32	2.11
3.66	7.33	322.0	11.93	23.34	24.15	24.95	25.76	1.26	2.02
3.75	7.50	346.3	12.83	25.11	25.98	26.84	27.70	1.20	1.92
3.83	7.67	369.0	13.67	26.74	27.67	28.59	29.51	1.15	1.84
3.92	7.83	395.6	14.66	28.68	29.67	30.66	31.65	1.10	1.76
4.0	8.0	420.3	15.56	30.47	31.52	32.57	33.62	1.06	1.70

SOURCE: Tribars, Inc.

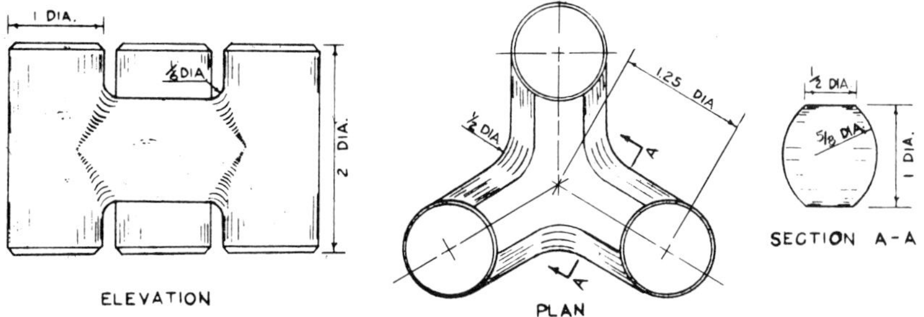

The crane hook must be positioned at the grid intersection, with a permissible tolerance of 0.30 m in all directions.

The tetrapods should be laid at random, i.e., their position does not have to be located exactly. The position of the hook is the only position requiring to be accurately fixed.

The blocks constituting the first layer automatically come to rest on the rock pile on three of their legs.

The second-layer blocks should preferably be laid "one leg down" in order to obtain a better fit.

The tetrapods must be laid, i.e., brought into contact with the rock pile or with the other tetrapods, before being released.

It is recommended first laying a row of tetrapods starting from the foot of the structure and extending over the widest possible front and then following up by a second layer, above the first, but extending over a slightly narrower front (one tetrapod less), and then by a third row, again slightly shorter.

After 3 or 4 rows have been positioned in this way, the second layer should be placed, fitting into the first and completing tne revetment.

The object of this method is to ensure that the tetrapod facing is not left in an uncompleted state (1 layer). Two layers that do not extend up to the top of the embankment in fact afford the most efficient protection if gale conditions occur while work is going on. The essential points to observe are as follows:

1. Start at the bottom.
2. Avoid leaving the structure exposed to the sea with only one layer of tetrapods in position.

On the upper part of the structure, the last tetrapods should be placed after the protection wall has been built, so as to ensure proper keying between this wall and the rest of the revetment.

Table 4.1 gives the physical characteristics of tribars, and the number of tribars required for 100 sq ft of armor cover for a single layer and for two layers.

4.7 Examples of Tetrapod and Tribar Construction

The first tetrapods actually used in construction were placed for the protection of a dyke in Sousse, Tunisia, which was finished in 1952 and required 1,550 four-ton units. By the beginning of 1959 more than 35 installations had either been completed or were under construction, including installations for such important projects as the base for the United States Navy at Rota, Spain; the extension of the main breakwater at Safi, Morocco; the extension of the main breakwater at Crescent City, California; the protection of a breakwater at Vera Cruz, Mexico; and several others of no less importance. The construction of the installations at Rota, Spain, and Safi, Morocco, will be described in some detail.

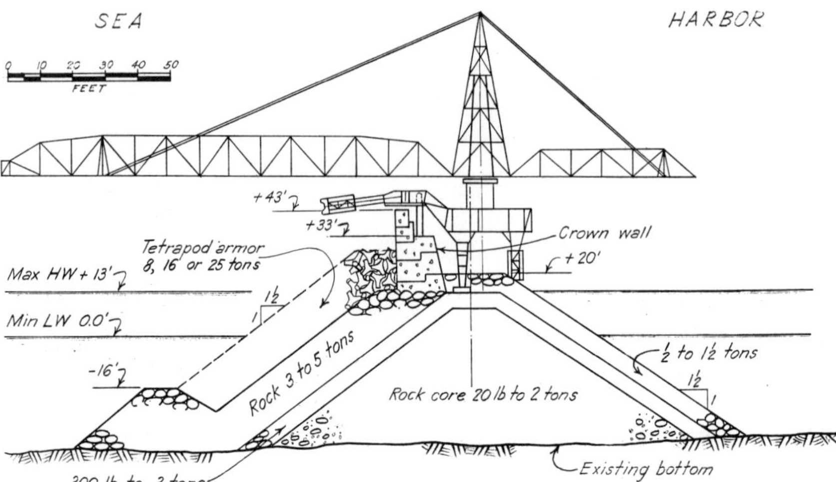

FIG. 4.41 Cross section through breakwater at Rota, Spain. (*From article by R. H. Corbetta and H. W. Hunt, Civil Engineering, October,* 1958.)

The principal port of entry for the United States bases in Spain, which was substantially completed in 1958, is Rota on the Bay of Cadiz, which is described in Sec. 3.6. The harbor is protected by a breakwater which extends out approximately 2,000 ft normal to the shore and then turns about 45° to more or less parallel the shore for a length of about 5,000 ft. The latter section is perpendicular to southwest ocean storms, which create waves up to 16 ft in height, and is slightly skewed to reflect waves towards shore rather than out towards the breakwater head.

Figure 4.41 shows a cross section through the outshore arm of the breakwater, with a 400-ton crane used for placing the tetrapods. Availability of suitable rock was a major consideration in the design. A hard limestone was available at a quarry about 35 miles from the harbor, but, because of fissures in the rock, the maximum size armor did not exceed 7 to 8 tons in quantity. A quarry of soft rock was located nearer the site and this was used to build the core to about 8 ft above low water, the material being placed by end dumping from trucks. The core is protected with secondary armor layers, and on the sea side by an armor course of tetrapods up to 25 tons in weight. The breakwater is capped with a cast-in-place crown wall varying in height from El +33 ft to El +43 ft above low low water.

More than ten thousand tetrapods, weighing up to 25 tons each, were placed on the breakwater. These were placed, at a distance of up to 125 ft from the center of the breakwater, by a full-revolving, hammerhead-type crane, which has a 360-hp diesel-electric generator mounted on its gantry to supply electric power for traveling, hoisting, swinging, and lighting. The crane runs on double rails spaced 20 ft apart. An auxiliary

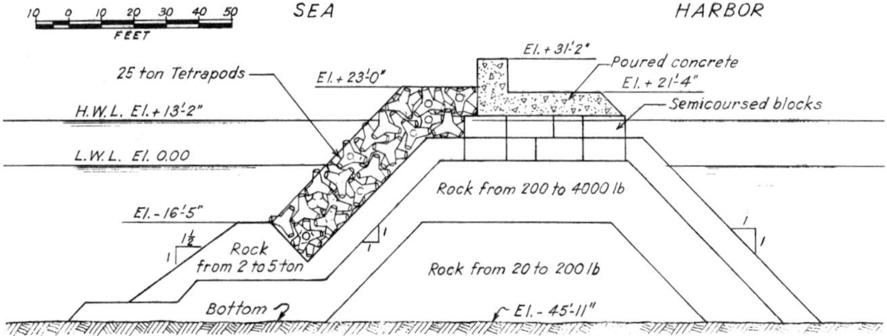

FIG. 4.42 Cross section through tetrapod armored breakwater at Safi, Morocco. (*Courtesy of NEYRPIC, Grenoble, France.*)

support, 20 ft further out, was used to give added stability for heavy lifts. The crane placed the outer armor rock and tetrapods up to about 100 ft in front of the wall construction, completing placement except for the space immediately adjacent to the wall. After the crown wall was concreted, and the forms removed, the crane returned to place the remaining tetrapods, which extend about halfway up the face of the wall. The crane was completely wrecked during a storm in December, 1958. The outshore rounded end of the breakwater was protected with 120-ton concrete blocks.

In 1955 the main breakwater at Safi, which has been described in Sec. 4.5, was extended. The new construction utilized 25-ton tetrapods, placed on a 1-on-1 slope on a rock-mound embankment, for armoring the sea side of the breakwater. Figure 4.42 shows a cross section through this breakwater.

Extensive model tests were performed to demonstrate the stability of the breakwater against waves up to 24 ft in height, both normal and oblique to the axis of the breakwater. Further tests were carried out to determine the stability of the structure at various stages of completion, and to give some idea of the probable extent of damage likely to be inflicted by storms during the period of construction. Studies were also carried out to determine the necessity of reinforcing the tetrapods, and, while the tests were inconclusive, it was decided to reinforce all of the tetrapods with 42 lb of steel per cu yd. Prestressed concrete tetrapods were also tested at Safi, and the conclusion was reached that the few advantages associated with prestressed units would not justify the additional heavy expense involved in their construction.

The tetrapods were laid haphazardly on the rock-fill embankment, the only precautions being to let them rest on the embankment before releasing them and to see that the unit density amounted to 22 tetrapods per 1,076 sq ft. In all 1,400 tetrapods were placed.

At the close of 1959 the largest tribars used were 18 tons. They were installed at Nawiliwili Harbor, Kauai. Tribars were used on the breakwater there for repair work and withstood satisfactorily the force of Hurricane Dot. Tribars weighing 5 tons were the smallest to be used. These were installed on jetties in northern Taiwan.

4.8 Experimental Design Studies of Mound Breakwaters

Model tests of breakwater stability are without question the best tool of the designer in arriving at a safe and economical design for a breakwater of the mound type, particularly where artificial blocks are involved; also, experimental values have been developed for the coefficient K' in the Iribarren formula and the coefficient K_D in the United States Waterways Experiment Station formula for stability of natural armor rock slopes, which enable the designer to use these formulas with better understanding and more confidence than was the case with the original Iribarren formula. Model tests have aided in the development of the tetrapod and tribar as two of the most economical and stable forms of artificial blocks for breakwater armor. They have aided in the planning and economical development of such harbors as Zonguldak, Turkey; Safi, Morocco; Taconite Harbor, Lake Superior; and others of equal importance. Such well-known laboratories as the United States Waterways Experiment Station at Vicksburg, Mississippi, the Saint Anthony Falls Hydraulic Laboratory of the University of Minnesota, and the NEYRPIC Hydraulic Laboratory at Grenoble, France, have pioneered in this field of work, and the publication of their experimental tests and studies has resulted in placing the design of breakwaters on a sound engineering basis. No longer need a breakwater be designed by rule of thumb.

The making of model tests is a special field of work and great care must be exercised in carrying out these tests to see that they simulate the prototype. The scale relationship of the hydraulic model is dependent on the controlling forces which produce critical conditions in the actual breakwater. Although initially generated by winds, the forces exerted by breaking waves on the breakwaters are established by the earth's gravitation. Analytically this leads to the Froude model law in arriving at motion and force relationships between the models and the breakwater counterparts. The sizes of the models are chosen to give accurate results in simulating field conditions, and they are made as small as practical for reasons of economy. If the model is too small, such secondary forces as surface tension and fluid friction would become of sufficient magnitude relative to the force of gravity to preclude scale reproduction of wave forces. Models made to the scale of 1:40 or 1:50 have been found generally satisfactory. Models are designed and operated in accordance with the Froude model law, which leads to the specifications that the velocity ratio between model and prototype must be proportional to the square root of the length ratio between model and prototype. The following tabulation gives the relationship of the properties of a model at a scale of 1:50 to the actual breakwater.

Dimensional	*Breakwater model, scale*
Units	1:50
Length	1:50
Area	1:2,500
Volume	1:125,000
Time	1:7.07
Velocity	1:7.07
Unit pressure	1:50
Force	1:125,000
Weight	1:125,000

4.9 Examples of Breakwater Models

In recent years a considerable amount of work has been done on model tests of important breakwaters prior to their construction. One of the more important and comprehensive investigations was performed on the harbor layout and breakwater stability for the harbor which was constructed in 1956 for the Erie Mining Company on the north shore of Lake Superior for the purpose of shipping iron ore. The harbor is described in Sec. 3.7. The layout of the breakwaters is shown in Fig. 3.22, and the typical cross section is given in Fig. 4.14. The model test of the over-all layout and alignment of the breakwaters to obtain an optimum harbor design with regard to quietness of water and economy of construction was performed at the Waterways Experiment Station of the Corps of Engineers in Vicksburg, Mississippi, and has been described in Sec. 3.6. The model tests on the stability of the breakwaters were performed at the Saint Anthony Falls Laboratory under the direction of Dr. Lorenz G. Straub, who issued a report dated December, 1955, on these tests.

The model studies were conducted in a glass-sided channel 20 in. wide, 28 in. deep, and 40 ft long. A pendulum-type wave generator was used. The wave generator was capable of producing waves with a maximum height equivalent to 24 ft for a wave period of 8.5 seconds and a water depth of 75 ft. The wave period and height could be adjusted as desired. A wave filter was placed between the generator and the model and could absorb an appreciable amount of the reflected wave energy.

The tests were conducted on models, accurately constructed to a scale of 1:50. The models were subjected to various wave heights and periods corresponding to those computed to occur on Lake Superior for various wind directions and intensities, the maximum wave height being 20 ft, with a period of 8.5 seconds.

The models were constructed of basalt rock having a specific weight of 170 lb per cu ft, which was shipped to the laboratory from the harbor site. The weights of the armor stones used in the model tests and equivalent weights of the prototype stones, as shown in Fig. 4.14, were as shown in Table 4.2.

***Table* 4.2 Weight of Rock in Prototype and Model of Breakwater**

Class	Weight of model stone, lb	Equivalent weight of prototype stone, tons
D	0.24–0.28	15–17.5
C	0.13–0.15	8– 9.4
B	0.03–0.06	2– 3.7

SOURCE: Report by Lorenz G. Straub on Experimental Design Studies, Taconite Harbor Project.

The core material, class A stone, as specified for the prototype breakwater, is composed of run-of-quarry rock, dumped by trucks and having a maximum size of 5 tons. It was recognized at the start of the tests that considerable importance must be attached to the mechanical composition of the core material in order to judge with assurance the relative vulnerability of the breakwater to various types of wave action. In order to bracket within reasonable limits the character of the class A stone, two extremes in size were provided for the model study, and a third graded size was made up by a composition of each of the two materials referred to as small class A and large class A stone. These three different compositions of core materials were used in various tests performed on the stability of the breakwater. The core materials averaged 3 tons, 400 lb, and 50 lb for the large, medium, and small categories, respectively.

In addition to performing tests to determine the effect of the size and permeability of the core material on the stability of the breakwater, tests were performed to determine the amount of overtopping of the breakwater for various wave heights and the effect of increasing the specific weight of the armor stone from basalt (170 lb per cu ft) to taconite (210 lb per cu ft).

Stability tests were made on two different sections of the east breakwater, one being in 75 ft and the other in 25 ft of water. The latter section was selected for test purposes because the 25-ft depth is the approximate computed value for the breaking of an 8.5-second 20-ft wave which was used for testing the models.

Stability of the models was studied by subjecting them to continuous wave action for a period of time equivalent to 24 hours. Waves of 20-ft height produced some movement of the armor stones, particularly in the initial stages of the test, but the damage was slight, being somewhat of a back-and-forth rocking with each wave. It was evident that the stability would be improved by extending the larger stones to greater depths on the exposed slope. The initial design was based on the 15-ton and larger stones extending to 5 ft below low lake level and the next smaller size of 8 to 15 tons, to 15 ft below this level. The tests indicated that the above armor stone should be extended to -15 ft and -25 ft, respectively, relative to the water surface.

The tests indicated that the east breakwater in a depth of 75 ft or more would be overtopped when the waves in the lake reached a height of 15 ft. Since the top of the breakwater is 12.8 ft above this water level, it follows that the ratio of the height of crest to height of wave is 0.8. This figure checks fairly closely the tests recently made by the United States Waterways Experiment Station at Vicksburg, Mississippi, on breakwater overtopping, which are shown in Fig. 4.7. Where the depth of water is 25 ft, overtopping would start when the waves reached heights of about 14 ft.

Tests indicated that the core material had a noticeable influence on the stability of the armor stone, particularly where the slope was approximately 1 on 1½ or about the angle of repose of this material dumped in water. It was shown that for a core of fine impermeable material, waves of about 8 ft would start a slide of the armor stone, whereas in the case of the coarser and more permeable core material, the armor was not so vulnerable to sliding. Further, when using fine core material it was noticeable that some of this was washed out between the voids in the armor stone, and that this had an effect on the stability of the slope.

Tests confirmed theoretical studies which were made to determine the effect on stability of using armor stone of greater specific gravity than the basalt found on the site. Since taconite rock was available at the mines for producing iron ore, it was used to make this comparison. Taconite has a specific weight varying between the extremes of 174 and 242 lb, and averaging about 210 lb per cu ft, whereas basalt rock has a specific weight of only 170 lb per cu ft. Using the modified Iribarren formula, it is apparent that to obtain the same degree of stability, with the wave characteristics and the slope of the breakwater fixed, the weight of stone will vary with the specific gravity as follows:

$$\frac{W_1}{W_2} = \frac{S_{1r}\,(S_{2r} - 1)^3}{S_{2r}\,(S_{1r} - 1)^3}$$

where W_1 = weight of basalt armor stone
W_2 = weight of taconite armor stone
S_{1r} = specific gravity of basalt (2.72)
S_{2r} = specific gravity of taconite (3.36)

Using the numerical values for the specific gravities of the two different weights of rock, the above equation becomes

$$\frac{W_1}{W_2} = \frac{2.72}{3.36}\,\frac{2.36^3}{1.72^3} = 2.10$$

Thus, all other factors being the same, basalt armor stone must be 2.1 times as heavy as taconite stone to provide the same stability or protection.

Figure 4.43 shows the result of a test run involving a 48-hour wave attack, with 20-ft waves at 8.5-second intervals, on a section of breakwater composed of part taconite stone and part basalt of 0.473 times the weight called for in the specified design, which were separated by a thin dividing wall placed on the center line of the channel. It is quite noticeable that the section composed of basalt was unstable, while that consisting of taconite showed only a small amount of displacement from the wave action. It was felt that the disturbance which occurred in the taconite armor near the top of the breakwater was due to the large variation which exists in the specific gravity of the taconite rock. In general, the tests confirmed the theoretical calculations made in accordance with the modified Iribarren formula.

In 1950 the NEYRPIC Hydraulic Laboratory at Grenoble, France, performed extensive experimental investigations on models of the harbor and breakwaters proposed for the construction of the Port of Zonguldak, Turkey. The layout of the port and breakwaters has been described in Sec. 3.7, and a section through the north breakwater is shown in Fig. 4.30.

The models of the breakwaters were constructed to a linear scale of 1 on 40. The tests were carried out in a 27-meter-long flume, which is 0.60 meter wide and 1.20 meters high. Figure 4.44 is a longitudinal section through the experimental channel or flume. The far end of this flume

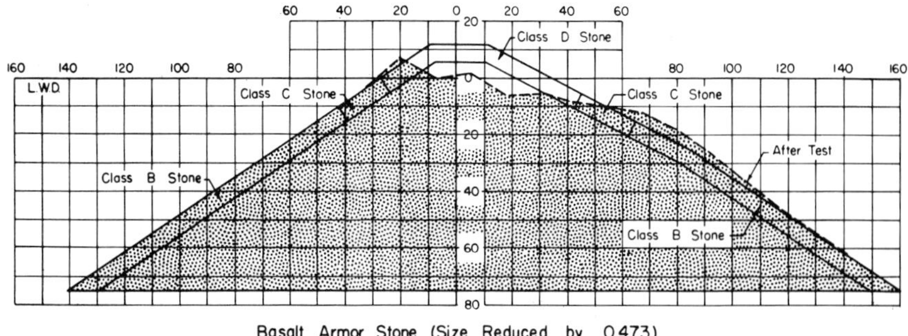

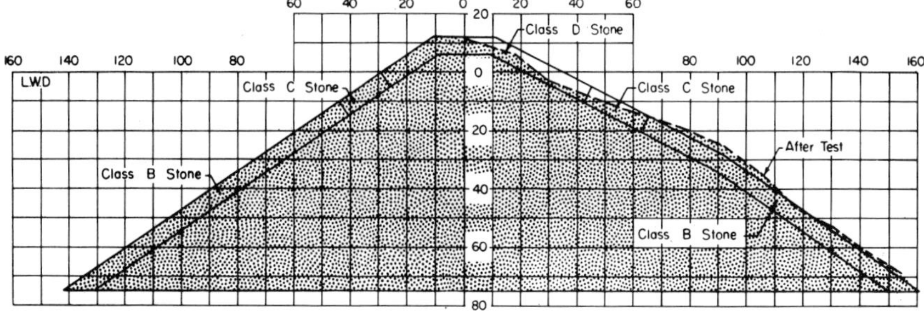

FIG. 4.43 Test run showing comparison of basalt and taconite armor stone for stability, both with stone weights approximately half those called for in the project design. (*From report by Dr. Lorenz G. Straub, Saint Anthony Falls Laboratory, on Model Tests for Taconite Harbor.*)

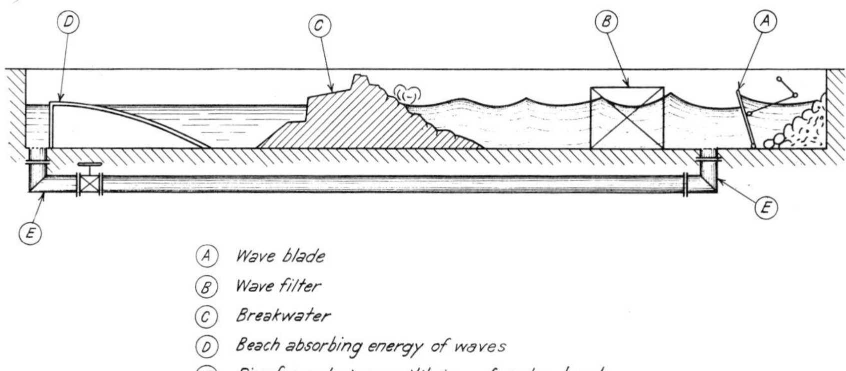

FIG. 4.44 Section through experimental flume for model tests of breakwater at Zonguldak, Turkey. (*From report of NEYRPIC Hydraulic Laboratory, Grenoble, France.*) (*A*) wave blade; (*B*) wave filter; (*C*) breakwater; (*D*) beach absorbing energy of waves; (*E*) pipe for restoring equilibrium of water levels.

is fitted with a wave-generator blade which is made to oscillate about a bottom horizontal axis by a variable eccentricity crank and connecting rod, driven by a motor-speed regulator and speed-reducer unit, as shown in Fig. 4.45.

The 2-hp electric motor drives a speed regulator and reducer which

FIG. 4.45 View of flume and wave maker for model tests of breakwater at Zonguldak, Turkey. (*From report of NEYRPIC Hydraulic Laboratory, Grenoble, France.*)

enables the period of wave-blade oscillations, and hence the wave length of the waves produced, to be adjusted as required. The amplitude of the waves varies with the eccentricity of the crankshaft setting, which may be adjusted between limits of zero and 19 cm.

The wave thus produced is purified in a set of filters, the wave form being rendered perfectly regular in this way by the elimination of higher-order harmonics. These filters, which are patented, consist essentially of a series of thin, vertical metal sheets, equidistant from one another and suspended parallel to the side of the flume. They absorb an appreciable proportion of the energy of the waves, which traverse them without causing any marked reflection.

On one side of the flume, where the model is located, there is a 4-meter-long glass window. It is through this window that the action of the waves on the breakwater structure can be observed and photographed. To provide good photographic conditions, an observation room, measuring 8 meters long by 4 meters high, is located in front of the glass-enclosed section of the flume.

The rock available at the site had a specific gravity of about 2.4 to 2.5. It was crushed and subsequently placed in a concrete mixer to eliminate the sharp edges in order to assimilate the actual condition of the stones in the breakwaters, which are subjected to the wearing action of the sea. The material was then graduated and separated into different categories of rock, within the limits fixed by the design, in accordance with Table 4.3.

Table 4.3 Weight of Rock Used in Prototype and Model of Breakwater

Category	On site		Model	
	Minimum metric tons	Maximum metric tons	Minimum kilograms	Maximum kilograms
1st.......	0	0.40	0	0.006
2d.......	0.40	2.00	0.006	0.032
3d.......	2.00	4.00	0.032	0.062
4th.......	4.00	13.60	0.062	0.212

SOURCE: NEYRPIC Hydraulic Laboratory Report on Model Tests of Breakwater at Zonguldak Harbor, Turkey.

In preparing the concrete blocks for the model tests, the weight was calculated on the assumption that the specific gravity of concrete is 2.2. The blocks used for the test were made from pure cement and were weighted at their center of gravity in order to bring them up to the required weight. All blocks were checked for weight and a tolerance of 5 per cent was allowed.

The sizes and weights of the different blocks used for the tests are given in Table 4.4.

The tests were divided into two main divisions: (1) tests to ascertain the best profile to meet the worst wave attack, and (2) endurance tests of the selected profile.

The exhaustive nature of the tests was indicated in that for (1) 115 tests were made, and for (2) the selected profile *N* for the north break-

***Table* 4.4 Sizes and Weights of Concrete Blocks Used in Prototype and Model of Breakwater**

On site		Model	
Size, meters	Weight, metric tons	Dimensions, cm	Weight, kg
3 x 3 x 3	60	7.5 x 7.5 x 7.5	0.935
2 x 3 x 4.5	60	5.0 x 7.5 x 10.1	0.935
3 x 3 x 3 (beveled edge)	52.5	7.5 x 7.5 x 7.5 (beveled edge)	0.820
2 x 4 x 2.5	44	5.0 x 10.0 x 6.2	0.690
2 x 4 x 2	35	5.0 x 10.0 x 5.0	0.550

SOURCE: NEYRPIC Hydraulic Laboratory Report on Model Tests of Breakwater at Zonguldak, Turkey.

water was subjected to a continuous storm of 36 hours, under the wave attack found to be most severe, i.e., 8½ meters in height and 125 meters in length. The profile selected for the endurance tests is shown being tested in Fig. 4.46.

During the construction of the breakwaters it was determined that sufficient heavy armor rock could be obtained from the quarry to replace the concrete crown wall and bedding blocks under the crown wall for the north breakwater and, therefore, a new profile *L*, as shown in Fig. 4.47, was tested. This model was subjected to the same endurance test as in profile *N*. It is the profile which was finally adopted for construction of the north breakwater.

FIG. 4.46 Endurance tests on profile *N* of north breakwater, Zonguldak, Turkey. (*From report of NEYRPIC Hydraulic Laboratory, Grenoble, France.*)

FIG. 4.47 Endurance tests on profile *L* of north breakwater, Zonguldak, Turkey. (*From report of NEYRPIC Hydraulic Laboratory, Grenoble, France.*)

4.10 Vertical-wall Breakwaters

Vertical-wall breakwaters differ from the sloping mound type in their manner of resisting wave action, i.e., the vertical wall reflects the wave without freeing any destructive energy, producing the stationary undulation known as "clapotis"; whereas the sloping mound type dissipates the energy through run-up on the sloping surface, and friction and eddies caused by the irregular surface play a large part in the ultimate destruction of the wave force.

In the mound type the wave will eventually reach a point on the sloping surface where the depth of water will be less than the height of the wave, and it will break. The vertical-wall breakwater, which is generally located in water of greater depth than the height of the wave, will reflect the oscillatory wave causing it to rise up the wall to a height equal to approximately twice its original height above still-water level. Therefore, the height of the breakwater above highest tide should be not less than 1⅓ to 1½ times the height (trough to crest) of the maximum wave, and the depth below lowest water level to the bottom of the wall should be not less than 1¼ to 1½ and preferably 2 times the height of the wave. However, this depth generally does not exceed 50 to 60 ft; otherwise, the size of the gravity wall becomes unwieldy, as the width of the wall usually will be not less than three-fourths of, and may be equal to or greater than, its height in order to provide adequate stability. In greater depths of water the gravity-wall structure usually is founded on a base of rubble, which may extend to such extreme depths as 130 ft below water level.

Unless the bottom is extremely hard and resistant to scour, the gravity wall always should be placed on a foundation mat of rubble or other suitable material, which will be of sufficient depth to distribute the load to a safe bearing pressure on the underlying soil, and which will extend beyond the toe a sufficient distance to prevent scour and undermining of the breakwater. As a general rule this distance should be not less than one-fourth the length of the wave, if scour is to be completely avoided. Very few breakwaters have failed due to structural weakness; their

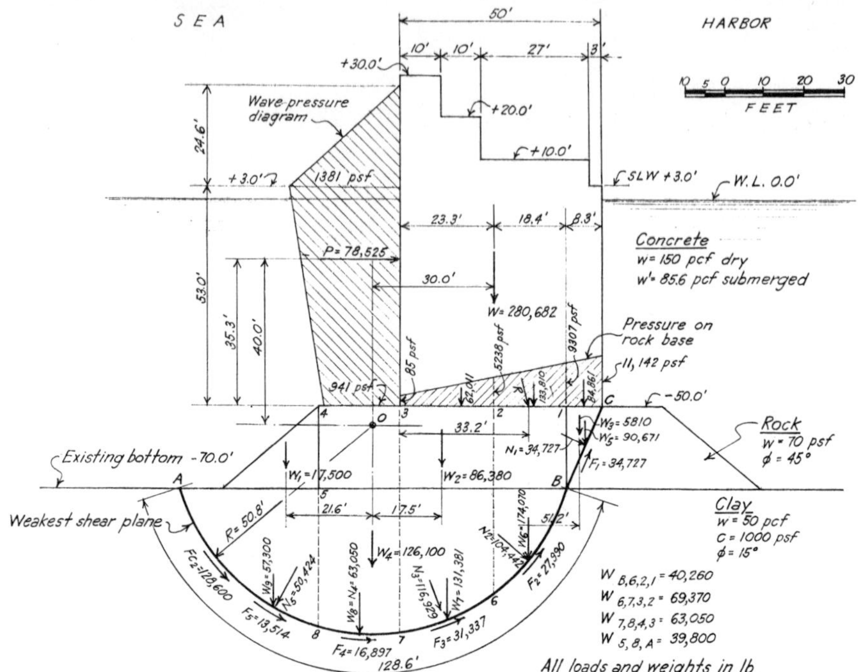

FIG. 4.48 Vertical-wall breakwater foundation stability analysis.

vulnerability to wave forces has been more often a result of scour and undermining of the toe, or overloading and shear failure of the foundation soil. Such a failure is demonstrated in the following example.

Example. Assume the breakwater wall, as shown in Fig. 4.48, is acted upon by a 20-ft wave; the rubble base rests on a clay bottom having a shearing value of $c + n \tan \phi$, in which c, the cohesion, is equal to 1,000 lb per sq ft, and the angle of internal friction is 15°. From a number of trial planes it is found that *ABC* is the weakest shear plane. The wave force, as derived by the Sainflou method, is a horizontal pressure of 78,525 lb per lin ft of wall, the center of gravity being located 35.3 ft above the base. The total submerged weight of the wall is 280,682 lb, and, when combined with the horizontal wave force of 78,525 lb, the resultant strikes the base 16.8 ft from the toe on the harbor side. This results in the pressure diagram indicated, and the maximum pressure of 5.6 tons per sq ft does not exceed the allowable on the rock base. However, by taking moments about point O, the driving and resisting moments must be equated to each other to provide equilibrium, as follows:

Driving Moment

W :	280,682 × 30.0 =	8,420,460 ft-lb
P :	78,525 × 40.0 =	3,141,000 ft-lb
W_2:	86,380 × 17.5 =	1,511,650 ft-lb
W_3:	5,810 × 51.2 =	297,472 ft-lb
W_4:	126,100 × 0 =	0 ft-lb
		13,370,582 ft-lb

Resisting Moment

W_1:		= 17,500 lb	17,500×21.6=	378,000 ft-lb
Cohesion:				
F_c:	128.6×1,000	= 128,600 lb	128,600×50.8=	6,532,880 ft-lb
Friction:				
Rock: ϕ = 45°	tan ϕ = 1			
W_5:	84,861 + 5,810	= 90,671		
N_1:	90,671 sin 22°30′	= 34,727		
F_1:	34,727 × 1	= 34,727 lb	34,727×50.6=	1,757,186 ft-lb
Clay: ϕ = 15°	tan ϕ = 0.268			
W_6:	133,810+40,260	= 174,070		
N_2:	174,070×0.6	= 104,442		
F_2:	104,442×0.268	= 27,990 lb	27,990×50.8=	1,421,892 ft-lb
W_7:	62,011+69,370	= 131,381		
N_3:	131,381×0.89	= 116,929		
F_3:	116,929×0.268	= 31,337 lb	31,337×50.8=	1,591,920 ft-lb
W_8:	63,050	= N_4		
F_4:	63,050×0.268	= 16,897 lb	16,897×50.8=	858,368 ft-lb
W_9:	17,500+39,800	= 57,300		
N_5:	57,300×0.88	= 50,424		
F_5:	50,424×0.268	= 13,514 lb	13,514×50.8=	686,511 ft-lb
				13,226,757 ft-lb

Factor of safety: $\dfrac{13{,}226{,}757}{13{,}370{,}582} = 0.99$

The above indicates that the factor of safety is less than 1.0, and that the wall will fail from the force of a 20-ft wave by having the foundation base shear along the plane *ABC*.

The design of the gravity structure is a straightforward analysis of bearing and shear stresses on horizontal planes from the base level to the top of the wall. The determination of the magnitude and distribution of wave force is perhaps the most uncertain part of the design.

The vertical-type breakwater has certain advantages over the sloping type, among which are the following:

1. It provides a larger harbor area and enables a narrower entrance to the harbor, thereby providing greater protection to the sheltered area.
2. It enables the harbor side of the breakwater to be used for mooring ships.
3. It is subject to more exact analytical analysis.
4. The cost of maintenance is practically eliminated.
5. Where there is a shortage of rock within easy hauling distance of the breakwater, it will usually result in a saving of time and money.

However, the vertical-type breakwater has a number of disadvantages, which may be listed as follows:

1. It can be safely constructed only where foundation conditions are favorable or can be made so.
2. It does not have the structural flexibility which a mound-type breakwater has in adjusting itself to settlement and wave-force disturbances.
3. If damaged it is difficult to repair.
4. The top must be carried to a considerably higher elevation than for an irregular-surfaced sloping breakwater.
5. It requires much more extensive and heavier plant equipment, which may be expensive and difficult to transport and set up in remote locations.

4.11 Examples of Vertical-wall-type Breakwaters

These have been constructed of (1) concrete blocks, (2) concrete or steel caissons, (3) rock-filled steel sheet-pile cells, (4) rock-filled timber cribs, and (5) concrete or steel sheet-pile walls.

Concrete blocks have been used more often in Europe than in the Western Hemisphere for the construction of vertical-wall breakwaters. A good example of this type of design is the Granili breakwater, which was constructed in 1910 and forms the main protection for the docks at the east end of the Port of Naples, Italy. It parallels and is 600 meters from the shore and is 1,000 meters long. It is perpendicular to the waves coming from the open sea. The depth of water varies from 18 to 24 meters at its eastern end.

Figure 4.49 shows a cross section through the breakwater. The foundation of the breakwater, containing 1,157,000 tons, is built of run-of-quarry stone with heavy rock facing, which is leveled off at El −10.5 meters where it is 38 meters wide. The slope on the sea side is 1 on 1½ and on the harbor side 1 on 1. The top of the core was carefully leveled with broken stone and supports a substructure composed of cellular concrete blocks, measuring 9 by 5 meters in plan and 2.3 meters high. The blocks each contain two cells 3.5 by 3.5 by 2.3 meters. They are laid five high

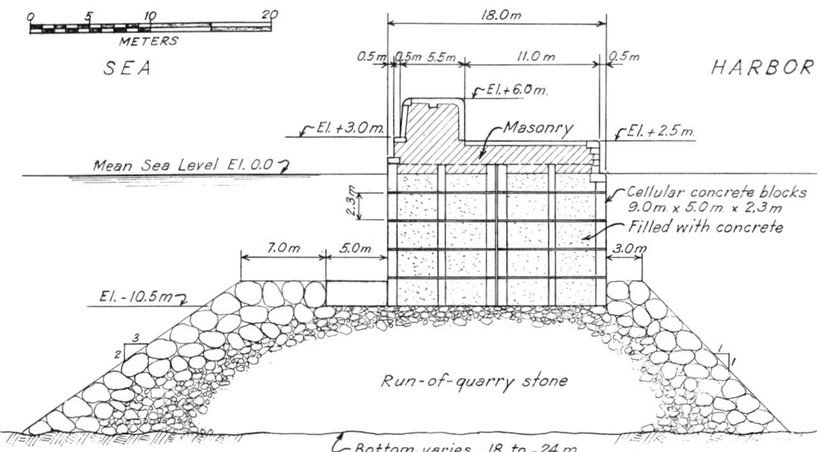

FIG. 4.49 Cross section through the Granili breakwater at the Port of Naples, Italy. (*From report by I. Inglese,* XII*th International Congress of Navigation, Philadelphia,* 1912.)

and two wide forming a substructure 18 meters wide by 11.5 meters high. The cells are filled with concrete.

In order to protect the foot of the substructure from scour from the backwash of the waves, there is a row of concrete blocks measuring 5 by 2.5 by 2.0 meters and weighing 50.5 tons each.

The superstructure from a level 0.5 meter above mean sea level is constructed of ordinary masonry laid in lime mortar, about 2 meters high, and is topped off on the sea side with a wall 5.3 meters wide at the top, rising to a height of 6 meters above mean sea level. This provides protection to the harbor side and enables the breakwater to be used as a quay to which vessels can tie up.

Figure 4.50 is a cross section through the Algiers breakwater which is better known for its failure and the studies which have been made by different engineers as to the cause of the failure.

When construction started in 1927 it was believed that all precautions had been taken in the design not to repeat the errors of past failures of this type of structure. As a result, the wall was constructed of huge blocks weighing 450 tons and keyed together with reinforced concrete dowels poured in place after the blocks had been set. The wall was capped with a heavy poured-in-place seawall. The foundation for the wall consisted of a rubble revetment placed on a firm fine-sand bottom. The toe and heel were protected with concrete blocks and the slopes of the revetment with natural-rock armor.

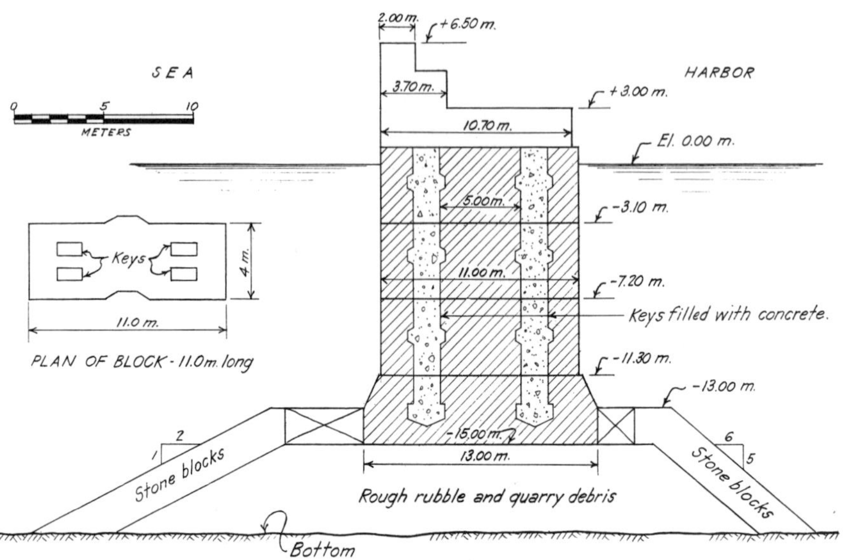

FIG. 4.50 Cross section through the Algiers, Morocco, breakwater.

Unfortunately, the information then available led to the design of the structure being based on a maximum wave height of only 16 ft. The construction had not been fully completed before it became evident that greater wave heights could occur in this locality, when, in the latter part of 1930, the wall was attacked by a severe storm producing waves over 20 ft high, and a portion of the wall, some 300 ft long, settled unevenly and tilted seaward. This led to remedial measures to prevent further movement of this portion of the wall and a rubble fill, extending on the sea side from the bottom to the top and on the harbor side to only half the height of the wall, was placed against the wall. Further measures, consisting of drilling and grouting, were taken to make the wall into as monolithic a structure as possible. In spite of all this, in the early part of 1934 the most severe storm yet struck the breakwater with waves estimated to be 30 ft high and 600 ft long, the waves passing completely over the top of the parapet.

Many figures and studies have been made to explain the reasons for the overturning of the breakwater, and these will not be repeated here. It must be kept in mind that the breakwater failed under a wave height almost twice that for which it had been designed, but the interesting and instructive feature of this is that it did not fail by overturning into the harbor but rather by tipping seaward, the direction in which, according to theory, the overturning force should have been a minimum. There are several explanations for this. First, while the parapet height of 21.5 ft above still water would have been high enough to have permitted a clapotis or complete obstruction of the designed wave height of 16 ft to take place, it was very much too low for a wave 30 ft in height. This wave then passed completely over the wall, raising the water level in the harbor and momentarily caused a very high static head against the harbor side of the wall, as the trough of the wave occurred on the seaward side. This, coupled with a suction force produced by the backwash of the waves, could have caused the failure to take place in the manner that it did. Also, there is evidence that this suction or undertow caused an erosion of the toe on the seaward side of the breakwater, which no doubt contributed to the failure.

This failure emphasizes the following very important points when designing a vertical-wall breakwater:

1. The design maximum wave height must be on the safe side since, unlike rubble-mound breakwaters, stability from overturning is an important factor.
2. The height of the wall or parapet must be sufficient to permit a clapotis or a complete obstruction of the wave to take place.
3. The foundation of the wall, whether it is a rubble-mound or concrete base, should extend either to firm material which cannot be eroded, or it should extend a sufficient distance below the sea bottom so that erosion will not undermine the toe, and the base should be correspondingly increased in width to maintain stability against overturning at the lower level. In lieu of the above, the foundation base should extend far enough beyond the toe of the wall, a distance generally considered to be one-fourth the wave length, to prevent erosion and undermining of the toe of the wall.

Concrete caissons. This type of construction has been used quite extensively for breakwaters in the Great Lakes and for the protection of harbors in Europe. It has the advantage of reducing considerably the construction working time on water. This is an important factor where the sea is rough and the working time of floating equipment is limited. The caisson-type construction enables a large amount of the work to be done on shore. A period of relatively good weather and calm water can be selected for the actual installation, which will require only a short interval of time for a single unit or caisson, thereby minimizing the possibility of storm damage.

The customary practice is to make these caissons of box-like units with a closed bottom and with diaphragm walls dividing the box into several compartments. The side walls may be either vertical or sloped so as to reduce the width at the top. An example of the latter is the south breakwater, built in 1926 to 1929, for the harbor of refuge at Milwaukee on Lake Michigan, a cross section of which is shown in Fig. 4.51. It consists

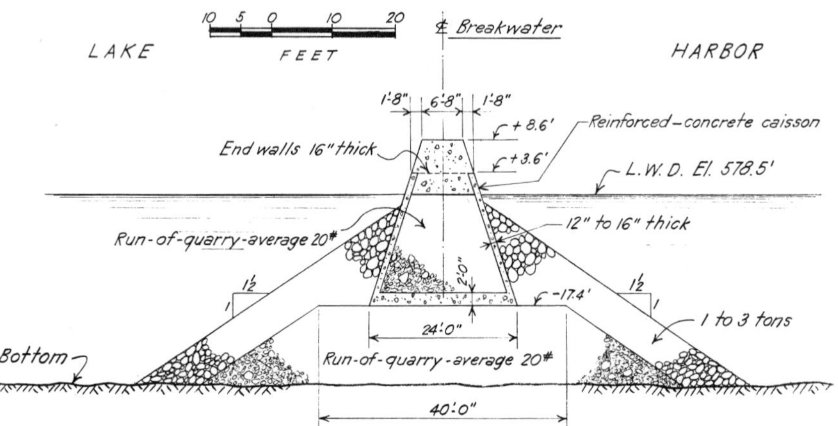

FIG. 4.51 Cross section through south breakwater at Milwaukee on Lake Michigan. (*From Paper* 79 *by Lt. Col. H. C. Tyler, Corps of Engineers, United States Army,* XVI*th International Congress of Navigation, Brussels,* 1935.)

of precast-concrete caissons each 54 ft long, 21 ft high, and 24 ft wide at the bottom and 10 ft wide at the top. The 54-ft-long caisson is divided into four compartments by 10-in.-thick cross walls. These sections were constructed on shore, launched, and towed to the site of the work. They were sunk in 24 to 35 ft of water on a prepared foundation consisting of run-of-quarry rock leveled off at a depth of −17.4 ft below lake level, filled with crushed stone, capped with a poured-in-place superstructure 6 ft 8 in. wide at the top and riprapped with stone laid on a 1-on-1½ slope on both sides.

A good example of a breakwater built with caissons having vertical sides is the north breakwater at Helsingborg, Sweden, which was built in 1918 to 1920. It is 340 meters in length and the depth of water varies from 5 to 13.5 meters. The bottom is of hard limestone covered with a 1.0 meter layer of sand. The sand was dredged away and a bed of stone chips, 0.5 to 3.0 meters thick, was placed over the rock and leveled by divers.

A cross section through the breakwater is shown in Fig. 4.52. The caissons vary in length from 21 to 29 meters. One longitudinal wall and cross walls every 3.5 meters divide the caisson into compartments. To prevent relative movement of individual caissons in a direction perpendicular to the axis of the breakwater, the end wall of one caisson is formed into a tongue which is fitted into a groove in the adjoining caisson.

The caissons were built in a dry dock consisting of a temporary coffer-

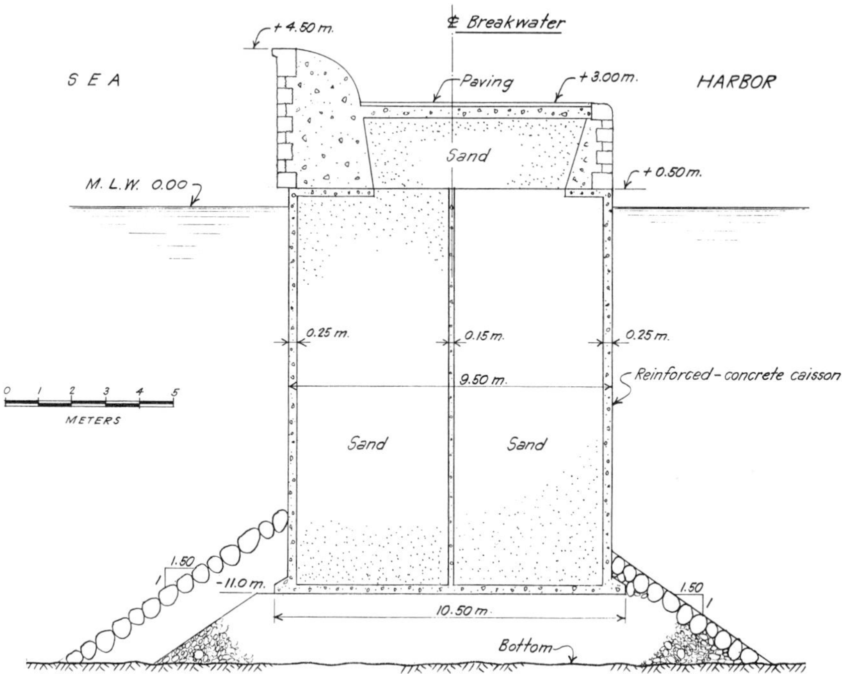

FIG. 4.52 Cross section through north breakwater at Helsingborg Harbor, Sweden. (*From Paper* 82 *by Alban Lange and Rikord V. Frost,* XVI*th International Congress of Navigation, Brussels,* 1935.)

dam. They were towed to the site, filled with water and sunk on to the prepared foundation bed of stone chips, and then filled with sand. The top of the caissons was constructed with a slab along each side on which a concrete seawall, faced with stone, was constructed. The space between the two walls was then filled with sand on which a paving was laid at elevation +3.0 meters.

Cellular sheet-pile breakwater. This type of breakwater has been used with considerable success on the Great Lakes. However, its use has never become widespread for the following reasons.

1. It is difficult, if not impossible, to construct in exposed locations where there is considerable wave action, as setting up the sheet piles and then holding them in place in rough water is a very difficult opera-

tion. The best approach is to make each cell self-supporting and to work from the completed cell, which has been filled with rock, to install the next cell, using a template to set the sheeting. However, until the circle is completely closed, the sheet-pile cell is very vulnerable to collapse by wave action. Since most breakwaters are built where there is rough water, it follows that a great many locations are not suitable for this type of construction, particularly as the operation of installing a cell usually takes a period of time of a week or more. It is only in those areas like the Great Lakes, where there are periods of relatively good weather and calm water at certain times in the year, that the use of sheet-pile cells becomes practical.

2. Corrosion is a problem which is not present when using concrete or rock for breakwater construction. There are some locations, such as Lake Maracaibo in Venezuela, where unprotected steel will have a life of only a few years and where cathodic protection below water level is of little value. Other places may require cathodic protection and concrete encasement below the low-water line.

3. Compared to a rock-mound breakwater which can be built in water of great depths, the use of a sheet-pile cellular breakwater is limited to a depth of water of about 50 to 60 ft, except where it is placed on rubble-mound foundation below that level.

Sheet-pile cells have been used for temporary installations where they serve not only as a cofferdam to permit unwatering of the harbor but also to protect the construction of the harbor facilities from the waves. Such an installation was used at Taconite Harbor on the north shore of Lake Superior and is described in Sec. 3.6. The cells, which were filled with sand to within about 3 ft of the top, were extended to a height of 12 ft above lake level and were capped with a layer of heavy rock.

Sheet-pile cells for breakwaters are generally the self-supporting type, i.e., each cell is stable by itself when filled with rock or other suitable material. The sheeting must extend to a sufficient depth below the bottom to prevent undermining of the cell by erosion of the bottom. The minimum depth of penetration is usually not less than 10 ft, unless the bottom is rock or other very hard material. It is customary to place riprap against the toe of the sheeting to protect the bottom against erosion. The top of the sheeting should extend to twice the height of the maximum wave above high water, although it may terminate at or just above mean high water and a seawall of poured-in-place concrete constructed to the required height. When the sheet piling is extended to the full height it may be capped with heavy rock, concrete blocks, or a poured-in-place concrete slab.

Figure 4.53 shows a cross section through the cellular sheet-pile breakwater at Calumet on Lake Michigan, which is 5,000 ft long and was constructed in 1935 as an extension of the existing timber-crib breakwater. The cells are 41 ft wide and the arcs have a radius of 38 ft 9 in., which makes a rise of 5 ft. The end walls of each cell are circular arcs with a radius of 35 ft 6 in. and a 3-ft 6-in. rise. The sheeting is 46 ft long, driven through 2 ft of sand and 6 ft of hard clay. The cells are in 32 ft of water and their top is 6 ft above lake level. They are filled with crushed rock and capped with large armor stone.

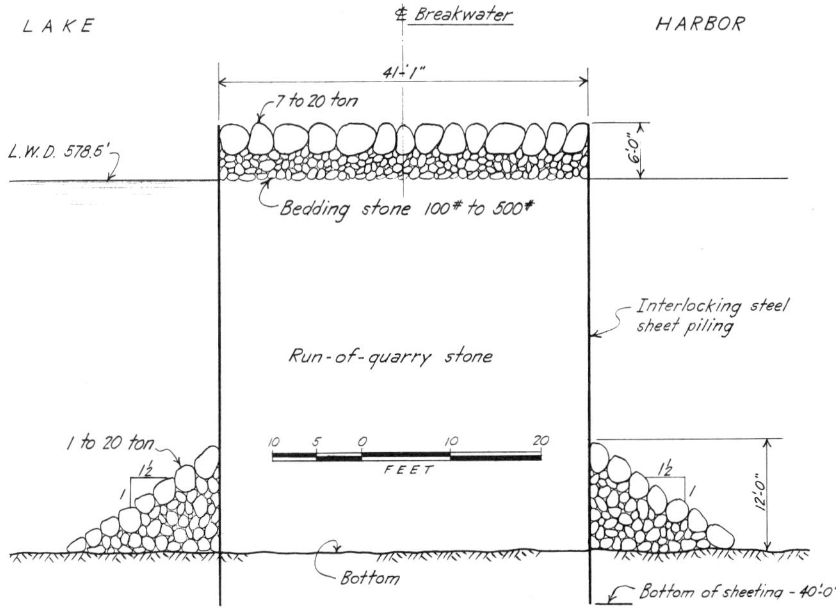

FIG. 4.53 Cross section through cellular sheet-pile breakwater at Calumet on Lake Michigan. (*From Paper* 79 *by Lt. Col. H. C. Tyler, Corps of Engineers, United States Army,* XVI*th International Congress of Navigation, Brussels,* 1935.)

Where the water is relatively shallow and the waves not too high, the breakwater may consist of two parallel lines of sheet piling with a rock or granular fill in between, the sheet piling being supported by steel walers and tie rods placed at or just above low-water level. The parallel lines of steel or concrete sheet piling are placed a distance apart equal to the depth of water plus twice the height of wave. The sheet piling in this type of construction is selected for its bending strength and usually one of the Z types of piling is used. The top may be capped with heavy rock or poured-in-place concrete depending upon whether the structure is also to be used as a quay for docking ships .

Rock-filled timber cribs. These have been used most extensively on the Great Lakes, particularly in the early days when timber was cheap in that area. The early construction consisted of cribs 30 to 35 ft square, divided into compartments by transverse and longitudinal wales and then filled with rock and sunk end to end along the line of the breakwater. The superstructure was of continuous wood decking, 7 to 8 ft above water level, which decayed and was badly damaged by storms. Later on, the tops of the cribs were cut off at about 3 ft below water level, and concrete

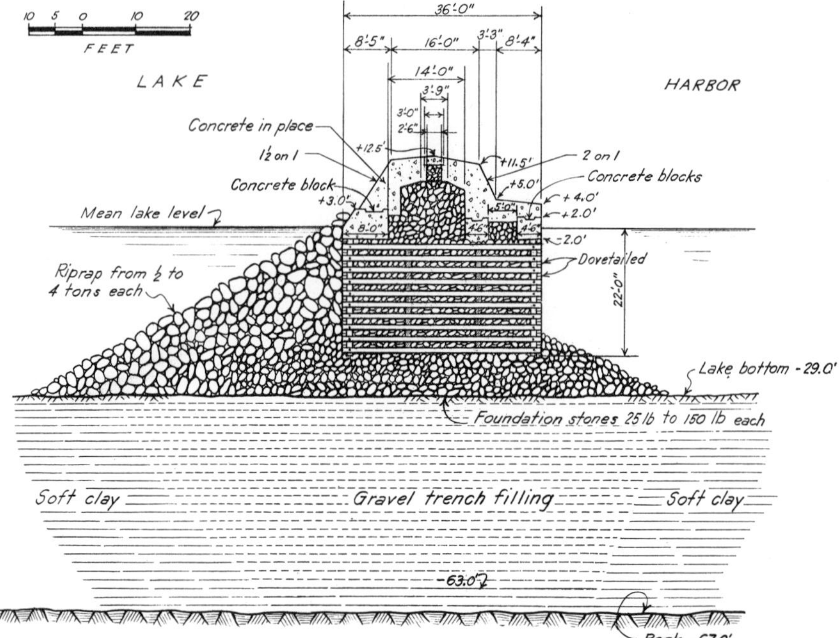

FIG. 4.54 Cross section through timber-crib breakwater at Buffalo, New York. (*From report by Joseph F. Hasskarl, XIIth International Congress of Navigation, Philadelphia,* 1912.)

blocks and poured-in-place concrete were used to rebuild the superstructure to 8 to 10 ft above lake level.

A good example of the above is the South Harbor breakwater at Buffalo, New York, which was originally built in 1898 to 1900. The superstructure of timber was badly wrecked by storms in the fall of 1900 and in 1902 a new superstructure of concrete was completed over a length of 1,800 ft. This is shown in Fig. 4.54.

Steel and concrete sheet-pile-wall breakwaters. There are some locations where the bottom is of soft material which extends to a great depth. It may be possible to keep dumping rock onto the bottom until a foundation is built up which will remain stable, and which will permit the building of a rock-mound breakwater. However, this may require a very large volume of rock and a considerable period of time may elapse before the bottom becomes stabilized. In such cases, and when the height of wave does not exceed 10 ft, it will be found more economical to use the type of bulkhead breakwater shown in Fig. 4.55. This consists of concrete sheet piling and concrete batter piles driven through the soft material to the underlying firm material. These are capped above low-water level with a poured-in-place wall.

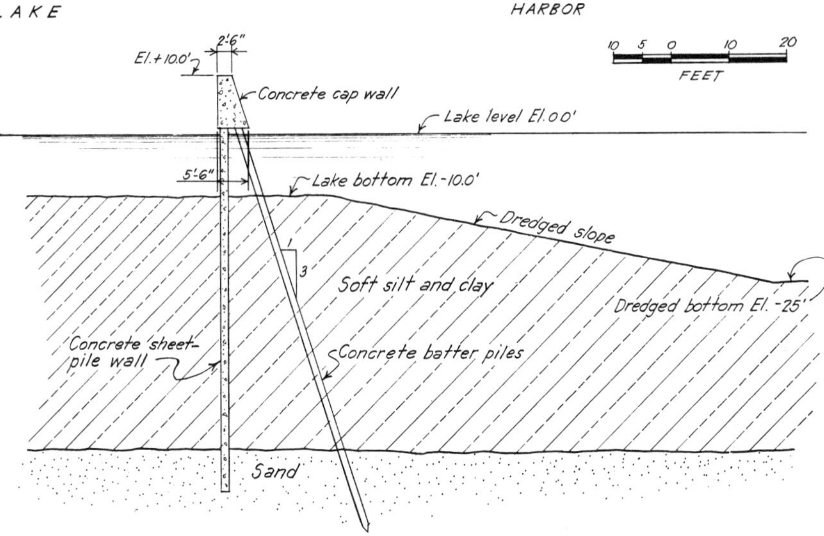

FIG. 4.55 Cross section of sheet-pile-wall breakwater.

4.12 Pneumatic and Hydraulic Breakwaters

A pneumatic breakwater is a method of controlling waves with compressed air; when the waves are controlled by water jets the method is termed a hydraulic breakwater. Figure 4.56 shows how these two breakwaters differ.

The principle of a pneumatic breakwater was developed by an American, Mr. Philip Brasher, who patented a process for calming waves by injecting air bubbles beneath the surface. His method was used with some success for several years after 1915 to protect from wave action the remaining inshore end of a pier of the Standard Oil Company at El Segundo, California, after the outshore portion had been destroyed by a severe storm. The phenomena of calming the waves by the air bubbles was not understood clearly then, and although some other installations followed in the ensuing years and a number of model tests were performed, the method has never become universally popular nor has full agreement been reached as to why the air bubbles produce this effect on the waves. Recently, however, there has been a renewed interest in developing and improving mechanisms for actual installations and in furthering a better understanding of its phenomena through more model tests and studies. A serious drawback to its use has been and still continues to be the wide divergence in the results of the model tests with respect to the amount of compressed air required, and, as a result, the

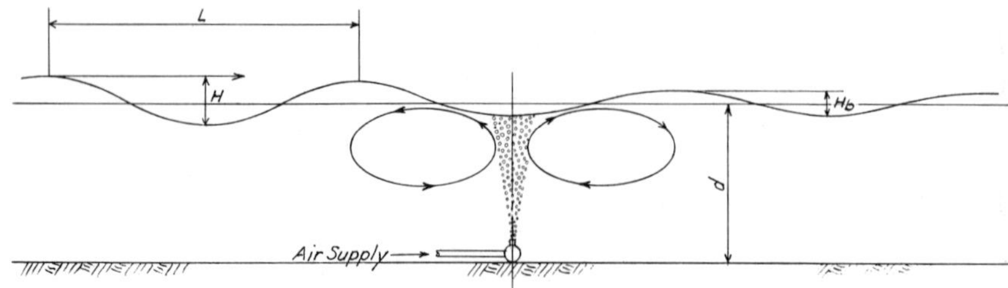

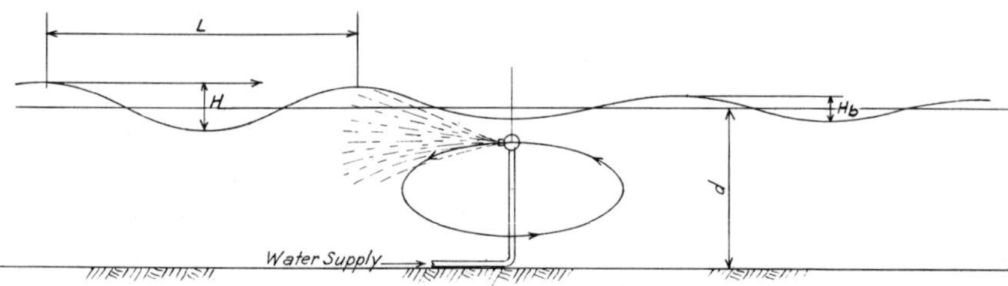

FIG. 4.56 Showing difference between pneumatic and hydraulic breakwater.

almost prohibitive amount of power and operating cost indicated as compared to experience obtained in the few prototype installations which have been made. This lack of confidence and inability to set up reliable information from a model of a proposed prototype installation has discouraged proceeding with any large project of this type. The result has been that the installations have been relatively small and on an experimental basis.

The following is a brief summary of the progress which has been made in understanding and developing the pneumatic and hydraulic breakwater. In 1936 Professor Thijsse, of Delft, experimented with the pneumatic breakwater and found that the quantity of air required for efficient damping would be very large. He proposed the theory that the calming of the waves is due not to the bubbles of air but to the currents of water set up by the bubbles first rising vertically from the air pipe laid parallel to the wave crests and then flowing out horizontally from each side of the rising column of air and water.

In 1950 Professor A. W. Carr of the California Institute of Technology carried out small-scale tests in a tank in which currents were produced both by air bubbles and by water jets. He concluded that the large amount of power required to dampen long waves made the method impractical.

In 1952, encouraged by the success in a small way of a pneumatic breakwater installed to protect the inner dock gate at Dover Train Ferry Dock, the British Transport Commission, Docks and Inland Waterways, undertook an investigation in the hydraulic laboratory to try to determine how the pneumatic breakwater works and the conditions under which it would be successful. From the observations, as reported by J. T. Evans, director of the Docks and Inland Waterways Research Station, it was concluded that the effect of air bubbles in calming waves is almost entirely due to the horizontal surface currents set up, that the bubbles themselves have a very small effect on the wave motion, their function being to entrain vertical currents of water which flow horizontally upon reaching the surface, and that the effect of the horizontal surface currents appears to shorten and to raise the waves until they break. Part of the tests were carried on with the use of water jets because with the equipment available more power could be supplied with water than with air.

The construction of the pneumatic breakwater to protect the lock of the Dover Train Ferry Dock led to the consideration of a pneumatic breakwater to calm the sea in Heligoland Harbor and to check the effect of such a breakwater by means of model tests. As reported by Professor Walter Hensen in the June, 1955, issue of the *Dock and Harbour Authority*, a meeting was held between representatives of the waterways and shipping authorities and the Franzuis Institute in Hanover, Germany, in March and June, 1954, at which a program of tests was laid out to develop information on the effectiveness of the pneumatic breakwater, the way in which it works, its effect on the internal motion of a wave passing through it, and other important considerations.

For the first time it was brought out that Froude's law of similitude for the scale of the model is not permissible in the case of a pneumatic breakwater since it is necessary to take into account not only the forces of gravity and inertia but also the properties of the water and air mixture, so that model experiments cannot provide accurate information on the quantities of air required for the reduction of waves under natural conditions. The model tests appear to indicate a quantity of air some 500 to 750 times greater than that actually required.

The test results showed that it is possible to obtain a reasonably good reduction in the height of steep waves with an L/H ratio below 15 to 20, but for flatter waves the height is not markedly reduced by the pneumatic breakwater. Unless the waves form surf in passing through the breakwater, the tendency is to re-form behind the breakwater. The research work carried out at the Franzuis Institute enabled a better understanding of how the pneumatic breakwater works, which can be briefly described as follows: The rising air bubbles entrain water upwards. On reaching the surface the rising current of water flows off and the loss of water is compensated by in-flows at the bottom, so that vortexes are formed. The waves run up against the surface flow of the vortex and if the vortex speed is high enough and the wave steep enough, the wave breaks, and surf is formed.

In Japan, between 1952 and 1956, as reported in the *Bulletin* of the Research Institute for Applied Mechanics, Kyushu University, a completely independent theoretical and water tank experimental study supplemented by two full-scale tests was carried out and developed the conclusion that the wave attenuation of an actual pneumatic breakwater is due not entirely to the surface current created by the vortexes of rising air-entrained water currents, as previously generally believed, but rather that turbulent viscosity plays an important part in the wave annihilation.

Hydraulic breakwaters are formed by forcing water through a perforated pipe or nozzles. The resulting discharge in the surrounding water induces a current which tends to increase the wave steepness and cause it to break, thereby causing it to lose its energy through turbulence.

In June, 1956, there was issued a report entitled Experimental Studies of Hydraulic Breakwaters, by Lorenz G. Straub, director of the Saint Anthony Falls Hydraulic Laboratory, covering the results of water jet model tests performed to determine the effect of various parameters on wave attenuation. Two wave channels were employed in these studies, which were geometrically similar. The small channel was 2 ft wide, 1 ft 3 in. deep, and 50 ft long, and the large channel was 9 ft wide, 6 ft deep, and 253 ft long. The experimental results indicated that the power requirements of a hydraulic breakwater are primarily dependent upon wave length, water depth, wave steepness, submergence of the nozzles, spacing and size (or area) of nozzles, and the number of manifolds.

Of unusual interest in the above tests was the scale-effect study on the two geometrically similar channels, which at the time was believed to be the first test of its kind. The report indicates that the comparative data obtained agree quite well when compared on the basis of Froude's law, which is the power ratio $P_r = L_r^{7/2}$ where L_r is the length ratio of the two models, for values of L/d between 1.22 and 1.78, indicating that little scale effect exists over this range and tending to substantiate extrapolation of the data to the prototype condition.

The report develops curves for horsepower requirements for 100 per cent attenuation of a 4-ft wave, 100 ft long, for a breakwater 50 ft long, for varying diameters of supply pipe and jet area per foot of breakwater. It is the author's interpretation that the large power required would prohibit an actual installation of this type of breakwater.

It was reported in *Engineering News-Record,* the January 22, 1959, issue, that the Pneumatic Breakwaters, Ltd., of London has developed a method of controlling waves with compressed air which is being used successfully at the entrance to the inner harbor at Dover, England. The breakwater consists of two parallel rows of air-bubble distributors placed across the 300-ft gap between the two breakwaters. When wave action becomes heavy, usually not exceeding 12 ft in height or 80 ft in length, air bubbles are released by the distributors at regular intervals which result in reduction of wave heights up to as much as 50 per cent. As the bubbles rise to the surface, they disturb the harmonic motion of the waves and create a turbulent zone some 20 to 40 yd wide, through which the waves cannot pass without losing a substantial amount of their force and height.

Unlike most previous installations which used a constant discharge of air through submerged perforated tubes, requiring an enormous amount of air, the claim is made that this new type of air distributor system makes the method economically feasible.

Each of the two lines of the Dover pneumatic breakwater, which are spaced 100 ft apart, is made up of distributors mounted on a series of 45-ft rails, each of which has two cross arms to provide stability on the sea bottom.

The distributors are bell-shaped polyethylene units mounted on legs on the rails. Air pumped into the distributor at the bottom enters a water-filled chamber, and, when the water is forced out of the chamber, the air bursts forth as a large bubble. As the bubbles rise, they create vortexes of air and water. Distributors of the size used at Dover, spaced at 7-ft intervals, produce vortexes about 7 ft in diameter, and this has proved to be the most efficient arrangement.

Compressors on shore supply air to the distributor sections through 1.5-in. flexible lines on the harbor bottom, from which individual distributors are fed by ½-in. tubes. The time interval between bubbles is controlled at the compressor, the average time between bubbles being about 7 seconds for the breakwater at Dover. The interval is shortened as the size of the waves increases.

The Dover breakwater uses six 500-cu-ft-per-min compressors which are rated at 100 lb per sq in. but are operated at 30 lb per sq in. because high pressures are not needed. The cost of setting up the breakwater in England, exclusive of the compressors, was reported to be about $85 per foot, and the operating expense for one line is about $2 an hour, which is a very reasonable cost.

A submerged reef-type breakwater is a barrier which has its top at or below the still-water level. The breakwater causes some of the wave energy to be reflected out to sea and, in addition, if high enough, causes the wave to break with a dissipation of energy.

The American Society of Civil Engineers published in March, 1959, in the *Journal* of the Waterways and Harbors Division, vol. 85, no. WW 1, part 1, paper 1979, by C. M. Snyder, entitled Model Study of a Hydraulic Breakwater over a Reef. Experimental tests were made in the laboratory to determine wave attenuations without the submerged reef in place and then for various combinations of the submerged reef and hydraulic breakwater, i.e., varying the location of the jets with respect to the submerged reef and varying the height and width ratio of the reef. The following conclusions were reached.

1. Shallow-water waves in the laboratory studies can be attenuated by the use of hydraulic-jet-induced currents; however, the power required to attenuate such waves is relatively high, and the cost to operate such a breakwater would be prohibitive in a prototype installation.

2. The large power and flow rate required for a prototype installation would make such an installation almost physically impossible to construct.

3. The use of the combination of jets with a submerged reef increases the efficiency of the jets; however, the increased efficiency obtained would not justify combining the jets with a submerged reef to form a practical breakwater system, except possibly as a wartime emergency.

4. For a practical type of hydraulic breakwater, the energy required to attenuate a wave would be of the same order of magnitude as the energy lost by the wave.

It is interesting to note that the prototype values of jet discharge and power requirements were computed using Froude's modulus.

The experimental work and full-scale installations cannot help but further the use of pneumatic and hydraulic breakwaters. However, from a practical standpoint their use appears to be limited to secondary installations such as (1) the quieting of the water at the entrance to harbors, (2) the improvement of conditions inside harbors, (3) the improvement of offshore loading conditions, and (4) the creation of temporary sheltered areas to permit landing on exposed beaches. Their limitation appears to stem from the fact that at best they only produce partial attenuation of the waves, and even this is very sensitive to wave height and length. While the development of better equipment and methods for the application of the air or water streams for calming the waves may lower the cost of operation to a point which will make the pneumatic breakwater economical over a wider range of uses, it is doubtful if it will ever become a major element in the permanent formation and protection of large harbors.

4.13 Floating Breakwaters

A sheltered area may be required as a harbor for the protection of ships or beach-landing craft so that personnel or cargo may be transferred to the shore. One method of accomplishing this has been investi-

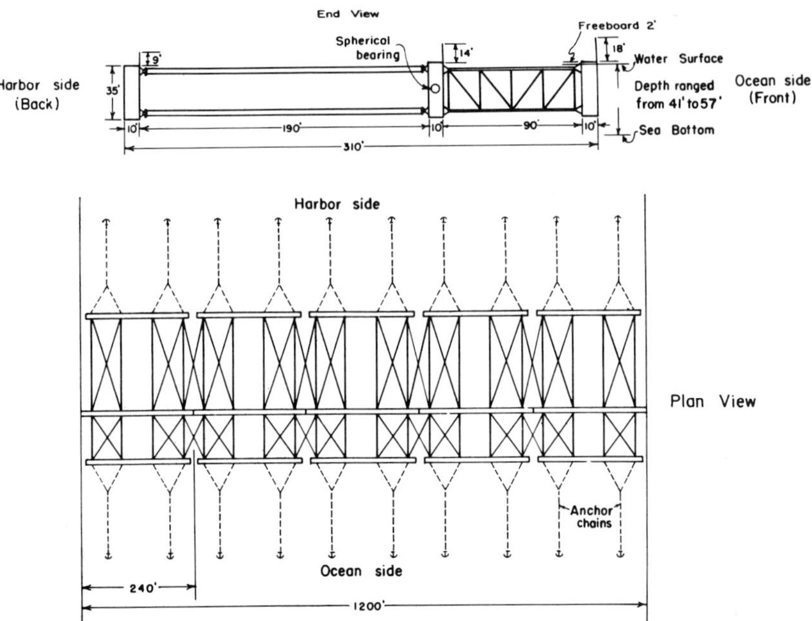

FIG. 4.57 Arrangement of floating breakwater. (*From report of Beach Erosion Board, September,* 1957.)

gated by the Beach Erosion Board which in 1952 was requested by the United States Navy, Bureau of Yards and Docks, to perform certain tests on a particular design of a floating breakwater at the California Institute of Technology. The results of these tests were given in a report by the Beach Erosion Board in September, 1957.

The prototype floating breakwater, for which the model was constructed, consisted of five sections, each 240 ft long, forming a breakwater with a total length of 1,200 ft. Figure 4.57 shows the arrangement of the floating breakwater, and Fig. 4.58 is an isometric view of one of the five sections. Structural steel was used for its construction.

The front and center bulkheads of each section were held in position relative to each other by four rigid trusses, 90 ft long, which constrained them to move as a unit. The center and rear bulkheads of each section were joined by eight pin-connected struts, 190 ft long, which allowed the rear bulkhead to move vertically independent of the other two, but constrained it to the same angular departure from the vertical as that of the other two bulkheads. The bulkheads were cross-braced against relative longitudinal motion. The sections were fastened to one another at the center bulkhead to form a continuous breakwater, a spherical bearing surface being provided at the ends of the center bulkhead. Each section was anchored with two anchors in front and two in back.

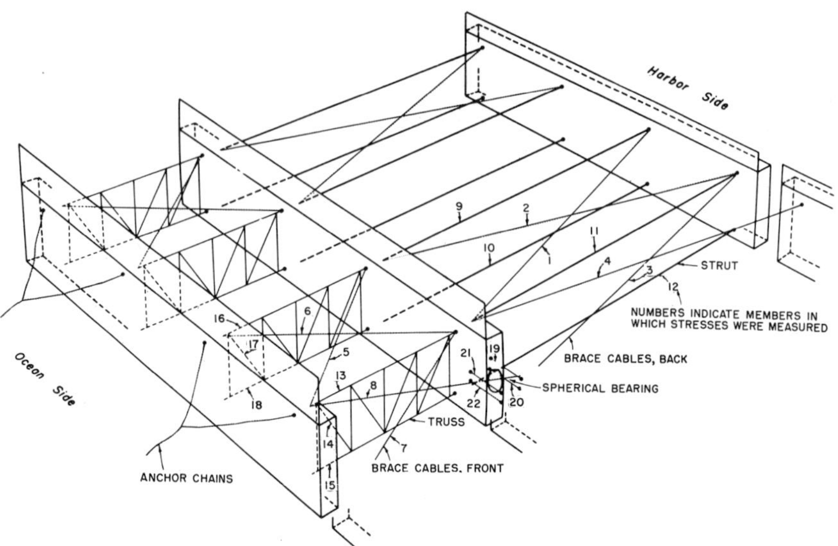

FIG. 4.58 Isometric view of a section of floating breakwater. (*From report of Beach Erosion Board, September, 1957.*)

The report of the Beach Erosion Board indicates that the breakwater was effective in reducing wave height (75 to 90 per cent) for wave periods of less than 8.5 (prototype) seconds and water depths from 41 to 53 (prototype) ft. The efficiency drops off rapidly with an increase in wave period beyond 8.5 seconds, or where the wave length approximates the width of the breakwater from front to back. The forces required to hold the breakwater in place against the larger waves (greater than 9 or 10 ft) exceeded 200,000 lb per anchor chain, and the stresses in some of the brace cables and struts exceeded 2 million lb with waves 9 ft high (prototype). These stresses appear to be beyond present practical design limits.

Another observation in the model tests was that each wave tends to move the breakwater in the direction in which the wave is traveling. If the stress in the anchor cable is not enough to bring the breakwater back to its original position between waves, the anchor chain soon becomes nearly straight, resulting in large stresses in the anchor chain of the model. In the prototype structure this would no doubt result in broken chains or dragging anchors.

Judging from the results of the tests it is doubtful that this type of breakwater will have much practical application, as it is not only costly to construct, but its installation raises an uncertainty as to whether it will remain in its anchored position over a period of time and under varying wave conditions. A pulling of the anchors or a failure in any of the members would probably result in the complete destruction of the breakwater in a short time. Its main applicability may be in its use to provide a temporary arbor for a short duration of time to permit the loading or unloading of a vessel, close to shore where docking facilities are lacking. Even here its use appears to be limited.

Chapter 5 WHARVES, PIERS, BULKHEADS, DOLPHINS, AND MOORINGS

5.1 Introduction

A *dock* is a general term used to describe a marine structure for the mooring or tieing up of vessels, for loading and unloading cargo, or for embarking and disembarking passengers. More specifically a dock is referred to as a pier, wharf, bulkhead, or, in European terminology, a jetty, quay, or quay wall. In Europe, where there are large variations in tide level, it is commonly known as an artificial basin for vessels and is called a *wet dock*. When the basin is pumped out, it is termed a *dry dock*.

A *wharf* or *quay* is a dock which parallels the shore. It is generally contiguous with the shore, but may not necessarily be so. On the other hand a *bulkhead* or *quay wall*, while similar to a wharf and often referred to as such, is backed up by ground, as it derives its name from the very nature of holding or supporting ground in back of it. In many locations where industrial plants are to be built adjacent to water transportation, the ground will be low and marshy and it is therefore necessary to fill this in, which is often done by dredging the adjacent waterway, creating a navigable channel or harbor along the property. To retain the made ground which will now be at a much higher elevation along the waterway, a bulkhead is usually installed. This or a part of its length may be used as a wharf for docking vessels, by the addition of mooring appurtenances, paving, and facilities for handling and storing cargo. It is then termed a *bulkhead wharf*.

A *pier* or *jetty* is a dock which projects into the water. Sometimes it is referred to as a *mole* and in combination with a breakwater it is termed a *breakwater pier*. As contrasted to a wharf, which can be used for docking on one side only, a pier may be used on both sides, although there are instances where only one side is used owing to either the physical conditions of the site or the lack of need for additional berthing space.

A pier may be more or less parallel to the shore and connected to it by a mole or trestle, generally at right angles to the pier. In this case it is commonly referred to as a *T-head pier* or *L-shaped pier,* depending upon whether the approach is at the center or at the end.

Dolphins are marine structures for mooring vessels. They are commonly used in combination with piers and wharves to shorten the length of these structures and are a principal part of the fixed-mooring-berth type of installation now being used extensively in bulk cargo loading and unloading installations. Also, they are used for tying up ships and for transferring cargo from one ship to another when moored along both sides of the dolphins. Dolphins are of two types: breasting and mooring.

Breasting dophins are usually the larger of the two types, as they are designed to take the impact of the ship when docking and to hold the ship against a broadside wind. Therefore, they are provided with fenders to absorb the impact of the ship and to protect the dolphin and the ship from damage. They usually have bollards or mooring posts to take the ship's lines, particularly springing lines for moving the ship along the dock or holding it against the current. These lines are not very effective in a direction normal to the dock, particularly when the ship is light, and, therefore, to hold the ship against a broadside wind blowing in a direction away from the dock, additional dolphins must be provided off the bow and stern, located some distance in back of the face of the dock. These are called *mooring dolphins* and are not designed for the impact of the ship, as they are located in back of the face of the dock where they will not be hit. Mooring dolphins, located about 45° off the bow and stern, and so that the mooring lines will be not less than 200 ft nor more than 400 ft long, are most effective if only two mooring dolphins are to be used. The largest ships may require two additional dolphins, off the bow and stern, and these are usually located so that the mooring lines will be normal to the dock, which makes them most effective in holding the ship against an offshore wind. Mooring dolphins are provided with bollards or mooring posts and with capstans when heavy lines are to be handled. The maximum pull on a single line will usually not exceed 50 tons, or 100 tons on a single bollard if two lines are used.

A *fixed mooring berth* is a marine structure consisting of dolphins for tying up the ship and a platform for supporting the cargo-handling equipment. The platform is usually set back 5 to 10 ft from the face of the dolphins so that the ship will not come in contact with it and, therefore, it does not have to be designed to take the impact of the ship when docking.

Moorings for ships consist of ground tackle placed in fixed positions for attaching the ship's lines. Each unit of ground tackle will consist of one or more anchors with chain, sinker, and buoy to which the ship's line is attached. These mooring units are usually located so as to take the bow and stern lines and, if the ship is large, one or more breasting lines. For some moorings, where the wind is in one direction, the ship may use its own bow anchor and the fixed tackle off the bow may be omitted.

5.2 Factors Controlling Selection of Type of Dock

A dock is usually constructed to serve a definite use. Its main function may be to handle passengers or general cargo or a combination of both; or it may be required to handle a specific type of cargo, particularly bulk cargo such as oil, ore, cement, and grain. The function which it is to serve will be of paramount importance in selecting the type of dock to be used. However, there are other factors which will enter into the determination of the type of dock to be constructed, such as whether a temporary or permanent installation is required, the size of ships to use the dock, the direction of waves and wind, soil conditions, particularly if dredging is to be considered, and last but of considerable importance—the determination of the most economical type of construction.

Municipal docks will usually be piers or wharves projecting out from or paralleling the shore, respectively. Finger piers are generally preferred as they provide berths on both sides, or double the berthing space for the same length of wharf. However, in some locations the slope of the bottom is so steep that a pier cannot be projected out from the shore without having the outshore end in water so deep that foundations are either unpractical or very expensive. A wharf may be found to be less expensive under this condition. In some locations shallow water may exist for some distance offshore and it may be found cheaper to place the pier out in deep water where little or no dredging will be required. For this condition T-head or L-shaped piers, with approach trestles from shore, as shown in Fig. 5.1, will be found suitable and economical, particularly for bulk cargo handling as the approach trestle will be a relatively cheap type of construction because of the light loads which it usually has to support.

Oil docks and some forms of bulk-handling cargo docks are of lighter construction than general cargo-handling docks, as they do not require warehouses, nor do they have to support railroad tracks or extensive cargo-handling equipment. Since the main products handled over oil docks are usually unloaded at fixed points and transported by pipelines, the required area of solid deck is very much reduced, as are the width and length of the dock, if supplemented by dolphins to take the bow and stern mooring lines. For this reason, a full-length pier or wharf is not economical or essential, and this together with the trend in recent years to the use of larger and deeper draft tankers has resulted in the adoption of the *fixed mooring berth.* This type of construction is economical because the large mooring forces, which the large ships impose upon the dock, can be concentrated at certain definite points, i.e., the pull of the mooring lines can be taken by dolphins off the bow and stern of the vessel and by breasting dolphins each side of the fixed platform. The breasting dolphins also keep the ship away from the platform and take the impact of the ship when docking.

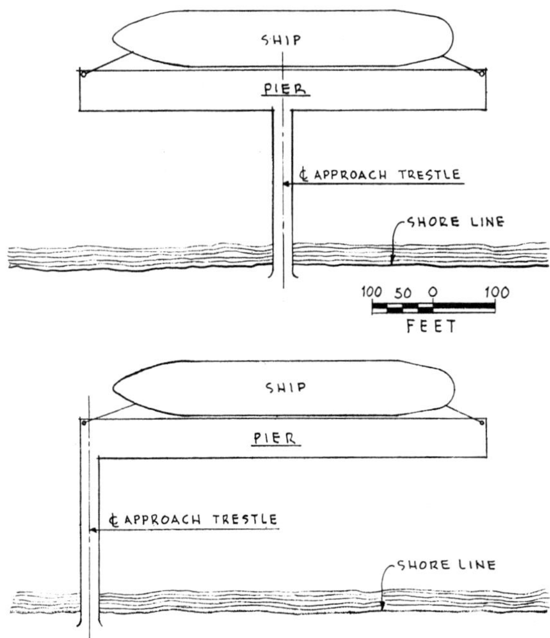

FIG. 5.1 Typical T-head and L-shaped piers.

In some locations it is impossible or not economical to provide a pier, wharf, or fixed mooring berth owing to site conditions or the deep draft of some of the recently constructed supertankers and ore carriers, in which case an offshore mooring may be provided and the cargo transferred to shore either by lighters, long conveyors, or ropeways or by submarine pipeline, if the product is a liquid such as oil, gasoline, and molasses.

Direction of waves and wind may have a bearing on the type of dock selected. In general, the dock should not be broadside to the prevailing wave front and, therefore, if the terminal is in an exposed location, and the wave front is generally paralleling the shore, a wharf type of dock may have to be ruled out. Also, all things being equal, it is better to have the ship anchored parallel to the direction of prevailing winds or, if this can not be accomplished, so that the wind is holding the ship off the dock.

Soil conditions will, of course, have an important bearing on the type of dock selected. The bottom may be more favorable in close to shore, thereby favoring a wharf or bulkhead installation. However, rock may be encountered which would make it very costly to obtain the required depth of water along the dock. In such a case a pier with an approach trestle or mole may be the solution to eliminate the need for costly excavation.

5.3 Types and Materials of Construction

The construction of wharves, piers, bulkheads, and fixed mooring berths falls generally into two broad classifications: (1) docks of open construction with their decks supported by piles or cylinders, and (2) docks of closed or solid construction, such as sheet-pile cells, bulkheads, cribs, caissons, and gravity (quay) walls.

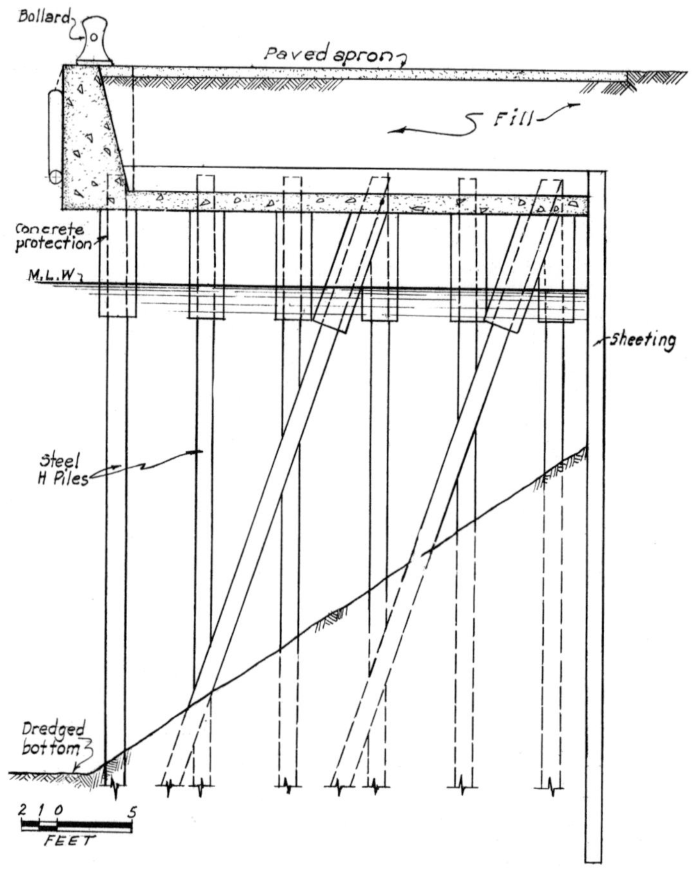

FIG. 5.2 Relieving-platform-type wharf.

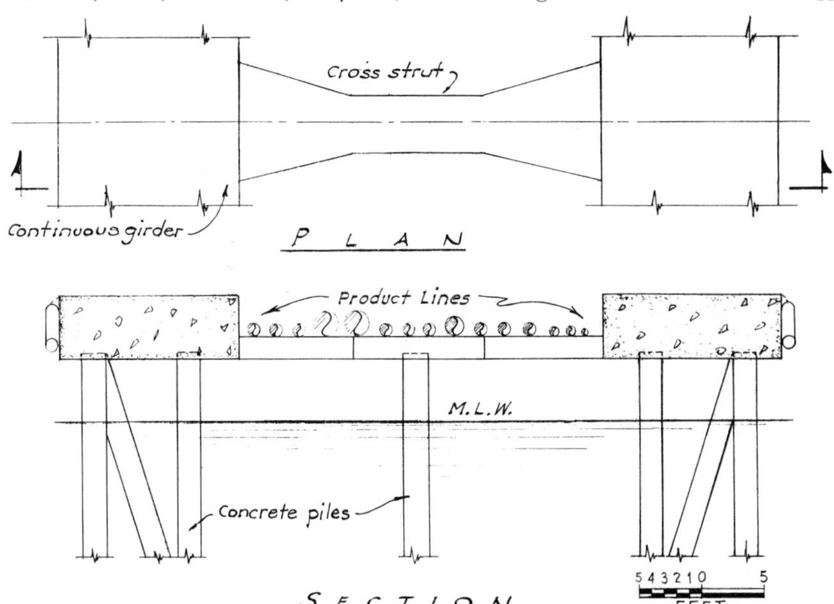

FIG. 5.3 Oil pier of skeleton construction.

Docks of open construction may be further subdivided into what are commonly referred to as (1) high-level decks and (2) relieving-type platforms in which the main structural slab is below the finished deck and the space between is filled to provide additional weight for stability, as shown in Fig. 5.2. High-level decks usually have a solid deck slab, but for oil piers, the slab may be of skeleton construction, being omitted at the pipeway, as shown in Fig. 5.3.

In the *open type of construction* quite prevalent in the construction of piers in the Western Hemisphere, the deck may be of wood, usually creosoted, or of reinforced concrete or a combination of concrete and steel or wood. Figure 5.4 shows a typical type of poured-in-place concrete deck construction. Piles are located in transverse rows or bents and are capped by concrete girders which distribute the load to the piles from the deck framing. The latter consists of a slab of T-beam construction which is poured monolithically with the transverse pile girders. Longitudinal beams are placed at points of concentrated loads, such as under railroad and crane rails and warehouse walls. Where concentrated loads do not exist and the bents are not spaced too far apart, the longitudinal beams may be omitted, and a flat slab may be used spanning between the transverse pile-cap girders. In some designs where the piles are spaced closely together, which sometimes results when wood piles are used with their lower loading, the pile cap will become a flat slab. This is particularly de-

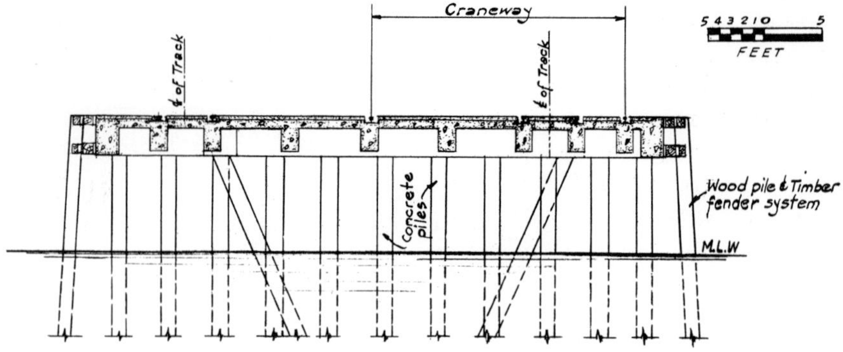

FIG. 5.4 Pier of poured-in-place concrete.

sirable if a relieving-type platform is used and the piles are cut off at or a short distance above low water, otherwise the removal of soffit forms becomes difficult, if not impossible.

In recent years precast- or prestressed-concrete slabs and beams have come into use and have proved to be an economical form of construction when working over water, owing to the large saving in form cost. Pier 40, recently built for the Department of Marine and Aviation, New York City, and leased to the Holland-American Line, consists of 6,000 prestressed-concrete slabs 1 ft thick, about 5 ft wide, and 20 to 25 ft long, resting on a poured-in-place concrete beam and pile-cap system, all supported on steel H piles driven to rock. The sides of the slabs are keyed so that they can be concreted together in place. An asphaltic-concrete wearing surface was placed on top of the slabs. In 1954 pier C in Hoboken, which consists of a prestressed-concrete deck of prestressed stringers and post-tensioned pile-cap bents, was constructed for the Port of New York Authority. The prestressed stringers are flat slabs, 2 ft 5 in. wide, 1 ft 0 in. deep, and 19 ft 6 in. long. The stringers span between the pile caps, which are spaced at 21 ft 6 in. on centers, and are provided with longitudinal keys, that were filled with concrete after the stringers were placed. The pile-cap beams were cast in place, and, to provide lateral compression in the deck slab, they were posttensioned after the poured-in-place stringer keys had set. The concrete deck is supported on steel H piles, with cathodic protection against corrosion. Figure 5.5 shows a plan and section of the deck construction. A somewhat different type of prestressed-concrete deck construction consists of long-span prestressed-concrete I beams and a poured-in-place concrete slab. This type of construction is suitable where the bents may be spaced quite far apart due to the use of heavy supporting members, such as piers or caissons. Figure 5.6 shows a typical cross section of this type deck structure.

The deck may be supported on piles which may be wood (usually creosoted), steel (H section or pipe), or reinforced concrete; or on large cylinders or caissons which may be of steel or reinforced concrete. Recently, prestressed- or posttensioned-concrete piles and cylinders have been used with success, particularly in deep water and where soft bottom conditions exist requiring very long foundation supports. The prestressing or posttensioning simplifies the handling of long piles and reduces cracking, because the compression in the pile from prestressing is made sufficient to overcome the tensile bending stress in handling the pile or to reduce it to an amount which will not cause the concrete to crack.

Creosoted-wood piles and wood-deck construction have been used very extensively in the past. Good examples of this type of construction are the docks along the waterfront of New York. However, these are gradually

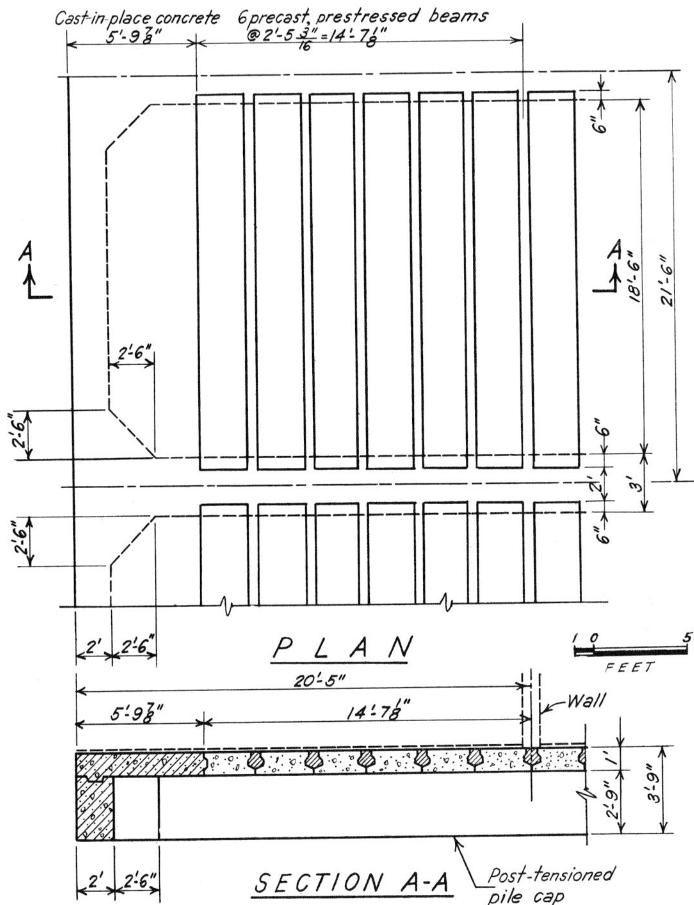

FIG. 5.5 Deck construction at pier C, Hoboken, New Jersey. (*From article by T. O. Blaschke and D. O. Hopkins, Civil Engineering, February,* 1954.)

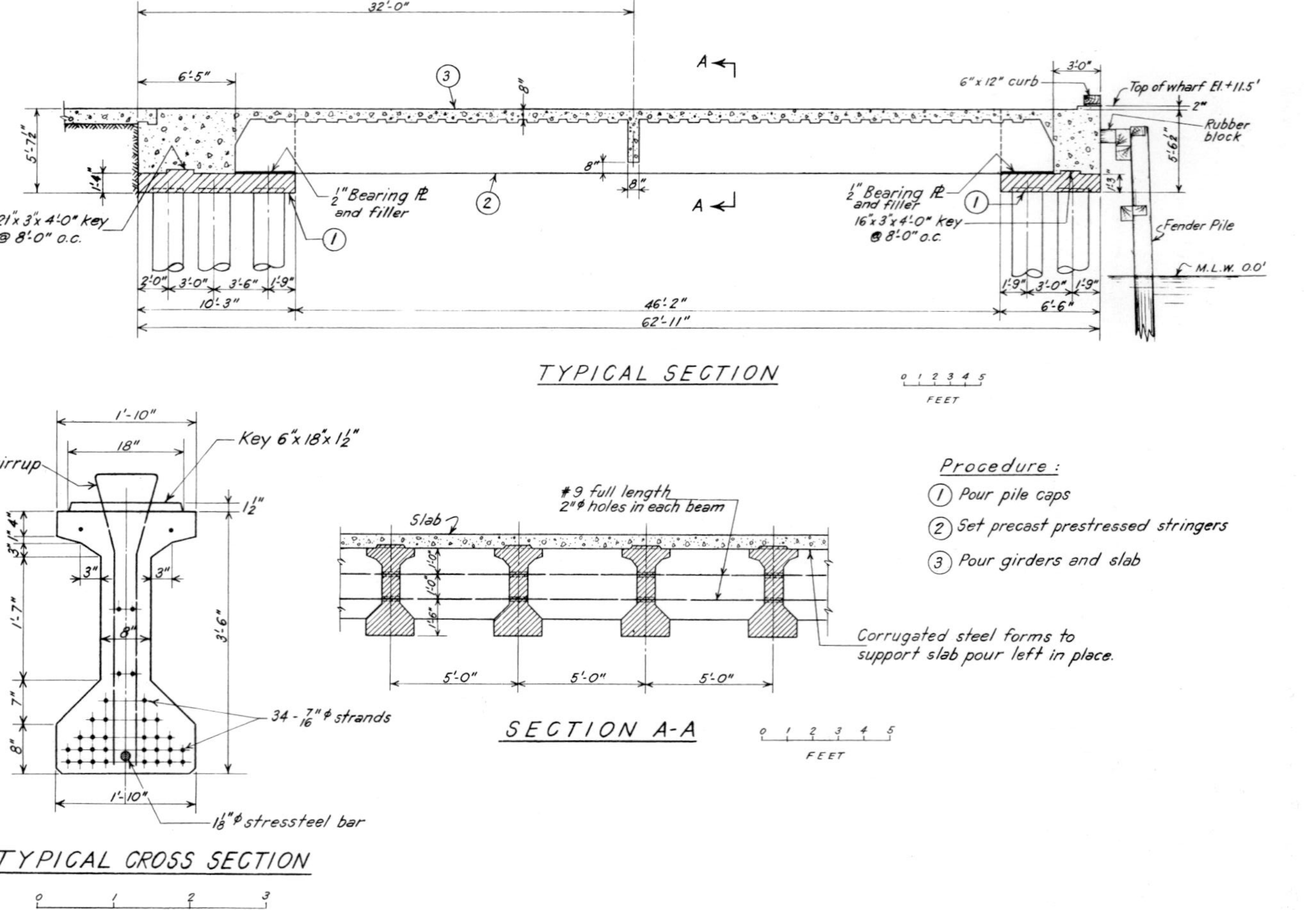

FIG. 5.6 Deck construction at pier 10, Brooklyn, New York. (*Courtesy of the Port of New York Authority.*)

being replaced with stronger and more permanent types of construction. This change has been brought about because of the great advances which have been made in reinforced- and prestressed-concrete design and in the greater use of steel piling which can now be adequately protected from corrosion; also, because of the necessity of designing stronger structures to support the lateral forces from the larger ships and to maintain stability in the increased depth of water required alongside the dock. Wood, how-

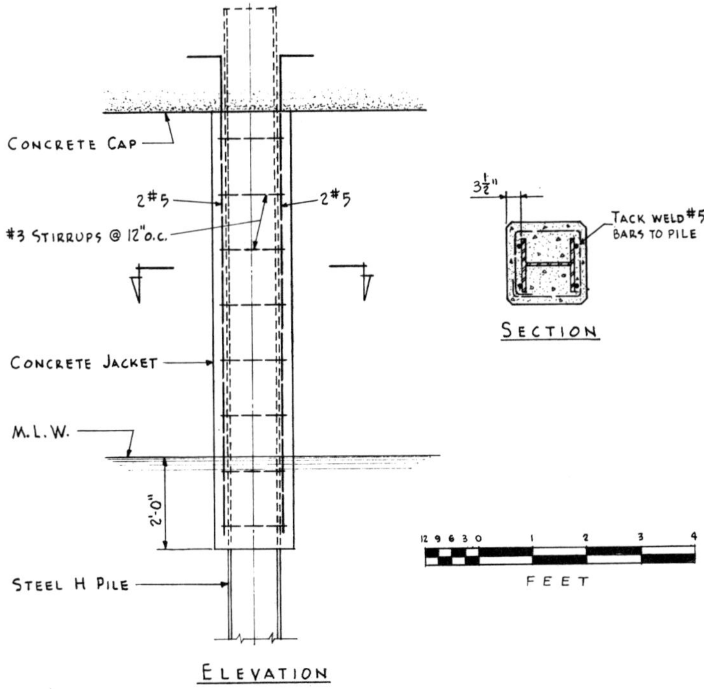

FIG. 5.7 Typical concrete encasement for steel H piles.

ever, is still a very important material in dock construction as it is used quite extensively for small docks, dolphins, fenders, walkways, etc. It is one of the cheapest types of construction although lacking in permanency as compared to reinforced concrete. In certain locations local hardwood or greenheart piles may be substituted for creosoted piles. However, greenheart is not recommended for deck construction as the wood is very hard to work.

Protection of steel piling from corrosion can be accomplished by encasing the pile with concrete from the underside of the deck to 2 ft below low-water level, as shown in Fig. 5.7, which is the area where the most severe corrosion is expected to take place. Below low water, corrosion is usually slow, and except in very corrosive water, may be ignored providing an allowance is made in the design of the piles for loss of area, and the piles are given not less than two coats of bitumastic paint prior to driving. Usually the stress is limited to a maximum of 9,000 lb per sq in., which is considered to provide a reasonable allowance for corrosion, although some building codes specify that an allowance of 1/16 in. be made for corrosion in figuring the cross-section area. Steel-pipe piles which are usually filled with concrete are subject to corrosion on the exterior surface only. Where more severe corrosion is expected, particularly in salt water, cathodic protection may be employed, as described in Sec. 5.16. However,

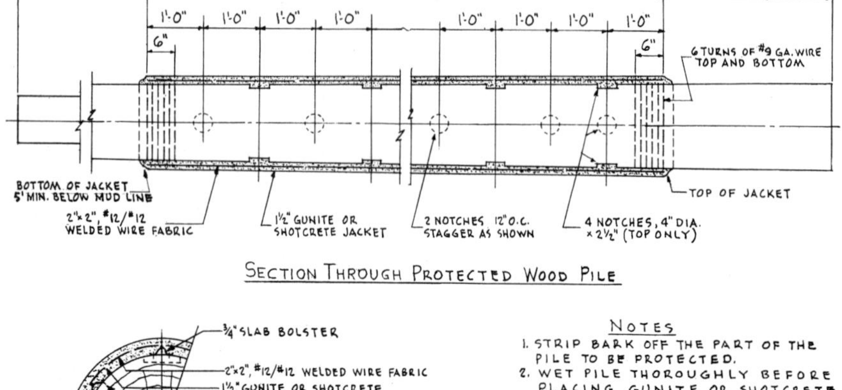

FIG. 5.8 Gunite or Shotcrete protection for wood piles.

there are waters, such as Lake Maracaibo, which are not very saline and which are very corrosive. Under such conditions cathodic protection and paint or other types of protection, other than concrete, are of little value. Good dense concrete made with sulfate-resisting cement is probably the best and most economical material for use in corrosive water.

Where wood piles are subjected to severe marine borer attack, they may be protected by guniting before driving. This has been successfully accomplished without cracking the gunite protection in driving. A satisfactory detail for placing the gunite on the wood pile is shown in Fig. 5.8.

The connection between the deck and the supporting piles or cylinders is of considerable importance. Piles of concrete should be cut off 4 in. above the bottom of the girder or cap, leaving the reinforcement projecting into the cap. Reinforced-concrete piles are sometimes driven with the rods projecting; in which case, if they can be driven or jetted to the specified grade, the piles do not need to be cut off. Steel H piles may be cut off 4 in. above the bottom of the concrete girder and capped with a steel plate or they may project into the girder sufficiently far to transfer the load to the piles in bond. The embedment of the pile has the added advantage of enabling it to take uplift and in fixing the end so as to reduce its unsupported length if it is acting as a long column in deep water. In figuring the bond, the entire surface area of the pile in contact with the concrete is used, but the bond stress should be kept low and should not exceed $0.02 \times f'_c$, where f'_c is the 28-day compressive strength. If the

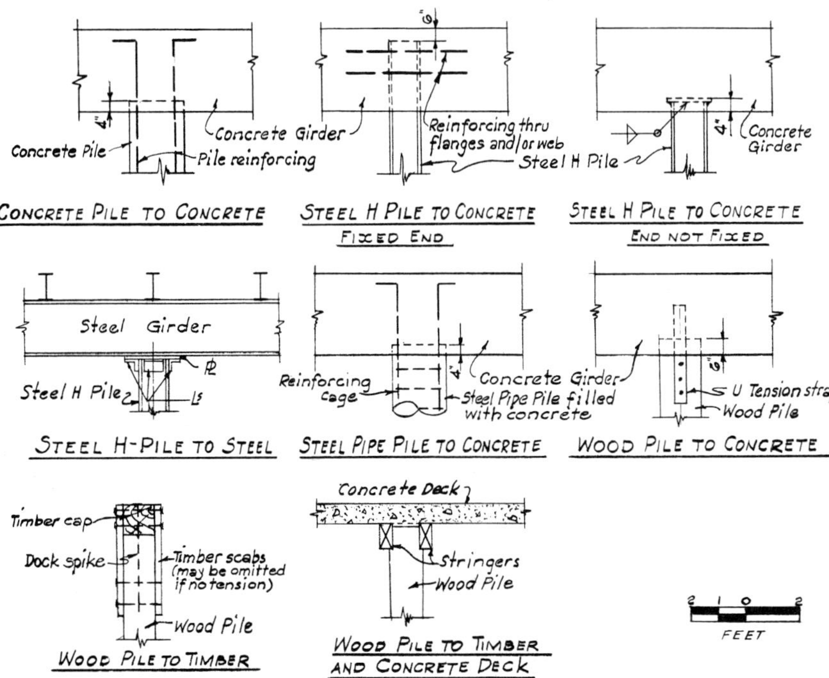

FIG. 5.9 Typical connections of piles to superstructure.

deck is supported by steel beams and girders, the steel pile may be burned off at the elevation of the underside of the steel girder, and the connection made by welding or bolting. Pipe piles or steel cylinders, which are usually filled with concrete, are cut off 4 in. above the bottom of the girder and dowels inserted into the pile, which project into the cap. Wood piles are usually cut off 6 in. above the bottom of the girder or cap, and if they are to take uplift or tension they are anchored into the concrete with a U-shaped strap which is bolted to the pile. If the cap is timber the pile will be connected to it with a drift pin and either wood or steel side plates. However, if the deck is a concrete slab which is supported on wood stringers bolted to the wood piles, the piles will be cut off 4 in. below the top of the stringers. Typical connections discussed above are illustrated in Fig. 5.9.

In the *solid type of dock construction* steel sheet-pile cells are quite commonly used where the depth of water does not exceed 50 ft and the bottom conditions are suitable for the support of gravity-type structures. The cells are generally capped with a concrete slab and bulkhead wall above water level, as shown in Fig. 5.10. Cells utilize flat web-steel piling which acts in tension to retain the fill inside, thereby forming a gravity wall of sufficient weight and shearing strength to resist overturning or sliding at the base. Cells may be circular in shape, or they may have circular ends and straight walls. The circular type is used more often as each individual cell may be filled to the top and is stable in itself. Therefore, it may be used as a base in which to construct the next cell.

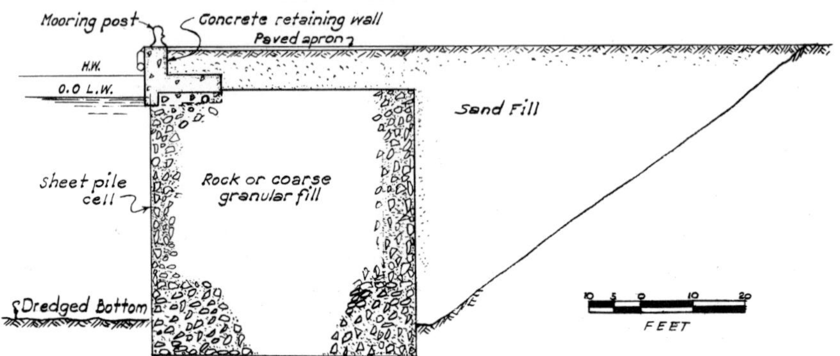

FIG. 5.10 Solid-type bulkhead wharf using sheet-pile cells.

Sheet-pile bulkheads may be constructed of wood, steel, or concrete sheet piling which may be supported by tie rods attached to an anchor wall or anchor piles located a safe distance in back of the face of the bulkhead, as shown in Fig. 5.11, or by batter piles along the rear of the piling, as shown in Fig. 5.12. In shallow installations and where the bottom is of good supporting value the sheet piling may be driven deep enough to act as a cantilever without benefit of additional support.

Rock-filled timber cribs were used quite extensively in the early construction of piers and wharves, particularly on the Great Lakes. The top of the timber crib is usually terminated at low-water level, and dock walls above are constructed of masonry or concrete to retain a fill on which the dock paving is placed. Figure 5.13 shows a typical section through a timber-crib wharf. One of the main criticisms of this type of construction has been the settlement which has taken place where these heavy cribs have been founded on soft bottoms. It is not unusual to scan along the elevation of the side of a pier and note a considerable difference in the elevation of the top of the cribs from the inshore to the outshore end of the pier.

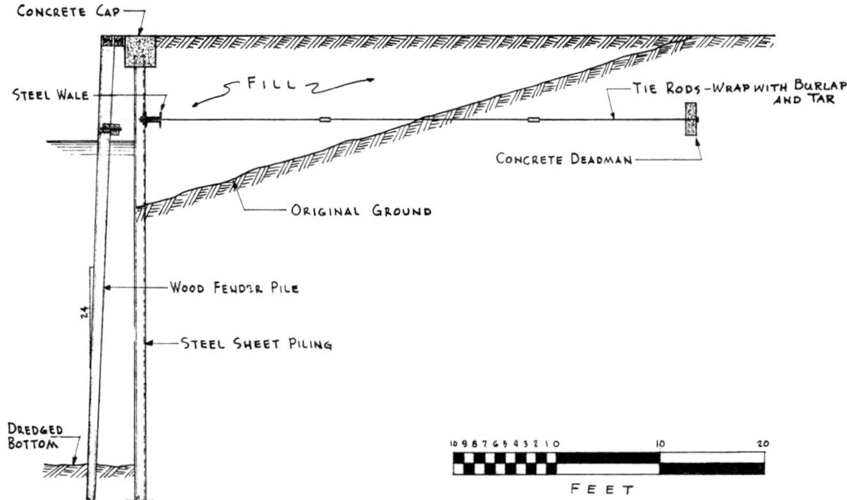

FIG. 5.11 Sheet-pile bulkhead supported by tie rods and anchor wall.

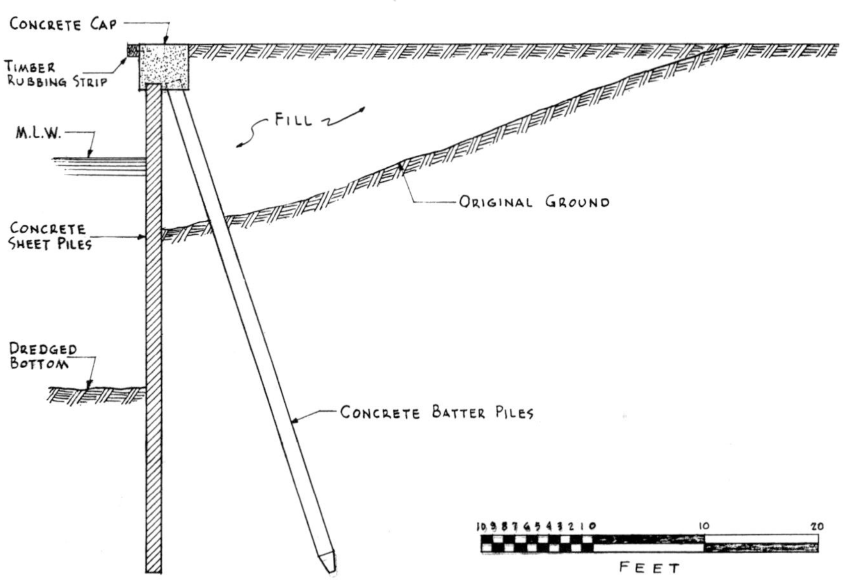

FIG. 5.12 Sheet-pile bulkhead supported by batter piles.

Concrete caissons have been used quite extensively for the construction of wharves or quay walls, especially in Europe. A striking example of this type of construction is the 7,500-ft-long quay built at Southampton, England, in 1934, which consists of 146 concrete caissons sunk to from 7 ft to 30 ft below dredged bottom. Caissons may have open wells and cutting edges so that they may be sunk below the dredged bottom in order to obtain a firm support, or they may have a closed bottom, as shown in Fig. 5.14, in which case they are lowered on to a prepared bottom usually consisting of a gravel or crushed-stone bed or leveling course. The latter type of caisson is usually filled with rock or granular material so as to provide added weight for stability. Caissons are generally constructed of such height that their tops will be at or a little above low-water level and are surmounted by a gravity dock wall of cast-in-place concrete. This permits

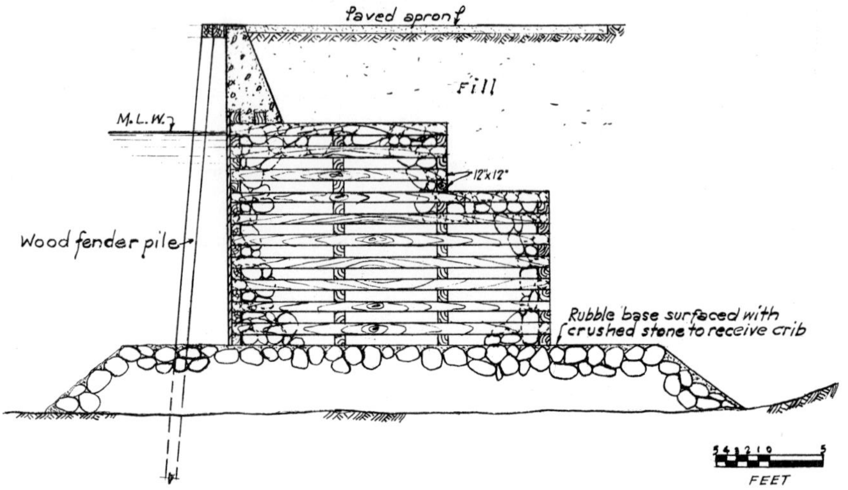

FIG. 5.13 Typical timber-crib wharf.

the upper part of the dock face to be constructed to true alignment and grade, as well as enabling provision to be made for the attachment of the fender system, backing log, etc., and the installation of railroad track, crane rails, utilities, and foundations, if required, in the fill above the caissons and in back of the dock wall or parapet, before laying the apron paving.

Gravity-quay walls are usually constructed of heavy precast-concrete blocks. This is a type of construction which is associated with European practice in dock construction, and is very seldom used in the United States. A typical section through a quay wall of the type most commonly used is shown in Fig. 5.15. The individual blocks of concrete may weigh from 50 to 200 tons and are laid so as to give the wall a slight backward inclination. The bottom course of blocks is usually laid on a rubble base and a rock fill is placed in back of the wall so as to reduce the lateral earth pressure. Above low-water level the wall or parapet is usually constructed of cast-in-place concrete.

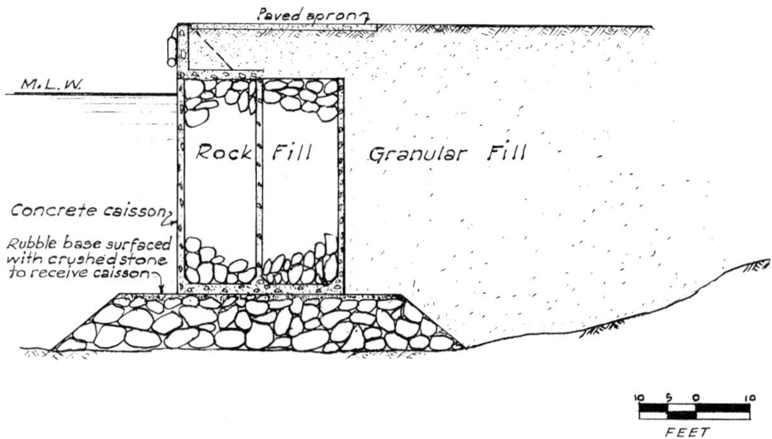

FIG. 5.14 Solid-type bulkhead wharf using concrete caissons with closed bottom.

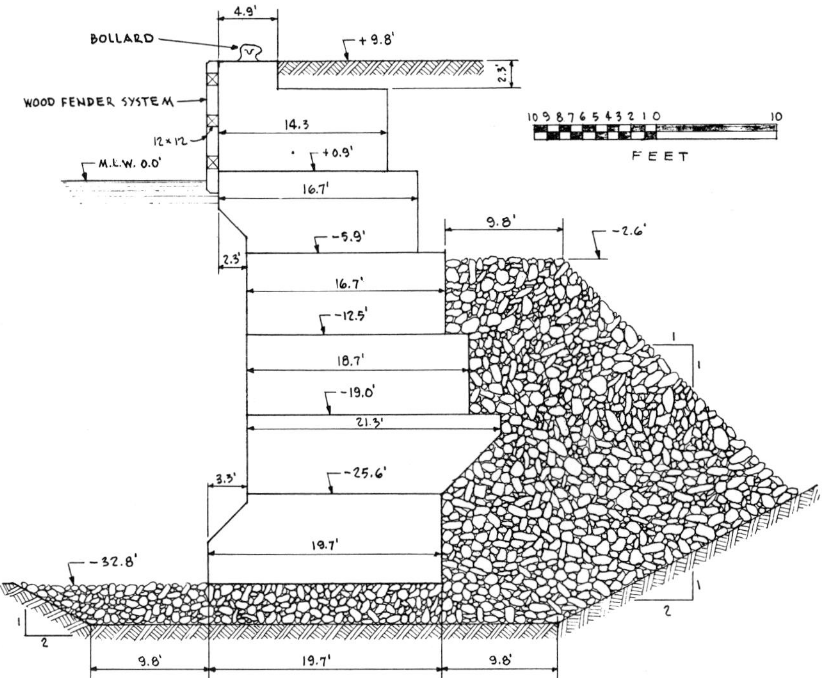

FIG. 5.15 Quay wall constructed of precast-concrete blocks at Zonguldak, Turkey. (*Courtesy of Netherlands Harbor Works Co., Ltd.*)

Table 5.1 Principal Dimensions of Ocean

Port	Facility	Type	Pier—Wharf—Wharf berth			
			Length, ft	Width, ft	Width of aprons, ft	Number of apron railroad tracks
Boston	Mystic Pier 1	Pier	890—south 620—north	468—east	25—south 25—north 20—east	1 1 ...
	Hoosac Pier 1	Pier	520—west 530—east	490—south	25—west 25—east 20—south	1 1 ...
	East Boston Pier 1	Pier	603	390	25—west 25—east 20—south	1 1 ...
New York	Pier 57, North River	Pier	750	150	12—upper and lower	...
	Pier C, Hoboken	Pier	700	328	25—upper 20—lower 20—face	1 ... ...
	Waterman Terminal (Port of Newark)	Marginal wharf	1,650 550	... ...	50 50	2 ...
Norfolk	Pier N	Pier	1,100	390	35—upper 35—lower 25—face	2 2 ...
Wilmington, N.C.	State docks	Marginal wharf	1,500	...	46	2
Savannah	State docks	Marginal wharf	2,047	...	46 35	2 1
Mobile	State docks—berths 6, 7, and 8	Marginal wharf	1,012 550	... ...	31 31	... ...
Long Beach	Berths 6 and 7 (municipal wharves)	Marginal wharf	1,200 (2 berths)	...	52	2
	Pier C—typical berth (municipal wharves)	Slip wharf	600 (berth)	...	45	2
Los Angeles	Berths 195 and 198 (municipal wharves)	Marginal wharf	1,650	...	38	2
San Francisco	Mission Rock Terminal (pier 50)	Double pier	1,480—lower 1,100 plus 582—upper	1,000—face	Open-face 31-29—upper 31-29—lower	2 2 2
Seattle	Pier 42	Double pier	1,019	396	32—north 32—south 40—face	2 2 ...

NOTES: † Non-inclusive listing.
‡ All transit sheds one-story except where otherwise noted under "Remarks."
§ Excludes track areas—includes aisles and other non-storage areas.
SOURCE: Maritime Administration, Division of Port Development, September, 1956. Published *Marine News*, June, 1959.

Terminals Constructed in the Last Decade †

Transit sheds ‡				Individual berth length, ft	Area § of transit shed per berth, sq ft	Remarks
Length, ft	Width, ft	Clear inside piling height, ft	Inside area, gross sq ft			
608	418	....	254,144	890 620 468	84,714	3 railroad tracks in depressed well in shed
480	462	....	221,760	520 530 490	73,920	2 railroad tracks in depressed well in shed
575	340	....	196,000	603	98,000	2 railroad tracks in depressed well in shed
700	125	28.5	175,000 (2 floors)	750	87,500	Two-story transit shed—Grace Line combination cargo and passenger terminal with passenger accommodations in headhouse
680	283	20	192,000	700	96,000	2 railroad tracks in depressed well in shed (temporarily filled in and paved to grade of shed floor)
1,020/460 460	200 200	20 20	367,000 (both sheds)	550	91,750	2 railroad tracks at platform level at rear of larger shed. Open berth not considered in this compilation
1,050	320	32	336,000	550	84,000	2 railroad tracks in depressed well in shed. Provision for semiportal gantry cranes on upper pier apron
450 450	162 162	16 16	145,800 (both sheds)	750	72,900	2 railroad tracks at platform level at rear of both sheds Provision for full-portal gantry cranes on wharf apron
450 450 360	165 165 165	22.5 22.5 22.5	74,250 74,250 59,400	680	2 @ 74,250 1 @ 59,400	2 railroad tracks at platform level at rear of all sheds Provision for full-portal gantry cranes on wharf apron
1,500	00	21	312,000	2 @ 506 1 @ 550	104,000	2 railroad tracks at platform level at rear of shed
1,152	200	Up to 33	230,400	600	115,200	2 railroad tracks at platform level at rear of shed
600	150	Up to 33	90,000	600	90,000	2 railroad tracks at platform level at rear of shed
1,208	200	....	241,600 (1st floor)	2 @ 825 or 3 @ 550	120,800 or 80,500	Matson Navigation Co. combination cargo and passenger terminal 2 floors and mezz. 704 lin ft first floor (140,800 sq ft), used solely for cargo; 504 lin ft (100,800 sq ft), used for passengers and general cargo. Upper floor—passengers only 3 railroad tracks at platform level at rear of shed
640 640 612 700	110 110 140 140	17 17 17 17	70,000 70,000 85,000 97,000	2 @ 740 1 @ 582 1 @ 1,100 or 2 @ 550	2 @ 70,000 1 @ 85,000 1 @ 97,000 or 2 @ 48,500	Open berths not considered in this compilation. Railroad tracks at platform level at rear of all sheds. 80 ft between edges of platforms at rear of two inshore (parallel) sheds
981 981	110 110	16 16	107,900 107,900	510	53,950	5 railroad tracks at platform level between sheds. 96 ft between edges of platforms at rear of sheds. This pier was built in 1942

5.4 Design Considerations

These will consist of, first, the determination of the size and layout of the pier or wharf; secondly, the general type of design to be used; and thirdly, the loads to be used in the design.

Size and Layout of General Cargo Terminals. Bulk shipping terminals, including berths for tankers, are covered in Chap. 8. These vary with the type of material and the machinery and other facilities required for the

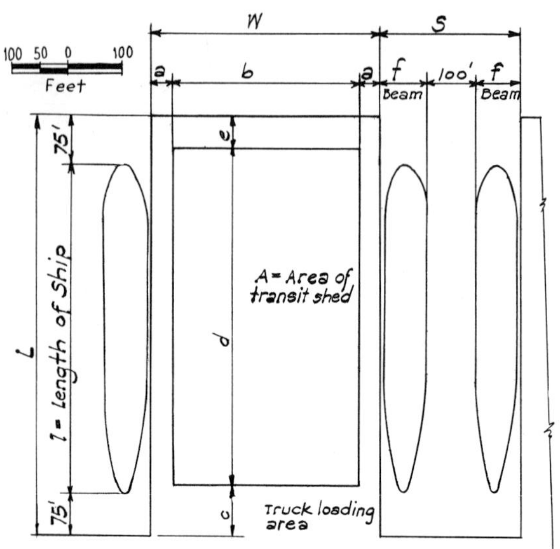

FIG. 5.16 Dimensions of two-berth pier and slip. $A = 90{,}000$ sq ft per berth; $L = l + 150$ ft; $W = 2a + b$; $S = 2f + 100$ ft; $d = L - (c + e)$; $b = A/d$; for a, c, and e see Fig. 5.19.

particular cargo to be handled. On the other hand general cargo terminals are quite conventional and have changed little over the years, other than to become larger and to place greater emphasis on the handling of cargo by truck, resulting in wider aprons. Because of larger ships with greater cargo capacity, transit sheds have become larger, and the storage height has become greater because of the practice of handling and stacking cargo on pallets by the use of fork-lift trucks and other high-stacking equipment. All of this has resulted in longer and wider piers and wharves. Table 5.1, which is reproduced from a paper written by Howard J. Marsden, chief, Division of Port Development, Maritime Administration, in the June, 1959, issue of *Marine News,* gives the principal dimensions of a number of ocean-going terminals constructed in the last decade.

Figures 5.16 and 5.17 give the dimensions for two- and four-berth piers and slips, respectively. The four-berth slip must be wide enough to maneuver a ship in and out of the inside berth, past ships moored at the outside berths, with the aid of a tug. Figure 5.18 shows the dimensions for a wharf. The area of the transit shed is based on the cargo storage capacity of the ship, based on measurement tons at 40 cu ft to the ton, al-

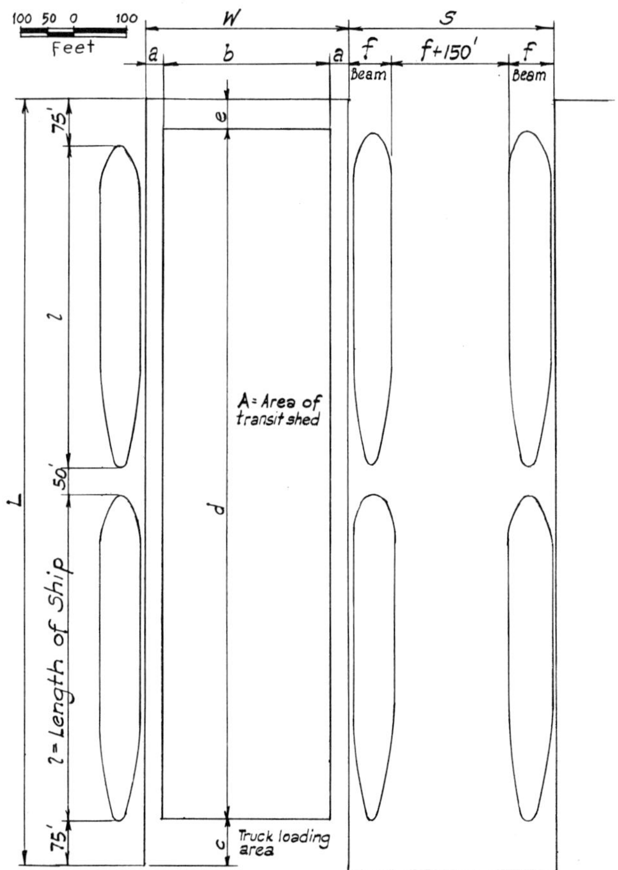

FIG. 5.17 Dimensions of four-berth pier and slip. $A = 90{,}000$ sq ft per berth; $L = 2l + 200$ ft; $W = 2a + b$; $S = 3f + 150$ ft; $d = L - (c + e)$; $b = A/d$; for a, c, and e see Fig. 5.19.

lowing 50 per cent for aisle space and assuming the cargo is piled in the transit shed to a net average height of 13 ft 6 in. For a typical dry-cargo ship an area of 90,000 sq ft has been found to be about the minimum space needed for one berth (see Sec. 6.2). Loading platforms and track areas are not included. The width of apron will depend upon the use of portal or semiportal cranes, and the number of railroad tracks and truck lanes, if any. Figure 5.19 gives the various widths of apron for these different operating conditions.

Referring to Table 3.3, it will be seen that the C-4 class cargo vessels are the largest afloat. However, the Mariner class, although not as heavy, has the greater length of 563 ft 8 in. Based on this size vessel the length of the two-berth pier in Fig. 5.16 would become 713 ft 8 in. (700 ft nominal) and the width would vary between 340 ft and 420 ft depending upon the width of apron. The width of slip would have to be 252 ft.

A departure from the more conventional pier and single-transit-shed layout is the twin-transit-shed design, in which the two sheds have loading platforms along their rear and are separated by a depressed area for the use of trucks and railroad cars. Access to the depressed area between

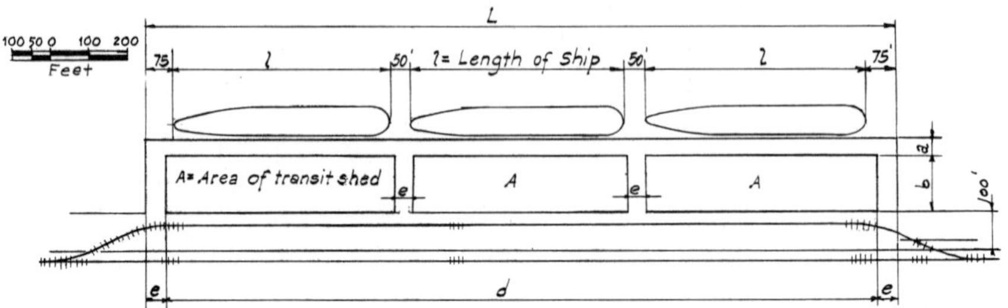

FIG. 5.18 Dimensions of wharf. $A = 90{,}000$ sq ft per berth; $L = 3l + 250$ ft; $d = L - 2e$; $b = 3A/(d - 2e)$; for a and e see Fig. 5.19.

the transit sheds is by means of a ramp at the inshore end of the pier. Access can also be had to the pier apron at the outshore end by means of ramps from the lower level. To provide space for loading and unloading trailer trucks along both platforms and for trucks going in and out of the area, a clear width of between 130 to 140 ft is required. This, of course, increases the width of pier considerably and is generally not economical if the depressed area has to be supported on piles.

Type of design. A pier may be designed as a rigid structure in which the lateral forces are taken by batter piles or by rigid-frame action. However, due to elastic deformation and bending, some movement may take place, but this is usually ignored in absorbing the impact of the ship. Some installations are designed to be flexible so as to absorb the docking impact. Wood-pile clusters are an example of this type of flexibility, as they absorb the energy of impact through the large movement which they are capable of undergoing without permanent distortion taking place. Their use, however, is usually confined to docks for barges and small vessels. Where large vessels are to be berthed against a flexible structure it will have to be designed of structural steel framing and steel piles to provide an adequate resisting force. An example of this type of construction is shown in Fig. 5.20.

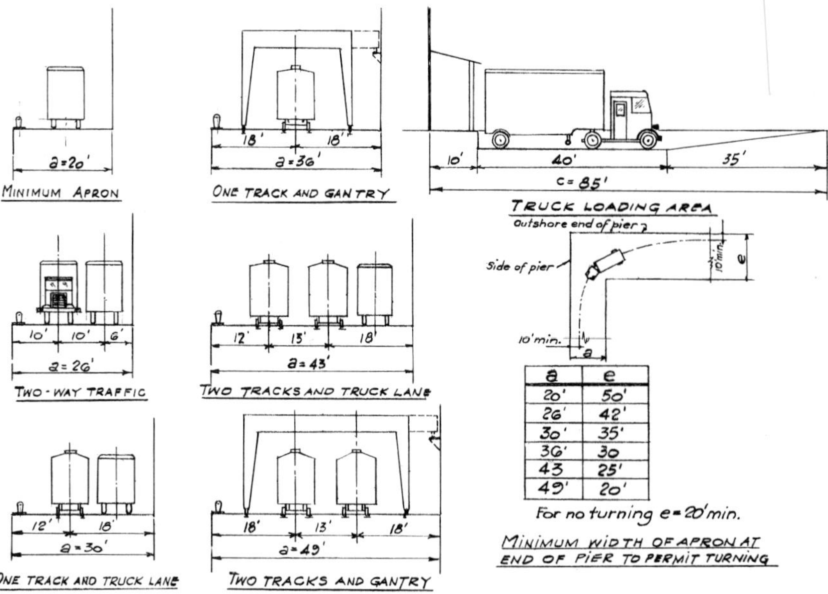

a	e
20'	50'
26'	42'
30'	35'
36'	30
43	25'
49'	20'

FIG. 5.19 Various widths of apron for different operating conditions.

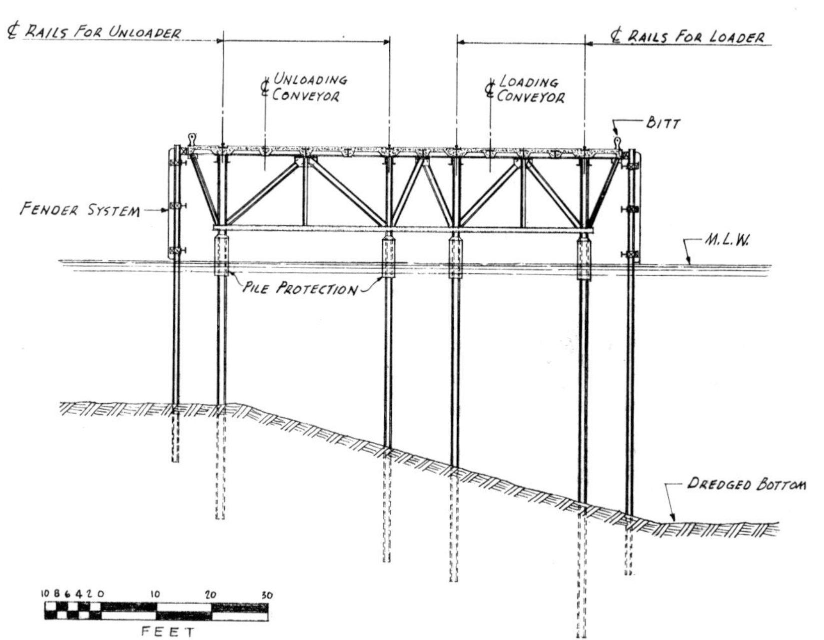

FIG. 5.20 Pier of rigid-frame construction.

Loads to Be Used in Design. When the type of dock and its general construction features have been determined, it will be necessary to establish the lateral and vertical loads for which the dock is to be designed. These will consist of the following.

Lateral loads from the mooring lines pull the ship into or along the dock or hold it against the force of the wind or current. The maximum wind force will equal the exposed area, in square feet, of the broadside of the ship in a light condition, multiplied by the wind pressure in pounds per square foot to which a shape factor 1.3 has been applied, which is a combined factor taking into consideration the reduction due to height and the increase for suction on the leeward side of the ship. The wind force varies with the location but is usually assumed to be not less than 10 nor more than 20 lb per sq ft, corresponding to wind velocities of about 55 to 78 miles per hour, respectively, based on the wind-pressure formula $p = 0.00256v^2$, multiplied by the shape factor 1.3, where p is the pressure in pounds per square foot, and v is the wind velocity in miles per hour. When ships are berthed on both sides of a pier, the total wind force acting on the pier, as a result of wind on the ships, should be increased by 50 per cent to allow for wind against the second ship. The author believes that a wind pressure higher than 20 lb per sq ft against the side of the ship is not warranted because a ship would not remain alongside the dock, in a light condition, in a storm approaching hurricane intensity. The ship would either put to sea or take on ballast, so as to reduce its exposed area to the wind. Wind against the pier structure and a warehouse or transit shed on the pier may be a more severe condition than wind on the ship, as the surface area may be larger and the wind intensity greater. The wind pressure in this case should be figured for the maximum wind velocity in the area and the proper shape factor applied for the type of structure on the pier. This factor may vary between 1.3 and 1.6, and the total wind pressure, in a hurricane area where the wind velocity is figured at 125 miles per hour, may amount to as much as 64 lb per sq ft.

The force of the current in pounds per square foot will equal $w/2g \times v^2$, where w is the weight per cubic foot of water, v is the velocity of the current in feet per second, and g is 32.2 ft per sec per sec. For salt water this results in a pressure per square foot equal to v^2. The velocity of current will usually vary between 1 and 4 ft per sec which will result in a pressure of 1 to 16 lb per sq ft, respectively. This pressure will be applied to the area of the ship below the water line when fully loaded. Since the ship is generally berthed parallel to the current, this force is seldom a controlling factor.

Docking impact is caused by the ship striking the dock when berthing. For the purpose of design the assumption is usually made that the maximum impact to be considered is that produced by a ship fully loaded (displacement tonnage) striking the dock, at an angle of 10° with the face of the dock, with a velocity normal to the dock of 0.25 to 0.5 ft per sec. A few installations have been designed for as much as 1.0 ft per sec but this is considered excessive as it corresponds to a velocity of approach of approximately 3½ knots, at an angle of 10° to the face of the dock, and could damage the ship. Fender systems are designed to absorb the docking energy of impact, and the resulting force to be resisted by the dock will depend upon the type and construction of the fender and the deflection of the dock, if it is designed as a flexible structure. The determination of the energy of impact and resulting force on the structure and a description of the different types of fenders and their energy-absorbing ability will be found in Sec. 5.6.

Earthquake forces will have to be considered if in an area of seismographic disturbance. The horizontal force may vary between 0.025 and 0.10 of the acceleration of gravity g times the mass, applied at its center of gravity, which can be expressed as 0.025 to 0.10 of the weight, respectively. The weight to be used is the total dead load plus one-half of the live load. Unless the dock is of massive or gravity-type construction, the effect on the design will usually be small as the allowable stress, when combined with dead- and live-load stresses, may be increased by 33⅓ per cent. If batter piles are used to take the lateral forces, they will need to be checked to see that they will carry the horizontal earthquake force without increasing the allowable loading by more than 33⅓ per cent; otherwise, additional piles will need to be added.

Vertical loads consist of the dead weight of the structure, termed the *dead load,* and the *live load* which will usually consist of a uniform load and wheel loads from trucks, railroad cars or locomotives, cargo-handling cranes, and equipment. The uniform live load may vary from 250 to 1,000 lb per sq ft of deck area, the smaller figure being used for oil docks and similar structures which handle bulk materials by conveyor or pipeline, where general cargo is of secondary importance. The tendency in recent years has been to design general cargo piers for heavier live loads, ranging from 600 to 800 lb per sq ft. Piers handling heavy metals such as copper ingots may be designed for 1,000 lb or more per sq ft. The uniform live load will control the design of the piles and pile caps, whereas the concentrated wheel loads, including impact, will usually control the design of the deck slab and beams. A reduction of 33⅓ per cent is sometimes made in the uniform live load in figuring the pile loads and in designing the pile caps or girders. This is based on the assumption that the entire deck area of adjoining bays will not be fully loaded at one time.

5.5 Design of Piles and Cylinders for the Support of Docks

General Design. In designing a pile to carry a certain load it is necessary to determine the condition of support at both the top and the bottom because in dock construction the piles have to be designed as long columns. The pile may be considered fixed if its ends are prevented from rotating. This means that for a vertical pile the axis of the pile must

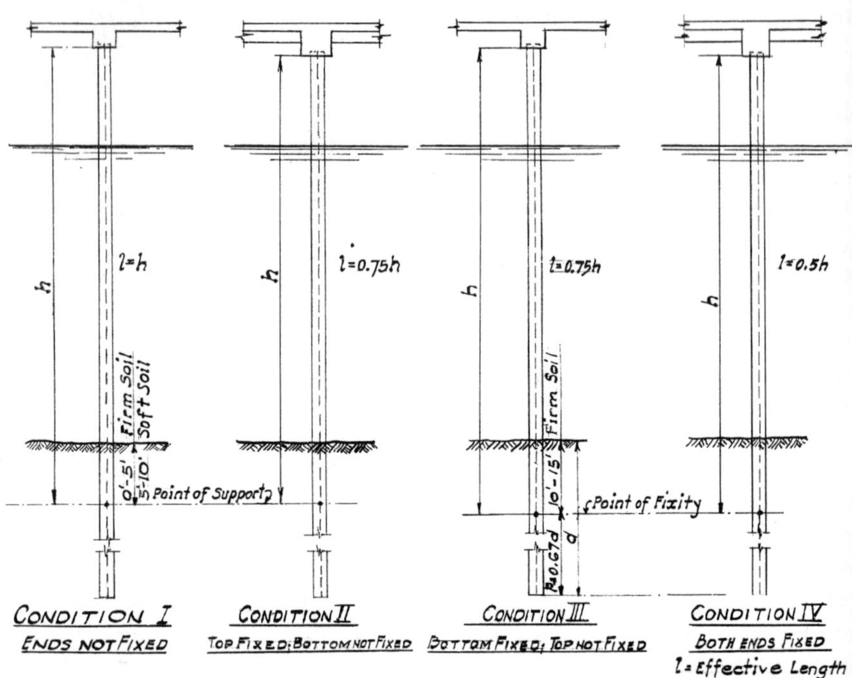

FIG. 5.21 Effective length of pile for various end conditions.

remain vertical at its ends. For fixity at the top of the pile it is essential that the deck be of heavy construction and that the pile be rigidly fastened to the deck either by embedding it, if an H pile, or by extending the reinforcing into the supporting cap or girder, if a concrete pile. To fix the pile at a point not too far below the bottom, the soil must be a firm material such as compact sand or hard clay into which the pile is driven a substantial distance below the point of fixity. The point of fixity in this case is assumed to be 10 to 15 ft below the bottom, and, with both ends fixed, the effective length of the pile is taken to be 0.5 of its length between the points of fixity. If it is a soft bottom, such as silt, a point of fixity would occur, if at all, not much above a depth of 20 to 25 ft below the bottom, whereas the pile may be considered as being supported from buckling at a depth starting 5 to 10 ft below the bottom.

Most soils, even though of relatively low strength, will provide sufficient support to prevent the pile from buckling. If the material is firm, and the pile is not driven sufficiently deep to provide a point of fixity, the pile may be assumed to be supported from 0 to 5 ft below the bottom. In the case of soft rock, hardpan, or hard clay, the support may be taken at the surface, but, for other materials that are less dense, and which may be eroded or disturbed near the surface, the point of support should be assumed 5 ft below the bottom. Therefore, if the pile is fixed at the top but not at the bottom, the effective length for design is 0.75 of its length figured from the point of fixity at the top to the point of support at the bottom. If the deck is of light construction such as wood or light steel, the top of the pile cannot be considered as fixed, and the effective length of the pile then becomes the distance between the point of support at the top (usually the underside of the deck) and the point of support at the bottom. These various conditions are shown in Fig. 5.21. Once the effective length of the pile is determined the allowable load may be figured.

Precast-concrete Piles. These are probably used more extensively for dock construction than any other type of pile. When properly constructed and driven, they provide a very permanent type of construction, even in salt water, without the need of maintenance. Generally, they utilize local materials, except that cement and reinforcement may have to be brought in at some locations. However, they have certain limitations, length being one of the more important ones, since handling stresses and weight become excessive for very long piles. Recently, prestressing has increased the length at which these piles can be used. Since a solid-concrete pile will displace an equal volume of soil it will disturb and remold clay soils, which may result in a considerable loss in shearing strength and frictional resistance to support the pile. Open-end pipe and steel H piles, which are essentially nondisplacement piles, are, therefore, favored for use in clay soils which lose their strength when remolded.

The following formula of the ACI Building Code, for the design of axially loaded reinforced-concrete columns, having an effective length l not greater than ten times the least lateral dimension t, may be used to determine the maximum allowable pile load:

$$P = 0.8A_g(0.225f'_c + f_s p_g)$$

where P = maximum allowable load, lb

A_g = gross area of tied column, sq in.

f'_c = compressive strength of concrete at 28 days, lb per sq in.

f_s = nominal allowable stress in vertical column reinforcement, lb per sq in., to be taken at 40 per cent of minimum specification value of yield point; viz., 16,000 lb per sq in. for intermediate-grade steel and 20,000 lb per sq in. for rail or hard-grade steel (nominal allowable stresses for reinforcement of higher-yield point may be established at 40 per cent of yield-point stress, but not more than 30,000 lb per sq in., when the properties of such reinforcing steels have been definitely specified by standards of ASTM designation)

p_g = ratio of effective cross-sectional area of vertical reinforcement, sq in., to the gross area A_g

Since the effective length of a pile used in dock construction will usually exceed 10 times the least lateral dimension, the maximum allowable load P derived from the above formula for short columns will be reduced to P', the maximum allowable load in pounds for a long column, in accordance with the ACI formula for long columns, in which

$$P' = P\left(1.3 - \frac{0.03l}{t}\right)$$

where l = effective length or height, in. (see Fig. 5.21)
t = least dimension, in.

Table 5.2 gives the maximum loads in short tons for different unsupported lengths of piles varying in size from 12 to 24 in. square, for concrete strengths f'_c of 3,000, 3,500, and 4,000 lb per sq in. The reinforcement is based on a minimum of 2 per cent ($p_g = 0.02$) and a maximum of 4 per cent ($p_g = 0.04$). Although the ACI Code permits a minimum of 1 per cent of reinforcement in tied columns, it is considered good practice to limit this to a minimum of 2 per cent for precast-concrete piles.

Moreover, it is considered good practice for the following reasons to use somewhat lower loads for piles than would be allowed for reinforced-concrete columns, particularly for the larger and heavier piles.

1. Piles have to withstand the impact stress from driving. This will greatly exceed the static stress for which the maximum pile load is figured, as the pile should be driven to a resistance of three times the design load to provide an adequate factor of safety. The impact stress may be assumed to be R_u/A_g, and should not exceed 50 per cent of the ultimate strength $0.85f'_c$ of the concrete.

2. There is a maximum resistance to which a pile of a certain weight can be driven with a hammer without damage to the pile. Unless a load test is to be performed, the maximum design loads should not exceed those indicated in Table 5.3, for the size of single-acting hammers and the concrete stress indicated. These loads have a factor of safety of 3 based on the ultimate resistance of the pile driven to the indicated set per inch for the last 6 in., as derived from the Redtenbacher pile-driving formula, which in turn is derived from the Terzaghi formula by considering the hammer and the pile to act as inelastic bodies during the period of impact.

$$R_u = \frac{AE}{L}\left[-s + \sqrt{s^2 + \frac{W_r^2 H}{W_r + W_p}\frac{2L}{AE}}\right]$$

where R_u = ultimate resistance of the pile, lb
A = gross area of the pile, sq in.
E = modulus of elasticity of the concrete = 1,000 f'_c
L = length of pile, in.
s = set, in.
W_r = weight of striking parts of hammer, lb
W_p = weight of pile, lb
H = fall of ram, in.

3. The handling of the pile from the casting bed, until it is in an upright position to be driven, is an important step in the installation of a precast pile and again emphasizes the need for a more conservative design than for concrete building columns which are cast in place and are not subjected to the bending stresses in handling. Experience has demonstrated that unless the reinforcing stress is kept low, not exceeding 12,000 lb per sq in., fine cracks may appear in the surface of the concrete pile during handling. These cracks may close up and be almost invisible when the pile reaches an upright position ready to be driven, but they will usually become enlarged and plainly visible during the driving of the pile, as a result of the impact stresses set up by the hammer. These fine cracks are undesirable for piles in salt water, and, therefore, the piles should be designed and handled in such a manner that cracking will not occur.

Piles are handled with a two-, three-, or four-point pickup, as shown in Fig. 5.22. Steel pipe sleeves are cast in the pile at the pickup points so that pins can be inserted, to which the wire rope is attached when picking up the piles. In lieu of pins, screw anchor sockets may be cast in the piles at the points of pickup and eyebolts used when picking up the piles. This is not as common a method as using pins, but it facilitates picking up the piles from the casting bed, as it eliminates having to jack the piles apart in order that the pins may be inserted and the wire rope attached.

In order to keep the handling stress in the steel to below 12,000 lb per sq in. it may be necessary for long piles to have additional rods at the pickup points; also, for the pile to be picked up at a sufficient number of points so that the amount of steel to be added will not become excessive. Table 5.4 shows the maximum handling lengths of piles for different pickup arrangements and various combinations of reinforcing steel so that the stress in the steel will not exceed 12,000 lb per sq in. In figuring the weight of the pile, 25 per cent of the weight should be added for impact.

Table 5.2 Maximum Design Loads in Short Tons on

24" square concrete piles – maximum load = 100 tons												
Effective length-ft.	f'_c = 4000 psi				f'_c = 3500 psi				f'_c = 3000 psi			
	Main reinforcing steel				Main reinforcing steel				Main reinforcing steel			
		12-#11 3.28%	12-#10 2.66%	8-#11 2.18%		12-#11 3.28%	12-#10 2.66%	8-#11 2.18%		12-#11 3.28%	12-#10 2.66%	8-#11 2.18%
55											119	111
60			121	114		120	111	104		110	100	94
65		106	98	93		98	90	84		89	82	76
70		82	76	72		75	69	65		68	63	59
75		57	53	50		52	48	46		48	44	41
80		33	30	29		30	28	26		27	25	24

18" square concrete piles – maximum load = 80 tons												
Effective length-ft.	f'_c = 4000 psi				f'_c = 3500 psi				f'_c = 3000 psi (70T max.)			
	Main reinforcing steel				Main reinforcing steel				Main reinforcing steel			
	8-#11 3.90%	8-#10 3.17%	8-#9 2.51%	8-#8 1.98%	8-#11 3.90%	8-#10 3.17%	8-#9 2.51%	8-#8 1.98%	8-#11 3.90%	8-#10 3.17%	8-#9 2.51%	8-#8 1.98%
35				94			91	85			82	76
40	98	90	83	78	90	83	76	70	83	76	69	64
45	78	72	67	62	72	66	61	56	67	60	55	51
50	58	54	50	47	54	50	46	42	50	45	41	38
55	39	36	33	31	36	33	30	28	33	30	28	25
60	20	18	17	16	18	17	15	14	17	15	14	13

14" square concrete piles – maximum load = 50 tons												
Effective length-ft.	f'_c = 4000 psi				f'_c = 3500 psi (45T max.)				f'_c = 3000 psi (40T max.)			
	Main reinforcing steel				Main reinforcing steel				Main reinforcing steel			
	8-#9 4.18%	4-#11 3.26%	4-#10 2.65%	4-#9 2.09%	8-#9 4.18%	4-#11 3.26%	4-#10 2.65%	4-#9 2.09%	8-#9 4.18%	4-#11 3.26%	4-#10 2.65%	4-#9 2.09%
25				62								
30	64	58	54	50	59	53	49	46		49	45	41
35	48	44	41	38	44	40	37	34	41	37	34	31
40	33	30	28	25	30	27	25	23	28	25	23	21
45	17	15	14	13	16	14	13	12	14	13	12	11

FORMULAS:

Allowable load: $P' = 0.8\, A_g (0.225\, f'_c + 16{,}000\, p_g) \times (1.3 - 0.03\, l/t$

Maximum allowable load: $P' = A_g \dfrac{0.85\, f'_c}{6}$, except as noted.

Precast-concrete Piles for Different Effective Lengths

20" square concrete piles - maximum load = 100 tons												
Effective length-ft.	f'_c = 4000 psi				f'_c = 3500 psi				f'_c = 3000 psi			
	Main reinforcing steel				Main reinforcing steel				Main reinforcing steel			
	12-#10 3.85%	8-#11 3.15%	8-#10 2.56%	8-#9 2.02%	12-#10 3.85%	8-#11 3.15%	8-#10 2.56%	8-#9 2.02%	12-#10 3.85%	8-#11 3.15%	8-#10 2.56%	8-#9 2.02%
35											115	106
40				112		118	110	102	118	108	100	92
45	118	109	101	95	109	100	93	86	100	91	84	78
50	96	89	83	77	89	82	76	70	82	74	69	63
55	74	69	64	60	69	63	59	55	63	58	53	49
60	53	49	46	42	49	45	42	39	45	41	38	35
65	31	29	27	25	29	27	25	23	27	24	22	21

16" square concrete piles - maximum load = 60 tons												
Effective length-ft.	f'_c = 4000 psi				f'_c = 3500 psi				f'_c = 3000 psi (55T max.)			
	Main reinforcing steel				Main reinforcing steel				Main reinforcing steel			
	8-#10 4.03%	8-#9 3.18%	4-#11 2.48%	4-#10 2.02%	8-#10 4.03%	8-#9 3.18%	4-#11 2.48%	4-#10 2.02%	8-#10 4.03%	8-#9 3.18%	4-#11 2.48%	4-#10 2.02%
30								70			67	62
35		72	67	63	74	67	61	57	68	61	55	51
40	62	57	52	49	58	52	48	45	53	48	43	40
45	45	41	38	37	42	38	35	32	39	35	31	29
50	28	26	24	22	26	23	21	20	24	21	19	18

12" square concrete piles - maximum load = 40 tons												
Effective length-ft.	f'_c = 4000 psi				f'_c = 3500 psi (35T max.)				f'_c = 3000 psi (30T max.)			
	Main reinforcing steel				Main reinforcing steel				Main reinforcing steel			
	4-#11 4.46%	4-#10 3.64%	4-#9 2.87%	4-#8 2.26%	4-#11 4.46%	4-#10 3.64%	4-#9 2.87%	4-#8 2.26%	4-#11 4.46%	4-#10 3.64%	4-#9 2.87%	4-#8 2.26%
20				50				45				
25	50	46	42	39	46	42	38	35		38	35	32
30	36	33	30	28	34	30	28	26	31	28	25	23
35	23	21	19	18	22	19	18	16	20	18	16	15
40	9	8	8	7	8	8	7	6	8	7	6	6

NOTE:

Pile loads above heavy line exceed max. allowable P' or limit dictated by generally accepted practice.

Table 5.3 Maximum Design Loads to Which Precast-concrete

24" square concrete piles - maximum load = 100 tons																
Pile Hammer	Length of pile - ft.	f_c' = 4000 psi					f_c' = 3500 psi					f_c' = 3000 psi				
		Set per blow - in.					Set per blow - in.					Set per blow - in.				
		0	0.05	0.1	0.2	0.3	0	0.05	0.1	0.2	0.3	0	0.05	0.1	0.2	0.3
W_r = 14,000 lb $W_r H$ = 37,500 ft. lb	50				88	68			116	86	66			111	83	65
	60			105	77	59			100	74	58		111	96	72	56
	70			93	68	52		106	88	66	51	113	97	84	64	50
	80		103	83	61	47	108	95	79	59	46	100	87	75	57	45
	90	105	93	75	56	43	98	86	72	54	42	91	78	68	52	41
	100	95	85	68	51	39	88	78	65	50	38	82	71	62	48	37
	110	88	78	63	47	36	82	72	60	46	36	76	66	57	44	35
	120	80	71	58	43	34	75	66	55	42	33	70	60	52	40	32
W_r = 10,000 lb $W_r H$ = 32,500 ft. lb	50		116	93	65	48		110	90	63	47		103	86	61	46
	60		99	80	56	42	114	94	77	54	41	106	88	74	53	40
	70	107	87	70	49	36	100	82	67	48	36	92	76	64	46	36
	80	95	77	63	44	33	88	72	60	43	32	82	68	57	42	32
	90	85	69	57	40	30	80	66	54	39	30	74	62	52	38	29
	100	77	63	51	36	27	72	60	49	35	27	67	56	47	34	27
	110	71	58	47	34	25	66	54	45	33	24	61	51	43	32	24
	120	65	53	44	31	23	60	50	42	30	22	56	47	40	29	22

18" square concrete piles - maximum load = 80 tons																
Pile Hammer	Length of pile - ft.	f_c' = 4000 psi					f_c' = 3500 psi					f_c' = 3000 psi (70^T max.)				
		Set per blow - in.					Set per blow - in.					Set per blow - in.				
		0	0.05	0.1	0.2	0.3	0	0.05	0.1	0.2	0.3	0	0.05	0.1	0.2	0.3
W_r = 14,000 lb $W_r H$ = 37,500 ft. lb	50					82					79					76
	60				88	72				84	70					68
	70				79	65				76	63				72	61
	80			87	71	59			82	68	57				65	55
	90		88	79	65	54		82	75	62	52			71	59	50
	100	89	80	73	60	50	83	76	69	57	48		71	65	55	47
W_r = 10,000 lb $W_r H$ = 32,500 ft. lb	50				78	62				76	61				72	59
	60			87	68	55			83	66	54			78	63	52
	70		88	77	61	49		83	74	59	48		79	70	56	46
	80	89	78	69	55	44	83	74	66	53	43	77	69	62	50	41
	90	80	71	63	49	40	75	67	60	48	39	69	62	56	46	38
	100	73	65	57	46	37	69	61	54	44	36	64	57	51	42	35
W_r = 8000 lb $W_r H$ = 26,000 ft. lb	50		93	79	59	46		88	76	57	45			72	55	43
	60		80	69	51	40	87	75	65	50	39		71	63	48	38
	70	82	70	61	46	35	77	66	58	44	35	72	62	55	43	34
	80	73	63	54	41	32	68	60	52	40	31	63	55	49	38	30
	90	66	57	49	37	29	61	53	46	36	28	57	50	44	34	28
	100	60	52	45	34	27	56	49	43	33	26	52	46	40	31	25

14" square concrete piles - maximum load = 50 tons																
Pile Hammer	Length of pile - ft.	f_c' = 4000 psi					f_c' = 3500 psi (45^T max.)					f_c' = 3000 psi (40^T max.)				
		Set per blow-in.					Set per blow-in.					Set per blow-in.				
		0.1	0.2	0.3	0.4	0.5	0.1	0.2	0.3	0.4	0.5	0.1	0.2	0.3	0.4	0.5
W_r = 8000 lb $W_r H$ = 26,000 ft. lb	30					51					50					
	40				52	44				51	44					43
	50			54	45	39				44	38				43	38
	60			48	40	35			46	39	34			44	38	33
	70		51	43	36	31		49	42	35	30			40	34	30
	80	56	46	39	33	28	52	44	38	32	28		42	36	31	27
W_r = 5000 lb $W_r H$ = 16,250 ft. lb	30		53	41	33	27		52	40	32	27			40	32	27
	40	59	44	34	28	23		42	34	28	22		41	33	27	22
	50	50	37	29	23	20	48	36	28	23	20	45	35	28	23	19
	60	43	33	25	21	17	41	32	24	20	17	39	30	24	20	17
	70	38	29	23	18	15	36	28	22	18	15	34	27	21	18	15
	80	34	26	20	16	14	32	25	20	16	14	30	24	19	16	13

Piles May Be Driven with Various Single-acting Hammers

20" square concrete piles – maximum load = 100 tons																
Pile Hammer	Length of pile - ft.	f'_c = 4000 psi					f'_c = 3500 lbs					f'_c = 3000 lbs (85^T max.)				
		Set per blow - in					Set per blow - in					Set per blow - in				
		0	0.05	0.1	0.2	0.3	0	0.05	0.1	0.2	0.3	0	0.05	0.1	0.2	0.3
W_r = 14,000 lb, $W_r H$ = 37,500 ft. lb	50				97	77				94	75				90	73
	60			108	85	68			103	82	66				79	64
	70		109	96	76	61		102	91	73	59			86	70	57
	80	110	98	86	68	55	103	92	82	66	54		86	77	63	52
	90	100	88	78	62	51	93	83	74	60	49	86	78	70	57	47
	100	91	81	72	57	46	85	76	68	54	44	79	71	64	52	43
W_r = 10,000 lb, $W_r H$ = 32,500 ft. lb	50		117	100	75	58		110	95	72	56			90	70	55
	60		100	86	65	50	110	94	82	62	49		89	78	60	48
	70	103	88	76	57	45	96	83	72	55	44	89	78	68	53	43
	80	92	79	68	52	40	86	74	64	50	39	79	70	61	48	38
	90	82	71	61	47	37	76	66	58	45	36	71	62	55	43	35
	100	75	65	56	43	34	70	61	53	42	33	65	57	50	40	32
W_r = 8000 lb, $W_r H$ = 26,000 ft. lb	50	114	94	78	55	42	106	88	74	54	41	98	83	70	52	40
	60	97	80	66	47	36	90	76	63	46	36	84	71	60	45	35
	70	83	70	58	42	32	80	66	56	41	32	78	62	53	40	31
	80	75	62	52	38	29	70	58	50	36	28	65	55	47	35	27
	90	67	56	47	34	26	62	53	44	33	26	58	50	42	32	25
	100	61	51	43	31	24	57	48	41	30	24	53	45	39	29	23

16" square concrete piles – maximum load = 60 tons																
Pile Hammer	Length of pile - ft.	f'_c = 4000 psi					f'_c = 3500 psi					f'_c = 3000 psi (55^T max.)				
		Set per blow - in.					Set per blow - in.					Set per blow - in.				
		0	0.05	0.1	0.2	0.3	0	0.05	0.1	0.2	0.3	0	0.05	0.1	0.2	0.3
W_r = 10,000 lb, $W_r H$ = 32,500 ft. lb	50					67					65					63
	60					57					56					55
	70				64	53				61	51				58	49
	80				57	48			66	54	46				52	44
	90			64	52	45		66	60	50	43			57	48	41
	100		65	58	48	40	66	60	55	46	38		56	52	44	37
W_r = 8000 lb, $W_r H$ = 26,000 ft. lb	50				63	50				60	49				58	48
	60				55	44			66	53	43			63	51	42
	70			62	49	39		66	58	47	38		62	54	45	37
	80		62	55	43	35	66	58	52	42	34		55	49	40	33
	90	64	57	50	40	32	60	54	48	38	31	56	50	45	37	30
	100	59	52	46	38	30	55	49	44	36	29	51	46	41	34	28
W_r = 5000 lb, $W_r H$ = 16,250 ft. lb	50		59	48	34	26	66	56	46	33	26	62	52	44	32	25
	60	61	50	41	29	22	56	47	40	28	22	52	44	38	28	21
	70	53	44	36	26	20	50	41	34	25	20	46	39	33	24	19
	80	46	38	32	23	17	43	36	30	22	17	40	34	29	22	17
	90	42	35	29	21	16	40	33	28	20	16	37	31	27	20	15
	100	38	32	26	19	15	36	30	25	18	14	33	28	24	18	14

12" square concrete piles – maximum load = 40 tons																
Pile Hammer	Length of pile - ft.	f'_c = 4000 psi					f'_c = 3500 psi (35^T max.)					f'_c = 3000 psi (30^T max.)				
		Set per blow - in.					Set per blow - in.					Set per blow - in.				
		0.1	0.2	0.3	0.4	0.5	0.1	0.2	0.3	0.4	0.5	0.1	0.2	0.3	0.4	0.5
W_r = 5000 lb, $W_r H$ = 16,250 ft. lb	30			44	37	31				36	30				35	30
	40		47	37	31	26			36	30	26			35	30	26
	50		40	33	27	23		38	32	26	22			30	26	22
	60	44	35	29	24	20		34	28	24	20		32	27	23	20
	70	39	31	25	21	18	37	30	24	20	18	35	29	24	20	18
	80	35	28	23	19	17	32	27	22	18	16	30	26	22	18	16

FORMULAS:

Allowable load: $P' = \frac{R_u}{3} = \frac{A}{3}\frac{E}{L}\left[-s + \sqrt{s^2 + \frac{W_r^2 H}{W_r + W_p} \times \frac{2L}{AE}}\right]$

Maximum allowable load: $P' = A_g \frac{0.85 f'_c}{6}$, except as noted.

NOTE:

Pile loads above heavy line exceed max. allowable P' or limit dictated by generally accepted practice.

Details of precast-concrete piles are shown in Fig. 5.23. Main reinforcing rods should have a 3-in. cover. All corners should have a 1-in. chamfer. Bands should be spaced 12 in. on center except at the ends of the pile and at the pickup points where a closer spacing is required. Long piles will require splicing the main rods. This may be done by butt-welding the ends of the rods or by using short splice bars with full tension laps on each side of the splice. Corner rods should not be lapped as this requires offsetting the rods.

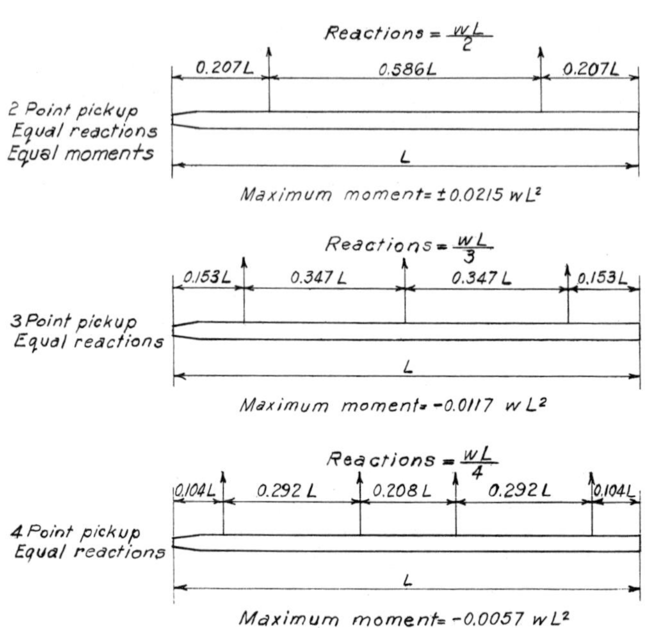

FIG. 5.22 Location of pickup points for precast-concrete piles.

Example. Design a precast-concrete pile to support a load of 60 tons. Assume that the depth of water is 40 ft and that the deck will be of reinforced-concrete slab and girder construction, with the bottom of the pile-cap girder 8 ft above low water; that the bottom is soft mud or silt to a depth of 15 ft and is then underlaid with a firm clay into which the pile is estimated to develop a safe load of 60 tons with a factor of safety of 3, after a penetration of 25 ft into the clay.

The pile will be fixed at the top by the concrete girder at El +8 ft and will be supported at a point in the mud, 5 ft below the bottom, at El −45 ft, a total unsupported length of 53 ft. This is condition II in Fig. 5.21, and the unsupported length as a column will be reduced by the fixity at the top to an effective length of $0.75 \times 53 = 39.8$ ft. The total length of the pile will be 91 ft, allowing 3 ft additional at the top for

***Table* 5.4 Maximum Handling Lengths, Ft, of Precast-concrete Piles for Different Pickup Arrangements and Various Combinations of Reinforcing Steel**

Pile size	Main reinforcing steel	Regular reinforcement		Two additional bars, three-point pickup
		Two-point pickup	Three-point pickup	
24-in. square	12 no. 11	90.0	122.1	144.0
	12 no. 10	82.2	111.3	131.0
	8 no. 11	76.7	104.0	130.0
20-in. square	12 no. 10	87.6	118.6	140.0
	8 no. 11	81.0	110.0	138.5
	8 no. 10	73.9	100.2	124.5
	8 no. 9	66.1	89.7	112.0
18-in. square	8 no. 11	83.9	114.0	143.5
	8 no. 10	76.0	103.0	128.5
	8 no. 9	68.2	92.5	116.5
	8 no. 8	61.3	83.4	104.0
16-in. square	8 no. 10	78.6	106.8	133.0
	8 no. 9	70.5	95.6	120.0
	4 no. 11	67.5	91.6	129.0
	4 no. 10	61.3	83.1	115.5
14-in. square	8 no. 9	73.0	99.0	*
	4 no. 11	70.0	94.9	134.0
	4 no. 10	63.5	86.0	120.5
	4 no. 9	57.0	77.3	108.5
12-in. square	4 no. 11	72.2	98.0	138.5
	4 no. 10	65.8	89.4	125.5
	4 no. 9	59.0	80.1	113.0
	4 no. 8	52.5	71.2	100.5

Additional bars are same size as regular reinforcement.
Lengths are based on 12,000 psi tension in reinforcement.
Load is pile weight plus 25% impact.
For details of concrete piles, refer to Fig. 5.23.
* Insufficient clearance for additional bars.

cutoff to provide for embedment of the rods in the pile-cap girder. From Table 5.2 it is seen that the pile, as a long column to support 60 tons, will need to be 18 by 18 in. with 8 no. 8 rods, with $f'_c = 3{,}000$ lb per sq in. The weight of the pile is 15.4 tons and Table 5.3 indicates that it will require an S-10 hammer to drive it to a safe load of 60 tons with a final penetration of 0.07 in. per blow, or about 14 blows per in. Table 5.4, shows that a three-point pickup will be required, with two additional no. 8 rods required at the pickup points.

In designing batter piles, the bending stress from the weight of the

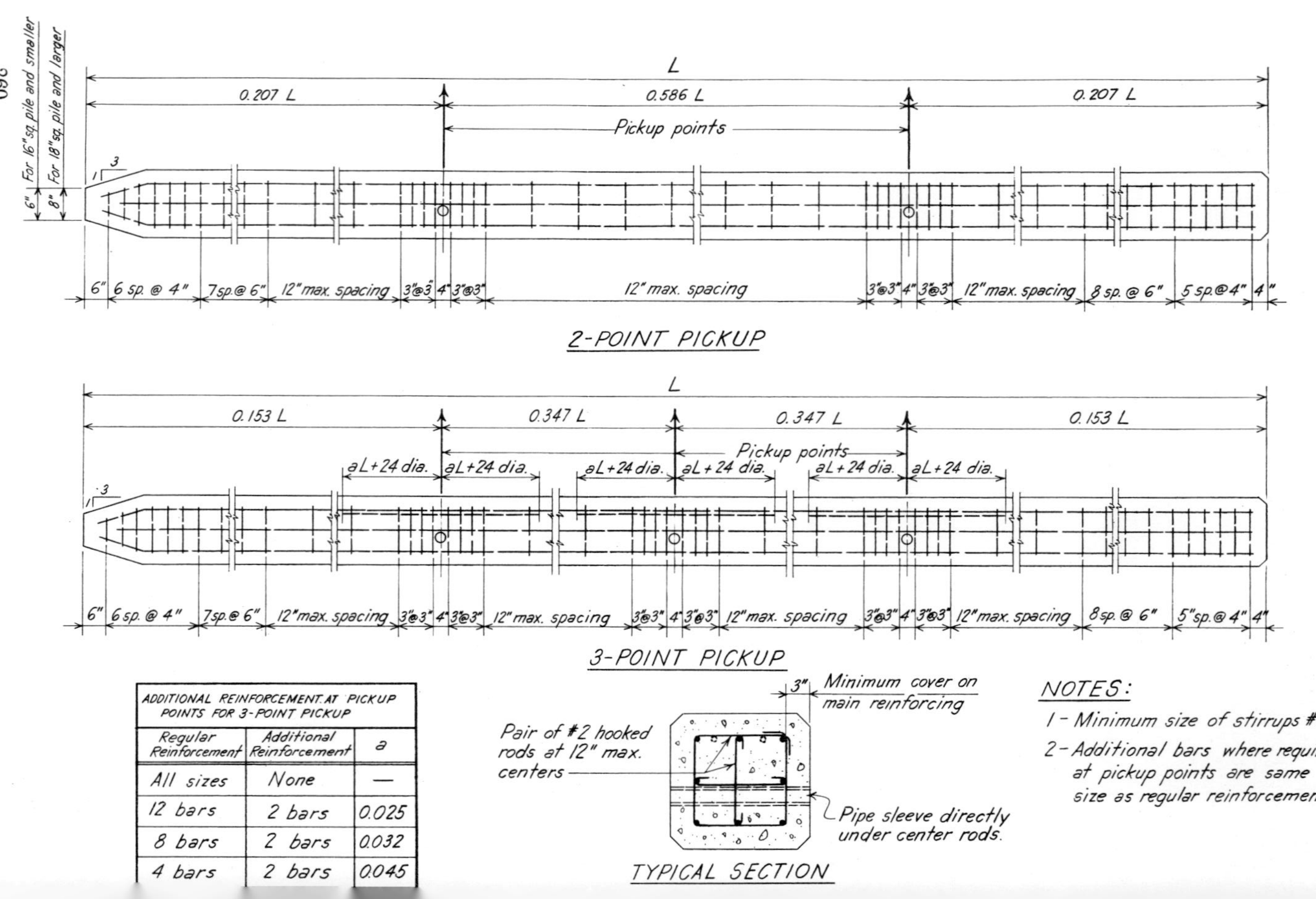

ADDITIONAL REINFORCEMENT AT PICKUP POINTS FOR 3-POINT PICKUP

Regular Reinforcement	Additional Reinforcement	a
All sizes	None	—
12 bars	2 bars	0.025
8 bars	2 bars	0.032
4 bars	2 bars	0.045

pile must be combined with the direct stress in determining the safe pile load. This may be done by using the ACI formula for combined stresses in concrete columns

$$\frac{f_a}{F_a} + \frac{f_b}{F_b} \leqq 1$$

where f_a = axial unit stress = actual axial load, lb divided by gross area A_g

f_b = actual unit bending stress due to weight of pile

F_a = allowable axial unit stress = P/A_g or P'/A_g

F_b = allowable bending unit stress in reinforcing steel that would be permitted if bending stress only existed, 20,000 lb per sq in. for intermediate grade and 18,000 lb per sq in. for structural grade

Precast-concrete sheet piles are designed for the bending moments from the earth pressure when the piling is in its permanent position, unless the piles are to carry vertical loads, in which case they will be designed for combined bending and direct stresses, as previously described for batter piles. The principal reinforcement will have to be checked for handling stresses, but the driving stresses will usually not be a controlling factor, unless the piles are to take direct load, as in most cases they may be jetted down to the required depth. Typical sheet-pile details are shown in Fig. 5.24.

A precast-concrete pile with a steel H-pile lower section, as shown in Fig. 5.25, has proved very effective at certain locations where concrete is needed because of the severe corrosive condition of the water and where the bottom is of sand and boulders, hard clay, or soft rock which would prevent the required penetration of a displacement type of concrete pile. The concrete section should extend to a depth of 2 to 10 ft below the bottom, depending on whether there is first a layer of soft material, in order to provide adequate protection from corrosion. The length of steel section may extend from as little as 5 to more than 30 ft below this level depending on how firm the material is and how important it is to develop a maximum amount of tension or pull-out value in the pile. The safe-working pull-out value may be estimated by taking the frictional value of the soil (the shearing strength) times the area comprising the depth of penetration in the firm material by the periphery of the square section of the pile, and dividing this value by 2 to allow for a factor of safety. This value should always be checked by making a pull-out test on one or more representative piles.

Prestressed-concrete Piles and Cylinders. These have come into favor for marine installations where the length requirements are such as to make regular precast piles difficult, if not impossible, to handle and

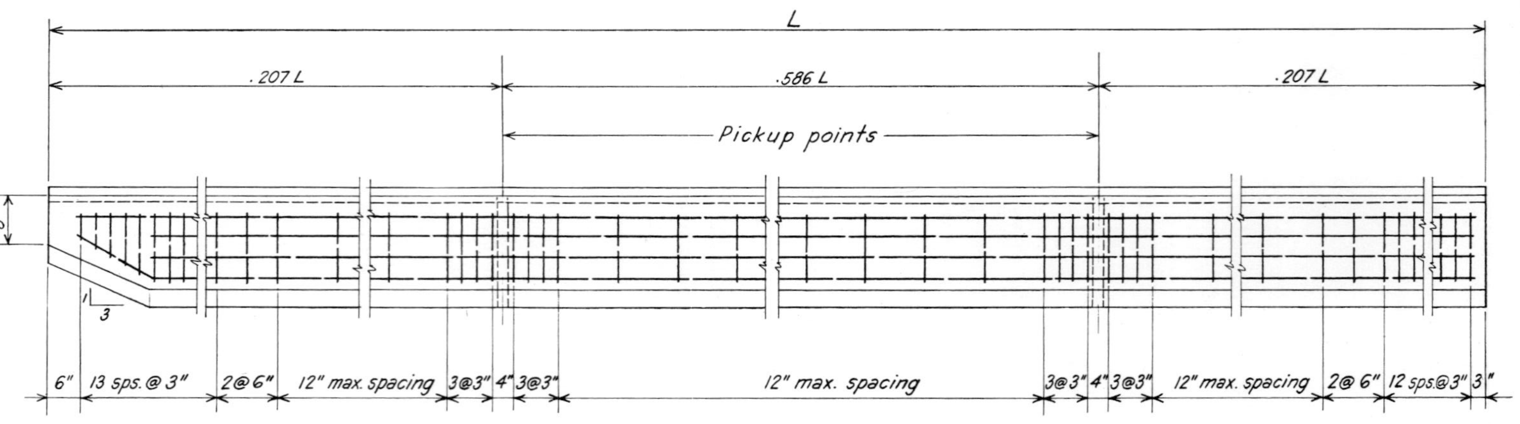

NOTES:

1- Minimum size of stirrups # 2.

2- Details shown for 2-point pickup.

Minimum cover on main reinforcing

3"

2"

$2\frac{1}{2}$"

3"

1

3

Pipe sleeve at pickup points

TYPICAL SECTION

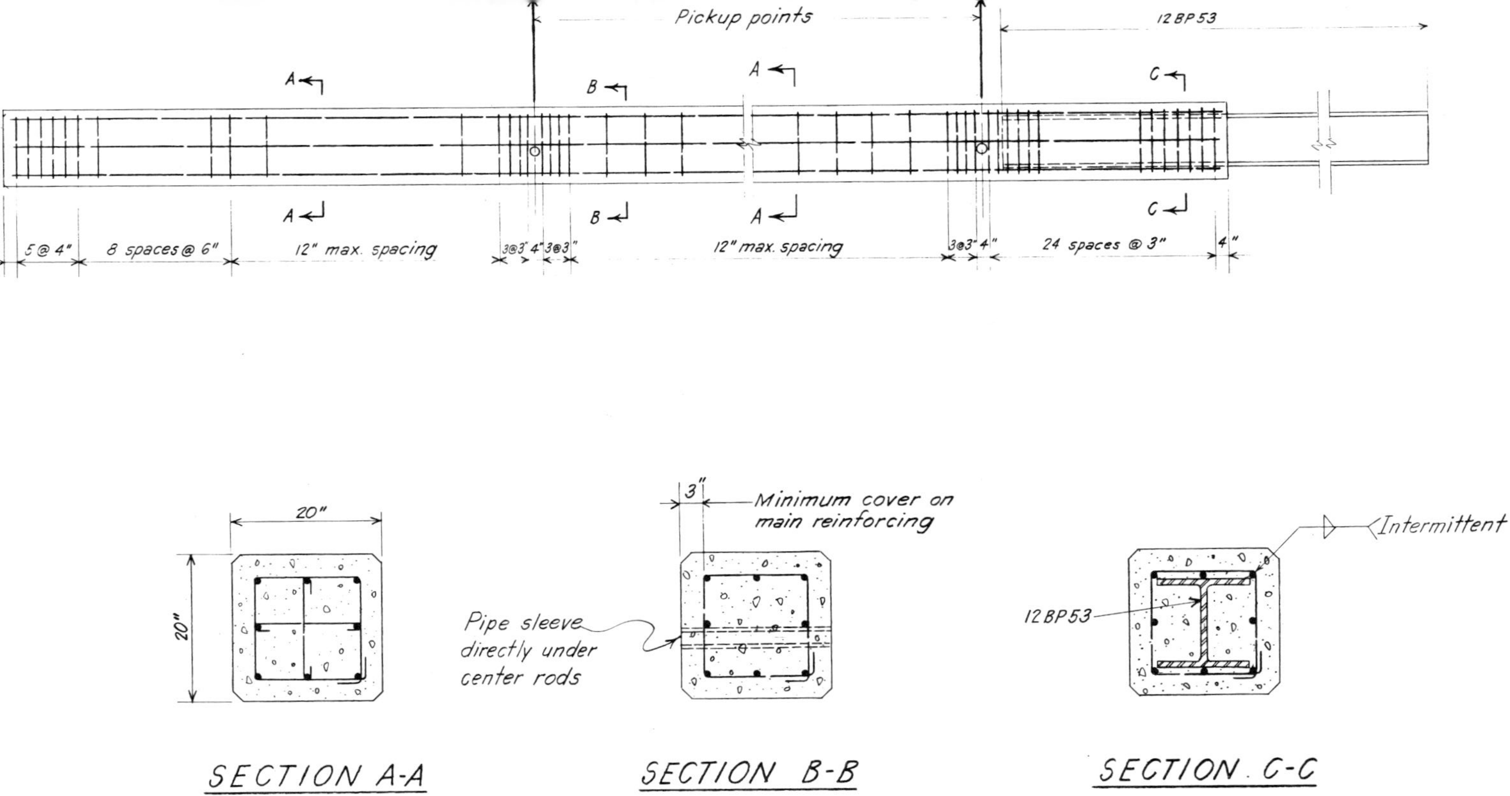

FIG. 5.25 A typical precast-concrete pile with H-pile point.

drive, and uneconomical to use. Prestressed hollow cylinders, 3 ft 0 in. in diameter and approaching 200 ft in length, with unsupported lengths exceeding 100 ft, have been successfully installed to support loads of 200 tons. Prestressing the concrete to 500 to 800 lb per sq in. makes it possible to handle these long piles and cylinders with little danger of cracking.

In designing prestressed piles and cylinders the driving stress or soil-carrying capacity will usually control the design load to be used, except for long unsupported lengths. It has been found economical and desirable to use high-strength concrete, usually 5,000-lb-per-sq-in. 28-day cylinder strength, for which an ultimate design stress of $0.85 \times 5{,}000 = 4{,}250$ lb per sq in. is permitted. It follows that after deducting the effective prestress, assumed to be a maximum of 800 lb per sq in., but reduced to 0.7 of this value to allow for shortening of the prestress wires from the compression of the concrete under direct load, and dividing the remainder by 2 to provide a proper safety factor for impact stress, the driving stress should not exceed $(4{,}250 - 560)/2 = 1{,}845$ lb per sq in. The ultimate load to which the pile is driven, as derived from the Redtenbacher formula, page 253, is divided by 3 to provide an adequate factor of safety; therefore, the design stress must not exceed $1{,}845/3 = 615$ lb per sq in. For an 18-in.-square pile the allowable load-carrying capacity would be $P = (615 \times 324)/2{,}000 = 99.6$ tons. Table 5.5 gives the maximum design loads for various sizes of piles and lengths, when driven with the size of single-acting hammers indicated.

For long unsupported lengths the load-carrying capacity of the pile will be limited to that of a long column. Using Euler's formula for the critical buckling load for a long column and allowing a factor of safety of 4, safe design loads for different unsupported lengths and sizes of piles and cylinders may be determined as follows:

$$P' = \frac{k\pi^2 EI}{4h^2}$$

where P' = allowable safe load, lb

I = moment of inertia of concrete, in.^{4}

E = modulus of elasticity of 5,000 lb per sq in. concrete, taken as 5,000,000 lb per sq in. for a short-term load and reduced to 2,000,000 lb per sq in. for sustained loading over a period of years; for equal dead load and live load E = 3,500,000 lb per sq in.

k = factor for end condition, taken as 1.0 for pin-connected ends, 2.25 for one end fixed, and 4.0 for both ends fixed

h = unsupported length, in.

In the above example, where the allowable short column load $P = 99.6$ tons, the maximum unsupported length would be

$$h = \pi \sqrt{\frac{3{,}500{,}000 \times 8{,}748}{4 \times 99.6 \times 2{,}000}} = 615 \text{ in. or } 51.2 \text{ ft}$$

Instead of computing the safe load by means of the foregoing formula, Table 5.6 may be used, which gives the safe load in tons for different effective lengths, determined from Fig. 5.21, for various sizes of piles and cylinders. Using the effective length, the table will give somewhat lower load-carrying capacities for one end fixed than would be obtained from Euler's formula by inserting the factor $k = 2.25$, but will give the same loads for both ends fixed as would inserting the factor $k = 4.0$, and for pin-connected ends using the factor $k = 1.0$.

In designing the pile or cylinder for pickup the maximum bending stress should not exceed the prestress, so that there will be no tension in the concrete when treated as an uncracked section, in which

$$f = \frac{Md/2}{I}$$

where f = the extreme fiber stress in concrete (which should not exceed the prestress f_p), lb per sq in.
M = bending moment, in.-lb
d = depth of pile section, in.
I = moment of inertia of concrete section, in.^{4}

Practice has varied on the amount of tension to be allowed in the concrete, some designers permitting no tension, i.e., the extreme fiber stress must not exceed the prestress, while others allow up to the maximum tensile value of the concrete on the basis that the section can be designed to have a factor of safety of at least 2 against ultimate failure, even though the section becomes cracked. It can be argued that any cracks occurring will be fine and will be closed up by the prestress, as soon as the temporary handling load is relieved. The author prefers to have the pile free of cracks when driven, as this is one of the advantages of the prestressed over the precast pile. By limiting the maximum flexural stress in handling to the prestress, there will be a factor of safety of close to 2 before the modulus of rupture will be exceeded, as this is equal to $7.5\sqrt{f'_c}$. Although the prestress may tend to prevent the enlargement of cracks during the driving, it is considered better practice to avoid this condition for piles which are exposed to the atmosphere and possibly corrosive conditions.

Table 5.5 Maximum Design Loads to Which Prestressed-concrete Piles May Be Driven with Various Single-acting Hammers

48" O.D., 36" I.D. ◎ Maximum load = 240 tons

Pile Hammer	Length of Pile-ft.	Set per blow-in. 0	0.05	0.1	0.2	0.3
W_r = 40,000 lb, $W_r H$ = 113,478 ft. lb	100		259	236	196	165
	110		240	218	182	153
	120	244	223	202	169	143
	130	228	208	190	159	135
	140	215	195	178	150	126
	150	202	185	168	142	120
	160	190	174	159	134	114
	170	181	165	151	127	108
	180	172	157	144	121	103
	190	164	150	138	116	98
	200	156	143	131	111	94
	210	149	137	126	106	90
	220	143	131	121	102	87
	230	138	126	116	98	84
	240	132	121	112	94	81
	250	128	117	108	91	78
W_r = 20,000 lb, $W_r H$ = 60,000 ft. lb	50		244	203	147	112
	60	252	210	177	128	98
	70	220	184	156	113	87
	80	196	165	139	102	78
	90	177	149	126	92	72
	100	161	135	114	85	65
	110	148	125	106	78	60
	120	136	115	98	73	56
	130	127	107	91	68	52
	140	118	100	85	63	49
	150	111	94	80	59	46
	160	104	88	76	56	44
	170	98	84	71	53	42
	180	93	79	68	50	40
	190	89	76	65	48	38
	200	85	72	62	46	36
W_r = 14,000 lb, $W_r H$ = 37,500 ft. lb	50	201	156	122	78	58
	60	172	134	104	69	50
	70	151	117	92	61	44
	80	134	104	82	54	40
	90	121	94	74	50	36
	100	109	85	67	45	33
	110	100	78	62	42	30
	120	92	72	57	38	28
	130	85	67	53	36	26
	140	80	62	50	33	24

42" O.D., 30" I.D. ◎ Maximum load = 200 tons

Pile Hammer	Length of Pile-ft.	Set per blow-in. 0	0.05	0.1	0.2	0.3
W_r = 40,000 lb, $W_r H$ = 113,478 ft. lb	100				200	171
	110				185	159
	120			203	173	148
	130		207	191	163	140
	140	210	193	178	153	132
	150	198	183	169	145	125
	160	187	173	160	137	119
	170	178	164	152	131	113
	180	169	156	144	124	107
	190	161	149	138	119	103
	200	154	143	132	114	98
	210	147	137	127	109	95
	220	141	131	122	105	91
	230	136	126	117	101	88
	240	131	121	113	97	84
	250	126	117	109	94	81
W_r = 20,000 lb, $W_r H$ = 60,000 ft. lb	50			208	154	119
	60		210	179	134	104
	70	216	185	159	120	94
	80	192	164	143	107	84
	90	174	149	129	98	77
	100	159	137	118	90	71
	110	145	125	108	83	65
	120	134	116	101	77	61
	130	125	108	94	72	57
	140	117	101	88	67	53
	150	110	95	83	63	51
	160	103	89	78	60	48
	170	98	85	74	57	45
	180	92	80	70	54	43
	190	88	76	66	51	41
	200	84	73	63	49	39
W_r = 14,000 lb, $W_r H$ = 37,500 ft. lb	50	201	159	127	87	64
	60	171	136	109	75	55
	70	150	119	96	66	49
	80	132	106	86	59	44
	90	119	95	77	53	40
	100	108	87	71	49	36
	110	99	80	65	45	34
	120	91	74	60	42	31
	130	85	68	56	39	29
	140	79	64	52	36	27

36" O.D., 26" I.D. ◎ Maximum load = 150 tons

Pile Hammer	Length of Pile-ft.	Set per blow-in. 0	0.05	0.1	0.2	0.3
W_r = 20,000 lb, $W_r H$ = 60,000 ft. lb	50				165	133
	60				145	118
	70			162	130	106
	80		163	146	117	96
	90		149	133	107	88
	100	152	136	122	99	81
	110	140	126	113	91	76
	120	129	116	104	85	70
	130	121	108	98	80	66
	140	113	102	91	75	62
	150	107	96	86	70	59
	160	100	90	81	66	55
	170	94	86	77	63	52
	180	90	81	73	60	50
	190	86	77	70	57	47
	200	82	74	67	55	45
W_r = 14,000 lb, $W_r H$ = 37,500 ft. lb	50		158	133	97	74
	60	162	137	115	85	65
	70	143	121	102	75	58
	80	127	108	91	68	53
	90	114	97	83	61	48
	100	104	89	76	57	44
	110	96	82	70	53	40
	120	88	75	65	48	38
	130	82	70	60	45	35
	140	77	66	57	43	33
	150	72	62	53	40	31
	160	68	58	50	38	29
	170	64	55	47	36	28
	180	61	52	45	34	27
	190	58	50	43	32	25
	200	55	48	41	31	24
W_r = 10,000 lb, $W_r H$ = 32,500 ft. lb	50	158	128	104	73	54
	60	135	109	90	63	47
	70	118	96	79	56	42
	80	104	85	70	50	37
	90	94	77	64	45	34
	100	85	70	58	41	31
	110	78	64	53	38	28
	120	72	59	49	35	27
	130	67	55	46	33	25
	140	62	52	43	30	23

30" O.D., 20" I.D. ◎ Maximum load = 120 tons

Pile Hammer	Length of Pile-ft.	Set per blow-in 0	0.05	0.1	0.2	0.3
W_r = 20,000 lb, $W_r H$ = 60,000 ft. lb						
	60					124
	70					111
	80				121	101
	90				111	93
	100			122	102	86
	110		123	113	94	80
	120	126	114	105	88	75
	130	117	107	98	83	70
	140	110	101	92	78	66
	150	103	95	87	73	63
	160	98	89	83	70	60
	170	93	85	78	66	56
	180	88	81	74	63	54
	190	84	77	71	60	51
	200	80	74	68	57	49
W_r = 14,000 lb, $W_r H$ = 37,500 ft. lb	50			135	102	81
	60		135	118	90	71
	70		120	104	81	64
	80	123	107	94	73	58
	90	111	95	85	66	53
	100	103	89	78	61	49
	110	94	82	72	56	45
	120	86	76	67	52	42
	130	81	71	63	49	40
	140	76	66	59	46	37
	150	71	62	55	43	35
	160	67	59	52	41	33
	170	63	56	49	39	31
	180	60	53	47	37	30
	190	57	50	45	35	28
	200	54	48	43	34	27
W_r = 10,000 lb, $W_r H$ = 32,500 ft. lb	50		128	102	78	60
	60	131	110	93	69	53
	70	114	97	82	61	47
	80	101	86	73	54	42
	90	92	78	66	49	38
	100	83	71	61	45	35
	110	76	65	56	42	32
	120	71	60	52	39	30
	130	66	56	48	36	28
	140	61	52	45	34	26

24" Octag. 12" Dia. Core ◎ Maximum load = 110 tons

Pile Hammer	Length of Pile-ft.	Set per blow-in 0	0.05	0.1	0.2	0.3
W_r = 14,000 lb, $W_r H$ = 37,500 ft. lb	50				104	82
	60			118	91	73
	70		119	104	82	66
	80	123	107	95	74	60
	90	110	97	86	67	54
	100	101	89	79	62	50
	110	93	82	73	57	47
	120	86	76	67	53	43
	130	80	71	63	50	41
	140	75	67	59	47	38
	150	70	62	56	44	36
	160	66	59	52	42	34
	170	63	56	50	40	32
	180	60	53	47	38	31
	190	57	51	45	36	30
	200	54	48	43	35	28
W_r = 10,000 lb, $W_r H$ = 32,500 ft. lb	50		128	109	81	62
	60		110	94	70	55
	70	114	97	83	62	49
	80	100	86	74	56	44
	90	91	78	67	51	40
	100	83	71	61	47	36
	110	76	65	56	43	34
	120	70	60	52	40	31
	130	65	56	49	37	29
	140	61	53	46	35	27
	150	57	49	43	33	26
W_r = 8000 lb, $W_r H$ = 26,000 ft. lb	50	125	103	84	60	45
	60	107	88	73	52	39
	70	93	77	64	46	35
	80	83	68	57	41	31
	90	74	61	52	37	28
	100	68	56	47	34	26
	110	62	52	43	31	24
	120	57	48	40	29	22
	130	53	44	37	27	21
	140	50	42	35	25	19
	150	47	40	33	24	18

22" Octag. 12" Dia. Core ◎ Maximum load = 90 tons

Pile Hammer	Length of Pile-ft.	Set per blow-in. 0	0.05	0.1	0.2	0.3
W_r = 14,000 lb, W_rH = 37,500 ft-lb	50					88
	60				95	78
	70				85	70
	80			95	77	64
	90		95	86	70	58
	100	97	88	79	65	54
	110	90	82	74	61	51
	120	83	76	68	56	47
	130	78	70	64	53	44
	140	73	66	60	50	42
	150	69	62	57	47	39
	160	65	59	54	44	37
	170	62	56	51	42	36
	180	59	53	49	40	34
	190	55	50	46	38	32
	200	53	48	44	37	31
W_r = 10,000 lb, W_rH = 32,500 ft-lb	50				85	68
	60			95	74	60
	70		96	85	66	53
	80	98	86	76	60	48
	90	89	78	69	55	44
	100	81	71	63	50	41
	110	75	66	59	46	38
	120	69	61	54	43	35
	130	64	57	50	40	33
	140	60	53	47	38	31
	150	56	50	44	36	29
W_r = 8000 lb, W_rH = 26,000 ft-lb	50		102	87	65	50
	60		88	75	56	44
	70	91	77	66	50	39
	80	81	69	60	45	35
	90	73	63	54	41	32
	100	66	57	49	37	29
	110	61	53	46	35	27
	120	56	49	42	32	25
	130	52	45	39	30	24
	140	49	42	37	28	22
	150	46	40	34	26	21

20" Square □ Maximum load = 120 tons

Pile Hammer	Length of Pile-ft.	Set per blow-in. 0	0.05	0.1	0.2	0.3
W_r = 14,000 lb, W_rH = 37,500 ft-lb	50			136	103	81
	60			118	91	71
	70		121	104	80	64
	80	123	108	94	72	58
	90	112	98	85	66	52
	100	103	89	78	61	48
	110	94	82	72	56	45
	120	87	76	67	52	42
	130	81	71	62	49	39
	140	76	66	58	46	37
	150	71	62	55	43	35
W_r = 10,000 lb, W_rH = 32,500 ft-lb	50		128	108	78	60
	60	132	110	93	68	52
	70	115	97	82	60	46
	80	102	86	73	54	42
	90	92	78	66	49	38
	100	84	71	60	45	35
	110	77	65	56	41	32
	120	71	60	52	38	30
	130	66	56	48	36	28
	140	62	52	45	33	26
	150	58	49	42	31	25
W_r = 8000 lb, W_rH = 26,000 ft-lb	50	127	102	83	57	43
	60	108	88	71	50	37
	70	94	76	62	44	32
	80	84	68	56	39	29
	90	75	62	50	36	27
	100	68	56	46	32	24
	110	63	51	42	30	23
	120	58	47	39	28	21
	130	53	44	36	26	19
	140	50	41	34	24	18
	150	47	39	32	23	17

18" Square □ Maximum load = 100 tons

Pile Hammer	Length of Pile-ft.	Set per blow-in. 0	0.05	0.1	0.2	0.3
W_r = 14,000 lb, W_rH = 37,500 ft-lb	50				106	86
	60				94	76
	70			105	84	68
	80		106	95	76	62
	90	107	97	86	69	57
	100	99	89	79	64	53
	110	92	82	73	59	49
	120	84	76	68	55	45
	130	79	71	64	52	43
	140	74	66	59	48	40
	150	70	63	56	46	38
W_r = 10,000 lb, W_rH = 32,500 ft-lb	50			109	82	65
	60		109	94	72	57
	70	111	97	84	64	51
	80	99	86	75	58	46
	90	90	78	68	53	42
	100	82	71	62	49	39
	110	75	66	57	45	36
	120	69	61	53	41	33
	130	65	57	50	39	31
	140	60	53	47	36	29
	150	57	50	44	34	27
W_r = 8000 lb, W_rH = 26,000 ft-lb	50		102	86	62	47
	60	105	88	74	55	42
	70	92	77	66	48	37
	80	82	69	58	43	34
	90	74	62	53	39	30
	100	67	57	48	36	28
	110	62	52	44	33	26
	120	57	48	41	31	24
	130	53	45	38	29	22
	140	49	42	35	27	21
	150	46	39	33	25	20

16" Square □ Maximum load = 80 tons

Pile Hammer	Length of Pile-ft.	Set per blow-in. 0	0.05	0.1	0.2	0.3
W_r = 10,000 lb, W_rH = 32,500 ft-lb	50				87	70
	60				76	62
	70			85	68	55
	80		85	76	61	50
	90	87	77	70	56	46
	100	80	70	64	52	42
	110	75	66	59	48	39
	120	68	61	54	44	36
	130	63	57	51	41	34
	140	59	53	48	39	32
	150	56	50	45	37	31
W_r = 8000 lb, W_rH = 26,000 ft-lb	50			88	67	53
	60		89	76	58	46
	70	89	77	67	51	41
	80	79	69	60	47	37
	90	72	63	55	43	34
	100	66	57	50	39	31
	110	60	53	46	36	29
	120	56	49	43	33	27
	130	52	46	40	31	25
	140	48	42	37	29	23
	150	45	40	35	28	22
W_r = 5000 lb, W_rH = 16,250 ft-lb	50	80	64	52	36	27
	60	67	54	44	31	23
	70	59	48	39	27	20
	80	53	43	35	24	18
	90	47	38	31	22	17
	100	43	35	29	20	15
	110	39	32	26	19	14
	120	36	30	24	17	13
	130	33	27	22	16	12
	140	31	25	21	15	11
	150	29	24	20	14	10

14" Square □ Maximum load = 60 tons

Pile Hammer	Length of Pile-ft.	Set per blow-in. 0	0.05	0.1	0.2	0.3
W_r = 10,000 lb, W_rH = 32,500 ft-lb	60					65
	70					58
	80				63	53
	90				58	49
	100			64	54	46
	110		65	59	50	43
	120		60	55	47	40
	130	61	56	52	44	37
	140	57	53	48	41	35
	150	54	50	46	39	33
W_r = 8000 lb, W_rH = 26,000 ft-lb	50					57
	60				61	50
	70				55	45
	80			61	50	41
	90		62	56	45	37
	100	63	57	51	42	34
	110	58	52	47	39	32
	120	54	49	44	36	30
	130	50	45	41	34	28
	140	47	43	38	32	26
	150	44	40	36	30	25
W_r = 5000 lb, W_rH = 16,250 ft-lb	50		64	54	39	29
	60	65	55	47	34	26
	70	57	48	41	30	23
	80	51	43	37	27	21
	90	46	39	33	25	19
	100	42	36	31	23	18
	110	39	33	28	21	16
	120	35	30	26	19	15
	130	33	28	24	18	14
	140	31	26	22	17	13
	150	29	25	21	16	12

FORMULAS:

Allowable load: $P' = \frac{R_u}{3} = \frac{AE}{3L}\left[-s + \sqrt{s^2 + \frac{W_r^2 H}{W_r + W_p} \times \frac{2L}{AE}}\right]$

Maximum allowable load: $P' = A_g \frac{4250 - 0.7 f_p}{6}$

Compressive strength of concrete: $f_c' = 5000$ psi.

NOTE:

Pile loads above heavy line exceed maximum allowable P' or limit dictated by generally accepted practice.

***Table* 5.6 Safe Load in Short Tons on Prestressed-concrete Piles for Different Effective Lengths**

EFFECTIVE LENGTH (FT.)	48" O.D. 36" I.D.	42" O.D. 30" I.D.	36" O.D. 26" I.D.	30" O.D. 20" I.D.	24" OCTAG. 12" DIA. CORE	22" OCTAG. 12" DIA. CORE	20" SQ.	18" SQ.	16" SQ.	14" SQ.
40										60
45									82	47
50								106	65	39
55						104	132	87	54	32
60					127	87	111	73	46	27
65					108	74	95	62	39	23
70					93	64	82	54	33	
75					81	56	71	47	29	
80					72	49	62	41		
85				133	63	43	55	36		
90				118	56	39	49			
95				106	51	35	44			
100				96	46					
105			164	87	41					
110			149	79	38					
115			136	72						
120			125	66						
125		217	115	61						
130		200	106	57						
135		186	98	52						
140		174	92	49						
145	253	161	85	45						
150	237	151	80	43						
155	222	142	75							
160	208	133	70							
165	196	125	66							
170	185	118	62							
175	174	111	59							
180	164	105	55							
185	157	100								
190	148	94								
195	141	90								
200	133	85								
205	126	81								
210	121	77								
215	116	74								
220	110									
225	105									
230	101									
235	96									
240	92									
245	89									
250	86									

FORMULAS:

Allowable load: $P' = \frac{\pi^2 EI}{4 \ell^2}$

Maximum allowable load: $P' = A_g \frac{4250 - 0.7 f_p}{6}$

Compressive strength of concrete: $f'_c = 5000$ psi

$E = 3{,}500{,}000$ psi (modulus of elasticity of concrete for $DL = LL = \frac{P'}{2}$)

NOTE: Pile loads above heavy line exceed max. allowable P' or limit dictated by generally accepted practice.

The area of prestress steel A_s is determined from the formula

$$A_s = \frac{f_p A_g}{0.56 f'_s}$$

where A_g = gross area of concrete, sq in.
f_p = prestress in concrete, lb per sq in.
f'_s = ultimate strength of prestress cable or wire, usually specified to be 250,000 lb per sq in.

The factor 0.56 is derived as follows. From ACI-ASCE Joint Committee 323, January, 1958, Recommendations for Prestressed Concrete, initial prestress equals 0.70 f'_s and loss in steel stress may be assumed to be 35,000 lb per sq in. Therefore, design stress equals $0.7 \times 250{,}000 - 35{,}000 = 140{,}000$ lb per sq in., which is $0.56 \times f'_s$ when $f'_s = 250{,}000$ lb per sq in.

It can be shown, as follows, that the permissible prestress f_p will vary within the limits of 500 to 800 lb per sq in. for 5,000-lb-per-sq-in. concrete. Table 5.7 gives the maximum handling lengths for two-, three-, and four-point pickups for a prestress of 500, 600, 700, and 800 lb per sq in.

The maximum bending-moment capacity for the uncracked section of pile is

$$M_1 = f \frac{I}{d/2}$$

where f = prestress f_p plus the modulus of rupture (530 lb per sq in. = f_t for 5,000-lb-per-sq-in. concrete).

The ultimate bending moment for a cracked section of pile, $M_2 = A_s f'_s jd$, where j equals approximately 0.39 for cylinders and 0.37 for solid square and hollow octagonal piles.

Assume a factor of safety K against failure; then $M_2 = KM_1$, and by substituting the above values for M_1 and M_2 and assuming a square pile with

$$A_s = f_p d^2/0.56 f'_s, \quad I = d^4/12, \quad f = f_p + 530$$

the following expression is derived:

$$K = \frac{4.5 f_p}{f_p + 530}$$

For prestress

$$\begin{aligned} f_p &= 800, & K &= 2.71 \\ f_p &= 700, & K &= 2.56 \\ f_p &= 600, & K &= 2.39 \\ f_p &= 500, & K &= 2.18 \\ f_p &= 400, & K &= 1.93 \end{aligned}$$

Table 5.7 Maximum Handling Lengths of Prestressed-concrete Piles

Pile section	Effective prestress (psi)	Maximum pile length - ft. 2-point pickup	3-point pickup	4-point pickup	Pile section	Effective prestress (psi)	Maximum pile length - ft. 2-point pickup	3-point pickup	4-point pickup
48" O.D. 36" I.D.	800	149.0	202.2	290.0	22" OCTAG. 12" DIA. CORE	800	88.0	119.2	170.8
	700	139.1	189.1	271.0		700	83.0	112.7	161.1
	600	129.0	175.2	251.0		600	76.8	104.1	149.0
	500	117.8	160.0	229.0		500	70.0	95.0	136.0
42" O.D. 30" I.D.	800	137.0	186.0	267.0	20" sq.	800	89.4	121.1	173.5
	700	128.6	174.5	250.0		700	83.3	112.8	161.5
	600	119.0	162.1	230.2		600	77.2	104.8	150.0
	500	109.0	147.5	211.5		500	70.5	95.6	137.0
36" O.D. 26" I.D.	800	127.0	172.5	247.0	18" sq.	800	84.5	114.8	164.2
	700	118.8	161.6	231.5		700	79.0	107.2	153.5
	600	110.2	149.8	214.5		600	73.2	99.1	142.0
	500	100.8	136.3	195.2		500	67.0	90.7	130.0
30" O.D. 20" I.D.	800	113.2	154.0	220.5	16" sq.	800	79.8	108.2	155.0
	700	105.7	144.3	206.7		700	74.5	101.0	144.5
	600	98.5	133.5	191.0		600	69.0	93.8	134.1
	500	89.6	121.5	174.0		500	63.0	85.5	122.3
24" OCTAG. 12" DIA. CORE	800	91.0	123.2	177.0	14" sq.	800	73.8	100.2	143.5
	700	85.1	115.2	165.4		700	69.7	94.4	135.5
	600	80.0	108.9	156.1		600	64.5	87.6	125.3
	500	72.0	97.7	140.0		500	59.1	80.2	114.9

Compressive strength of concrete at the time of handling: 3750 psi.
Lengths are based on handling without tension in concrete.
Load is pile weight plus 25% impact.

The factor of safety should be not less than 2.0; therefore, f_p should be not less than 430 lb per sq in., or in round numbers 500 lb per sq in.

However, there is an upper limit to which the pile should be prestressed, so as to provide an equivalent factor of safety of 2.0 against failure in compression, on the basis that the compressive stress should not exceed

$4{,}250/2.0 = 2{,}125$ lb per sq in.

$$f_t + 2f_p = 2{,}125 \qquad \text{or} \qquad f_p = \frac{2{,}125 - f_t}{2} = \frac{2{,}125 - 530}{2}$$

$$= 798 \text{ or } 800 \text{ lb per sq in.}$$

Figure 5.26 shows typical details of square, octagonal, and hollow cylindrical prestressed-concrete piles. Figure 5.27 illustrates the general

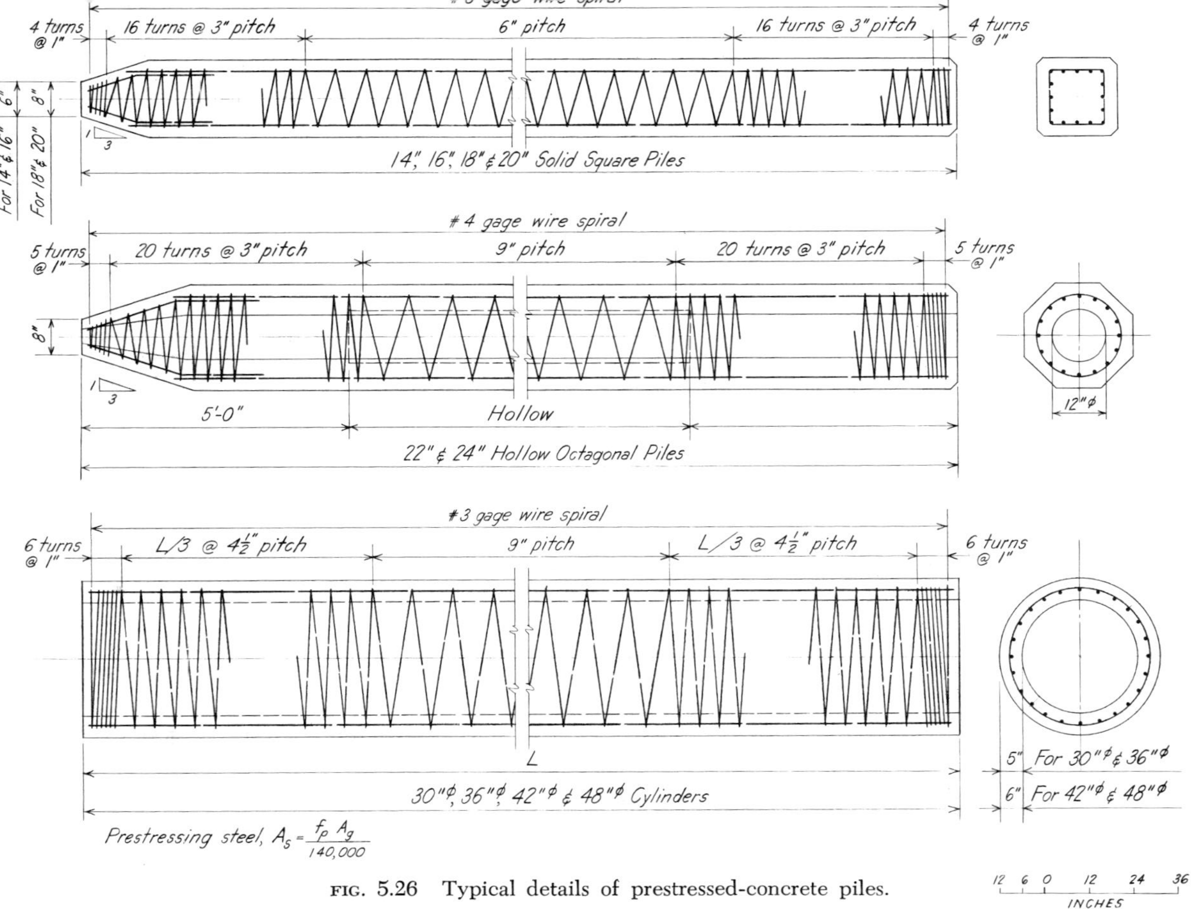

FIG. 5.26 Typical details of prestressed-concrete piles.

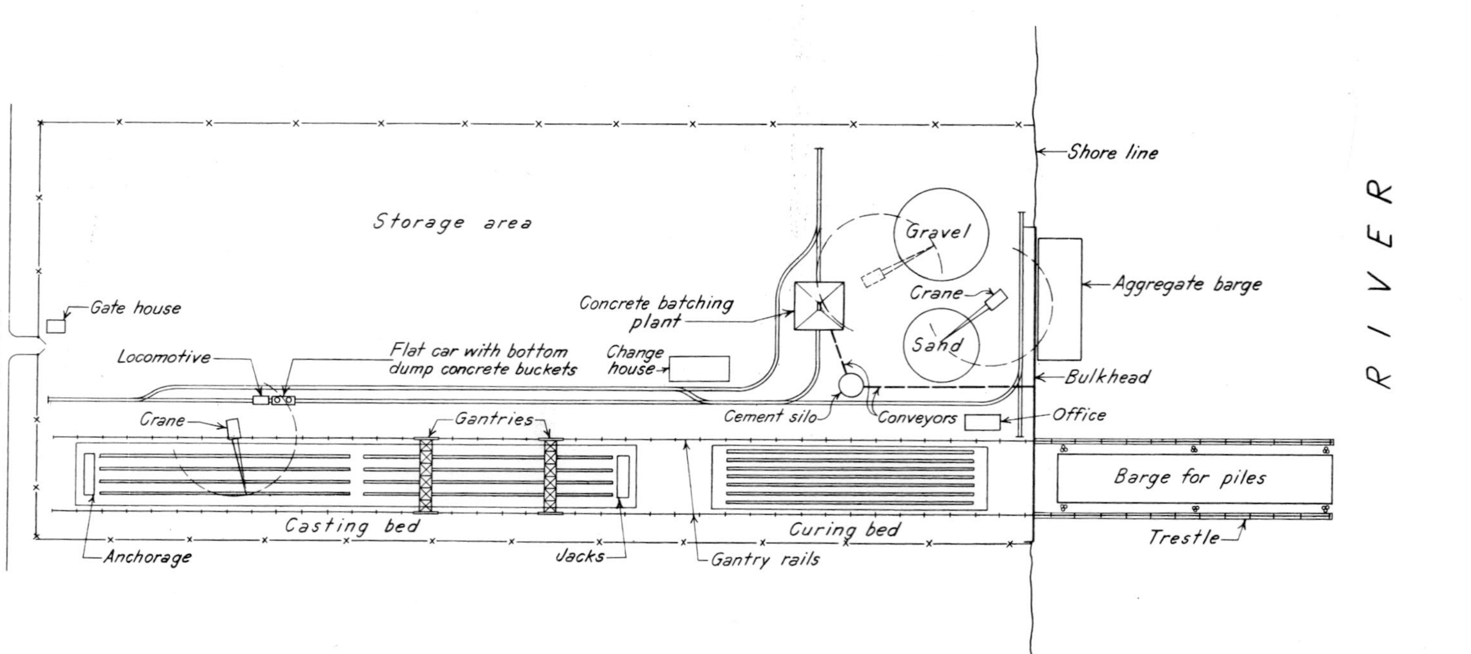

FIG. 5.27 Layout of casting yard for prestressed-concrete piles.

layout of a prestressed-pile-casting yard. The casting bed must be supported by unyielding ground or on piles, and the anchorages at the ends must be unyielding when subjected to the prestressing loads. If these rules are carefully followed little difficulty will be encountered in producing satisfactory piles.

Steel H Piles. In recent years the increase in draft and size of vessels has led to the construction of larger and stronger docks in which steel piling, particularly the H pile, has been used extensively. The following are some of its advantages.

1. It is suitable for driving in extremely long lengths, as it is relatively light and can be easily spliced by butt welding to develop its full strength. It can be readily seen that large supertankers, requiring a minimum depth of 50 ft of water alongside a dock, make it necessary to use very long piles, particularly if there is a wide range of tide and the bottom is soft. Piles over 200 ft in length have been driven, although it is usually considered more economical, if possible, to limit driving to extreme depths by the addition of lagging to the piles. This may consist of bolting wood members to the flanges of the pile a short distance from the tip, as shown in Fig. 5.28*a*, or of welding steel plates between the flanges and adding short steel H sections to the flanges as shown in Fig. 5.28*b*. The purpose of the lagging is to increase the bearing and skin friction area in the lower part of the pile.

2. The H pile has a very small soil displacement which makes it ideal to use in clay soils which lose strength when remolded.

3. It can withstand very hard driving, and if the head is damaged it can be cut off, and driving continued. The fact that it is often used as a "spud" to make a hole through boulder formations, into which a concrete pile can be driven, is evidence of its ability to withstand hard driving.

4. It is one of the easiest piles to frame or fix to the deck of a dock, as its large surface area enables the pile to develop a large amount of bond when embedded in concrete, or it can be welded to steel pile-cap girders if the deck is of steel construction. In this respect, it is easily adaptable to rigid-frame construction.

5. With respect to permanency, there is ample evidence that when embedded for its full length in soil, except loose fill, cinders, and peat bog, the H pile will suffer little, if any, loss in section from corrosion over a great number of years. However, when exposed to salt water, as is the case in most dock installations, the H pile, unless properly protected, may be subjected to severe corrosion, particularly within the tidal range. Fortunately, engineers and dock constructors have learned how to cope with this problem and, except in rare locations, H piles can be protected so that the dock may be considered a permanent installation.

This may be accomplished by coating the piles with bitumastic paint before they are driven, removing any paint remaining above the low-water level after the piles are driven, and encasing the piles with concrete from the underside of the deck to 2 ft below low water. The remaining portion of the pile may be given cathodic protection, as described in Sec.

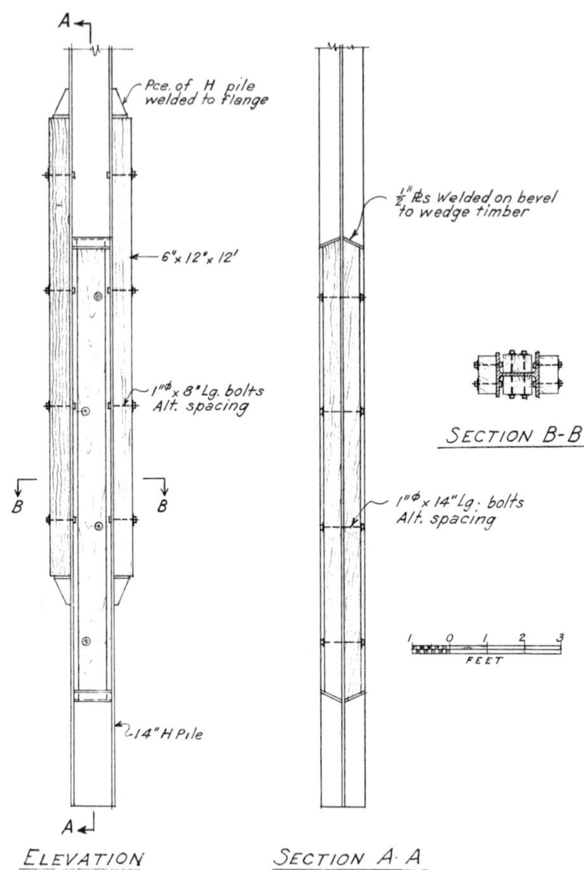

FIG. 5.28 (*a*) Typical lagging for H piles using timber.

5.14, although this is not always necessary. Unless experience from previous installations indicates the necessity of providing cathodic protection, provision may be made for its later installation, if found necessary. For temporary dock installation, where the use of the dock is not expected to extend over more than a period of 15 to 20 years and no extreme corrosion conditions are known to exist, painting the piles with two coats of bitumastic paint before they are driven and renewing this above low water about once every five years will usually provide adequate protection. If a doubtful situation exists, and concern is felt about the integrity of the portion of the pile under water, which cannot be painted, a pile section of heavier weight than required to carry the load as a column may be selected on the basis that the loss in section from corrosion over the 15- to 20-year period will not exceed the additional area which has been provided. This rate of corrosion may be estimated to amount to from 0.001 to 0.005 in. per year.

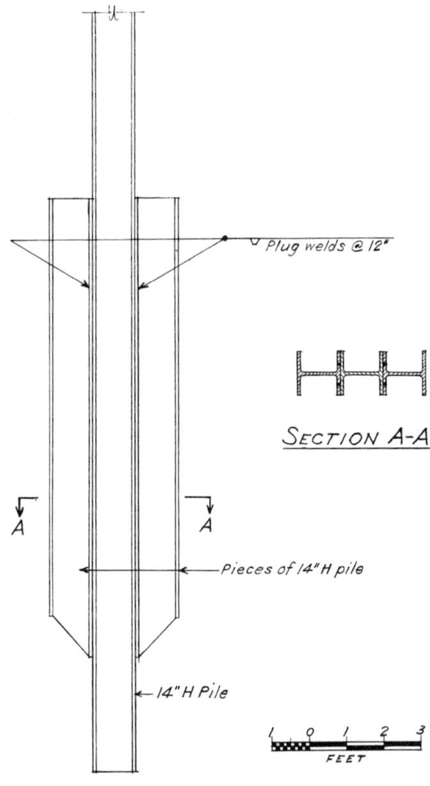

FIG. 5.28 (*b*) Typical lagging for H piles using pile cutoffs.

Allowable loads for the different standard sections of H piles are shown in Table 5.8, for different effective lengths, from Fig. 5.21. These are the loads allowed on a column and, because of the uncertainties which are connected with the installation of piles, the stress is usually limited to 9,000 lb per sq in. and a maximum load of 120 tons, if driven to rock, or 70 tons for friction piles.

H piles are usually driven with a single-acting steam hammer, to develop safe load-carrying capacities in accordance with one of the recognized pile-driving formulas. Because H piles are generally not so heavy

***Table* 5.8 Allowable Loads in Short Tons on H Piles for Different Effective Lengths**

Effective Length Feet	14" BP				12" BP		10" BP		8" BP
	117 lb	102 lb	89 lb	73 lb	74 lb	53 lb	57 lb	42 lb	36 lb
	r = 3.59	r = 3.56	r = 3.53	r = 3.49	r = 2.91	r = 2.86	r = 2.45	r = 2.40	r = 1.95
20									51
22									44
24								62	37
26							76	54	31
28							67	48	27
30					104	72	59	42	22
32					94	65	52	37	19
34					84	58	46	32	
36			127	102	75	52	40	28	
38			117	94	68	47	35	24	
40		124	107	86	60	42	30	21	
42		114	98	79	54	37			
44	122	104	90	72	48	33			
46	111	95	82	65	43	29			
48	102	87	75	59	38				
50	93	79	68	54					
52	85	72	62	49					
54	77	66	56	45					
56	70	59	51	40					
58	63	54	46	36					
60	57								

Below this line, $\frac{l}{r} > 120$

Below this line, $\frac{l}{r} > 200$

FORMULAS

For $\frac{l}{r} \leq 120$, $f = 17000 - 0.485\frac{l^2}{r^2}$

For $\frac{l}{r} > 120$, but < 200, $f = \frac{18000}{1 + \frac{l^2}{18000 r^2}} \times \left(1.6 - \frac{l}{200 r}\right)$

Values above this line exceed 120 tons and/or a maximum stress of 9000 psi (Use 70 tons max. for friction piles)

as concrete piles, but considerably heavier than wood piles, the author considers the second modification of the Engineering News formula to give good results and to be simple to use, as it takes into consideration the weight of the pile with respect to the ram of the hammer, as follows:

$$R = \frac{2E}{s + 0.3P/W}$$

where R = safe load, lb
s = average penetration per blow for last 5 blows, in.
E = energy per blow, ft-lb
P = weight of pile, lb
W = weight of ram of hammer, lb

It is readily seen that, when the weight of the pile equals the weight of the ram, the above formula becomes the first modification of the Engineering News formula, $R = 2E/(s + 0.3)$, which is often used when driving heavy precast-concrete piles; whereas if the pile is one-third the weight of the ram of the hammer the formula becomes the regular Engineering News formula, $R = 2E/(s + 0.1)$, which is used for nearly all wood-pile driving.

In using the second modification of the Engineering News formula, the size of the hammer should be selected so that the final inch of penetration will not require more than 20 blows ($s = 0.05$). Prolonged hard driving may damage the pile as well as the hammer. Particular care and judgment must be exercised when driving to refusal on rock. Refusal is ordinarily considered to be reached when five blows of the hammer do not produce a penetration of greater than ¼ in.

There are certain silt and clay soils in which excessive penetrations of H piles will result if driven in accordance with the pile-driving formulas. These soils have the characteristic of "setting up" around the pile once driving and vibration have stopped, and it is common knowledge that it takes many more blows per foot to start these piles moving again than it did at the time driving was stopped. A load test will generally prove that the pile will carry several times the load indicated by the pile-driving formulas. When this type of soil condition exists the piles should be driven to fixed penetrations determined by taking undisturbed soil samples and arriving at the allowable soil-shear value and friction between the pile, the latter being taken usually as the maximum shear value. The total skin friction thus derived, plus an allowance for end bearing based on the gross area of the pile and soil, should be divided by 2 to arrive at the allowable load based on a factor of safety of 2. Designed penetrations should be checked by making load tests, and the results should be correlated with the pile-driving formulas to arrive at the proper factor to use as a guide in evaluating the results of further pile driving, keeping in mind that soil formations are not always uniform, and that soil tests will represent the true condition of the soil only at the point at which they are taken.

In addition to corrosion, erosion is a factor which must be considered in some areas. This may be severe where there is loose, shifting sand carried by the current and the waves, in which case the surface of the piling should be protected with creosoted-wood plank or the pile encased in concrete.

H-pile splices should be designed to develop the full strength of the section in bearing and in bending. This can be done by butt welding as shown in Fig. 5.29. With the improvement in welding technique and reliability in recent years, this method of butt splicing has now superseded the use of splice plates, except for occasional jobs where splice plates or a combination of splice plates and butt welding may be specified. The butt weld is usually made with only one end of the pile beveled. The piles may be ordered from the mill with one end beveled for welding, although this can be easily and accurately done on the job by means of a jig and flame cutting torch.

Steel-pipe Piles and Cylinders. Pipe piles are generally purchased in nominal sizes ranging from 8 to 24 in., in 2-in. increments of diameter, and in various wall thicknesses ranging from 5⁄16 in. for the smaller sizes to ½ in. for the larger diameters, except that spiral-welded pipe is available in a minimum thickness of 9⁄64 in. in the smaller diameters. Starting with a 14-in. diameter, the outside diameter is the nominal size of the pipe and remains constant for all thicknesses of wall. Above 24 in. in diameter, the pipe, when used as a foundation, is commonly referred to as a cylinder.

Pipe for piles is customarily specified as seamless or longitudinally welded, ASTM designation A 252, grade 2 (minimum tensile strength 60,000 lb per sq in.) or grade 3 (minimum tensile strength 75,000 lb per

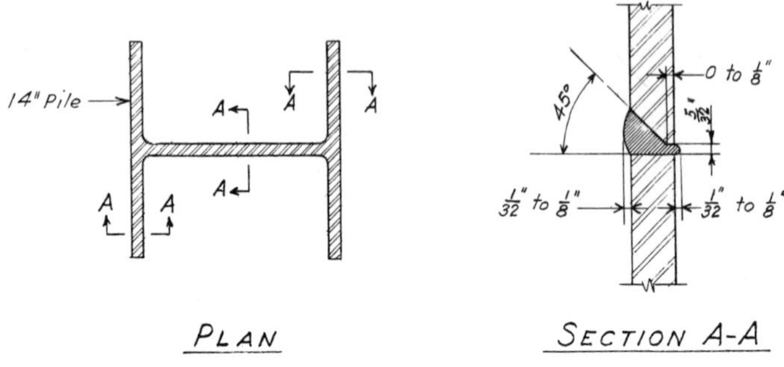

FIG. 5.29 Butt-weld splice for H piles.

sq in.). Electric-fusion-welded spiral-seamed steel pipe, ASTM designation A 252, grade 2, is sometimes used although not recommended for hard driving conditions. Unless ordered cut to specified lengths, at additional cost, seamless pipe is purchased either in single random lengths, 16 to 25 ft, inclusive, or double random lengths, over 25 ft with a minimum average of 35 ft, the latter practice being most common so as to keep the number of splices to a minimum. Spiral-welded pipe can be purchased in standard lengths up to 60 ft and up to 90 ft by special order.

Pipe piles are driven either with open or closed ends depending upon soil conditions. The latter method predominates in marine work and dock construction where rock is usually not encountered except at excessive depths. Open-end pipe piles are usually driven to rock or other hard stratum, cleaned out, and filled with concrete. Skin friction is ignored in figuring the load-carrying capacity of the pile. If the soil formation is such that the major part of the load is carried in skin friction, it is obvious that there is no advantage in driving the pile with an open end and incurring the additional expense of cleaning it out, unless the following conditions exist: (1) a displacement type of pile is not desirable because of loss in shearing strength due to remolding of the soil; (2) a boulder formation exists in which it may be necessary to drill inside the pile to obtain the proper penetration. Unless the above conditions exist, a closed-end pipe pile will prove more economical.

Except for temporary installations pipe piles and cylinders are filled with concrete. In addition to increasing the load-carrying capacity of the pile it protects the shell from corrosion on the inside.

Pipe piles for docks are usually spliced by butt welding, using a back-up ring or plate. Welding is essential if the piles are to take uplift or bending. Standard cast-steel splice sleeves may be purchased and are commonly used when pipe piles are driven from the ground surface and act only in compression. Closed-end pipe piles require points. Standard cast-steel driving points may be obtained, or if unavailable a special steel point may be fabricated by welding.

Pipe piles are usually driven with a single-acting steam hammer, and when driven with open ends to rock, a penetration of not more than ¼ in. in the last five blows of the specified hammer will be considered refusal. The allowable load for closed-end friction piles may be determined as for H piles (page 276).

Pipe piles or cylinders for dock construction will usually have to be designed as long columns. The allowable load on columns consisting of steel pipe filled with concrete, in accordance with the ACI Building Code, is

$$P' = 0.25f'_c\left(1 - 0.000025\,\frac{l^2}{K_c}\right)A_c + f'_rA_s$$

where P' = allowable axial load, lb
f'_c = compressive strength of concrete at age of 28 days
l = effective length of column, in.
K_c^2 = radius of gyration of concrete
A_c = area of concrete
A_s = area of steel pipe
f'_r = allowable unit stress in steel pipe which is 17,000 − 0.485 l^2/K_s^2 when the pipe has a yield strength of at least 33,000 lb per sq in. and an l/K_s ratio equal to or less than 120, where K_s = radius of gyration of the metal pipe section

Table 5.9 gives the maximum loads in short tons for different effective lengths, from Fig. 5.21, of pipe piles filled with 3,000 lb per sq in. concrete.

Wood Piles. These have been used in the past more extensively for dock construction than any other type of pile. However, the trend of recent construction, except for temporary use, has been away from the use of wood piles, due to the stronger and larger piers which are required for the huge liners and tankers of today. In general, where wood piles can be used, they are still the most economical type of construction.

Table 5.9 Maximum Loads in Short Tons on Concrete-filled Pipe Piles for Different Effective Lengths

Effective length ft	Outside Diameter and Wall Thickness of Pipe Pile																					
	24"	22"	22"	22"	20"	20"	20"	18"	18"	18"	16"	16"	16"	14"	14"	14"	$12\frac{3}{4}$"	$12\frac{3}{4}$"	$12\frac{3}{4}$"	$10\frac{3}{4}$"	$10\frac{3}{4}$"	$10\frac{3}{4}$"
	.500"	.500"	.438"	.375"	.500"	.438"	.375"	.500"	.438"	.375"	.500"	.438"	.375"	.500"	.438"	.375"	.500"	.438"	.375"	.500"	.438"	.365"
20																				125	112	98
22																				120	108	95
24																			123	116	103	91
26																			119	110	98	86
28																			114	104	93	82
30																		125	110	98	87	77
32																		120	105	91	81	71
34																122	127	114	100	84	75	65
36																117	120	108	94	77	68	59
38															126	111	113	101	88			
40															120	105	106	95	82			
42														127	113	99	98	88	76			
44														120	106	93						
46													126	111	98	86						
48													119	103	91	80						
50												127	112									
52												119	105									
54											124	111	97									
56																						
58										124												
60										116												
62								139	123	111												
64																						
66																						
68					164	146	129															
70																						
72																						
74																						
76		178	162	140																		
78																						
80																						
82	205																					

Above this line $P > 120$ tons

Below this line $\frac{h}{K_s} > 120$

FORMULAS

$$P = 0.25 f_c' \left(1 - 0.000025 \frac{h^2}{K_c^2}\right) A_c + f_r' A_s$$

$$f_r' = 17000 - 0.485 \frac{h^2}{K_s^2}$$

NOTES

Minimum yield strength of pipe $\geqq$ 33000 psi.

Outer $\frac{1}{16}$" of pipe thickness deducted in computing A_s.

$f_c' = 3000$ psi.

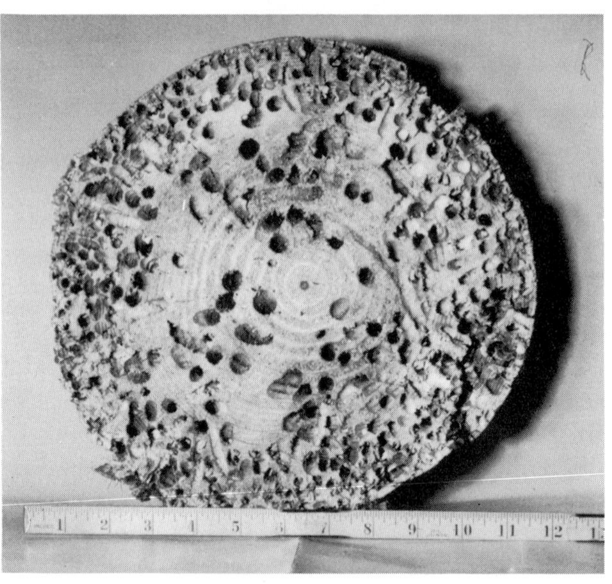

FIG. 5.30 Marine borer attack on uncreosoted-wood pile.

Practically all wood piles used for permanent dock construction are creosoted. Figure 5.30 shows the condition of a plain wood pile, attacked by marine borers, which was in the water less than one year, and although the structure was considered temporary (2 years use), most of the piles had to be replaced. Of course, all waters are not inhabited with marine

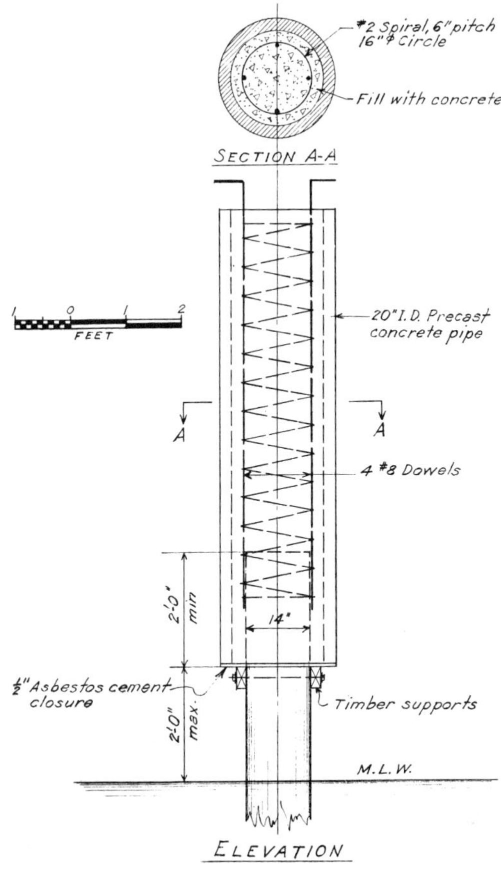

FIG. 5.31 Concrete pipe encasement for wood piles. (*Courtesy of the Port of New York Authority.*)

organisms which attack wood, and some lakes and rivers have structures supported on plain wood piles, cut off and capped at low-water level, which have been in service many years. Greenheart piles have been found to be highly resistant to marine organism attack and decay and have been used quite extensively for dock construction, particularly for fender piles, because of their very high strength in bending and crushing. In addition to creosoting wood piles, recent practice has been to further protect them above the water level, particularly from fire, by encasing them with concrete pipe sleeves, as shown in Fig. 5.31.

The load on wood piles for dock construction is usually kept somewhat lower than for general foundation use, where the pile is supported by the ground for most, if not all, of its length, and where good supporting soil is usually found at somewhat higher levels than at the locations of marine structures. Piles which will be unsupported for a considerable part of their length will have to act as long columns in which the average diameter will probably not exceed 12 in. It can be readily demonstrated that a load of 15 to 20 tons is the most a pile of average unsupported length (35 ft) will safely support. However, greenheart piles, because of their exceptional strength, may support as much as 30 tons per pile. It must be kept in mind that wood piles used for dock construction will, in general, receive no reduction in unsupported length, as they are seldom fixed by the deck or low-water bracing at the top or by the soil at the bottom. Piles for foundations on land, which are designed to support 25 to 30 tons each, would normally be designed for 15 to 20 tons, if used in dock construction.

Wood piles may be driven with single- or double-acting steam hammers to safe bearing loads in accordance with the straight Engineering News formula, $R = 2E/(s + 0.1)$.

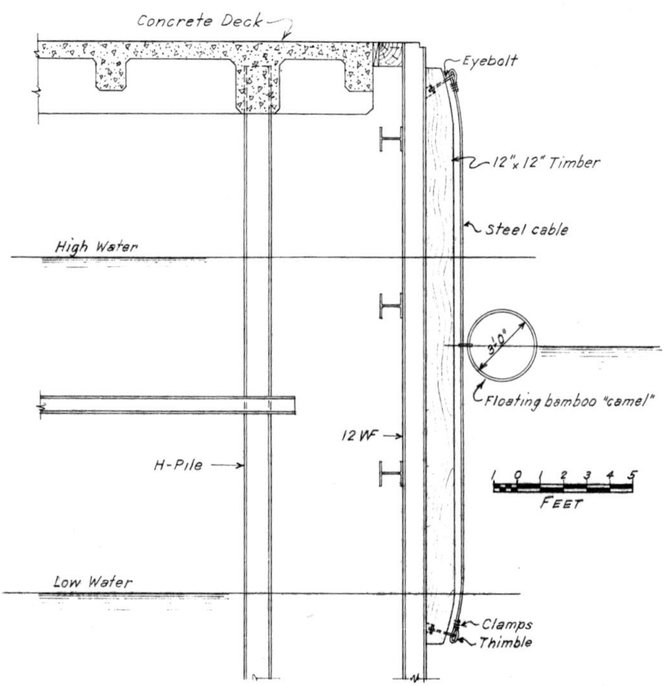

FIG. 5.32 Floating camel fender.

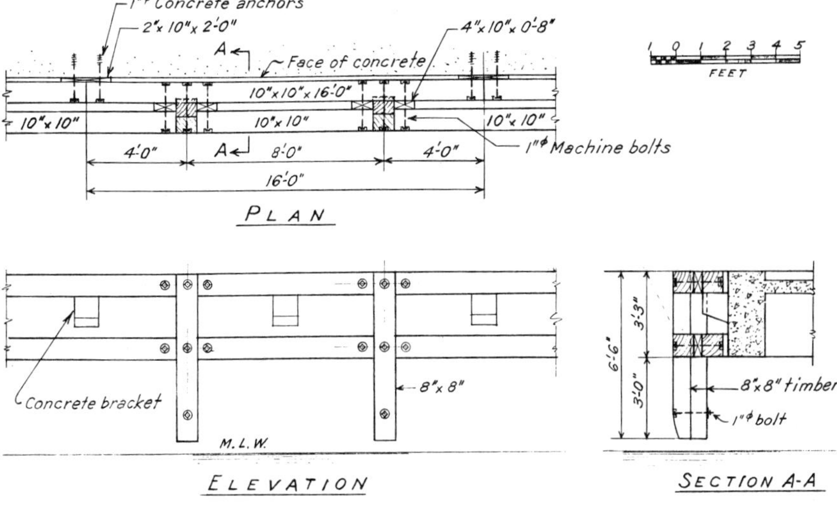

FIG. 5.33 Typical hung-wood fender.

5.6 Dock Fenders

The principal function of a dock fender is to prevent the ship and/or the dock from being damaged during mooring. Under ideal conditions and under perfect control a ship might approach a dock without striking a severe blow, but it is still essential to separate it from the dock with some form of rubbing strip of wood or rubber which will prevent the paint from being damaged on account of the relative motion between the dock and the ship, caused by the wind and waves. A floating log or "camel," as shown in Fig. 5.32 is sometimes placed between the ship and the fender system or face of the dock. This accomplishes two purposes: i.e., it holds the ship off the face of the dock, and it helps to distribute the load along the fender system. The latter is of particular importance when a large ship is docking alongside a wood pier with wood-fender piles.

Types of Fenders. In its simplest form the fender may be a horizontal wood member or a number of vertical wood members or rubbing strips fastened to the deck or face of the dock. For these vertical members, wood piles may be used or they may be timbers terminating at the water level and hung from the deck, in which case the fender is called a "hung fender," as shown in Fig. 5.33. Care must be taken to see that the weight of the fender is supported on brackets from the face of the dock; otherwise, the long bolts which hold the timbers in place will bend and allow the fender to sag. The wood in itself can absorb a certain amount of energy due to being compressed, and, if this is built up into a substantial thickness, the force of impact will be considerably reduced.

Wood-fender piles, which are placed away from the dock on a slight batter of about 1 on 24, will absorb energy due to the deflection which will take place when struck by the ship. However, as the ships became larger it was found that something additional was needed to absorb more of the energy, and various types of flexible-fender systems have been designed and have functioned with a considerable amount of success.

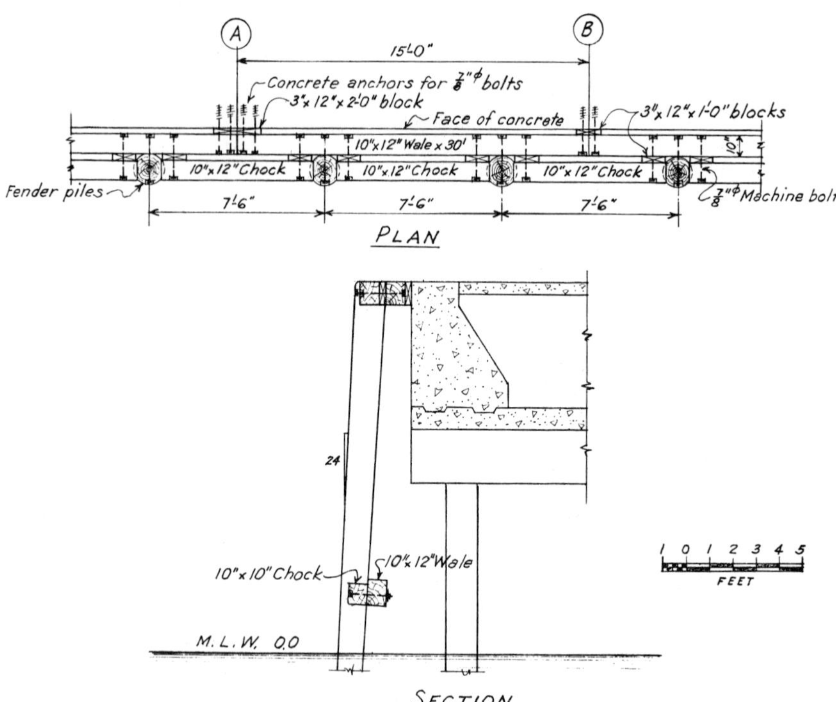

FIG. 5.34 Typical springing-type wood fender.

Figure 5.34 shows a springing type of wood fender in which energy absorption is obtained not only from the deflection of the wood piles but from the deflection of a horizontal wood wale which is blocked out from the deck so that the ship cannot strike at a point which is rigidly connected to the deck. This is accomplished by locating the wood piles at the quarter points of the span and by blocking out the chocks between the piles. The wood wale must be carefully proportioned to give the proper deflection without failing in shear or bending.

In designing fender systems involving primarily the use of wood, only stress grade timber should be specified and it is customary to creosote this to a retention of 12 to 16 lb per cu ft, or to refusal in the case of oak.

Bolt holes should be drilled the same diameter as the bolt, and all holes on the face of the fender should be countersunk. All cuts made in the field should be painted with creosote oil, and the remaining space around the heads of all countersunk bolts should be filled with mastic. Fender piles should be creosoted to a retention of 14 to 20 lb per cu ft. All fender hardware should be galvanized.

FIG. 5.35 Rubber-tired truck-wheel fenders at Government Pier, Miragoane, Haiti.

Rubber has come into extensive use for fender systems. Rubber tires hung over the side of a dock are an example of its utilization as a fender. A unique use of the rubber tire as a fender is shown in Fig. 5.35, in which truck tires on wheels are placed in a horizontal position along the face of the dock and rotate on their axles set in the concrete deck, thereby eliminating longitudinal friction between the ship and the face of the dock. This type would only be suitable for locations where the water is calm and the tide range is small.

From the use of rubber tires have sprung the hollow-cylindrical or rectangular fenders, rectangular rubber blocks, and the sandwich type known as the Raykin fender buffer. The hollow-cylindrical type was originally used as a draped fender, as shown in Fig. 5.36. This requires a solid fascia wall for a depth of at least 6 ft, as it is desirable to spread the load over at least a 3-ft height of the ship's plate. In this respect, it is important to have the fenders precurved to the specified radius. The

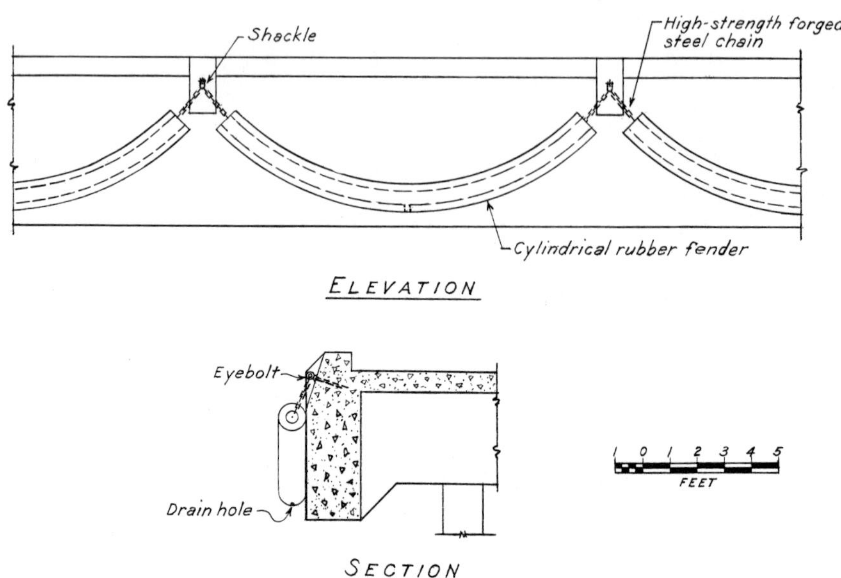

FIG. 5.36 Typical draped rubber fender.

draped fender is particularly adaptable to the solid type of dock construction, such as sheet-pile cells capped with a heavy concrete dock wall, quay walls, or bulkheads; or to the open relieving-platform type of construction with a deep fascia wall; or to the heavy-concrete platform-type dolphins. Figure 5.37 shows an actual installation of the largest size, 18-in.-O.D. cylindrical rubber fenders on concrete breasting dolphins designed for the impact of 100,000-ton supertankers. Draped rubber fenders are supported by wire rope or chain attached to eyebolts set in the concrete dock wall. The eyebolts are set in recesses so that they do not protrude beyond the face of the wall. Table 5.10 indicates suggested chain sizes for draped rubber fenders. The lowest point of each curved fender should be provided with a drain hole.

Where it is not practical to drape the fender, as at a curved surface at the corner of a pier or the rounded end of a dolphin, either the square or the cylindrical fender may be attached to the concrete with bolts, as

FIG. 5.37 Cylindrical rubber-fender system at Mene Grande oil dock, Puerto La Cruz, Venezuela. (*Courtesy of the Goodyear Tire and Rubber Co.*)

Table 5.10 Suggested Chain Sizes for Cylindrical and Rectangular Draped Rubber Fenders

Cylindrical fender size	Rectangular fender size	Trade size of chain, in.	Material size, in.	Inside length link, in.	Inside width link, in.	Weight per 100 ft, lb	Proof test, lb	Working load, lb
5″ x 2½″ 7″ x 3″	5″ x 6½″ x 2½″ 7″ x 10″ x 3″ 8″ x 8″ x 3″	½	17/32	1 15/32	13/16	285	14,000	7,000
8″ x 3½″	8″ x 10″ x 3″	⅝	21/32	1 11/16	15/16	435	20,250	10,125
10″ x 5″	10″ x 10″ x 4″ 10″ x 12″ x 4″	¾	25/32	1 15/16	1⅛	635	28,000	14,000
12″ x 6″	12″ x 12″ x 5″	⅞	29/32	2¼	1¼	870	38,250	19,125
15″ x 7½″ 18″ x 9″		1	1 1/32	2 9/16	1⅜	1,125	48,500	24,250

NOTE: Chain made of carbon steel heat-treated to an average tensile strength of 85,000 psi.

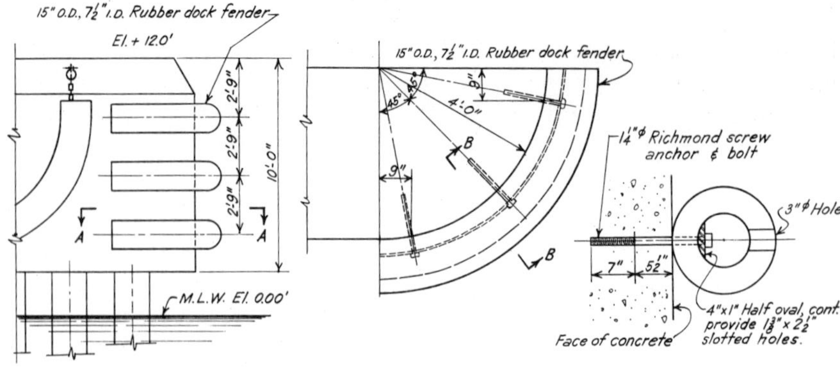

FIG. 5.38 Typical details of rubber fender at curved corner.

FIG. 5.39 Combination rubber and wood-pile corner fender. (*Courtesy of the Goodyear Tire and Rubber Co.*)

shown in Fig. 5.38, curved plate washers or a continuous half-oval bar being placed under the bolt heads, and holes being provided in the wall opposite the bolts to permit their insertion. Figure 5.39 shows a combination rubber and wood-pile corner fender being used on one of the New York City piers.

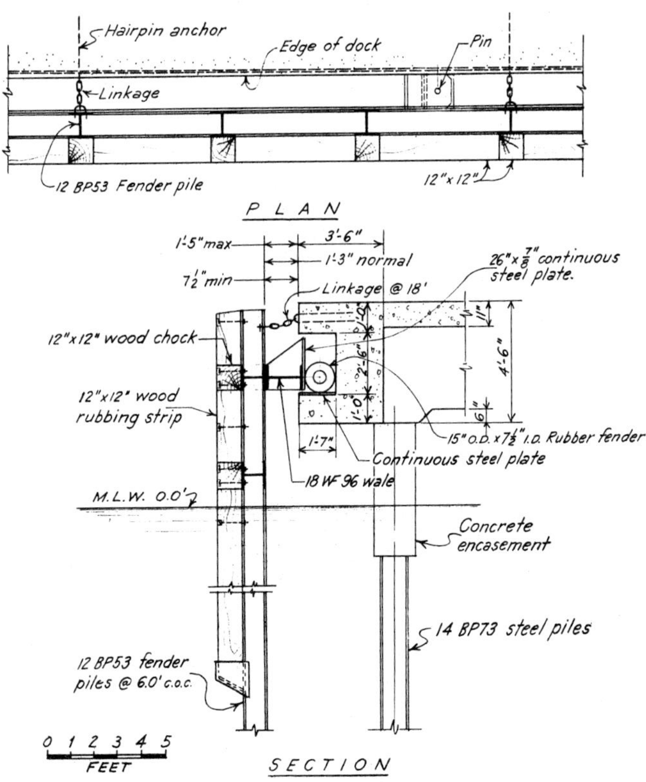

FIG. 5.40 Combination steel-beam and rubber-fender system with steel-fender piles.

Where it is not practical to use a deep-dock fascia beam or wall, the cylindrical rubber fender may be placed in back of a horizontal steel beam to which are attached fender piles, as shown in Fig. 5.40. If the steel beam is longer than about 30 ft, it should be articulated by inserting pin-connected splices which will transmit shear but not moment. Piles may be either wood or steel, but if the latter are used they should be provided with wood rubbing strips.

Cylindrical rubber fenders come in sizes ranging from 5 in. O.D. by 2½ in. I.D. to 18 in. O.D. by 9 in. I.D. Figure 5.41 gives the energy absorption and resulting force with respect to deflection for each of the above sizes of cylindrical rubber fenders, and Fig. 5.42 gives the corre-

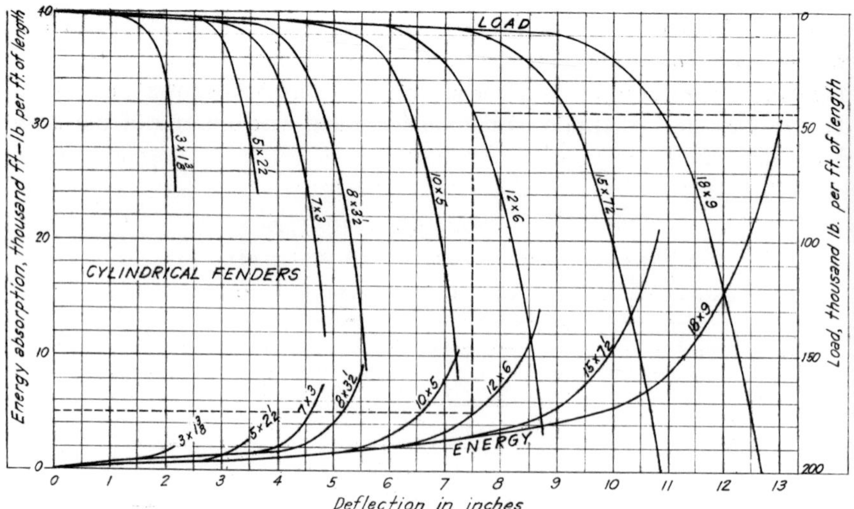

FIG. 5.41 Energy absorption and load versus deflection curves for cylindrical rubber fenders. (*Courtesy of the Goodyear Tire and Rubber Co.*)

Example. For an energy of 5,000 ft-lb and a 12- by 6-in. fender, the load per ft will be 43,000 lb, and the deflection will be 7½ in.

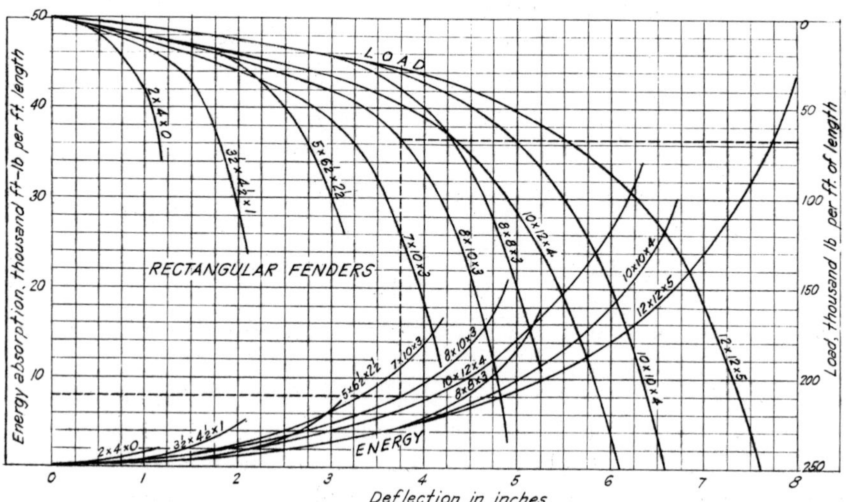

FIG. 5.42 Energy absorption and load versus deflection curves for rectangular rubber fenders. (*Courtesy of the Goodyear Tire and Rubber Co.*)

Example. For an energy of 8,000 ft-lb, and an 8- by 10- by 3-in. fender, the load per ft will be 68,000 lb, and the deflection will be 3¾ in. The energy and load curves are plotted for loads applied to the wider face.

sponding information for rectangular rubber fenders. The energy absorption of the cylindrical rubber fender is directly proportional to the force until the deflection equals approximately 50 per cent of the external diameter. Beyond this point the force increases much more rapidly than the absorption of energy, and it is usually desirable to use a fender large enough so that the energy of the striking ship will be used up without requiring a deflection of such magnitude as to result in a disproportionate increase in the force.

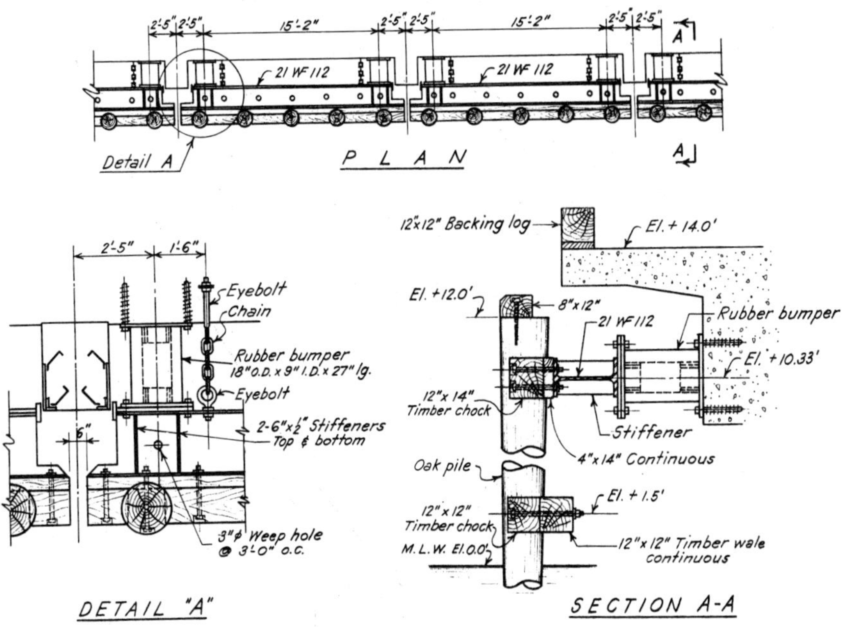

FIG. 5.43 Fender system using cylindrical rubber blocks in end compression.

Cylindrical or rectangular rubber blocks are used in compression behind steel wales or piles to absorb the ship's impact, as shown in Fig. 5.43. The energy and force-deflection curves for end compression of cylindrical rubber blocks are shown in Figs. 5.44 and 5.45, respectively.

Raykin fender buffers consist of a series of connected sandwiches made of steel plates cemented to layers of rubber, as shown in Fig. 5.46. They can be obtained in various sizes and the energy-absorbing capacities are given in Table 5.11.

Steel springs have been used in dock fender systems. Figure 5.47 shows a typical installation. Rubber fenders have generally replaced the use of springs as the former have a longer life and require less maintenance. Also, the cylindrical type of rubber fender is better able to take longitudinal forces parallel to the dock.

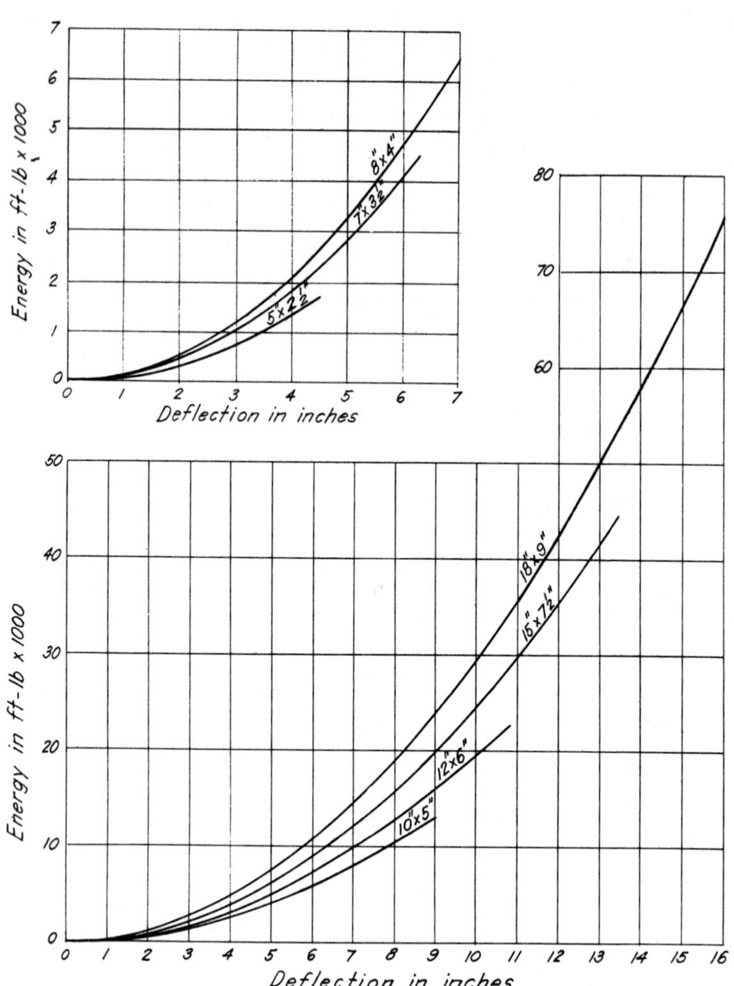

FIG. 5.44 Energy-deflection curves for cylindrical rubber fenders in end compression. (*Courtesy of the United States Rubber Co.*)

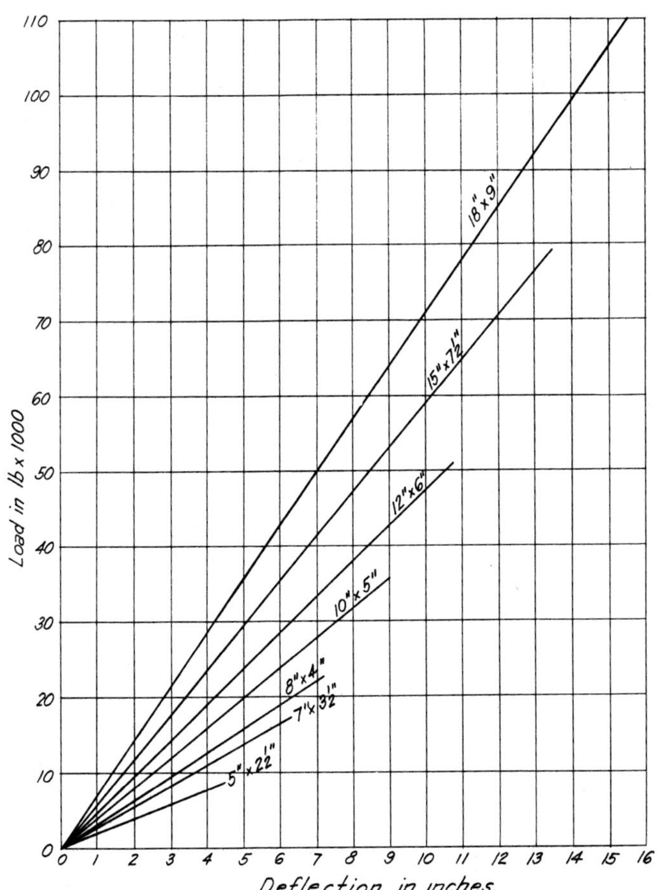

FIG. 5.45 Load-deflection curves for cylindrical rubber fenders in end compression. (*Courtesy of the United States Rubber Co.*)

Gravity-type fenders have been used for many years in Europe but have never become too popular in the United States. These are designed on the basis of transforming the kinetic energy into potential energy by means of raising weight. This is accomplished in a number of ways: (1) by a system of cables and sheaves, (2) by a pendulum, or (3) by trunnions.

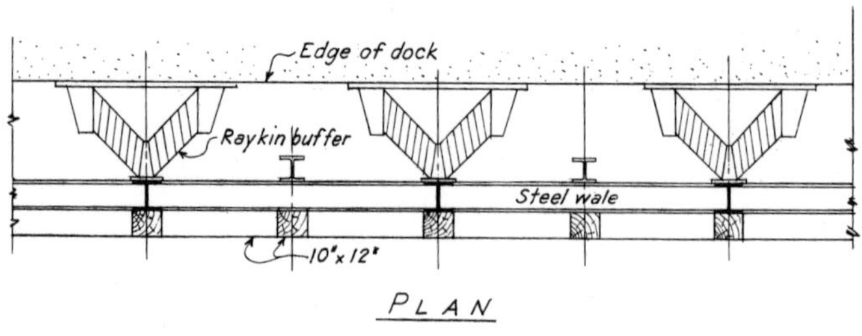

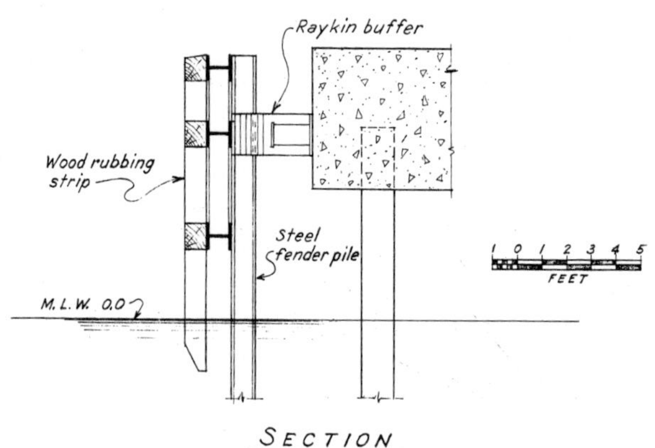

FIG. 5.46 Fender system using Raykin fender buffers.

The first gravity fenders were installed at Heysham, England, in 1942, at a special wartime oil pier. The site is exposed to severe sea and weather conditions and a 27-ft tidal range. The ends of the pier are protected by bell dolphins as shown in Fig. 5.48. The ballasted outer frame or bell can rotate and when pushed laterally the center of gravity of the bell, which weighs 170 tons, is raised by 11 in. The work done is, therefore, $170 \times 11 = 1{,}870$ in.-tons, which is sufficient to absorb the entire energy of impact of a vessel with a displaced weight of 28,000 long tons, traveling at a speed of 0.5 ft per sec.

A common type of gravity-fender unit suitable for use along the face of a dock is shown in Fig. 5.49. These units of steel tubes filled with concrete, with a facing of wood rubbing strips, weigh in the order of

Table 5.11 Technical Data for Raykin Fender Buffers

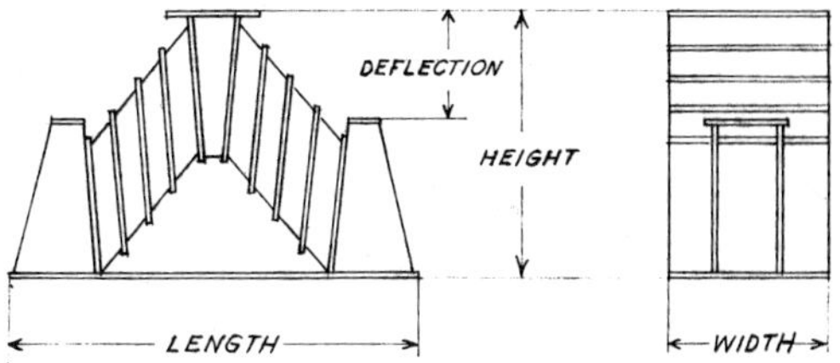

	PART NO	LOAD LB.	ENERGY ABSORPTION FT-LB	PART NO.	LOAD LB.	ENERGY ABSORPTION FT-LB	DEFLECTION	DIMENSIONS IN INCHES		
								LENGTH	WIDTH	HEIGHT
20-25 TON SIZE (SAME OVERALL DIMENSIONS)	A-20	40,000	5,800	A-25	50,000	7,250	3	33 1/8	18	20 9/16
	B-20	40,000	11,600	B-25	50,000	14,500	6	39 1/2	18	23 13/16
	C-20	40,000	17,400	C-25	50,000	21,750	9	45 3/4	18	27 1/8
	D-20	40,000	23,200	D-25	50,000	29,000	12	51 7/8	18	30 3/8
	E-20	40,000	29,000	E-25	50,000	36,250	15	58 1/8	18	33 5/8
	F-20	40,000	34,800	F-25	50,000	43,500	18	64 1/8	18	36 7/8
30-35 TON SIZE (SAME OVERALL DIMENSIONS)	A-30	60,000	8,700	A-35	70,000	10,150	3	38 3/4	21 1/8	23 11/16
	B-30	60,000	17,400	B-35	70,000	20,300	6	45	21 1/8	26 15/16
	C-30	60,000	26,100	C-35	70,000	30,450	9	51 1/4	21 1/8	30 1/4
	D-30	60,000	34,800	D-35	70,000	40,600	12	57 1/2	21 1/8	33 1/2
	E-30	60,000	43,500	E-35	70,000	50,750	15	63 3/4	21 1/8	36 3/4
	F-30	60,000	52,200	F-35	70,000	60,900	18	70	21 1/8	40
40-45 TON SIZE (SAME OVERALL DIMENSIONS)	A-40	80,000	11,600	A-45	90,000	13,050	3	45 1/4	24 1/2	26 3/16
	B-40	80,000	23,200	B-45	90,000	26,100	6	51 3/4	24 1/2	29 1/2
	C-40	80,000	34,800	C-45	90,000	39,150	9	58 1/4	24 1/2	32 3/4
	D-40	80,000	46,400	D-45	90,000	52,200	12	64 7/8	24 1/2	36 1/16
	E-40	80,000	58,000	E-45	90,000	65,250	15	71 1/4	24 1/2	39 1/8
	F-40	80,000	69,600	F-45	90,000	78,300	18	78 1/4	24 1/2	42 5/8
50-60 TON SIZE (SAME OVERALL DIMENSIONS)	A-50	100,000	14,500	A-60	120,000	17,400	3	51 1/4	27	28 15/16
	B-50	100,000	29,000	B-60	120,000	34,800	6	57 3/4	27	32 1/4
	C-50	100,000	43,500	C-60	120,000	52,200	9	64 3/4	27	35 1/2
	D-50	100,000	58,000	D-60	120,000	69,600	12	70 3/4	27	38 13/16
	E-50	100,000	72,500	E-60	120,000	87,000	15	77 1/4	27	42 1/8
	F-50	100,000	87,000	F-60	120,000	104,400	18	84 1/4	27	45 3/8

SOURCE: General Tire and Rubber Company.

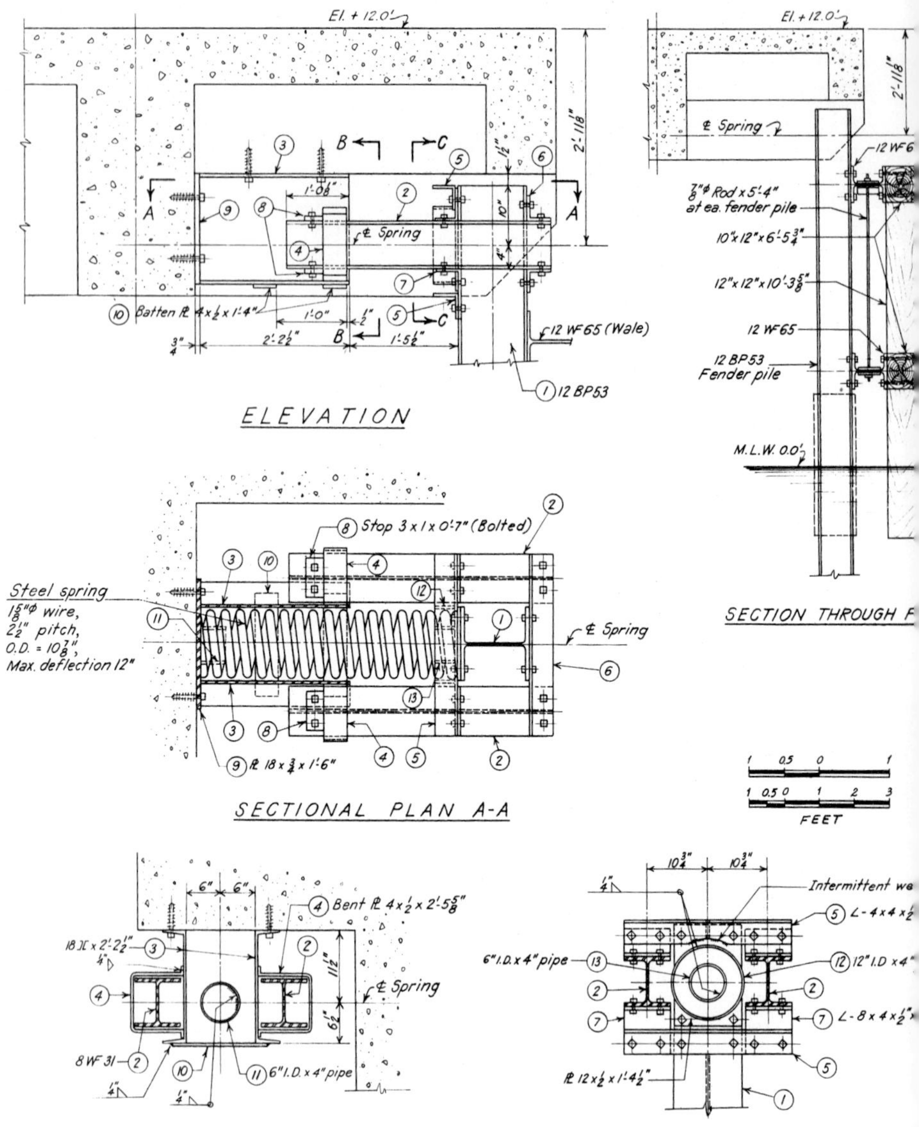

FIG. 5.47 Fender system using steel springs.

15 tons and have a maximum vertical movement of about 2 ft, thereby absorbing 30 ft-tons of energy. By providing a sufficient number of units along the face of the dock, the impact energy of the ship may be absorbed, taking into consideration that the amount of energy absorbed by each unit will vary directly with its movement, which will depend upon the curvature of the hull and the angle with which the ship strikes the dock, as shown in Fig. 5.50.

Another design utilizing the principle of transferring kinetic energy

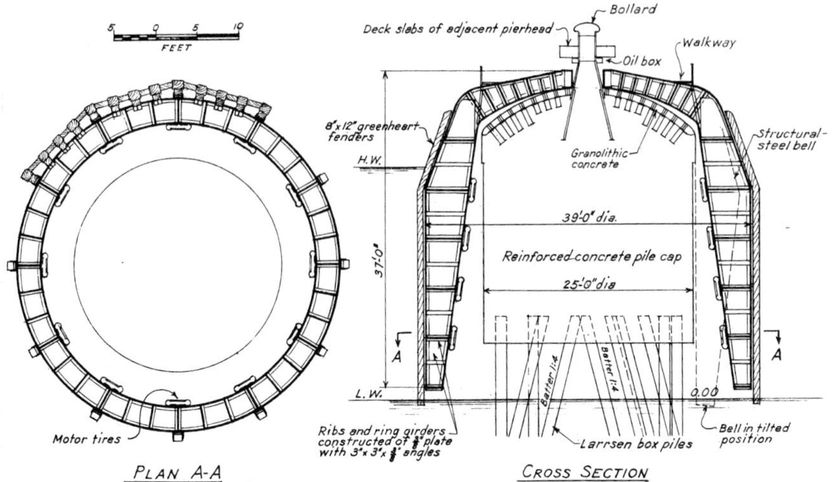

FIG. 5.48 Baker bell dolphin. (*From Dock and Harbour Authority, January,* 1947.)

of impact to potential energy of position is shown in Fig. 5.51, in which a large block of concrete is suspended horizontally by two sets of cables or chains inclined in a transverse and longitudinal direction from the deck of the pier. The front face of the concrete block is provided with wood rubbing strips.

Operating on a somewhat similar gravitational principle, Virgil Blancato, manager, structural branch, Public Works Department, New York Naval Shipyard, has designed a fender unit, as shown in Fig. 5.52. A unit 88 ft long of this type of fender was installed in the Brooklyn Navy Yard in 1955. This fender unit when struck by a ship is moved inward and upward on inclined supports, thereby utilizing the weight of the fender to absorb the kinetic energy of impact.

General Design of Fenders. The maximum impact caused by a ship striking the dock when berthing is based upon certain assumptions as to the ship's operation with respect to the angle and speed with which it approaches the dock. It is customary to assume that the ship is fully loaded (displaced tonnage) and approaches at an angle of 10° to the

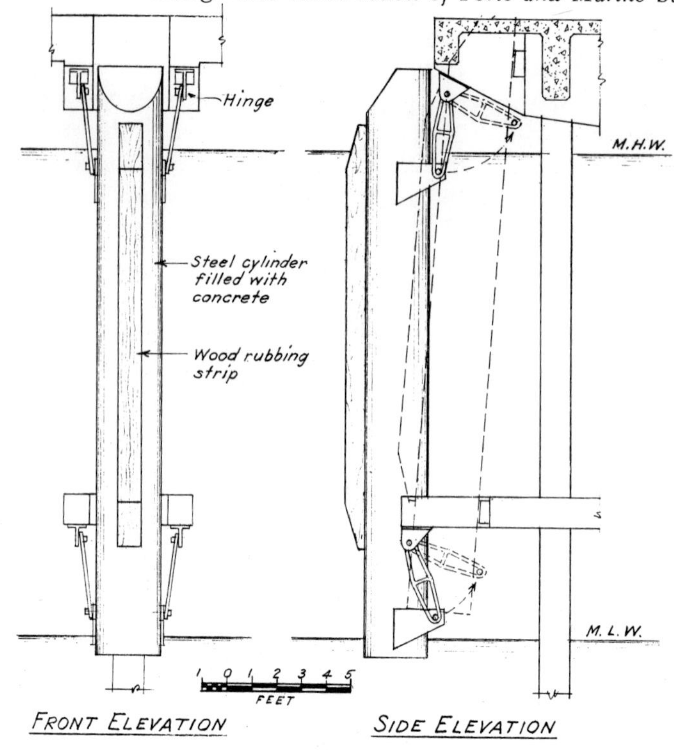

FIG. 5.49 Suspended-gravity fender, tubular type. (*From Dock and Harbour Authority, January,* 1947.)

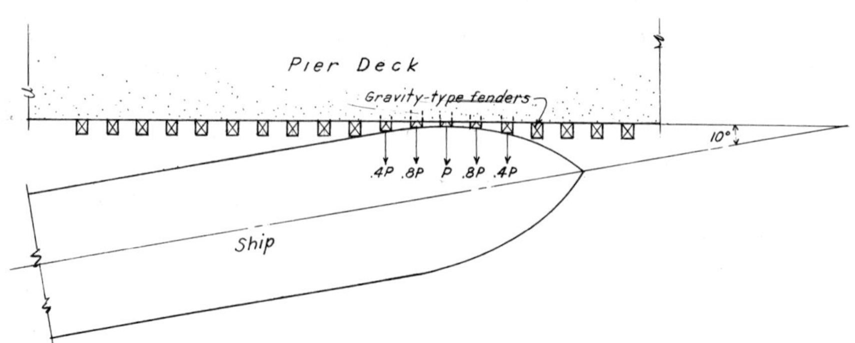

FIG. 5.50 Ship striking dock with suspended-gravity fender system.

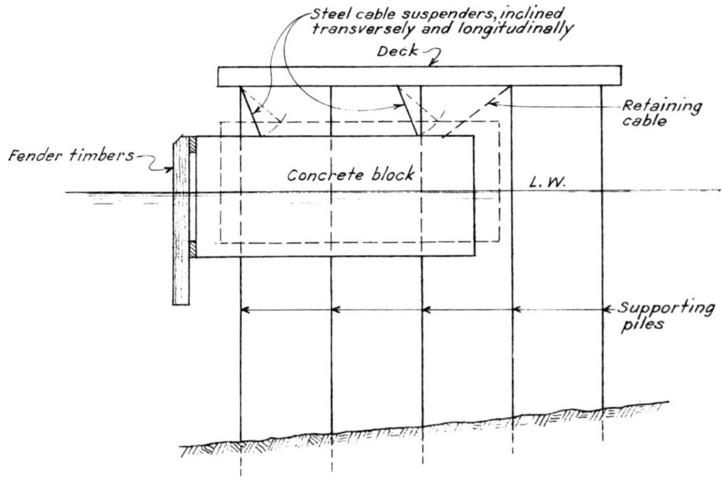

FIG. 5.51 Suspended-gravity fender, concrete-block type. (*From Dock and Harbour Authority, January,* 1947.)

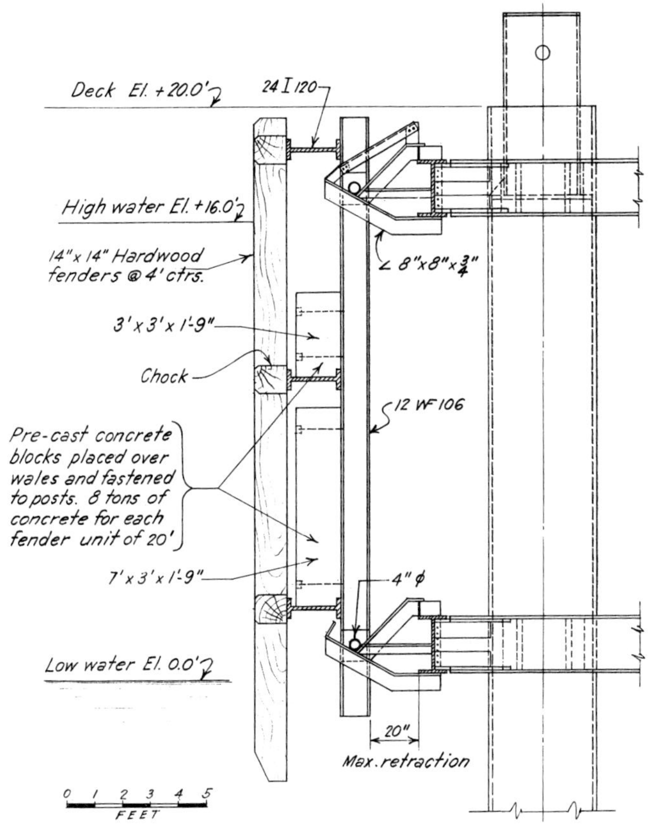

FIG. 5.52 Suspended-gravity fender, Blancato type. (*From A Breasting Dolphin for Berthing Supertankers, by J. M. Weis and V. Blancato, Journal of the Waterways and Harbor Division, ASCE, September,* 1959.)

face of the dock, as shown in Fig. 5.53. It is readily seen that the bow of the ship will strike the fender, and that only approximately one-half the tonnage will be effective in creating energy of impact to be absorbed by the fender and pier. The speed of approach will have to be assumed and it is here that the greatest uncertainty exists, particularly since its effect on the energy varies as the square of the velocity. The speed of the ship must be converted into the component normal to the dock, and experience has indicated that this velocity will be between 0.15 and 1.0 ft per sec, the latter figure corresponding to a velocity of approach of approximately 3½ knots at an angle of 10° to the face to the dock. In

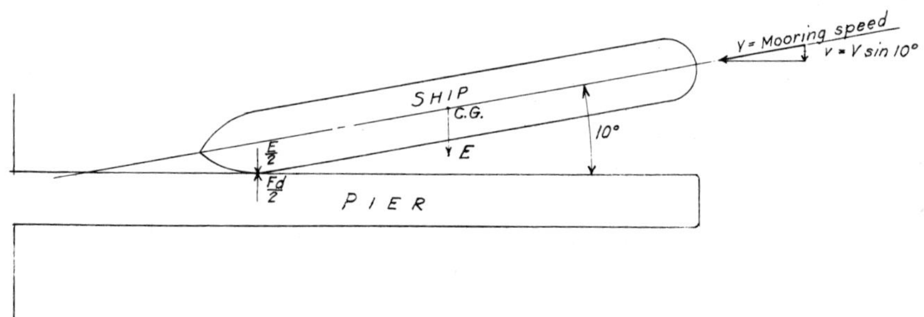

FIG. 5.53 Design assumptions for ship striking dock.

general, the velocities of 0.5 to 1.0 ft per sec normal to the dock are assumed for more exposed locations, where ships dock without the aid of tugs, and for ships of lighter tonnage, whereas velocities below 0.5 ft per sec are applicable to the heavier ships docking in protected locations or with the assistance of tugs.

The kinetic energy of impact is $E = \frac{1}{2}Mv^2$, and, substituting W/g for the mass M, E becomes

$$\tfrac{1}{2} \times (W/g) \times v^2$$

where E = energy, ft-tons (2,240 lb)
W = displaced weight of ship, long tons
v = velocity of ship normal to dock, ft per sec
g = acceleration due to gravity, 32.2 ft per sec per sec

The energy to be absorbed by the fender system and dock is $\frac{1}{2}E$, as the remaining one-half is assumed to be absorbed by the ship and water, because of the rotation of the center of mass of the ship around the point of contact of the bow with the fender. This energy, $\frac{1}{2}E$, must be absorbed by the fender system and dock in bringing the ship to rest. The resistance increases from zero to a maximum, and the work done by the pier is $\frac{1}{2}F \times d$. Therefore, $\frac{1}{2}E = \frac{1}{2}F \times d$, which is the work done by the dock in absorbing the energy, where F = force to be resisted in long tons, and d = distance through which the force moves, in feet, and is the elastic compression of the fender and/or the deflection of the fender and structure. The assumed d for timber is the thickness, in feet, divided by 20. Fender systems are designed to absorb this energy, and the resulting force to be resisted by the dock will depend upon the type and construction of the fender and the deflection of the dock, if it is designed as a flexible structure.

Typical Examples of the Design of Fenders.

Wood-springing-type fender. A ship of 14,000 long tons displaced weight is to dock with a maximum speed of 0.15 ft per sec normal to the dock. The dock is to be protected by a wood-fender system of the type shown in Fig. 5.34. It is desired to determine the size of wood wale to be used.

$$E = \frac{Wv^2}{2g} = \frac{14{,}000 \times 2{,}240 \times 0.15^2}{2 \times 32.2} = 10{,}950 \text{ ft-lb}$$

The energy to be absorbed by the fender system is $E/2$ = 5,475 ft-lb

$$F\frac{d}{2} = \frac{E}{2}$$

Therefore, $Fd = E$ = 10,950 ft-lb = 1.31×10^5 in.-lb. Assume a 10- by 12-in. wale supported on 3-in.-thick blocks located at 15-ft centers. The assumption can be made that the impact force is distributed over two fender piles.

Where the two piles are in the same span, the wale is subjected to two equal forces $P = F/2$. They compress the timber of the wale and of the fender piles. Its amount can be estimated as d_1 = thickness/20 = 24/20 = 1.2 in. The forces also cause a bending deflection d_2 in the wale:

$$d_2 = \frac{Pa}{24EI}(3l^2 - 4a^2)$$

where l = 180 in.
$a = l/4$ = 45 in.
$E = 1.76 \times 10^6$ lb per sq in.
I = 1,000 in.^{4} (10 by 12 rough lumber)

obtaining $$d_2 = 9.5 \times 10^{-5}P$$

and $$2P(9.5 \times 10^{-5}P + 1.2) = 1.31 \times 10^5$$

or $$P = 20{,}670 \text{ lb}$$

The bending deflection is $d_2 = 9.5 \times 20{,}670 \times 10^{-5}$ = 1.96 in.

The stresses in the wale under the loads P must be within allowable limits. Assuming that southern pine, dense structural no. 86 grade, is used for the fender system, the following are the allowable stresses in pounds per square inch according to the National Design Specification of the National Lumber Manufacturers Association:

	Normal loads	Impact loads
Bending	2,400	4,800
Compression perpendicular to grain	455	910
Horizontal shear	150	300

The actual stresses in the wale are as follows:

Bearing (assuming 5 in. for the width of contact between fender pile and wale):

$$f = \frac{20,670}{12 \times 5} = 344 < 910 \text{ lb per sq in.}$$

Bending: $M = P \times 45 = 20,670 \times 45 = 930,000$ in.-lb

$$f = \frac{M}{S} = \frac{930,000}{200} = 4,650 < 4,800 \text{ lb per sq in.}$$

Horizontal shear:

$$v = \frac{V}{bh} \times 1.5$$

where V = shear force = 20,670
b = height of wale = 12 in.
h = depth of wale = 10 in.

$$V = \frac{20,670}{12 \times 10} \times 1.5 = 258 < 300 \text{ lb per sq in.}$$

Where the two fender piles are in two adjacent spans, the deflection d_2 in each wale is

$$d_2 = \frac{Pa^2b^2}{3EIl}$$

where $a = 0.75 \times 15 \times 12 = 135$ in.
$b = 45$ in.

obtaining $$d_2 = 3.88 \times 10^{-5}P$$

and $$2P(d_2 + d_1) = E$$

$$2P(3.88 \times 10^{-5}P + 1.2) = 1.31 \times 10^5$$

or $$P = 28{,}500 \text{ lb} \qquad \text{and} \qquad d_2 = 1.11 \text{ in.}$$

The reactions of the wale are:

$$R_A = 0.75P = 21{,}400 \text{ lb} \qquad \text{and} \qquad R_B = 0.25P = 7{,}100 \text{ lb}$$

Bearing: $$f = \frac{28{,}500}{12 \times 5} = 475 < 910 \text{ lb per sq in.}$$

Bending: $$M = 21{,}400 \times 45 = 963{,}000 \text{ in.-lb}$$

$$f = \frac{963{,}000}{200} = 4{,}820, \text{ say } 4{,}800 \text{ lb per sq in.}$$

Shear: $$v = \frac{21{,}400}{10 \times 12} \times 1.5 = 268 < 300 \text{ lb per sq in.}$$

Draped round rubber fender. A ship of 13,800 long tons displaced weight is to dock with a maximum speed of 30 ft per min normal to the pier. A draped round rubber fender, as shown in Fig. 5.36, has been selected, and it is desired to find the size to be used.

The energy of the docking ship is

$$E = \frac{Wv^2}{2g} = \frac{13{,}800 \times 2{,}240 \times 0.50^2}{2 \times 32.2} = 120{,}000 \text{ ft-lb}$$

One-half of this energy, 60,000 ft-lb, is absorbed by the fenders. The length of the portion of the fender that is compressed by the impact depends largely on the shape of the ship's hull and the inclination of its approach to the dock. For this size of ship the impact may be assumed to be distributed over a length of 20 ft. Therefore, each linear foot of fender must absorb 60,000/20 = 3,000 ft-lb. For a 15- by 7½-in. rubber fender, the corresponding deflection and load are found from the charts of Fig. 5.41 as 7½ in. and 9,000 lb per lin ft, respectively.

Cylindrical rubber fender, steel-wale design. Figure 5.40 shows a fender system in which the ship's impact is absorbed mainly by a continuous cylindrical rubber fender placed in a horizontal slot in the concrete fascia beam or dock wall, in back of an articulated steel wale which is attached to, and supported by, steel-fender piles with wood rubbing strips on their outside flanges. The wale is made up of 30-ft sections, with pin connections which will transmit shear, but not moment, between the sections. Chain linkages connect every third fender pile to the pier, limiting the possible outward movement of the assembly to 2 in.

The fender is to be designed for the impact of a ship of 46,400 long tons (52,000 short tons) displacement, docking at an angle of 10° with a speed of 1 knot (1.689 ft per sec). Its velocity perpendicular to the pier

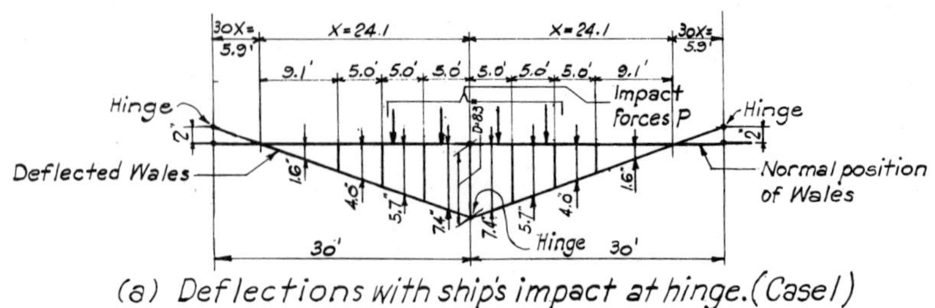

(a) Deflections with ship's impact at hinge. (Case 1)

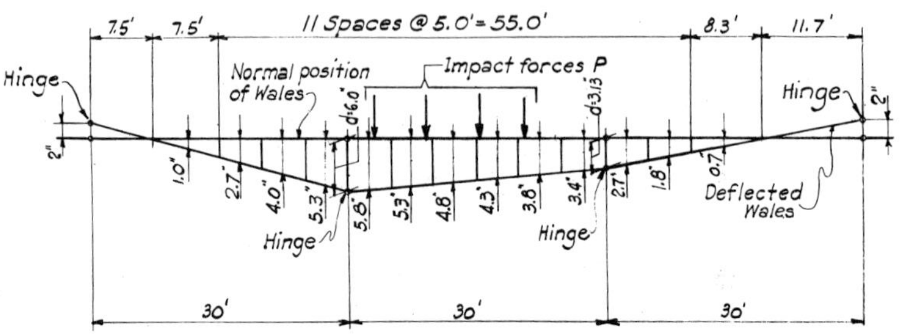

(b) Deflections with ship's impact near center of wale. (Case 2)

FIG. 5.54 (*a*) Cylindrical rubber fender, steel-wale design; deflections with ship's impact at hinge (case 1). (*b*) Cylindrical rubber fender, steel-wale design; deflections with ship's impact near center of wale (case 2).

is then $1.689 \times \sin 10° = 1.689 \times 0.174 = 0.29$ ft per sec, and the energy developed in stopping the ship is

$$E = \frac{Wv^2}{2g} = \frac{52{,}000 \times 2{,}000 \times 0.29^2}{2 \times 32.2} = 136{,}000 \text{ ft-lb}$$

One half of this energy, or 68,000 ft-lb, is absorbed by the fender system.

If the ship should hit at a point where the wale is hinged (case 1), the deflection will take the form shown in Fig. 5.54*a*, if the wale is assumed infinitely stiff as compared to the rubber fender. Note that the wale cannot move more than 2 in. outward from its normal position due to the linkage. The energy absorption and the corresponding load as functions of the deflection are given in Fig. 5.41 for rubber fenders of different sizes. The deflection d which brings about the given energy absorption of 68,000 ft-lb can be found by trial and error. First x can be found in terms of d as

$$x = \frac{30d}{2 + d}$$

Assuming a value $d = 8.3$ in., x becomes equal to 24.1 ft. The average deflection of sections of suitable length, in this case 5 ft, can next be determined, Fig. 5.54*a*. Finding the energy absorption and the load at each section, we obtain for a 15- by 7½-in. rubber fender:

L	d	E/lin ft	E, ft-lb	P/lin ft	P, lb
2 × 5	7.4	3,000	30,000	8,000	80,000
2 × 5	5.7	1,800	18,000	5,000	50,000
2 × 5	4.0	1,100	11,000	3,000	30,000
2 × 9.1	1.6	500	9,100	1,500	27,300
			68,100		187,300

If the total energy absorption had not been close to the given 68,000 ft-lb, the computation would have to be repeated with a different assumed value for d, until close agreement is reached.

If the ship hits near the center of a 30-ft length of wale (case 2), the wale takes the form shown in Fig. 5.54*b*. The maximum deflection can be found again by trial and error: $d = 6.0$ in. The deflections of sections of suitable length are shown in Fig. 5.54*b*. The energy absorption and load are then

L	d	E/lin ft	E, ft-lb	P/lin ft	P, lb
7.5	1.0	300	2,300	1,000	7,500
5	2.7	700	3,500	2,500	12,500
5	4.0	1,100	5,500	3,000	15,000
5	5.3	1,700	8,500	4,500	22,500
5	5.8	1,900	9,500	5,000	25,000
5	5.3	1,700	8,500	4,500	22,500
5	4.8	1,400	7,000	4,500	22,500
5	4.3	1,200	6,000	3,500	17,500
5	3.8	1,000	5,000	3,000	15,000
5	3.4	900	4,500	3,000	15,000
5	2.7	700	3,500	2,500	12,000
5	1.8	400	2,000	1,500	7,500
8.3	0.7	200	1,700	500	4,000
			67,500		199,000

The steel wale distributes the impact forces from the fender piles into the rubber fender. The loads, shear forces, and moments in the wale are given in Fig. 5.54*c* and *d* for cases 1 and 2, respectively. The wale consists of an 18-WF beam and a ⅞-in. distribution plate, with a total section modulus of 212 in.³ The maximum moment of 367,200 ft-lb results

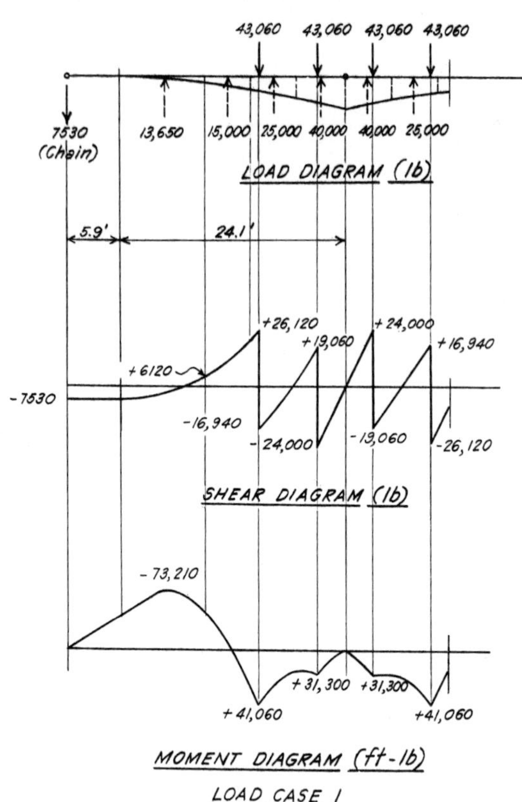

FIG. 5.54 (*c*) Cylindrical rubber fender, steel-wale design; load, shear, and moment diagrams for case 1.

in a stress of 367,200 × 12/212 = 20,800 lb per sq in., which is considered satisfactory for this type of loading. The maximum shear force of 57,300 lb causes a stress of 57,300/18.16 × 0.512 = 6,160 lb per sq in. in the web of the wale.

Steel-spring-fender system. A dock is to be designed for the impact force of a ship of 34,000 long tons displacement, approaching at a velocity of 10 ft per min (0.167 ft per sec) normal to the face of the dock. A steel-spring-fender system, as shown in Fig. 5.47, is to be provided to absorb the energy of the docking ship. It is desired to determine the size and spacing of the springs and the resulting force to be taken by the dock.

$$E = \frac{Wv^2}{2g} = \frac{34{,}000 \times 2{,}240 \times 0.167^2}{2 \times 32.2} = 33{,}000 \text{ ft-lb}$$

$$F\frac{d}{2} = \frac{E}{2} = \frac{33{,}000}{2} = 16{,}500 \text{ ft-lb}$$

Assume a maximum spring deflection of 12 in. or 1.0 ft = d

$$\frac{F \times 1.0}{2} = 16{,}500 \qquad F = 33{,}000 \text{ lb}$$

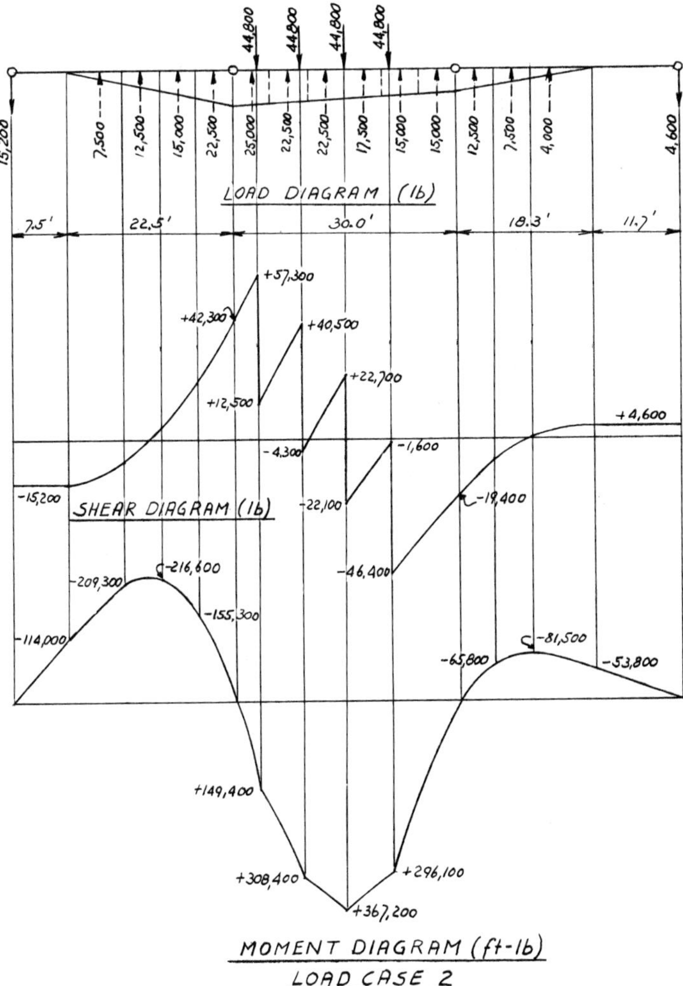

FIG. 5.54 (*d*) Cylindrical rubber fender, steel-wale design; load, shear, and moment diagrams for case 2.

Assume that the impact of the ship will be distributed over four springs, spaced 15 ft on centers. Therefore, the load on each spring = 33,000/4 = 8,250 lb, with a deflection of 12 in.

The design of the spring is based on the criteria given in Formulas for Stress and Strain, pages 187 and 188, by Prof. R. J. Roark.

$$P = \frac{\pi d^3 \times S}{16rk} = \frac{0.1963\, d^3 \times S}{rk} \tag{1}$$

$$f = \frac{64nr^3\, P}{d^4 G} = \frac{4\pi nr^2 S}{dGk} \tag{2}$$

$$k = \frac{4c - 1}{4c - 4} + \frac{0.615}{c} \tag{3}$$

where S = safe-shearing stress, lb per sq in.
P = safe load, lb
d = diameter of wire (or rod), in.
r = mean radius of coil, in.
n = number of coils
G = shearing modulus of elasticity = 10,500,000 lb per sq in.
k = a constant to be used for closely coiled helical springs
$c = 2r/d$
L = free length of spring, in.
f = deflection of spring, in.

Use hot-rolled carbon steel, double heat-treated, with a maximum S = 60,000 lb per sq in., approximate L available = 43 in. Assume $d = 1\frac{5}{8}$ in. and pitch = $2\frac{1}{2}$ in. Required deflection f = 12 in.

$(n - 1)(2.5 - 1.625) + n \times 1.625 = 43$ in. $\qquad n = 17.6 \qquad$ say 18 coils

From Eq. (1), $k = \dfrac{0.1963\, d^3 S}{rP} = \dfrac{0.1963 \times 4.3 \times 60{,}000}{r \times 8{,}250} = \dfrac{6.14}{r}$

From Eq. (2), $k = \dfrac{4\pi nr^2 S}{dGf} = \dfrac{4\pi \times 18 \times r^2 \times 60{,}000}{1.625 \times 10{,}500{,}000 \times 12} = 0.0662r^2$

Equating, $\dfrac{6.14}{r} = 0.0662r^2$ and $r^3 = 92.6$

$r = 4.53$ in. $\qquad$ say $4\frac{5}{8}$ in.

$$c = \frac{9.25}{1.625} = 5.7$$

From Eq. (3), $k = \dfrac{4 \times 5.7 - 1}{4 \times 5.7 - 4} + \dfrac{0.615}{5.7} = 1.27$

From Eq. (1),
$$S = \frac{8{,}250 \times 4.625 \times 1.27}{0.1963 \times 4.3}$$
$$= 57{,}300 \text{ lb per sq in.} < 60{,}000 \text{ lb per sq in.}$$

Actual free length of spring $L = 18 \times 1.625 + 17 \times .875 = 44$ in.

Compressed length $= 29.2$ in.

Available for deflection $= 14.8$ in. > 12 in.

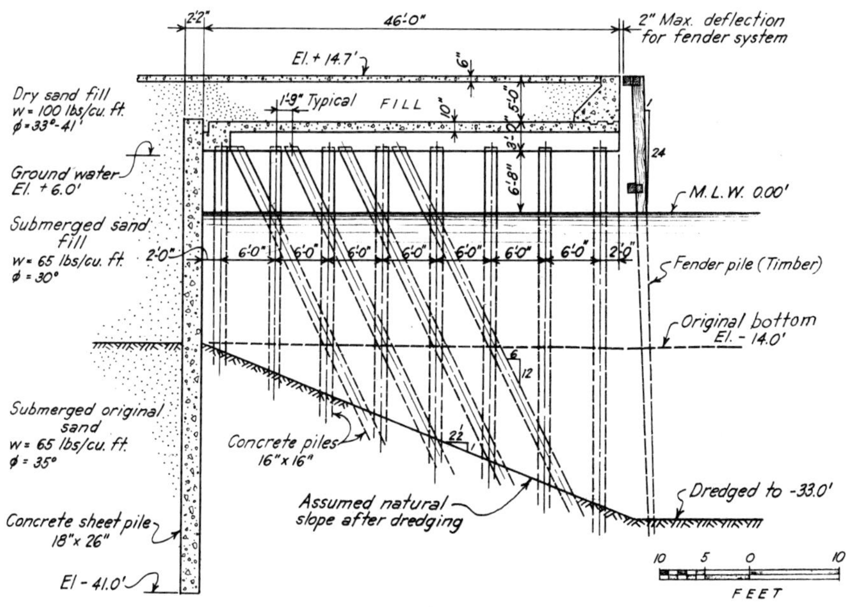

FIG. 5.55 (*a*) Wharf design, relieving-platform type; typical section.

5.7 Typical Examples of the Design of Docks

Wharf Design, Relieving-platform Type. Figure 5.55*a* shows a cross section through a relieving-platform type of wharf which consists of a concrete platform, 46 ft wide, carrying 4 ft 6 in. of sand fill and a 6-in. concrete pavement, supported by concrete piles. A concrete fascia wall retains the sand fill at the outshore edge.

The original ground is at approximately El -14 ft, referred to mean low water at El 0.0, and is to be dredged to El -33 in front of the wharf, leaving the bank on a 1-on-2½ slope to the original ground level. A line of reinforced-concrete sheet piling is to be driven along the rear of the platform to retain a fill to the established wharf grade at El $+14.7$ ft.

Batter piles will be designed to resist the horizontal reaction at the top of the sheet-pile wall, plus the additional pressure from the earth and surcharge of 600 lb per sq ft above the platform level. A wood-wale springing type of fender system with wood piles will protect the wharf against damage from docking ships.

Soil and water pressures acting on a linear foot of sheet-pile wall are

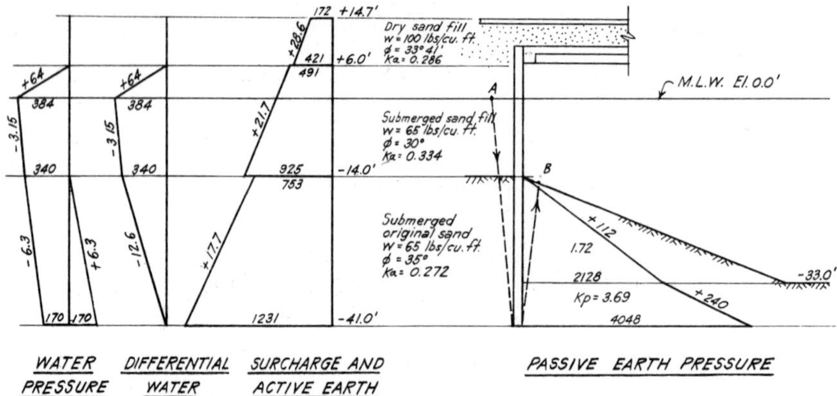

FIG. 5.55 (*b*) Wharf design, relieving-platform type; soil and water pressures.

given in Fig. 5.55*b*. The earth pressures are determined by using Rankine's formulas, as follows:

$$p_a = w \times K_a \qquad \text{where } K_a = \tan^2 (45° - \phi/2)$$

$$p_p = w \times K_p \qquad \text{where } K_p = \tan^2 (45° + \phi/2)$$

or

$$p_{p_1} = w \times K_{p_1} \qquad \text{where } K_{p_1} = \left[\frac{\cos \phi}{1 - \sqrt{\sin \phi\,(\sin \phi - \cos \phi \tan \theta)}}\right]^2$$

where p_a = active unit pressure, lb per sq ft

p_p = passive unit pressure, lb per sq ft

p_{p_1} = passive unit pressure, lb per sq ft for surface sloping away from wall

w = unit weight of soil, lb per cu ft

ϕ = angle of internal friction

K_a = coefficient of active lateral earth pressure

K_p = coefficient of passive lateral earth pressure for horizontal surface

K_{p_1} = coefficient of passive lateral earth pressure for surface sloping away from wall

θ = angle between surface of soil sloping away from wall and the horizontal

The mean daily fluctuation in tide is from MLW (mean low water) at El 0.0 to MHW (mean high water) at El +10.0 ft, and as a result the ground-water level in back of the sheet piling will fluctuate as well, but in a narrower range, flowing back and forth through the porous fill and underlying soil. It is assumed that at MLW the ground-water level will be at El +6.0 ft, which will cause a differential water pressure at El 0.0 approximately equal to $6 \times 64 = 384$ lb per sq ft. Since the water has the tendency of establishing the same level on both sides of the wall, there will be a flow of water around the bottom of the wall, as approximately shown in Fig. 5.55*b*. Because of this flow the pressure differential will drop from its maximum at point *A* to zero at point *B*. Between points *A* and *B* the water has to flow through 14 ft of fill and through $(27 + 27)$ ft of the original sand bottom. Assuming permeability coefficients of $k_1 = 1 \times 10^{-2}$ cm per sec and $k_2 = 5 \times 10^{-3}$ cm per sec, respectively, for the two materials, and assuming further that the velocity of flow, $v = kS$, is constant along line *AB* we obtain $v = k_1S_1 = k_2S_2$, or $S_2 = (k_1/k_2) \times S_1 = 2.0S_1$, where S_1 and S_2 are the hydraulic gradients in the fill and sand, respectively. The condition that the total pressure loss must be equal to 384 lb per sq ft yields a second equation

$$S_1L_1 + S_2L_2 = 384$$

Therefore

$$S_1 \times 14 + 2.0S_1 \times 54 = 384$$

$$S_1 = 3.15 \text{ lb per sq ft per ft}$$

$$S_2 = 2.0S_1 = 6.3 \text{ lb per sq ft per ft}$$

The pressure at El −14 then becomes

$$384 - 14 \times 3.15 = 340 \text{ lb per sq ft}$$

The pressure at El −41 becomes

$$340 - 27 \times 6.3 = 170 \text{ lb per sq ft}$$

The resultant differential water pressure acting on the wall is shown in Fig. 5.55*b*.

The previously determined forces tend to push the wall outward. It is held in place at the top by the concrete platform and at the bottom by the passive pressure of the soil in front of the wall.

By substituting the values of $\cos \phi = 0.819$, $\sin \phi = 0.574$, and $\tan \theta = 0.40$ in the equation for the coefficient K_{p_1}, a value of 1.72 is obtained, and $p_{p_1} = 65 \times 1.72 = 112$ lb per sq ft for the passive pressure of the soil sloping away from the wall.

Below El −33 the soil surface is horizontal. By substituting the value of $\phi = 35°$ in the equation for the coefficient K_p, a value of 3.69 is obtained and $p_{p2} = 3.69 \times 65 = 240$ lb per sq ft.

The depth to which the sheet piling must be driven is determined from the condition that the moment of the passive pressures about the point

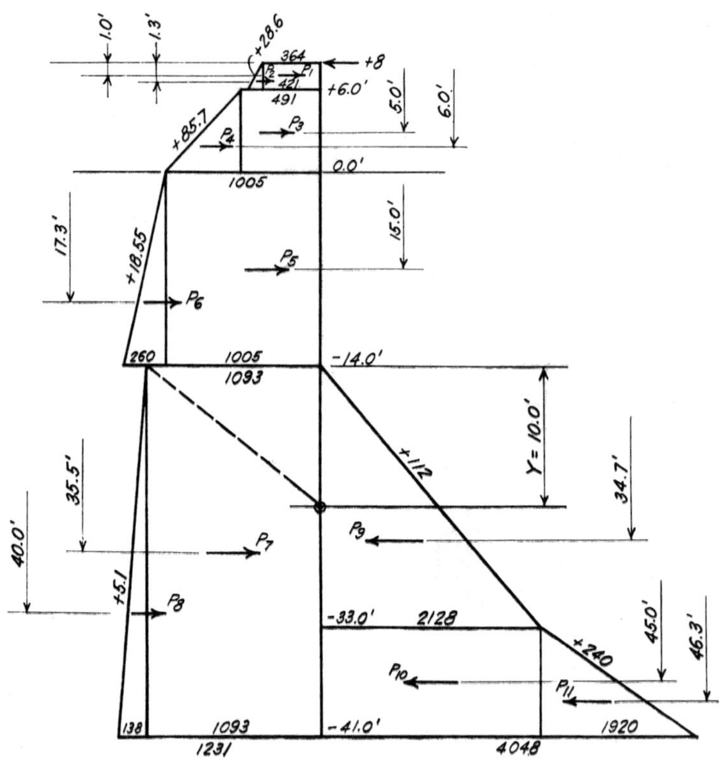

FIG. 5.55 (*c*) Wharf design, relieving-platform type; passive and active forces and moment arms.

of support at the top of the sheet piling must exceed the moment of the active pressures by an amount sufficient to provide a reasonable factor of safety, usually considered to be from 1.25 to 1.50, against the sheet piling moving outward at the bottom. Several trial depths will usually have to be figured before arriving at the one which will give the desired factor of safety. A satisfactory solution is found with the sheet piling driven to El −41. The forces and moment arms for this condition are shown in Fig. 5.55*c*, and the moments for the active and passive pressures are as follows:

Active pressures:

P_1:	364 ×	2 =	728 ×	1.0 =	728
P_2:	57 ×	2/2 =	57 ×	1.3 =	74
P_3:	491 ×	6 =	2,946 ×	5.0 =	14,730
P_4:	514 ×	6/2 =	1,542 ×	6.0 =	9,252
P_5:	1,005 ×	14 =	14,070 ×	15.0 =	211,050
P_6:	260 ×	14/2 =	1,820 ×	17.3 =	31,486
P_7:	1,093 ×	27 =	29,511 ×	35.5 =	1,047,640
P_8:	138 ×	27/2 =	1,863 ×	40.0 =	74,520
					1,389,480 ft-lb

Passive pressures:

P_9:	2,128 ×	19/2 =	20,216 ×	34.7 =	701,495
P_{10}:	2,128 ×	8 =	17,024 ×	45.0 =	766,080
P_{11}:	1,920 ×	8/2 =	7,680 ×	46.3 =	355,584
					1,823,159 ft-lb

Factor of safety: $$\frac{1,823,159}{1,389,480} = 1.31$$

The sheet piling will be designed according to H. Blum's equivalent-beam method. The sheet piling is assumed supported at the top (+8) and at a depth Y below the original bottom where the pressure diagram passes through zero. At this depth the active pressure is $1,093 + 5.1Y$ and the passive pressure is $112Y$. Equating the two values, we obtain

$$Y = 10.2 \text{ ft}; \qquad \text{use } Y = 10.0 \text{ ft}$$

The sheet piling can be treated as a simple beam, if it is driven deep enough to allow the earth pressures below to develop a large enough constraining moment.

$$X = K_2 \left(Y + \sqrt{\frac{6R_2}{2p_p - p_a}} \right)$$

where X = depth of penetration below outside bottom elevation
K_2 = 1.1
R_2 = bottom reaction of simple beam at El −24 = 12,674 lb
p_p = passive earth pressure = 240 lb per sq ft
p_a = active earth pressure = 5.1 lb per sq ft

Substituting,

$$X = 1.1 \left(10 + \sqrt{\frac{6 \times 12,674}{2 \times 240 - 5.1}} \right) = 25.0 \text{ ft}$$

With the sheet piling driven to El −41, the actual value is $X = 41 - 14 = 27$, which is more than the required depth.

The load diagram can now be drawn (Fig. 5.55*d*), and the reactions and moments determined, as follows:

P_1:	364 × 2 =	728 ×	1.0 and	31.0 =	728 and	22,568
P_2:	57 × 2/2 =	57 ×	1.3	30.7 =	74	1,750
P_3:	491 × 6 =	2,946 ×	5.0	27.0 =	14,730	79,542
P_4:	514 × 6/2 =	1,542 ×	6.0	26.0 =	9,252	40,092
P_5:	1,005 × 14 =	14,070 ×	15.0	17.0 =	211,050	239,190
P_6:	260 × 14/2 =	1,820 ×	17.3	14.7 =	31,486	26,754
P_7:	1,093 × 10/2 =	5,465 ×	25.3	6.7 =	138,264	36,616
		26,628 lb			405,584 ft-lb	446,512 ft-lb

$$R_2 = \frac{405{,}584}{32.0} = 12{,}674 \text{ lb} \qquad R_1 = \frac{446{,}512}{32.0} = 13{,}954 \text{ lb}$$

The maximum moment occurs at the point of zero shear, which is Z_1 ft below El 0.0.

$$R_1 - P_1 - P_2 - P_3 - P_4 - 1{,}005Z_1 - \frac{18.55Z_1^2}{2} = 0 \qquad Z_1 = 8.0 \text{ ft}$$

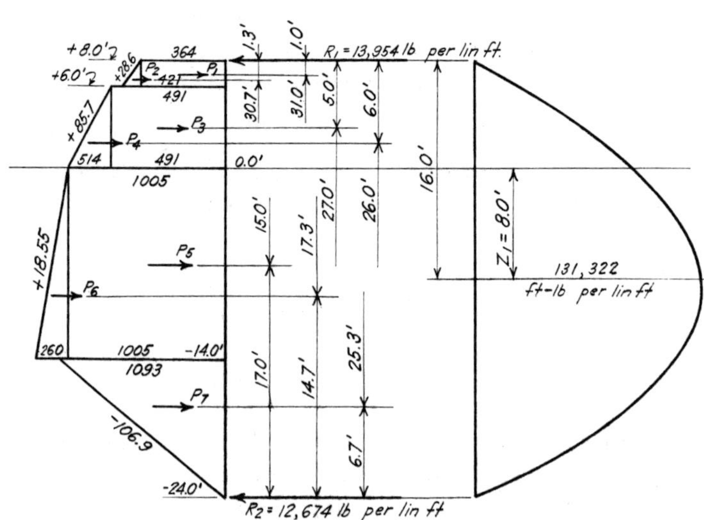

FIG. 5.55 (*d*) Wharf design, relieving-platform type; load and bending moment diagrams.

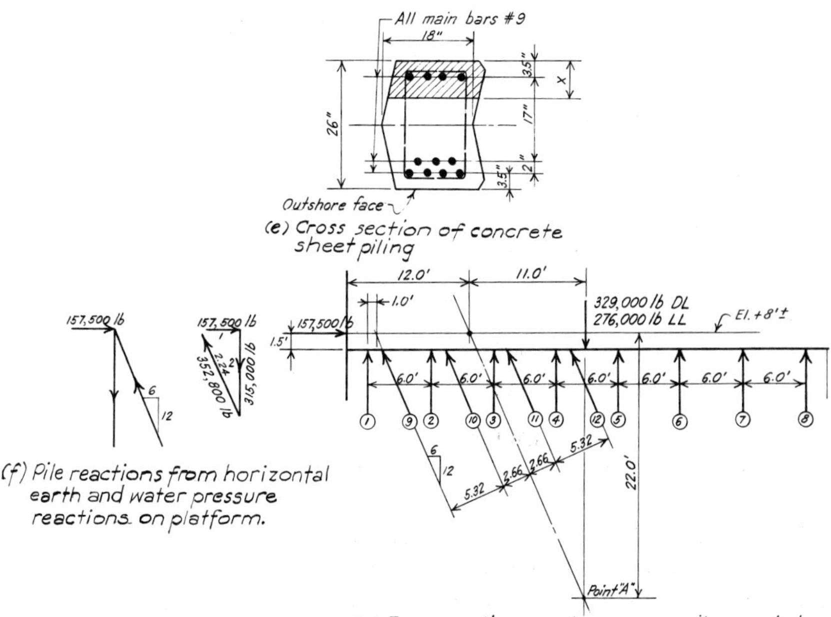

FIG. 5.55 (*e*) Wharf design, relieving-platform type; cross section of concrete sheet piling. (*f*) Wharf design, relieving-platform type; pile reactions from horizontal earth- and water-pressure reactions on platform. (*g*) Wharf design, relieving-platform type; forces acting on a transverse pile-cap girder.

The moment diagram is shown in Fig. 5.55*d* and the maximum positive moment is

$$M = 13{,}954 \times 16.0 - 728 \times 15.0 - 57 \times 14.7 - 2{,}946 \times 11.0$$
$$- 1{,}542 \times 10.0 - 1{,}005 \times 8.0 \times \frac{8.0}{2} - 18.55 \times \frac{8.0}{2} \times \frac{8.0}{3}$$
$$= 131{,}322 \text{ ft-lb}$$

The sheet pile must be designed for a moment of 131,322 ft-lb per lin ft of sheet piling. Assume a section as shown in Fig. 5.55*e*. The moment for one pile is $131{,}322 \times 1.5 \times 12 = 2{,}364{,}000$ in.-lb. Assuming a concrete of $f'_c = 4{,}000$ lb per sq in. ($n = 7.5$), the neutral axis is determined as the center of gravity of the equivalent section

$$18\,x\frac{2}{2} + 4 \times 6.5(x - 3.5) = 3 \times 7.5(26 - x - 5.5)$$
$$+ 4 \times 7.5(26 - x - 3.5) \qquad x = 8.1 \text{ in.}$$

The moment of inertia of the equivalent section is

$$I = 18 \times \frac{8.1^3}{3} + 4 \times 6.5(8.1 - 3.5)^2 + 4 \times 7.5(26 - 8.1 - 3.5)^2$$

$$+ 3 \times 7.5(26 - 8.1 - 5.5)^2 = 13{,}410 \text{ in.}^4$$

The section moduli are then found:

$$S_c = \frac{13{,}410}{8.1} = 1{,}660 \text{ in.}^3 \quad \text{and} \quad S_s = \frac{13{,}410}{7.5 \times 14.4} = 124 \text{ in.}^3$$

and finally

$$f_c = \frac{2{,}364{,}000}{1{,}660} = 1{,}420 \text{ lb per sq in.}$$

$$f_s = \frac{2{,}364{,}000}{124} = 19{,}060 \text{ lb per sq in.}$$

The horizontal reaction from the sheet piling at El +8, $R_1 = 13{,}954$ lb, must be resisted by the platform. The reaction is increased by the lateral pressure exerted against the platform by the fill above +8, which acts against the front retaining wall, transferring the load into the platform, and which is equal to $6.7(172 + 364)/2 = 1{,}796$ lb, making a total of $13{,}954 + 1{,}796 = 15{,}750$ lb.

Assuming a bent spacing of 10 ft, the total thrust per bent is 157,500 lb. As shown in Fig. 5.55*f*, this force causes a load of 352,800 lb or 176.4 tons in the batter piles and an uplift of 315,000 lb or 157.5 tons, which must be resisted by the dead load of the structure and the pull-out value of the vertical piles.

The weight of the platform, fill, and paving is

Sand fill:	$4.5 \times 100 =$	450
Top slab:	$0.5 \times 150 =$	75
Deck Slab (10 in.):	$0.83 \times 150 =$	125 lb per sq ft
		650 lb per sq ft

The transverse girder or pile cap, which distributes the vertical and horizontal loads to the vertical and batter piles in each bent, is assumed to act as a stiff member.

The forces acting on the girder are shown in Fig. 5.55*g*. The total dead load is $650 \times 46 \times 10 = 299{,}000$ lb plus 30,000 lb for the weight of the girder or 164.5 tons. The total live load is $600 \times 46 \times 10 = 276{,}000$ lb or 138.0 tons. Assuming that only the vertical piles carry the vertical loads, the dead load on each is $P_1 = 164.5/8 = 20.6$ tons and the live load is $P_2 = 138.0/8 = 17.2$ tons. The uplift reduces the direct load by $P_3 =$

157.5/8 = 19.7 tons in each pile. The direct load on each batter pile is P_4 = 176.4/4 = 44.1 tons. Since the resultants of the vertical and batter piles intersect at point *A*, 22.0 ft below the line of action of the horizontal force, the direct loads on the piles must be adjusted by the effect of the moment of the horizontal force about point *A*, which is M = 157,500 × 22.0 = 3,460,000 ft lb or 1,730 ft-tons. The effect of this moment is to add or deduct from the direct load in the piles in accordance with the formula Mc/I where I = moment of inertia of pile group with respect to point *A*, c = the perpendicular distance from point *A* to the center line of each pile.

Pile no.	c^2, ft^2	I/c	Mc/I, tons
1, 8	$21^2 \times 2 =$ 882	78.7	21.9
2, 7	$15^2 \times 2 =$ 450	110.2	15.7
3, 6	$9^2 \times 2 =$ 162	183.7	9.4
4, 5	$3^2 \times 2 =$ 18	551.0	3.1
9, 12	$7.98^2 \times 2 =$ 127	207.1	8.4
10, 11	$2.66^2 \times 2 =$ 14	621.4	2.8
Total	I = 1,653		

The summary of pile loads in tons follows:

Pile no.	P_1	P_3 or P_4	Mc/I	Case 1, total load, tons (lb)	P_2	Case 2, total + P_2, tons (lb)
1	+20.6	−19.7	−21.9	−21.0 (−42,000)	+17.2	− 3.8 (−7,600)
2	+20.6	−19.7	−15.7	−14.8 (−29,600)	+17.2	+ 2.4 (+4,800)
3	+20.6	−19.7	− 9.4	− 8.5 (−17,000)	+17.2	+ 8.7 (+17,400)
4	+20.6	−19.7	− 3.1	− 2.2 (−4,400)	+17.2	+15.0 (+30,000)
5	+20.6	−19.7	+ 3.1	+ 4.0 (+8,000)	+17.2	+21.2 (+42,400)
6	+20.6	−19.7	+ 9.4	+10.3 (+20,600)	+17.2	+27.5 (+55,000)
7	+20.6	−19.7	+15.7	+16.6 (+33,200)	+17.2	+33.8 (+67,600)
8	+20.6	−19.7	+21.9	+22.8 (+45,600)	+17.2	+40.0 (+80,000)
9		+44.1	− 8.4	+35.7 (+71,400)		+35.7 (+71,400)
10		+44.1	− 2.8	+41.3 (+82,600)		+41.3 (+82,600)
11		+44.1	+ 2.8	+46.9 (+93,800)		+46.9 (+93,800)
12		+44.1	+ 8.4	+52.5 (+105,000)		+52.5 (+105,000)

\+ indicates compression in pile.
− indicates tension in pile.

The vertical piles must be designed to carry 40 tons, and the batter piles to carry 52.5 tons. The vertical and batter piles are fixed at the top by the transverse girders and are supported 5 ft below the bottom. The effective length as a long column, from Fig. 5.21, is, therefore, $44 \times 0.75 = 33.0$ ft. From Table 5.2, a 16- by 16-in. pile with 4 no. 10 bars and 3,000 lb per sq in. concrete will carry a load of 55 tons.

The vertical inshore pile in each bent must resist a maximum uplift of 21.0 tons, or approximately 50 per cent of the load to which it is to be driven. Assuming an average value of 800 lb per sq ft for the friction between the pile and the surrounding sand, and taking the perimeter of the pile as $4 \times 1.33 = 5.33$ ft, the pile, to have a factor of safety of two against pull-out, must have a minimum embedment of

$$L = \frac{2 \times 21.0}{5.33 \times 0.4} = 19.7 \qquad \text{say, 20 ft}$$

to resist the pull-out force.

From the outshore side the wharf is subjected to the impact force of a docking ship. The fender system, which is a wood-pile and double-wood-wale springing type, as shown in Fig. 5.34, is designed on page 303. The maximum docking force of the ship is $2 \times R_a = 2 \times 21{,}400$ lb $= 42{,}800$ lb, and assuming this is distributed by the lower slab of the wharf over a length of 50 ft, or 5 bents, the force at each bent is $42{,}800/5 = 8{,}560$ lb. Since this is much less than the horizontal thrust from the earth pressure, it is unnecessary to provide batter piles in the opposite direction.

The platform consists of four main elements: slab, inshore longitudinal girder, outshore longitudinal girder, and transverse girder or pile cap. They are designed according to standard methods for reinforced-concrete design. Assume $f_s = 20{,}000$, $f'_c = 3{,}000$, $n = 10$, $K = 236$, and $j = 0.87$.

Slab. From Fig. 5.55*i* the span of the slab is 8 ft. The load was previously found to be 650 lb per sq ft dead load and 600 lb per sq ft live load, giving a moment of $M = 1{,}250 \times 8^2/12 = 6{,}670$ ft-lb. A slab thickness of 10 in. and no. 5 reinforcing bars at 5 in. spacing, top and bottom, will be found satisfactory.

Inshore longitudinal girder carries the sheet-pile reaction of 13,954 lb per lin ft to the transverse pile-cap girders. $M = (13{,}954 \times 10^2)/12 = 116{,}100$ ft-lb. A cross section of 3.0 by 3.0 ft and 4 no. 7 bars on each side of the section will develop this moment within allowable stresses.

Outshore longitudinal girder acts as a retaining wall for the fill on top of the platform and to take the reaction from the fender system. From Fig. 5.55*j*, the loads from the fill and surcharge are $P_{15} = 172 \times 5/2 = 430$ lb and $P_{16} = 315 \times 5/2 = 788$ lb, and the overturning moment is $P_{15} \times 3.33 + P_{16} \times 1.67 = 2{,}748$ ft-lb per lin ft of wharf. The weight of the girder furnishes the righting moment. $W_1 = 2 \times 4 \times 150 = 1{,}200$ lb,

$W_2 = 3 \times 3 \times 15\%_2 = 675$ lb, and $W_3 = 5 \times 1 \times 150 = 750$ lb. The moments $W_1 \times 1 + W_2 \times 3 + W_3 \times 2.5 = 5{,}100$ ft-lb, which gives a factor of safety of 5,100/2,748 = 1.85 against overturning.

The impact of the ship produces a concentrated horizontal load of

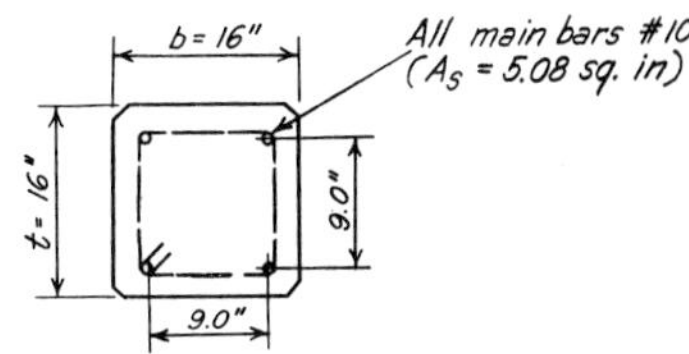

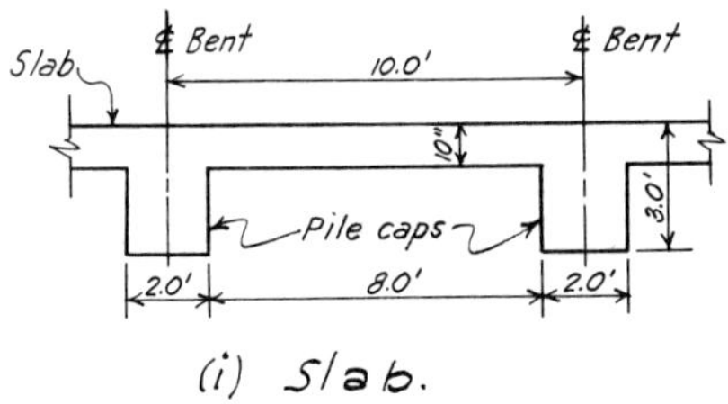

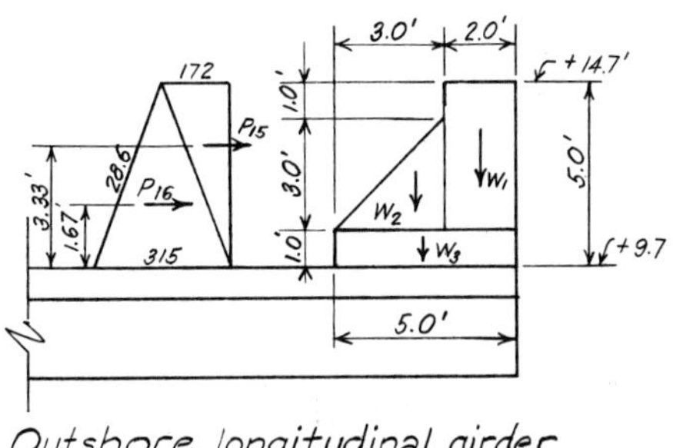

FIG. 5.55 (*h*) Wharf design, relieving-platform type; cross section of concrete pile. (*i*) Wharf design, relieving-platform type; slab. (*j*) Wharf design, relieving-platform type; outshore longitudinal girder.

$2 \times 21{,}400 = 42{,}800$ lb either at a transverse pile-cap girder or in midspan, acting at the top of the longitudinal girder. It can be shown that this load would overturn the girder if it were designed as a gravity-retaining wall. This load produces a maximum vertical moment of $42{,}800 \times 5 = 214{,}000$ ft-lb. The weight of a 10-ft length of wall can be assumed to produce a righting moment of

$$10(W_1 \times 4 + W_2 \times 2 + W_3 \times 2.5) = 80{,}250 \text{ ft-lb}$$

The balance of 214,000 − 80,250 = 133,750 ft-lb is transmitted into the pile-cap girder. The required reinforcing steel in the outshore girder is

$$A_s = \frac{133{,}750 \times 12}{20{,}000 \times 0.87 \times 55} = 1.7 \text{ sq in.} \qquad \text{or 3 no. 8 bars}$$

Where the load falls in the center of the span, it produces a horizontal moment in the girder of

$$\frac{2 \times 21{,}400 \times 10}{4} = 107{,}000 \text{ ft-lb}$$

requiring a horizontal reinforcement at the inside face of

$$A_s = \frac{107{,}000 \times 12}{20{,}000 \times 0.87 \times 20} = 3.7 \qquad \text{or 5 no. 8 bars}$$

Transverse-pile-cap girder. The pile cap is a girder carrying a uniform dead load from the slab equal to 650 × 10 = 6,500 lb per lin ft, and a live load of 600 × 10 = 6,000 lb per lin ft. The weight of the girder is

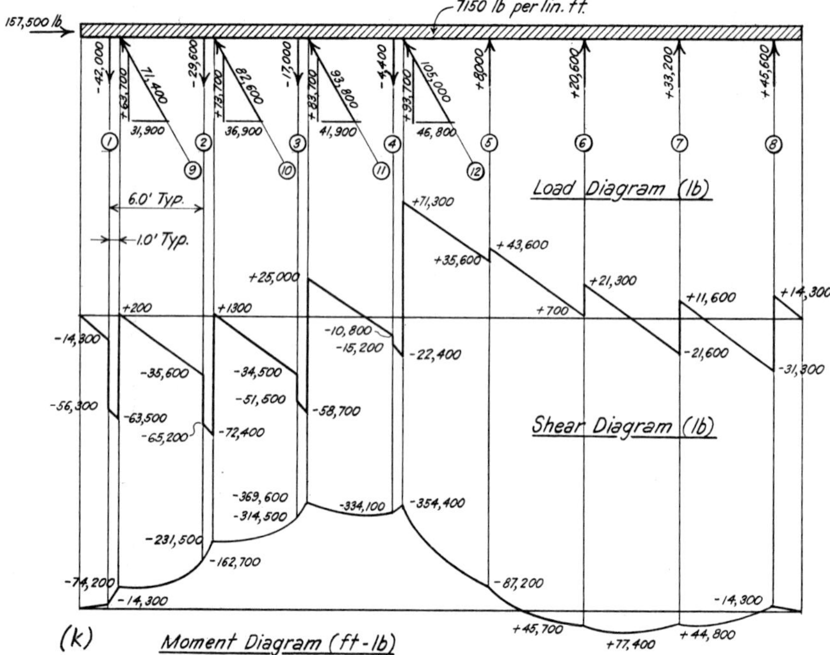

FIG. 5.55 (*k*) Wharf design, relieving-platform type; transverse pile-cap girder load, shear, and moment diagrams for case 1.

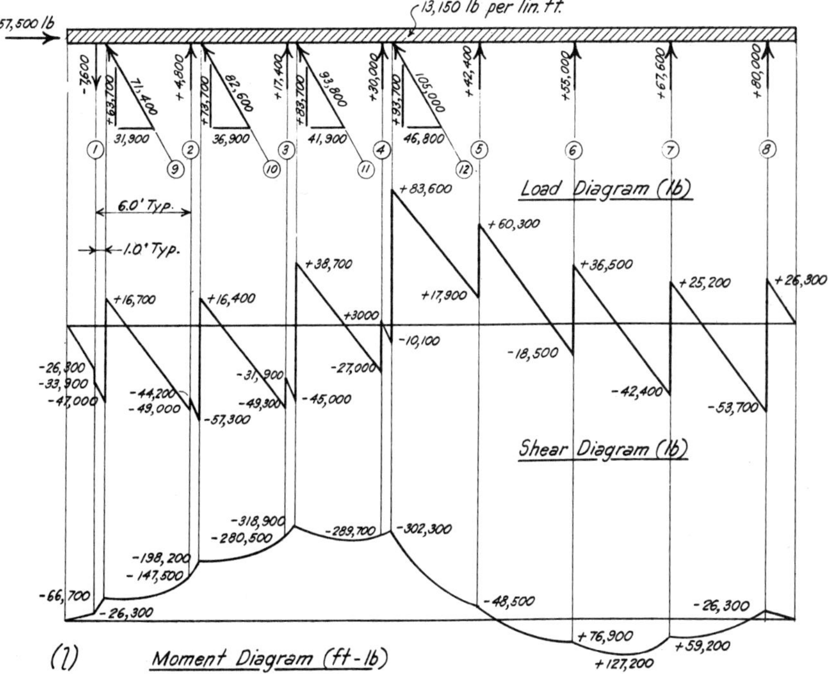

FIG. 5.55 (*l*) Wharf design, relieving-platform type; transverse pile-cap girder load, shear, and moment diagrams for case 2.

650 lb per lin ft. The total dead load is 7,150 lb per lin ft (case 1), and the dead load plus live load is 7,150 + 6,000 = 13,150 lb per lin ft (case 2). The girder is supported by the piles. Their loads have already been determined for the two load cases. In Fig. 5.55*k* and *l* the loads are summarized for each load case and the corresponding shear diagrams are developed. From these data the moments are computed, adding the moments of all forces to one side of a certain section by using the formula:

$$M_n = M_{n-1} + V_{n-1}\,a + P_m a_m$$

where M_n = moment at section n

M_{n-1} = moment at previous section

V_{n-1} = shear at previous section

a = distance from previous section

P_m = loads and reactions between previous section and section n

a_m = distance of P_m from section n

For example, for case 1 the moment M_3 at pile 2 is found as

$$M_3 = M_2 + 200 \times 5 - 35{,}800 \times 2.5$$

$$= -74{,}200 + 1{,}000 - 89{,}500 = -162{,}700 \text{ ft-lb}$$

Having found the maximum negative moment as −369,600 ft-lb and the maximum positive moment as +127,200 ft-lb, the necessary maximum reinforcement for top and bottom of the section will be found as

$$A_s = \frac{369{,}600 \times 12}{20{,}000 \times 0.87 \times 32} = 8.0 \text{ sq in.} \qquad \text{or 8 no. 9 bars in top}$$

$$\text{and } A_s = \frac{127{,}200 \times 12}{20{,}000 \times 0.87 \times 32} = 2.7 \text{ sq in.} \qquad \text{or 5 no. 7 bars in bottom}$$

This reinforcing steel also takes care of the moment from the ship impact which occurs at the outshore end of the girder.

A Finger Pier. This will be located in a protected harbor and is to be designed to handle general cargo to be loaded on or unloaded from ocean-going vessels having the following characteristics: dead-weight tonnage, 35,000 long-tons; displacement tonnage, 46,400 long-tons; loaded draft, 37 ft 6 in.; length, 700 ft; and exposed area when light, 30,000 sq ft. The vessels will dock without the aid of tugs and it is estimated that they will approach the pier at a velocity which will not exceed 0.29 ft per sec normal to the face of the pier. The cargo will be transported to and from the pier by truck, with warehouses located on shore. Mean high tide is 6 ft above low-water datum taken as El 0.0. The bottom is very soft silt, extending to about El −50 where a stiff clay is encountered extending to a depth of over 100 ft. The maximum wind velocity is 70 miles per hour in a direction normal to the pier. The location is in an earthquake zone with an acceleration of 10 per cent of gravity. A plan view and typical bent of the pier are shown in Fig. 5.56*a*.

General design. Since the loaded draft is 37 ft 6 in., the bottom will need to be dredged to El −40. The pier length will need to be 50 ft longer at each end than the length of the ship, or a total length of 800 ft, to provide for bow and stern mooring lines. Since a transit shed or warehouse is not required on the pier, the width will be controlled by the minimum space for operating trucks and transferring cargo from ships moored on both sides of the pier at one time. A width of 60 ft is considered to be satisfactory for this purpose and will also provide adequate stability for the lateral forces which will be imposed upon the pier. The deck will be designed of reinforced concrete, and the bents will be spaced on 18-ft 0-in. centers so as to permit the use of a one-way slab spanning between the pile-cap girders. The only longitudinal beams will be the fascia girders along the face of the dock, which will support the fender system. Piles will be steel H piles encased with concrete above 2 ft below low-water level to provide protection from corrosion.

Vertical and horizontal loads. The pier is to be designed to support a uniform live load of 600 lb per sq ft and concentrated wheel loads from an H-20 truck. The uniform live load over the entire deck will cause the maximum pile load, and for this condition a reduction in load of 25 per cent will be assumed on the basis that the two adjacent bays contributing to a pile bent will not be fully loaded over more than 75 per cent of the total area. The H-20-truck rear-axle load will be 16 tons distributed on two wheels, 6 ft on centers, but for the design of the deck slab this may

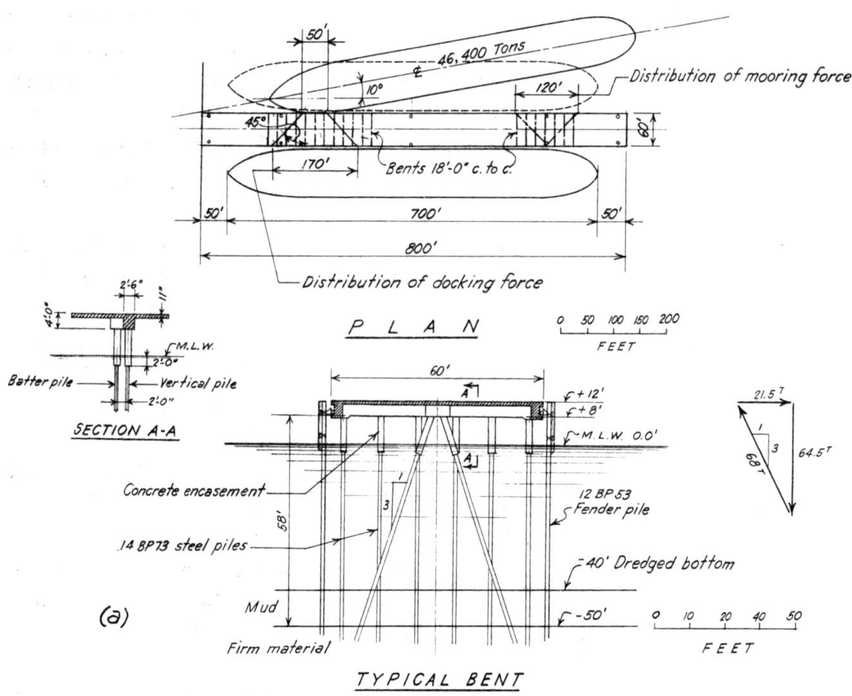

FIG. 5.56 (*a*) Finger pier; plan and typical bent.

be reduced to one axle load of 12 tons or two axle loads of 8 tons each spaced 4 ft apart, whichever produces the greater stress, in accordance with Art. 3.2.8 of the Standard Specifications for Highway Bridges of the American Association of State Highway Officials. These loads are to be increased by 25 per cent to allow for impact.

The fender system is shown in Fig. 5.40. The force of impact from the docking ship is 100 tons, as derived on page 305, Fender Systems. This force may be considered to be distributed by the ship over a 50-ft length of the fender system and then to be further distributed by the diaphragm action of the concrete deck at an angle of 45°, making the total participating length of pier equal to $50 + 2 \times 60 = 170$ ft or 9 bents. Therefore, the docking force per bent is equal to $^{100}/_{9} = 11.1$ tons.

The intensity of wind velocity pressure is

$$p = 0.00256v^2$$

where p = velocity pressure, lb per sq ft
v = velocity of wind, miles per hour

Therefore $p = 0.00256 \times 70^2 = 12.54$ lb per sq ft

This pressure is usually multiplied by a factor of 1.3 to allow for suction on the leeward side of the ship, which increases the pressure to 16.3 lb per sq ft. The total wind force P which one ship exerts against the pier will then be $16.3 \times 30{,}000/2{,}000 = 244.5$ tons. If a second ship is berthed on the opposite side of the pier, the additional wind force is taken as $\frac{1}{2}P$ or $0.5 \times 244.5 = 122.2$ tons. The total horizontal wind force on the pier is, therefore, $244.5 + 122.2 = 366.7$ tons.

If the ship is moored on the windward side of the pier, it will bear against the pier for a length of about 400 ft, and, with a further distribution at 45° through the deck at each end, the total participating length of pier is equal to $400 + 2 \times 60 = 520$ ft or 28 bents. Therefore, the wind force per bent is equal to $244.5/28 = 8.8$ tons. If the ship is moored on the leeward side the wind force tends to pull the ship away from the pier, and the force is transmitted to the pier by the mooring lines. Assuming four mooring lines and a 45° distribution through the pier deck at each mooring line, the number of bents absorbing the pull $= 4 \times {}^{120}/_{18} = 26$. The force per bent in this case is $244.5/26 = 9.4$ tons. If, finally, two ships are moored at the pier, one on each side, the one on the windward side will exert 8.8 tons per bent, and the one on the leeward side $9.4/2 = 4.7$ tons. The maximum force per bent due to mooring forces is thus $8.8 + 4.7 = 13.5$ tons.

The horizontal force from earthquake = 0.1 (D.L. + ½ L.L.).* A 33⅓ per cent increase in stress and allowable pile load is permitted when combined with dead- and live-load stresses.

Deck slab. Assume an 11-in. slab and a clear span of 15 ft 6 in.

CASE 1. Uniform live load of 600 lb per sq ft.

$$\text{D.L.} + \text{L.L.} = 138 + 600 = 738 \text{ lb per sq ft}$$

$$-M = \frac{738 \times 15.5^2}{11} = 16{,}100 \text{ ft-lb}$$ (negative moment at interior support)

$$A_s = \frac{16{,}100 \times 12}{20{,}000 \times 0.87 \times 9} = 1.23 \text{ sq in.}$$ no. 7 bars at 5½ in. (A_s = 1.31 sq in.) in top of slab

$f_c = 1{,}180 < 1{,}350$ lb per sq in. allowable for $f'_c = 3{,}000$ lb per sq in.

$$+M = \frac{738 \times 15.5^2}{16} = 11{,}100 \text{ ft-lb}$$ (positive moment at center of interior span)

* Dead load plus one-half live load.

$$A_s = \frac{11{,}100 \times 12}{20{,}000 \times 0.87 \times 9} = 0.85 \text{ sq in.}$$ no. 7 bars at 8 in. (0.90 sq in.) in bottom of slab.

Shear: $$V = 1.15 \frac{738 \times 15.5}{2} = 6{,}570 \text{ lb}$$

$$v = \frac{6{,}570}{12 \times 0.87 \times 9} = 70 < 90 \text{ lb per sq in.}$$

Web reinforcement is not required because shear stress is below 90 lb per sq in.

CASE 2. One axle load of 12 tons, which has two wheel loads of 6 tons, 6 ft apart. The main reinforcement is parallel to the pier traffic. Wheel loads can be assumed distributed over half a lane width or 5 ft.

$$W = 1.25 \frac{6 \times 2{,}000}{5} = 3{,}000 \text{ lb}$$ on a 1-ft-wide strip

$$L = 18.0 \text{ ft}$$

By using moment coefficients from influence-line tables for continuous beams the following moments may be derived.

$$+M = 0.1708 \times 3{,}000 \times 18.0 = 9{,}200 \text{ ft-lb}$$ from live load

$$+M = 0.0417 \times 138 \times 18.0^2 = 1{,}860 \text{ ft-lb}$$ from dead load

$$11{,}060 \text{ ft-lb}$$ (maximum positive moment, interior span)

This moment has been determined using center-to-center span. Because of the width of support it can be reduced by $\frac{1}{6}V \times a$,

where a = width of support = 2.5 ft

$V = 1{,}500 + 1{,}240 = 2{,}740$ lb

Therefore, $+M = 11{,}060 - 2{,}740 \times 2.5/6$

$= +9{,}920 < 11{,}100$ ft-lb moment for uniform live load

For maximum shear, place wheel load 1 ft outside of face of pile cap. Width of distribution = $1.25 + 2 \times 1.0 = 3.25$ ft.

$$W = 1.25 \frac{6 \times 2{,}000}{3.25} = 4{,}610 \text{ live load}$$

$$138 \times 15.5/2 = 1{,}070 \text{ dead load}$$

$$5{,}680 < 6{,}570 \text{ lb shear}$$ for uniform live load

CASE 3. Two axle loads of 8 tons each, 4 ft between axles, each axle having two wheel loads of 4 tons each, 6 ft apart.

$$W = 1.25\,\frac{4 \times 2{,}000}{5} = 2{,}000 \text{ lb each of 2 wheel loads, 4 ft apart, on 1-ft-wide strip}$$

$$M = 0.2372 \times 2{,}000 \times 18.0 = 8{,}550 \text{ ft-lb} \quad \text{from live load}$$

$$M = 1{,}860 \text{ ft-lb} \quad \text{from dead load}$$

$$10{,}410 < 11{,}060 \text{ ft-lb} \qquad \text{(see case 2)}$$

Vertical piles. Assume a 30-in.-wide by 48-in.-deep pile-cap girder and a 42-in.-wide by 54-in.-deep fascia girder (net area = 11.8 sq ft due to slot) (see Fig. 5.40).

D.L. per bent = 15.5 × 53.0 × 0.92 × 150 = 113,000-lb slab
2.5 × 4.0 × 60.0 × 150 = 90,000-lb pile cap
2 × 11.8 × 15.5 × 150 = 54,900-lb fascia girders

Total D.L. per bent = 257,900 lb
L.L. per bent = 18.0 × 60.0 × 0.75 × 600 = 486,000 lb

Total D.L. + L.L. = 743,900 lb = 372 tons
Total D.L. + ½ L.L.
= 257,900 + ½ × 486,000 = 500,900 lb = 250 tons

Assume six vertical piles per bent.
Load per pile = $^{372}/_{6}$ = 62.0 tons
Assume a 14-in. 73-lb pile, 90 ft long.

Weight of pile = $90 \times \frac{73}{2{,}000}$ = 3.3 tons

Weight of concrete protection:

$1.83 \times 1.83 \times 10.0 \times \frac{150}{2{,}000}$ = 2.5 tons

Total load on pile = 67.8 tons

The pile may be considered fixed at the top at El +8.0 and supported at the bottom at El −50.0, a total effective length (Fig. 5.21) of 0.75 × 58 = 45.0 ft. From Table 5.8, the allowable load is 68.5 tons.

Batter piles. The horizontal loads, which can act on either side of the pier, are as follows:

Docking force = 11.1 tons per bent
Wind = 13.5 tons per bent
Earthquake = 0.1 × 250 × ¾ = 18.8 tons per bent

The above loads do not act concurrently, and, therefore, the earthquake force controls the design of the batter piles. As shown in Fig. 5.56*a*, a pile, with a batter of 1 horizontal to 3 vertical, driven to a safe-load capacity of 68 tons, is capable of resisting a horizontal force of 21.5 tons which is in excess of the maximum horizontal force of 18.8 tons per bent acting on the pier. Therefore, it is unnecessary for the batter pile in the opposite direction to take part of the horizontal force by acting in tension, although the shearing strength of the clay indicates that it can safely take up to 50 per cent of its 68-ton bearing capacity in tension, thereby providing

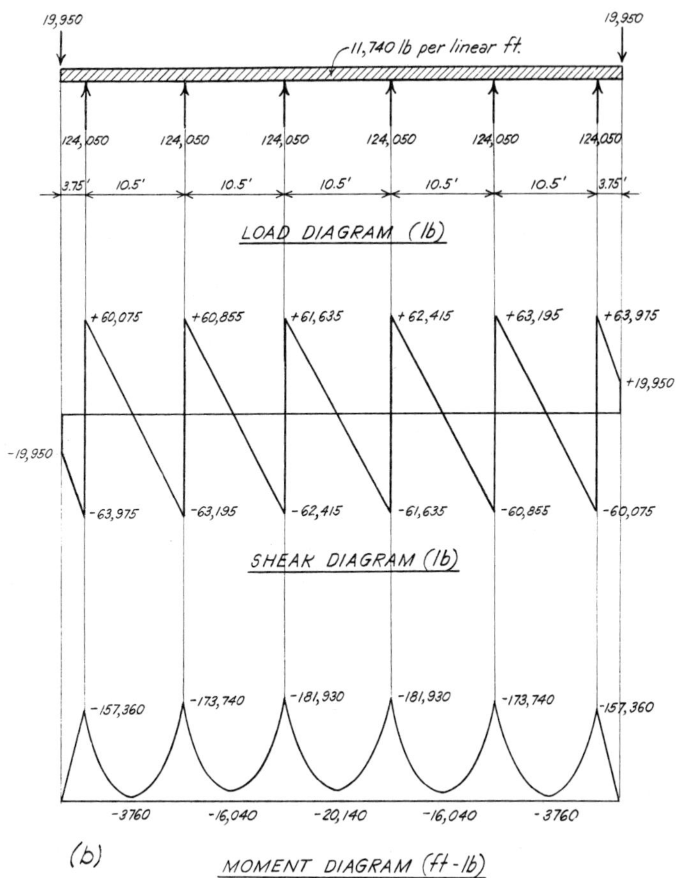

FIG. 5.56 (*b*) Finger pier; load, shear, and moment diagrams for pile-cap girder.

an additional factor of safety. The uplift from the batter pile, which amounts to $3 \times 18.8 = 56.4$ tons, is counteracted by the dead load of the deck and the pull-out value of the batter pile in the opposite direction.

Pile-cap girder is to be designed as a stiff member to distribute the dead and live loads of the deck to equal pile reactions of 62.0 tons each. The vertical piles are spaced as shown in Fig. 5.56*b* and the batter piles are located at the center of the pier, but offset 2 ft from the center line of the vertical piles to provide space for the stay-lathing timbers which hold the vertical piles in line.

The maximum bending moment and shear in the pile-cap girder are determined and are shown in Fig. 5.56*b*.

$$-M = 181{,}930 \text{ ft-lb}$$

$$A_s = \frac{181{,}930 \times 12}{20{,}000 \times 0.87 \times 44} = 2.85 \text{ sq in.}$$

Use 4 no. 8 bars (3.16 sq in.) top.

$$f_c = 560 < 1{,}350 \text{ lb per sq in. allowable}$$

$$+M = 0$$

$$A_{s,\min} = 0.005 \times 30 \times 44 = 6.6 \text{ sq in.}$$

Use 9 no. 8 bars (7.11 sq in.) bottom.

$$V_{\max} = 63{,}975 \text{ lb} \qquad v = \frac{63{,}975}{0.87 \times 30 \times 44} = 56 < 90 \text{ lb per sq in.}$$

Use minimum web reinforcement, no. 4 stirrups at 12-in. centers.

Fascia girder is designed for the dead and live load of the deck and the horizontal reaction of the docking of the ship which is equal to $(100 \times 2{,}000)/50 = 4{,}000$ lb per ft.

Uniform live loads are carried by the slab directly into the pile cap. Wheel loads can come within one foot of the curb or almost on top of the fascia girder.

Vertical moment:

$$W = 1.25 \times 6 \times 2{,}000 = 15{,}000 \text{ lb}$$

$$L = 18.0 \text{ ft}$$

$$+M = 0.1708 \times 15{,}000 \times 18.0 = 46{,}100 \text{ ft-lb} \quad \text{from live load}$$

$$+M = 0.0417 \times 11.8 \times 150 \times 18.0^2 = 24{,}000 \text{ ft-lb} \quad \text{from dead load}$$

$$70{,}100 \text{ ft-lb}$$

Less $\frac{1}{6}Va$

$$= \frac{1}{6}\,\frac{15{,}000 + 11.8 \times 150 \times 18}{2} \times 2.5 = 9{,}750 \text{ ft-lb}$$

Reduced moment at center of span $= 60{,}350$ ft-lb

$$A_s = \frac{60{,}350 \times 12}{20{,}000 \times 0.87 \times 50} = 0.84 \text{ sq in.}$$

$$A_{s,\min} = 0.005 \times 23 \times 50 = 5.75 \text{ sq in.}$$

Use 8 no. 8 bars in bottom.

Vertical shear:

$$V = 15{,}000 + \frac{11.8 \times 150 \times 15.5}{2} = 28{,}700 \text{ lb}$$

$$v = \frac{28{,}700}{0.87 \times 23 \times 50} = 29 < 90 \text{ lb per sq in.}$$

Horizontal moment:

$$-M = \frac{4{,}000 \times 15.5^2}{11} = 87{,}200 \text{ ft-lb} \qquad \text{(negative moment at support)}$$

$$A_s = \frac{87{,}200 \times 12}{20{,}000 \times 0.87 \times 38} = 1.6 \text{ sq in.}$$

Use 4 no. 7 bars (2.40 sq in.) at outside face.

$$+M = \frac{4{,}000 \times 15.5^2}{16} = 60{,}000 \text{ ft-lb} \qquad \text{(positive moment at center of span)}$$

$$A_s = \frac{60{,}000 \times 12}{20{,}000 \times 0.87 \times 38} = 1.1 \text{ sq in.}$$

Use 3 no. 7 bars (1.80 sq in.) at inside face.

Horizontal shear:

$$V = \frac{4{,}000 \times 15.5}{2} = 31{,}000 \text{ lb}$$

$$v = \frac{31{,}000}{0.87 \times 24 \times 38} = 39 < 90 \text{ lb per sq in.}$$

No stirrups are required, but use nominal no. 4 stirrups at 12-in. centers.

Wharf Design, Sheet-pile-cell Type. The plan layout of a cellular sheet-pile wharf is shown in Fig. 5.57*a* and a cross section through a typical cell is given in Fig. 5.57*b*. The wharf consists of a series of sheet-pile circular cells connected by sheet-pile arcs. The piling is cut off at El +4 ft. A concrete wall on the bulkhead line provides a straight dock wall for the support of the fender system and protects the sheet piling down to 2 ft below mean low water.

The soil formation at the location of the wharf consists of silty clay overlying a sand stratum at El −30. The silty clay will be removed completely to 10 ft in back of the cells and then on a 1-on-5 slope, when dredging the harbor to a depth of 35 ft below low water. The cells and the area behind them will be backfilled with coarse sand and gravel.

Design of cells. The earth-pressure forces are computed in accordance with Rankine's theory and act on the cells as shown in Fig. 5.57*b*.

Assume a cell 52.52 ft in diameter. To simplify the analysis of the structure with its irregular shape in plan, it is customary to introduce an equivalent rectangle. In this case the width of the equivalent rectangle

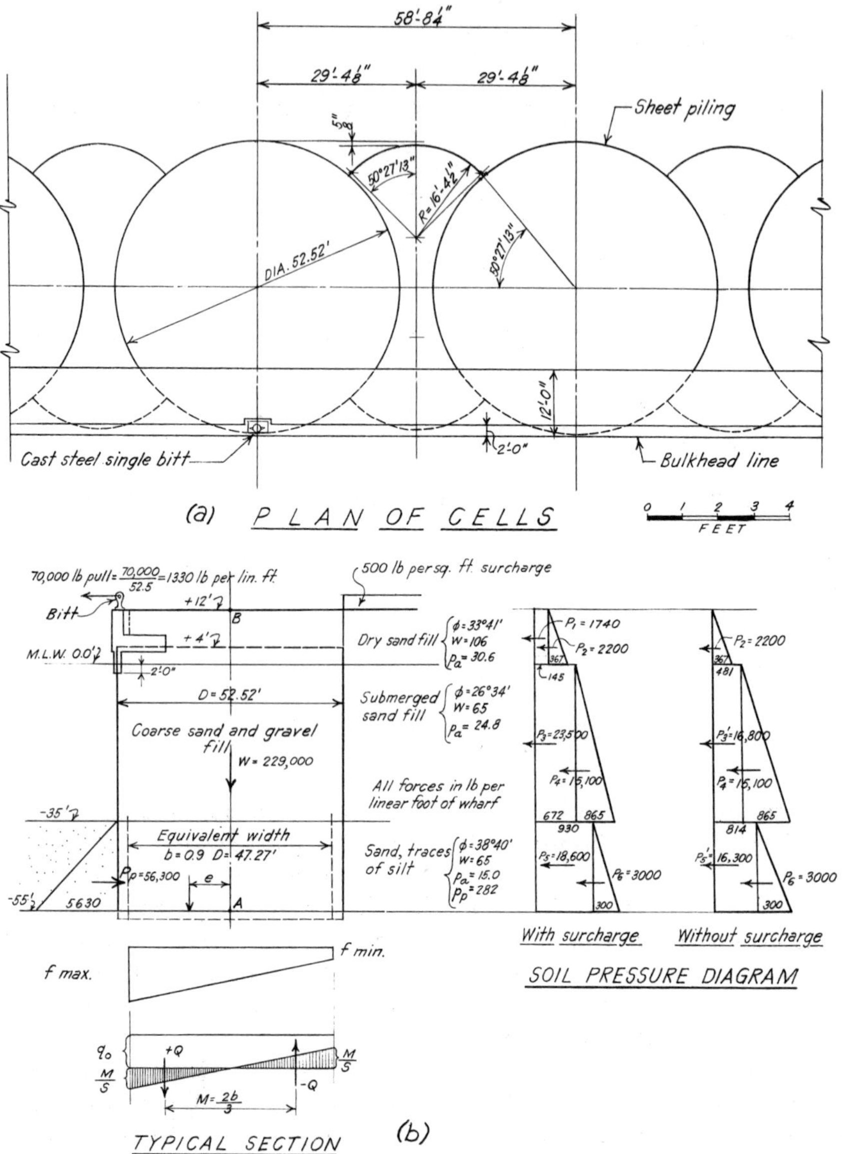

FIG. 5.57 (*a*) Cellular sheet-pile wharf; plan of cells. (*b*) Cellular sheet-pile wharf; typical section and soil-pressure diagram.

can be taken as $b = 0.9 \times 52.52 = 47.27$ ft. The weight of the sand and gravel fill inside the cell is $(106 \times 12 + 65 \times 55) \times 47.27 = 229{,}000$ lb per lin ft of wharf.

The overturning moment about point A is derived as follows:

1,330 lb × 69.5 ft =	92,460 ft-lb
1,740 lb × 61.0 ft =	106,140 ft-lb
2,200 lb × 59.0 ft =	129,800 ft-lb
23,500 lb × 37.5 ft =	881,250 ft-lb
15,100 lb × 31.7 ft =	478,670 ft-lb
18,600 lb × 10.0 ft =	186,000 ft-lb
3,000 lb × 6.7 ft =	20,100 ft-lb
65,470 lb	1,894,420 ft-lb
−56,300 lb × 6.7 ft =	−377,210 ft-lb
9,170 lb	1,517,210 ft-lb

The resultant of all forces should fall within the middle third of the equivalent width at the base $(e < b/6 = 7.9 \text{ ft})$

$$e = \frac{M}{W} = \frac{1{,}517{,}210}{229{,}000} = 6.6 < 7.9$$

The maximum toe pressure f_{max} is

$$f_{max} = \frac{229{,}000}{1 \times 47.27} + \frac{1{,}517{,}210}{S} \qquad \text{where } S = \frac{1 \times 47.27^2}{6} = 372.4 \text{ ft}^3$$

$$f_{max} = 8{,}920 \text{ lb per sq ft}$$

The minimum toe pressure $f_{min} = 4{,}846 - 4{,}074 = 772$ lb per sq ft.

The sliding resistance of the sand at the base of the cell is $W \tan \phi = 229{,}000 \times 0.800 = 183{,}200$ lb. The horizontal shearing force at the base is 9,170 lb which is only a fraction of the resistance at this level.

The overturning moment will produce shear forces in the fill. K. Terzaghi, in his paper, Stability and Stiffness of Cellular Cofferdams, in the 1945 *Transactions* of the American Society of Civil Engineers, describes a method for evaluating these shear forces. In Fig. 5.57*b* the normal stress diagram at the base is shown as composed of a uniform stress q_o due to direct weight of the wharf and two triangles (crosshatched areas) due to the overturning moment. Each triangle represents a force Q, and the moment of these internal forces must be equal to the external overturning moment

$$Q = \frac{3M}{2b} = \frac{3 \times 1{,}517{,}210}{2 \times 47.27} = 48{,}100 \text{ lb per lin ft}$$

A vertical plane AB (Fig. 5.57*b*), 1 ft wide, must resist this internal force Q in shear. The maximum allowable shear on such a plane is $V = P \times \tan \phi$ where P is the force normal to the plane, and $\tan \phi$ the coefficient of friction of the soil. Tan ϕ varies vertically, as plane AB passes through different strata, and the total friction force becomes the sum of partial forces at the various levels. At each level the normal force is equal to the horizontal active Rankine pressure. This is computed the same as for the horizontal earth pressure against the cell, but without the surcharge, and is shown in Fig. 5.57*b*. Not only the soil inside the cell but also the walls of the sheet piling resist shear. A very close approximation of the influence of the sheet piling is obtained by adding a coefficient of interlock friction, usually $f = 0.3$, to the coefficient of soil friction. This is derived from the assumption that the total tension in the two sheet-pile walls, which are cut by a longitudinal section through a cell, is equal to $P \times D$, and the friction in the interlocks is, therefore, $P \times D \times f$ where f is the coefficient of friction in the interlock, assumed equal to 0.3. By dividing $P \times D \times f$ by the diameter of the cell D, the additional shearing resistance per ft of width of cell is equal to $P \times f$.

Therefore: $$V = \Sigma P_n(\tan \phi_n + f)$$

P_n	ϕ_n	$\tan \phi_n$	$\tan \phi_n + f$	V_n
2,200	33°41′	0.667	0.967	2,130
31,900	26°34′	0.500	0.800	25,520
19,300	38°40′	0.800	1.100	21,230
				$V = V_n = 48{,}880$ lb

V is only slightly greater than the force Q, and the safety factor is 48,880/48,100 = 1.02. However, many cofferdams have been built for which the safety factor as computed by this method is below unity, and they have not failed. The explanation is that the soil pressure and consequently the friction force inside a cell is probably considerably greater than the value given by the Rankine formula, or the friction in the interlocks may be greater than assumed.

The tension in the interlock is determined by the formula for hoop tension in a pipe subject to internal pressure.

$$T = p \times \frac{D}{2}$$

where T = tension, lb per ft of interlock
p = horizontal earth pressure, lb per sq ft
D = diameter of cell, ft

The maximum earth pressure occurs at El −35 and is equal to 1,537 lb per sq ft. Therefore, $T = 1{,}537 \times 52.52/2 = 40{,}400$ lb per lin ft or 3,360 lb per lin in. The recommended maximum working stress in the interlocks for the flat-web sheet piling, weighing either 28 or 32 lb per sq ft, is 8,000 lb per lin in. and for the flat-arch section (usually not used for major structures), weighing 23 or 28 lb per sq ft, is 3,000 lb per lin in. Therefore, the flat-web section, weighing 28 lb per sq ft and having a ⅜-in.-thick web, will be selected. The sheet piling below the concrete protection will be given cathodic protection.

Dock wall. The stem of this wall will be designed for the outward pressure of the earth and surcharge load, for the 70,000-lb outward pull of a mooring line, and for the impact of a vessel with a displacement of 13,800 long tons, striking with a velocity of 30 ft per min normal to the dock. A 15-in. draped round rubber fender will be used, and the resulting force against the dock wall will amount to 9,000 lb per ft over a length of 20 ft, as derived in the design of the fender system on page 303. The fender system is illustrated in Fig. 5.36.

A cross section through the L-shaped dock wall is shown in Fig. 5.57*c* together with the loads per ft of length. The wall is supported by the sheet piling and the sand fill. It is assumed that by the time the wall is built the sand fill inside the cells will be consolidated and will support the wall without appreciable settlement. The soil pressure will vary from zero at the sheet piling to a maximum at the interior edge of the footing on the center line of the cell. The increase in soil pressure will be assumed to follow a straight line in both directions, as shown in Figs. 5.57*c* and *e*. The maximum soil pressure for permanent loads and surcharge can then be found from the condition that the moment of all forces about point A must be zero.

$$R_2 \times 7.33 = 4{,}500 \times 5.00 + 6{,}360 \times 6.00 + 6{,}000 \times 5.00 - 1{,}230 \times 4.25 - 1{,}105 \times 2.83 = 82{,}300 \text{ ft-lb}$$

$$R_2 = 11{,}230 \text{ lb}$$

$$R_1 = 4{,}500 + 6{,}360 + 6{,}000 + 1{,}800 - 11{,}230 = 7{,}430 \text{ lb}$$

$$f = \frac{11{,}230 \times 2}{11} = 2{,}040 \text{ lb per sq ft}$$

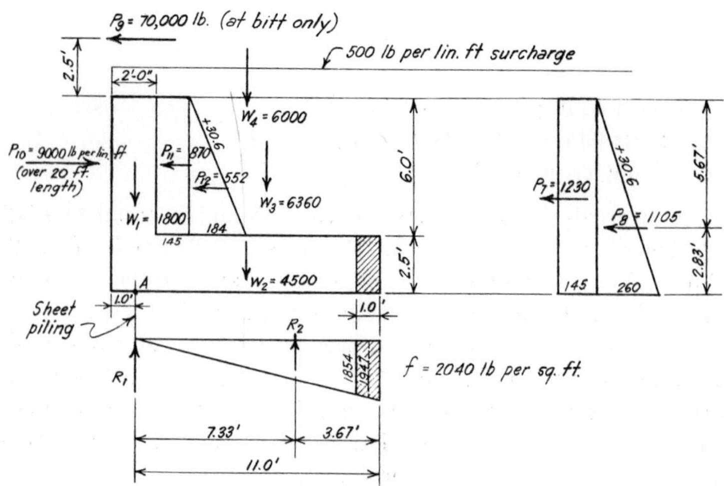

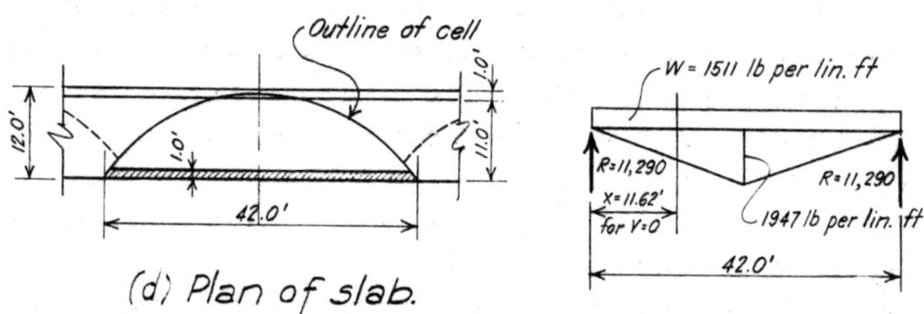

FIG. 5.57 (c) Cellular sheet-pile wharf; cross section and soil-pressure diagrams for dock wall. (d) Cellular sheet-pile wharf; plan of slab. (e) Cellular sheet-pile wharf; load diagram for design of slab.

The innermost 1-ft-wide strip of the bottom slab, indicated by cross-hatching in Fig. 5.57*d*, carries the loads shown in Fig. 5.57*e*. The direct load, including surcharge, is $p = 500 + 6 \times 106 + 2.5 \times 150 = 1{,}511$ lb per lin ft. The sum of all vertical forces must be zero; therefore,

$$R = 1{,}511 \times 21 - 1{,}947 \times \frac{21}{2} = 11{,}290 \text{ lb}$$

The maximum moment occurs where $V = 0$, 11.62 ft from the support

$$M = 11{,}290 \times 11.62 + \frac{1{,}947 \times 11.62^3}{21 \times 2 \times 3} - 1{,}511 \frac{11.62^2}{2} = +53{,}570 \text{ ft-lb}$$

which requires a reinforcement, at the bottom and parallel to the face of the wharf, of

$$A_s = \frac{53{,}570 \times 12}{20{,}000 \times 0.87 \times 26} = 1.42 \text{ sq in.} \qquad \text{no. 8 bars at 6-in. centers}$$

The bottom slab can be divided into 1-ft-wide strips, and each strip can be designed in a similar manner.

The stem of the wall has to resist the earth pressure and either the outward mooring force or the inward docking force. The docking force is assumed to be carried down into the stem at an angle of 45°, or a distributed length of 17 ft. The maximum outward moment at its base is

From earth pressure:	$552 \times 2 =$	1,104 ft-lb
and	$870 \times 3 =$	2,610 ft-lb
From mooring force	$70{,}000 \times \frac{8.5}{17} =$	35,000 ft-lb
		38,714 ft-lb

The maximum inward moment is

From docking force:	$9{,}000 \times 3 =$	27,000 ft-lb
Less minimum earth pressure:	$552 \times 2 =$	1,100 ft-lb
		25,900 ft-lb

The required vertical reinforcing in the stem is then

$$A_s = \frac{38{,}714 \times 12}{20{,}000 \times 0.87 \times 20} = 1.33 \text{ sq in.} \qquad \text{no. 8 bars at 7 in. at inside face}$$

$$A_s = \frac{25{,}900 \times 12}{20{,}000 \times 0.87 \times 20} = 0.90 \text{ sq in.} \qquad \text{no. 8 bars at 10 in. at outside face}$$

The same moments are carried into the bottom slab where they require no. 8 bars at 9 in. and no. 7 bars at 10 in., top and bottom, respectively, perpendicular to the face of the wharf.

5.8 Unusual Dock Construction

The following are a few examples of recently constructed docks which are unique in their design and method of construction.

Pier at Ilo, Peru, for the Southern Peru Copper Company. Figure 5.58 shows a cross section through a pier constructed in 1957 for ocean-going vessels, which had to be designed for a foundation condition in which the sea floor in this area is a granitoid rock with some small pockets and pinnacles, and which is bare in most areas except for some thin sand and shell deposits. The bottom slopes seaward from −30 ft at the inshore end of the pier, which is connected to the mainland by a 900-ft rock mole, to −62 ft at the outer end of the pier. Since the use of conventional piling was not feasible and since the large earthquake forces had to be taken care of in the design of this heavy pier structure, it was decided to use concrete-filled steel cylinders founded directly on the rock bottom. These cylinders are 5 ft in diameter, with ¼-in. steel walls in the straight section, flaring out into a bell section of ⅜-in. steel walls, 11 ft in diameter at the bottom.

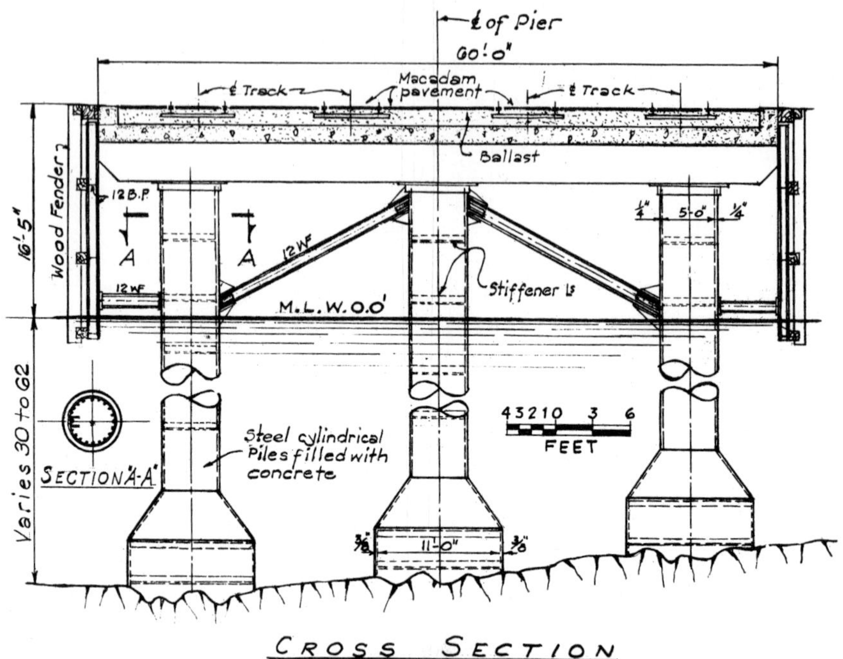

FIG. 5.58 Cross section of pier for the Southern Peru Copper Company at Ilo, Peru.

Each of the 30 pier bents is composed of three cylinders which are heavily reinforced, and which are capped with a large transverse reinforced-concrete girder. Each bent was designed as a rigid frame to take the force of the earthquake (0.1g) and the lateral docking and wind forces from a 40,000-dead-weight-ton ship.

The pier was constructed by the overhead method, i.e., without the use of floating equipment. This procedure consisted of using a pair of heavy steel mats designed to rest on top of the cylinders after they had been braced and concreted, to support a large crane, and to permit it to advance offshore, as work progressed, by picking up the rear mat, swinging it around and placing it in position on the cylinders in the next bent in front and then walking forward onto this mat.

The cylinders were of welded construction and the bottoms of the belled-out sections were cut to fit the contours of the rock bottom. Determination of these contours was accurately done with a measuring device composed of a telescoping pipe shaft with an angle-iron ring attached to the bottom. The ring had the same diameter as the bell, i.e., 11 ft. It was fitted at its third points with leveling screws, 2 in. in diameter by 3 ft in length, with handles to enable manual operation. In holes on 1-ft centers around the ring, ¾-in. by 3-ft pins were held in place by large thumbscrews. The device was handled by the crane and located in its exact position with a transit, with those above working in conjunction with divers handling the three leveling screws on the measuring device. With the template in exact position, the divers loosened the thumbscrews and dropped the pins to the rock bottom and then tightened the thumbscrews. The template was then withdrawn, and the relative position of the pins was measured and plotted on a chart, after which the chart was sent to the fabrication yard where the contour was marked off on the bell, which was then burned with a torch to trim the cylinder bottom to the proper contour. When the cylinders were lowered in their designated position on the sea bottom, divers checked the fit of the cylinder bottom against the rock and, where necessary, closed any openings with sandbags.

Each cylinder was filled with tremie concrete to approximately one-half its height. When the tremie concrete had set a sufficient length of time, the remaining water in the cylinder was pumped out, the laitance removed, a key cut in the top surface of the concrete, and concrete placed in the dry to within 4 ft of the top of the cylinder. The remaining height of the cylinder was filled at the time of concreting the transverse girder.

The pier is intended to berth one ship on each side, which will be loaded with copper ingots transported out on the pier on flat railroad cars. The initial installation provides for two railway tracks which will be eventually increased to four tracks.

Ore Dock for Erie Mining Company at Taconite Harbor, Minnesota. The long and comparatively narrow shape of the harbor, which is restricted to about 1,500 ft in width by two islands paralleling the shore, pointed to a bulkhead type of dock for this location. This, together with the necessity of supporting a very considerable tonnage of iron-ore pellets stored as close as possible to the ore carriers alongside, in order to expedite and simplify loading operations, suggested cutting back the comparatively straight, rocky shore line in such a way as to widen the harbor and at the same time provide suitable foundations for storage bins.

In order to make it possible for boats to dock along the wall it was necessary to excavate rock and overlying sand and gravel to a depth of 30 ft below lake level. This meant the removal of one million cubic yards of material either by underwater blasting and dredging or in the dry

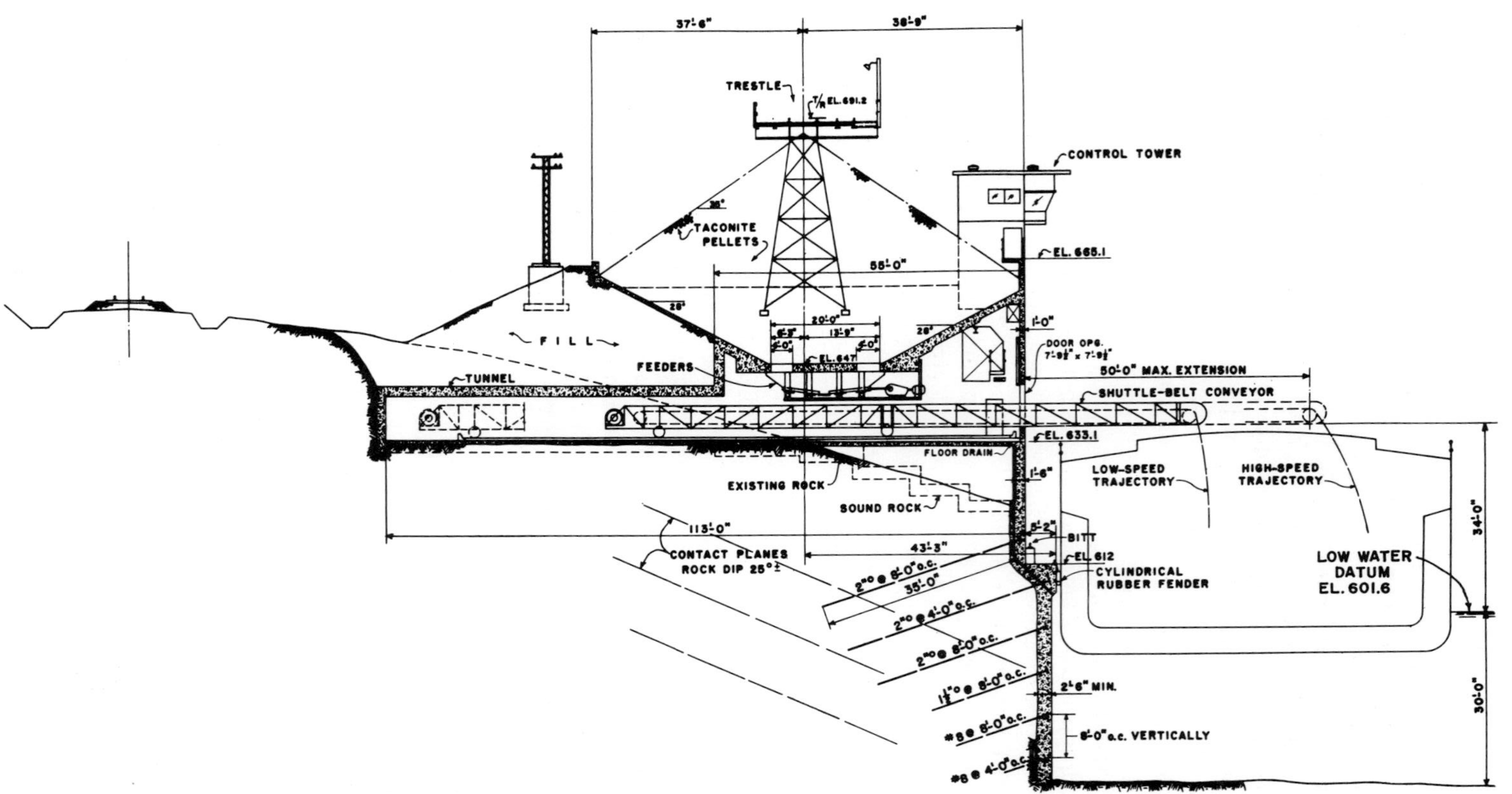

FIG. 5.59 Cross section of ore dock for Erie Mining Company at Taconite Harbor, Lake Superior.

behind a cellular cofferdam to shut out the lake. The latter method was adopted by the contractor and proved to be the most economical as well as simplifying the excavation for the dock wall and its construction. In excavating for the dock wall the dock face was first line-drilled on 1-ft centers. As the rock, a volcanic basalt, was removed from the face, there was evidence of contact planes, some of which were filled with fine-grain elastic materials or rock fragments, which could be removed with a pick. Many of them were water bearing, being fed from the high ground above. The rock in back of the face was cement grouted both before and after the excavation was made.

The original design of the dock wall had been based on using a relatively thin concrete lining which would be anchored to massive rock by short dowels of close spacing. Consequently, the condition of the rock face as uncovered gave some cause for concern, particularly since it had to support a surcharge of about 3 tons per sq ft from the weight of the storage bin, and contained iron-ore pellets.

From the geology of the area and from earlier exploratory drilling, it was known that the rock was a fairly good amygdaloidal basalt which had been laid down in successive surface flows having a strike almost parallel to the shore and a dip of roughly 25° toward the lake. In order to study more fully the condition of the rock immediately in back of the face of the dock and on which the proposed ore-storage bins were to be supported, it was decided to make additional core borings on lines every 48 ft perpendicular to the dock face; the holes being located 10, 30, and 50 ft back of the face. The information obtained from the borings enabled geological cross sections to be plotted, and from the observations made on the exposed rock face, which had already been excavated, it was possible to determine the extent and depth of the contact planes.

After further study and consultation with a geologist, the original design for anchoring the dock-face wall to the rock with short dowels and close spacing was modified to one using a fewer number of larger and longer rods so as to anchor the wall farther back into the rock and to make it and the rock act as a monolithic mass. As shown in Fig. 5.59, some of these rods penetrated as much as 35 ft into the rock and were 2 in. in diameter.

Since the dock face extended for a length of around 2,000 ft, the contractor developed efficient mobile drilling and grouting platforms, moving along the rock face on rails, to facilitate the drilling, placing of rods, and grouting. Two such towers as shown in Fig. 5.60 were used, having a platform for each horizontal row of dowels. The first tower was used to drill the holes and the second one to set and grout the anchor rods. The holes were drilled on an incline of about 20° below the horizontal. Before placing the anchor rods, the holes were partly filled with grout consisting of one part cement, one part sand, and one part Embeco (an expanding agent to prevent shrinkage).

Prefabricated panels were used to form the concrete dock-lining wall. They were handled by crane and were attached to the anchor rods projecting from the rock face, making it unnecessary to brace the exterior form. The concreting of the 42-ft-high wall was done in two vertical lifts and horizontal pours 48 ft long.

FIG. 5.60 Mobile drilling and grouting platform at Taconite Harbor, Lake Superior.

New Pier 57, New York City. This pier, which replaced the old Grace Line pier burned down in 1947, is a complete departure from the conventional type of pier construction. Designed by Emil H. Praeger, then of Madigan-Hyland, Long Island City, New York, it is a concrete and steel structure that has a buoyant hollow-box foundation resting on sand-drain consolidated silt, in which some 3,000 timber piles which supported the old pier were cut off at El −34.0 and left in place to transfer the live load to the silt when the pier is fully loaded.

About 90 per cent of the total dead load is carried by the buoyancy of the pier's three submerged reinforced-concrete boxes (Fig. 5.61), which were constructed in a basin some distance up the Hudson River and towed down the river to the pier site.

Before sinking the boxes, concrete girders, 150 ft long, were poured on 20-ft centers on the top of the boxes to support the main pier deck consisting of prestressed trapezoidal-shaped concrete stringers placed edge to edge in the longitudinal direction and covered with a poured-in-place concrete slab with integral finish. The girders span the box width and cantilever out 35 ft beyond it on each side to form a pier 150 ft wide and 725 ft long.

When the concrete had been completed, the boxes were sunk onto a prepared sand and gravel bed, which had been placed over the silt after the wood piles had been cut off at El −34, by pumping fresh water into them. The overload thus applied further consolidated the silt. When the

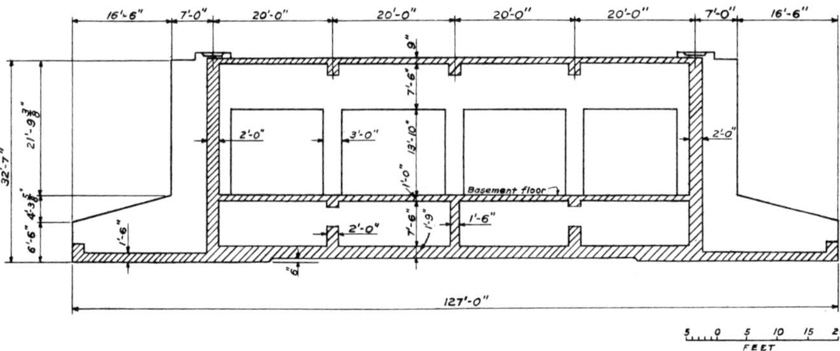

FIG. 5.61 Cross section of submerged reinforced-concrete box, pier 57, New York City. (*From Engineering News-Record, January* 11, 1951.)

boxes had finally come to rest, 30-in.-diameter steel caissons, filled with concrete, were dropped through 36-in.-diameter vertical wells in the box walls, sunk into the river bottom, and concreted into the wells. These caissons act as spuds to resist the horizontal loads which come on the pier. The boxes were then dewatered in increments, as additional dead load was supplied by the erection of the superstructure, a two-story shed 700 ft long and 120 ft wide. The bulkhead box at the inshore end of the pier carries a 375- by 135-ft two-story shed. Figure 5.62 shows a cross section through the pier.

5.9 Dolphins

Dolphins are designed principally for the horizontal loads of impact and/or wind and current forces from a ship when it is docking and during the time that it is moored. These forces are determined in the same manner as for the design of docks (page 248).

Dolphins may be of the flexible or rigid type. Wood-pile clusters are examples of the former type. These are driven in clusters of 3, 7, 19, etc., piles, which are wrapped with galvanized cable, as shown in Fig. 5.63. The center pile of each cluster is usually permitted to extend about 3 ft

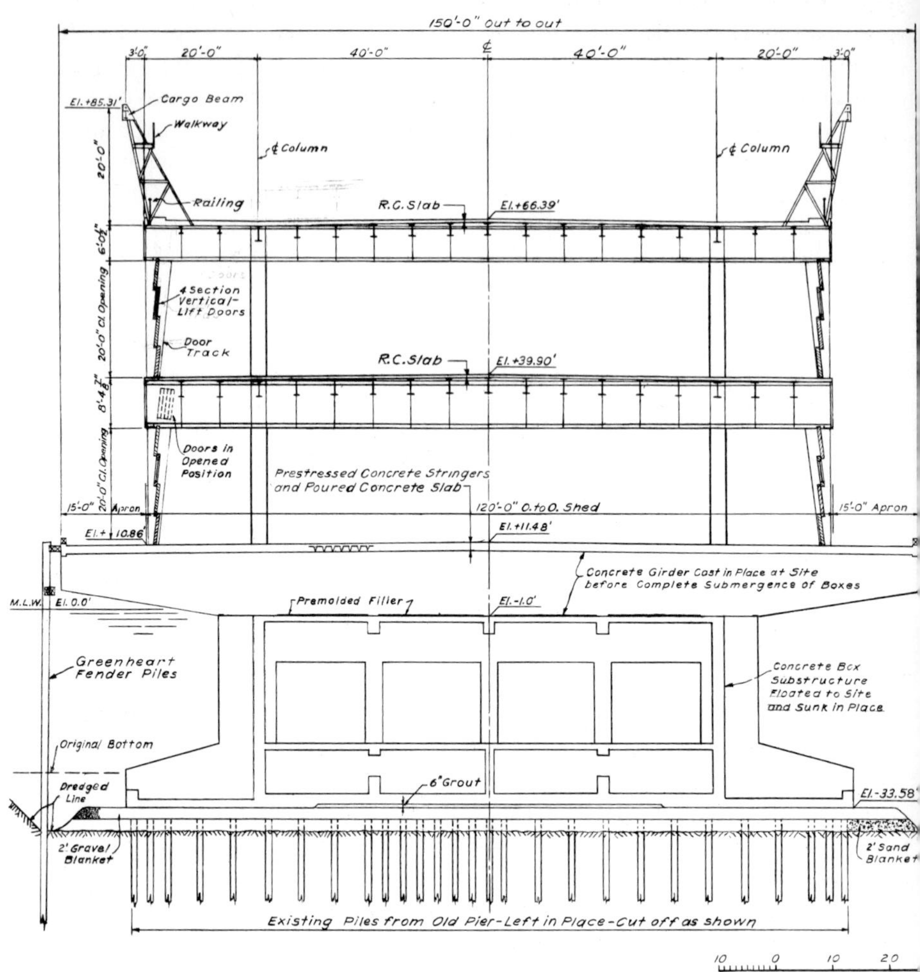

FIG. 5.62 Cross section of pier 57, New York City. (*Courtesy of the Department of Marine Aviation, New York City.*)

above the other piles to provide a means of attaching the ship's mooring lines. A modification of this type of dolphin is to arrange the piles in a symmetrical pattern, so that they are on a slight batter and bolted to wood cross members located just above low-water level, and with wood framing at the top, as shown in Fig. 5.64. Large steel cylinders and groups of steel-pipe piles have also been used to provide flexible dolphins, as shown in Fig. 5.65*a*, *b*, *c*. In general, dolphins of the flexible type have

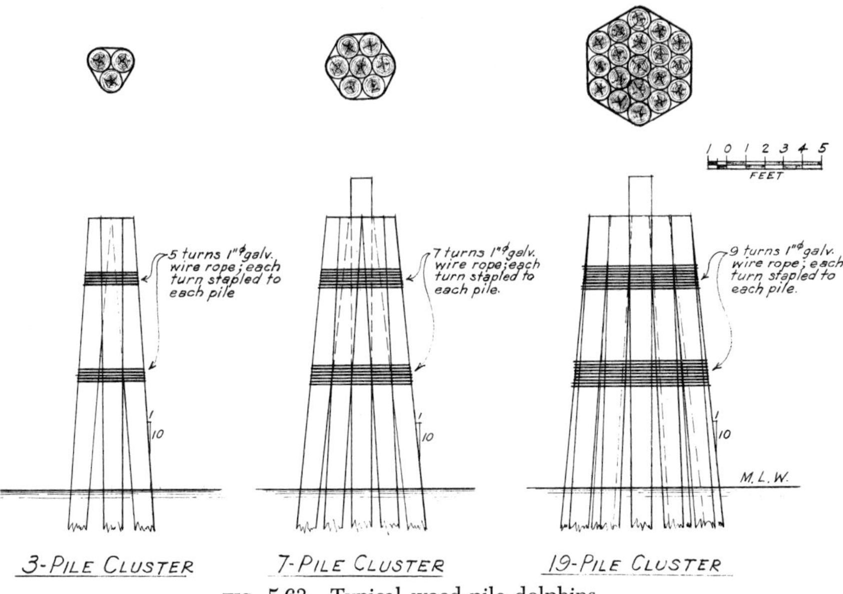

FIG. 5.63 Typical wood-pile dolphins.

been used for mooring small vessels not exceeding 5,000 DWT (deadweight tonnage), or as an outer defense for the protection of docks or for breasting off somewhat larger vessels from loading platforms and structures not designed to take the impact of ships. The bottom soil conditions must be suitable for this type of installation; otherwise, if the soil is too soft, the dolphins or pile clusters will not rebound to their original positions after being struck by the vessel, and their energy absorbing ability through deflection will be gradually dissipated.

For larger cargo ships and tankers of the T-2 class (9,000 to 17,000 DWT) a wood-platform type of rigid dolphin, utilizing wood batter piles, may be used for mooring and breasting the ship. Such a dolphin is shown in Fig. 5.66. Since the wood platform is relatively light in weight, its lateral stability depends to a large extent on the pull-out value of the wood piles. In general, a lateral force of about 40 to 50 tons is about

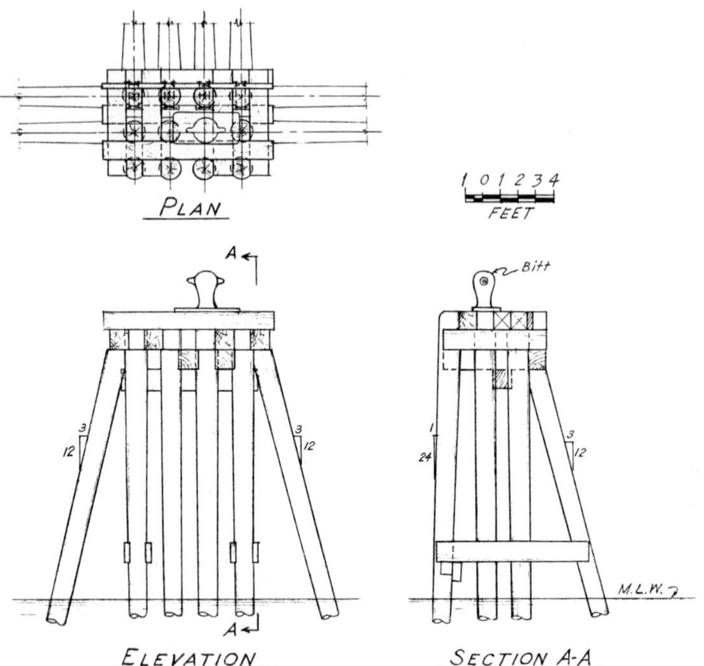

FIG. 5.64 Typical wood-pile dolphin with timber framing.

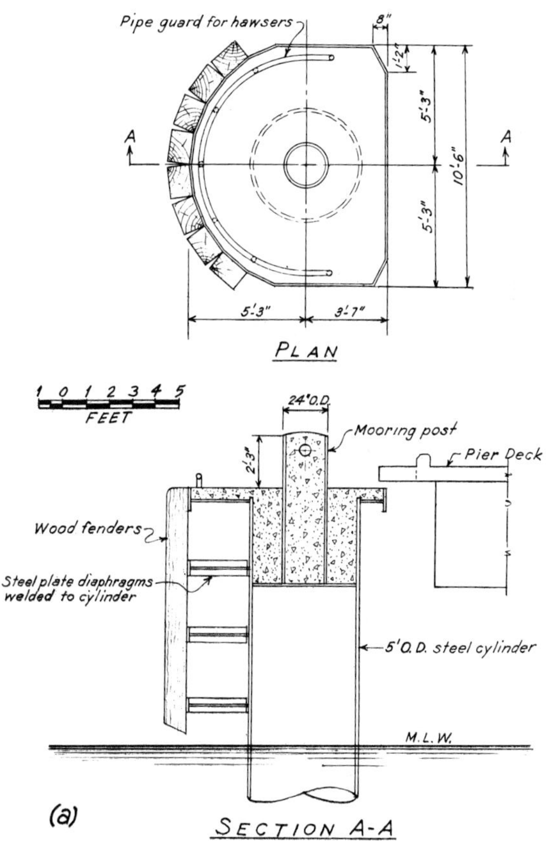

FIG. 5.65 (*a*) Flexible steel-cylinder dolphin at Puerto Miranda, Venezuela. (*Courtesy of the Cia Shell de Venezuela.*)

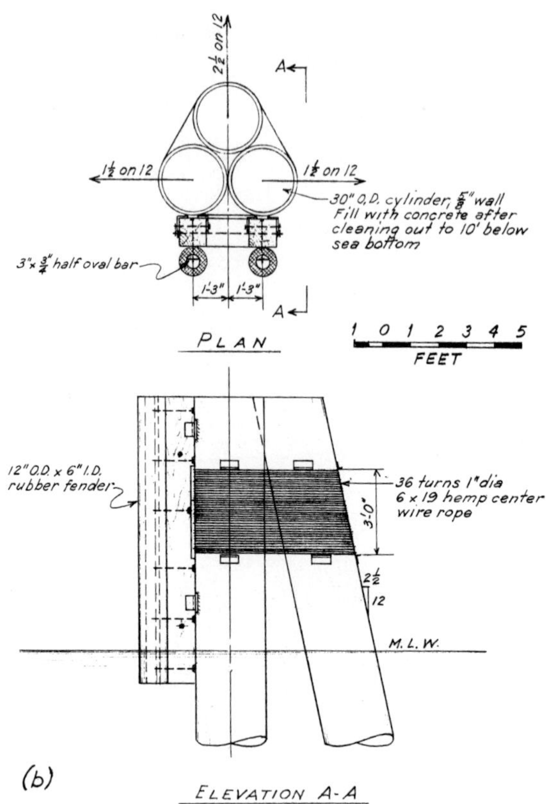

FIG. 5.65 (*b*) Flexible dolphin with steel-pipe piles at Miragoane, Haiti. (*Courtesy of Reynolds Haitian Mines, Inc.*)

FIG. 5.65 (*c*) Flexible dolphin with steel-pipe piles and steel framing. (*Courtesy of Mannesmann, Dusseldorf, West Germany.*)

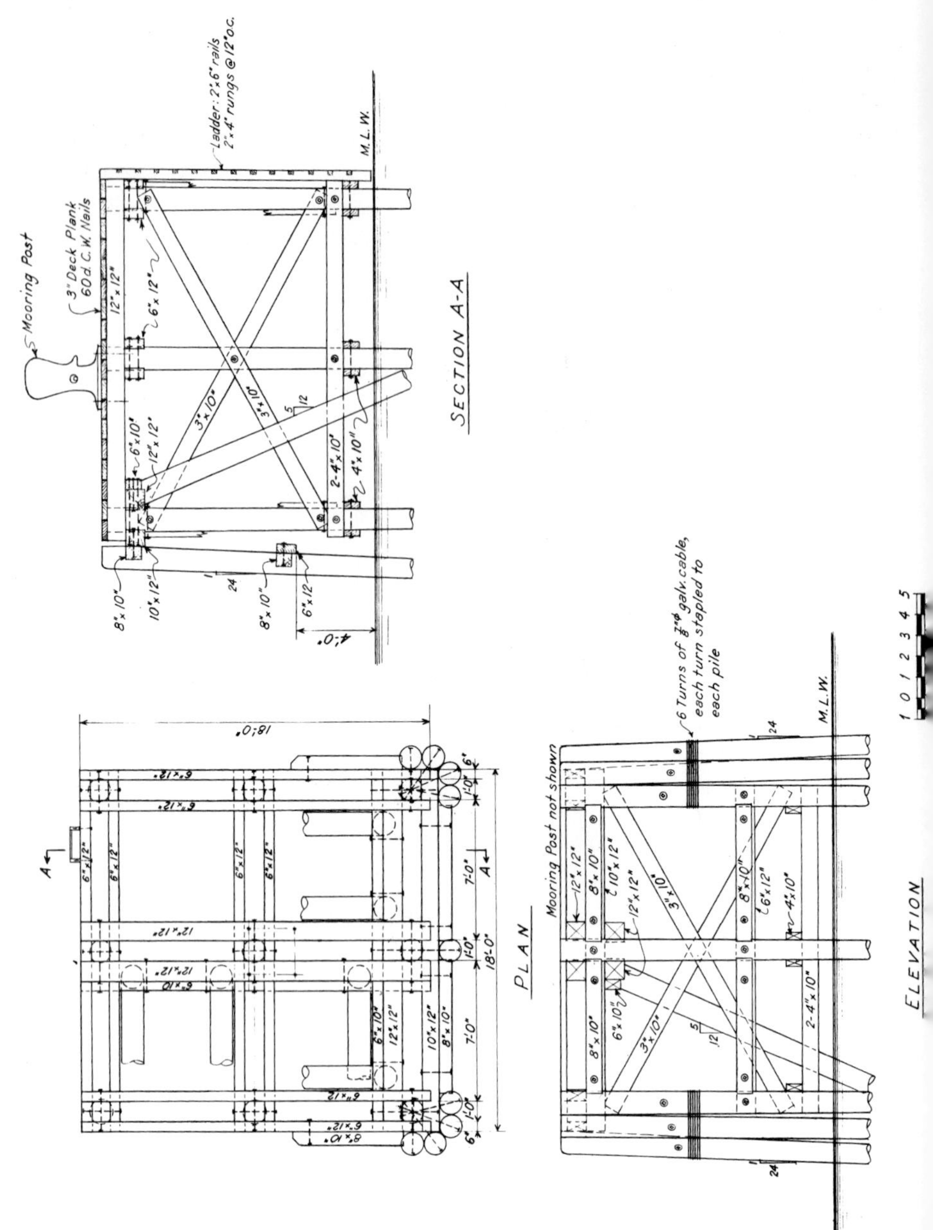
Mooring Post
3" Deck Plank
60 d. C.W. Nails
Ladder: 2"x6" rails
2"x4" rungs @ 12" o.c.
M.L.W.
SECTION A-A
PLAN
Mooring Post not shown
6 Turns of 7/8"φ galv. cable,
each turn stapled to
each pile
ELEVATION

the most that a dolphin of this type can resist without becoming too large and unwieldy.

If bottom soil conditions are suitable, sheet-pile cells make excellent dolphins and can be designed to withstand the forces from the largest ships, if provided with adequate fenders. Cells, because of their circular

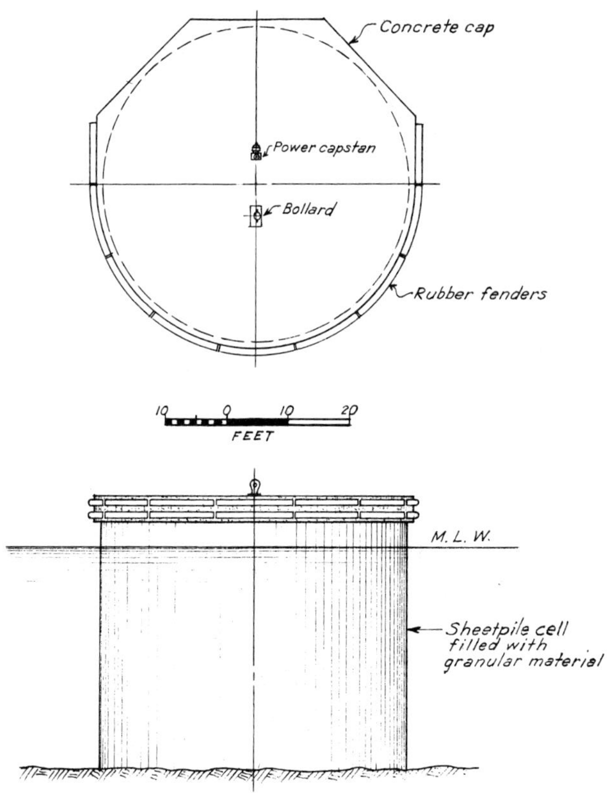

FIG. 5.67 Cellular sheet-pile dolphin.

shape, are well suited for turning dolphins, for warping or turning the ship around at the end of the dock. Such a dolphin, with fender system, is shown in Fig. 5.67 and will accommodate a 35,000-DWT ship. Cellular dolphins are usually capped with a heavy concrete slab to which the mooring post or ballard is anchored. When large ships are to be handled, a powered capstan should be provided to draw in the heavy wire-rope mooring lines.

As the ships have become larger, the design of dolphins has turned to the use of heavy concrete platform slabs supported by vertical and batter piles usually of steel, although precast concrete is also used. This type of dolphin has been designed to take the docking and mooring forces from the largest supertankers (110,000 displacement tons) and will resist lateral forces up to 450 tons. This requires the use of a large number of batter piles, the uplift from which, in turn, makes it necessary to have a considerable amount of dead weight, as the vertical piles will in general resist only a relatively small proportion of the uplift. This dead weight is supplied by the concrete slab which may be 5 to 6 ft in thickness. A sufficient number of vertical piles must be provided to support this dead weight. In addition, the vertical piles must not be spaced too far apart; otherwise it will be difficult and expensive to provide forms for the support of the concrete when it is poured. When the depth of slab exceeds 4 ft 6 in., it is usually economical to pour the slab in two lifts, providing horizontal shear keys at the construction joint. This greatly reduces the cost of the forms. Figure 5.68 shows a large concrete dolphin supported on steel H piles and protected with a cylindrical rubber-fender–steel-wale type of fender system, which will take the docking and mooring forces of a 70,000-displacement-ton vessel.

The following is the design of the dolphin shown in Fig. 5.68.

The dolphin is one of two similar dolphins placed on each side and 10 ft in front of a petroleum hose-handling platform, for the purpose of taking the docking force of the ship and holding the ship away from the platform when an offshore wind is blowing. It is to be provided with a mooring post to take the springing and mooring lines.

The dolphin is to be designed for docking a ship with a displacement of 70,000 long tons, with an approach speed of 20 ft per min (0.333 ft per sec) normal to the face of the dolphin; for a mooring-line pull of 100 tons parallel to the face of the dolphin, in either direction, or normal to the face in an offshore direction; and for breasting a ship off the dock against an offshore wind of 75 miles per hour. The exposed area of the ship when light is 40,000 sq ft.

The wind force $p = 0.00256v^2 \times 1.3 = 0.00256 \times 75^2 \times 1.3 = 18.7$ lb per sq ft; use 20 lb per sq ft. The total wind force against the side of the ship $= 20 \times 40{,}000 = 800{,}000$ lbs $= 400$ tons, which is divided equally between the two breasting dolphins, or 200 tons per dolphin.

The energy of the docking ship is

$$E = \frac{Wv^2}{2g} = \frac{70{,}000 \times 2{,}240 \times (0.333)^2}{64.4} = 270{,}000 \text{ ft-lb}$$

$$\frac{E}{2} = 135{,}000 \text{ ft-lb} \qquad \text{energy to be absorbed by the fender system}$$

If possible the docking force should not exceed the wind force. Therefore, the length of distribution of the energy of the striking ship and the size of fender should be selected within practicable limits to obtain

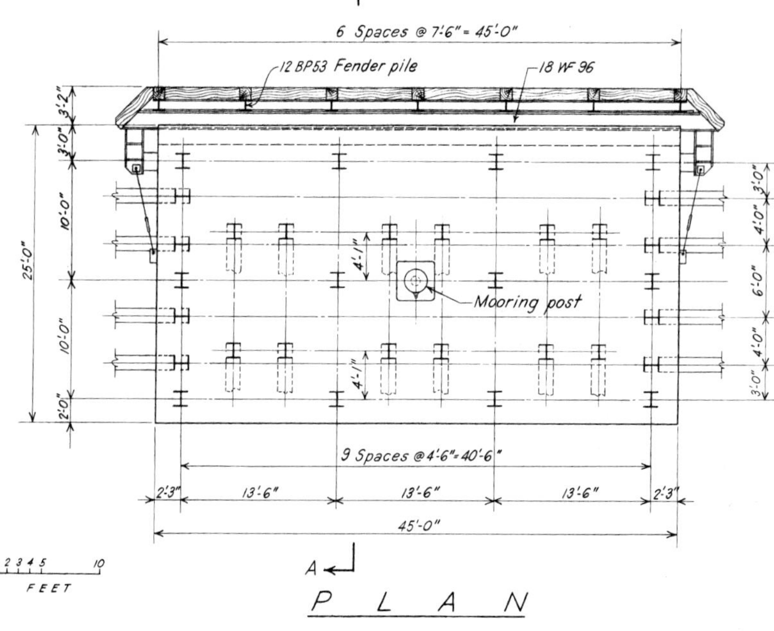

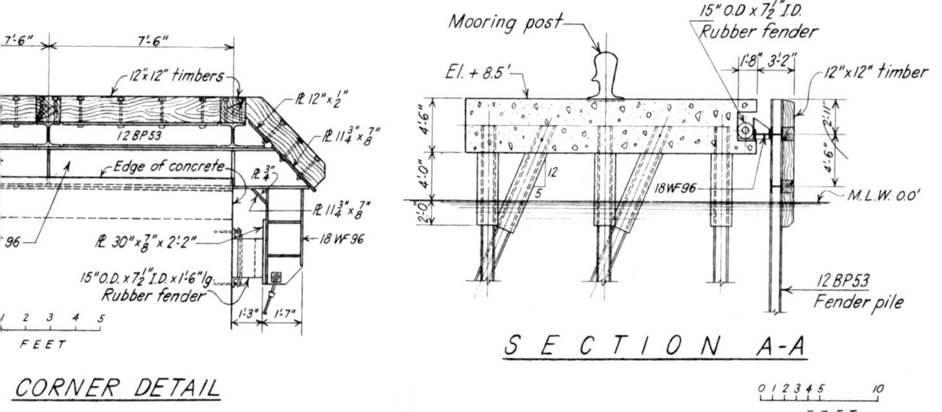

FIG. 5.68 Breasting dolphin with steel H piles and concrete platform.

this result. If we assume a 15- by $7\frac{1}{2}$-in. cylindrical rubber fender and a maximum deflection of 50 per cent or $7\frac{1}{2}$ in., and referring to Fig. 5.41, it will absorb an energy of 3,000 ft-lb per lin ft. The required length of distribution would then be 135,000/3,000 = 45 ft. The resulting force per linear foot will be 9,000 lb, and the total force from the docking ship will be $9{,}000 \times 45 = 405{,}000$ lb = 202.5 tons. For this size of ship a length of 45 ft is considered to be about the maximum length over which the impact of the ship will be distributed. For a smaller ship, such as a T-2 tanker, about one-half of this length would normally be used for this distribution.

A 14-in. 73-lb H pile, driven to a safe load not to exceed 70 tons, has been selected for the support of this dolphin. Since the H piles are to be protected with concrete jackets, their effective load-carrying capacity will be reduced by this weight, which amounts to 1.4 tons, and their own weight of 2.9 tons, assuming a total length of 80 ft, or a total reduction of 4.3 tons.

Assume a pile cap 25 ft wide and 4 ft 6 in. thick. The length of 45 ft has already been determined. The weight = $(25.0 \times 45.0 \times 4.5 - 1.67 \times 2.5 \times 45.0)\ 150 = 731{,}000$ lb = 365.5 tons. This weight plus the downward component of the mooring-line pull will have to be supported by vertical piles. The vertical piles should be spaced not more than 12 to 14 ft on centers in order to support the forms for concreting the caps. An inspection of the plan of the cap (Fig. 5.68) indicates that piles spaced 13 ft 6 in. on centers in three longitudinal rows will provide 12 vertical piles. This group of piles will have a moment of inertia I around the longitudinal center line equal to $4 \times 10^2 \times 2 = 800$ ft² and S = $^{800}/_{10} = 80$ ft. From Fig. 5.69 it is seen that the line of force of the ship impact passes through the intersection of the resultants of the group of vertical and batter piles and, therefore, the moment is zero. However, the 100-ton mooring-line pull acts 4.0 ft about this point of intersection, resulting in a moment = $100 \times 4.0 = 400$ ft-tons. It can be shown that the maximum pile load in the outshore row of vertical piles occurs when the mooring-line pull is normal to the face of the dolphin and is equal to $100 \times {}^{12}/_5 \times {}^{1}/_{12} + {}^{400}/_{80} + 365.5/12 = 20 + 5 + 30.5 = 55.5$ tons. The required bearing capacity is $55.5 + 4.3 = 59.8$ or 60 tons.

The maximum upward component from the batter piles resisting the docking force is ${}^{12}/_5 \times 202.5 = 486$ tons. This is partly resisted by the weight of the cap, leaving $486 - 365 = 121$ tons to be taken by the vertical piles in tension or ${}^{121}/_{12} = 10.1 < 35$ tons per pile allowable in tension. This would indicate the possibility of reducing the thickness of the cap since the vertical piles are capable of taking more of the uplift force in tension. However, 4 ft 6 in. is the minimum thickness which will accommodate the fender and which will insure a rigid cap and distribution of pile loads.

In the longitudinal direction there will be the 100-ton pull of the mooring line, in either direction, or the longitudinal component of the docking force, acting at the wood rubbing strip and equal to $0.3 \times 202.5 = 60.8$

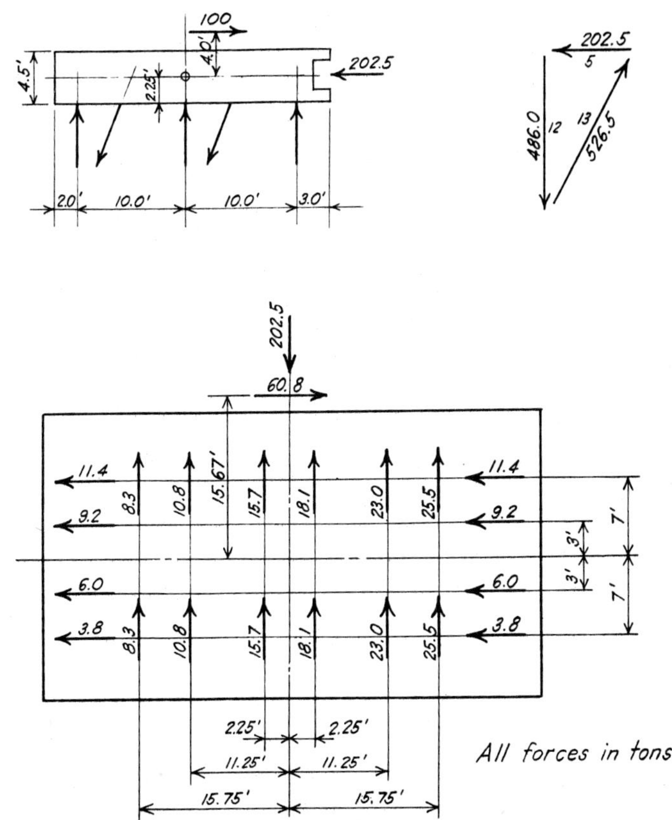

FIG. 5.69 Plan and section showing forces acting on breasting dolphin.

tons. A pair of batter piles, one taking compression and the other tension (50 per cent of compression), will resist a horizontal force $= \frac{5}{13} \times (70.0 - 4.3) + \frac{5}{13} \times 35 = 25.3 + 13.5 = 38.8$ tons. The required number of batter piles in the longitudinal direction $= 100/38.8 \times 2 = 5.2$; but use 8, 4 in each direction, for symmetry around the longitudinal center line of the cap and to allow for additional load due to eccentricity of the longitudinal docking force, as follows.

Assume 12 transverse batter piles located as shown in Fig. 5.68. The moments of inertia of the horizontal components of the longitudinal and transverse batter piles (see Fig. 5.69) about the longitudinal and transverse axes, respectively, are $(2 \times 7^2 + 2 \times 3^2)\ 2 = 232\ \text{ft}^2$, and $(2 \times 15.75^2 + 2 \times 11.25^2 + 2 \times 2.25^2)\ 2 = 1{,}518\ \text{ft}^2$. Therefore, $232 + 1{,}518 = 1{,}750\ \text{ft}^2$. The moment of the longitudinal component of the docking force $= 60.8 \times 15.67 = 953$ ft-tons. Referring to Fig. 5.69, it will be noted that the longitudinal component of the docking force tends to produce a clockwise rotation in the dolphin which is resisted by two couples, one in the longitudinal batter piles and one in the transverse batter piles. The maximum and minimum horizontal components in a longitudinal batter pile are therefore $60.8/8 \pm 953 \times 7/1{,}750 = 7.6 \pm 3.8$, or a maximum of 11.4 tons and a minimum of 3.8 tons. The maximum compression or tension in a longitudinal batter pile would be $11.4 \times {}^{13}/_{5} = 29.6$ tons. This is less than the allowable 35 tons in the case of a pile in tension. The maximum and minimum horizontal components in a transverse batter pile would be $202.5/12 \pm 953 \times 15.75/1{,}750 = 16.9 \pm 8.6$, or a maximum of 25.5 tons and a minimum of 8.3 tons. It then follows that the maximum compression in a transverse batter pile is $25.5 \times {}^{13}/_{5} = 66.3$ tons. The piles would be driven to a safe load of $66.3 + 4.3 = 70.6$, say 70 tons.

The batter piles are assumed to be 50 per cent effective in tension. Therefore, ${}^{70}/_{2} = 35$ tons, and the horizontal and vertical components are 13.5 and 32.3 tons, respectively. For the mooring-line pull of 100 tons normal to the face of the dolphin, the tension in the batter piles $= {}^{13}/_{5} \times 100 = 260$ tons total and ${}^{260}/_{12} = 21.7 < 35$ tons allowable per pile.

5.10 Moles, Trestles, and Catwalks

Many piers are located a considerable distance offshore, where the water at the inshore end of the pier is deep enough to accommodate the loaded draft of the largest vessel to use the pier, or where it is no longer economical to extend the required depth by dredging toward shore. In such instances, access from the mainland to the inshore end of the pier will have to be provided by a mole or a trestle or a combination of both.

A mole is a fill, usually rock, extending out from shore, with its side slopes protected from erosion by riprap or armor rock, and with its upper surface of the required width and grade to accommodate the facilities which may be required to serve the pier, such as roadway, sidewalk, railroad tracks, utilities, pipelines, and conveyor. Figure 5.70 shows a typical cross section through a mole. In general, it will be found more economical to use a mole rather than a trestle out from shore to where the depth of water is approximately 10 ft, assuming that suitable fill material is readily available and that the top of the mole will not be above the normal height of 12 to 15 ft above low water, making the maximum height of mole about 25 ft. It must be kept in mind that 8 to 10 ft is about the minimum depth of water in which floating equipment can safely operate; therefore, if a trestle is to be constructed in shallower water, it will have to be done by the overhead method. The mole will have to be constructed with stable slopes, protected with armor rock of a size depending upon the degree of exposure. The interior fill or core, unless in a very protected area, should be of run-of-quarry rock so that it will not be washed away by waves and swells before it can be properly protected. In general, the requirements for the design will conform to that for breakwaters, keeping in mind that since the core material may

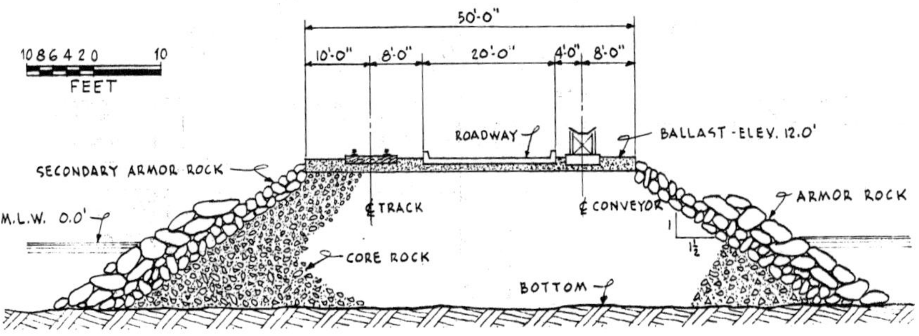

FIG. 5.70 Typical cross section of a rock mole.

have to support a roadway, tracks, etc., it must not become eroded or undergo future settlement.

A trestle will usually be of lighter construction than the pier, as it does not have to withstand the ship's docking and mooring forces. Vertical loads will be the principal forces to be considered, although sufficient lateral stability will have to be provided to take care of current, wind, ice and earthquake forces, and sway from equipment, where these exist. Generally, it will be found that batter piles may be omitted where the height above firm bottom is 25 ft or less and the trestle is not subject to earthquake or unusual forces from equipment. In deeper water, batter piles will be required, in all or in alternating bents. Vertical live loads may consist of one or more of the following: H-10 to H-20 trucks, railroad loads, mobile or truck cranes (dead-weight only), pipelines filled with liquid, loaded conveyor, or 250 lb per sq ft uniform live load.

Precast- and prestressed-concrete deck slabs have been found economical for trestle roadway construction. Figure 5.71 shows a trestle using the precast type of construction. The roadway for an entire bay is precast in one unit and lifted into place on the supporting transverse pile-cap girders. The roadway slab units are tied together and to the pile-cap girders by cast-in-place concrete, which embeds the hooked ends of projecting reinforcing rods from each of these units.

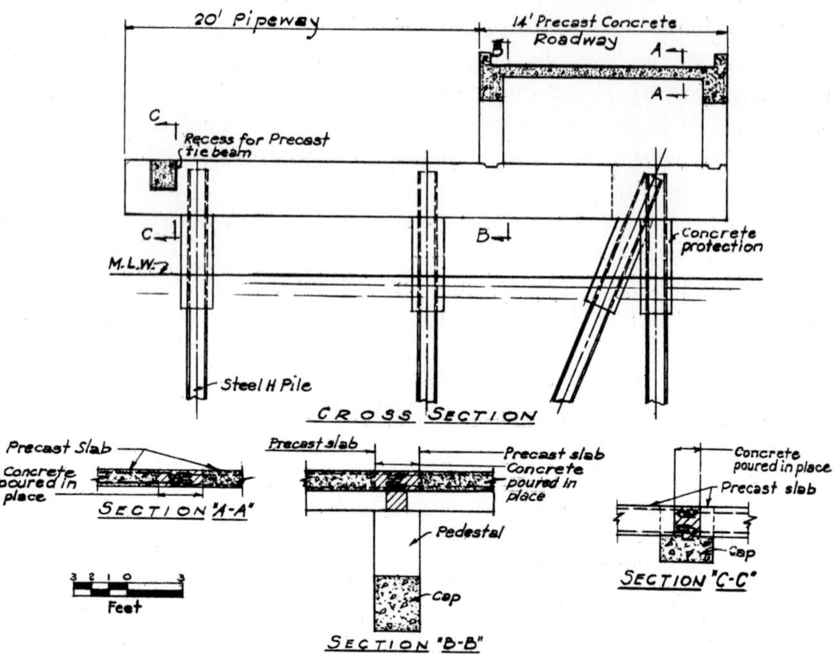

FIG. 5.71 Cross section and details of trestle with precast-concrete roadway slab and tie beams.

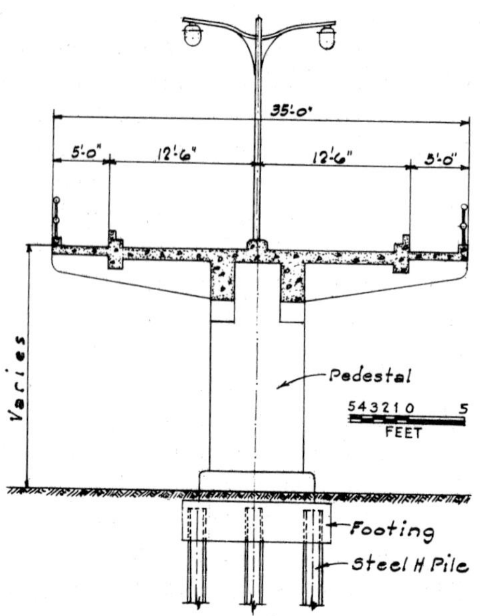

FIG. 5.72 Cross section of approach viaduct to the passenger terminal at the port of La Guaira, Venezuela.

Figure 5.72 is a cross section through a concrete viaduct leading to the second floor of the passenger terminal at the Port of LaGuaira, Venezuela. This design embodies the center-pier and cantilever-deck type of construction.

A typical cross section through a wood trestle is shown in Fig. 5.73. This type of construction is very economical and is particularly suitable for temporary or short-term use.

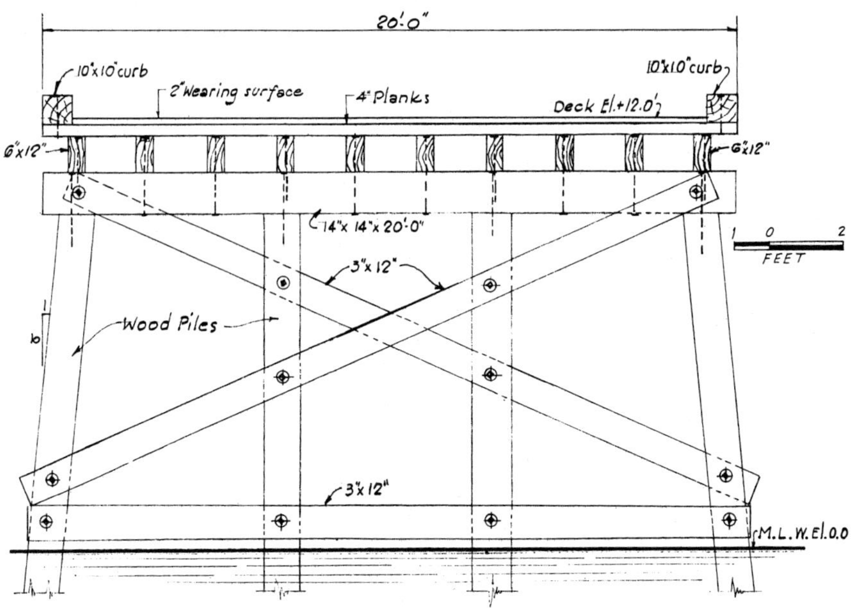

FIG. 5.73 Cross section of timber trestle on wood piles.

Catwalks are used to provide access to and between dolphins. These walkways provide a convenient means of running out ships' lines to their moorings; otherwise these must be handled by boat. In its simplest form, as shown in Fig. 5.74, these catwalks consist of a light wood walkway, with railing, supported on pairs of wood piles. A live load of 100 lb per sq ft is usually adequate for the design of these catwalks. Therefore, it is readily seen that the supporting piles are very lightly loaded. This leads to the economical use of longer spans, utilizing light steel or wood trusses, where foundation conditions require the use of long piles. These light trusses may have spans of around 80 to 100 ft, the length being limited by the lateral stiffness of the deck since the walkway usually does not exceed 4 to 5 ft in width. Welded-pipe construction is ideal for these trusses. Figure 5.75 shows a catwalk of this type of design. In locating the walkways, it is very important to place them far enough in

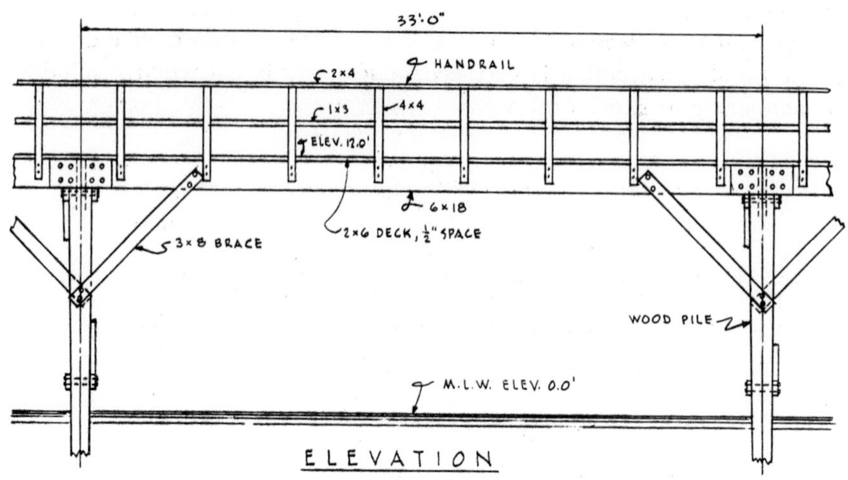

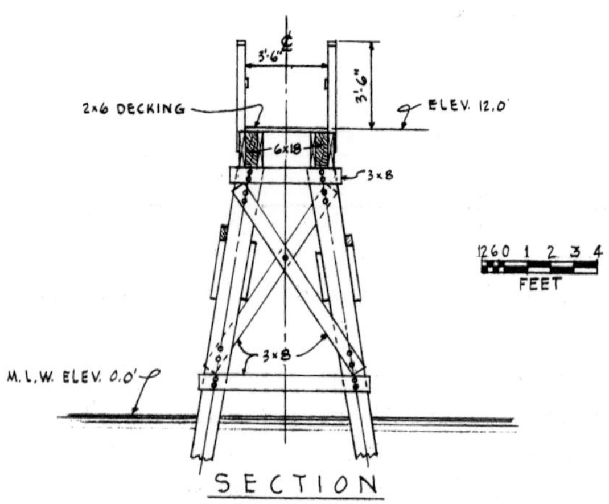

FIG. 5.74 Timber catwalk on wood piles.

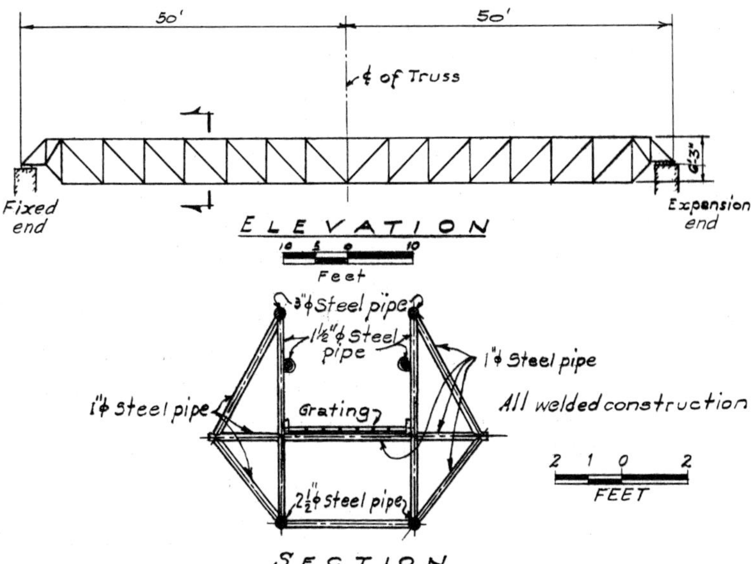

FIG. 5.75 Long-span catwalk of steel-pipe construction.

back of the face of the dock or mooring so that they will not be struck and damaged by a ship.

5.11 Offshore Moorings

For over a quarter century the petroleum industry has made use of the submarine-line sea terminal to provide a means for the transfer of oil through underwater pipelines between shore storage and tanker. The last few years have witnessed unprecedented growth of tanker construction, and the problem now is to design facilities to handle tankers of 100,000 DWT and larger. One of the major difficulties is the lack of harbors and channels with water of sufficient depth to accommodate these large vessels which draw 49 ft when fully loaded. One solution to the problem has been to transfer sufficient cargo to lighters in deep water to reduce the draft sufficiently to enable the vessel to use available channels, harbors, and docking facilities. This is a costly procedure and is to be avoided if possible. However, the cost of constructing conventional piers may be prohibitive due to the large amount of dredging required or the distance offshore and depth of water in which they must be located. Furthermore, exposed conditions may make it unsafe to dock against a fixed type of structure. When one or more of these conditions exist, and the cargo to be handled is bulk material, an offshore mooring may be the most economical and satisfactory solution to the problem.

A vessel may be moored offshore with its own anchors, or to a buoy or group of buoys, or by a combination of its own anchors and buoys. When moored only with its anchor it will swing at anchor to be generally parallel with the wind or current. Such a mooring is not suitable for a sea loading or unloading cargo terminal if the wind and current vary in direction from time to time, although a mono-mooring type of floating buoy or structure has been studied and is believed to be feasible, under most conditions, as a marine offshore facility for oil transfer. The most serious problem connected with its use is the possibility of the ship overriding the mooring under certain current and wind conditions.

Sea terminals are used primarily for the loading and/or discharging of petroleum, although other bulk cargo is sometimes handled in this manner, as described in Chap. 8. Regardless of the type of cargo being handled, it is essential that the vessel maintain a more or less fixed position with respect to the loading point during the transfer. Therefore, the vessel must put out a sufficient number of mooring lines to hold it against the forces of wind, current, and waves.

There is a difference of opinion among sea-terminal operators as to the number of mooring buoys required at a sea berth, with the result that moorings at different terminals vary somewhat in this respect. They may range from two to eight buoys, the number being determined by the size of vessels to use the terminal; the wind, current, and waves; the condition of the sea bottom; and economic conditions. Figure 5.76 shows different arrangements of moorings consisting of three to eight buoys, supplemented in most cases with either one or both of the ship's anchors. The most common arrangement for vessels up to the T-2 tanker class is the three-buoy berth having two quarter lines and one stern line, supplemented by the ship's anchors placed at an angle of 30 to 45° off the bow. Where strong winds may occur broadside to the ship, two additional breasting lines may be added making a five-buoy berth. For the supertankers up to 100,000 DWT, six to eight buoy berths have been found necessary to assure a safe mooring. Where the prevailing wind direction may vary at different times of the year, it may be necessary to provide an eight-buoy berth with buoys for quarter lines at both ends of the berth, so as to tie up the vessel on either heading.

In general, the vessel will want to approach the berth heading into the wind and will drop either its port or starboard anchor first, depending on which direction the wind is from. At the same time, the harbor boat will take out the corresponding quarter line off the stern and make it fast to the buoy. After this, the ship will maneuver into position to drop its second anchor, and the corresponding quarter line off the stern will be run out. Next in order will be the attachment of the breasting lines, and the ship will then be drawn into proper position with respect to the loading point by the ship's mooring winches, the large ships carrying up to as much as 1,500 ft of wire rope on a winch. Since conditions will vary at different sea loading terminals, a careful mooring procedure, in conjunction with the location of the buoys, will have to be worked out for each site. Range lines will have to be established so that the ship's

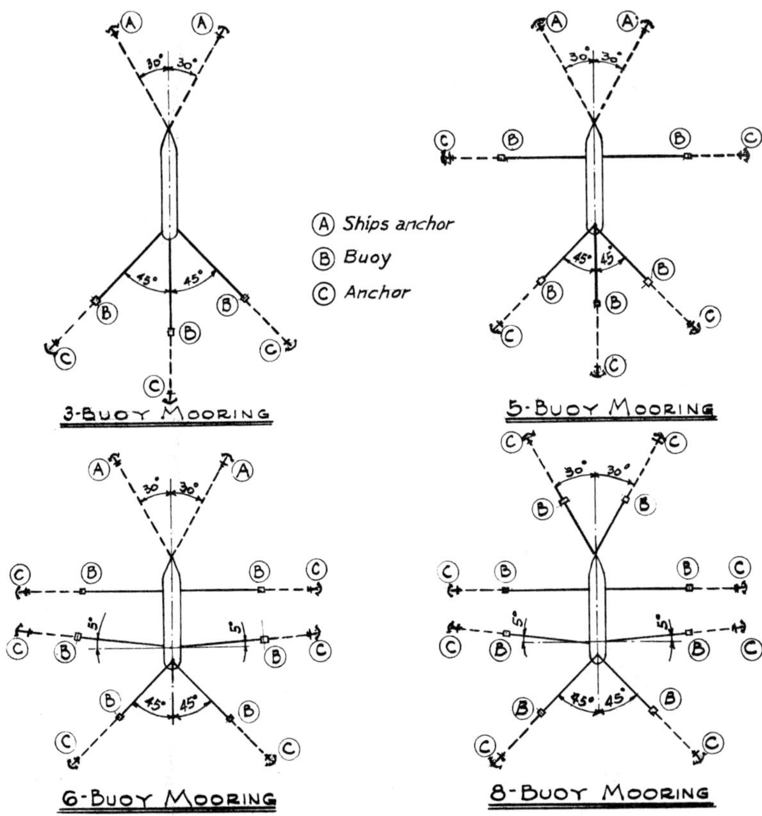

FIG. 5.76 Various arrangements of offshore moorings.

captain will know how to approach the berth and where to drop the ship's anchors.

The mooring should be located as close to the shore as possible, consistent with the required water depth. For the large supertankers a depth of about 60 ft at the loading point is required to provide adequate depth toward shore for the safe maneuverability of the vessel. Most major sea terminals are located within about one mile of the shore line and the moorings are laid out, insofar as possible, for the vessels to head into the wind, waves, and current. However, this is not always possible, and the berth may require a two-directional heading, or the vessel may lay off the end of a loading-out conveyor platform, in a direction more or less parallel to the shore. This will have an important bearing on the space to be allotted if the sea terminal is to have more than one berth. Aside from this factor, the dimensions of a multiple sea berth will depend upon the layout of the buoys and the size of vessels to be berthed. In general, the supertankers of 35,000 to 100,000 DWT will require a center-to-center berth spacing of 3,500 to 5,000 ft. The over-all length, from bow to stern

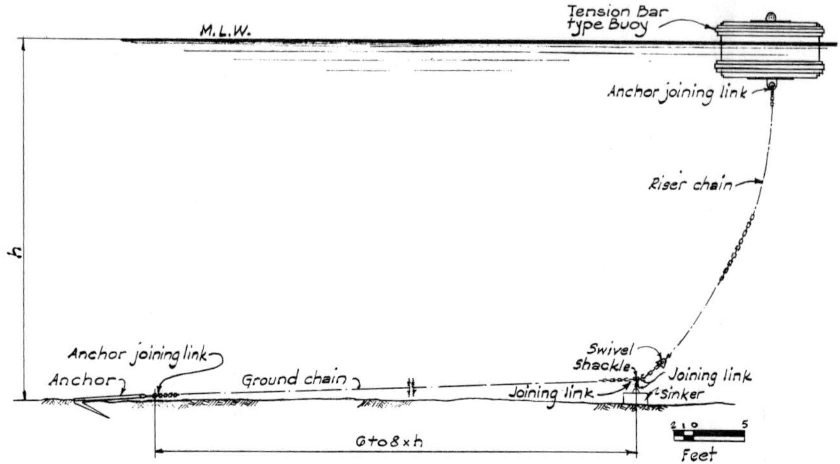

FIG. 5.77 Typical mooring-buoy unit or anchorage.

anchors, may vary from 2,200 to 2,600 ft depending upon whether a one- or two-directional heading is provided for in the buoy layout.

The components of a mooring-buoy unit or anchorage consist of the mooring buoy and sinker, the anchor or anchors, and the connecting or ground chain between the anchors and mooring buoy. Figure 5.77 shows a typical mooring-buoy unit.

Mooring buoys are usually large cylindrical cans or drums, as shown in Fig. 5.78, which are provided with through-stays to which the mooring hook is secured at the top end and the anchor chain at the underwater end. The ship's line is attached to the mooring hook on the buoy, which is quite often a self-releasing type of hook, which enables the ship's mooring line to be unhooked from the buoy by a man on a launch or on the ship itself. Mooring buoys are designed to have sufficient buoyancy to take the resultant downward component between the pull of the ship's mooring line and the ground chain. This will submerge the buoy to the general position shown in Fig. 5.79. To maintain the top of the buoy in a more or less horizontal position, a type of buoy known as the "Lamgar eccentric mooring buoy," patented by Lambert Garland Moor-

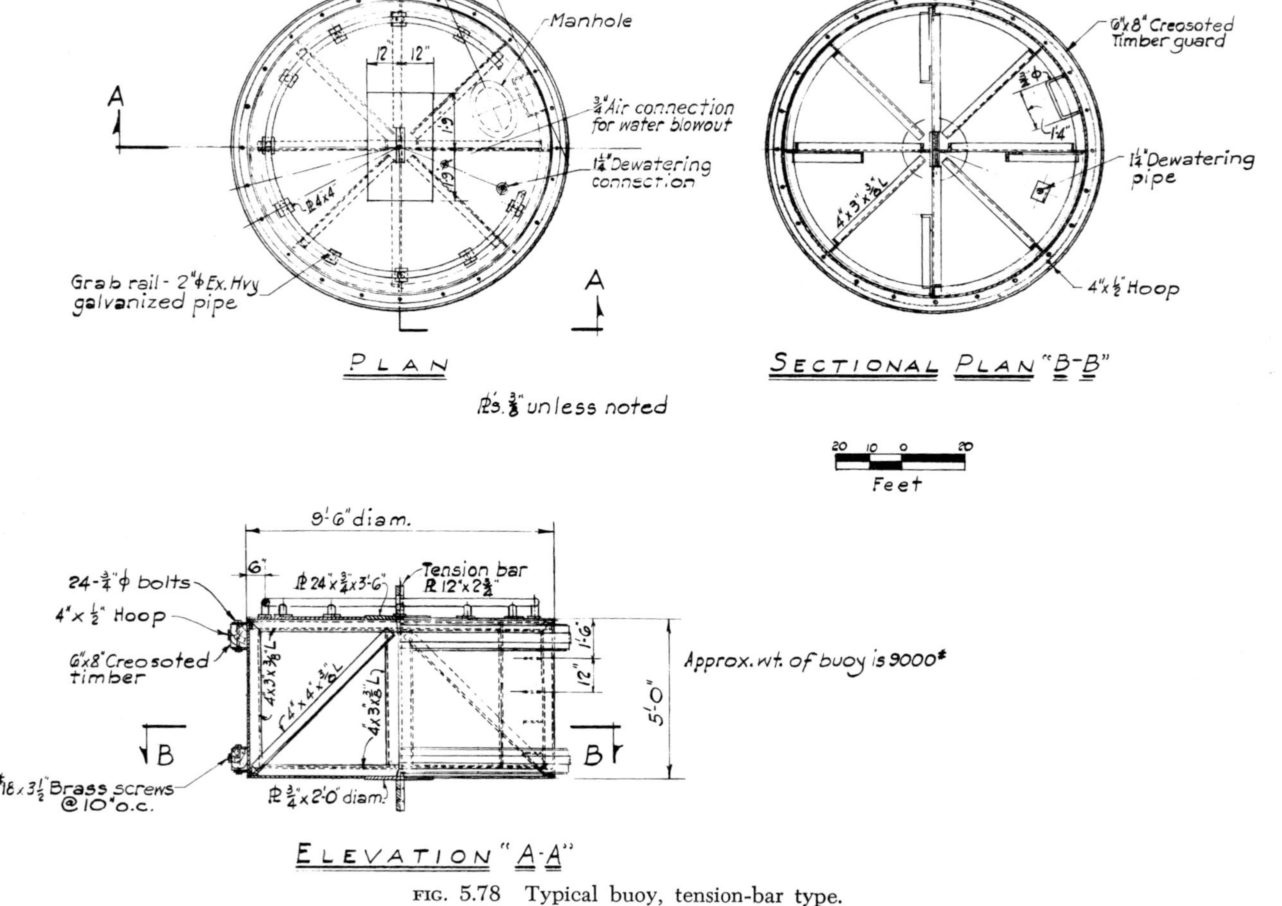

FIG. 5.78 Typical buoy, tension-bar type.

ings, Ltd., may be used. This type of buoy is shown in Fig. 5.80. Buoys of the drum type vary up to 18 ft in diameter and 9 ft deep. The ratio of depth to diameter is usually made 1:2.

Mooring-buoy anchors are usually cast-steel Navy stockless or Danforth. The former has a holding power in firm sand of about $7W_a$ and the latter $65(W_a)^{0.82}$, provided the load is applied at less than 3° above the horizontal, where W_a is the weight of the anchor in air. These values may be increased up to 50 per cent where the bottom is a stiff plastic

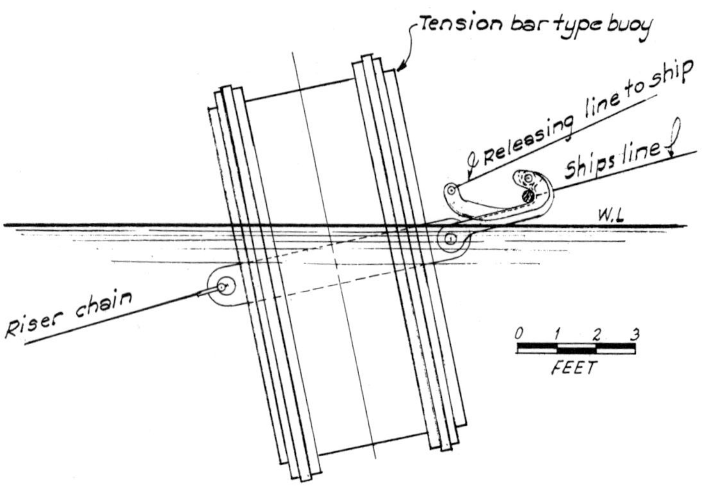

FIG. 5.79 Buoy partially submerged by pull from ship's line.

clay. Where the bottom is soft mud, the values will be reduced to about one-third to one-fourth of those for sand. Where the bottom is very soft, it is advisable to use precast-concrete anchors of the design shown in Fig. 5.81. These anchors are provided with jet pipes so that they can be jetted deep into the mud bottom, preferably into underlying firmer material if it exists. The pull-out value of such an anchor should be based on the shearing value of the surrounding soil. The anchor shown in Fig. 5.81 weighs 25 tons and is designed to resist an anchor-chain pull of 100 tons. Where stockless or Danforth anchors are used in a soft bottom, it may be necessary to use two anchors to each buoy, laid in bridle formation, with a triangular yoke piece connecting the buoy ground chain and the two individual anchor chains. The largest available Navy stockless and Danforth anchors are 16 and 7 tons (weight in air), respectively.

Anchor chain most commonly used is cast-steel stud-link, and the size generally does not exceed 2¾ in. for vessels up to the T-2 size and 3⅜ in. for supertankers up to 100,000 DWT. The dip sections are sometimes

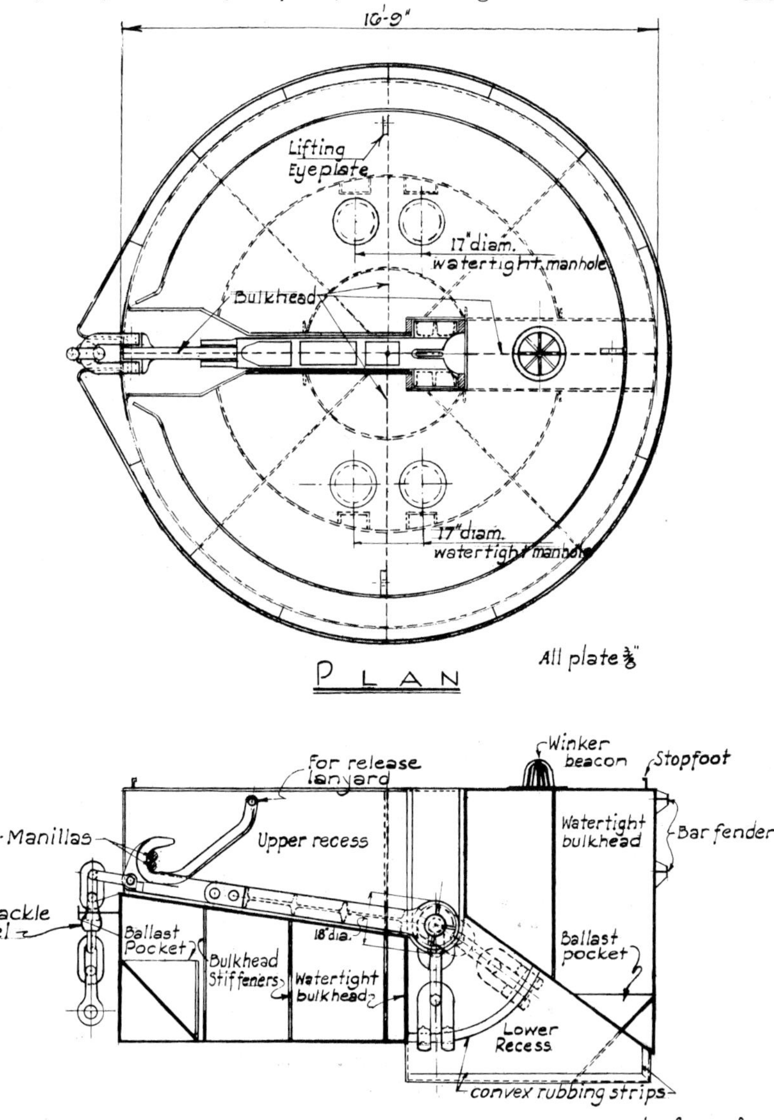

FIG. 5.80 Lamgar eccentric mooring buoy. (*Courtesy of Lambert Garland Moorings, Ltd., Stirling, Scotland.*)

made ⅛ in. larger in diameter to allow for wear. Mooring wire rope is usually galvanized plow steel up to 1½ in. in diameter for the large supertankers. To obtain the maximum pull-out of the anchor, it must not be subjected to a pull more than 3° above the horizontal. With this

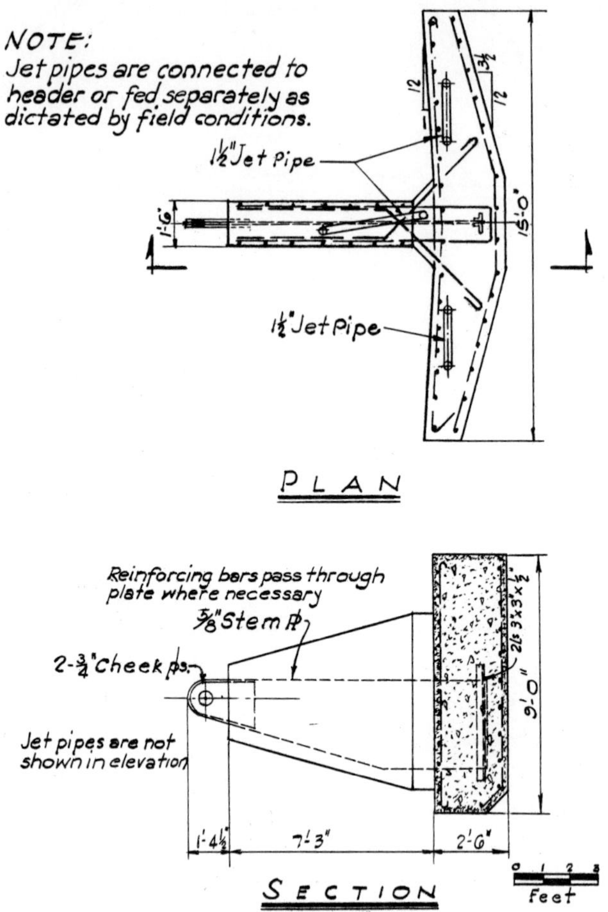

FIG. 5.81 25-ton precast-concrete anchor.

as a basis, the length of chain can be obtained for a certain pull and depth of water, as illustrated in the example which follows. The horizontal distance from the buoy to the anchor will usually vary between six and eight times the depth of the anchor below water level, the shorter distance being applicable if the concrete weight for holding the buoy is attached to the ground chain.

A concrete weight is used to position the mooring buoy. It may be attached separately to the buoy by chain or to the ground chain at a distance from the buoy of approximately 1½ times the depth of water.

The concrete weight, which may be from 2 to 10 tons depending on the size of anchorage, reduces the length of chain required by adding to the dead weight of the chain.

The following example illustrates the procedure of designing a multiple-buoy mooring for a supertanker at the terminal end of a submarine pipeline. A general layout of the anchorage is shown in Fig. 5.82. Data on the vessel and site is as follows.

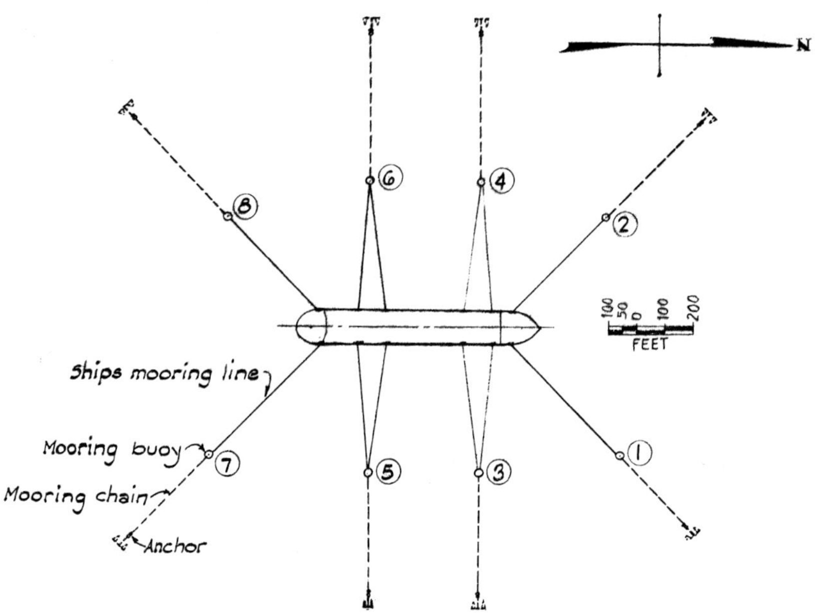

FIG. 5.82 Layout of multiple-buoy mooring.

Ship characteristics. Length, 856 ft; beam, 122 ft; draft, 47 ft maximum and 17 ft minimum; exposed wind areas for light ship, 10,000 sq ft on end and 46,500 sq ft on side; dead-weight tonnage, 87,000 long tons; number of winches, 12; and size of wire-rope mooring lines, 1½ in.

Climatic conditions. Wind velocity is 60 miles per hour maximum for a 5 minute gust from any direction. Hurricanes occur almost every year during the season, but it is assumed that the vessel will get underway during such conditions.

Oceanographic conditions. Current velocity, 2 knots from one direction (north); depth of water, 65 ft below low water; tidal range, 5 ft; sea bottom, firm sand; anchorage area is protected and waves are a maximum of 4 ft high. Waves 4 ft high in 65 ft of water would be of the oscillatory rather than of the translating type.

The *wind forces* may be determined from the formula $p_w = 0.00256\ v^2k$, where p_w = wind pressure in pounds per square foot of projected area, v = velocity in miles per hour, and k = shape factor = 1.3. Therefore, for a wind velocity of 60 miles per hour the pressure $p_w = 0.00256 \times 60^2 \times 1.3 = 12$ lb per sq ft. The total wind force on the side of the ship = 12 × 46,500 = 558,000 lb. The load on each mooring line = 558,000/(4 + 2 × 0.707) = 103,000 lb. The total wind force on the end of the ship = 12 × 10,000 = 120,000 lb.

The total *current force* on the ship's hull is composed of two parts. The dynamic head P_d of the current striking the vertical projection of the submerged part of the hull and the frictional resistance P_f of the wetted perimeter. The values of these forces are given by the following expressions:

$$P_d = A_d \times k_s \times 2.86 \times v^2$$

$$P_f = A_f \times k_l \times v^2$$

where P_d = dynamic force, lb
P_f = frictional force, lb
A_d = area of vertical projection of hull under water, sq ft
A_f = area of wetted surface, sq ft
k_s = constant, which varies from 0.75 to 1.00 and depends on the shape of the underwater part of the hull
k_l = constant, which depends upon the length of the vessel and is commonly assumed as 0.01
v = velocity of current, knots

$P_d + P_f = P_t$ = total force of current against the ship. Therefore, the total force of the current on the end of the ship in the light condition for a 2-knot current = $P_t = 17 \times 122 \times 0.75 \times 2.86 \times 2^2 + (122 + 2 \times 17)\ 830 \times 0.01 \times 2^2 = 23{,}000$ lb. Adding the force of the wind, the total force on the end of the ship then becomes 23,000 lb + 120,000 lb = 143,000 lb. The load in each head line = 143,000/2 × 1.414 = 101,000 lb.

Wave forces for this mooring condition may be safely neglected. Referring to the paper entitled The Energy Problem in the Mooring of Ships Exposed to Waves, by Basil W. Wilson of Agricultural and Mechanical College of Texas, which was presented at the 1958 Princeton University Conference on Berthing and Cargo Handling in Exposed Locations, we find that the heaving and swaying motion from the mean position of an unmoored 80,000-ton-DWT tanker in a beam sea with 15-ft oscillatory waves is less than one-half the wave height in both vertical and lateral directions. Since the wave height while the ship is moored is not expected to exceed 4 ft, the sway and heaving should not exceed about 2 ft from the mean position. It can be seen that this movement would result in a negligible increase in stress in the long anchor chain.

From Fig. 5.82, it is seen that buoys 3, 4, 5, and 6 each take two mooring lines and are, therefore, subjected to a total horizontal force H = 103,000 × 2 = 206,000 lb. The required anchor weight W_a = 206,000/7 = 29,430 lb. Use a standard Navy stockless anchor weighing 30,000 lb.

The chain should be designed for the holding power of the anchor selected; so H = 30,000 × 7 = 210,000 lb. It is considered good practice to limit the allowable working load of the chain to 35 per cent of the breaking strength. To approximate the breaking strength, use the formula $F_b = 1.12H/0.35 = 3.2H$. Therefore, F_b = 3.2 × 210,000 = 672,000 lb. From the table of breaking strength of cast-steel stud-link chain, a 3-in.

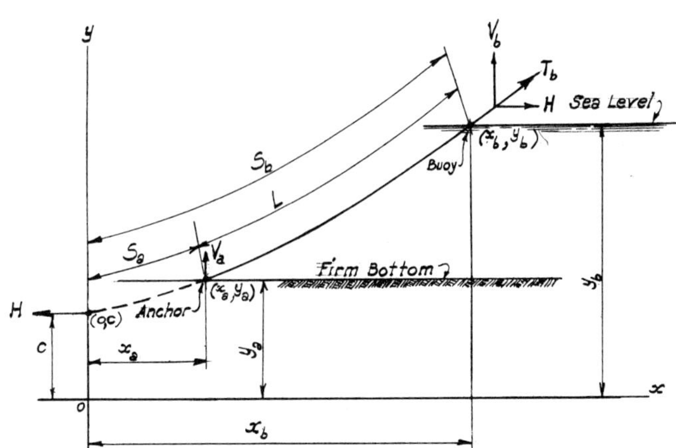

FIG. 5.83 Diagram showing forces acting on a chain.

chain is required, which has a breaking strength of 693,000 lb. The weight of 3-in. chain is 7,500 lb per shot. The weight of the chain in air, w_a = 7,500/90 = 83.3 lb per lin ft, and the weight in water, w_w = 83.3 × 0.87 = 72.5 lb per lin ft. Referring to Fig. 5.83 and using the formula for a catenary, $c = H/w_w$ = 210,000/72.5 = 2,897. The anchor must not be subjected to a pull more than 3° above the horizontal to develop its full pull-out value. Using this as a maximum, the slope of the catenary at point x_a, y_a (Fig. 5.83) is the tangent of 3°. Since H = 210,000 lb, V_a = 210,000 × 0.0524 = 11,000 lb.

$$S_a = \frac{V_a}{w_w} = \frac{11{,}000}{72.5} = 152 \text{ ft}$$

$$y_a = \sqrt{S_a^2 + c^2} = \sqrt{152^2 + 2{,}897^2} = 2{,}901 \text{ ft}$$

$$y_b = 2{,}901 + 70 = 2{,}971 \text{ ft}$$

$$S_b = \sqrt{2{,}971^2 - 2{,}897^2} = 659 \text{ ft}$$

$$L = S_b - S_a = 659 - 152 = 507 \text{ ft}$$

Number of shots of chain required = $^{507}/_{90}$ = 6 shots. The stress in the chain at the buoy = $T_b = y_b w_w$ = 2,971 × 72.5 = 215,400 lb. The allowable working load for 3-in. chain is 693,000 × 0.35 = 242,500 lb > 215,400 lb. Therefore, the 3-in. chain selected is satisfactory.

5.12 Mooring Accessories

A large ship will tie up to a dock with bow and stern lines, spring and breast lines, as shown in Fig. 5.84. These lines will be fastened to mooring fittings known as bollards, single or double, which are located along the face of the dock on 50- to 80-ft centers. Larger fittings called corner

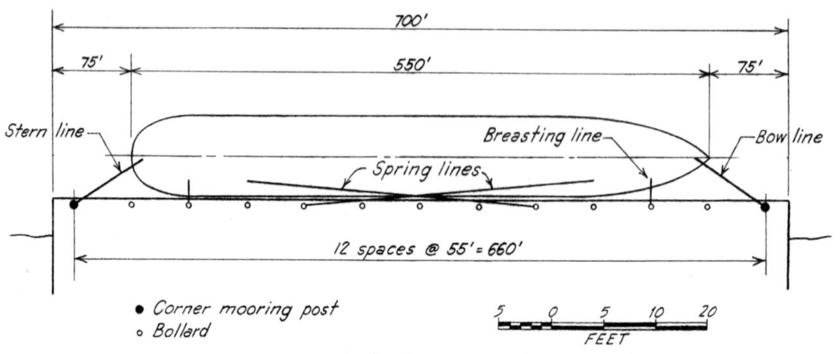

FIG. 5.84 Method of tying up ship to dock.

mooring posts are sometimes located at the outshore corners of a pier or at the ends of a wharf. They are used principally while bringing the ship into the dock or while it warps around the corner of the pier or turning dolphin.

Bollards or single bitts are usually designed to take line pulls of 35 tons and corner mooring posts of 50 tons, although special designs may be made for line pulls of up to 100 tons. These fittings are fastened to the deck, if of concrete, by galvanized bolts passing through pipe sleeves set in the concrete, which enables the bolts to be removed at a later date, if damaged. The base of the fitting is grouted in a recess formed in the deck, which permits the shear from the line pull to be transmitted directly in bearing to the concrete deck. When large and long wire-rope lines are to be handled, particularly when attached to dolphins, the lines are pulled in to the mooring fittings by means of capstans which may be either electrically or air operated. Where mooring lines are attached to buoys or dolphins which are reached only by a service boat, the steel hawsers may be provided with releasing hooks, which will enable the ship's lines to be detached by tripping the hook with a small manila line from the ship.

Small ships, tugs, and work boats are usually tied up to cleats which are spaced about 30 to 40 ft on centers along the face of the dock.

Open or closed chocks are used for directing lines, the latter being used when there is a change in the vertical as well as the horizontal direction of the line. The various mooring accessories described above are shown in Fig. 5.85.

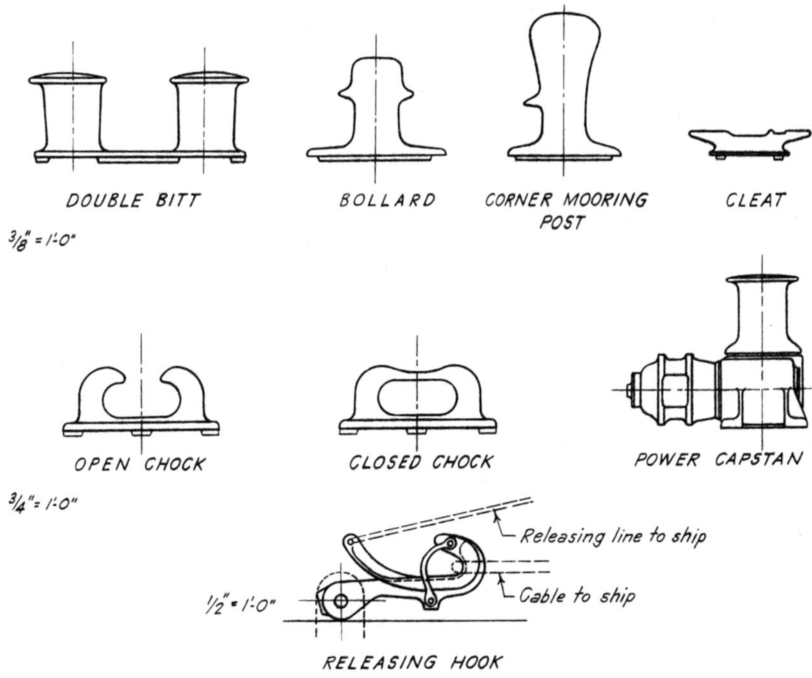

FIG. 5.85 Typical mooring accessories.

5.13 Shipping-terminal Utilities

Lighting. Shipping terminals are usually required to function at night as well as during daylight hours, and, therefore, satisfactory illumination must be provided for night operation. For open working areas on the pier where ship loading or unloading occurs, a lighting intensity of at least 5 ft-candles should be maintained. This may be achieved by locating outdoor floodlights at strategic points. Warehouses or storage buildings in the terminal area are supplied with incandescent or fluorescent lighting fixtures, which also will furnish about 5 ft-candles. Other port buildings or areas, such as administration, passenger waiting rooms, customs and security offices, and restaurant will require higher illumination levels, between 20 to 50 ft-candles, depending on the type of work performed therein.

In addition to the open-working-area lights, which need be turned on only during night operating periods, security illumination must be provided for all roads and walkways every night that they are accessible. Here an illumination level between 0.2 and 0.5 ft-candles is generally supplied by street-lighting luminaires mounted on poles or standards.

Since a shipping terminal functions as part of a port system, the Coast Guard, or other local shipping authority, usually requires certain specific signal lights, serving as aids to navigation, to be located on the pier, or inshore, or mounted on buoys in the harbor. Where the location of these navigation lights has no readily available electric service, it is customary to furnish each navigation light with an independent low-discharge battery, which has a long life and provides assured continuity of operation.

Electric Power. In the shipping terminal, the mechanical equipment required for the loading and unloading of vessels and for storage varies, depending on the kind of materials handled. It may include large ore bridges, traveling cranes, conveyors, pumps, hose-handling equipment, dump cars, or trucks. While some of these may be driven by diesel, gasoline, gas, or steam engines, the tendency today is to use electric motors for operating this equipment because of the better control resulting therefrom. Where a large number of motors are required one or more motor-control centers are usually provided at convenient locations, each containing the starters, protective devices, and relays required for a number of motors. Equipment operation will be controlled from remote push-button stations or from limit switches located at the equipment so that automatic or sequential operation can be provided.

The electrical design of a shipping terminal must take into consideration the type of material to be handled. Where explosive or combustible materials are involved they may create atmospheric mixtures of hazardous gases, vapors, or dusts. Therefore, only specially designed electrical equipment may be used within areas designated as hazardous locations. The National Electrical Code requires the adherence to special, rigid design standards for motors, starters, transformers, switches, lighting fixtures, receptacles, and other electrical equipment installed within their designated hazardous locations. Generally described as "explosion-proof," this type of electrical equipment is required where the terminal handles gasoline, benzine, alcohol, or other flammable, volatile liquids.

While grounding the frames of electrical equipment and other non-current-carrying metal at any shipping terminal is a normal safety requirement, special grounding considerations are necessary where gasoline or other volatile flammable liquids are being pumped to or from the pier to which the vessel is tied. The danger arises from the fact that the vessel may have picked up an electric static charge while sailing enroute to its present location. This charge could be transmitted to the ship's hose, and when it is connected to the grounded coupling on the pier, a spark could ensue in the presence of a combustible atmospheric mixture with disastrous results. To eliminate such possibility a disconnecting ground switch is provided. One terminal of the switch is permanently connected to the pier ground, and the other terminal connected to a flexible length of insulated cable with a clamping hook fastened to the end of the cable. When a vessel is tied up, and before any hose connections are made, the clamp is connected to the steel hull of the ship with the switch in the open position. The switch is then closed, thus grounding any static charge on the ship, and the hose connections can then be safely made.

Communications. In the course of normal operation of a terminal it is often necessary for information to be exchanged between the ship's captain on board and the loading-tower operator on the pier while the hold of the ship is being loaded. Using their voices to communicate directly would be difficult while the loading operation is in progress owing to the machinery and conveyor noise. Hand signals could be used, but this would limit the information that could be imparted and certainly is a very primitive method. Furthermore, it may be necessary for the tower operator to converse with the remotely located operator of the feeder conveyor which is bringing material from the storage area to the tower, and finally the terminal manager located in the pier office may want to speak to one of the operating staff. It has, therefore, been found advantageous to install an intercommunication system with telephones located at strategic points. This is usually a simple phone system where one can pick up a receiver and use a push button (or crank with a magneto phone) and by code rings call the person to whom he wishes to speak. The problem arises with connecting the ship captain's phone into the communication circuit. This is often accomplished by having phone outlet receptacles located at various points along the side of the pier. A portable telephone with a long extension cable and a plug at its end is furnished. When a ship is tied up, the telephone plug is connected to the receptacle nearest the hold to be loaded, and the portable telephone is put on board, thus making possible a conversation between the man stationed at the ship's hold and any of the terminal's operating staff. Where the ship in port is a passenger and/or cargo vessel, ship-to-terminal communication is achieved by connecting a plug attached to a wire extension emanating from the ship's telephone system to one of the pier phone-outlet receptacles.

Power Supply. All the electric power requirements for a shipping terminal are generally supplied by one or more feeders emanating from a nearby substation. Where the demand includes large power machinery and lighting for a considerable area, a primary feeder of 2,400 volts, three phase, is usually employed. Where the power requirements are small and lighting is the primary need only, a secondary feeder of 440 volts, three phase, is installed with step-down transformers to provide lighting service. As an alternative, where just a small area is involved, the secondary feeder may supply 208-volt three-phase four-wire service which can be used directly for lighting without requiring the step-down transformers.

Where shiploading facilities are to be constructed in remote coastal areas, there may not be a nearby substation or even a public utility serving the area. In such instance it becomes necessary to include in the port development a power plant to furnish electric power. This plant usually comprises 2 or more generators of 50- to 500-kw capacity each, directly coupled to diesel engines, gasoline engines, or gas engines. The choice of a prime mover will depend on the availability of the various types of fuel required. Today, in remote areas where neither fuel nor water are readily available, the possibility of installing an atomic power plant should be considered. All types of power plants will include the associated engine-starting and speed-regulating equipment as well as the generator control and synchronizing devices, meters, and the necessary fuel-storage tank.

Electrical Distribution. The running of distribution feeders and other electrical conductors out on a pier often presents special problems. Since overhead conductors are usually undesirable because of their possible interference with cranes or other shiploading equipment, it is customary to install the electric distribution and branch circuit conductors in galvanized-steel conduits or asbestos-cement ducts. When steel conduits are used, they may be located exposed under the pier or preferably embedded in the pier deck or beams, if this is a concrete structure. Asbestos-cement ducts should always be embedded since this material is not considered satisfactory for exposure to mechanical damage. The conduit or duct installation requires the inclusion of embedded or exposed pull boxes and splice boxes. These are usually made of galvanized cast iron and are mounted in accessible locations. Because of the presence of moisture a moisture-resistant insulation with a neoprene jacket for mechanical protection is considered desirable for the conductor covering.

Large movable loading towers or cranes are mounted on track rails. The electric energy for propulsion and other power requirements for the tower or crane are supplied by trolleys or by a retractable cable reel, the choice usually being dependent on the comparative costs of these two types of installation. The cable reel is mounted on the movable structure. Where the cables are small, spring-retractable cable reels are satisfactory. However, where the cable is of large diameter, the cable reel is motor-operated. Cables as large as triple-conductor 500 MCM (thousand circular mil) can be used on motor-operated reels. In fact, such a cable reel was used on the shiploader tower for a pier built at San Juan Bay, Peru, in 1959: a 270-ft length of triple-conductor 500-MCM type G cable was mounted on the drum of the cable reel, as shown in

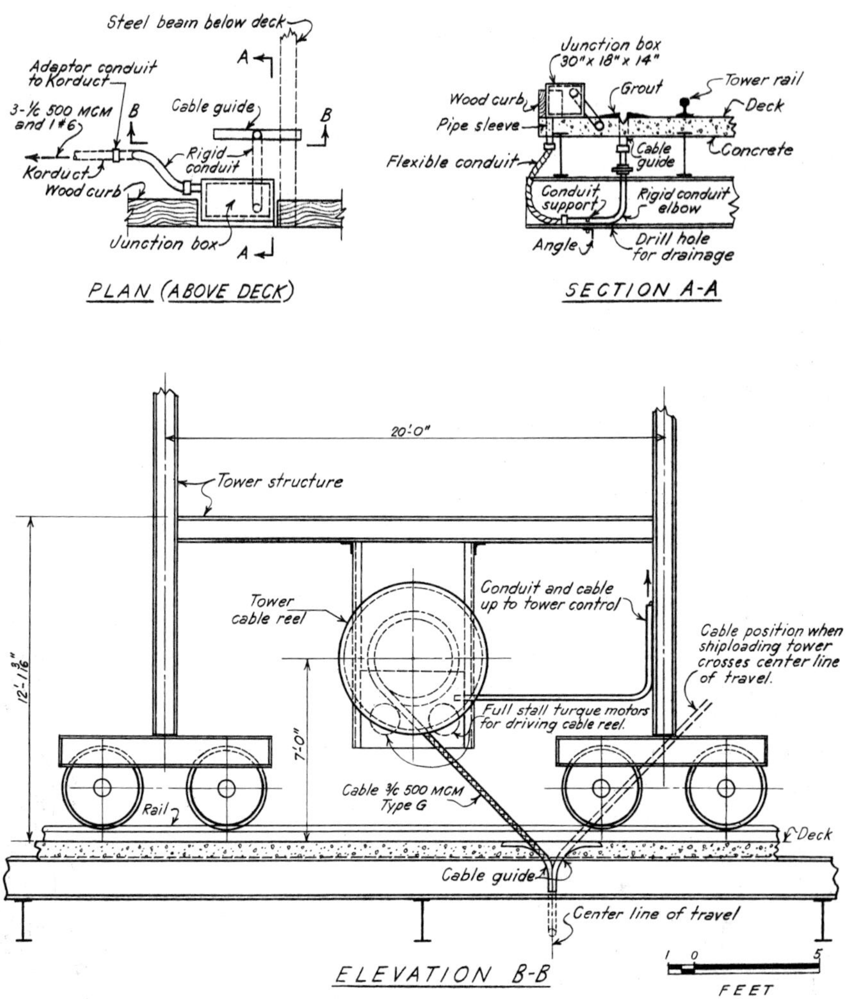

FIG. 5.86 Cable reel mounted on traveling shiploader.

Fig. 5.86. A 440-volt feeder which is carried in a 3-in. asbestos-cement duct (Korduct) embedded in the concrete deck of the pier is run to a 30- by 18- by 14-in. junction box. This cast-iron box is located at the midpoint of the approximately 500-ft distance that the rail-mounted loading tower can travel along the pier. The feeder (three single-conductor 500-MCM insulated cables and 1 no. 6 bareground wire) is spliced to the triple-conductor 500-MCM type G cable in the junction box. The triple-conductor cable then runs up to the reel drum. Running this 3-in.-diameter cable from the box to the reel presented a problem, particularly because of its large size. Furthermore, in order to avoid excessive strain and wear on the cable insulation, as the loading tower passes the point where the cable comes up through the pier deck, a specially designed cable guide made up of two 3½-in. standard 90° steel-conduit elbows was fabricated as shown in Fig. 5.86. This figure also indicates the manner in which the conduit and cable connections between the junction box and cable guide were installed.

Potable Water Supply. For the use of the terminal personnel for sanitary purposes and also for replenishment of water supply on shipboard, potable water is an important commodity. This presents no problem where the terminal is located in an urban area or in conjunction with other installations which are supplied with drinking water. There are, of course, many cases where terminals are remotely situated beyond the reach of any established water supply. In such cases water may be obtained from wells or other sources but, lacking such, water may have to be shipped in by tanker or ship's ballast, in which event adequate storage will be required to maintain supply between shipments. Generally, water is obtainable from some local source and the necessity for its importation is rare.

Sanitary facilities are usually confined to such buildings as warehouses and transit sheds, administration and customs, passenger waiting rooms, restaurants, and the like. On open bulk cargo piers, certain loading or unloading operations, which operate for prolonged periods, may necessitate the installation of sanitary facilities in control towers. Flow requirements for such facilities are very small, of the order of 5 to 10 gal per min, and are very intermittent in use. Depending upon the nature and magnitude of terminal operations, the potable water requirement may vary widely and can only be determined by analysis of the component units of the terminal facilities.

Hose connections, usually 2½ in., are provided either amidship or fore and aft at the berthing space or spaces of the pier. On covered piers the piping is usually confined within the shed, and the hose connections project through the walls. This arrangement is quite satisfactory if the ship's hose which is draped over the apron does not interfere with pier operations. Should it interfere, it then becomes more desirable to provide hose connections along the outer edge of the apron. Connections of this type, as well as connections on open piers, are usually located below the deck in pits covered by removable grating or plates and designed for convenience of operation (see Fig. 5.87).

Supply piping on open piers may be supported either above or below the deck depending upon the design of the pier and its purpose. Where thermal expansion is a problem, proper provision must be made for expansion joints or loops. Expansion joints in the structure must also be considered when designing the piping. Piping with rigid joints requires nominal guiding while piping with bell and spigot or mechanical friction joints should be guided at each joint and restrained at ends, elbows, and branches.

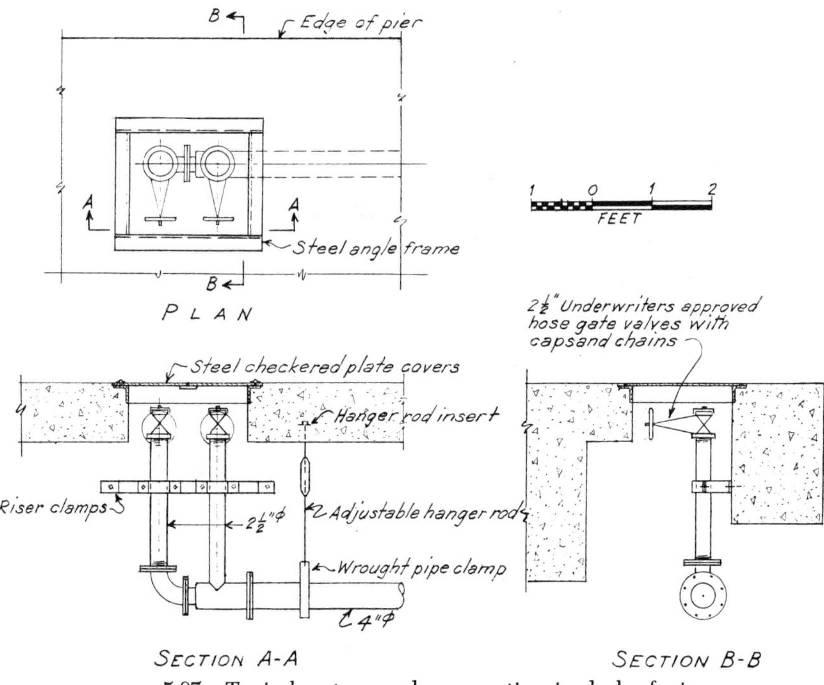

FIG. 5.87 Typical water-supply connection in deck of pier.

Ships' water supplies are usually metered, and a charge is made for water taken aboard. The meter or meters should be easily accessible for reading by both terminal and ships' officers and therefore should be conveniently located on the pier. On covered piers the meters are logically placed overhead indoors, while on open piers the meters should be located below deck in pits with proper covers so as not to interfere with pedestrian or vehicular traffic.

In cold climates water lines should be protected against freezing by insulation and steam tracing or electric heating.

Fire Protection. Outdoor fire protection for terminal areas on land is no different than for any other installation involving similar facilities. A water-distribution system, tailored to the layout of roads and buildings, should be looped, if possible, for maximum safety and assurance of continuity of service. Normally the pipelines should be buried to a depth sufficient to prevent freezing in cold climates and to a nominal depth to prevent mechanical damage from traffic in any climate. Sectionalizing valves should be so located as to minimize isolated areas in the event part of the system must be shut off owing to damage or repairs. Conventional fire hydrants with 4½-in. pumper connections as well as 2½-in. hose connections are desirable. Where mobile pumpers are not used the pumper connections would be eliminated.

Since the layout of a terminal may form a quite irregular pattern, it is difficult to qualify protection in terms of hydrant spacing. A good criterion is to locate hydrants so that any potential fire can be reached from two hydrants, each serving not more than 300 ft of hose. In the case of warehouses it is desirable to have four hydrants accessible, two on each side. Hydrants should not be located too close to buildings since a fire therein may make such a hydrant unapproachable. Twenty-five ft is considered the absolute minimum, 50 ft or more is preferable.

Fire water requirements should be determined on the basis of the various hazards involved. However, one might use 2,000 gal per min for 4 hours as a fair minimum for developments involving large warehouses. This premise allows 1,000 gal per min for sprinklers and 1,000 gal per min for hose streams. The system should be designed to insure adequate residual pressure as follows: 10 lb per sq in. at a pumper hydrant, 15 lb per sq in. at the level of the highest sprinkler heads, and, in cases where neither sprinklers nor pumpers are involved, sufficient pressure at the hose nozzles to throw a forceful stream upon the tallest objective.

Where potable water is available in the vicinity, it is usually good policy to provide a combined system for both fire and drinking water. Since the demand for fire fighting is likely to greatly exceed the demand for other purposes, the availability of adequate flows in case of fire is a primary consideration in system design. Where potable water is in limited supply, it may be necessary to provide separate systems and use sea water for fire fighting.

Fire protection on open piers usually can be provided by a single main with branches at strategic points along its length. Branch risers topped with a pair of 2½-in. hose valves are usually more practical than conventional hydrants. A lightweight hose cart or buggy, stored in a shed on the open pier, can readily be hand-drawn to the hose stations. Openings in the deck with removable covers permit use of fog nozzles in combating under-pier fires.

Foam is used for fighting petroleum fires and various types of apparatus are available for this purpose. Foam can be produced from two separate dry chemicals, a single dry mixture, or from concentrated solutions. Perhaps the simplest method of application is the eduction of solution from a pail into an eductor at the base of the foam nozzle where water from the hose line mixes with the chemical to generate foam. Another system consists of a foam generator with a hopper for dry chemical. Here the powder is drawn into the generator where it mixes with the water, and foam is discharged through the hose line to the nozzle. Single or double hoppers are used for the mixed dry chemical or the separate chemicals, respectively. Where a foam truck is used the concentrated solution is stored aboard in a fairly large tank. The liquid is metered to the generator through a proportioner insuring proper mixture of chemical and water. Where the water pressure is 125 lb per sq in., no pump is required. For lower pressures, a pump mounted on the truck boosts the pressure to the proper level.

When sea water is used for fire protection, the pumps may be located in a variety of ways. If the locality has clean water without suspended sand or mud, the pumps can be placed wherever convenient. They may be horizontal, self-priming type with suction pipe and foot valve or vertical type for direct immersion into the water. The latter type when electrically driven requires a minimum of space. Where the pier is built out from a beach, it may prove desirable to place the pumps at the offshore end to get into deep, clear water. It may be advisable in some cases to clarify the water before pumping by providing two chambers, one to function as a settling basin and the other as a pump-suction pit. The settling basin should be arranged so that accumulated sand may be removed by clamshell, eduction, or some other means. It is always desirable to prevent floating or suspended materials from entering the pump suction. Where electric power is available, the fire pumps would of course be electrically operated with remote control at strategic locations. Otherwise, diesel or gasoline engines would be used, probably with storage-battery-operated starters, this arrangement resulting in a much more complicated system. The sea-water system is normally pressurized only when the fire pumps are operating.

Indoor fire protection naturally depends upon the character of a building and its contents. A sprinkler system, hose stations, and chemical hand extinguishers may be used. Modern covered piers are frequently equipped with all three. In cold climates water lines are steam traced, and sprinkler systems are of the dry-pipe type. Figure 5.88 is a typical section and plan of the passenger pier at La Guaira, Venezuela, showing the potable-water and fire-protection systems.

Miscellaneous. *Steam.* Aside from any process use that may be involved in the terminal installations, steam is usually required only in cold climates for space heating and protection of piping against freezing. Storage

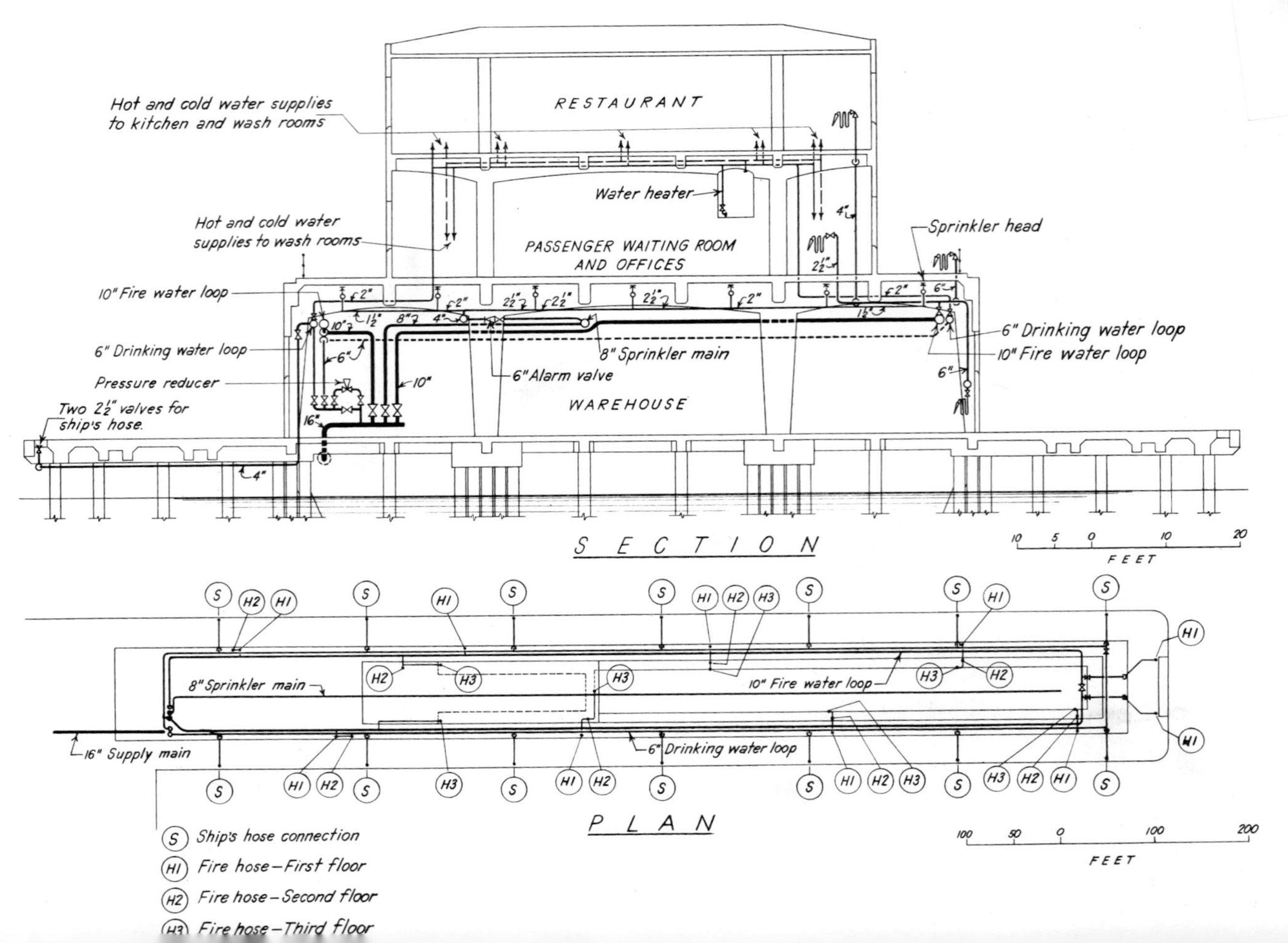
RESTAURANT
Hot and cold water supplies to kitchen and wash rooms
Water heater
Hot and cold water supplies to wash rooms
PASSENGER WAITING ROOM AND OFFICES
Sprinkler head
10" Fire water loop
6" Drinking water loop
Pressure reducer
Two 2½" valves for ship's hose.
8" Sprinkler main
6" Alarm valve
WAREHOUSE
6" Drinking water loop
10" Fire water loop
SECTION
FEET
8" Sprinkler main
10" Fire water loop
16" Supply main
6" Drinking water loop
PLAN
FEET
S Ship's hose connection
H1 Fire hose–First floor
H2 Fire hose–Second floor
H3 Fire hose–Third floor

or handling areas are not ordinarily heated. In certain special cases, steam is available for cleaning tanks and piping and also for smothering fires in bilges, tanks, or other confined spaces.

Bunkering facilities. Passenger and cargo piers in urban areas normally are not provided with bunkering facilities on the piers themselves. Bunkering is accomplished from the water side from barges or oilers. However, at the Port of San Diego, the construction of the 10th Avenue Marine Terminal included berthside bunkering. Here vessels may bunker at any of the nine berths and load and unload cargo at the same time.

In remote localities, piers designed primarily for other purposes may also provide facilities to unload bunker C or diesel fuel required for land operations. In such cases it may be quite convenient to bunker ships by using the same facilities in reverse. Such facilities usually consist of storage tanks on land, pumps, fuel pipelines, and cargo hose connections at convenient locations on the pier. As in the case of other piping the installation should be planned to avoid interference with pier operations.

Compressed air is sometimes used for operating air motors or cylinders in connection with hose-handling structures on petroleum piers and in other hazardous operations where electrical apparatus may be undesirable.

Sanitary waste originating on a pier can sometimes be carried by gravity to a sewer on shore if the run is short and sufficient difference in elevation exists. In most cases it is necessary to pump the sewage back to shore, and this is accomplished by collecting the sewage in tanks or chambers under the deck and pumping off automatically with float-controlled sewage ejectors.

5.14 Cathodic Protection

The corrosive effect on steel and other metals when submerged in water or embedded in moist soil is primarily due to galvanic action. This phenomenon is analogous to the conditions prevalent in an electric battery cell, i.e., the presence of two dissimilar metals in an electrolyte. In the case of the water-submerged or soil-embedded steel structure, the dissimilar metal consists of the nonuniformities or nonferrous impurities in the steel or other adjacent metal structures in electrical contact with the steel, while the water or moist soil acts as the electrolyte. This establishes a flow of current from the steel (the anode) through the water or soil to the dissimilar metal (the cathode). This action is similar to that of a galvanic cell battery where the dissimilar materials are generally zinc and carbon (see Fig. 5.89).

Actually, the phenomenon of the current leaving the steel (anode), flowing through the electrolyte, and entering the nonferrous impurity (cathode) is carried on by particles of iron called iron ions, which are emitted by the anode and go into solution in the water. The iron ions are then exchanged for hydrogen ions leaving the iron behind as a rusty formation. The hydrogen ions now form a film deposit on the cathode. This pitting action gradually causes a decrease in the steel cross section with a resulting weakening of the structure to the point of failure (see Fig. 5.90).

It has been estimated that the corrosion losses on buried and submerged metal structures has been costing American industry about a billion dollars annually. In order to reduce or practically eliminate this loss, cathodic protection is being resorted to by many builders of submerged or buried steel structures. This protection has been satisfactorily achieved by changing the direction of the flow of electric current, i.e., *to* the steel and not *from* the steel, thus preventing the iron ions from flowing out of the steel and causing its decomposition (galvanic action). Cathodic protection, as now applied, makes the protected metallic structures cathodic in an electric circuit, thus counteracting the normal corrosive action. This is accomplished by establishing a d-c voltage between the protected metallic structure and an auxiliary anode, so that the current flows through the water or moist soil to the structure.

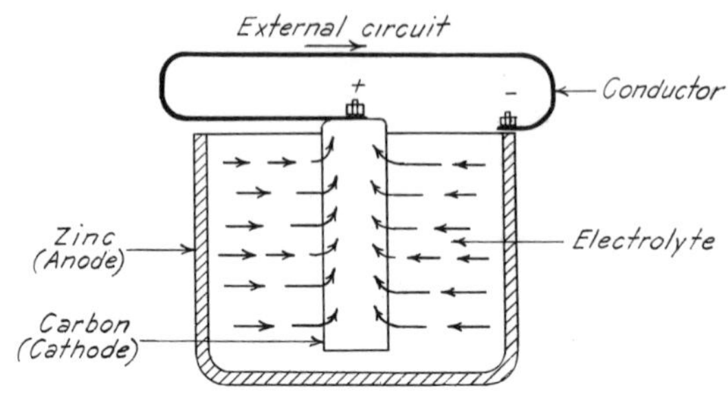

FIG. 5.89 Typical galvanic-cell battery.

A sacrificial, i.e., expendable, metal, such as aluminum, zinc, cadmium, or magnesium, may be used for the anode as the source of the direct current. These are described as galvanic anodes. However, to gain better control of the current and regulate the magnitude thereof more accurately, an impressed external source of current is usually applied for the protection of structures consisting of steel piles and pipelines where large quantities of current are required. Here, a soluble metal, such as iron, or an insoluble material, such as graphite, generally serves as the anode. However, even graphite becomes decomposed in time, primarily due to electrochemical oxidation, and must be replaced in 5 to 15 years, depending on the quantity, size, and location of the anodes. Theoretically, when applying the recommended current density, the graphite anode life is in the order of 20,000 to 80,000 amp-hr per lb. Assuming the lower 20,000 amp-hr as a conservative value, a 70-lb graphite anode submerged in salt water would be completely consumed only after providing 7 amperes continuously for $(20{,}000 \times 70)/(7 \times 24 \times 365)$, or 23 years. Practically, however, replacement must be made before the anode is greatly reduced in size in order to avoid an excessive current density as the exposed surface of the anode diminishes. Also, in addition to the decrease of the quantity of graphite due to the oxidation of the carbon, there is a material loss in the submerged anode caused by water action. The realistic useful life of the 70-lb graphite anode described above would be between

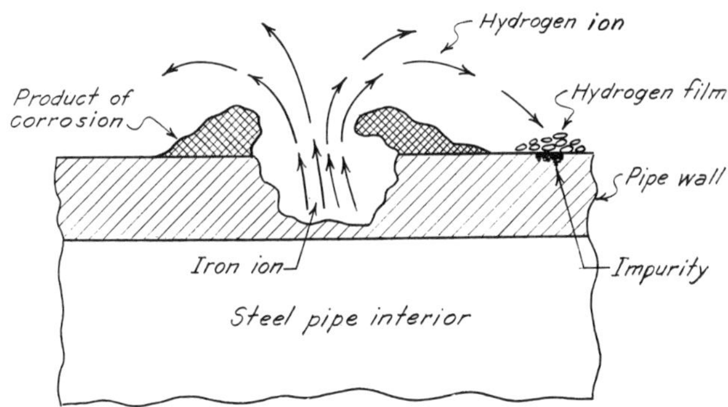

FIG. 5.90 Corrosion of the wall of a steel pipe immersed in water.

5 and 15 years. Although the initial cost of the external impressed current system is greater, the long-range economics over a 10-year period indicate that the impressed-current type costs considerably less than the galvanic-anode type for such installations as steel piles, submarine pipelines and offshore drilling platforms.

A schematic diagram of an external-impressed-current cathodic-protection installation, with two different methods of arranging the anodes, is shown in Fig. 5.91. This is a typical application for the protection of steel piles under a pier. The suspended submerged graphite anodes are usually equally spaced under the full length of the pier. This is known as the "distribution anode" arrangement. The underwater ground-bedded graphite anodes usually consist of one or more groups of anodes with each anode in the group held in a supporting block of wood or concrete, resting on the bottom but holding the anode above the bottom in order to prevent it from becoming covered with mud or silt. The anode beds are generally located on both sides of the structure to be protected. This is described as the "semiremote anode-bed" arrangement.

In the application of cathodic protection to submerged steel structures such as piles and pipelines, the most frequently selected equipment to provide the required d-c power consists primarily of a transformer and a rectifier mounted inside a protective housing. This enclosure is usually weatherproof, although explosion-proof housings are provided where required. The operation of this equipment is indicated in the wiring diagram shown in Fig. 5.92. The primary of the transformer is connected to

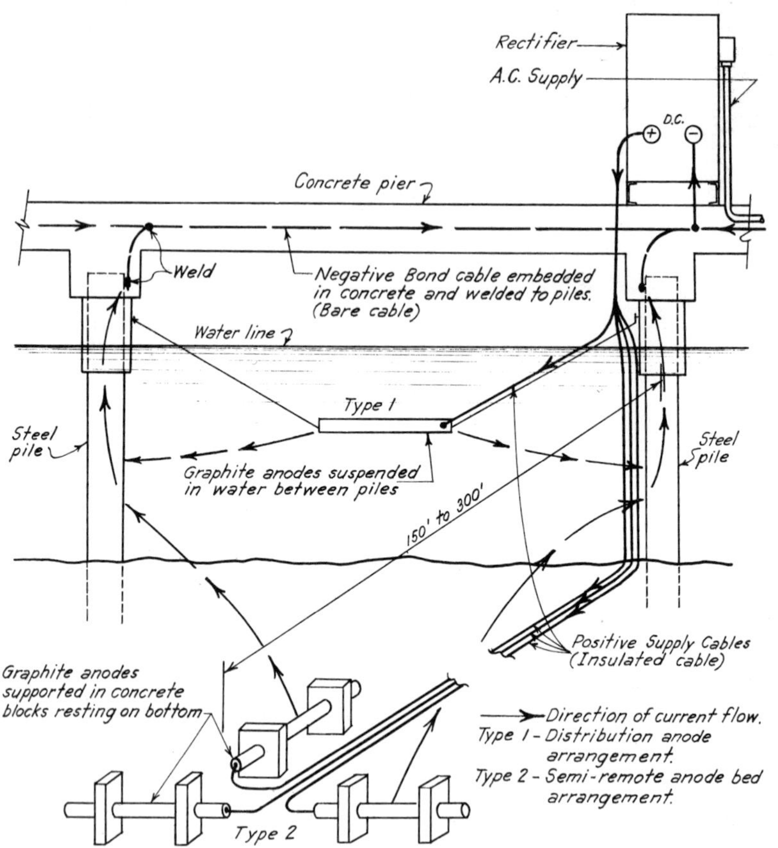

FIG. 5.91 Schematic diagram of a cathodic-protection installation.

the external a-c electric supply which is preferably 440 or 220 volts, three phase, but may be 220 or 110 volts, single phase. The secondary of the transformer is provided with variable taps so that the proper a-c voltage may be applied to the rectifier, which, in turn, supplies the relatively low d-c voltage and high current required to protect the submerged steel structure against corrosion. The three types of rectifiers commonly in use are described as copper oxide, selenium, and copper sulfide rectifiers. Their capacity for converting alternating to direct current is the result of the electrical check-valve properties of certain metals. This characteristic is usefully applied in the copper oxide rectifier where a pure-copper disc is coated on one side with a film of copper oxide. One electric connection is made to the metallic copper, and another connection to a lead disc in contact with the copper oxide formed on the surface of the copper. A unidirection current will encounter less resistance and flow more readily from the copper oxide film to the copper than in the reverse direction. Basically, the selenium and copper sulfide rectifiers operate in a similar manner.

Any structural steel member or steel pipeline, submerged below the surface of the water, can be protected when an adequate current density

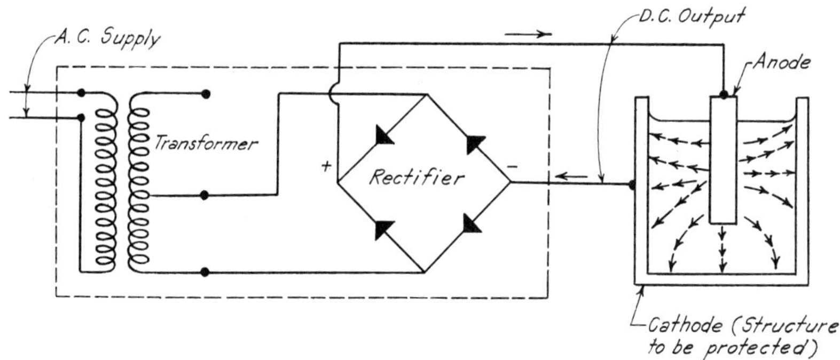

FIG. 5.92 Wiring diagram of a transformer and rectifier for cathodic protection.

is supplied by a properly designed cathodic-protection system. However, because of the specialized problems involved and the additional considerations that must be given to the resistance, temperature, and dissolved oxygen content of the water, a comprehensive study of all conditions must be made in order to design a satisfactory and economical system.

The initial installed cost of cathodic protection, as applied to the underwater steel in a pier, trestle, or pipeline, is small compared to the cost of the structure being protected. The annual operating costs consisting of maintenance, power, and eventual replacement of the anodes have been found to be less than other methods of corrosion protection. A five-million-dollar pier supported on steel piles was recently constructed in Hoboken, New Jersey, and provided with cathodic protection. This is expected to furnish complete protection from corrosion below the mean low-water line for the life of the pier, at an estimated cost of approximately $3 per pile per year for electric current and maintenance.

Sometimes a pier is to be located in an area where there are no historical data in reference to the corrosion action on similar piers in the vicinity. At the time of the design of such a pier on steel piles, and even after the driving of piles has begun, there may be doubt as to whether an installed cathodic-protection system is necessary. Because the prevailing conditions of the water and its corrosive action on the steel piles are not completely known, the owner may wish to avoid the expenditure incurred by a complete cathodic-protection system until it is definitely established that this protection is necessary.

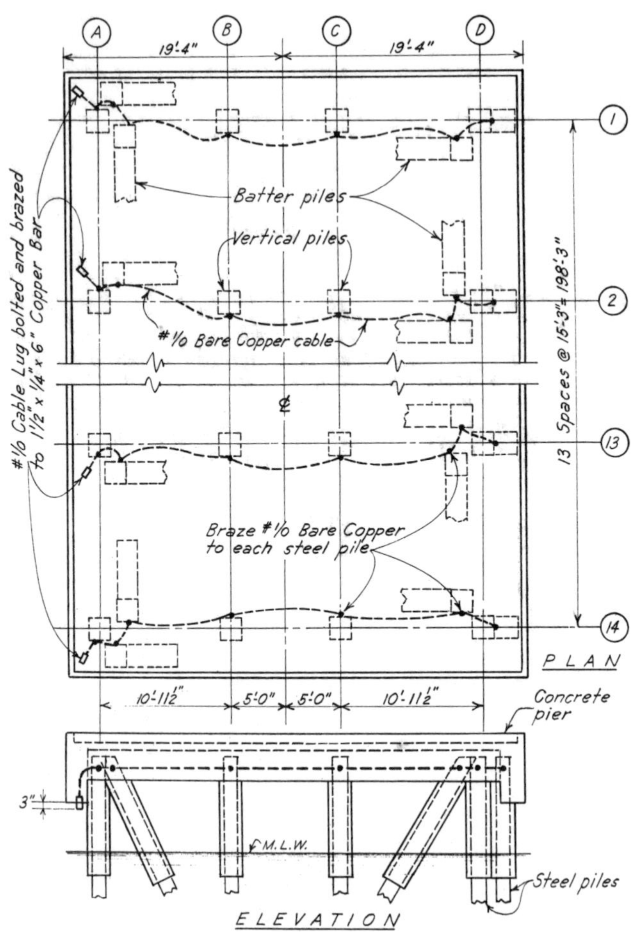

FIG. 5.93 Cathodic protection for Texas Company pier with steel H piles at Santiago, Cuba.

In this instance it is often desirable to install an embedded negative-bond cable connecting the steel piles electrically, so that if the installation of a cathodic-protection system is eventually required, the embedded negative cable is in place. This cable usually consists of bare-stranded copper, varying in size from no. 1/0 to no. 4/0, depending on the anticipated current-capacity and voltage-drop requirements. It is of course obvious that, if this cable had not been installed prior to the time the concrete deck, beams, and pile caps were poured, it would become practically a prohibitive cost to attempt to provide a satisfactory cable tie subsequently. However, the additional cost, if this negative-tie cable is installed before pouring concrete, is not great and has the favorable advantage of permitting the application of cathodic protection to the pier at any future date.

Such an installation was provided for a tanker-berthing pier recently constructed in Santiago, Cuba, and is shown in Fig. 5.93. The embedded negative-bond conductor consisted of a no. 1/0 bare-stranded copper cable brazed to all the steel H piles in each bent and terminating in a 6- by 1½- by ¼-in. copper-bar connection which protrudes 3 in. beyond one end of each bent. The purpose of this 3-in. exposed extension is to permit the connecting of all the protruding copper bars to an exterior tie cable in order to provide the negative return to the rectifier at any future time that the installation of a cathodic-protection system is deemed necessary.

Chapter 6 PORT BUILDINGS

6.1 Introduction

The buildings in a port may comprise one or more of the following: transit sheds, warehouses, cold-storage building, administration building, customs building, police station, guard houses, stevedores gear and change house, repair shop and garage, firehouse, and powerhouse. In addition, bulk cargo shipping terminals, which are covered in Chap. 8, may contain grain elevators, silos, storage tanks, and sheds for covering sugar, fertilizer, bauxite, etc.

Some of the above facilities may be contained in one building; for instance the transit shed may house the customs offices, the stevedores gear room, and locker and washroom facilities. The transit shed is the logical location for these facilities as it is the place where these services are required. Likewise the transit shed may contain the administration and shipping companies' offices. On the other hand, the trend in large ports has been to place the general offices for port administration, shipping companies, customs, and port security within one centrally located administration building. It is here that one will find the port captain, chief customs inspector, chief of police, general manager of warehousing, personnel director, accounting department, paymaster, etc. Direct communication is maintained from here to all parts of the port: the offices in the transit sheds and warehouses, customs inspection counters and rooms, guard houses, firehouse, etc.

6.2 Transit Sheds and Warehouses

General cargo docks are provided with transit sheds the purpose of which is to provide temporary storage for (1) goods discharged from vessels and awaiting clearance through customs, and distribution to warehouses or points of destination by means of trucks or railway carriers; and (2) goods arriving by land and awaiting export. Transit sheds should not be used as warehouses for long-term storage, although there are some instances of multistory sheds in which the upper floors are used as warehouses, because (1) the space available alongside a berth is usually limited to that required for unloading and loading a single ship; (2) the operation of a transit shed is entirely different from that of a warehouse, the former requiring a greater amount of aisle space for rapid handling of goods by mobile equipment; and (3) economical considerations usually do not justify the construction of warehouses on or alongside docks, as their structures are generally heavier than are required for transit sheds, and the soil conditions at these locations normally require expensive pile foundations.

Since the transit shed is the interchange point in a cargo marine terminal between goods moving by water and by land and functions to temporarily store these goods during the short interval of time between receiving and discharging them, it follows that the design of transit sheds has changed considerably in recent years to keep in step with (1) the revolutionary changes in land transportation, in which the motor truck has become as important as the railroad, if not more so, for not only local delivery but long-haul transportation as well; (2) the greatly increased cargo-carrying capacity of ships, without a corresponding increase in length of berth; and (3) the laborsaving devices for cargo handling such as fork-lift trucks and mobile cranes (see Chap. 7).

Obviously, transit sheds cannot be standardized in design. There may be considerable variation from port to port and even within ports. Finger piers with their restricted widths and lengths limit to a large extent the area of the transit shed per berth, as well as its width, and may as a result be the determining factor as to whether more than a one-story shed will be required. Recent practice in the New York area has been to replace several old narrow piers and two-story pier sheds with one wide pier and a single-story transit shed, more or less square or broadly rectangular in plan. As contrasted to the pier, the marginal wharf, if not in a build-up or restricted area, will have adequate space behind the wharf, particularly if the terminal is being designed in accordance with modern practice, to construct a single-story transit shed of the required area, and with present-day cargo-handling equipment the width will not be a limiting factor. Cargo-handling practices, which vary in different parts of the world, also have their effect on the design of the transit shed. The long-boom wharf cranes, particularly of the level-luffing type, are more commonly used in Europe than in the United States, which results generally in the use of wider aprons and the construction of multistory sheds with setbacks or aprons at each floor, facing the dock, within reach of the wharf cranes. Certain commodities, such as fruit and particularly bananas, and newsprint, may be imported in sufficient quantities at certain locations to warrant special sheds and handling equipment for their exclusive use. Bulk cargo shipping terminals, which are covered in Chap. 8, are prime examples of this specialization, as it is the exception when more than one material is handled at a shipping terminal.

Recent construction in transit sheds has leaned toward providing a greater area per berth for the storage of incoming and outgoing cargo. A minimum area of 90,000 sq ft per berth is now considered desirable for terminals at which an entire shipload is to be handled. For smaller terminals where a ship may discharge and take on only a partial load, a proportionately smaller area may be used. The 90,000 sq ft requirement is based on discharging and loading a typical dry-cargo ship carrying 6,250 measurement tons of cargo. The total cargo to be handled per berth is, therefore, 12,500 measurement tons which at 40 cu ft per ton will occupy a space of 500,000 cu ft. With the use of fork-lift trucks and greater headroom in the modern transit sheds, the storage height may be conservatively figured at 15 ft or a net height of cargo equal to 13 ft 6 in. after the thickness of the pallets is deducted. This would require a storage area equal to 37,000 sq ft, if packed solidly, but since some space is lost between stacks of pallets, this figure is increased about 25 per cent to 45,000 sq ft. However, the shed must have ample aisle space leading to the doors along both sides of the shed and it has been found that approximately 50 per cent of the floor area must be allowed for this purpose if fork-lift trucks are to operate efficiently in sorting, stacking, and moving the cargo. Therefore, a gross area of 90,000 sq ft of transit shed is required per berth.

The length of the transit shed is generally governed by the length of berth and should not be shorter than the out-to-out length between the fore and aft hatches since the efficient moving of the cargo from ship to shed and vice versa requires for each hatch at least one door, which should be ideally located opposite the hatch. Based on an average length of transit shed equal to 500 ft per berth, the required width will be 180 ft to obtain an area of 90,000 sq ft. Therefore, a finger pier with berths on both sides will require a one-story transit shed to be 360 ft wide. Where space is not available for this width of shed, the two-story or multistory shed must be resorted to.

There is a great divergence of opinion as to the merits of a one-story versus a two-story shed, except perhaps where the second story is used for a passenger terminal and customs clearance of general baggage. For this purpose the two-story shed is generally looked upon with favor because (1) the upper-floor apron is usually ideally located for the landing of passenger ramps or gangplanks; (2) the vertical lift of the passengers and baggage is usually not a problem; and (3) the lower floor is left free to function as a regular one-story cargo-handling transit shed. Aside from its use as a combination cargo and passenger terminal, there appears to be no general rule which can be laid down as to the most suitable type, the one-story or two-story shed. The divergence of opinion between many authorities of many countries only emphasizes the necessity of studying all the problems and local factors which vary from port to port and even within a port, before reaching a decision as to the best and most economical type of shed to use with respect to initial capital and con-

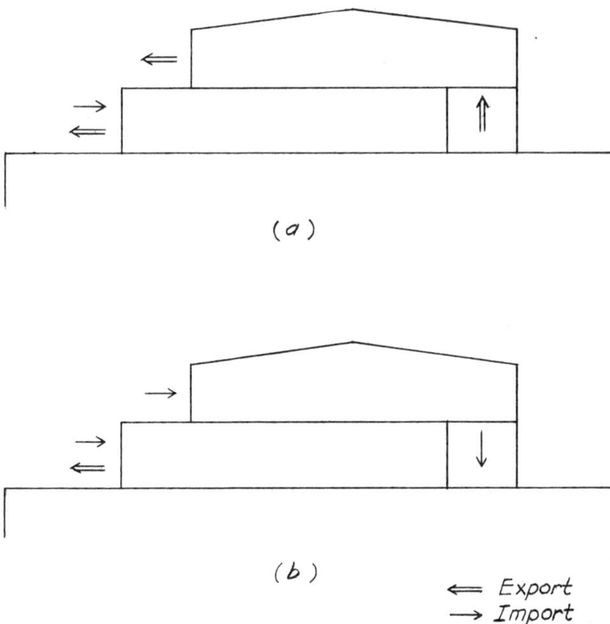

FIG. 6.1 Possible methods of operation for two-story sheds.

tinuing operating costs. One thing which most authorities appear to agree on is the unsuitability of using more than two stories as a transit shed because of the difficulty in providing for rapid vertical flow of the cargo. A two-story shed does not present the same problem because at least three-quarters of the handling of the goods can be done by regular mobile equipment operating in a horizontal direction. Figure 6.1 illustrates various methods of operation by which this can be accomplished. In (*a*) the upper floor is used for exports and the lower floor for both imports and exports. The operation can be reversed in the case of imports exceeding exports, as in (*b*). In this respect the two-story shed has a distinct advantage over the one-story shed in that a large proportion of the cargo for import and export can be kept separate, thereby avoiding the necessity of segregating the cargo. Note that in Fig. 6.1 the cargo moves horizontally, except for transporting it to and from the upper floor at the rear of the shed, which is done by means of elevators, hoists, chutes, etc. Ramps have been used for truck access to the upper floor, but these and the open space which must be provided on the upper floor for their operation, result in a considerable reduction in the space available for the storage of cargo. As a result, the net storage area may be reduced from 50 per cent to as little as 35 per cent of the total floor area. Two-story sheds make it desirable to have wharf cranes along the apron so that cargo can be handled directly from the upper floor to the hold of the ship, the upper story being stepped back about 15 ft to provide a continuous platform for the landing and handling of goods in this manner.

The two-story shed is more expensive per square foot than the one-story shed because (1) heavier foundations are generally required; (2) the upper floor will need to be of strong suspended construction to support the heavy live loads; (3) elevators, hoists, chutes, etc., must be provided to move cargo to and from the upper floor. Operational costs are also less for the one-story shed. The main offsetting factor in cost for the two-story shed is the reduction in roof area. In general, a transit shed should be of the lightest and cheapest type of construction possible without incurring high maintenance costs. The one-story shed is more adaptable to this type of construction.

The one-story shed enables the number of columns to be reduced to a minimum. The use of the fork-lift truck and mobile crane for handling cargo has placed greater emphasis on wider spacing of interior columns and even their elimination in some instances. Whether the latter is economical or necessary is open to question. However, the use of prestressed-concrete, rigid-frame construction and long-span trusses or arches, plus lightweight types of roof covering, such as gypsum, lightweight concrete, and aluminum, has brought the clear- or long-span type of shed construction into greater favor and use. In general, it is believed advisable to limit the spacing of interior columns to not less than 30 ft.

The clear height of transit sheds should be not less than 16 ft and preferably 20 ft. If mobile cranes are to be used inside the shed it will be desirable to have a clear height of 24 ft.

Doors are a very important part of the transit shed. They are located along the front and back and should be directly opposite each other. In addition there should be one or two large doors at each end of the shed. The doors along the front and back may form a continuous opening, except for the columns, if of the vertical-lift or rolling-shutter type, or they may be located in every second or third bay. As a general rule, they should be located not more than 60 ft apart. The narrower the apron, the closer the spacing of the doors should be. For a minimum-width apron of 15 ft, the doors should be in every bay or at most in every other bay, which will insure that at least one door will be available for each hatch of the ship, and very little, if any, lateral movement of the cargo will be required along the apron. Doors should be not less than 12 ft in width and 16 ft in height, and present-day practice is to make these openings even larger, an 18- by 20-ft door being not unusual. Transit-shed doors are usually one of three types: rolling shutter, sectional vertical lift, or horizontal sliding. These are shown in Fig. 6.2. Swinging and what is termed "up and over" doors should not be used as they interfere with the storage of cargo. Lift doors may be motor-operated but are more commonly hand-operated by means of a continuous chain. A 25-lb pull will usually suffice to operate the heaviest door. Sliding doors should be suspended from overhead rollers in preference to running on tracks set in the concrete deck. The tracks may become clogged with dirt or damaged, making it difficult for the workmen to slide the doors. In large doors it is often desirable to provide a small pass door so that the main door does not have to be opened each time a workman wants to go in and out of the warehouse. This is particularly true in cold climates. Doors should be provided with locks or bolts which can be operated only from the inside. Jambs should be protected with wheel guards so that the frames will not be damaged by trucks. There appears to be no general rule for providing glazed doors, and whether or not this is done is more a matter of preference. Generally, the glazed panel is small and high up on the door where it will not get broken. In the southern warmer climates, where doors are kept open a large amount of the time, there appears to be little reason for installing glazed panels in the doors.

Although it is quite common for warehouse floors to be built at truck-platform height above the surrounding grade, this is not suitable for transit sheds where the cargo is transported between the ship's side and the shed by means of fork-lift trucks or mobile cranes. The advantages of being able to run the mobile cargo-handling equipment directly into or from the shed without raising or lowering the cargo are so obvious that transit-shed ground floors are generally built at the same level as the apron along the dock or as a continuation of its slope. Sloping the floor of the shed upward between $\frac{1}{8}$ in. and $\frac{1}{4}$ in. per ft will usually enable a truck or railroad-car loading platform to be established along the rear of the building at a height of 3 ft 2 in. to 3 ft 6 in. above the roadway or top of rail. If the shed is not wide enough to obtain this height without exceeding the maximum slope of $\frac{1}{4}$ in. per ft, the roadway or track along the rear of the shed can be depressed, but this should be avoided, if possible, as it may present a drainage problem. The slope of the floor also facilitates washing down and cleaning the floor. Floors are usually constructed of concrete with either integral or separate cement finish which should contain a floor hardener, or iron filings where

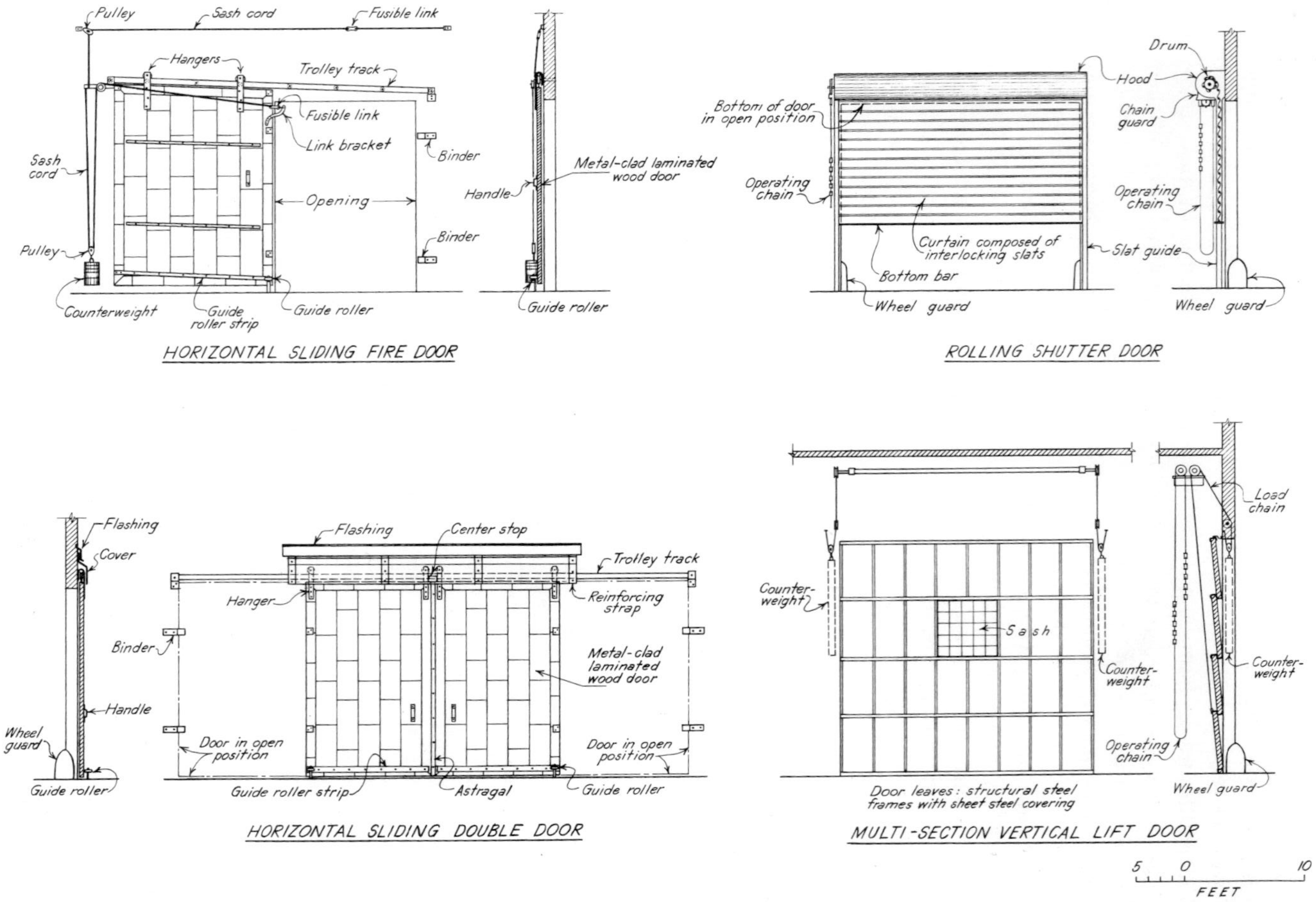

FIG. 6.[illegible] Types of transit shed doors

the floor will be subjected to severe wear. An asphaltic-concrete surface course, generally $1\frac{1}{2}$ in. thick, may be placed over precast- and prestressed-concrete floor slabs to provide a smooth wearing surface. Wood blocks set in asphalt form a clean, dry wearing surface which does not absorb smells, but this type of surfacing is more expensive than most other types. The use of fork-lift trucks, tractors, and mobile cranes for handling cargo makes it important to have a smooth, even surface on the floor.

Truck-loading platforms along the rear and at the inshore end of the shed should be at least 12 ft in width to enable cargo to be moved along the platform to a truck parked between two doors. Since the movement of cargo is more rapid into and out of a transit shed than it is at a warehouse, the loading platform should be continuous; whereas it need be only in front of the doors of a warehouse and may be reduced in width to 5 or 6 ft or eliminated altogether. Referring to the basis of establishing the minimum area of the transit shed as 90,000 sq ft per berth, which will store enough cargo to unload and load a ship containing 6,250 measurement tons in 5 days, and if it is assumed that two-thirds of the total cargo handled will be moved by truck, the amount to be moved each day will be $\frac{2}{3} \times 2 \times 6{,}250 \times \frac{1}{5}$ or 1,666 tons. This will equal 208 tons per hour, based on an 8-hour day. If it is assumed that the average truck load is 15 measurement tons (600 cu ft), and that it takes 3 hours to load or unload a truck, the number of trucks to be accommodated at the loading platform will equal $208 \times 3 \times \frac{1}{15}$ or 42 trucks. This will require a loading platform 504 ft long, based on a 12-ft parking width, which is the approximate length of the transit shed and demonstrates why the loading platform should be continuous along the rear of the transit shed. In some ports where most of the cargo is carried by rail, a fewer number of truck-loading docks may be provided. If space is not available to load along the rear of the shed, which is often the case on finger piers, the trucks will have to be loaded at the inshore end of the pier or within the shed itself. The loading platform should be covered, and the canopy or roof should extend beyond the edge of the platform a sufficient distance (about 6 ft) to cover the end of the trucks. In a two-story shed the upper floor may extend out over the platform, which in addition to providing protection from the weather enables cargo to be lowered through hatches in the floor onto the lower platform or directly into open trucks or railroad cars. A second track or truck-loading area may be provided at the rear of a two-story transit shed for direct loading of goods by cranes or hoists from and to the upper floor. Platforms are sometimes cantilevered out from the upper floor to provide space on which to land the cargo handled by crane. Figure 6.3 illustrates the above arrangement for handling cargo at the rear of a two-story transit shed.

In addition to providing open floor storage the transit shed should contain a lockup for housing highly pilferable or very valuable cargo, as well as highly dutiable goods to be examined by customs officials and held pending payment of duty. The lockup should be constructed of heavy wire mesh and steel frame extending to the ceiling or roof of the shed, or provided with a ceiling of the same or solid type of construction, about 8 ft above the floor. This enables the guards on duty to see the inside of the lockup when they are making their rounds. Some transit sheds are provided with a separate closed room or annex for the storage of "dirty cargo," such as paint and oil, so as to prevent contamination of the other cargo and to keep the main floor of the shed as clean as possible.

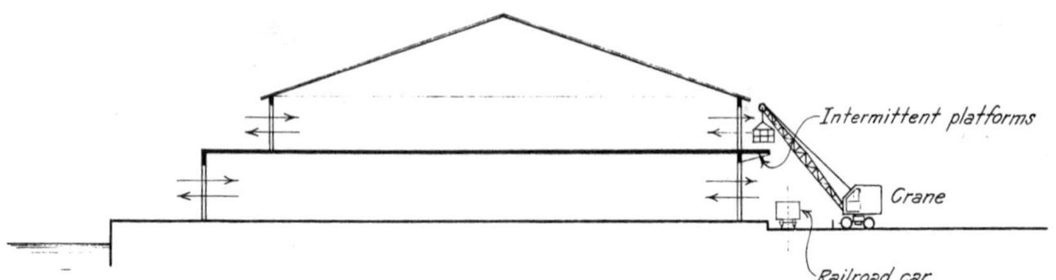

FIG. 6.3 Crane handling cargo to and from upper story of transit sheds.

A room should be provided for storing the stevedore's gear, and, since this need be only 10 ft high, the space over may be used as a locker room. Washroom and toilet facilities should be provided within the shed, and on each floor if a two-story shed. General offices for the dock staff and customs officials should be located at the head end of the shed, and additional small portable offices may be provided within the shed at convenient locations for the shipping clerks and customs inspectors.

Floor live loads will vary considerably, depending on the type of cargo and the method of handling it. General cargo will average about 70 cu ft to the long ton or about 32 lb per cu ft. In modern sheds with the use of fork-lift trucks the cargo may be expected to be piled on pallets to a net height of 13.5 ft, which would impose an average load of 432 lb per sq ft on the floor slab. Assuming that over a floor slab panel the unit weight might vary by as much as 50 per cent from the average, but that it will not be possible to stack the pallets close enough together to cover more than about 75 per cent of the floor area, the unit load of 432 lb per sq ft might be increased to 648 lb per sq ft, but would probably not average more than 75 per cent of this, or 486 lb per sq ft over the entire floor-slab panel. Therefore, a design uniform live load of 500 lb per sq ft should be satisfactory for general cargo transit-shed floors. This load may be either lighter or heavier for transit sheds or warehouses which are assigned to handle or store a specific commodity, such as cotton and

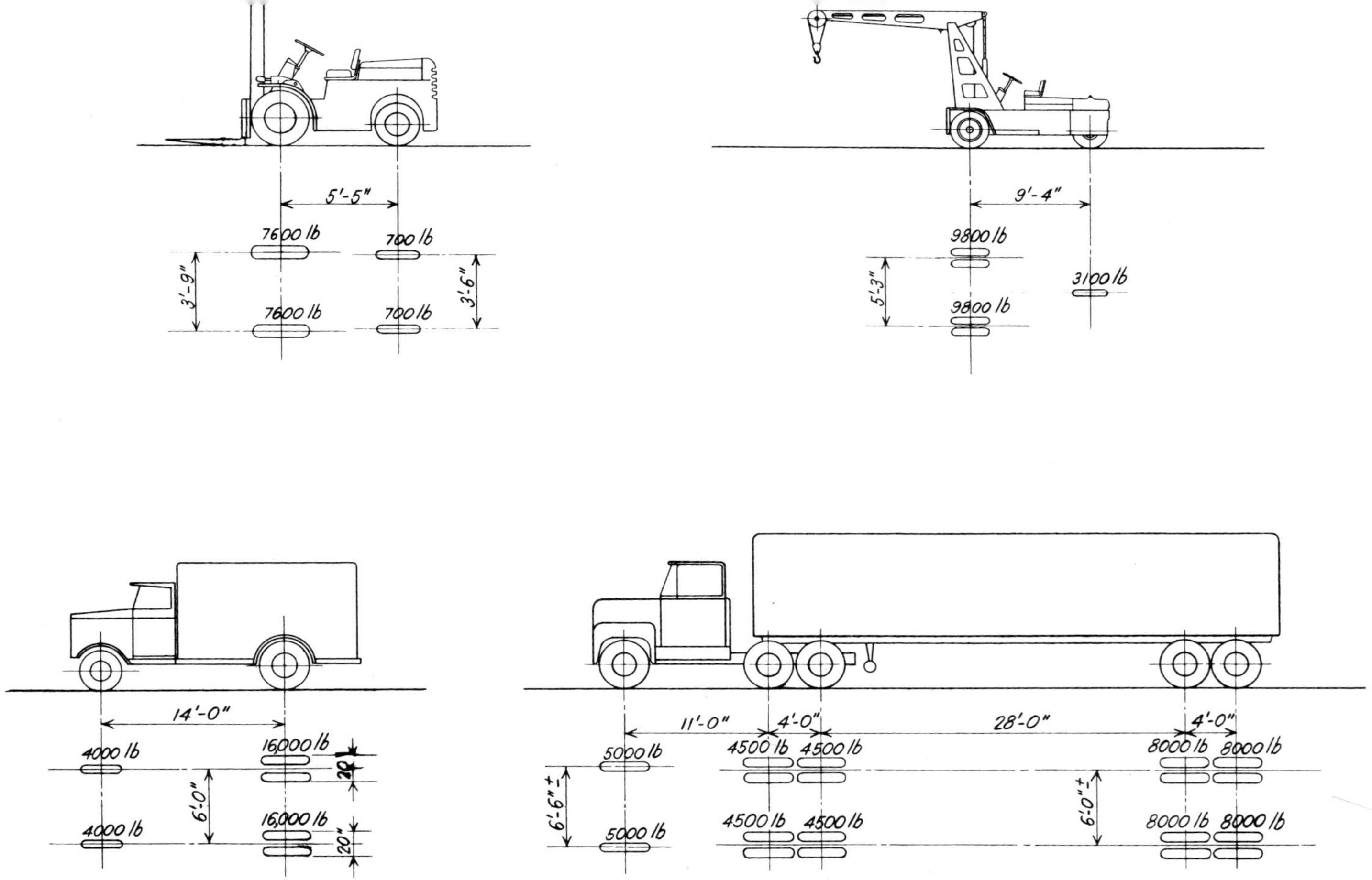

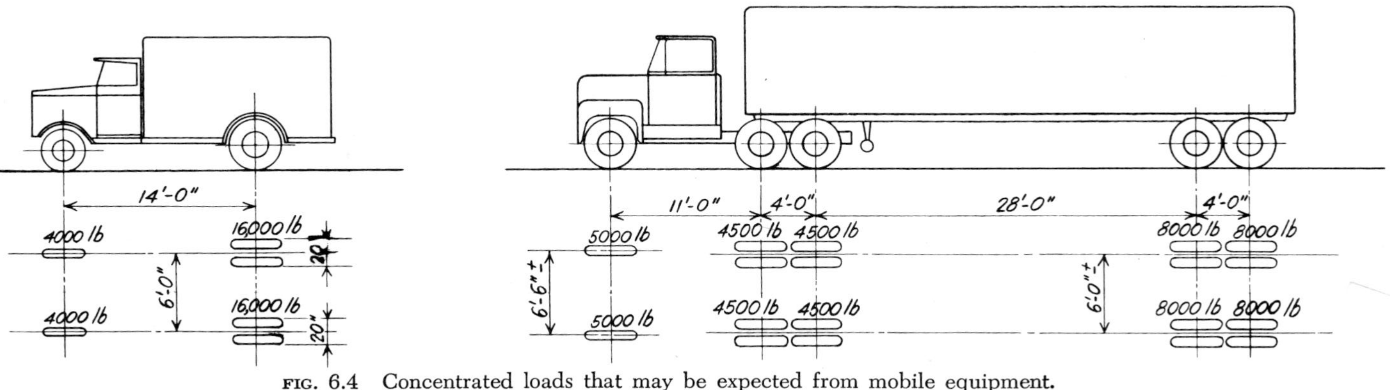

FIG. 6.4 Concentrated loads that may be expected from mobile equipment.

wool (300 to 400 lb per sq ft) and metal products (600 to 800 lb per sq ft).

The uniform live load will usually control the design of the beams or girders and the supporting foundations, but the slab should be checked for concentrated wheel loads from fork-lift trucks, tractors, mobile cranes, or trucks, whichever are to be used for handling the cargo in and out of the transit shed, and which will give the most severe loading condition. Figure 6.4 gives the wheel loads and their spacing for (1) 3-ton-capacity fork-lift truck, (2) 5-ton-capacity mobile crane, (3) 20-ton truck (gross), and (4) 30-ton trailer truck (gross).

When it comes to the construction of modern transit sheds, they present wide variations in design and materials of construction as will be seen in the following section covering a number of well-known installations.

6.3 Examples of Modern Transit-shed Construction

The following are only a few of the transit sheds which have been built in various parts of the world in the last ten years. They have been selected not because they are the most outstanding but to illustrate the different types of construction. Four of these transit sheds are combination passenger and cargo-handling terminals.

Passenger and Cargo-handling Terminal, La Guaira, Venezuela. In 1952, as a part of the expansion of the Port of La Guaira, Venezuela, a transit shed was completed which is noteworthy for the facilities it contains for the convenience and pleasure of ocean travelers and for the speedy and efficient handling of cargo.

The passenger terminal building of rigid-frame reinforced-concrete construction is mostly two stories high, but a third story, housing a restaurant and cocktail lounge, tops part of it. The main-deck level is devoted to cargo storage. On the second floor are a waiting room, customs inspection, a parking area, and additional cargo space.

Reinforced-concrete beams 13 ft apart support the second and third floors. The beams span 26 ft between reinforced-concrete rigid frames.

The base of each first-story column is supported on a cast-steel rocker so as not to cause bending in the pier deck. The lower half of the casting is bolted to the pier, and the upper half is doweled into the column. Rocker-bearing surfaces were carefully machined to a tolerance of 0.004 in. Upper and lower surfaces are separated by a $\frac{1}{64}$-in. lead sheet to prevent freezing and binding when the column deflects.

Second- and third-story columns are doweled into the frames below, and their fixed-end moments are taken by the structure.

The general arrangement of facilities for handling passengers and cargo are shown in Fig. 6.5.

When a ship docks, a self-powered platform moves along the apron of

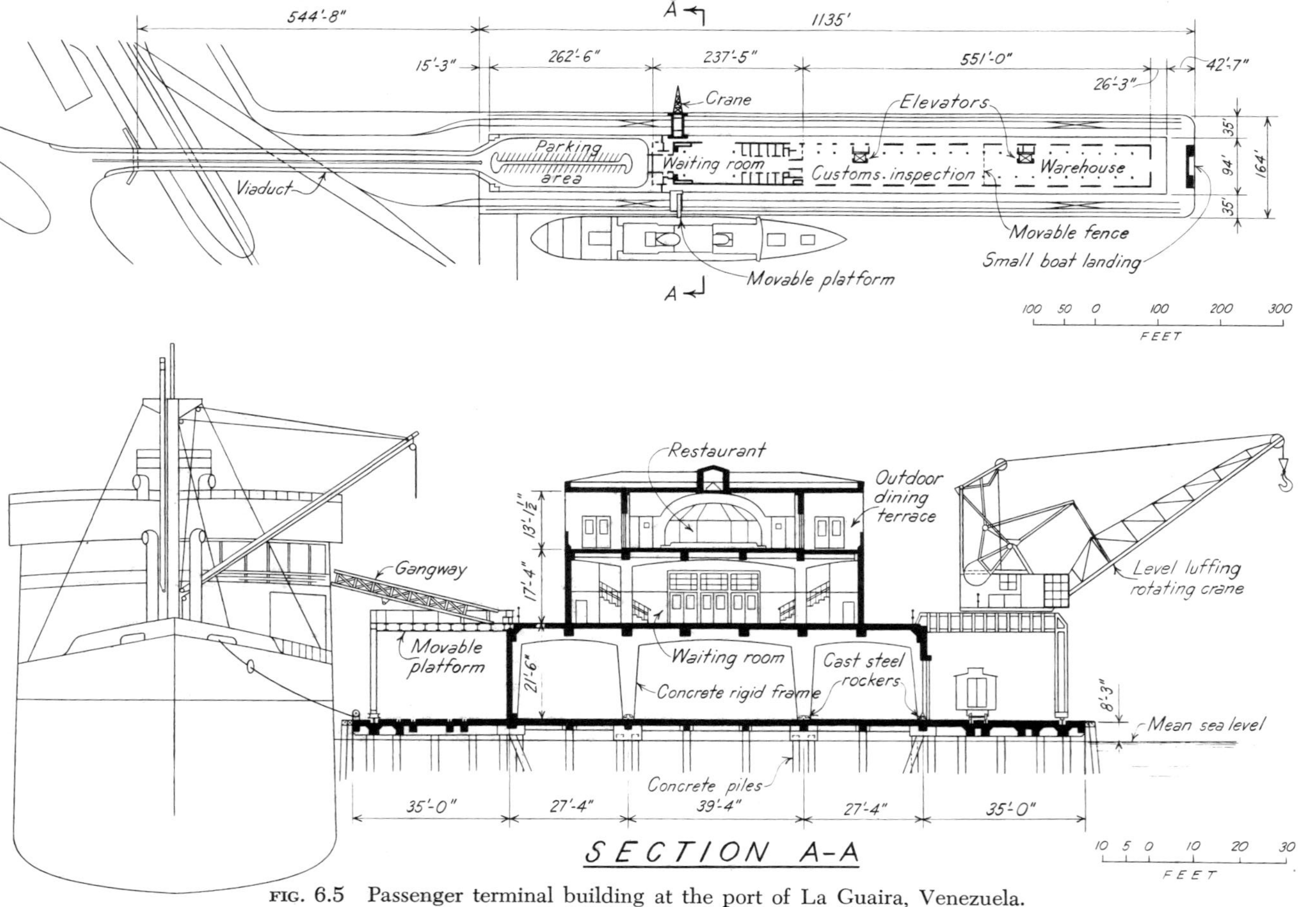

FIG. 6.5 Passenger terminal building at the port of La Guaira, Venezuela.

the pier, on the same rails installed for the gantries, to a position opposite the passenger disembarkation point on the ship. A portable gangplank is then placed between the ship and the platform, which is at second-floor level. Cargo is loaded on lift trucks on this platform by ship's tackle, and the trucks in turn transport it along the second-floor apron into the shed.

When passengers disembark, they walk along the second-floor apron to the nearest entrance to customs inspection. An area 65 ft wide by 551 ft long is allotted for this purpose. Since the space needed varies from time to time, a portable barrier is placed across the floor to define the inspection area, leaving the remainder of the floor for cargo storage.

From customs inspection, passengers pass through a gate into the waiting room, where are found steamship offices, rest rooms, concessions, and the main stairway to the restaurant above. The waiting room is attractively finished with terrazzo floor, blue-glass-tile wainscot, and acoustical-tile ceiling. A lobby at the far end leads directly to the main entrance.

Between the main entrance and the shore end of the pier, a distance of 260 ft, is a parking area with space for 46 cars. A two-lane roadway and sidewalk encircle the end of the parking space in front of the main entrance. Folding gates limit direct access to the second-floor apron, which extends along the sides and across the ends of the second story.

The two-lane roadway converges at the shore end of the pier into one exit lane and one entrance lane separated by a center island. A viaduct carries this roadway over the railroad and roadways in the port yard. It connects with the express highway to La Guaira and Caracas, which at this point is at about the same level as the second floor of the passenger terminal.

The viaduct is a reinforced-concrete structure about 560 ft long. It is supported at 52-ft intervals on a single, centrally located row of columns. The single-column construction offers less obstruction to the traffic below than would conventional multiple-column construction and presents a pleasing appearance.

Almost the entire first story of the building is given over to the storing and handling of cargo. Two 10-ton freight elevators transfer cargo from the first to the second floor for customs inspection and storage. These elevators are self-leveling, with automatic biparting doors. Platforms are large enough to accommodate a small automobile or two fully loaded lift trucks.

For movement of cargo in and out of the building at first-floor level, large sliding doors are provided in every other bay in the exterior wall along each side and end of the building. These open to the main deck, which has an apron 35 ft wide along each side of the building and 43 ft at the sea end.

Although provision was made for the installation of semiportal ganti cranes, these have not been put into service, and the cargo continues t be handled by the ship's gear.

Passenger and Cargo Terminal at Southampton Docks, England. The New Docks, constructed in 1930, which extend along Southampton waters for a distance of about one and one-half miles, are described in Sec. 3:7. In 1956 a new passenger and cargo building, which replaced a single-story transit shed destroyed in World War II, was put into operation to provide facilities for passengers and cargo carried by the Union Castle liners from South Africa. The new building at berth 102 was joined to a single-story transit shed at berth 101. The new terminal has demonstrated its ability to handle the heavy weekly cargo and to provide the passengers with a high standard of service. An excellent description of the terminal facilities and operation appeared in the December, 1957, issue of the *Dock and Harbour Authority*. Figure 6.6 shows the arrangement of these facilities, and the following are some of the unique features, which have created such a favorable impression of the efficiency of the operation of this two-story shed.

The new building is approximately 932 ft long and 162 ft at its widest portion. The minimum headroom on the lower floor, which is used for passengers and their baggage and for perishable cargo and wine, is 17.5 ft at the dock side and diminishes to 14.25 ft at the back of the building, owing to the upward slope of the floor, to provide a railroad car loading platform at a height of 3.25 ft above rail level. The minimum headroom on the upper floor, which is used primarily for cargo, is 18 ft.

Annexed to the building on the inshore side is a semiopen gantry crane bay, 442 ft long by 20 ft wide, containing four electrically operated traversing cranes, each of 3,000-lb lifting capacity, which are used for transferring cargo from the upper floor directly into railroad cars below, or onto the adjacent platforms. On the dock side is a single-story portion, about 640 ft long and 34 ft wide, the roof of which serves as a platform on which to land cargo unloaded from the ship by eight 3- or 6-ton-capacity electric level-luffing wharf cranes. The cargo on the upper-level platform is distributed into the shed by battery-operated 3,000-lb-capacity squeeze-clamp-type fork-lift trucks and 2-ton platform trucks.

The landward side of the lower floor terminates in a railroad well which continues through the adjoining shed 101 and is used for passenger and freight trains. On the outer side of the rail track is an island platform, about 515 ft long by 16 ft 3 in. wide, for the handling of cargo lowered from the upper floor by the overhead cranes. Provision is made for access to the loading platform island from the ground floor by means of three electrically operated lift bridges which span the well. These are of steel construction and wooden decks, 12 ft in width, capable of supporting

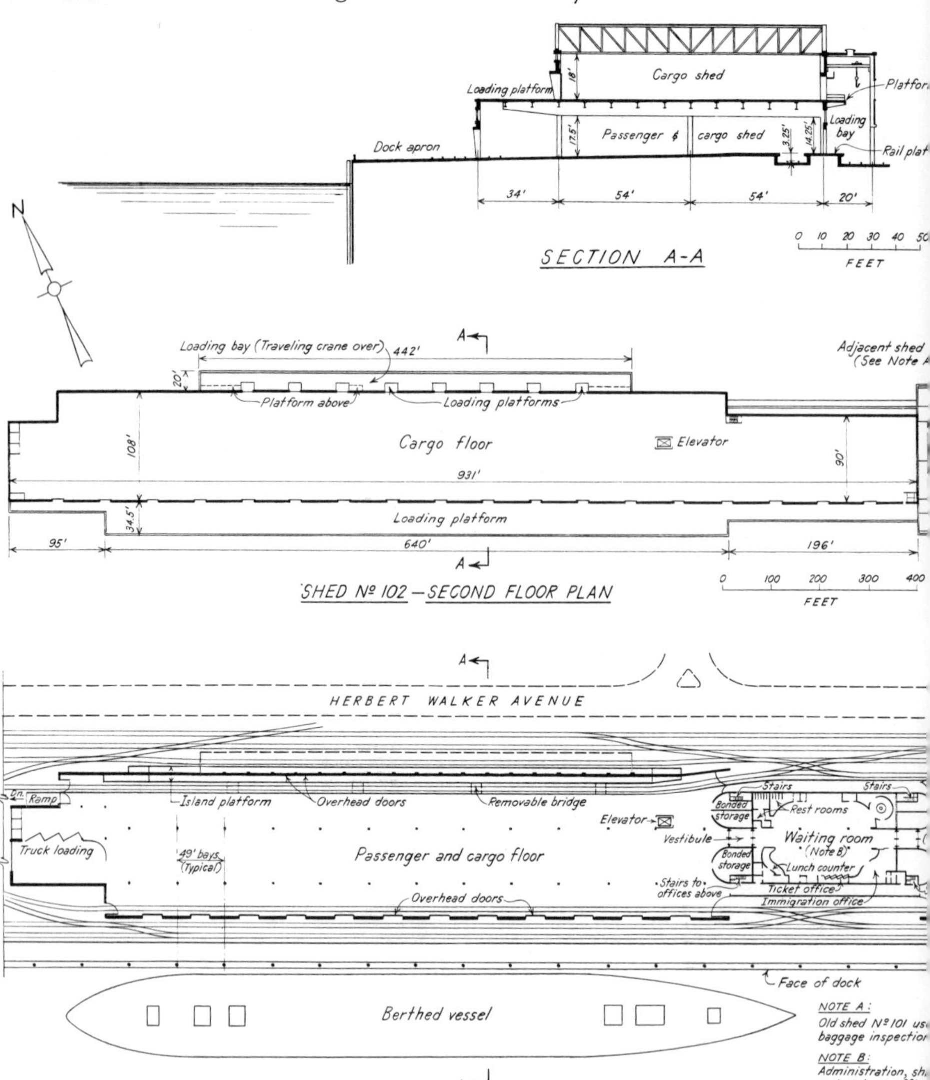

FIG. 6.6 Shed 102 at Southampton Docks, England. (*From Dock and Harbour Authority, cember,* 1957.)

fully loaded fork-lift trucks weighing 4½ tons. Automatic warning-signal lights on the railroad indicate whether the bridges are up or down.

Truck-loading facilities are provided at the west end of the building, where there is a platform for loading six trucks at one time. Three 3,000-lb traversing electric hoists, above wells in the upper floor, lower goods from the upper floor onto the lower truck-loading platform and directly into the trucks at two of the six locations.

An elevator of 3-ton capacity provides for the transfer of mechanical equipment between the upper and lower floors, and enables the battery-operated cargo-handling equipment to be removed from the upper floor for recharging and repair.

Two large enclosed areas are provided at the east end of the working area of the lower floor as lockups for bonded cargo and duty-paid goods, as well as stevedore's gear. Above one of these enclosures on the dock side are the offices for the shed-operating personnel.

The eastern section of the building, which is about 196 ft long and 90 ft wide, contains the passenger waiting room. Above the waiting room, at the mezzanine level immediately below the upper floor, are the offices for general administration, shipping companies, and customs. Passengers arriving or departing are routed through the waiting room, either to the ground-floor cargo area or to customs inspection in the adjoining single-story shed 101. The baggage examination tables are constructed of aluminum and can be quickly dismantled and stored when not needed.

The steel framework of the building is of particular interest because of its all-welded construction and the relatively small number of columns in the interior of the building, the upper floor having a clear span and the lower floor two transverse spans of 54 ft each across the building, with cantilever spans on the dockside and landward sides of 34 ft and 20 ft, respectively. These main transverse girders, which support a uniform live load of 300 lb per sq ft on the upper floor, are 134 ft in length and weigh 34 tons. They were brought to the job in two pieces and were assembled by butt welding. The roof trusses span 108 ft and are of the Howe type with 12 equal panels of 9 ft. They are located on 49-ft centers at the ridges, with rafters from the top-chord panel points extending downward on each side at an angle of 21½° to form valleys midway between the trusses. The rafters are supported at a distance of 13 ft from the trusses by struts rising from the lower-chord panel points. The main structure is roofed over with an aluminum alloy decking system spanning 9 ft between the rafters, which is covered with ½-in. insulating fiber-board bonded in bitumin and waterproofed with two layers of bitumin and felt. The gable ends of the main roof and the long side wall of the gantry crane bay on the landward side are covered with asbestos cement sheeting. The main exterior walls of the first story are faced with brown-colored brick. The upper and lower floors, landing platforms, and flat roofs are of poured-in-place reinforced concrete. Those floors on which cargo-handling equipment operates are surfaced with a $1\frac{1}{4}$-in. asphalt wearing course.

Pier 57, North River, New York City. The ceremonies officially opening the Department of Marine and Aviation Pier 57 (leased by Grace Line), which replaced the old Grace Line pier burned down in 1947, termed the massive structure of steel and concrete, with its unique buoyant type substructure, "The World's Most Modern Pier." A brief description of its unusual substructure is given in Sec. 5.8, and Fig. 5.62 shows a section through the pier and shed. The following are some of the features which were incorporated in the new pier shed design.

The two-story shed on the pier is 700 ft long and 120 ft wide and is backed up with a two-story bulkhead shed at right angles to it, which is 373 by 139 ft. These structures have 15-ft-wide aprons facing the water.

The two-story shed is in effect equivalent to four stories as it utilizes, in addition to the two main cargo decks, the flat roof for the storage of automobiles and the basement for storage, driveways, and elevators. Cargo is transported by trucks and trailers, which enter the structure directly from the street and may unload both in the bulkhead structure and the pier shed at street level. To avoid traffic congestion in front of the pier, the trucks and trailers can also reach the second deck directly by ramp as shown in Fig. 6.7. Large elevators serve all four decks of the pier. To facilitate truck traffic within the shed, both on the first and second decks, there are only two rows of columns in the width of the building, spaced 80 ft apart and 40 ft on centers along the pier shed.

Passenger cars, taxicabs, and small trucks enter the basement of the bulkhead structure directly by a ramp from the street, discharge their passengers and luggage, and then return to the street by ramp at the opposite end. Passengers reach the upper decks by means of stairs, escalators, and elevators, and luggage arrives by means of inclined luggage lifts.

The second floor of the bulkhead structure contains modern passenger accommodations and steamship offices, as shown in Fig. 6.7.

Both the second floor and roof are reinforced-concrete slabs on structural steel frames which will support live loads of 450 and 100 lb per sq ft, respectively. The main deck of prestressed-concrete beam and girder design will support a live load of 600 lb per sq ft.

Four-leaf vertical-lift doors, 20 ft wide by 18 ft high, enable the pier shed to be completely open along its sides at both the first- and second-floor levels, except for the door guides and framing. The lower leaf can be left in closed position, while the upper leaves are raised, to provide a

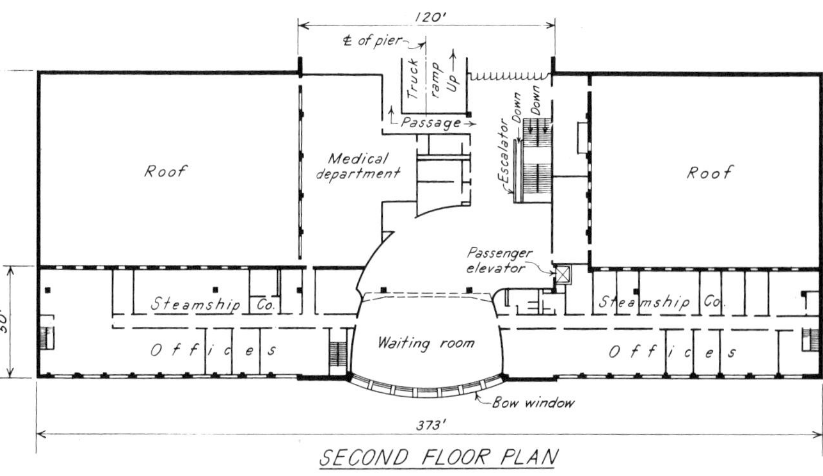

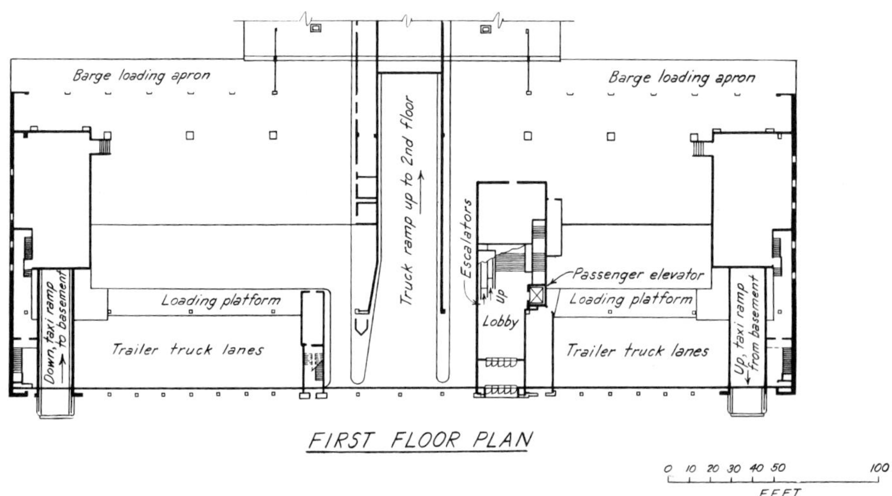

FIG. 6.7 Bulkhead shed, pier 57, North River, New York City. (*From Engineering News-Record, Jan.* 11, 1951.)

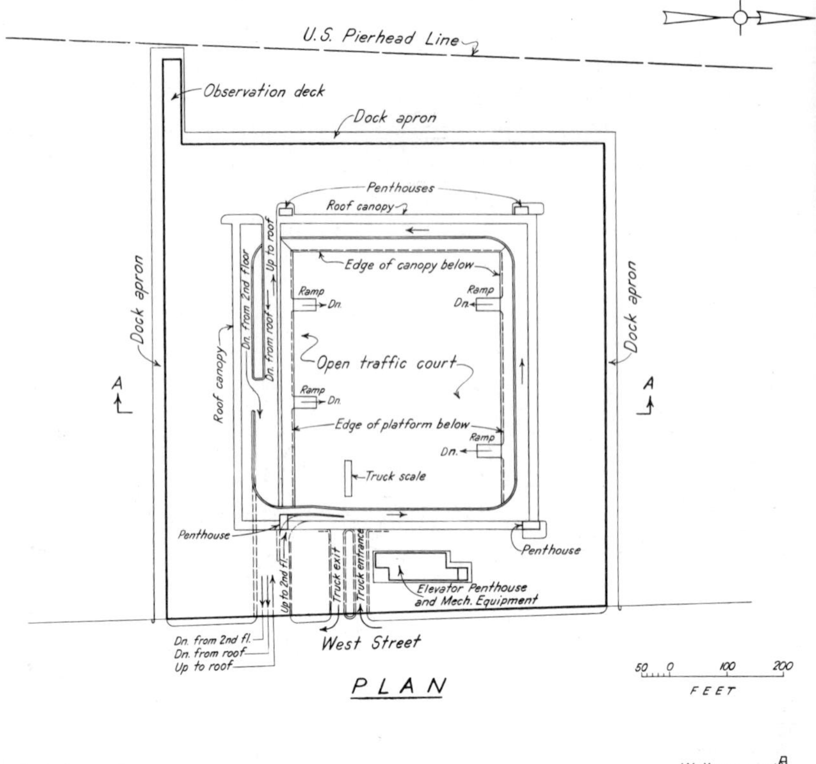

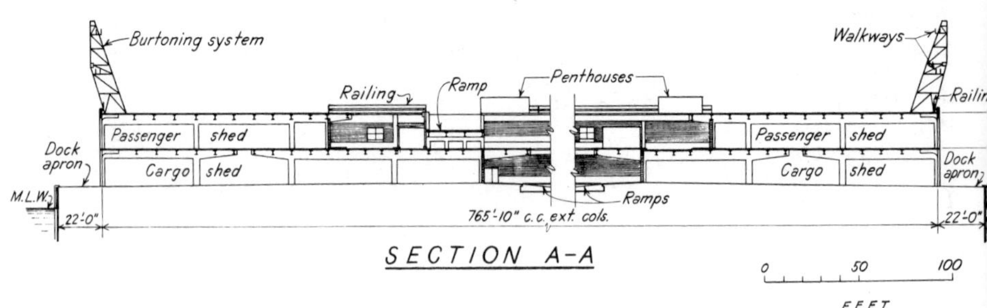

FIG. 6.8 Pier 40, North River, New York City. (*Courtesy of the Department of Marine and Aviation, New York City.*)

railing protection. Cargo hoist frames above the roof, along both sides of the shed, are typical of New York pier cargo-hoisting facilities.

New Pier 40, North River, New York City. To be completed in 1961, this pier will be the Department of Marine and Aviation's new square-shaped cargo and passenger terminal, for occupancy by the Holland-America Line. The new terminal, costing close to $19 million, will cover the area previously occupied by piers 37 to 41, inclusive.

FIG. 6.9 Aerial view of Port of New York Authority Pier 1, Brooklyn, New York. (*Courtesy of World Ports and the Mariner.*)

Unique features of the new terminal are its square shape, measuring about 810 ft on each side and providing berthing space for four vessels at one time; its huge, open interior truck court, with covered loading platforms on three sides for trucks and trailers loading and unloading cargo at the lower cargo-handling level; and its spacious passenger-handling facilities on the second deck and parking for approximately 725 private cars on the roof; all reached from the street level by a system of two-lane ramps, with a circumferential roadway at the second-floor level.

Figure 6.8 shows a plan and cross section through the building. The building frame is constructed entirely of reinforced concrete; a large part of which, including the columns, is either prestressed or precast. Bents are spaced 42 ft apart and columns in the bents are located, generally, 50 or 55 ft on centers. Exterior walls are concrete block.

Brooklyn, Port Authority Pier 1. An L-shaped pier on the East River just south of the Brooklyn Bridge was dedicated April 29, 1959, and was the third of ten new piers to be completed by the Port Authority in its $85-million plan of replacing 25 of the 26 obsolete piers along two

FIG. 6.10 Interior view of Port of New York Authority Pier 1, Brooklyn, New York. (*Courtesy of World Ports and the Mariner.*)

miles of Brooklyn waterfront. Figure 6.9 is an aerial view of the completed pier.

Pier 1 provides for two berths along its 1,090-ft westerly side and one berth along its 500-ft southerly end. The pier accommodates an L-shaped single-story cargo-terminal building with a 30-ft-wide apron, 1,040 ft long on the west side, 440 ft long on the south side, and 200 ft wide, providing 256,000 sq ft of covered space, equal to about 85,000 sq ft per berth.

The building is a light steel-framed structure, an interior view of which is shown in Fig. 6.10. Roof and sides are corrugated aluminum sheets. The roof is formed with five ridges, and about 5 per cent of the roof area is made of translucent plastic panels to provide natural lighting to the interior of the shed. The floor is of asphaltic concrete and is capable of supporting a live load of 500 lb per sq ft.

There are 22 doors on the west and south sides facing the wharf, each 20 ft wide and 18 ft high. On the land sides of the building, 16 doors, each 20 ft wide and 18 ft high, open on a 20-ft-wide covered truck platform capable of handling 70 trucks at one time. There are nine additional truck berths at the end of the building.

A paved upland area of 179,000 sq ft provides for outdoor storage and parking space for trucks and trailers, and contains a 14,000-sq-ft stevedore's garage for the storage and repair of cargo-handling equipment.

FIG. 6.11 Longshoremen's shelter at Port of New York Authority Pier 1, Brooklyn, New York. (*Courtesy of World Ports and the Mariner.*)

An unusual feature is a longshoremen's shelter, the first of its type in the Port of New York. A view of this structure is shown in Fig. 6.11. It is 47 by 33 ft, with brick walls and a corrugated aluminum roof. The shelter is furnished with long benches against the brick walls.

Rigid-frame Transit Shed for the Port of Long Beach, California. This one-story building erected in 1948 on a new wharf in one of the world's most modern ports is of unusual transit-shed design. Measuring 1,152 ft long by 200 ft wide, its outstanding feature is its rigid-frame construction, providing a clear working space nearly 1,100 ft long and almost 200 ft wide interrupted only by a fire wall at its mid-length. The cost of the shed compares favorably with small buildings of narrower width and the operating costs are lower.

Thirty-two rigid frames of all-welded construction, each 200 ft long and weighing 42 tons, were assembled on the ground and then lifted into position by three truck cranes to provide the framework for this huge structure. Figure 6.12 shows three of the rigid frames in place with some of the remaining ones on the ground ready to be lifted into position.

The rigid frames were designed with pin connections at each end, consisting of 6-in.-diameter steel pins, which transmit the loads from the frames to the footings through the base plates, each of which is anchored to the footing with four 1¾-in. bolts. The footings are supported on piles, since the entire structure is founded on a dredged fill. Opposite footings are connected by sets of 3-in.-diameter rods, which are encased in concrete for protection and to provide a strut as well as a tie between the footings.

The exterior walls of the shed are of 8- and 10-in.-thick poured-in-place concrete. The roof construction is of wood sheathing treated for fire resistance with chromated zinc chloride.

FIG. 6.12 200-ft-span rigid frames for transit shed at port of Long Beach, California. (*From Engineering News-Record, Dec.* 23, 1948.)

It is reported that the 200-ft clear-span building cost an average of 22 per cent less per sq ft than buildings the same in all respects except that their widths were 120 instead of 200 ft. The unit cost of structural steel fabricated and erected was $2.17 per sq ft of floor area, and the unit cost of the completed structure including steelwork, but exclusive of certain limited underground work and footings, was $6.15 per sq ft of floor area.

Twin Transit Sheds at the New Marine Terminal at San Diego, California. Erected in 1958, in back of a new marginal wharf approximately one-half mile long, these twin transit sheds provide nearly 400,000 sq ft of covered storage area. Each shed is 200 ft wide and 964 ft long, and is divided by fire walls into four rooms, each 240 ft long.

Figure 6.13 shows a typical cross section through the shed. Columns are spaced at 60-ft centers along the length of the building and are located to provide a 100-ft center aisle with two 50-ft side aisles. This wide column spacing makes for a minimum of interference with traffic inside the shed and provides great flexibility in storing cargo. The clear headroom varies from 22 ft on the water side to 20 ft on the land side, the floor sloping upward from the wharf apron to the height of the loading platform along the rear of the building. Since the floor was placed on a newly dredged fill a flexible type of payment was used, consisting of a 3-in.-thick asphaltic-concrete wearing course over a 9-in.-thick crushed-stone base course.

Side-wall panels of 6-in.-thick precast concrete, 20 ft wide and 28 or 30 ft high depending upon whether they are on the land or water side, were tilted into place by a crane using a vacuum-grip device. The panels rest

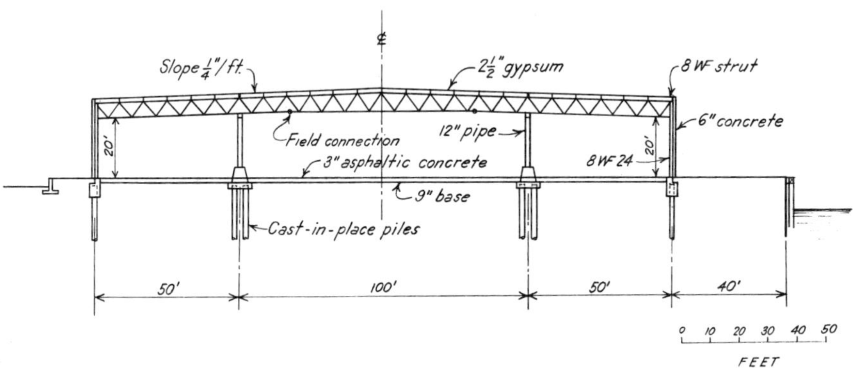

FIG. 6.13 Cross section of transit sheds at marine terminal, San Diego, California. (*From article by J. E. Liebmann and G. W. Ferver, Civil Engineering, November, 1958.*)

on the grade beam and are held against the steel columns by stud bolts fastened to the columns. The stud bolts pass through the space between adjacent panels. Galvanized steel plates, extending the full height of the wall, were placed over the studs and bolted in place. Plastic sealing compound placed along the edge of the steel plates provides a weather seal at the joints. The panels are attached at the top to the eave strut by clips. Fire walls between rooms are 12 in. thick, extend 5 ft above the roof, and are returned 20 ft in each direction at the side walls. Roller-shutter type doors are located in the center of each transverse wall and in every other bay along the side walls, except at the fire-wall returns. The roof is of poured-in-place gypsum supported by steel purlins and roof trusses. The gypsum roof consists of a 2-in. poured fill over a ½-in.-thick sheet-rock form, reinforced with 6-by-6 no. 10/10 galvanized wire mesh. The sheet-rock form is supported by steel-bulb tees welded on 32-in. centers to the purlins which are spaced 8 ft 4 in. on centers. The gypsum roof is waterproofed with 15-year bonded built-up roofing with stone-chip surfacing. The roof has no skylights or monitors, and lighting is entirely artificial, being furnished by fluorescent lights which are designed to give a lighting intensity of 7 ft-candles at floor level. One interesting feature of the steel roof-truss design was the determination of design stresses based on simple end connections and then making both chords continuous by connecting them after all dead loads were in place.

It is reported that the total weight of steel amounted to 1,047 tons or 5.4 lb per sq ft, and cost $1.08 per sq ft in place, based on an area of 387,882 sq ft, and that the total unit cost of the transit sheds was $4.86 per sq ft.

Transit Shed at the Port of Antwerp, Belgium. One of the most spacious sheds ever constructed for the complete loading and unloading

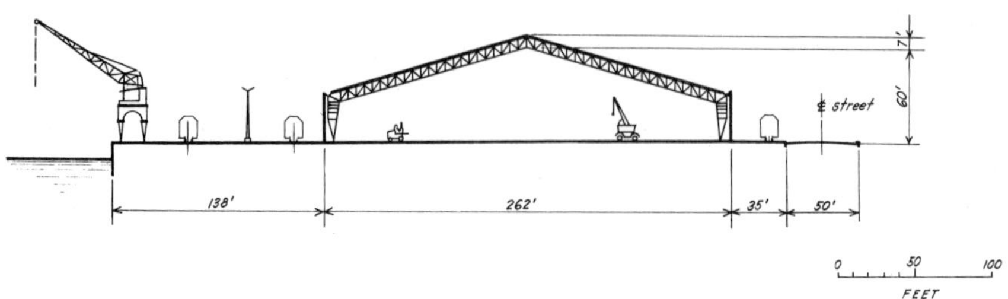

FIG. 6.14 Cross section of transit shed of light alloy at the port of Antwerp, Belgium. (*From Dock and Harbour Authority, November,* 1958.)

of vessels carrying general cargo is that at Antwerp, providing an area of 214,840 sq ft or 107,420 sq ft per berth.

As reported in the *Dock and Harbour Authority* issue of November, 1958, the shed is a one-story structure, 820 by 262 ft, consisting of a vast single bay spanned by pin-ended lattice-type portal frames, as shown in Fig. 6.14, spaced 65 ft 8 in. apart. The structural framework combines the use of aluminum and steel, the latter being used generally at the periphery of the building where the dead weight has little effect on the stresses in the spanning members. Aluminum alloy, containing about 1 per cent of silicon and magnesium, together with a small amount of manganese or chromium for improving the mechanical properties and corrosion resistance of the metal, was used for the lattice frames, the purlins, and roofing. The strength of the aluminum alloy is approximately the same as that of carbon steel. However, the modulus of elasticity is much lower, being only about one-third that of steel. This results in greater deformation of the aluminum compared to steel and makes it necessary to use structural members having a low slenderness ratio, if high working stresses are to be used. To accomplish this, it was necessary to use special extruded sections with bulbs or thickened sections at the ends and large fillets at reentrant angles. Light lattice-type purlins, spaced 5 ft 6 in. on centers, are supported on the portal frames and carry corrugated-aluminum sheeting. Natural lighting is obtained by twelve longitudinal strips of corrugated-transparent-plastic sheeting set in the roof. Artificial fluorescent lighting provides an illumination of 2.3 ft-candles at floor level. This type of construction resulted in the very low dead weight of approximately 2.5 lb per sq ft, which, with the long span, resulted in a cost which was less than a comparable building of conventional design.

The external walls of the shed are constructed of brick with continuous sash at the top. Large steel sliding doors are provided for ten openings along the front and six along the rear, each 19 ft 8 in. by 20 ft 4 in., and for three large openings in each gable end, the central opening being 25 ft wide by 23 ft high and the two side openings 21 ft wide. The floor was paved with removable 4-in.-thick reinforced-concrete slabs with a wearing surface containing iron filings, laid on a 4-in.-thick bed of sand. The edges of the slab are protected by steel angles.

Transit Sheds at the Port of Lagos, Nigeria, Africa. Behind a 2,500-ft extension of the Apapa Wharf and on part of 100 acres of reclaimed land created by the deposition of dredged sand in the area behind the wharf, four modern transit sheds were constructed and put into service in 1956. These together with other facilities make one of the largest harbor developments to be carried out on the West Coast of Africa since the war, and are described in the *Dock and Harbour Authority* issue of April, 1956. The port is being operated by the Nigerian Ports Authority.

The first shed is a two-story building, 487 ft 6 in. long and 100 ft wide, the upper story being used for passenger accommodations and mail, and the lower floor for cargo. Covered loading platforms for railroad cars and trucks are provided along the rear and at the ends of the building. Four electric elevators at the rear and one passenger elevator at the harbor side provide access between the upper and lower floors. A 12-ft-wide balcony at the upper-floor level and an aluminum gangway spanning between the balcony and the ship provide access for passengers. The passengers' accommodations comprise a waiting room with immigration counter, lunch counter, toilets, telephones, etc., and a customs examination room.

The other three sheds are single-story buildings for the import and export of general cargo. One is 350 and two are 425 ft long, and all are 150 ft wide. A typical cross section through one of the sheds is shown in Fig. 6.15. Steel roof trusses span the 150-ft width and give an unobstructed floor area for the storage and handling of cargo by mechanical equipment. The roof is covered with corrugated-asbestos cement sheeting and the walls are constructed of hollow precast-concrete blocks, 18 in. thick. Large sliding doors are provided in alternate 25-ft bays along the front and rear of the shed, with those in the rear leading to a continuous covered truck- and rail-loading platform.

Among the other important features of the port is the produce warehouse, which is 450 ft long and 150 ft wide, with truck and rail platforms along each of the long sides. The construction of the warehouse is similar to that of the transit sheds except that there are columns every 75 ft along the center of the building, which support a lattice girder carrying two intermediate transverse trusses.

This modern port also includes a second warehouse, 195 ft long by 80 ft wide; two small buildings for the storage of dangerous cargo; a two-story building, 233 ft long by 67 ft wide, for the Customs Depart-

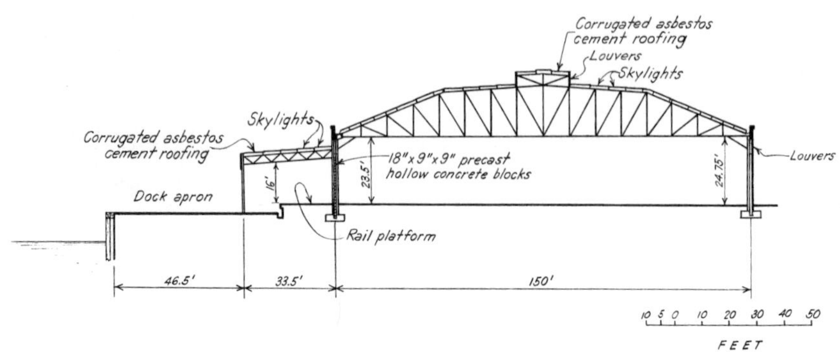

FIG. 6.15 Cross section of transit shed at the port of Lagos, Nigeria. (*From Dock and Harbour Authority, April,* 1956.)

ment; a second two-story building, 229 ft long by 19 ft wide, for the various shipping companies and importers; repair shops, police station, fire and ambulance station, and various comfort stations. Figure 6.16 shows the general arrangement of these port buildings.

Banana-handling Facilities at the Port of Rouen, France. In 1958, an up-to-date transit shed of reinforced and prestressed concrete was added to a newly constructed wharf in the port of Rouen, and is described in considerable detail in the November, 1958, issue of the *Dock and Harbour Authority.*

The facilities provide for the unloading of bananas from vessels up to 450 ft in length and moving a cargo of 1,500 tons, in about eleven working hours; the sorting and storing of the bananas in a modern shed, which is maintained at a temperature of approximately 55°F; and the shipping of the fruit inland by rail and truck. The shed has a storage capacity of 1,200 tons, but, since the bananas are shipped inland at the rate of 100 tons an hour, its size is adequate to handle the entire 1,500 tons unloaded from the vessel. Bucket elevators and conveyors transport the bananas from the ship's holds to the receiving area inside the shed. A continuous hatchway along the wharf side of the shed, with removable covers,

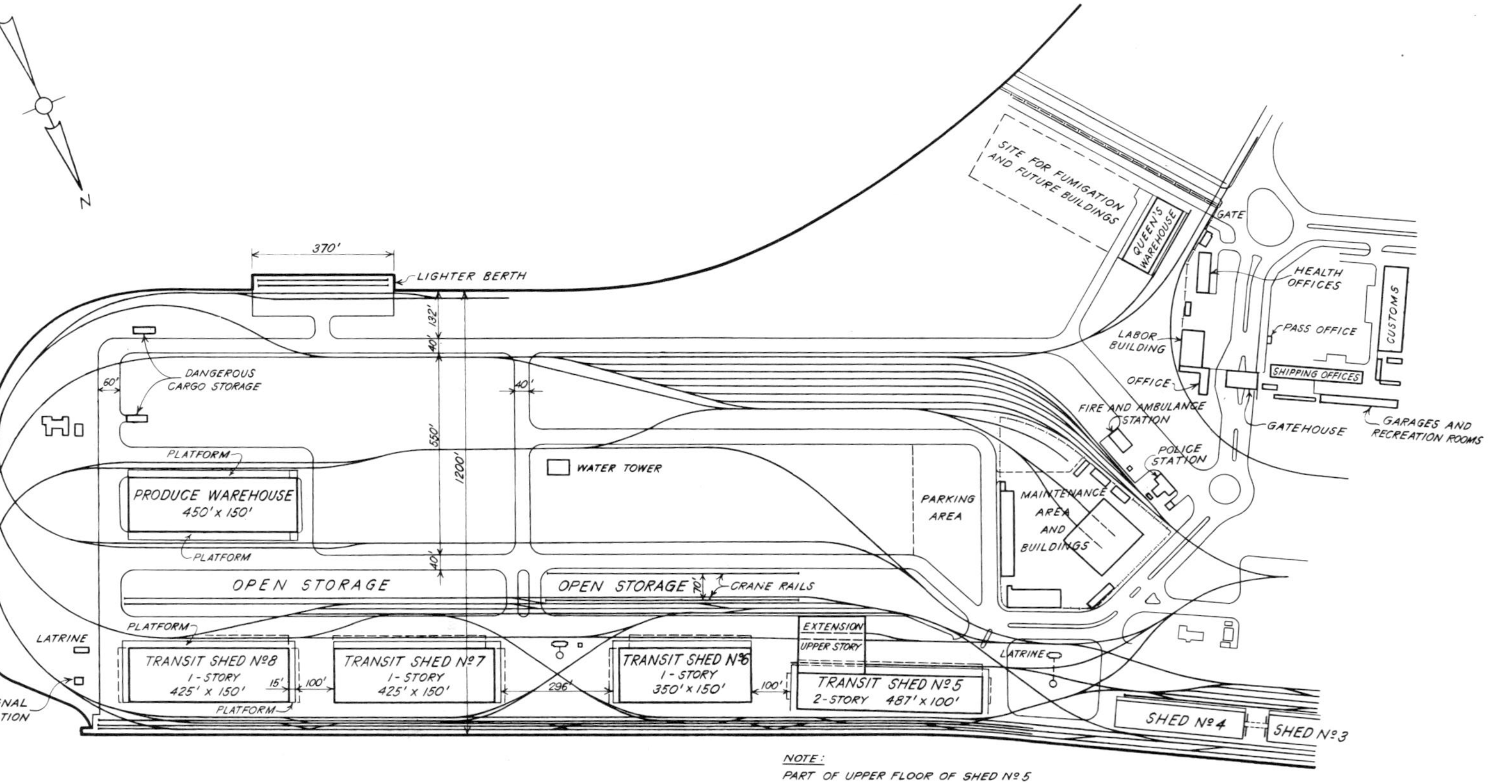

FIG. 6.16 General arrangement of port buildings at Lagos, Nigeria. (*From Dock and Harbour Authority, April,* 1956.)

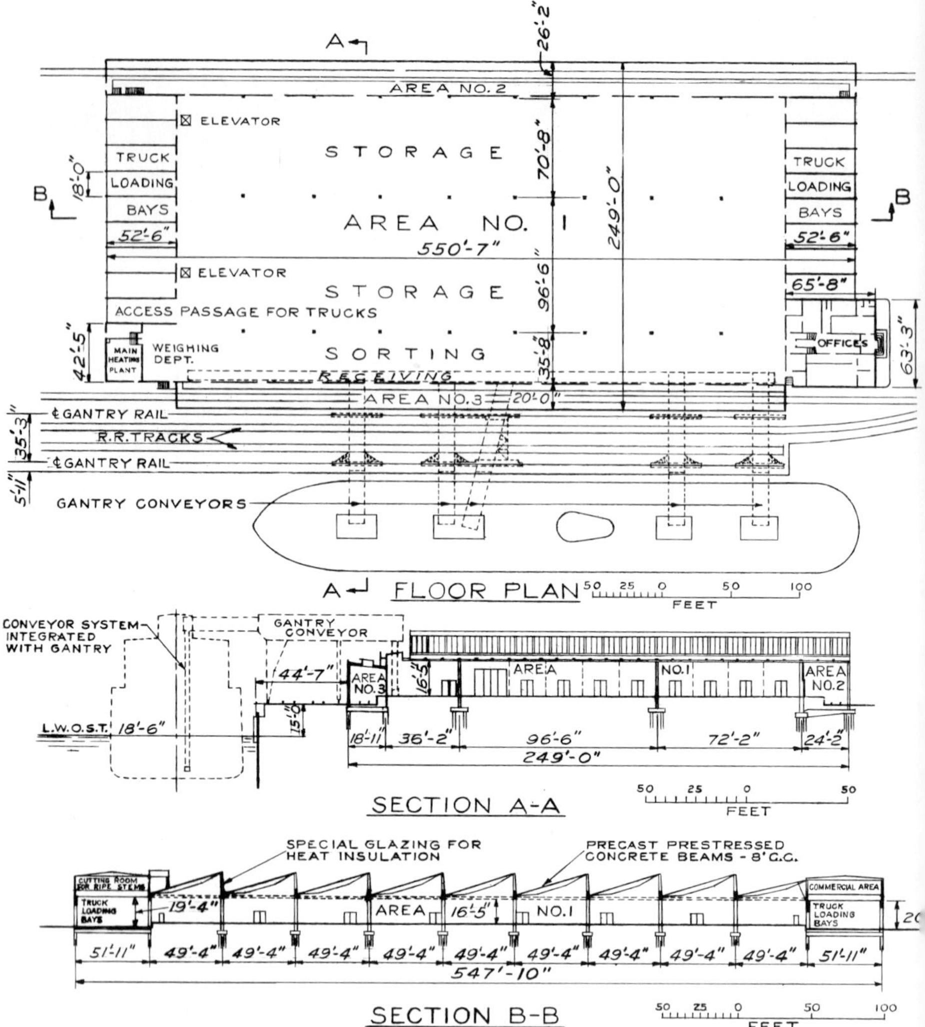

FIG. 6.17 Transit shed for banana handling at the port of Rouen, France. (*From Dock and Harbour Authority, November,* 1958.)

enables the bucket elevator at the inshore end of the banana unloader to be lowered into the building.

The ground-floor plan, transverse and longitudinal sections, is shown in Fig. 6.17. The building is a one-story structure, except for a two-story wing at each end, and has a ground-floor area of 136,000 sq ft, a length of 547 ft 10 in., and a width of 249 ft. The ground floor is at truck- and rail-loading platform height. A clear headroom of 16 ft 5 in. is provided within the main shed, the roof of which is of saw-tooth construction. The main flooring consists of a bituminous concrete surfacing laid on a macadam base. The roof is constructed of special precast units spanning 8 ft and insulated with approximately 2½ in. of expanded cork, which is made watertight by a bituminous covering surfaced with granulated slate. Flat portions of the roof are of reinforced concrete with two layers of asphalt.

The main shed, including the rail-loading gallery at the rear, comprises nine bays, 49 ft 4 in. in width, which are framed by prestressed-concrete beams 220 ft 9 in. in length, and which are continuous over three spans and cantilevered at one end. The framing of the saw-tooth roof consists of precast- prestressed-concrete beams with a span of 50 ft 10 in., which are spaced 8 ft on centers. These beams are supported at their lower end by the bottom flange of the main transverse prestressed I beam, and at their upper end by vertical posts, which, in turn, rest on the main girder. The vertical face of each saw-tooth section of the roof is glazed for a height of 9 ft 10 in.

The temperature inside the building is controlled at $55 \pm 2°F$ throughout the year by 34 thermostatically controlled air-heating units. In warm weather the building is artificially cooled at night by supplying fresh air to the heating units, the cool air being maintained during the daytime by the thermal insulation.

6.4 Cold-storage Buildings

When foods which require refrigeration are to be shipped by refrigerated boats and distributed inland by rail or truck, a cold-storage building must be provided on the dock in such a position that the frozen goods can be taken from the refrigerated ship and placed inside the cold-storage building in as short a time as possible, so as to keep the possible temperature change at a minimum. In this way deterioration of the foods can also be kept at a minimum, as the basic principle in the refrigeration of foods is to keep them at the same temperature and humidity as when first frozen. Most large cold-storage buildings will have to be multistory and should be designed with setbacks or balconies facing the dock, so that the frozen foods can be transferred directly from the ship to hand trucks, which will then take the commodities directly into the refrigerated rooms or to the elevators, if the upper floors do not have balconies.

The main commodities usually stored are meat, dairy produce, fish, fruit, and vegetables. All have what is known as a critical temperature which is governed by the water content, and as a result some foods can be frozen while others have to be chilled. Table 6.1, reproduced from the September, 1958, issue of the *Dock and Harbour Authority*, which describes the new cold-storage building at Southampton, shows the cold-storage temperature for various foods. The operation of the cold-storage plant is a very specialized one where the maintenance of correct temperature, air circulation, and humidity are of the greatest importance to keep the food of good quality.

Table 6.1 Cold-storage Temperatures for Various Foods

Commodity	Storage temperature, °F	Critical temperature, °F	Storage period
Meat:			
Chilled	30	28	10–15 days
Frozen	15	10	1–10 months
Dairy products:			
Butter	15	5	1–6 months
Frozen eggs	5	0	1–2 years
Shell eggs	31	30	6–10 months
Cheese	40	35	1–6 months
Fish	0	5	2–3 months
Fruit:			
Apples	36	31	1–6 months
Pears	32	30	1–4 months
Oranges	32	31	1–4 months
Vegetables:			
Green	35	32	10–20 days
Root	38	34	1–3 months

An excellent example of efficient and safe handling and storing of refrigerated foods at dock side is the new cold-storage building at Southampton Docks, England, which was completed in 1958 to replace the building destroyed in World War II. Figure 6.18 shows a cross section and second-floor plan of the new building.

The building is 250 ft long, 150 ft wide, and 60 ft high and has four floors. The ground floor is used for transit purposes, and accommodates both rail and truck traffic. Four 3,000-lb elevators, located in the middle of the building, serve the upper floors. The second and third floors are refrigerated, and the fourth floor is for refrigerating in the future, which will then provide a total storage capacity of 7,000 tons of frozen cargo.

The floors and columns are of reinforced concrete, and the exterior walls are 9-in. brick. Cork is used for insulation and is generally in 8-in.

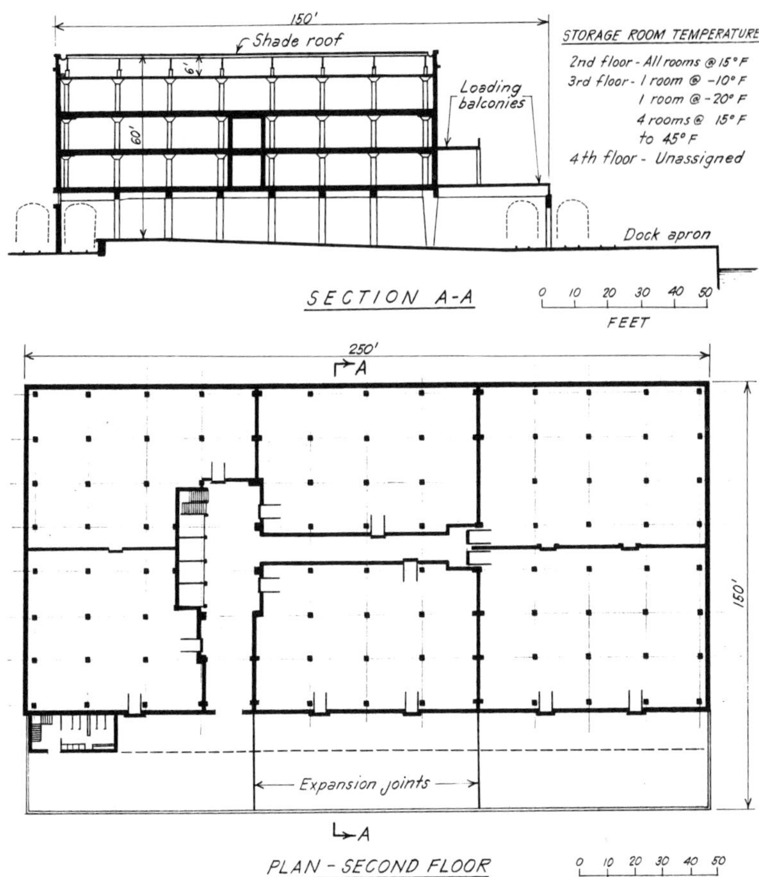

FIG. 6.18 Cold-storage building at Southampton Docks, England. (*From Dock and Harbour Authority, September,* 1958.)

thickness. Insofar as possible, the cork provides a complete envelope of insulation around the refrigerated space to stop heat leaking into the cold rooms from outside.

A feature of the construction is a double roof, the regular roof being a reinforced concrete slab, which is shaded with a light asbestos roof placed 6 ft above the slab. The latter is supported by steel trusses resting on reinforced-concrete stub columns.

The second floor is divided into six cold-storage rooms, approximately

80 by 60 by 10 ft high. Corridors provide access from the loading balconies and elevators to the various rooms. Two doors are provided for each room, leading to the corridors and connecting adjacent rooms, and in addition there are doors in the exterior front wall leading to the balconies. The remaining upper floors are similar in layout.

The floors are designed to carry a live load of 250 lb per sq ft. The second floor is a conventional beam and two-way slab design. The remaining floors are designed as flat slabs to provide flat surfaces on which to place the cork insulation.

The second floor is insulated with 8-in. thick cork on walls and floors, and the third floor 10-in. cork on walls and 8-in. cork on floors. The future insulation on the fourth floor will be similar to that on the first floor. The cork floor is protected by a 2½-in.-thick granolithic surfacing with a light wire mesh. The walls are protected by cement finish and 2- by 2-in. vertical wood battens with 7- by 1¼-in. horizontal bumper strips at hand-truck level. Columns are insulated and protected for a height of 4 ft above the floor in a similar manner. In addition to protecting the cork from damage, the wood battens provide a space for air circulation between the stored cargo and the wall.

The door openings are 4 ft 8 in. wide by 6 ft 6 in. high. The doors are approximately 10 in. thick, of wood construction with cork insulation, and metal clad with galvanized sheet metal. The doors weigh about 800 lb and can be operated from both sides. A heating element on the meeting faces of the door and frame prevents ice from forming, which would make it difficult to open the door. Each door is provided with an air lock on the inside of the room, which is constructed of wood and cork partitions, with self-closing rubber swing doors at the end of the lock. The air lock helps to reduce the loss of cold air from the room when the heavy insulated door is opened.

6.5 Port Administration Buildings

Facilities for the administration of the port will vary considerably depending upon the system of administration, the geographical location of the port, and its size. Comparing the methods used in various ports of the world it is difficult to find anything approaching a standard operation. It is becoming more generally recognized, however, that a centralized administrative agency with broad powers is essential for the efficient and economical operation of a port.

Administration of the port may be under the control of the national government, the municipality, port authority, private concern, or a combination of these various interests. However, jurisdiction over customs, immigration, and quarantine at ports of entry will be vested in the national government.

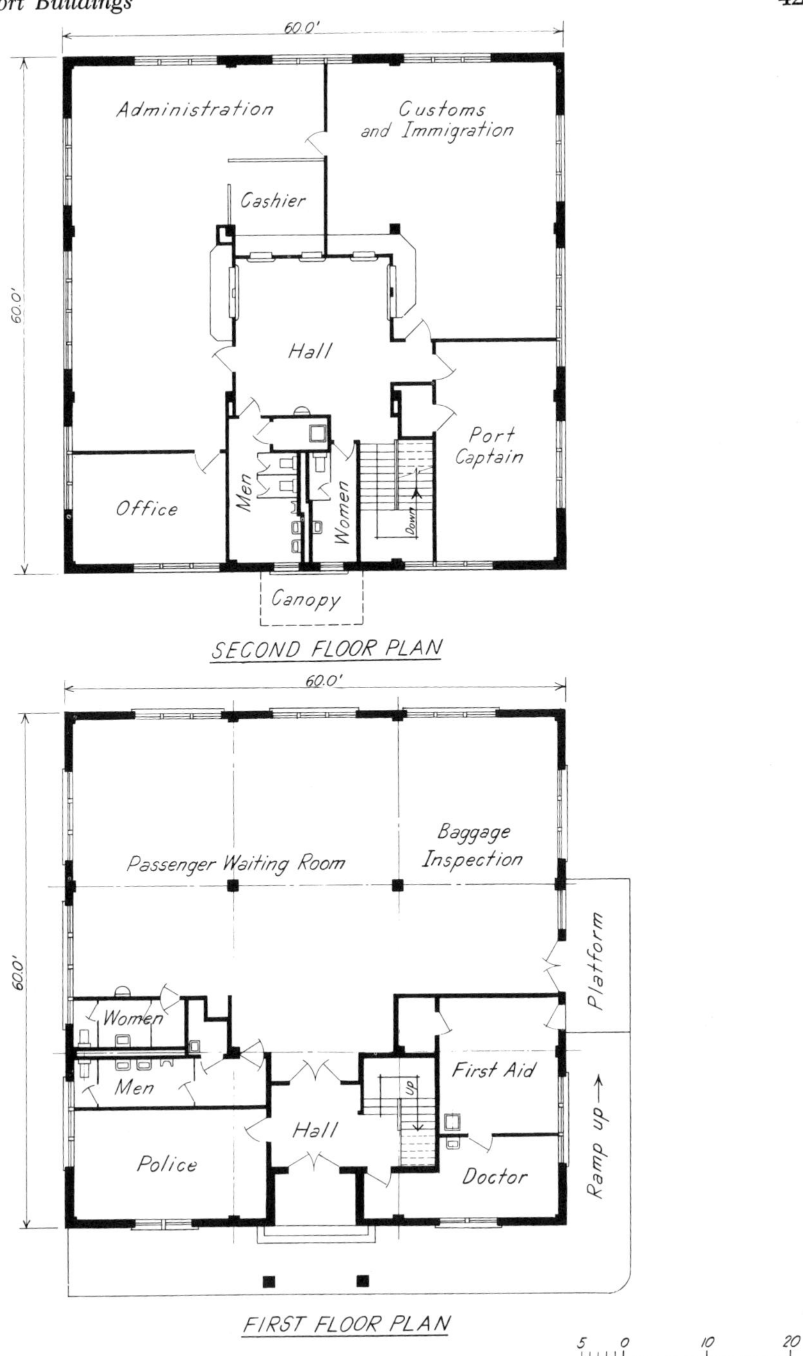

FIG. 6.19 Administration building for small government-owned port.

Figure 6.19 shows the floor plans of an administration building for a small government-owned port, which does not have a separate transit shed for passengers. The port administration under the direction of the port captain, the port security or police, customs inspection and immigration, waiting room, first aid, and rest rooms are all centralized in one building close to the docks. In marked contrast are the facilities for the administration of the port of New York, which is vested in the Port of New York Authority in its large office building in downtown Manhattan, and the Department of Marine and Aviation.

Chapter 7 GENERAL CARGO-HANDLING EQUIPMENT

7.1 Introduction

In this age of mechanical progress in all fields of commerce and industry, the field of cargo handling is no exception to the trend of mechanization. Great strides have been made, and are still being made, in increasing the efficiency of shiploading and unloading operations. A modern port should take advantage of every opportunity for mechanization, both to hold down labor costs and to minimize the time that a ship must remain in port.

With respect to the type of handling equipment required, the materials carried by ships can be classified in two general categories: general cargo and bulk cargo. *General cargo* includes items that are shipped as units, like automobiles and machinery, and materials in any kind of package, like bales, bags, barrels, or boxes. General cargo, as so defined, requires certain care in handling, to prevent damage, and in stowing, to trim the ship and to prevent shifting. *Bulk cargo,* on the other hand, can be defined as loose, unpackaged material that can be poured or pumped freely into the ship's holds. This category includes more or less free-flowing dry materials like grain, ore, and coal, and also liquids, of which the most important are petroleum and petroleum products. Since bulk handling is faster and cheaper than unit or package handling, many products, formerly packaged, are now being shipped in bulk. Examples of such materials are portland cement, sugar, and many liquids, including even orange juice and wine. For material unsuited to bulk shipment, once packaged in a size that could be handled by one man, the trend is to larger packages suited to efficient handling by machine. The handling of bulk cargo is discussed in Chap. 8; this chapter will concern itself with equipment for general cargo.

7.2 Loading and Unloading the Ship

With rare exceptions, ships are loaded and unloaded by hoisting cargo through the deck hatches. The hoisting equipment varies to suit the requirements of the cargo, the ship, and the port facilities.

General-purpose Equipment. The majority of general cargo is handled in lifts of 5 tons or less, generally considerably less. Equipment for this

FIG. 7.1 Loading palletized cargo with ship's gear. (*Courtesy of the Clark Equipment Co.*)

class of lifting has undergone little basic change in recent years, except for a trend toward larger capacities, and refinements leading to increased speed.

Ship's gear. Each hatch of a typical cargo vessel is equipped with a pair of cargo booms. For loading or unloading, one of these is stayed over the offshore edge of the hatch, the other overhanging the wharf. The cargo hook hangs from a link to which both hoisting lines are attached. By joint manipulation of two winches, the operator can drop the hook into either side of the hold and maneuver the load vertically and horizontally at high speeds. This method of handling is shown in Fig. 7.1. Some multistory sheds are equipped with cargo beams supported on a framework running the length of the shed above the roof. By reaving a line from one of the ship's winches through a block attached to this beam instead of over the shore-side boom, goods may be transferred between the hold and an upper story of the shed. The use of the ship's gear is the standard method for loading and unloading ships in the United States.

Wharfside cranes. The fast-acting, revolving, level-luffing crane is the popular device for shiploading and unloading in European and many

FIG. 7.2 Level-luffing cranes at the Port of Hamburg, West Germany.

other world ports. The port of Hamburg, for example, has nearly 900 in use. The term *level luffing* means that the crane is so rigged that the boom can be luffed (raised or lowered) without changing the height of the load. The fast action of the crane is partly due to the fact that the operator can hoist, swing, and luff all at once, and still keep his load under control. These cranes are mounted on portal or semiportal frames designed to clear railway or truck traffic on the apron. The frames move on tracks parallel to the wharf. The commonest crane sizes are in the capacity range of 3 to 5 tons (see Fig. 7.2). Special rubber-tired mobile cranes with gooseneck booms are also occasionally used for this purpose.

Heavy-lift Equipment. For heavy lifts, which may run up to 50 or 100 tons or more in the case of a locomotive or any other piece of heavy machinery, there are three classes of equipment that are commonly used.

Any one of these is necessarily much slower than the general-purpose equipment described above, which is the reason that ocean freight rates include a "heavy lift charge" for items weighing more than a specified limit.

FIG. 7.3 Slat conveyor loading baggage on passenger ship. (*Courtesy of the Link-Belt Co.*)

Ship's gear. Most general cargo ships are equipped, over at least one hold, with an additional boom, designed for lifting 50 tons or more. This boom can be swung over the ship's side by means of vang lines.

Wharfside equipment. Fixed derricks on the wharf, to which the ship must be brought, or mobile cranes operating on the wharf deck, are sometimes used. The latter piece of equipment requires special design of the wharf to support the heavy concentrated loads imposed by the crawlers, wheels, or outriggers.

Floating equipment. Some of the heaviest of loads are handled by floating cranes or derricks. These normally operate on the offshore side of the ships, transferring cargo to barges, for which it must be rehandled. The boom of a heavy-lift floating crane is visible in the background in Fig. 7.2.

Special equipment. There are many special-purpose ships and special-purpose wharves for which unusual and ingenious machinery has been developed. Some ships have openings in the side through which cargo can be handled by belt or slat conveyors; this method is useful for loading and unloading mail and baggage on passenger ships (see Fig. 7.3). Special conveyors are used to handle bananas and bagged goods. Large containers are hoisted by equipment individually designed for the particular sizes and shapes of containers used. This equipment may be either on the ship or on the wharf, and ranges in size up to overhead traveling cranes that carry loaded freight cars.

7.3 Handling on Land

A limited amount of material can be hoisted directly between the ship and highway trucks or railroad cars on the wharf. However, the greater part of the contents of a general cargo ship usually requires handling into and out of a transit shed for sorting and temporary storage. It is in this field that the greatest progress has been made in mechanization.

Fork-lift Trucks. The fork-lift truck, as developed during and since World War II, has done more than any other single device to revolutionize cargo handling on the wharf. This versatile little machine can pick up unit loads or palletized loads off the apron, run them into the shed, and there stack them up to 16 or 18 ft high. This operation is shown in Fig. 7.4. This stacking ability, of course, makes for much more efficient use of floor space. To take advantage of it, modern transit sheds are designed with at least 20 ft of clear headroom. Fork-lift trucks are considered efficient for horizontal travel up to about 150 ft. The most popular sizes have capacities of about 2 or 3 tons, although they are available, for special purposes, up to 20-ton capacity. These trucks can be fitted with clamps or other special handling devices for lifting certain unpalletized material, such as rolled paper or baled material, as shown in Fig. 7.5. They are available with side forks for long loads, like bundles of pipe or lumber, although straddle trucks are more generally used for such loads (see Fig. 7.6).

Mobile Cranes. Compact, agile, pneumatic-tired mobile cranes have been developed, some with hydraulically operated extensible booms, for operation in close quarters (see Fig. 7.7). They perform a function similar to that of the fork-lift trucks, and share their limitations with respect to horizontal travel. Since the boom and sling occupy at least 3 or 4 ft above the load, they are not able to stack material up close to the underside

FIG. 7.4 Fork-lift truck stacking palletized goods in transit shed. (*Courtesy of the Hyster Co.*)

FIG. 7.5 Fork-lift truck with attachment for lifting and turning rolls of paper. (*Courtesy of the Hyster Co.*)

FIG. 7.6 Straddle truck. (*Courtesy of the Hyster Co.*)

FIG. 7.7 Mobile crane. (*Courtesy of the Hyster Co.*)

of ceiling structures, as fork-lift trucks can. On the other hand, they are better able to handle long or awkwardly shaped objects.

Tractor Trains. Where distances between shipside and storage areas are too great for efficient use of fork-lift trucks, tractor-drawn trains of low-bed, small-wheeled trucks are used, as shown in Fig. 7.8. The trucks are loaded or unloaded at shipside by the shiploading gear, and in the storage area by fork-lift trucks. Of course, these trains are also useful for

FIG. 7.8 Tractor train. (*Courtesy of the Clark Equipment Co.*)

transporting material that cannot be palletized, or is otherwise unsuitable for fork-lift operation. Such a situation arises in the case of a mixed cargo containing many small packages consigned to many different addresses. In such a case there is no avoiding a hand-sorting operation.

Conveyors. It is in the field of bulk material handling that conveyors are best suited to perform their special function, which is the automatic movement of a continuous flow of material. However, certain types of conveyors have been found useful to some extent in general cargo movements on the wharf. Goods in units small enough for a man to lift may be transported horizontally for short distances on portable roller or belt conveyors. Spiral chutes bring material down from an upper to a lower floor. Portable inclined belt or slat conveyors are used for stacking bags and other packages. Overhead chain or monorail conveyors provide horizontal transportation within sheds. Nowadays most of these functions have been taken over by fork-lift trucks. It is only on old wharves, unsuitable for fork-lift trucks, or for special, single-purpose operations, like banana handling, that the conveyor remains an important means of general cargo handling.

Overhead Cranes. Traveling bridge or gantry cranes, so common in industrial plants and warehouses, are useful in transit sheds only in special cases where cargoes are uniformly shipped in large packages. As more and more goods are packed this way, their use may increase in the future. They require extra headroom in the shed, but they can pile high, and they take up no floor space and require no working aisles.

7.4 Handling in the Hold

The problems involved in stowing and recovering cargo in the hold of a ship are similar to those met with in the transit shed, but with the big difference that lack of space greatly reduces the opportunity for mechanization. Fork-lift trucks can be lowered into the hold, but their usefulness is limited by odd-shaped spaces, low headroom, and the impossibility of leaving an adequate working aisle as the hold fills. Portable roller conveyors are of some use for horizontal movement of cargo, but a great deal of this must still be done by manpower, using hand trucks or dollies. Modern ships, designed with these problems in mind, are much better suited to mechanized cargo handling than some of the older ones.

7.5 Pallets

The efficient use of fork-lift trucks requires the consolidation of small packages into suitable load units, which is done by stacking on pallets. The pallet is a double platform, separated a few inches by battens to permit the insertion of the fork. The top platform supports the load, and the bottom one provides a flat surface for stacking. Modern pallets are made with an eye at each corner, for convenience in attaching slings. Pallets are most commonly made of wood, and come, for general use, in sizes up to about 4 by 6 ft. Special sizes are made for special purposes. Material unsuitable for palletization is still handled in cargo nets.

Palletization at the Source. Sometimes the shipper straps or lashes his goods into unit loads on pallets which stay attached until the shipment reaches its ultimate destination. This method of packing eliminates all manhandling, and greatly speeds up operations at a properly equipped port. Its usefulness, however, depends on there being enough similarly packed cargo to justify special organization of the handling gangs, and also on whether the ship's hold is adapted for mechanical stowage. Prepalletization has not become a widespread practice, and probably never will until the steamship companies are able to offer a rate reduction adequate to repay the shipper at least part of the cost. At present its value to the shipper lies in the probability of a reduction of losses through damage and pilferage. The French Line estimates that reduction in thefts is enough to justify the entire expense of palletizing cases of cognac.

Palletization at the Port. Most pallets in use today are used as stevedores' tools. They are the property of the port-operating organization and never leave the port. In a typical import operation, such as shown

FIG. 7.9 Pallets and fork-lift trucks on wharf apron. (*Courtesy of the Clark Equipment Co.*)

in Fig. 7.9, pallets are lowered into the hold, loaded by hand, and transferred to the wharf apron. The loaded pallets are then picked up by fork-lift trucks and stacked in the transit shed. Later, they are recovered from the stacks by the same trucks and set on highway trucks or railway cars, where the goods are removed from the pallets and stowed by hand. The pallets are then returned to storage for re-use. This whole process, of course, is reversed for material being exported. Palletization at a busy port requires a large stock of pallets; the Port of Marseilles uses about 80,000.

7.6 Containers

"Containerization," the packing of small items or bulk materials into larger re-usable containers, is the technique that appears to offer the greatest promise for the future development of mechanized cargo handling. So-called "piggy-back" containers have been used successfully for many years for land transportation. They are made in modules of the lengths of railway cars and highway trucks, to be readily transferable from one to the other. For ocean shipment, similar containers are used, with the difference that they must be designed for stacking. Since some part of the journey of almost any shipment is by truck, the maximum size of containers is limited by highway clearance requirements. The largest size in common use is 8 by 8 by 35 ft. The most efficient size for load units to be shipped by any means of transportation, land or sea, is the maximum that can be handled by the equipment available at the shipping point, the final destination, and the intermediate transfer points. It would be futile to equip a port, which is by its very nature a transfer point, with machinery to handle lifts too heavy to be handled at the terminals or at other transfer points, such as a railroad station where goods are transferred between railway and highway carriers.

Containers in Western Europe. Containers have established themselves as a basic feature of the land transportation of goods in Great Britain and Western Europe, and are used to a lesser extent for coastwise shipping. A 1958 census showed over 250,000 containers of more than 35 cu ft in use, 75 per cent of them owned by the railroads. The larger ones tend to approximate a volume of 350 cu ft with a maximum weight of 3 to 5 tons. Containers of this size can be handled by standard port equipment. Ships have been, and are being, built or adapted for carrying containers of 350 and 700 cu ft.

Containers in the United States. Containers in the United States range from pallet size to van size. The United States Army Transportation Corps has developed a container of 295 cu ft to suit its special needs in world-wide service. The Corps uses about 80,000 of these containers. The Navy has its own system of containers on a smaller scale. Three major groups of sizes are in use in commercial maritime service:

275 cu ft, measuring 7 ft 9 in. by 6 ft 5 in. by 6 ft 10 in.

900 cu ft, measuring 17 ft 0 in. by 8 ft 0 in. by 8 ft 0 in. Two of these will go on a semitrailer truck chassis.

2,000 cu ft, measuring 35 ft 0 in. by 8 ft 0 in. by 8 ft 0 in. One of these becomes the body of a semitrailer truck.

Standardization. Dozens of local, national, and international associations and committees, both in this country and in Europe, have worked for years on the many problems involved in the design and standardization of shipping containers. These groups represent government agencies, technical societies, sea and land carriers, equipment manufacturers, and potential shippers. Containerization for land transportation, being an older development, and having somewhat less complicated problems to solve, is well ahead of sea transportation in its progress toward standardization. Much remains to be done before containers, particularly the largest sizes, become common in transoceanic international trade. Their present usefulness is mostly for coastwise trade, between ports having similar loading facilities and land transportation facilities available.

Customs Regulations. The United States and some European countries now permit temporary import of foreign containers and reimport of their

FIG. 7.10 Fork-lift and straddle trucks handling van containers. (*Courtesy of the Clark Equipment Co.*)

own containers without duty. Customs inspection of the contents is another problem. To unpack and repack a container for this purpose at a port would be to defeat its basic purpose. There is need for more widespread international agreements for passing sealed containers through ports without opening, perhaps by arranging for inspection at the source or at the destination. Such agreements are already in force in a limited way among European countries.

Port Equipment. Containers weighing up to about 5 tons can be handled by conventional port equipment. Efficient handling of larger containers requires special equipment on the ship or on the wharf, which can be justified only by a large-scale container operation. Large movable cranes on the wharf or traveling gantry cranes on the ship may be used for shiploading. If rehandling is necessary on land, cranes or special oversize fork-lift trucks may be used. There is a giant straddle truck on the market capable of setting a van-sized container on a truck, or of stacking the containers two high on the ground, as shown in Fig. 7.10.

Van Containers in United States Coastwise Trade. It is in th (including noncontiguous domestic ports) that most van-sized ma containers are in use today. They have been in use for some time between the west coast and Hawaii and between Seattle and Alaska. In Seattle,

FIG. 7.11 Van container being lifted from truck chassis to Pan-Atlantic containership. (*Courtesy of the Pan-Atlantic Steamship Corp.*)

they are loaded two deep on barges and towed to Alaska. The lifting is done by crawler cranes on the wharf. Seatrain Lines, a company that has for years been transporting loaded railway freight cars between Atlantic, Cuban, and Gulf ports, has also begun handling van containers.

The highest present development of the potentialities of containerization is illustrated by the Sea-Land Service operated by Pan-Atlantic Steamship Corporation, as shown in Figs. 7.11 and 7.12. This service provides door-to-door pickup and delivery throughout the eastern and southern United States and Puerto Rico by means of coordinated truck and ship operation. The service was inaugurated in its present form in October, 1957, and as of April, 1959, operated 6 "containerships," approximately 3,000 containers (35 by 8 by 8 ft), 1,740 semitrailer chassis, and

FIG. 7.12 Container being loaded into hold of containership. (*Courtesy of the Pan-Atlantic Steamship Corp.*)

175 tractors. The ships put in at a dozen Atlantic and Gulf ports from Boston to Houston, as well as Puerto Rico. A typical shipment is loaded on a trailer-mounted container at the shipping point, sealed, and hauled to the port, where the loaded trailer is parked in an open storage area to await the arrival of a ship. When a ship is being loaded, the trailer is hauled to the wharf apron, from which the container is hoisted directly into the hold. Opening a container at the port to rehandle its contents is necessary only in the case of LTL (less than trailer load) shipments

bound for different ports. At the unloading port the container is hoisted from the ship directly to a trailer chassis for delivery to its destination. Local pickups and deliveries in the port area are made by the company's own trucking equipment. Longer hauls are turned over to highway common carriers. The containerships are converted C-2 dry-cargo vessels, with the intermediate decks and bulkheads removed and the hatches enlarged. The large container hatches remaining are subdivided by open steel framing, which acts as guides for the containers. Spanning the hatches are two traveling gantries operating on rails along the sides of the ship. Each gantry carries an overhead traveling crane of 50-ton capacity which moves across the ship and out over the wharf on cantilever arms, which can be folded down when the crane is not operating. Each ship carries 226 containers with about 4,000 net tons of payload freight. The port requirements for this operation are a wharf apron suitable for truck traffic, a large open storage area, and a transit shed for sorting LTL shipments.

7.7 Roll-on Roll-off Service

Ships designed for this service have side or end doors through which vehicles can be driven. Either complete vehicles or trailers without their tractors may be shipped. As a method of transporting cargo, the usefulness of this system seems to be limited to special conditions, such as short ferry trips. It is used by the United States Army, but with limited success because most existing piers and wharves are not designed for it. For maximum efficiency, the port should be equipped with movable approach ramps, such as those commonly used at ferry slips, capable of adjustment to varying tides and varying ship draft.

Chapter 8 BULK CARGO SHIPPING TERMINALS

8.1 Introduction

For the handling of general cargo, as described in Chap. 7, a typical shipping terminal must be equipped to load and unload many different kinds of goods. A bulk cargo terminal, on the other hand, is usually designed for a single function, such as loading grain or unloading ore. A transfer station has both loading and unloading facilities; for example at many European ports, imported coal is unloaded from ships and reloaded on river barges for inland delivery; frequently ore is brought down to a port by river boats for transfer to ocean-going vessels. Sometimes, at an isolated bulk shipping terminal, facilities must be provided for bringing in supplies and equipment to carry on the operation.

8.2 Storage Facilities

Adequate storage capacity is a basic requirement in any bulk cargo terminal, but the definition of adequate varies widely, and must be determined individually for each terminal. The minimum requirement is surge capacity to take up the slack between the rate of shiploading or unloading and the rate of inland transportation. More and more emphasis is being placed on the rapid loading and unloading of ore carriers and tankers in order to cut down turn-around time. As these vessels have increased in size, it has become necessary to provide larger bulk-storage facilities and equipment capable of handling the materials at rapid rates; for example, the loading of iron ore at 15,000 tons per hour or the unloading of a supertanker at the rate of 50,000 bbl per hr, rates unheard of a few years ago. Larger capacities are made necessary by seasonal restrictions on the production or use of the material being shipped, or by a limited shipping season. The shipping season for Lake Superior iron ore is only seven months a year; the receiving ports must therefore be equipped to unload and store enough ore to keep the mills operating the other five months. Agricultural products like grain and sugar must be stored between harvests for year-round use; if the product is destined for water shipment, the shipping terminal is an efficient place to store it. The type of storage facilities varies according to the shipping requirements and the nature of the material. They may take the form of extensive railroad yards for storing loaded cars, tanks for liquids, silos or warehouses for material requiring protection from weather, or open ground storage for nonperishable materials, like crushed stone, ore, and coal.

8.3 Material-handling Equipment

Liquids, of course, are pumped and some lightweight powdered or fine granular materials, like cement and grain, can be transported pneumatically. However, most bulk materials are handled by conveyors or buckets and frequently by a combination of the two.

Conveyors. The materials-handling industry has developed an almost countless variety of conveyors for special functions in industry. Among these, the types most useful in the operation of a cargo terminal are, first and foremost, belt conveyors; second, bucket elevators; and, less frequently, apron or pan conveyors, oscillating or vibrating conveyors, flight conveyors, and screw conveyors. For rapid movement of a wide variety of powdered, granular, and lumpy materials, belt conveyors are the most

FIG. 8.1 4,500-ton-per-hour traveling shiploader handling blended limestone on Lake Huron. (*Courtesy of the Wellman Engineering Co.*)

versatile. They can carry large quantities for long distances, horizontally or up and down slopes of 15 to 20°. With appropriate auxiliary equipment, they can be loaded or discharged at their terminals or at intermediate points. They are used to move material into and out of storage and into the ship's holds. The material can be stock-piled in open storage

FIG. 8.2 Bucket elevator with marine leg. (*Courtesy of the Stephens-Adamson Manufacturing Co.*)

by a traveling stacker having an inclined boom conveyor which sometimes is designed to be able to rotate 360°, enabling the material to be stored in piles along both sides of the conveyor; or it may be elevated by inclined conveyor to a distributing conveyor above the storage pile, which may be supported on a trestle or from the roof of the storage shed or silo. Reclaiming the material may be done by means of a reclaiming conveyor in a tunnel underneath the storage, or it may be loaded into hoppers which feed a conveyor above ground. The conveyor from storage to shipside may be served by a stationary or traveling tower on the wharf, which may have a hinged or retractable boom conveyor supporting a chute at its end through which the material will drop into the hold of the ship. Figure 8.1 shows a traveling shiploader handling blended limestone at the rate of 4,500 tons per hour. Bucket elevators, usually of lower capacity than belts, convey material vertically or up steep inclines. They are used for operations like filling silos, and, when mounted on a "marine leg," can be lowered into the ship's hold for unloading, as shown

FIG. 8.3 Two 10-ton traveling bauxite-unloading towers at Point Comfort, Texas. (*Courtesy of the Wellman Engineering Co.*)

in Fig. 8.2. The other types of conveyors mentioned are usually found in a port operation as auxiliary equipment, such as feeders, in a belt conveyor system.

Buckets. The clamshell bucket is the most used piece of equipment for high-speed unloading of bulk cargo. One type of bucket is designed for handling by ship's gear, another by revolving cranes, but the greatest capacity is attained by a bucket working from a traveling trolley on the boom of an unloading tower on the wharf. The tower may be stationary or traveling; the traveling type is a timesaver because it can be moved from hatch to hatch faster than the ship can be moved to a new position in front of a fixed tower. In order to obtain higher unloading speeds, two or more traveling towers can operate on one ship. Figure 8.3 shows two 10-ton traveling bauxite-unloading towers with special twister-type bucket trolley designed to rotate on a gantry base to work either side of a finger pier. These towers are generally equipped with hoppers into which the buckets may dump, and which in turn feed the material into railroad cars or trucks or to a belt conveyor system for transfer to storage. Sometimes the towers take the form of bridges extending back over inshore storage areas, as shown in Fig. 8.4. In these cases, the same bucket can be used for reclaiming the stored material. Such buckets can be made in capacities up to about 25 tons of ore per bite.

Drag-scraper buckets are useful for storing and reclaiming bulk materials. In Fig. 8.5, coal is unloaded from barges by a grab bucket on the

FIG. 8.4 17-ton man trolley unloading, stocking, and reclaiming bridge for the Steel Company of Canada at Hamilton, Ontario. (*Courtesy of the Mead Morrison Division, McKiernan-Terry Corp.*)

traveling unloading tower in the left background. The boom on the shore side of this tower carries a belt conveyor, which stacks coal in a long ridge behind the wharf apron. This ridge is distributed over the storage area by a drag scraper, whose traveling tail tower is seen in the left foreground. The scraper bucket also reclaims the coal for use, delivering it to a hopper at the foot of the inclined conveyor gallery shown on the right.

The Hulett-type unloader is used extensively for unloading ore at the Great Lakes ports, and is shown in Fig. 8.6.

Aerial Ropeways. Belt conveyors are in a class by themselves for really large-scale movement of bulk materials. However, for economical long-distance transportation of moderate quantities of such materials, aerial ropeways have certain advantages. A ropeway is capable of delivering

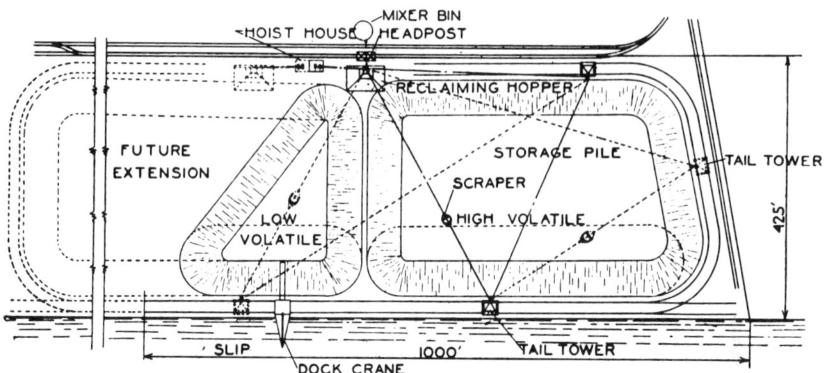

FIG. 8.5 A 7-cu-yd drag-scraper system for storing and reclaiming coal. (*Courtesy of Sauerman Bros., Inc.*)

FIG. 8.6 Wellman Hulett ore unloaders at a Great Lakes dock. (*Courtesy of the McDowell Co., Inc.*)

up to about 400 tons per hour over several miles of terrain impassable by other means. An appropriate application of a ropeway to marine purposes is to load ships that are forced to anchor a long distance from shore because of shallow water. This is illustrated in Fig. 8.7.

An example of such a facility is one that has been designed for a Caribbean location where salt is produced by the natural evaporation of sea water. In this design, a ropeway runs 3½ miles out to sea to reach

FIG. 8.7 Tramway used to load ships docked more than one mile offshore. (*Courtesy of the American Steel and Wire Division of the United States Steel Corp.*)

water deep enough for large ships. The support towers are 950 ft apart and rise 72 ft above water level. The owner's requirements are for the export of a million tons of salt a year, and the loading of a ship of 10,000 tons capacity in not more than 48 hours. To meet these requirements, the ropeway is designed for a capacity of 250 tons per hour.

Car Dumpers. Material brought to a port by rail is frequently unloaded by car dumpers which roll the cars over and pour out their contents. The material is usually received in a depressed hopper, from which it is transferred to storage by conveyors. One type of machine lifts the cars before dumping and delivers the material directly to the ship by means of an apron converging into a trimming chute.

8.4 Self-unloading Ships

There are many ships carrying crushed stone and coal on the Great Lakes which are loaded by conventional means, but which carry their own built-in unloading equipment. These ships have V-bottom hoppers built into their holds, with a series of bottom gates which feed material to two longitudinal pan or belt conveyors or drag scrapers operating in tunnels at the bottom of the ship. The material is transferred at one end of the ship to bucket elevators which in turn deliver it to a belt conveyor on a hinged boom capable of swinging out over either side of the ship. The boom conveyor can discharge directly to a storage pile, to a hopper

FIG. 8.8 Self-unloading ocean-going collier *Consolidation Coal.* (*Courtesy of the Stephens-Adamson Manufacturing Co.*)

feeding a conveyor system, or to barges. One of the largest ships of this type, and the first designed for ocean service, is the collier *Consolidation Coal,* which was built in 1958 (see Fig. 8.8). This ship has three parallel 42-in. belt conveyors under the holds, and a boom 250 ft long, carrying a 60-in. belt. The discharge rate is 3,600 tons per hour; the total capacity 24,000 tons.

Another form of self-unloading vessel is the cement barge, which is widely used for river traffic. In these barges, drag scrapers bring the cement to one end, from which it is discharged by cement pumps.

8.5 Terminal Facilities

Bulk cargo terminals vary widely; each one must be designed individually to meet the requirements of a number of variable conditions. Some of the major variables are:

Site conditions: the usual ones encountered in the location of cargo terminals, with somewhat less emphasis on quiet water and permanency of construction. Private ownership predominates.

Function: import or export of bulk material or both, with or without the handling of supplies and equipment.

Type of material to be handled: dry or liquid, powdered, granulated or lumpy, free flowing or sticky, perishable or durable.

Quantity requirements: annual, seasonal, or daily. Storage and shipping capacities are both interrelated with seasonal variations in use or production, and with the size and frequency of ships.

Available inland transportation: railroad, highway trucks, river craft, or conveyors.

Some bulk cargo terminals are built without a wharf or pier in the usual sense. In such a terminal the ships are moored offshore to dolphins or to fixed anchors, and served by a conveyor, a pipeline, or a ropeway. In another terminal, the ships may be moored to a wharf having a broad, heavily constructed apron capable of carrying railroad tracks and trucks as well as traveling loading or unloading towers. One common and efficient method of loading ships is by gravity chutes connected to high-level silos or bins. Grain silos are usually filled by pneumatic or bucket elevators, ore and coal bins by dumping from elevated railroad trestles.

Modern oil terminals of today are a specialized installation. They are discussed more fully in the following Sec. 8.6.

Minerals are being mined in more and more remote parts of the world. This sometimes leads to the establishment of shipping terminals in places so isolated that it is necessary to create self-sufficient communities for the housing of the operating personnel. In such a case the port designer is called on to lay out a complete town with streets, landscaping, power and water supply, sewers, homes, stores, and public buildings, such as an administration building, a town hall, a school, and a hospital.

8.6 Oil Terminals

In general, docking facilities or shore installations for tankers will consist of wharves, piers, or fixed mooring berths with mooring appurtenances and equipment for handling cargo hose to connect the ship's manifold to the pipelines on the dock, which will transport the products to and from the ship. However, the increase in size of tankers to where their draft now exceeds the depth of many of the navigable waters imposes a limitation on the use of such shore installations. In such cases, the tanker must either anchor in deep water and discharge its load by underwater pipeline or carry a reduced load which will keep its draft less than the depth of channel to be navigated to reach the dock. For instance, the tanker *Universe Leader* has a loaded draft of 46 ft 3 in. compared to an established minimum channel depth of 40 ft 0 in. in the Delaware River, 41 ft 0 in. in the Panama Canal, and 34 ft 0 in. in the Suez Canal.

The rate of loading and unloading has kept pace with the increase in size of tankers. The tanker's pumps are usually sized to enable it to be unloaded in about 16 hours. The pumping rate may vary from 10,000 bbl per hr for the T-2 tanker, to 25,000 bbl per hr for a 45,000-DWT supertanker, to 50,000 bbl per hr for an 87,000-DWT tanker like the *Universe Leader.*

Oil docks, in general, are of lighter construction than general cargo-handling docks as they usually do not require warehouses or extensive cargo-handling equipment. Since their main products are usually unloaded at a fixed point and transported by pipelines, the required area of solid dock is very much reduced, as are the width and length of the dock if supplemented by dolphins to take the bow and stern lines. For this reason, a full-length pier is not usually economical or essential, but if used it will usually be of skeleton construction, with the deck slab omitted at the pipeway.

The trend in recent years to the use of larger and deeper-draft tankers has resulted in the adoption of the fixed mooring berth, with its relatively small and light hose-handling platform, which is protected by breasting dolphins against which the tanker moors and is provided with separate dolphins to take the ship's mooring lines. The hose-handling platform may be connected to shore by a trestle which will support the pipelines, or, where the berth is a considerable distance offshore, the trestle may be omitted and the pipelines run out on the sea bottom.

In general, it may be said that oil-shipping terminals can be operated in less-protected water than would be required for general cargo-handling terminals. Installations have been found workable, although not recommended if it can be avoided, where the swells have been as high as 10 ft. In such unprotected waters the tanker is moored headed into the swells and is held 15 to 20 ft off the loading platform by mooring lines to dolphins or mooring buoys. The flexibility in the hose-handling structure permits a considerable amount of movement to take place without damaging either the ship or platform.

Another method of berthing and transferring liquid cargo in unprotected water is the offshore anchorage, which has been described in Sec. 5.11. This method is now used extensively for berthing the very large supertankers where there is not sufficient water within the harbor or alongside the dock for them to operate safely when fully loaded. The oil is transferred to or from shore by pumping through a submarine pipeline, the offshore end of which may be in water as deep as 60 ft and is connected with one or more hoses to the ship's manifold. This can be accomplished in the following manner.

1. The more conventional method is to have the hose lay on the sea bottom, the end being attached by chain to a hose-marker buoy (usually a small spherical or nun buoy). The end of the submarine line is also marked with a spar or nun buoy. The tanker, after mooring, then picks up the hose-marker buoy, using its own tackle, and the hose is hauled on board and is made fast to the manifold. The procedure is repeated in reverse order when the tanker is ready to cast off. This method has been used extensively and has worked well where the bottom is not too soft, and when the rate of transfer does not exceed that which can be handled through two 12-in. hose lines. Recently 16-in. hose has been used, and, to reduce its weight to within the lifting capacity of the supertanker's tackle, one of the hose manufacturers has developed a special pontoon-type hose which can be attached to the heavy 16-in. hose so as to give it added buoyancy. This size hose filled with oil weighs 172 lb per ft in air and 55 lb submerged in sea water. The submarine hose for a supertanker will be about 200 ft long, of which about 60 ft will be out of water when connected to the manifold at the time the ship is light. This length of hose will weigh 9 tons, which could be reduced to about 7 tons by the buoyancy of the pontoon, which is within the 7½-ton minimum lifting capacity of the boom on the 87,000-ton supertanker. The boom on the T-2 tanker has a lifting capacity of 3 tons which limits the maximum size hose to 8 in. A modification of the above arrangement is to use 12-in. hose for that part which will be out of water, thereby reducing considerably the load to be lifted by the ship's tackle, since 12-in. hose filled with oil weighs 114 lb per ft in air compared to 172 lb per ft for the 16-in. hose.

2. When the sea bottom is too soft to support the submarine hose, or when the unloading rate is so high that more than two hoses are required, the method of hose handling previously described becomes unsatisfactory. Suitable equipment for use where these conditions exist has been developed by Clifford Hartley, a renowned engineer in London, England, who has patented a submergible type of hose-handling structure known as the Hartley hoister. This piece of equipment, after undergoing extensive model testing, was first installed at Kuwait, a terminal in the Persian Gulf, but did not undergo any extensive use. A second installation was recently made in the Philippines for unloading an 87,000-deadweight-ton supertanker at the rate of 50,000 bbl per hr. Figure 8.9 illustrates this installation. Briefly, the hoister is a welded-pipe tower, the lower end of which is anchored by chain to a foundation in the sea bottom, which by means of air-controlled buoyancy tanks built into the structure can be made to lay on the sea bottom or to assume a nearly upright position with its top projecting some 40 ft above the water. The 18-in. pipes forming one side of the tower act as conduits for carrying the oil, the lower

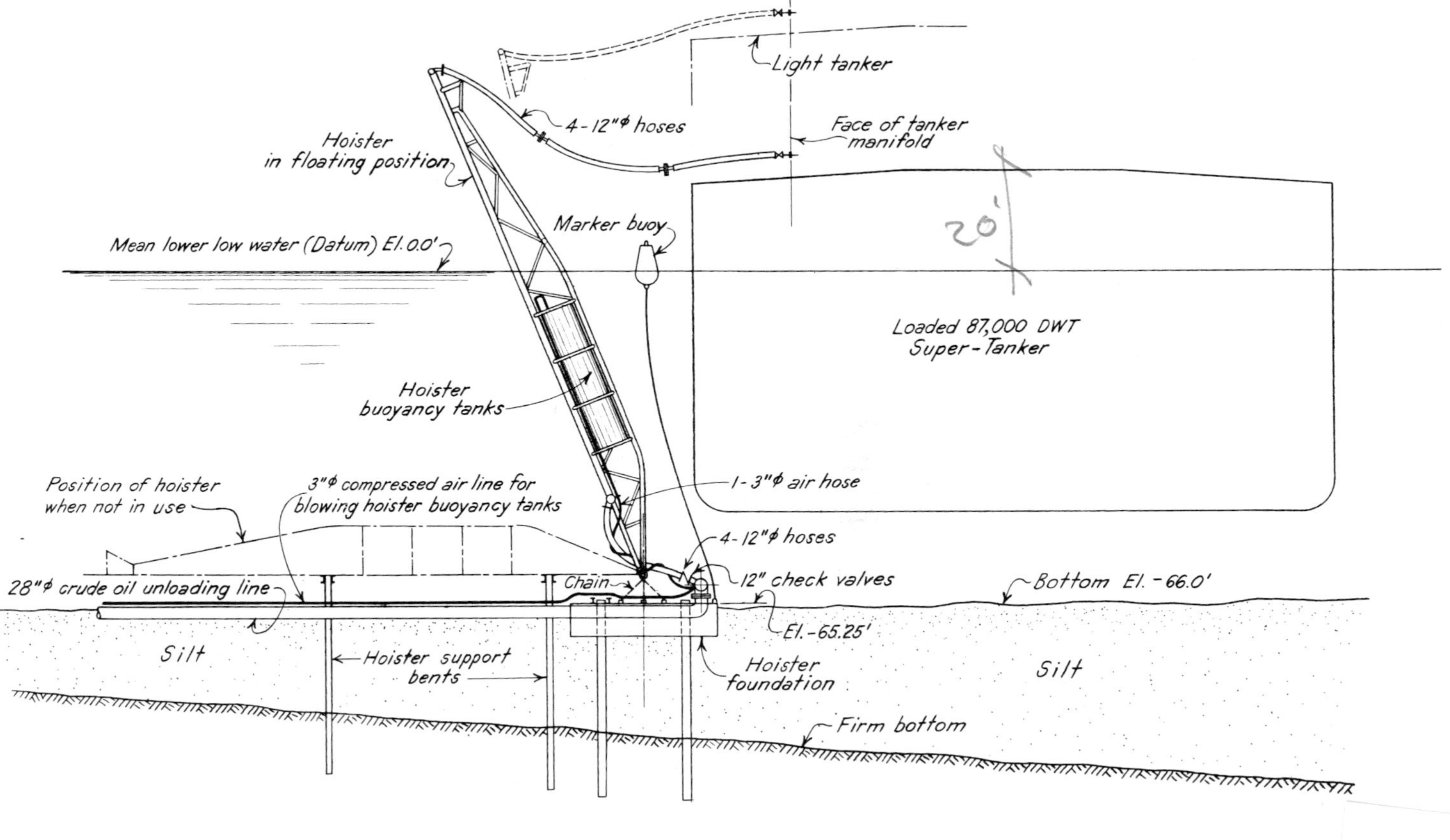

FIG. 8.9 "Hartley hoister" submergible hose-handling structure. (*Courtesy of the Collins Construction Co.*)

ends being connected by short pieces of hose to the manifold at the end of the submarine line and the upper ends being provided with sufficient length of hose to reach the ship's manifold.

To load or unload a tanker alongside a dock, it is necessary to make a temporary flexible connection between the ship's manifold at the pumps to the pipelines or their manifold on the dock. This is accomplished by means of cargo hose or by aluminum pipe with swivel joints known as

FIG. 8.10 Hose-handling frame at the marine terminal of the Tidewater Oil Refinery at Delaware City, Delaware. (*Courtesy of the Tidewater Oil Co.*)

Chiksan loading arms. The ship's manifold is usually located about midship and in the case of the very large supertankers there may be two manifolds located about 200 ft apart.

Until recent years, the usual method of handling cargo hose was to store individual lengths on racks on the dock or hang them from frames. When required for unloading a tanker, these lengths would be removed from the rack, coupled together on the deck, and the line lifted into position by a light hose-handling frame or derrick where it could be reached by the ship's cargo boom. This resulted in a considerable amount of spillage and drip on the deck.

With the advent of the larger supertankers requiring the use of larger and longer hose and as many as eight lines at one time, it became necessary to install hose-handling structures which would make it unnecessary to dismantle and store each length of hose. Several different types of structures have been developed to meet this need.

Figure 8.10 shows an installation for use where tankers berth only on one side of the dock. Each separate cargo hose line is of sufficient length to reach the tanker's manifold when the ship is in either a light or loaded condition and is connected to the manifold on the dock. The hose is held in a hanging position, when not in use, by means of a saddle which can be raised and lowered by an air hoist. The open end of the line hangs in a vertical position and drains into a drip trough. Each hose has its own individual hoist which is controlled from a central panel board.

FIG. 8.11 Hose-handling frame at the Esso marine terminal, Havana, Cuba. (*Courtesy of Esso Standard Oil, South America.*)

In addition, the frame supports a derrick, with air-operated hoist, for lifting the end of the hose so that it can be connected to the ship's manifold.

Figure 8.11 illustrates a somewhat similar installation to that shown in Fig. 8.10, but differing mainly in the way the hose is supported and handled. This structure is on a pier with tanker berths on both sides and consists of a tower with projecting arms for supporting the ends of the hose, which can be raised and lowered by means of air-operated hoists, the purpose being to raise the hose to a position in back of the face of the pier until after the ship has docked, when it can then be lowered to project out over the ship at the location of its manifold. The end of the hose can also be raised and lowered by means of air hoists so that the hose can be connected to the ship's manifold. The entire operation is controlled from a central panel board located just above the deck level. Hoists may also be operated by electric motors.

A more recent development in loading and unloading equipment is the Chiksan flexible arm, which is shown in Fig. 8.12 and is comprised of hydraulically controlled arms of aluminum pipe, with swivel joints which permit movement in any direction and thereby enable it to be attached to the tanker's manifold even though the ship is undergoing motion alongside the dock from the tide, wind, and waves. One or more arms may be used and they are supported on a platform about 15 ft above the deck

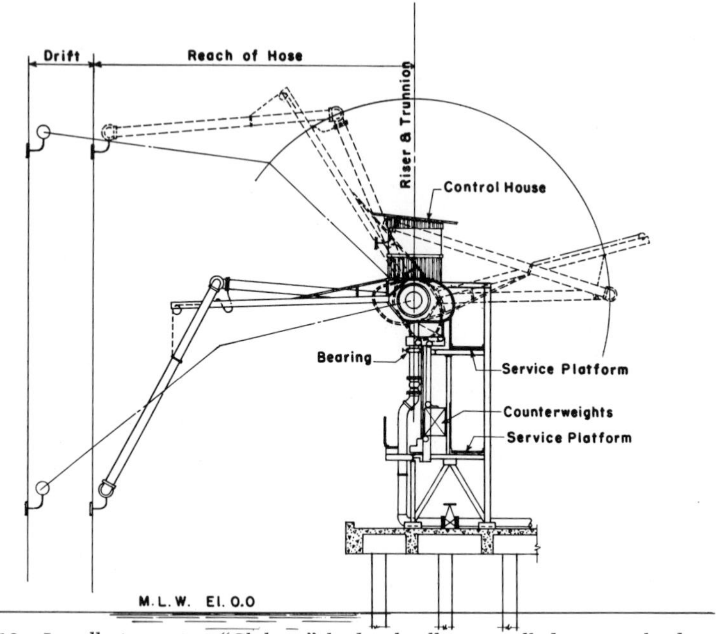

FIG. 8.12 Installation using "Chiksan" hydraulically controlled marine loading arm. (*Courtesy of the Chiksan Co.*)

and 8 ft in back of the face of the dock. A unit consisting of five 8-in.-diameter arms occupies 10 by 24 ft of dock space at the base. An electric motor, driving a pump, delivers hydraulic pressure at 750 lb per sq in. to power whichever arm is selected by the operator. The arms are counterweighted. Arms varying in size up to 12 in. in diameter have been installed, but 16-in.-diameter and larger sizes are contemplated.

8.7 Some Modern Bulk Cargo Terminals

The following are some of the modern installations for handling such commodities as beneficiated iron ore, lump iron ore, nitrates, bauxite, sugar, and oil.

A Beneficiated-iron-ore Shipping Terminal. Located at Taconite Harbor, Minnesota, this is a special-purpose harbor, built for the sole use of the Erie Mining Company in loading out taconite pellets from their mine and beneficiating plant 75 miles inland. The Sault Sainte Marie canal and locks are icebound for five months of the year, leaving only a seven-month shipping season in Lake Superior, while the mine and plant operate the year round. Since a whole year's production, which is eventually expected to reach 20 million long tons, must be handled in seven months, the material-handling equipment was designed for maximum practical speed. A special requirement, due to the nature of the material, is careful lateral trimming of the cargo in each hold. This is because the processed taconite is in the form of hard, round pellets from $\frac{1}{2}$ to $\frac{5}{8}$ in. in diameter. This forms a free-flowing cargo which could shift dangerously if it were left peaked amidship.

Pellets are brought to the harbor by a privately owned, standard-gauge railroad, equipped with powerful diesel-electric locomotives and bottom-dump cars of 100 tons capacity. One 94-car train making a round trip each eight hours, around the clock, during the shipping season can deliver the entire initial annual production of over five million long tons. At the harbor, the trains pass over a high-level trestle through which the pellets are dumped into a continuous row of concrete storage bins parallel with and immediately behind the dock face. The trains then pass around a return loop to the main line, having unloaded and returned without uncoupling. Berths are provided for three 600-ft ore vessels, but the bins behind one berth were omitted in the initial construction. The capacity of the bins as now built is 150,000 long tons. This is all live storage, as the bins are built with sloping bottoms.

Under the bins, at 48-ft spacing, are discharge openings over dual reciprocating feeders, which deliver pellets to 42-in. retractable shuttle-belt conveyors. At maximum extension these conveyors reach 50 ft beyond the dock face, and when retracted they are entirely under the shelter of the bins and protected from the weather by power-operated overhead doors. Since all Great Lakes ore vessels have a standard hatch spacing of 24 ft, the 48-ft spacing of conveyors is capable of loading alternate hatches simultaneously, and will completely load and trim all hatches with only one 24-ft movement of the vessel. Each conveyor, with its belt operating at 500 ft per min, will deliver 1,500 long tons per hour, and can be operated at half speed and half capacity for trimming. Only one of the two feeders is operated when the belt is run at half speed. Each belt is equipped with a weightometer which records weight on instruments located in the control towers. There are 25 of these conveyors for the 1,200-ft bin or a maximum of 13 for one vessel. The system is designed to load a 15,000-ton vessel in little more than one hour. Figure 5.59 is a cross section through the storage bin and dock and shows the shuttle conveyor extended in position to load the ship.

When a vessel is being loaded, the mate patrols the deck carrying a portable telephone by means of which he gives instructions to an operator in a control tower high up on the dock face over the center of the vessel. There is one control tower for each berth, and each tower contains a push-button console, controlling all the functions of the conveyors serving its berth. Also in each tower are indicating devices to show the operator the position of each belt, its state of operation, and the tonnage it has delivered. A typical cycle of operations in loading a vessel would be:

1. Operator opens all necessary shuttle-well doors while the vessel is being moored.
2. The mate reports to the operator that the vessel is ready for loading.
3. The operator presets a scale-timing device for each belt to the tonnage requested by the mate.
4. The operator positions the required shuttles as directed by the mate.
5. The operator starts belts and feeders and loading begins.
6. Loading operations continue as shuttle positions and belt speeds are adjusted for trimming as directed by the mate.
7. When each hatch is loaded, on signal from the mate, the operator stops the feeder, empties the belt, and retracts the shuttle.
8. The vessel is then shifted 24 ft to load intermediate hatches, repeating the cycle of operations 2 to 7.
9. After the vessel is completely loaded and trimmed, the mate signals the operator, who clears all conveyors, shuts them down, retracts the shuttle, and closes all the shuttle-well doors.
10. The operator records, by means of an automatic ticket printer, the total tonnage delivered by each conveyor.

With this rapid discharge of material into the hold of the ship, all under the control of one man, the vital importance of automatic safety controls is obvious. To eliminate as far as possible the chance of human error, interlocking controls are provided which automatically prevent:

1. Extending a shuttle before its door is open, or closing the door on an extended shuttle.
2. Operating a belt when the shuttle is not sufficiently extended to clear the dock.
3. Operating feeders when a belt is not operating.
4. Operating feeders at a higher capacity than that at which belts are operating.
5. Overloading a hatch. This is accomplished through the scale presetting device mentioned above, which, when the preset tonnage has been delivered, turns on a light on the dock face and another in the control tower, and stops the conveyor.

To supply power and light for the operations at the harbor and inland at the plant, a power plant was constructed adjacent to the dock so as to obtain the most economical supply of coal. To provide for unloading the coal, without interfering with the loading of ore, one end of the wharf was extended 500 ft to provide room for colliers to tie up and be unloaded. To accomplish the rapid unloading of the coal, a traveling unloading tower with 14-ton grab bucket, with an unloading rate of 1,500 tons per hour, was provided. The bucket dumps the coal in a hopper which in turn feeds a conveyor belt leading to the storage area in back of the

FIG. 8.13 14-ton traveling coal-unloading tower at Taconite Harbor, Lake Superior. (*Courtesy of the Wellman Engineering Co.*)

power plant. Figure 8.13 shows a view of the coal-unloading equipment.

An Iron-ore Shipping Terminal at San Juan Bay, Peru. This terminal started operation in 1959. Figure 8.14 shows a plan of the shipping terminal and a section through the pier.

Crushed ore is delivered from the mine in 40-ton bottom-dump trucks. Under the receiving hopper is a vibrating feeder loading a transfer belt, which in turn feeds a conveyor 966 ft long running through the ground storage area. Straddling this conveyor, on a pair of rails 24 ft apart, is a traveling stacker with a long tripper-trailer. The stacker has a boom conveyor on one side which discharges 50 ft above the ground and 75 ft away from the center line of the stacking conveyor. All the belts in this system are 36 in. wide. Storage is provided for 180,000 long tons of ore, with provision for doubling this capacity in the future by adding another boom on the other side of the stacker. Ore is graded at the mine

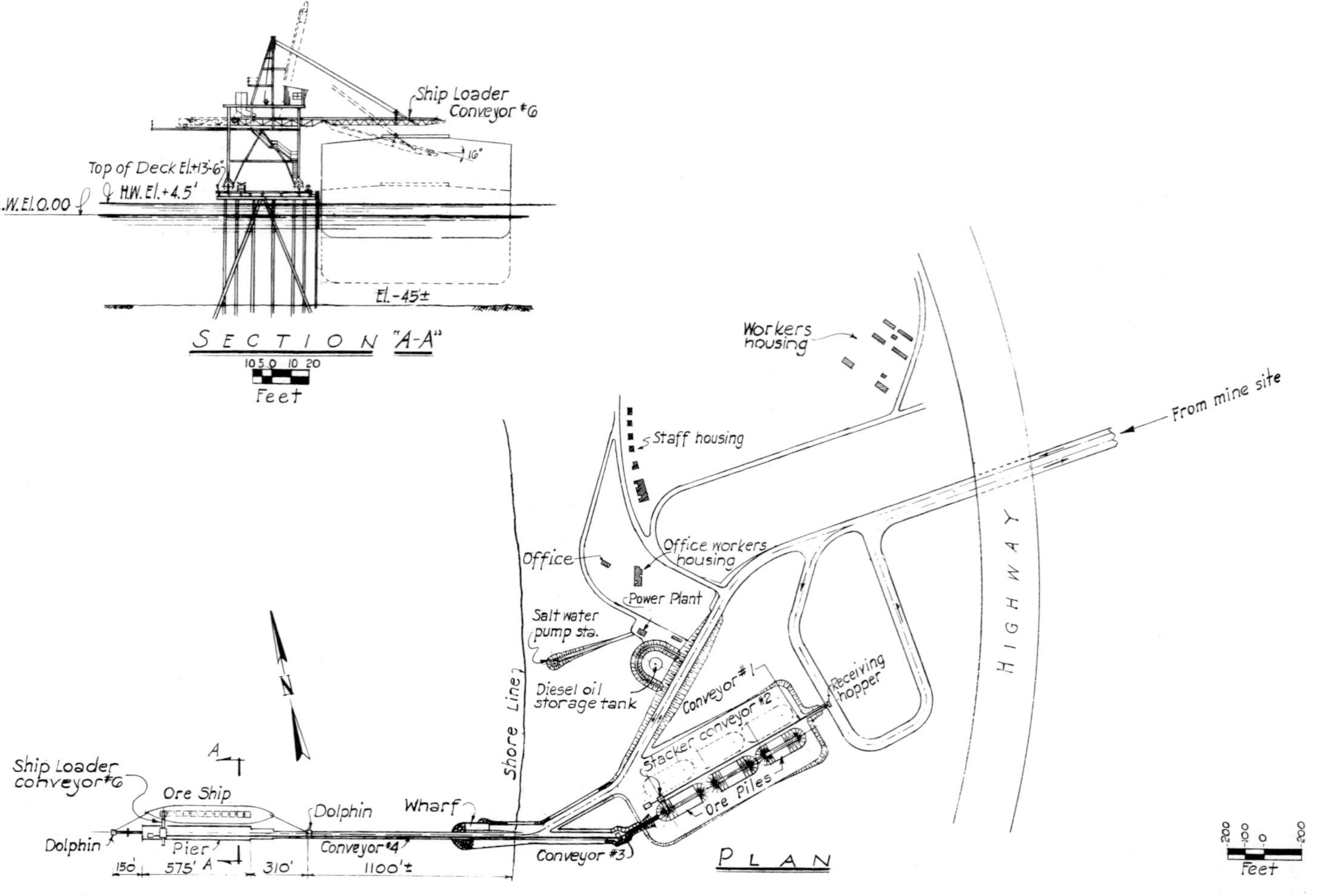

Ship Loader
Conveyor #6
16°
Top of Deck El.+13'-6"
H.W. El.+4.5'
L.W. El. 0.00
El.-45±
SECTION "A-A"
10 5 0 10 20
Feet
Workers housing
From mine site
Staff housing
Office
Office workers housing
Power Plant
Salt water pump sta.
Diesel oil storage tank
HIGHWAY
Receiving hopper
Conveyor #1
Stacker conveyor #2
Ore Piles
Shore Line
N
A
Ship Loader
conveyor #6
Ore Ship
Dolphin
Wharf
Dolphin
Pier
Conveyor #4
Conveyor #3
150'
575' A
310'
1100'±
PLAN
200 100 0 200
Feet

into three size classifications, having maximum lumps of 1, 5, and 8 in., respectively. The three sizes are kept segregated in the storage pile. The receiving and storing system operates at 660 tons per hour in the initial installation. When the operation is expanded, this can be increased to 880 tons per hour by adding a second receiving hopper and feeder. When this has been done, the two feeders can be operated jointly at 440 tons per hour each, or singly at 660 tons per hour.

Reclaiming from storage is by a belt conveyor in a tunnel under the storage pile. The tunnel roof is flush with the ground, and is provided with openings at 30-ft spacing. A vibrating feeder of 550-ton-per-hour capacity is suspended under each opening. Up to four of these feeders are operated at once, regulating the total output to the belt capacity of 2,000 tons per hour by adjusting the variable speed control which is provided on three of the feeders. The reclaiming conveyor transfers the ore to another conveyor which runs out over a short rock mole and a trestle to the beginning of the pier, where it in turn loads a conveyor running the length of the pier. Straddling this conveyor is a shiploading tower with another tripper-trailer, which feeds a belt on a boom extending out over the ship. The boom can be raised to clear the ship's superstructure, and, when in operating position, can be retracted for trimming. The tower has a travel of 490 ft. At the outshore end of the trestle, a weightometer automatically records the weight of ore delivered to each ship. The whole reclaiming and shiploading system operates at 2,000 tons per hour; all belts are 42 in. wide.

The pier and the trestle are supported on steel H piles, and have steel superstructures with concrete decks. They are designed to accommodate H-20 trucks, which handle imported supplies. For the import of very heavy equipment, a barge landing is provided alongside the mole. The terminal has its own power plant, and housing for administration, personnel, and workmen. The site is arid; fresh water must be brought in by tank trucks. Cooling water for the diesel-operated power plant is obtained from a large well dug on the sandy beach near the shore line.

Loading-out Nitrate by One of the World's Largest Revolving Conveyor Booms. This operation will soon be under way at Tocopilla, Chile. Figure 8.15 shows a plan of the storage and loading-out facilities and an elevation of the conveyor boom. This is an unprotected site, fully exposed to the Pacific swells. The shore is rocky and rugged, with many small islands and underwater rock pinnacles near shore. For many years, nitrate ships have been anchored well offshore and loaded by lighters operating from a small pier. There are many days when the swell is too heavy for lighters to operate. A more efficient port has long been needed, but the sea is too rough to permit mooring ocean vessels against a pier without breakwater protection, which would be quite costly. The loading facility

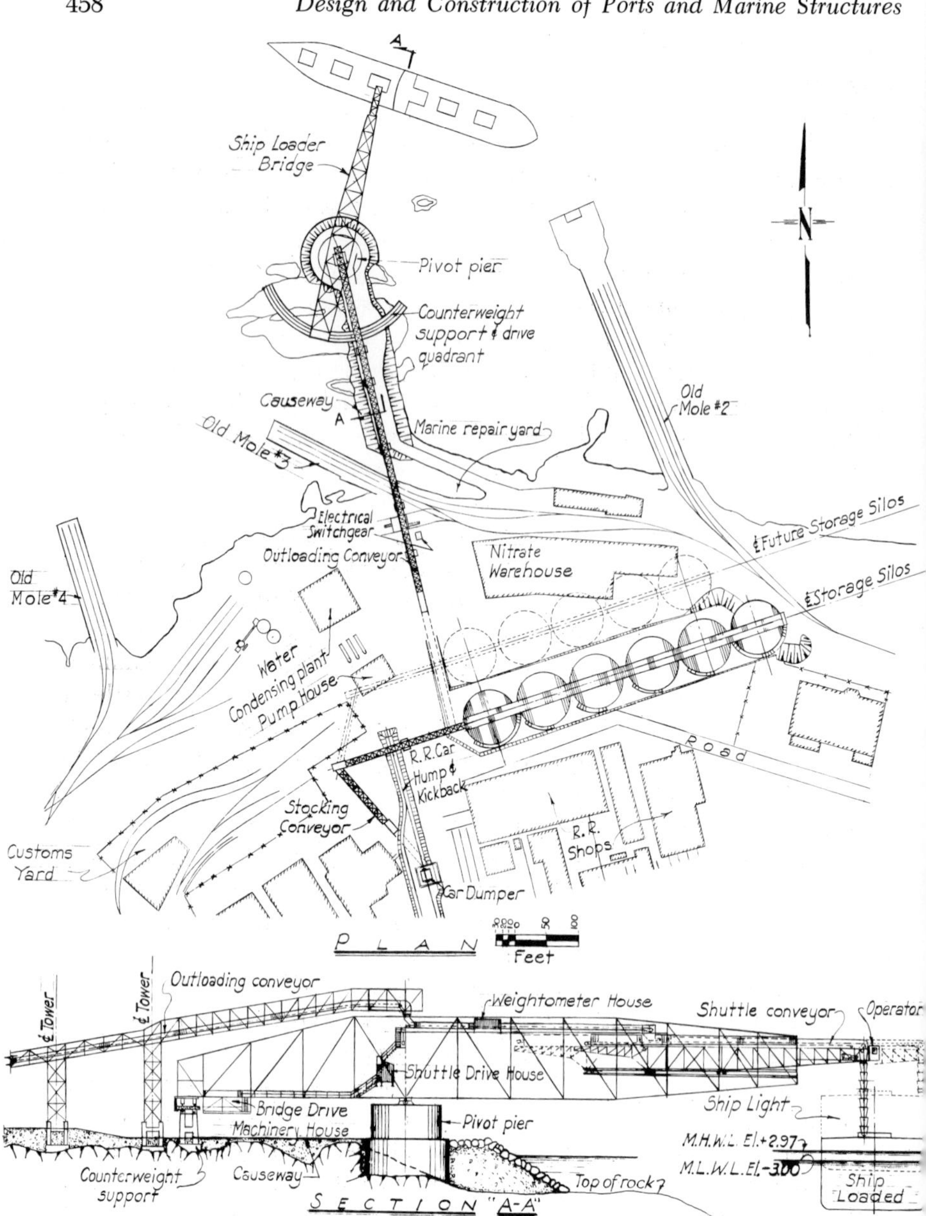

FIG. 8.15 Nitrate shipping terminal for Anglo-Lautaro Nitrate Corporation at Tocopilla, C

decided on, and now under construction, consists of a high-level revolving boom reaching out over a ship moored offshore. A belt conveyor on a shuttle truss at the end of the main boom will operate within the range of 232 to 306 ft from the pivot point, and will be able to reach all the holds without moving the ship being loaded. The shuttle belt will be 62 ft above mean sea level. The inshore end of the structure will be counterweighted and will be supported by motor-driven trucks operating on a curved track at a radius of 125 ft from the pivot point. Both the track and the pivot pier are being built on a partially submerged rock island near the shore.

The product to be handled is processed natural nitrate of soda in the form of hollow beads less than ⅛ in. in diameter. The material is free-flowing, with a weight of 81 lb per cu ft and an angle of repose of 26°. The beads are sufficiently fragile to create considerable quantities of dust when the material is dropped any great distance.

Nitrate will be received at the terminal in narrow-gauge gondola cars, which will be overturned by a car dumper into a transfer hopper. The material will be carried by inclined belt conveyors to a traveling tripper operating in a gallery over a row of six storage silos into any of which the tripper may dump at the option of the operator. Each silo has a capacity of 11,000 tons, or about a shipload. A reclaiming tunnel will run under the silos, with five roof openings under each silo. To load the reclaiming belt in the tunnel, five traveling belt feeders will be provided, of which three will be operated at a time to load the belt to capacity. Reclaimed material will be conveyed by inclined belts to a transfer chute at the top of the shiploader boom, directly over the pivot point. This chute will rotate with the boom, feeding a conveyor on the main boom, which in turn will load a conveyor on the shuttle truss extending out over the ship being loaded. The material will be dropped into the holds, through a retractable telescopic chute, to aid in trimming the cargo as well as to minimize degradation. The belts in the receiving and storing system are 36 in. wide and are designed for a rate of 660 tons per hour. The reclaiming and shiploading belts are 48 in. wide and will carry 1,400 tons per hour. There is provision in the design for increasing the live-storage capacity of the terminal from 66,000 to 121,000 tons by the future addition of five more silos.

Dust-collection systems, each with a cyclone separator, will be installed at the car dumper and in the tripper-conveyor gallery. For cleanup purposes, all the galleries and tunnels housing the various conveyors will be provided with vacuum outlets at frequent intervals. Five sets of vacuum-cleaning tools will be kept in cabinets conveniently located throughout the system.

A Transfer Station at Chaguaramas Bay, Trinidad. This station has been operating for nearly twenty years to transfer bauxite from river boats to ocean vessels. It illustrates a typical transfer facility involving ship-unloading, covered storage, reclaiming, and shiploading facilities for bulk material, using belt conveyors. Figure 8.16*a* shows the general layout and Fig. 8.16*b* typical sections of the loading and unloading facilities.

Separate berths are provided for loading and unloading ships. The unloading berth is equipped with two traveling unloading towers, each with a 4-ton grab bucket. Each bucket is suspended from a trolley traveling on a boom extending out over the ship and dumps into a hopper in the tower. Under the hopper is a belt feeder delivering the bauxite to a belt conveyor running along the back of the wharf. The capacity of this belt is adequate to permit simultaneous operation of the two towers.

The incoming bauxite is transferred, through an intermediate conveyor, to a conveyor suspended under the ridge of the storage building. A traveling tripper operates on this belt, distributing the material the whole length of the building. Reclaiming is through manually operated gates in the roof of a tunnel under the storage-building floor. A traveling feeder, which can be set under any desired gate, delivers material to a reclaiming belt in the tunnel.

The reclaimed material is carried, behind, and parallel to, the shiploading wharf, on an elevated conveyor equipped with a traveling tripper. This tripper is linked to a traveling loading tower, to which it delivers. The tower carries a belt conveyor on a hinged boom which reaches out over the ship being loaded. An adjustable telescopic chute, suspended from the end of the boom, delivers bauxite into the hold of the ship.

The bauxite is destined for an aluminum plant on the Saguenay River in Canada. Since this river is icebound for several months each winter, the transfer station must provide storage for all the bauxite produced while the ocean vessels are not operating. The storage building will accommodate 145,000 tons.

All the main conveyor belts, for both incoming and outgoing material, are 42 in. wide, and are capable of carrying 1,400 tons per hour.

A Modern Shiploading Sugar Terminal. At such a terminal, recently completed at Aguadilla, Puerto Rico, sugar is delivered in 10-ton side-dump containers, three of which are carried on one flat-bed trailer truck. The containers are dumped by overhead hoists into a hopper, from which the sugar is transported by a system of belts to a tripper conveyor under the peak of the roof in the storage building. Reclaiming is accomplished by a belt conveyor in a tunnel under the center of a warehouse floor, fed by gravity through a series of floor openings. Cleanup of the sugar not withdrawn by gravity is accomplished by scoop trucks. The reclaiming conveyor feeds a belt system which passes the sugar through

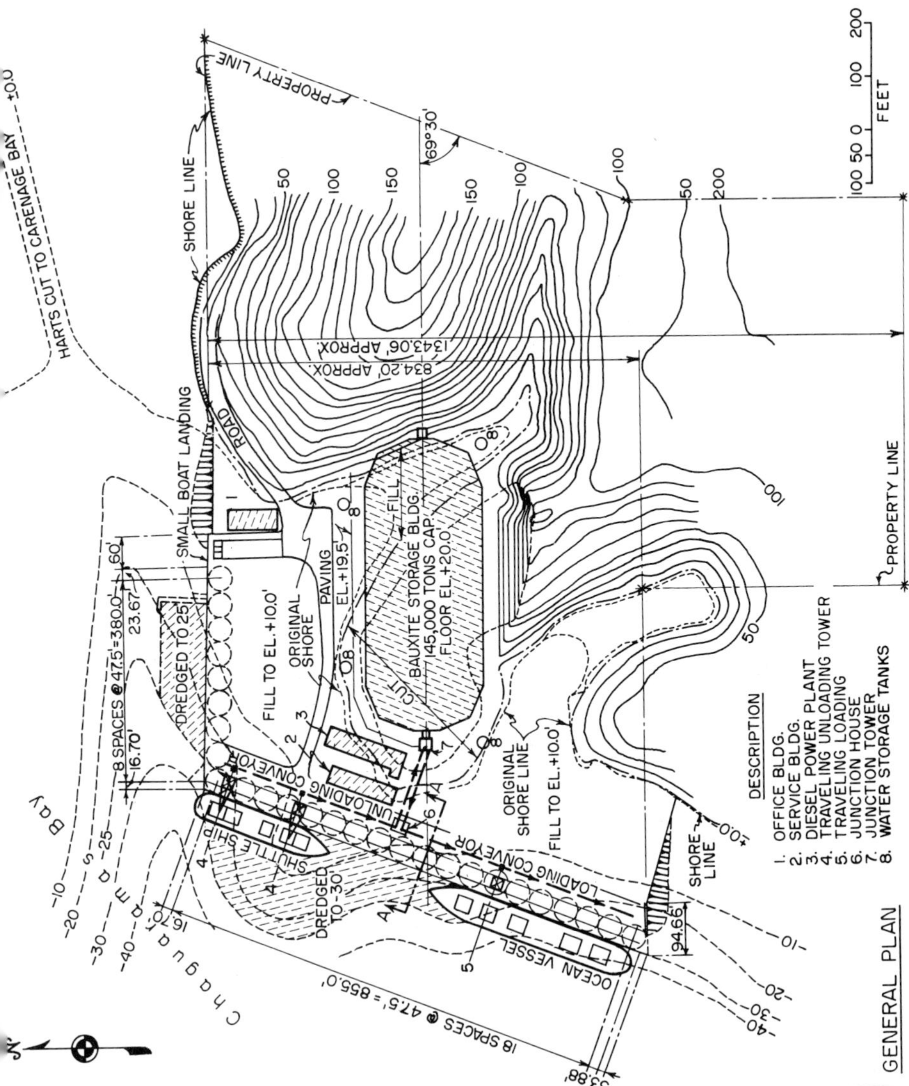

FIG. 8.16 (*a*) General layout of bauxite transfer station for Aluminum Company of Canada at Chaguaramas Bay, Trinidad, British West Indies.

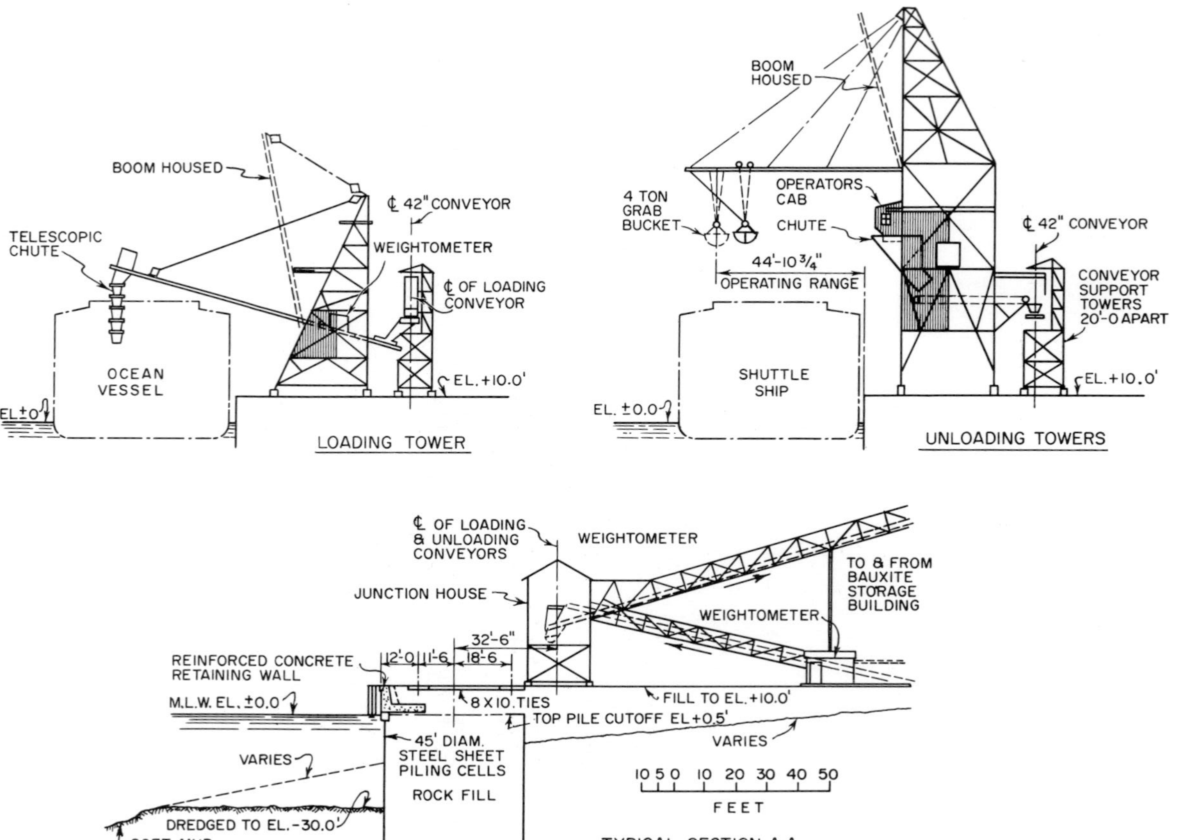

FIG. 8.16 (*b*) Typical sections of loading and unloading facilities at bauxite transfer station, Chaguaramas Bay, Trinidad, British West Indies.

a weigh house and over a trestle to an offshore loading tower, having a hinged boom carrying a belt conveyor which delivers to the ship. Delivery is through a retractable telescopic chute, at the lower end of which is a trimming device designed to cast the material to the farthest corners of the hold. The boom can be swiveled to load through two adjacent hatches without moving the ship. The ship is moored clear of the tower base by four permanent anchors attached to Navy-type mooring buoys.

FIG. 8.17 Sugar shipping terminal for Central Coloso, Inc. at Aguadilla, Puerto Rico. (*Courtesy of the Stephens-Adamson Manufacturing Co.*)

The receiving and storing system has a capacity of 400 tons per hour; the reclaiming and shiploading system operates at the rate of 700 tons per hour and can load 10,000 tons in about 18 hours, including time lost in respotting the ship. The warehouse capacity is 40,000 tons.

Accurate records are kept of sugar received and shipped. Each incoming truck is weighed on a 50-ton platform scale and reweighed empty as it leaves. The weigh house contains an automatic batch-type scale, which measures the tonnage delivered to the ship. Both scales have automatic recording and ticket-printing mechanisms.

In Fig. 8.17, the tall structure at the shore end of the trestle is the weigh house. To its right and farther inshore is the warehouse, with the transfer tower for incoming sugar at its left end. The truck-receiving building is hidden behind the warehouse.

The New Tidewater Oil Refinery at Delaware City. Situated on the Delaware River, about 15 miles below Wilmington, this refinery was completed in the fall of 1956, with a refining capacity of 100,000 bbl. It has a marine terminal which was designed to accommodate barges and tankers ranging in size from a T-2 to a 50,000-deadweight-ton supertanker. These tankers are handled at three separate T-head piers, with approach trestles from shore, and with breasting and mooring dolphins for docking the ships. Figure 8.18 shows the general layout of this terminal. Berth 1

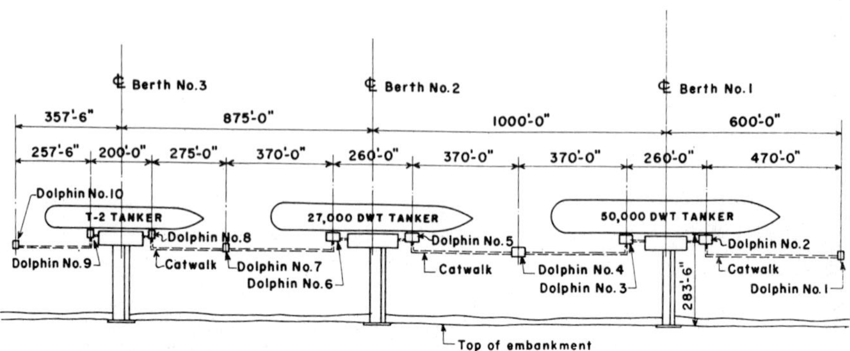

FIG. 8.18 Marine terminal for Tidewater Oil Company at Delaware City, Delaware.

is for the large supertankers of 50,000 tons; berth 2 handles T-2 and supertankers; and berth 3 is for T-2 tankers and smaller ships.

The structures are supported on H piles driven to predetermined tip elevations in the underlying silty clay. The piles in the dolphins were designed for a load of 50 tons in compression and 75 per cent of this in tension.

The breasting dolphins are provided with fenders (similar to Fig. 5.40) consisting of wood piles bearing against a steel waler which is backed up with a 15-in. cylindrical rubber fender supported in a recess in the face of the concrete cap of the dolphin.

The loading dock or platform for the supertanker berth is a concrete structure 45 ft wide by 135 ft long, set back 10 ft from the face of the breasting dolphins so that it will not be hit by the ship when mooring. It supports a hose-handling frame of the type shown in Fig. 8.10.

The trestle out from shore to the platform provides a roadway and pipeway.

Chapter 9 OFFSHORE MARINE STRUCTURES

9.1 Introduction

Military and industrial challenges of the past decade have resulted in the development of certain marine structures which are worthy of discussion here, namely, mobile wharves for military and commercial use; radar and lighthouse platforms for national defense and navigation aids, respectively; and offshore drilling structures for the petroleum and other industries.

The mobile wharf was developed for use in regions where construction equipment and materials were not readily available, or where time allowable for on-site construction was critically short. The great advantage offered by this type of structure lies in the ability to prefabricate a large portion of the wharf and to tow it with all of the required erection equipment and material to the site, where it can be installed in a relatively short period of time without the need of additional floating equipment. The completed installation can be used on a temporary basis and removed to a new location or may be completed in a permanent manner as occasion demands.

Radar platforms (Texas Towers), designed to serve as a part of our national air defense early-warning system, are permanent structures planned for five locations well off the North Atlantic Coast. Three of these have already been erected as of 1960, all similar, but each with unique features which distinguish it from the others.

Lighthouses erected upon offshore platforms are currently under consideration as replacements for lightships in the Coast Guard's system of aids to navigation. The adaptation of the Texas Tower to this use is predicated upon studies which indicate economic feasibility and important operational advantages. Of the 36 lightships now in service, it is contemplated that all but two could be replaced by such rigid towers.

Offshore-drilling structures have been in use for many years, but it was not until drilling expanded in a big way into the Gulf of Mexico that the severe wind and wave conditions there presented new and challenging problems in the development of this specialized field of activity. This region covers some 300 million acres of offshore waters less than 600 ft deep, of which perhaps only 12 per cent has undergone more than a minor amount of exploration. While Lake Maracaibo now leads overwhelmingly in over-water wells which number in the thousands, and probably will continue to hold its supremacy for some years to come, the potential

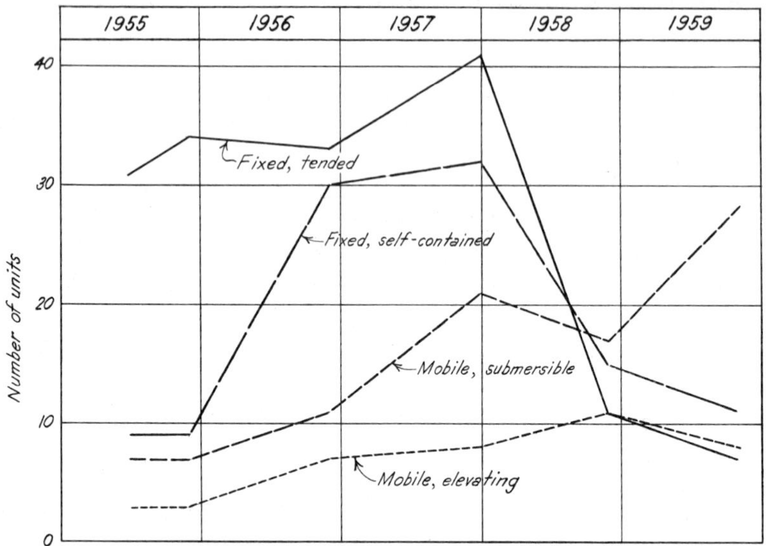

FIG. 9.1 Graph showing trends of types of drilling platforms used in the Gulf of Mexico since 1955.

possibilities of the Gulf of Mexico and contiguous waters appear to be limited only by the oil industry's ability to develop methods and structures to drill in deeper water. The search for oil has brought the drill rig to other offshore areas throughout the world, such as the Persian Gulf, South China Sea, Sea of Japan, the Bay of Bengal, and the Gulf of Paria off the coast of Venezuela.

Offshore-drilling methods and structure designs are in a continual state of change and development, popularity of any particular method generally being the result of currently favorable economic advantages which one may enjoy over another. Competition in the development of offshore-drilling structures, which is borne out by the hundreds of patent applications which have been filed over the past several years, has caused popularity to shift among the various methods, a significant factor in this probably being the consistent campaign to conquer deeper and deeper water.

While fixed platforms tended by barges have enjoyed popularity in Lake Maracaibo, the early use of this method of drilling has diminished in the Gulf of Mexico, and in 1959 mobile units accounted for over 60 per cent of the current drilling operations, with fixed, self-contained, and tended platforms sharing the remainder. Back in 1955 tended operations enjoyed a similar popularity. Figure 9.1 shows clearly the trends in the Gulf since 1955. Until recently, the legislative stalemate in California limited drilling to floating ships or artificial islands, but now the mobile unit has moved into the Pacific.

9.2 Mobile Wharves

The mobile wharf, a development of the De Long Engineering and Construction Company, was the forerunner of the elevating-deck-type mobile drilling rig. It was developed for use by the armed forces in Alaska and Greenland where adverse weather conditions made speedy on-site construction critically important.

In essence, the De Long wharf consists of a buoyant bargelike deck provided with openings for cylindrical steel columns or caissons which can be lowered to the bottom when the deck has been floated into final position. Unique circular pneumatic gripping jacks mounted on the deck above the openings permit the deck to be elevated in steps by climbing up on the vertical columns. The wharf, in process of installation, is shown in Fig. 9.2.

Subsequent to the initial military applications, a similar mobile structure was used commercially by the Orinoco Mining Company on the Orinoco River in Venezuela where it functions as a pier for the shipment of iron ore. The installation consisted of three sections of barge, each 337 ft long, 82 ft wide, and 15 ft deep, which together form a wharf over 1,000 ft long, which was elevated to a safe position above the seasonal high-water levels encountered on the Orinoco. The supporting cylindrical steel columns are 6 ft in diameter and 100 ft long, are fabricated from 1-in.-thick steel plate, and weigh about 40 tons each. A view of the completed dock is shown in Fig. 9.3.

The units were fabricated in Texas and towed 3,000 miles to the erection site. The hull structures were compartmented, reinforced to provide rigidity, and fitted with piping, tracks, mooring devices, etc., as required for their ultimate functioning as a wharf. Preparation for transit included loading on the hulls the cylindrical steel columns, the crawler crane for erecting them, and other tools and materials for the field work. Upon arrival at the site, the unit was moved into approximate position and moored, and the columns were dropped through the jacks and hull by the crane and temporarily supported by engaging the jacks to keep them suspended above the bottom. Once the columns were all hanging from

FIG. 9.2 De Long wharf in process of installation. (*Courtesy of the De Long Corp.*)

FIG. 9.3 De Long wharf for the Orinoco Mining Company on the Orinoco River, Venezuela. (*Courtesy of the De Long Corp.*)

the hull, the structure was moved into final position, and the columns lowered to rest upon the bottom where initial penetration was attained from dead weight.

At this stage the actual jacking of the deck began, the first phase being the further penetration of the columns until sufficient friction was

FIG. 9.4 De Long gripper-type jack. (*Courtesy of the De Long Corp.*)

developed in the bottom to support the weight of the deck. Once this was achieved the deck was raised to the desired elevation and locked with the jacks. One at a time the columns were released from the jacks, and the free column driven to refusal by a hammer swung from the crane on the deck. When all columns were thus driven, the hull or deck was welded to them, the jacking devices removed, and the columns cut off flush with the deck. They were filled with sand and capped with steel plates thus completing the installation.

The jacking device, a patented feature, comprises an upper and a lower cylindrical section surrounding the column and separated by a bellows. Each section is lined with a series of expansible rings which, under air pressure, force serrated gripper segments against the column. The deck hangs from the upper section. By alternately expanding and contracting the bellows, the whole deck can be moved upward or downward on the column, direction depending on whether the lower or upper sets of grippers are engaged. During the climbing cycle auxiliary jacks are used to lift the lower section for a fresh grip. When the deck is

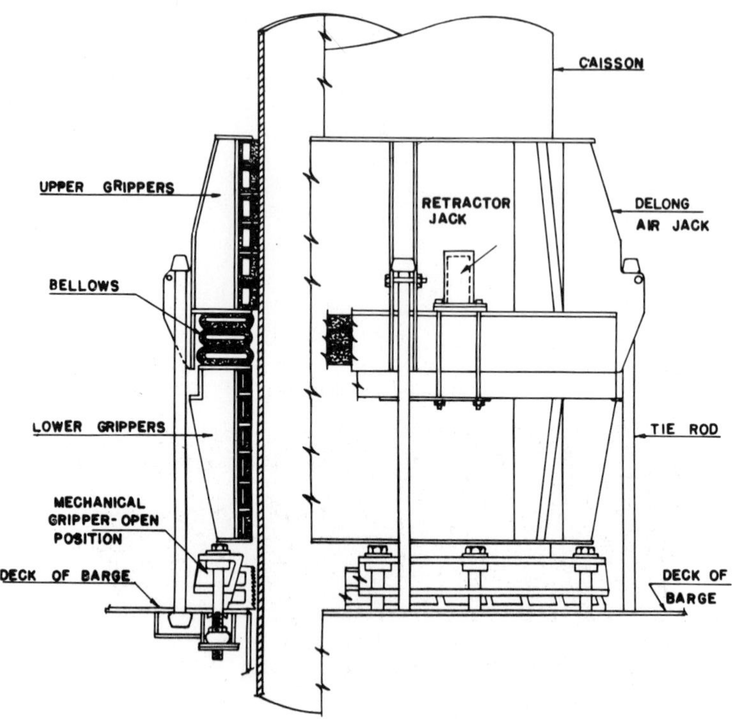

FIG. 9.5 Cutaway view of De Long gripper-type jack. (*Courtesy of the De Long Corp.*)

finally positioned, auxiliary gripping segments are wedged between the columns and deck projections to secure the deck and relieve the jacking units of their loads. The outward appearance of the jack is shown in Fig. 9.4 while a cutaway view is shown in Fig. 9.5.

9.3 Radar Platforms

In 1954, radar outposts, best known as "Texas Towers," were planned for shoal areas along the Atlantic Coast. The locations of the five sites selected for the radar platforms are shown in Fig. 9.6. Site 1 is on Cashes Ledge, 75 miles east of Portland, Maine; site 2 is on Georges Bank, 160 miles east-southeast of Boston, Massachusetts; site 3 is 80 miles southeast of Nantucket; site 4 is 70 miles east of Ambrose Light; and site 5 is on Browns Bank, 200 miles east of Boston. As of 1960, installations had been made at sites 2, 3, and 4.

While these structures are for the use of the Air Force, design and construction have been under the supervision of the Navy. The Woods Hole Oceanographic Institute contributed materially to the design which was handled by Anderson-Nichols and Company, and Moran, Proctor, Mueser, and Rutledge as a joint venture.

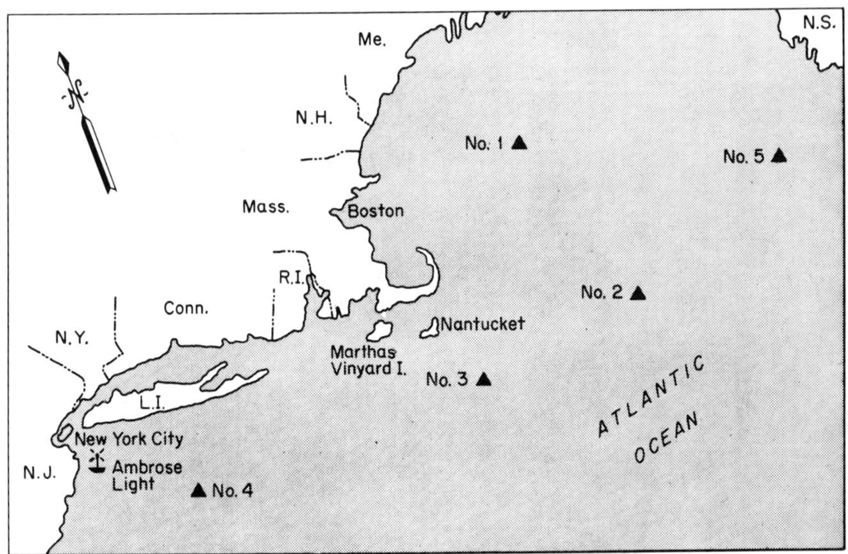

FIG. 9.6 Location of radar platforms off the coast of New England. (*From article by Gordon F. A. Fletcher, Civil Engineering, January,* 1956.)

Since very little was known about the condition of the bottom at the sites selected, core borings were made, except where the water was too deep. Because of excessive wave action the use of a conventional floating drill barge was ruled out and a De Long mobile wharf was used. The depth of water varied considerably at the different sites; being 56 ft at the first installation at site 2, 82 ft at the second installation at site 3, and 180 ft at site 4.

These platforms had to be designed to withstand waves up to 60 ft in height and to be installed under conditions where satisfactory construction weather was limited to the months of May, June, July, and early August—this period coming between the end of the northeasterly storm season and the beginning of the hurricane season—and even in this favorable period waves less than 4 ft in height could not be expected for more than a few days. From the information already developed in the design and operation of mobile drilling platforms in somewhat similar but less severe conditions in the Gulf of Mexico, the development of the Texas Towers followed a somewhat similar pattern; i.e., provision in the design for the maximum amount of prefabrication, rapid erection and elevation of the structure to a safe height above the waves, and minimum area of

FIG. 9.7 First radar platform erected off Cape Cod. (*From Engineering News-Record, Oct.* 25, 1956.)

obstruction to the waves. The shape of the platform was finalized as an equilateral triangle, approximately 200 ft on a side, which was designed as a watertight hull to be floated out to the erection site. It was to be elevated to clear mean sea level by 67 ft, so as to be above the crest of the highest wave, and to be supported on three cylindrical steel cylinders, 10 ft in diameter. (The first two installations used 10-ft diameters, but the third installation was increased to 12 ft 6 in. in diameter.)

The method of installation for the first two towers was generally the same and consisted of towing the platform hull with its permanent and temporary cylindrical supports, weighing approximately 6,000 tons, to the site, jacking the platform up to its permanent position on temporary supports, installing the permanent cylindrical caissons and transferring the load to them, and then completing the outfitting with as much prefabricated material and equipment as possible. The second installation differed mainly in the type of jacks used for lifting the platform; i.e., De Long jacks of the type shown in Fig. 9.4 were used for the first installation, whereas the Roebling cable-type jacking equipment was used for the second installation.

The third installation, which was in 180 ft of water, dictated a departure

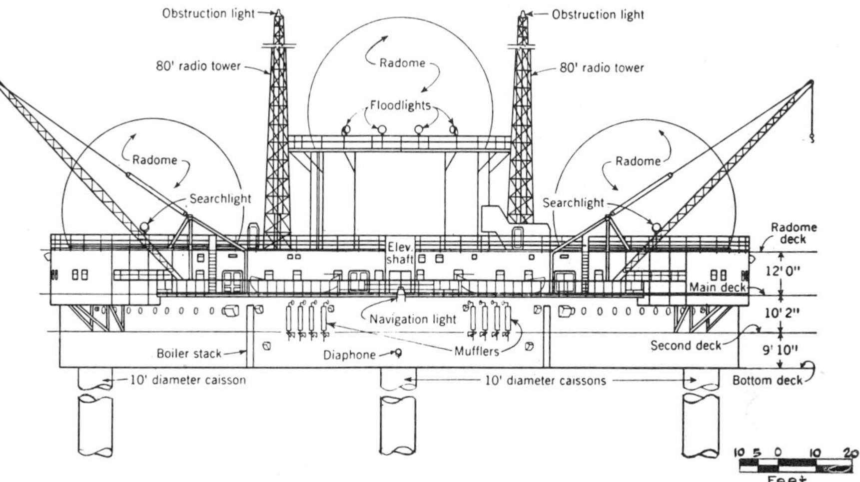

FIG. 9.8 Elevation of radar platform. (*From article by Gordon F. A. Fletcher, Civil Engineering, January,* 1956.)

from the unbraced caisson design that was used for the first two towers where the water was much shallower. Three caissons, 12 ft 6 in. in diameter by 288 ft long, with enlarged 25-ft-diameter "cans" at their lower ends, were connected together with struts to form a tripod, which was floated on its side to the site, then upended and sunk in the bottom. Unlike the two previous platforms, the watertight hull was arranged with slots at the three corners so as to allow it to be floated into engagement with the tripod structure, after it had been seated permanently.

The first Texas Tower erected off Cape Cod is shown in Fig. 9.7. Figures 9.8 and 9.9 show the radar platform in elevation and plan, respectively. The radar platform is a self-contained unit which houses a crew of about 70 Air Force officers and men. The deckhouse is 200 ft long by 60 ft wide with semicircular ends and contains operational facilities and offices. Atop the deckhouse on what is known as the radome deck are mounted the three radar domes, the middle one supported upon an enclosed two-story base approximately 25 ft high. Two radio towers, 80 ft high, are located between the domes. The weather deck is sufficiently large to provide a suitable landing area for a helicopter. Two stiff-leg cranes with 80-ft booms are located close to the deckhouse, one near each side of the triangular platform. They are used to transfer supplies, personnel, material, and equipment from vessels serving the radar station. The second deck is devoted mainly to quarters, mess and recreational facilities,

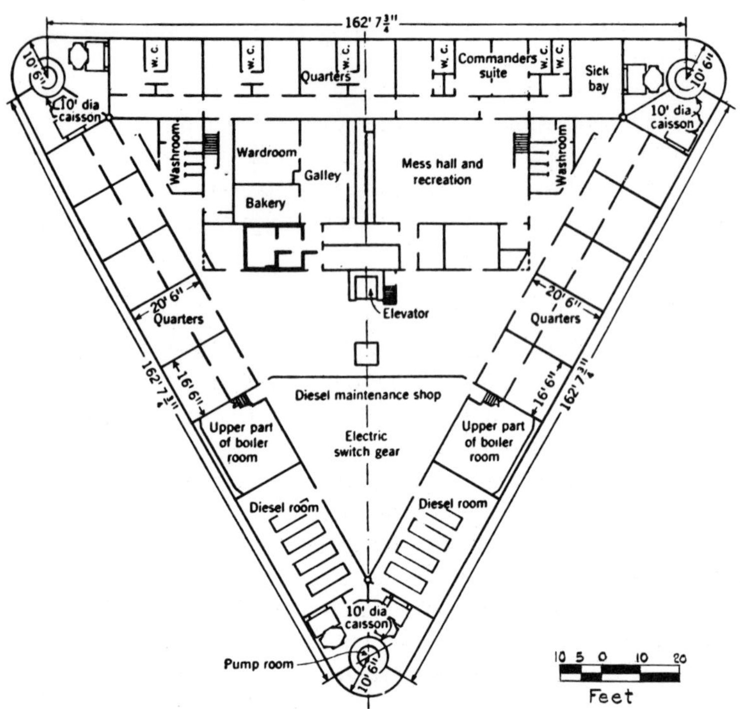

FIG. 9.9 Plan of second deck of radar platform. (*From article by Gordon F. A. Fletcher, Civil Engineering, January,* 1956.)

galley, bakery, refrigerated food storage, washrooms, diesel-electric generating equipment, switchgear, air-conditioning equipment, and maintenance shop. The lower deck houses the boilers and provides extensive storage space. The hollow space inside two of the legs is used for fuel storage, and the third is used for a salt water intake for cooling equipment on the platform.

9.4 Lighthouse Platforms

The use of lightships dates back to 1820, when the first one was used off Craney Island in Chesapeake Bay. Since that time the number has grown to 36, and today's powerful beacons are a far cry from the relatively feeble glow that guided mariners back in the nineteenth century.

Despite the technological advances that have marked progress in navigational aids, the lightships still have certain inherent disadvantages, such as cramped crew quarters and extremely limited recreational facilities, hazards of tearing loose from moorings in a storm, and limited height of light above sea. In addition to these physical aspects there is also the high operating cost that is normal with lightships.

The Coast Guard has sought through the years to improve efficiency and reduce costs, and the Texas Tower type of lighthouse structure appears to offer interesting possibilities in this respect. Range of visibility of the light itself can be considerably increased by elevating the light to about 150 ft above water, which of course is not possible on a lightship. Stability of the installation will also permit the wider use of directional equipment as well as more complete automation. It is believed that a crew of 5 men can operate the lighthouse, as opposed to 16 men presently constituting a crew for a lightship.

9.5 Permanent Drilling Islands

The Monterey Oil Company and the Texas Company built the first Pacific offshore-drilling island off Belmont, California. The initial installation was intended to permit the drilling of six wells and consisted of a circular cell of steel sheet piling, 75 ft in diameter, with a pier projecting on one axis which is supported on gunited wood piles. A mound of sand was first placed over the area on the ocean bottom, and the sheet piling was then driven through it into the natural bottom. The cell was filled with gravel to slightly above sea level, and the remaining space up to the top was then filled with sand. After completion of all pile driving, the original sand mound remaining outside the cell was covered with a heavy layer of trap rock to prevent scouring of the sand. Conductor pipes were driven through the fill at the selected well sites.

After producing wells had been completed, and the site proved out, it was intended that the island be enlarged to form a square about 800 ft on a side. Riprap type of construction was the contemplated method to be employed. High construction costs led the companies to reconsider their position, however, and a scheme was evolved whereby extremely close spacing of directional wells would permit as many as 70 to be drilled within the 75-ft-diameter island. Shutdown time was avoided by driving conductor pipes on one side while drilling continued on the other. Figure 9.10 shows a view of the drilling island during remodeling. An annular trench was dug around the entire circumference of the cell deep enough to expose the gravel layer. Grout pipes were driven into the ground, and grout forced into the voids. Ultimately, the trench was filled with concrete to form a continuous wall or ring around the inside face of the piling.

This change in plans resulted in complete development of the lease at a fraction of the cost of the original plan and also in a much shorter time.

Totally unlike the foregoing example is another drilling island which has been constructed in the Pacific off Rincon on the coast of southern

FIG. 9.10 Permanent drilling island for the Monterey Oil Company and the Texas Company off Belmont, California. (*From Offshore, May,* 1956.)

California. This island is constructed of natural materials, as opposed to the steel-sheet-piling wall which formed the perimeter of the island previously described.

The shape in plan, as can be seen in Fig. 9.11, is trapezoidal with sloping sides to simulate a natural island, which at the time of its inception was a requirement imposed by state legislation. Later legislation nullified this requirement and permitted the use of platform-type structures such as were being used in the Gulf of Mexico.

Rincon island is located 3,000 ft from shore in about 46 ft of water.

Consideration of direction and intensity of offshore swells and wave heights for all seasons of the year resulted in orientation of the island so that its long axis is approximately east and west rather than normal to the coast line which bears from east-southeast to west-northwest. The windward western face was designed for waves in excess of 20 ft, which called for armor rock weighing up to 40 tons, and was extended beyond the island at each end, in the form of jetties or short breakwaters, to provide protection against scour to the sides of the island. The sides of

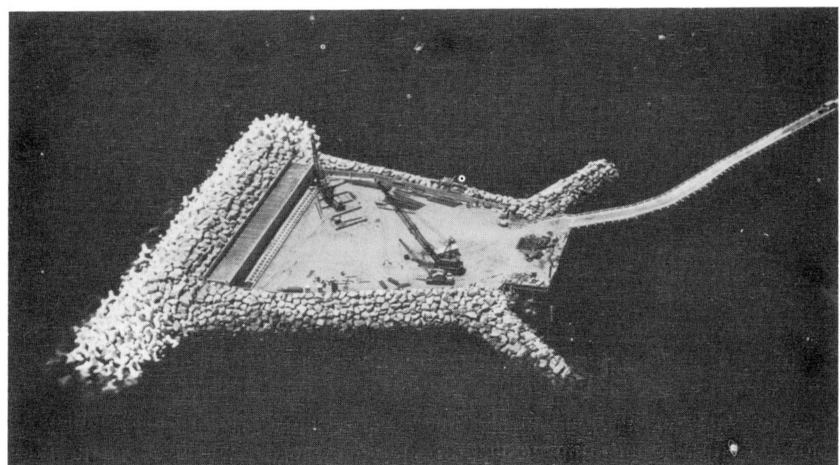

FIG. 9.11 Permanent drilling island for the Richfield Oil Corporation off Rincon, California. (*From Oil and Gas Journal, Aug.* 11, 1956.)

the island were extended in a similar manner to protect the wharf which was constructed on the leeward end of the island.

The general idea of the project was to provide a suitable sand-fill core through which conductor pipes could be driven, and protecting this with successive layers of rock graduated in size and terminating with armor rock. In lieu of using 40-ton armor rock, the windward side was ultimately faced with 1,130 concrete tetrapods, weighing 31 tons each, from a level 19 ft below water to the top of the fill 41 ft above water. The other three sides were constructed to 24 ft above water. An estimated 400,000 cu yd of fill were required for the project.

The method of construction was to place the material in layers starting with a peripheral dyke of small rock to retain the sand, which was placed next. Outer layers of graded rock were added, and the whole process was repeated again and again. A cross section through the face would show a lapping of rock over core material for each layer as the face slopes inward from the bottom extremities.

The area of the island at sea level is about three acres, and a working surface of slightly over one acre will permit drilling an estimated 68 wells. The drilling area, 16 ft above sea level, is enclosed by a concrete wall. The wharf is supported on 16-in. prestressed-concrete piles averaging 80 ft in length. A causeway with a deck 35 ft above water was constructed between the mainland and the island.

9.6 Fixed Drilling and Production Platforms

The world's first overwater oil well was drilled in Caddo Lake, 20 miles north of Shreveport, Louisiana. This took place in May, 1911, and the well produced 450 bbl per day, a most auspicious beginning for what has now grown to be a very large overwater operation. The derrick was set on a wooden platform supported by cypress piles driven in 10 ft of water. For construction of the platform and drilling of the well, Gulf Refining Company provided an offshore fleet consisting of a floating piledriver, 3 tugs, 10 barges, and 26 small boats.

In 1925 Creole Petroleum Corporation made the first attempt at oil drilling in relatively shallow water, 16 ft in depth, in Lake Maracaibo, Venezuela. Wood piles which supported the platform quickly fell prey to the toredo (see Fig. 5.30 as an example of toredo action on a plain wood pile in a temporary construction platform in Lake Maracaibo for less than 1 year), and as a result of this experience this type of construction was changed to standard precast-concrete piles in 1927. These piles were made in three sizes: 16 in. square up to 69 ft long; 20 in. square up to 99 ft in length; and 24 in. square in lengths up to 133 ft.

The general method of drilling in Lake Maracaibo consists of erecting a permanent drilling platform with derrick and draw works and mooring to it a tender or barge equipped with mud pumps, bits, casing, and all the miscellaneous materials and equipment required for the drilling. The foundations for these platforms have, in general, conformed to a pattern of either 24 or 30 ft square (size determined by the derrick), except for occasional multiple-well platforms which are rectangular, with a length equal to twice the square dimension. A steel superstructure, to provide a drilling floor about 30 ft above the lake level, is erected on the foundation platform, of which one side is usually cantilevered out about 25 ft to provide room for the draw works. Figure 9.12 shows a typical well-drilling platform used in the lake. When a well is completed the derrick and drilling superstructure may be removed, leaving in place only the lower production floor, which supports the well piping and blowout preventer, or the derrick may be left in place for future reworking of the well. The oil is piped directly from the well by an underwater system of piping leading to a collection or gathering platform, which serves a number of wells and which supports small storage tanks, separators, and pumps. The latter transfer the oil through a pipeline on the

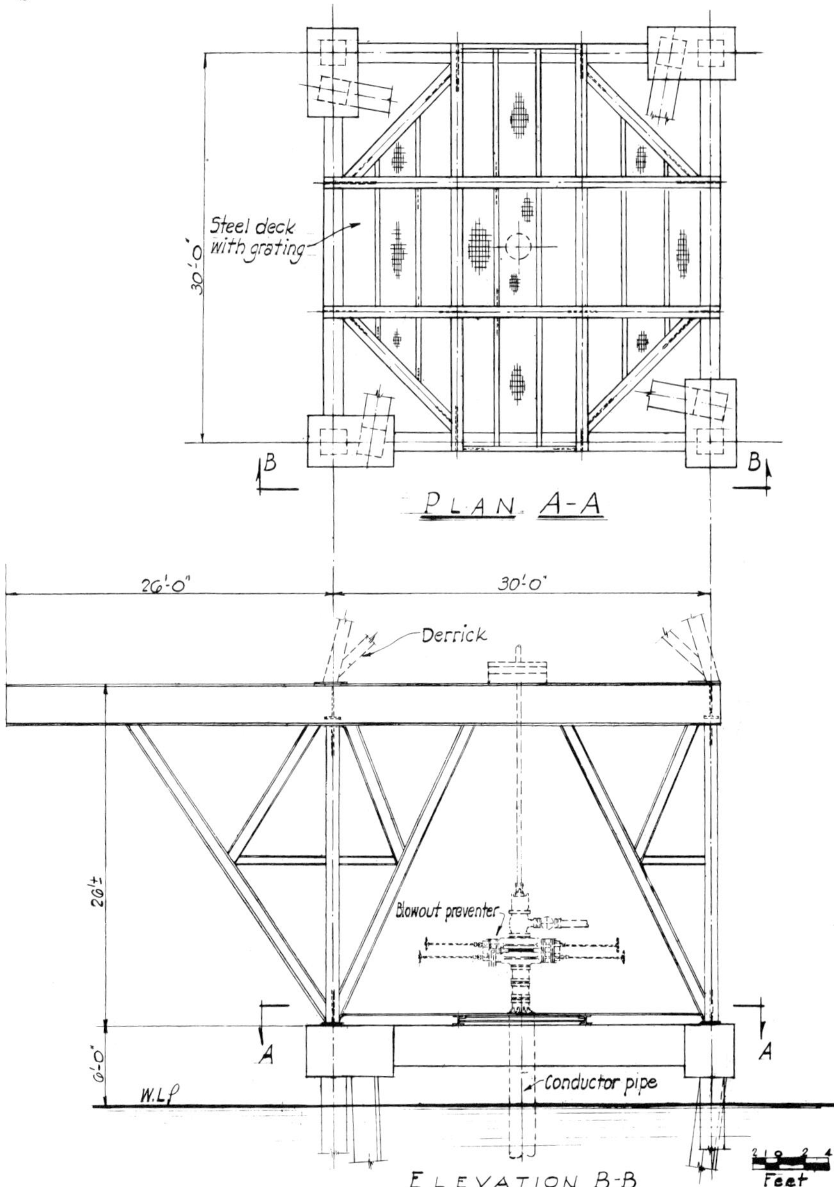

FIG. 9.12 Typical well-drilling platform used in Lake Maracaibo, Venezuela.

lake bottom to large storage tanks on shore or to pumping stations which pump the oil long distances to the refineries. A few years ago the inlet to Lake Maracaibo was deepened by dredging, which enables ocean-going tankers to enter the lake, and some of the oil is transferred directly into these tankers.

The earliest well-drilling platforms were in the shallow water along the shore, but in recent years the drilling has progressed to areas out toward the center of the lake, some 30 to 35 miles from either shore, and in water up to 110 ft in depth. In much of this area the bottom is a soft silt for a depth of 50 ft or more, the over-all combination of deep water and soft bottom requiring piles up to 200 ft in length. It is fortunate that, unlike the Gulf of Mexico, the maximum waves do not exceed a height of 8 ft, and the wind a maximum of 80 miles per hour; otherwise, the piles would have to be considerably longer and the platforms of much heavier construction.

Steel piles or cylinders would have been the natural solution to the foundation problem had it not been that the water in the lake is the most corrosive in the world owing to free carbon dioxide and low alkalinity, and cathodic protection is not very effective because of the lack of salinity. Nevertheless, one of the oil companies has used the steel template type of platform quite extensively, its installation being justified on the basis that its greatly reduced cost compared to conventional precast piles and poured-in-place caps would enable it to be renewed after five or more years, if necessary, without greatly exceeding the capital cost of the more permanent type of installation.

The template type of platform foundation is a prefabricated steel tower consisting of four tubular columns, one at each corner, connected with steel pipe bracing, all of which are welded together to form a structure of the approximate height of the depth of water in which it is to be installed. This tower or template is set on the lake bottom, if the material is not too soft, otherwise it is held in a suspended condition a few feet off the bottom by a derrick boat while a second derrick boat drives pipe piles through the corner members of the tower. The template is then welded to the piles and the space between the two is filled with grout which protects the main supporting members, but leaves the bracing members vulnerable to corrosion.

A recent noteworthy step forward in the template platform type of construction has been made in the development of an all-aluminum-alloy template of welded construction. The corner members of the template are 34-in.-diameter cylinders with ⅜-in.-thick walls. Most of the various cross-bracing members are 12-in.-O.D. by ⅜-in. wall pipe. The aluminum templates are fabricated in the United States, loaded upright on a flat deck barge, and towed to Lake Maracaibo. They are installed in a manner similar to the steel template platforms; driving 24-in.-diameter steel pipe piles through the corner aluminum cylinders, which have rubber gaskets at the bottom and top to prevent the steel from coming in contact with the aluminum and thereby causing bimetallic corrosion of the aluminum. The space between the outside of the steel pile and the aluminum cylinder is grouted. If a nonproducing well is encountered, it is planned to remove and re-use the aluminum templates by cutting

FIG. 9.13 Aluminum templates being transported by barge to Lake Maracaibo, Venezuela. (*Courtesy of J. Ray McDermott, Inc.*)

off the steel piles below the bottom of the template. When installing the template the second time, the steel piles would be reduced to 20 in. in diameter so that they can be driven inside the 24-in. steel piles which remain in the template. Figure 9.13 shows the aluminum templates being transported by barge to Lake Maracaibo.

Concrete being resistant to the corrosive water of Lake Maracaibo, it is only natural that a great deal of study has been made in developing its use in platform foundations which would be suitable for use in the deepest parts of the lake. Because the installations of drilling platforms in the lake involve many duplications it was all the more important that, in addition to a sound design, an economical method of installation be developed.

In 1939 the Creole Petroleum Corporation developed a concrete-encased steel-shell hollow cylinder or caisson, which lent itself to mass production, and which could be assembled into various lengths up to 185 ft to suit the condition at each drilling-platform location. The cylinders were manufactured in three different sizes with outside diameters of 4 ft 2 in., 4 ft 10 in., and 5 ft 6 in., with a wall thickness of 5 in., and were cast in a vertical form with an inside liner of ¼-in. steel plate.

FIG. 9.14 Prefabricated steel derrick base being lowered onto finished foundation. (*From Engineering News-Record, Dec.* 26, 1946.)

The cylinders were cast in 15-ft sections, with the steel liner plate protruding 4 in. at each end. The sections were laid flat, end to end, and were welded together to form a hollow cylinder of whatever length was required, the space between the ends of the concrete walls being filled with a low-shrinkage concrete. A precast-concrete point and a steel plate welded into the end of the top section completed the airtight hollow cylinder or caisson, which could be rolled down the ways from the casting yard into the water and floated out to the site of the platform. Virtually the entire foundation was prefabricated on land. It consisted of a 24-ft-square prefabricated steel derrick platform, with cantilevered wings on opposite sides, extending 10 and 15 ft, respectively, which rested on four concrete cylinders, as previously described, one located at each corner of a square that measured 21 ft center to center of cylinders. Arched box girders of welded steel were clamped to the caissons at the top to form a rigid-frame structure, which eliminated the need for batter piles or lateral bracing. The cylinders were sunk by filling them with water and loading them with 200 tons of precast weights. Figure 9.14

FIG. 9.15 Variable-section concrete pile at casting yard.

shows the prefabricated steel base on which the derrick is erected being lowered onto the finished foundation with portal braces attached.

Over 200 drilling-platform foundations utilizing the concrete steel-lined hollow cylinders were installed before this method was abandoned in favor of variable-section precast-concrete piles using four vertical and four batter piles for each drilling-platform foundation (Fig. 9.15). These piles, which are cast up to 160 ft in length and weigh as much as 60 tons, are being installed by huge derrick boats designed especially for this purpose. The vertical piles are pushed into the lake bottom by 50-ton concrete weights, a total load of 200 tons being placed by the derrick on the top of each pile, as shown in Fig. 9.16. The batter piles are driven on a 1-on-10 batter, and at each corner a vertical and batter pile are connected by a poured-in-place concrete pile cap. These caps serve as the supports for the lower production platform which ties the four corner pile caps together.

It was only natural that the development of the prestressed pile found a ready application for its use in the foundations of the drilling platforms and other structures in the lake. The Raymond prestressed cylinder file (produced by Raymond International, Inc.) is being used for the foundations of many of these structures. This pile is a hollow, cylindrical,

FIG. 9.16 Creole Petroleum Company constructing drilling platform in Lake Maracaibo, Venezuela, showing 200-ton weight pushing vertical pile into lake bottom.

precast- prestressed-concrete pile, made of a series of sections, normally 16 ft in length, placed end to end and held together by cables of high-strength steel wire. The pile sections are manufactured by a centrifugal casting method known as the CEN-VI-RO method, similar to the manner in which concrete pipe is commonly made. The longitudinal holes for the prestressing cables are formed by rubber tubes stiffened with steel rods. With this method of spinning the pile, 28-day concrete strengths of 8,000 to 10,000 lb per sq in. are obtained.

The individual pile sections, after being cured, are placed end to end on the prestressing bed so that the longitudinal holes line up. The ends of each section are spread with a special resin adhesive which, after assembly and prestressing, hardens and welds the sections together. Prestressing cables, usually consisting of 12 parallel wires of 0.192 in. diameter, are then placed by special machine in the 1⅜-in. diameter holes in the assembled pile. Once placed, the cables are stressed by jacks to approximately 25 tons each. After stressing, the wires are anchored with steel or aluminum anchor cones, which do not bear against the concrete but against special steel sleeve cages attached to the re-usable end-ring assembly. The pile is then rolled off the stressing bed and made ready for grouting of the cables. The normal procedure is first to flush the longitudinal holes with water and then to apply a neat cement grout, under a pressure of up to 150 lb per sq in., until the interstices are completely filled. After allowing the grout to cure for approximately 36 hours the stressed cables are cut, thereby transferring the force by the bonding action of the grout. The completed prestressed pile is then ready to be transferred to the storage yard.

The piles or cylinders can be manufactured in several sizes but the following two sizes are standard: 36 in. O.D. with 4-in. walls and 54 in. O.D. with 5-in. walls.

A typical drilling platform consists of eight 36-in. prestressed hollow-cylinder piles, one vertical and one batter pile at each of the four corners, which are connected by poured-in-place concrete pile caps. Several variations are being used in the construction of the deck or lower floor, which may consist of either a structural steel frame set directly on the pile caps or precast-concrete units.

A rigid-frame foundation utilizing one vertical 54-in.-diameter prestressed-concrete cylinder at each of the four corners has been constructed, but has met with less favor because of its lack of rigidity compared to the platforms supported by both vertical and batter piles.

Drilling-platform foundations similar to the above are being constructed in Lake Maracaibo, but they use prestressed cylinders cast in the conventional manner.

Since the water in the Gulf of Mexico is not so corrosive as that in Lake Maracaibo, the steel-template type of platform has continued to be one of the favored types of construction for both tender-type and self-contained drilling and production platforms. Figure 9.17 shows a template being transported on a barge with launching ways and the launching of the template. When the barge reached the drilling site in 136 ft of water it was partially flooded to bring one end about a foot below water, and the structure was launched from the ways. The tubular members, which had been previously sealed to provide buoyancy, permitted the structure to barely float. A 250-ton crane righted the structure, and

FIG. 9.17 Template for drilling platform in the Gulf of Mexico being transported to location and launched. (*Courtesy of J. Ray McDermott, Inc.*)

water was pumped into the members to cause it to sink to the bottom in an upright position. Pipe piles were then driven through the tubular columns of the template, and the prefabricated platform was then installed on top, as a single unit, as shown in Fig. 9.18. Outfitting of the tender-type platform with draw works and derrick followed.

To provide a platform which would be stable in 200 ft of water in the Gulf of Mexico, a template, 30 ft square at the top, 94 ft square at the bottom, and 230 ft high, was fabricated and barged out to the site, where it was lifted overboard by two 250-ton derricks as shown in Fig. 9.19. After placing it in its final upright position, piles were driven through the splayed tubular corners to the required penetration in the bottom. The prefabricated platform with draw works and other drilling equipment was lifted into place as a unit and secured to the supporting structure. The oil derrick was then lifted onto the platform completing the installation of the tender-type drilling platform.

FIG. 9.18 Installing prefabricated platform on template. (*Courtesy of J. Ray McDermott, Inc.*)

A monumental example of fixed offshore structures is the Freeport Sulphur Company's sulfur mining installation at Grand Isle, six or seven miles off the coast of Louisiana in the Gulf of Mexico, which is believed to be the world's largest steel island, nearly one-half mile long. This first offshore mining plant of its kind is to mine a major deposit of sulfur, which was discovered during oil explorations in the area. Sulfur is taken from the underwater deposit, some 1,700 ft below the floor of the Gulf, by liquefying it with superheated water. The liquid sulfur is then pumped by pipeline ashore where it will be solidified.

The site is in 50 ft of water. Erection of the huge structure was by means of steel templates which were placed in position in the water and pinned with piles up to 237 ft long. Deck sections of each tower were

FIG. 9.19 Template for use in 200 ft of water in the Gulf of Mexico being lifted overboard by two 250-ton derricks. (*Courtesy of J. Ray McDermott, Inc.*)

then placed on top and prefabricated 200-ft-long bridge spans were lifted into place between them, providing access between the platforms. Figure 9.20 shows a huge floating crane, rigged with double booms to provide lifting capacity of 800 tons, lifting a deck section for the power-plant platform, which weighed approximately 700 tons and is believed to be the largest single lift in overwater construction work.

One of the more pretentious fixed drilling structures is one that was installed for the Standard Oil Company of California offshore from Summerland, in the Pacific. The platform was designed to permit drilling of 25 wells without moving, and the rig was able to drill two wells at once. The supporting prefabricated structure was provided with four 27-ft-diameter by 40-ft high caissons, one at the bottom of each of the four vertical legs. These permitted the 167-ft-high frame to be floated and towed out to the drilling site about two miles offshore in 100 ft of water. A 250-ton floating derrick was brought alongside and supported the tower while the caissons were flooded, and the structure settled vertically until it rested upon the bottom. Rotating high-pressure jets in each of the caissons were operated to accomplish penetration of the caissons into the bottom while material was discharged by air lift. When the desired penetration was achieved the caissons were plugged with tremie-placed concrete at the bottom, followed by sand, then more con-

FIG. 9.20 800-ton capacity double-boom floating derrick lifting deck section for power-plant platform in the Gulf of Mexico for the Freeport Sulphur Company. (*Courtesy of the American Hoist and Derrick Co.*)

crete, and finally topped off with sand. About 6,000 tons of ballast were thus placed to anchor the tower firmly into the bottom. A 110-ft-square platform was then hoisted into place about 50 ft above the water. A novel feature of this unit is that it is all-electric in its operation, power being supplied from shore through a submarine cable laid on the ocean bottom. Two 200-kw diesel-electric units are provided for emergency drilling in case of power failure. The platform is self-contained except for crew quarters, only emergency facilities being provided for this purpose. Personnel is ferried back and forth by helicopter or service boat on an 8-hour-shift basis.

9.7 Mobile Drilling Units

Exploratory drilling in unproved fields is fraught with uncertainty, and means whereby this can be accomplished with a minimum expenditure of time and money is the goal of designers. A fixed platform is not needed until a well has been completed, and the expense of such a platform can be deferred, when using a mobile unit, until the well has been proved productive, or, in the case of a dry or unsatisfactory hole, can be eliminated entirely by capping the well on the bottom. If oil is discovered some operators find it economically desirable to move the mobile unit about in order to define the field, straight holes being less costly and more quickly drilled than directional holes from a fixed platform. Once the field is well defined, it may then be more desirable to install fixed self-contained or tended platforms from which directional holes can be drilled with reasonable assurance of success, and which ultimately can serve as production platforms after completion of the drilling.

The self-contained mobile unit, although of high initial cost (some have been reported as costing more than five million dollars when fully outfitted), appears to have established a place for itself in the oil industry's offshore-drilling operations, as it provides continuity of operation, owing to rapid installation and removal at each drilling site, which results in a minimum amount of lost time from storms. Over the years many designs have been made, some of which have been patented, but only a limited number of types of rigs have been constructed and operated with any great degree of success. While these differ widely in design, all have a common objective, i.e., to provide a temporary platform safe from wind, wave, tide, and current. This applies not only to those which can be readily moved from one location to another, but also to those which will remain stable regardless of the nature or conformation of the sea bottom.

Early designs produced a variety of mobile units which were suitable for relatively shallow waters. As new concessions were obtained farther offshore in deeper water, designers developed mobile units to fit this need and are continuing to study and to develop methods and equipment for exploratory drilling in deeper and deeper waters. When it is considered that in the Gulf of Mexico these mobile units must be designed to withstand hurricane winds up to 125 miles per hour and waves up to 40 ft in height, the problem confronting the designer is no small one.

Most mobile units fall within one of three general categories. First, there is the barge or vessel which remains in a floating state while drilling and is held in position by at least four anchors, widely spaced, and whose cables are held taut by winches on the deck. Secondly, there is the self-elevating type which consists of a buoyant bargelike deck with columns or legs arranged to drop through wells in the deck and furnish support when resting upon or penetrating into the sea bottom. By various means the deck is then raised upon these columns, until it is safely above the waves that may be anticipated, and then secured. Thirdly, there is the submersible type which consists of a buoyant structure which supports a tall rigid superstructure topped by a platform. By flooding the lower buoyant structure, the whole unit sinks and rests upon the bottom, leaving the platform still sufficiently elevated above the water. There are a number of variations of these fundamental principles, some of which have features which place them in an overlapping category.

Barges have long been used for core boring and probing of underwater

FIG. 9.21 *Cuss* I floating drill barge. (*From Oil and Gas Journal, June* 9, 1958.)

areas. Generally, such exploratory work is carried to limited depths depending upon the nature of the project for which the data are required. In the field of offshore-drilling operations, the work done by the boring rig is immensely magnified. Rigs must work to depths measured in thousands of feet often in very deep water. Since most exploration is carried out in totally unprotected locations, the vessel must be rugged and thoroughly seaworthy.

The drill ship is the ultimate in mobility. Self-propelled, it is able to maneuver itself into position and maintain its position with greater ease than is the case with a barge. Various types of vessels have been converted into drill ships, the majority being provided with open wells amidship through which the drilling is done. The structural frame of the ship is reinforced to carry the loads imposed by the mast or derrick and the drill string, as well as the pipe racks and other heavy loads. To compensate for the rolling motion of the ship, the traveling block is guided from the deck to the crown of the derrick, and the rotary is mounted similarly to a gyroscope and powered by hydraulic motors. Vertical motion is taken care of by providing several sections of drill pipe with vertical slip joints which assure continuous seating of the bit on the bottom of the hole, while the drill string lengthens or shortens as the ship rides the waves or fluctuates with the tides.

Off the coast of southern California, using drill ships such as described

FIG. 9.22 *Nola* 2 floating drill barge. (*Courtesy of the Zapata Off-Shore Co.*)

above, core holes have been successfully drilled in water as deep as 1,500 ft, and drilling costs have been found comparable to those of onshore operations. Typical of those ships is the *Cuss* I owned by the Continental, Union, Superior, and Shell group and illustrated in Fig. 9.21.

The first ship ever to drill for oil in the Gulf of Mexico, Zapata Off-Shore Company's *Nola* 1, similar to *Nola* 2 shown in Fig. 9.22, has been equipped in a slightly different manner from those already described and has a derrick mounted on a portside overhang counterbalanced by a ballast tank overhanging the starboard side. Ballast pumps are used to compensate for changes in equilibrium brought about by variations in weight of drill pipe and casing handled by or racked in the derrick. Eight 10,000-lb anchors, four on the bow and four on the stern, serve to moor the vessel. One time, on location off the Louisiana coast, 7-ft waves resulting from a sudden storm gave the *Nola* 1 a 5° roll, but drilling continued without interruption. The water depth at this location was 26 ft, although the ship can operate in 200 ft of water. Here, blowout preventers and other equipment were mounted on the casing several feet above water, and no structure of any sort was necessary.

For deep water, a tripod structure pioneered by Zapata was used, the perpendicular leg serving as a conductor through which the well was drilled. The ship is equipped to set and erect fixed platforms as required for drilling or production, a feature made possible by the over-the-side mounting of the derrick.

Offshore drilling used to be done by first sinking a casing to the required depth and terminating it above the water surface. Sometimes a protective conductor pipe was used. Attached to the top of the casing was the well head equipment consisting of control gates, blowout preventers, mud crosses, strippers, etc., which, although above the water, nevertheless functioned just as though the well was being drilled on land. However, with this arrangement, it was not possible to readily move the rig from one site to another, and, therefore, mobile rigs with drilling slots or overhanging drilling equipment were developed.

The use of casing to set the well head equipment above water is limited to sites where water depth is such that this is structurally and economically feasible. For those locations where water is too deep for above-water completion, or where, for any reason, the well is to be completed below the surface in shallow water, subsea well head equipment, such as that manufactured by Shaffer Tool Works, is now available and can be utilized by any type of drilling unit including drill ships or barges with hull wells. With this type of underwater drilling equipment, if it is necessary for any reason to move from the site during the drilling operation, the procedure is to remove the drill string, close the full shut-off gate, release guide cables and mud and hydraulic lines from the rig, and fasten them to buoys. The drilling ship is then free to leave and return as desired.

The idea of well completions on the bottom of the sea is one which, if and when reduced to practice, might well alter the over-all concept and economics of drilling and result in the use of floating rigs in preference to all others. Whereas the completion of wells on platforms is limited to water depths within the feasibility of bottom-supported structures, the sea-bottom completion has no specific depth limitations and might well prove to be the key to an unprecedented expansion of offshore drilling and production.

The second category of mobile, or self-elevating, units was pioneered by De Long, by adjusting the mobile wharf design already described in Sec. 9.2 to accommodate the requirements of well drilling. One of the earliest of the mobile units, Offshore Company's no. 1, had a hull 70 by 203 ft by 8 ft 6 in. and was supported on twelve 6-ft-diameter caissons with De Long pneumatic gripper-type jacks. These jacks, with a stroke of 6 in. and a cycle of 2 minutes, provide a jacking speed of 15 ft per hr.

Another De Long design was developed utilizing hydraulic jacks and open-trussed towers instead of the pneumatic jacks and circular caissons of the earlier designs. Instead of friction grips around a circular caisson,

FIG. 9.23 Two mobile drilling platforms of the Offshore Company. (*Courtesy of Offshore.*)

positive engagement was accomplished by sliding pins into recesses in two of the four vertical members of the towers. Figure 9.23 is typical of this type of platform when in a floating condition ready for transport. The two units in the illustration, no. 54 and no. 55, were built by the American Bridge Division of the United States Steel Corporation for the Offshore Company and have hulls measuring 200 by 104 by 15 ft deep.

Each unit was provided with eight towers 223 ft tall. At the bottom of each tower was a vertical steel spud tank, 11 ft 9 in. in diameter by 50 ft high, with a convex dished head at the top and a concave dished head recessed about 2 ft at the bottom. The bottom construction was designed to prevent excessive penetration of the sea floor when the towers were fully loaded. The four vertical members of the openwork towers were welded to the tanks and consisted of a pair of circular pipe columns diametrically opposite and a pair of triangular columns on the other axis.

The triangular members were provided with square openings on 25-in. centers, into which the pins mentioned above were slipped to provide support for the towers when the hull was afloat or support for the hull when the towers were resting on the bottom, during the elevating or lowering cycles, or while drilling. These members were trussed together by tubular cross bracing. Each tower weighed about 200 tons and was designed to carry live and dead loads in combination with maximum wind and wave forces.

The hull was provided with wells which guided the towers vertically and a pair of jack-mounting elements were incorporated into the hull structure on the fore and aft axis of each well. Hydraulic jacks were hung from the tops of the mounting elements, the guided lower ends being provided with heads carrying the pins to engage the slots in the towers. Similar pins were provided on the top of each mounting element. These upper and lower pins were hydraulically operated and interlocked so that neither could be retracted unless the other was engaged. One of these jacking assemblies is shown in Fig. 9.24.

Operational procedure for installation of the unit at the drilling site follows the pattern described under Sec. 9.2, Mobile Wharves. The mechanics of the jacking cycle consist of having the upper pin on the jack support in the retracted position, the jack retracted, and the lower pin on the jack engaged with the tower leg. The jack is extended 25 in., the hull rises a similar distance, and the upper pin is engaged. This permits retraction of the lower pin, whereupon the jack is retracted 25 in., the lower pin reengaged, the upper pin retracted, and the cycle repeated. For lowering the platform the procedure is reversed. The equipment was designed to provide a jacking speed of 16 ft per hr.

The first mobile drilling platform to arrive at the Pacific Coast was Pacific Driller 1 of Offshore Constructors, Inc., designed by De Long. This unit has the distinction of being equipped with the salvaged caissons and pneumatic gripper jacks that were used off Cape Cod to raise the platform of the first Texas Tower. In most respects it was similar to the other De Long pneumatic units that were built for use in the Gulf, except two jacking units were used in tandem for each caisson. The hull, 200 by 100 by 13 ft deep, was supported on eight steel caissons 6 ft in diameter and 195 ft long. Each caisson weighed 80 tons, the hull 1,100 tons, and the whole unit fully equipped weighed 4,000 tons.

Design criteria for units to be used in the Pacific vary somewhat from those governing Gulf designs. Average bottom in the Pacific is firm sand over firmly consolidated silt. Wave and wind forces are less critical but the earthquake factor must be considered.

R. G. LeTourneau, Inc., first adapted the tripod-support principle to mobile drilling units in Zapata Off-Shore Company's Scorpion shown in Fig. 9.25. The platform of the Scorpion was constructed around three horizontal steel cylinders which served as the main structural members and also provided buoyancy to float the unit. Guides or spud wells for

FIG. 9.24 De Long hydraulic jacking assembly. (*Courtesy of the De Long Corp.*)

the three towers were bracketed out from the main structure and were enclosed by semicylindrical shells to streamline the contours of the hull. The two outer cylinders or floats were extended at the aft end of the structure to provide a drilling slot to accommodate the derrick, which was supported on transverse brackets welded to the cylinders. Corrugated-steel bottom plates were used to add strength to the platform which measures 185 by 150 by 20 ft deep.

In addition to having the triangular arrangement of tripod legs or towers, the pattern was carried further by constructing each leg with three main vertical members to form an open truss of triangular cross section 151 ft high. These towers, at the bottom, embrace a spud tank, 30 ft in diameter by 16 ft high, which forms a footing for the leg. Each of the main vertical members is provided with an integral toothed rack and pinion, extending from top to bottom, which enables the platform to climb up or down the tripod support. Each pinion is driven by an

FIG. 9.25 Mobile drilling platform Scorpion. (*Courtesy of the Zapata Off-Shore Co.*)

individual electric gear motor equipped with an integral motor-load brake which automatically sets when power is interrupted, thus locking the platform to the legs in case of power failure. This gear-driven mechanism, which has the advantage of providing continuous vertical motion as opposed to the step-by-step motion which characterizes most jacking systems, is shown during construction in Fig. 9.26. The vertical speed of one foot per minute minimizes the time the hull spends being lifted from or lowered to the water surface and during which wave action tends to pound the hull while it is neither floating upon nor out of reach of the waves. Equipment on this as well as other heavy-duty LeTourneau units has a capability of drilling to 20,000 ft.

The Vinegaroon, also built for the Zapata Off-Shore Company, differs from the Scorpion in that the horizontal floats or cylinders were omitted, and the hull took on a more triangular shape, as can be seen in Fig. 9.27. Corrugated steel plates were used for the sides, another feature which distinguished it from its predecessor and which is a novel type of hull construction. The Vinegaroon measures 194 by 152 by 20 ft deep. The trussed triangular spuds are 145 ft high, including spud tanks 35 ft in

FIG. 9.26 Rack and pinion drive. (*Courtesy of R. G. LeTourneau, Inc.*)

diameter by 32 ft high. A distinctive feature of the LeTourneau design is the provision of a helicopter deck atop the forward spud tower where it is more easily and conveniently supported than is the case with decks which are cantilevered out from the hull. The complete unit weighs about 4,000 tons. A typical LeTourneau unit is shown in plan and elevation in Fig. 9.28.

Other platforms built to the same dimensions include Mr. Cap owned by Barnwell Offshore, Inc., a unit for Japanese Petroleum Company, Ltd., and Julie Ann for Dixilyn Drilling Corporation. The latter differs only in the height of the legs, which is 175 ft, permitting drilling in at least 125 ft of water.

Another LeTourneau platform, the C. E. Thornton, owned by Reading and Bates Offshore Drilling Company, follows the familiar pattern of tripod legs and triangular hull but is much lighter and less expensive than the other platforms mentioned. Nevertheless, it is capable of drilling to 15,000 ft in 85 ft of water and provides the usual self-contained features that are found in all the others. The hull measures 146 by 139 by 15 ft deep. The legs are 140 ft tall with 24-ft-diameter spud tanks, 20 ft

FIG. 9.27 Mobile drilling platform Vinegaroon. (*Courtesy of R. G. LeTourneau, Inc.*)

high. The complete unit weighs about 3,000 tons, which is considerably less than the heavy-duty types.

In addition to the self-contained platforms described above, LeTourneau has also produced a novel mobile platform which depends upon the services of a tender. The design is essentially similar to the larger units but accommodates only the derrick, draw works, and diesel-electric generators to operate the electric motor-driven elevating mechanism. All other equipment, supplies, quarters, etc., are provided by the tender. One unit owned by Arabian-American Oil Company operates in the Persian Gulf and measures only 92 by 104 by 10 ft deep. The triangular towers are 103 ft tall, with spud tanks 18 ft in diameter by 10 ft high.

A novel design by LeTourneau utilizes the mobile platform as the support for a 250-ton revolving crane with 200-ft boom. The supporting legs provide a stable base which greatly improves its lifting characteris-

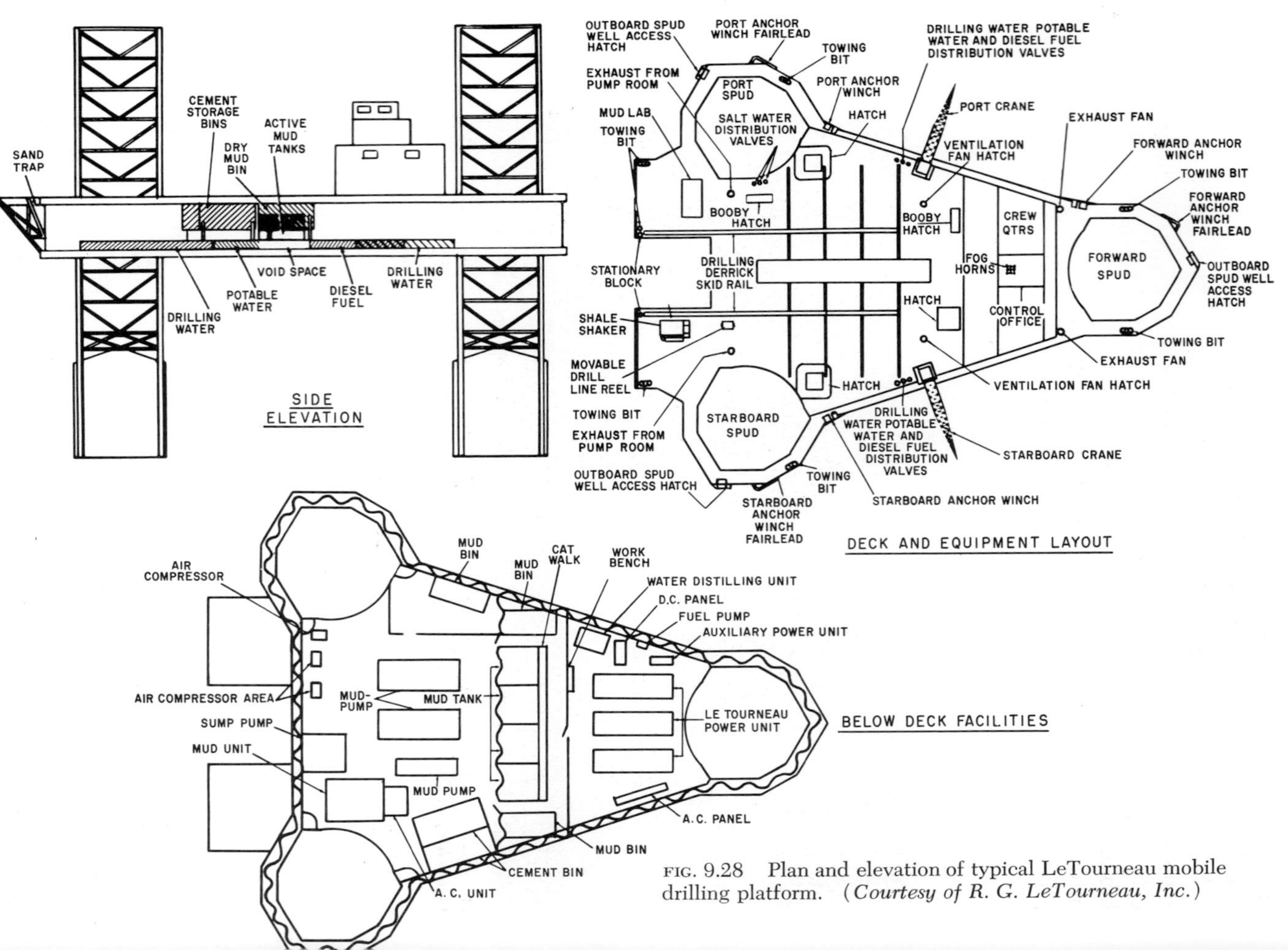

FIG. 9.28 Plan and elevation of typical LeTourneau mobile drilling platform. (*Courtesy of R. G. LeTourneau, Inc.*)

tics as compared with conventional floating cranes. As of 1960, this rig was being used to construct the Lake Maracaibo bridge.

LeTourneau has also prepared a design for a mobile drilling unit, shown in various phases of erection in Fig. 9.29, which is capable of extending its tripod towers to bottom in 600 ft of water. The legs are fabricated in sections which can be added as they are sunk. In order to provide adequate stability for a structure so high, the spud guides are pivoted to allow the splaying of the legs, after they have been extended

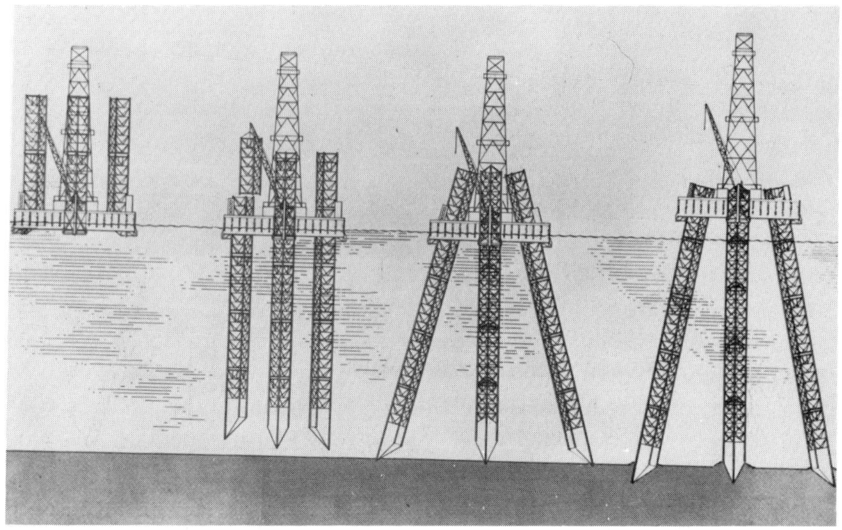

FIG. 9.29 Mobile drilling platform for deep water in various stages of erection. (*Courtesy of R. G. LeTourneau, Inc.*)

to full length and just before they touch bottom. This results in a unit closely resembling the tripod for a transit or level. Jacking apparatus holds the legs thus spread, while the gear motors drive the tripod into the bottom in the usual manner. When resistance equals the sinking force, the hull elevates upon the legs, the changing vertical angle being constantly compensated for by adjustment of the jacks.

The versatility of mobile platforms is well illustrated in the George F. Ferris, a self-elevating De Long design which was constructed for use in laying a 12-ft-diameter submarine outfall sewer for the City of Los Angeles. The unit has four square trussed towers 275 ft high, which allow it to work in the 200-ft water depth at the site. It is moored in its floating position by anchors, and when in exact position the towers are lowered to bear upon the bottom. The platform is then elevated upon the towers just as is done in self-elevating drilling units. After that portion of the submarine pipe which can be installed from this location has been completed, the platform is lowered to its floating position, the towers raised slightly, and the unit moved along to the next position. Upon completion of the outfall line, the owners planned to convert the unit into an offshore drilling rig, the design having been developed in order to permit this to be done.

Mr. Gus was one of the more publicized mobile platforms because of its untimely overturning and destruction in a hurricane in 1957. It was a 4,000-ton self-elevating rig consisting of an upper drilling section and a lower submersible foundation section or hull. When the rig was being towed, the upper section rode piggy-back on the lower section. The drilling platform was supported by four columns attached to the lower hull and by eight piles, 5 ft in diameter, which were pushed into the bottom through wells in the lower hull. All 12 supports were actuated by slip-type hydraulic jacks attached to the upper platform.

When the unit was properly located at the drilling site, the eight spuds were lowered until they penetrated the bottom sufficiently to support their own weight. The platform was then raised to drilling level, approximately 67 ft above the water, by jacking upon four of the spuds. As the platform load was applied to the four spuds they were forced downward to refusal, and the platform started its climb. After full height was reached, the other four spuds were also jacked down to refusal, and the platform was finally leveled off. The hull was then flooded and, together with its four columns, settled slowly to the bottom guided by the eight spuds. The jacks on the four columns forced the hull firmly into the bottom, and the unit was ready for drilling.

Mr. Gus II is the heaviest and costliest mobile platform ever built, weighing 9,000 tons and costing $6.5 million. Its design was based on experiences gained from the first Mr. Gus. It is capable of drilling in 150 ft of water in the calm season and is supported by four huge columns, each 10 ft in diameter by 235 ft high, with a wall thickness varying from 1¼ in. to 2 in., on a lower hull or foundation mat which is 200 by 180 by 10 ft. The drilling platform is 173 by 104 by 22½ ft.

Drilling is done through one leg of a permanent triangular prefabricated well structure which is set in place, before drilling, by use of the two 75-ton stiffleg derricks which are a part of the platform's equipment.

The third category of mobile units is the submersible type, which covers a rather broad field. Some examples of units having secondary submersible features, in addition to their primary mechanical features, have already been covered under the self-elevating category. Other examples, having secondary mechanical features in addition to primary submersible features, will be covered here in conjunction with other conventional submersible designs.

The Kerr-McGee rigs 46 and 47 consist of 14-ft 6-in.-diameter cylinders forming a buoyant grid-pattern pontoon which measures 202 by 242 ft. At the corners, vertical stabilizing columns, 22 ft 0 in. in diameter, extend from a level 6 in. below the bottom of the pontoons to a height of 64 ft 6 in. and are topped by conical caps 36 ft high. Twenty 42-in.-diameter columns and two 48-in.-diameter columns provide additional support for the deck structure, which is 100 ft above the bottom of the pontoon.

FIG. 9.30 Kermac submersible-type mobile drilling platform 46. (*Courtesy of Offshore.*)

The rig is submerged by flooding the pontoon until it rests on the bottom where its stability depends upon the sheer size and mass of the whole structure, its minimum width at the base being more than twice the height of the structure. It was designed for operating in water 70 ft deep, with the main deck about 30 ft above water. In this depth of water it can be submerged to rest on the bottom in about 45 minutes.

The deck is tee-shaped and utilizes only about 60 per cent of the area of the rig. The derrick and derrick substructure are cantilevered 55 ft off the end of the leg of the tee. Six wells can be drilled without moving the rig. Deckhouses at the top of the tee accommodate equipment and crew quarters and provide a helicopter deck. Figure 9.30 shows a view of Kermac 46 rig.

The Offshore Company's no. 53 is a 200-ft-long by 74-ft-wide submersible drilling barge. The drilling platform is supported by twenty-three 30-in. tubular columns which rest upon a submersible pontoon. In addition, there are four 72-in.-diameter spuds which are operated by De Long jacks. On location, the four spuds are jacked down first to position the unit, and then the hull is flooded and sunk to the bottom. Spacious two-

FIG. 9.31 Submersible drilling barge 53 of the Offshore Company.

deck air-conditioned housing has accommodations for 40 men. The low floor has seven 4-man rooms, an air-conditioning machinery room, a laundry, and a shower room. The upper floor has three staterooms, an office with radio equipment, a recreation room, and a modern equipped galley and mess hall. Figure 9.31 shows the Offshore Company's no. 53 submerged at the drilling location.

Ocean Drilling and Exploration Company's Margaret is a twin-hull submersible. Each hull measures 300 by 60 by 12 ft, and the two are separated by an 80-ft-wide gap. Along the outside edge of each hull, there are five stabilizing columns, each 15 ft in diameter by 75 ft high. Tubular truss work supports the deck high above the hulls and is composed of 20-in.- and 50-in.-diameter members. The unit is designed to operate in water up to 65 ft deep. The large hull area lends itself to use at sites with a soft bottom, such as would be encountered near the mouth of the Mississippi.

9.8 Self-contained Platforms

When a structure is referred to as "self-contained," it is implied that it will function as an independent unit serviced only by transport vessels bringing supplies and material and crew boats or helicopters which periodically ferry the crews back and forth. No auxiliary support is required for its full operation.

The self-contained principle has been applied to both fixed and mobile offshore units, the latter being of more particular interest. The features which comprise self-containment in a mobile offshore-drilling unit may be summarized as follows: derrick or mast with rotary table and draw works; mud and jet pumps; mixers and storage tanks; shale shaker and cementing equipment; dry mud, baroid, and cement storage; casing and drill-pipe racks; fuel and water storage; power plant; repair shop; platform elevating and lowering equipment; air-conditioned personnel accommodations, including office, laboratory, sleeping quarters, mess galley, laundry, recreation and sanitary facilities; refrigerated and dry food storage; fire protection; helicopter landing deck; and cranes to handle material and supplies.

These self-contained units usually have accommodations for 40 to 50 men. Figure 9.32 shows the arrangement and space allocation of the facilities on the Offshore Company's no. 54, which illustrates quite well the features of self-containment found on these drilling platforms. Figure 9.28 shows the layout for a triangular shaped self-contained mobile platform of the LeTourneau design.

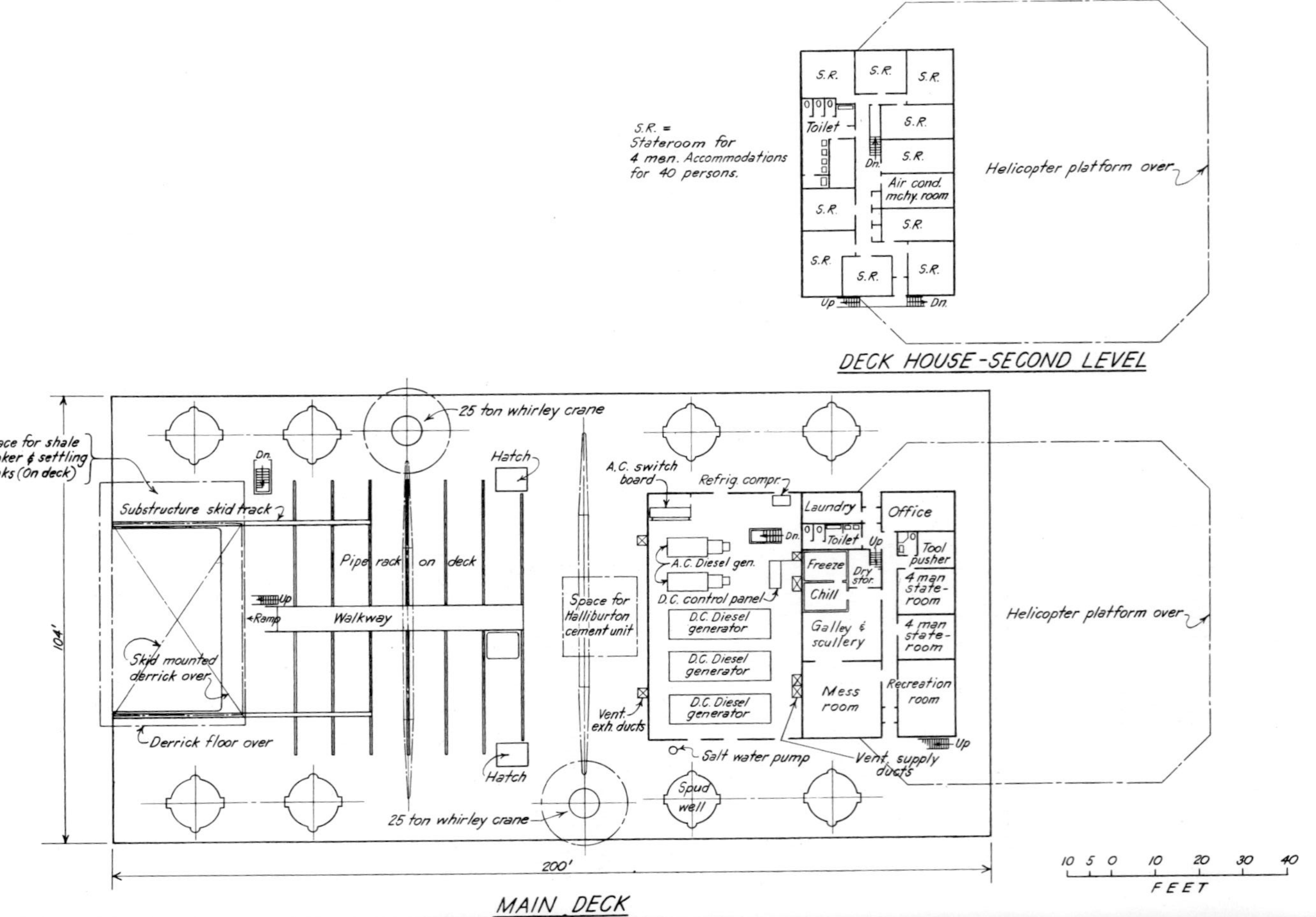

S.R. = Stateroom for 4 men. Accommodations for 40 persons.
S.R.
Toilet
Dn.
Air cond. mchy. room
Up
Dn.
Helicopter platform over
DECK HOUSE-SECOND LEVEL
25 ton whirley crane
Space for shale shaker & settling tanks (On deck)
Dn.
Hatch
A.C. switch board
Refrig. compr.
Laundry
Office
Substructure skid track
Toilet
Up
Tool pusher
Pipe rack on deck
A.C. Diesel gen.
Freeze
Dry stor.
4 man state-room
Up
Ramp
Walkway
Space for Halliburton cement unit
D.C. control panel
Chill
Helicopter platform over
D.C. Diesel generator
Galley & scullery
4 man state-room
Skid mounted derrick over
D.C. Diesel generator
Mess room
Recreation room
Vent. exh. ducts
D.C. Diesel generator
Derrick floor over
Up
Salt water pump
Vent. supply ducts
Hatch
Spud well
25 ton whirley crane
104'
200'
MAIN DECK
10 5 0 10 20 30 40
FEET

Chapter 10 NAVIGATION AIDS

10.1 Introduction

Navigation aids are necessary in rivers, channels, and harbors, and along lake and ocean shores to enable ships using these waterways to travel safely and rapidly to their points of destination. The type of aids required will vary with the kind of waterway they are to serve and their function in this waterway. Navigation aids may be either floating or fixed structures which are equipped with the necessary type of beacon lighting, bells, or other sound-warning devices, and radar reflectors. The type of aid, beacon lighting, sound-warning devices, numbering, and painting are governed by the United States Coast Guard, under a chief administrative officer, with headquarters at Washington, D.C.

10.2 Purpose

The purpose of these aids is to give the ships warning of hidden dangers, such as rocks, shoals, sand bars, and important turns in channels, and to guide the ships safely along the coast, through rivers and channels, into harbors and to their berth or anchorage. Navigation aids include the following:

1. Floating buoys and fixed-structure channel markers to outline the navigable portions of channels and harbor entrances
2. Navigation lights on piers, wharves, and dolphins to outline their limits, and on any other objects projecting into navigable waters
3. Fixed-structure light beacons on shore, breakwaters, etc.
4. Lighthouses
5. Lightships
6. Range-light installations on framed structures on shore to guide the ships through the channels and harbor entrances

These various types of navigation aids will be described in the following sections.

10.3 Buoys

Buoys are floating markers which are anchored in their proper locations and may be lighted or unlighted in accordance with the required purpose of each type of marker. They also may have radar reflectors and bells or other sound-warning devices as required at their particular locations. The marine beacon-light lanterns, to be mounted on the buoys, should be of the required color and intensity, and may be fixed, occulting, or flashing in accordance with the navigational requirements. The lighting power may be provided by electric storage batteries or acetylene gas. The buoys are painted in accordance with their location and use. The various types of floating buoys are spar, can, nun, spherical, lighted, sound warning, etc. Spar, can, and nun buoys are unlighted. Spherical buoys may be lighted or unlighted. Light buoys are beacon lighted, and sound-warning buoys may also be lighted. Sound-warning buoys are equipped with the required sound devices such as bells, whistles, or horns.

The coloring and numbering of buoys are uniform in all United States waters and conform to what is known as the lateral system. Briefly, this is as follows: the coloring and numbering of buoys are determined by their positions in the navigable channel, i.e., right or left side of the vessel, entering from seaward and following the channel toward the head of navigation. Since all channels do not lead from seaward, such as the Great Lakes, along the coasts, and the Intracoastal Waterway, the following additional rules govern: On the Great Lakes the buoys are colored and numbered from the outlet of each lake toward its upper end. Proceeding in a southerly direction along the Atlantic Coast, in a northerly and westerly direction along the Gulf Coast, and in a northerly direction along the Pacific Coast is considered the same as proceeding from seaward. The Intracoastal Waterway is marked proceeding from the north to the south.

Typical buoys used as aids to navigation are shown in Fig. 10.1. Their numbering, coloring, chart symbols, lighting, and other characteristics are indicated in Table 10.1. Some of the various types of buoys are described as follows.

Spar Buoys. Spar buoys are floating unlighted long thin masts of wood or metal, 20 to 50 ft in length and appropriately painted, which show above water and are anchored in place by chain and sinker. They are generally used in channels where high-velocity currents or tides are prevalent and also in channels where floating ice is present during seasonal periods. They can also be used as temporary markers.

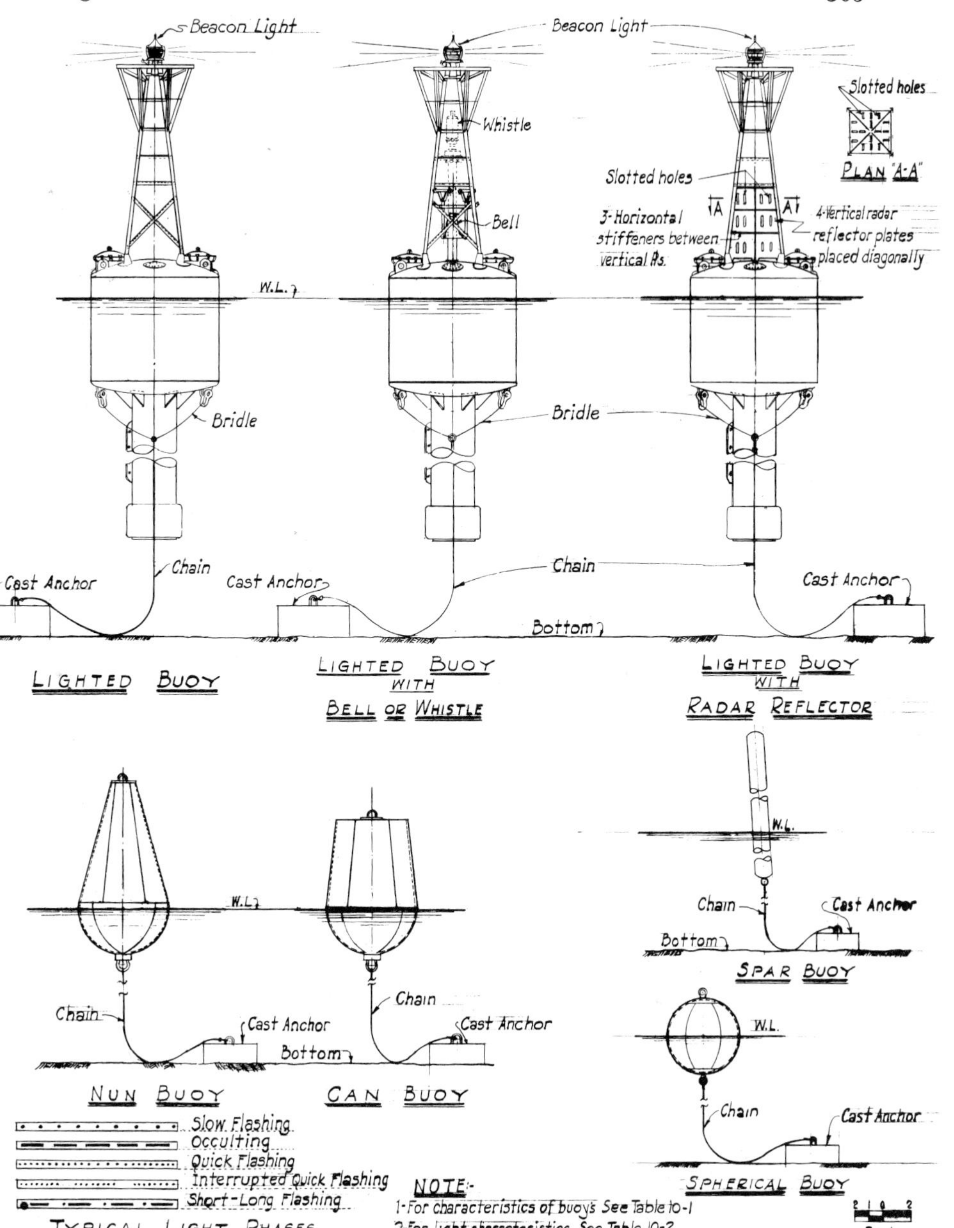

FIG. 10.1 Typical buoys used as aids to navigation.

Table **10.1 Characteristics of Buoys**

Type of buoy and location	Buoy or lightship symbol	Numbering	Paint color	Light color	Usual light phases
Lighted—port		Odd	Black	White or green	Slow flashing, occulting, quick flashing
Lighted—starboard		Even	Red	White or red	Slow flashing, occulting, quick flashing
Lighted bell, gong, or whistle—port	Bell, gong or whis.	Odd	Black	White or green	Slow flashing, occulting, quick flashing
Lighted bell, gong, or whistle—starboard	Bell, gong or whis.	Even	Red	White or red	Slow flashing, occulting, quick flashing
Lighted—fairway—mid-channel	BW	Optional	Black and white vertical stripes	White	Short-long flashing
Lighted—junction, isolated danger or obstruction	RB	Optional	Red and black horizontal bands	White, red or green	Interrupted quick flashing
Bell, gong or whistle—port	Bell, gong or whis.	Odd	Black	None	
Bell, gong or whistle—starboard	Bell, gong or whis.	Even	Red	None	
Can—port	C	Odd	Black	None	
Nun—starboard	N	Even	Red	None	
Spherical	SP	Optional	Optional	None	
Spar	S	Optional	Optional	None	
Checkered		Optional	Colors optional, checkered	None	
Fairway—mid-channel	BW	Optional	Black and white vertical stripes	None	
Junction, isolated danger or obstruction	RB	Optional	Red and black horizontal bands	None	
Quarantine	Y	Optional	Yellow	None	
Fish trap	BW	Optional	Black and white horizontal bands	None	
Lightship		Name	Superstructure white, masts and stacks buff	Optional	Optional

Can Buoys. Can Buoys are floating and unlighted, have a flat top projecting above the water, and are positioned on the port or left side of the channel when entering from seaward in United States waters. They are constructed of metal, painted black, and numbered with odd numbers.

Nun Buoys. Nun buoys are floating and unlighted, have a conical top projecting above the water, and are positioned on the starboard or right side of the channel when entering from seaward in United States waters. They are constructed of metal, painted red, and numbered with even numbers.

Spherical Buoys. Spherical buoys have a domed top projecting above the water and are usually placed to mark special positions in the channels, such as shoals. They may be lighted but are usually unlighted. They are constructed of metal and are painted in accordance with their position and use in the channels.

Lighted Buoys. Lighted buoys are floating and lighted and have tall metal central-framed or tower structures mounted on broad metal floating bases of such proportions as to provide adequate buoyancy and stability in stormy weather. The bases are also designed to contain the required fuel supply, which is generally acetylene gas, in steel tanks. Storage batteries are also used. Marine beacon-light lanterns are mounted on top of the central structures. Radar reflector plates may also be attached to the central structures when required. Light phase characteristics may be either flashing or occulting. Flashing lights have a period of light shorter than the period of darkness while occulting lights have a light period equal to or greater than the period of darkness. The light characteristics are indicated in Table 10.2. These buoys may be used on

***Table* 10.2 Light Characteristics**

Light	Abbreviation	Characteristic phases
Fixed	F.	Continuous
Occulting	Occ.	Long periods of light at regular intervals with equal or short periods of intervening darkness
Flashing	Fl.	Short periods of light at regular intervals with longer periods of intervening darkness
Quick flashing	Qk. Fl.	Light flashing continuously with more than 60 flashes per minute
Interrupted quick flashing	I. Qk.	Light flashing continuously with more than 60 flashes per minute and with total eclipses at regular intervals
Alternating	Alt.	Light that changes color in each period
Group occulting	Gp. Occ.	Light occulting more than once in each period
Group flashing	Gp. Fl.	Light flashing more than once in each period
Short-Long flashing	S.-L.	Short and long flashes at regular intervals with periods of intervening darkness between each group
Fixed and group flashing	F. Gp. Fl.	Fixed light varied at regular intervals by a group of two or more flashes of relatively greater brilliancy
Rotating	Rot.	Rotating light

both sides of channels or in special locations, according to the navigational requirements. They are painted and numbered in accordance with their positions along the channel or at other locations.

Sound-warning Buoys. Sound-warning buoys are floating and may be lighted or unlighted. They have tall metal central-framed structures mounted on broad metal floating bases of such proportions as to provide adequate buoyancy and stability in stormy weather. The bases are also designed to contain the required fuel supply. When marine beacon-light lanterns are used, they are mounted on top of the central structures, and the sounding devices are mounted below. When no lights are used, the sounding devices are mounted on top of the central structures. The sound-warning devices may be bells, gongs, whistles, or horns, which are operated by the movement of the buoy or by automatic mechanical devices. These buoys are referred to as bell buoys, gong buoys, or whistle buoys. They may be used at isolated or special locations to warn shipping in fog or low visibility by day and night. Gong buoys are used to give a distinctive sound when there are several bell buoys in one vicinity. Buoys are painted and numbered in accordance with their locations. They may also be equipped with radar reflector plates when required.

10.4 Fixed-structure Channel Markers

Fixed-structure channel markers are lighted and are fixed into the channel bottom at the proper locations. The structures are generally supported on pipe or H piles driven into the bottom, and have concrete or steel decks. The tops of the decks are set high enough to be out of the tidal range and well above the crest of storm waves. Marine beacon-light lanterns are mounted on top of the decks at the required elevations and above the fuel supply and the radar reflector boxes when required. In general, when the radar reflectors are used, the lights are mounted directly above them with the fuel supply to one side. These markers may be used on both sides of the channel. When floating ice is liable to be present in the channels, adequate provisions must be made to prevent the ice from damaging or destroying them. They are painted black and numbered with odd numbers on the port or left side, and are painted red and numbered with even numbers on the starboard or right side when entering from seaward.

10.5 Navigation Lights on Piers, Wharves, Dolphins, etc.

One marine beacon-navigation-light lantern is generally placed at each end of all piers, wharves, long mooring dolphins, etc., in order to outline their limits. One light may be used on narrow dolphins or other narrow objects projecting into navigable waters. These lights are generally fixed white lights and are fastened directly to the structures. They are generally powered by shore electric current.

10.6 Fixed-structure Beacon Lights on Breakwaters, Shore, etc.

Fixed-structure beacon lights are erected on the projecting ends of breakwaters, on salient points of land projecting into navigable waters, at harbor entrances, and on other points of special danger to shipping. The structures are metal-framed towers with marine beacon-light lanterns mounted on top of the structures. The lights must be high enough to be easily sighted by approaching vessels. The lights may be fixed, occulting, or flashing, and of the color required. The lights may be powered by shore electric current, electric storage batteries, or acetylene gas. Radar reflector plates may be erected on the tower structure, where required.

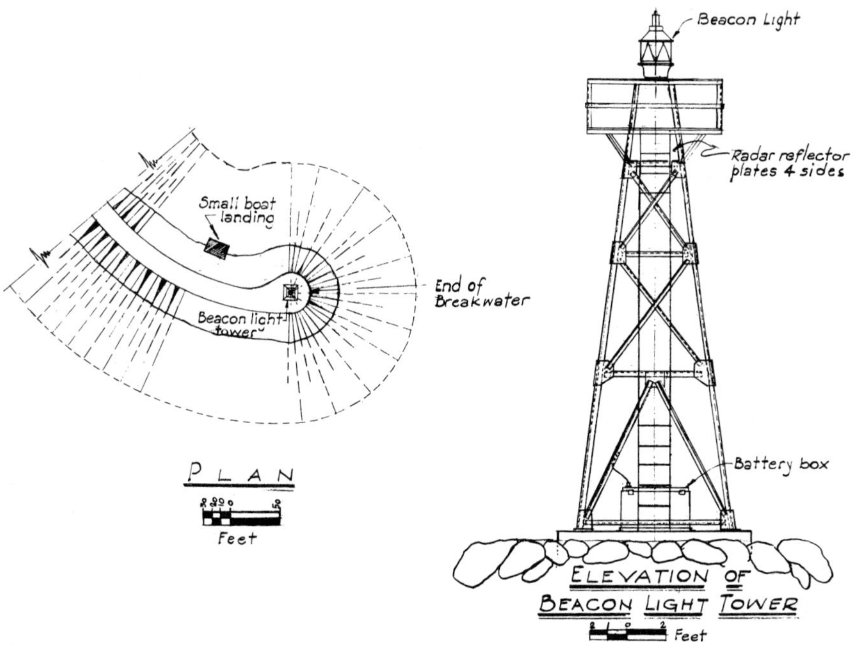

FIG. 10.2 Typical beacon light at end of breakwater.

These towers are painted the colors required by their locations. They also may be galvanized and unpainted. Figure 10.2 shows a typical installation of a fixed-structure light at the end of a breakwater.

10.7 Lighthouses

Lighthouses are tall tower structures with a marine beacon-light lantern on top. They are usually erected on points along the shore to guide shipping to a nearby port, as well as on reefs, shoals, or other points of danger to shipping. They are usually constructed of masonry and are built to withstand heavy wave action and weather. The towers must be high enough, because of the earth's curvature, so that the beacon lights may be sighted by approaching vessels at a considerable distance offshore, a visibility of 20 miles being not unusual. Care should be taken so that the lights are not too high to be more frequently obscured by clouds, mist, etc., than would those nearer to sea level. Figure 10.3 gives a method of determining the required height of a lighthouse to be visible at a certain distance out to sea.

The lights may be white or colored, and flashing or occulting as required; they are powered by shore electric current, electric batteries, or acetylene gas. The flashing characteristics which distinguish many of the lighthouses are produced by revolving the entire lens by electric motor.

The larger lighthouses are also equipped with fog signals produced

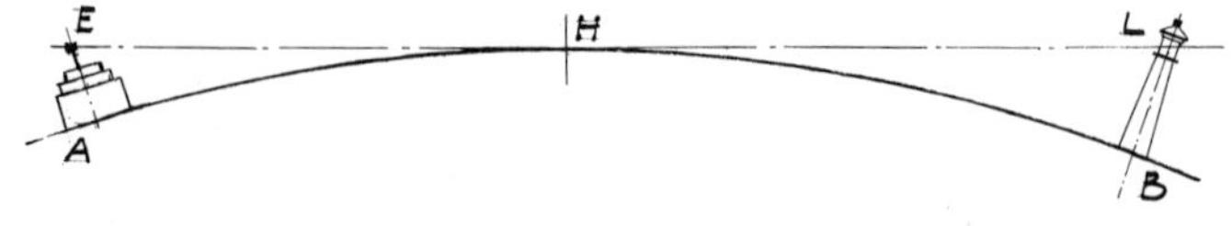

AHB = Earth's serface
BL=Height of light
AE=Height of eye
H=Horizon

HL [nautical miles] = $\frac{8}{7}\sqrt{BL\text{ (feet)}}$
HE [nautical miles] = $\frac{8}{7}\sqrt{AE\text{ (feet)}}$
HL + HE = Total range of visibility

FIG. 10.3 Method for determining height of lighthouses.

by various types of sounding devices. The light and fog signal characteristics are distinct for each lighthouse and are given in the Light Lists, and many also are given on the charts.

Certain lighthouses are also radio beacon stations, being part of the system established along the coasts, and are published in the Light Lists. They are radio stations for sending out radio signals in all directions for the guidance of ships. Each radio beacon is located at a definite point on the charts and has its own characteristic signal which distinguishes it from other radio beacons, as does a lighthouse by its distinguishing light beams. There are more than 140 of these stations operated by the United States Coast Guard, some of which are on lightships, as well as on lighthouses, which operate within a frequency range set aside for this purpose. The lighthouse may be attended or unattended, depending upon its size and location. Many of the larger lighthouses are operated automatically. The lighthouses may be painted white or a combination of colors such as red and white, black and white, etc.

10.8 Lightships

Where it is impracticable to build lighthouses, lightships serve the same purpose. The lightships may vary in size from fully manned ones to small unmanned ones having automatic lights and fog signals, etc. Hulls of lightships in the United States are generally painted red with the name of the station in white on both sides. Superstructures are white, with the masts and stacks in buff. Hulls are built of steel and propulsion is either steam or diesel. Auxiliary generators supply power for operation of the signals. The masthead lights, fog signal, and radio beacon have distinctive characteristics, as given in the Light Lists, which identify the lightship under all conditions. The lightships also will show storm warning signals and will observe all passing ships and any floating navigational aids in the vicinity. Lightships are usually held in position by a single anchor. Relief lightships, painted red, with the word "Relief" on the sides, replace regular lightships when they are being overhauled.

10.9 Range-light Installations

Range-light installations are necessary to guide shipping safely through hazardous narrow or twisting port entrances and channels, in addition to channel markers, buoys, and other navigational aids. These range lights are unidirectional and are installed in pairs on extensions of the channel or port entrance center lines. The range-light towers are generally erected on shore, and the rear lights are set considerably higher and back a considerable distance from the front lights. The structures are metal-framed towers with unidirectional marine range-light lanterns mounted on top of the structures. The lights of ranges may be of any color, and may also be fixed or flashing, the principal requirements being that they stand out distinctly from the surroundings. The lights may be powered by shore electric current, electric batteries, or acetylene gas. These towers are painted in accordance with the location requirements. Radar reflector plates may be attached to the structures when required. The design of a range-light installation depends on various conditions such as the navigable width of channels, the distance from front lights to the limits of usefulness of the range, the distances between the front and rear lights, the difference in elevations of the front and rear lights, and the coefficient of sensitivity.

The primary objectives in the design of range-light installations are as follows:

1. The rear light must be high enough above the front light so that they do not appear as one single light at the minimum distance at which a ship will be using the range. However, the distance between the front and rear lights should be as great as necessary to provide the desired sensitivity.

2. The navigable width of the channel is important in the calculations since this determines the minimum and maximum distances between the front and rear lights. The minimum distance between lights should be

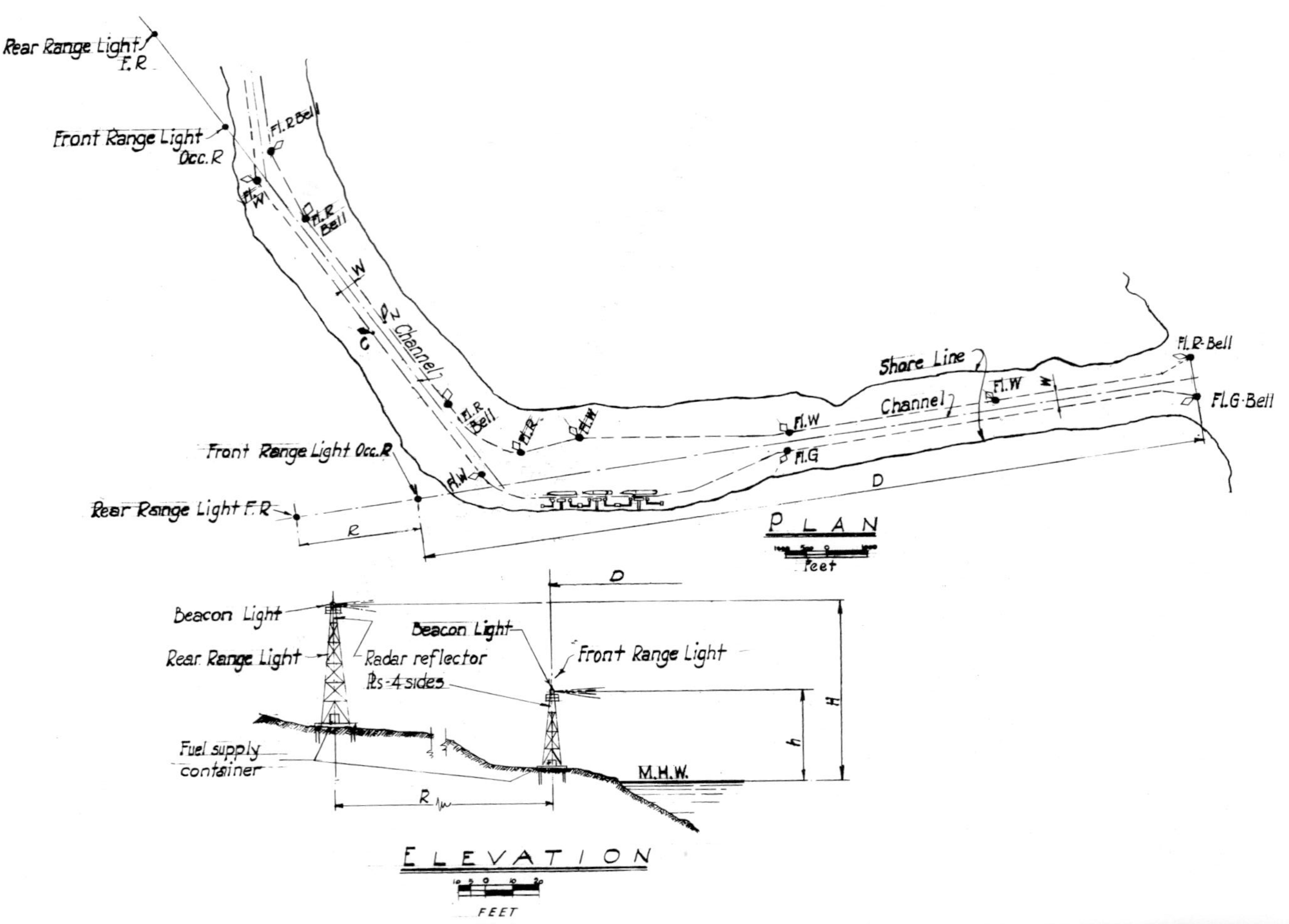
Rear Range Light F.R
Front Range Light Occ.R
Fl.R Bell
Fl.W
Fl.R Bell
W
Channel
C
N
Fl.R Bell
Fl.R
Fl.W
Front Range Light Occ.R
Fl.W
Rear Range Light F.R
R
Fl.W
Fl.G
D
Shore Line
Channel
Fl.W
W
Fl.R-Bell
Fl.G-Bell
PLAN
Feet
D
Beacon Light
Rear Range Light
Radar reflector
Rs-4 sides
Beacon Light
Front Range Light
H
h
Fuel supply container
M.H.W.
R
ELEVATION
FEET

such as to provide sufficient sensitivity to keep the ships within the channel, and the maximum should be such that the sensitivity will not be high enough to cause the ship's pilot to use the outer portions of the channel.

3. When more than one range is involved in an installation which requires a series of turns, the ranges should have the same sensitivity as far as possible.

4. The candle-power output should be as required for adequate visibility, and the candle-power output of both front and rear lights should be approximately the same.

Figure 10.4 shows a typical range-light installation.

The formulas for determining the lateral distance between the front and rear range lights and the difference in elevation between them are as follows

(1) $$H - h = \frac{D}{650}$$

(2) $$R = \frac{KD(H - h)}{W}$$

where H = elevation above mean high water of rear light, ft
h = elevation above mean high water of front light, ft
D = distance from front light to the limit of the usefulness of the range, ft
R = distance between front and rear lights, ft
W = width of channel, ft
K = coefficient of sensitivity (values listed in Table 10.3)

Table 10.3 Coefficient of Sensitivity for Range Lights

Value of K	Description of Sensitivity	Remarks
Under 0.6	Not acceptable	Range should be improved as it is unworkable
0.6–1.0	Poor	Increase sensitivity if possible
1.0–1.5	Fair	
1.5–2.5	Good	
2.5–3.5	Very good	
3.5–4.5	Excellent	Upper limit above which sensitivity shall not be increased

10.10 Radar Reflectors

Radar reflectors may be used on all types of buoys, except spar, can, and nun buoys, and on fixed-structure channel markers and beacon lights, and range towers. They are used to reflect an echo back to the transmitting vessels so as to warn shipping of their presence or to mark a particular location. The reflectors are usually steel plates which are attached to the structures to form a distinctive pattern. Some of the various designs are as follows:

1. The older type of radar reflector on buoys had circumferential plates attached to the buoys' superstructures so as to present a conical form when viewed on a ship's radar screen.

2. The later type of radar reflector plates on buoys consists of four vertical steel plates, which are attached to the buoy's superstructure and fitted so as to present a conical form from all angles when viewed on a ship's radar screen. The plates are slotted toward the base in order to prevent damage by wave action. These plates are interconnected by three horizontal steel plates. This type increases the radar range of the ships by about 50 per cent over the previous type described.

3. Radar reflectors used on fixed-structure channel markers are usually constructed of an angle frame in the form of a cube with vertical diagonal plates. These boxes are usually fastened directly to the decks with the marine beacon-light lanterns erected above them.

4. Radar reflectors, used on tall fixed structures, beacon lights, and range-light installations on breakwaters, shore, etc., are usually constructed of four steel plates which are usually attached to all four sides of the towers in order to present a prismatic form when viewed on a ship's radar screen and are located on the upper sections of towers directly under the light beacons.

10.11 Marine Beacon-light Lanterns

Marine beacon lanterns are constructed of metal frames, with glass or plastic lenses and the necessary lighting, and are operated by electricity or acetylene gas. Electric-powered lights are being used more extensively than the acetylene gas-powered lights due to the lower operating cost per candle-power unit and lower cost of the lanterns. The high intrinsic brilliance of 1,300 to 7,800 candles per sq in. of the incandescent filament, compared to 33 to 53 candles per sq in. of acetylene, makes it possible to use smaller electric lanterns with less expensive lenses to obtain the required candle-power output. They are generally equipped with flasher mechanisms, sun switches, or valves when required and automatic lamp changers for electric installations.

Types of Lanterns. There are various types of lanterns such as closed- or open-top single lanterns, and closed- or open-top duplex lanterns.

The closed-top types are used exclusively for marine traffic. The open-top types have dual-purpose lenses which primarily serve marine traffic but also divert a portion of the beams upward to serve air traffic. The candle-power distribution of the open-type lanterns should be sufficient for marine traffic. Duplex electric lanterns have two separate lenses and lighting power, and have a candle-power output equal to the sum of the two beams. The duplex types are used in locations difficult to reach, to provide the required candle power without resorting to large-diameter lenses, and to allow use of two different-colored lenses when required.

Lenses. Marine lantern lenses are the medium for transmitting, directing, and increasing light. They are arranged to conform to one of the following optical systems or a combination of them.

Catoptric. In this system, the light is only reflected, and the reflector is a highly polished surface.

Dioptric. In this system, the light is refracted or bent by a glass agent in the required direction. This type of lens is generally known as the Fresnel type and is generally used on marine lanterns where the lights require wide vertical divergence. These lenses are usually drum type in closed-top lanterns or may be a dual-purpose type in open-top lanterns which allow a beam of light to be projected vertically.

Catadioptric. This system is a combination of both the catoptric and dioptric systems. It uses both refraction and reflection to bend the rays of light in the required direction. The lens usually consists of both dioptric and catadioptric elements formed in rings and set around a common focus. They may be arranged in a cylindrical form to give a beam of light in all directions horizontally, or in panels in order to concentrate light both horizontally and vertically.

The lenses are generally made of cut or pressed glass, but in some cases Stimsonite plastic is used. The shapes are generally drum type for closed-top lanterns, or a combination type for open-top lanterns. There are also plain Spredlite or bulls-eye lenses used for unidirectional lanterns such as employed on range-light towers. The plain or bulls-eye type is used when the approach to the range is nearly head-on while the Spredlite type is used when the ships normally approach the range from the sides or at acute angles. The degree of divergence to be selected generally depends upon the points at either side of the channel from which approaching ships should first see the lights distinctly. The lenses may be clear or colored in accordance with the requirements.

Sun Switches or Valves. Sun switches or valves may be installed on unattended shore beacon lights and buoys when required. They are operated by atmospheric light and automatically extinguish the lights at dawn and relight them at twilight.

A sun switch is used on an electrically lighted lantern and is operated by a photoelectric cell, which actuates a switch, thus turning the light off and on.

A sun valve is used on an acetylene-gas-lighted lantern and is operated mechanically by the difference in thermal expansion between a polished and a dull rod which actuates a valve thus turning the light off and on.

Flasher Mechanisms. Flasher mechanisms are used for both electric and acetylene-gas installations and can be regulated to obtain any desired flashing characteristics.

The flasher mechanism for an electric installation is operated by means of a motor-driven circuit interrupter. The flasher may be either single- or triple-circuit type. The triple-circuit type may be used for simultaneous operation of beacon light, fog signal, radio beacon, etc.

The flasher mechanism for an acetylene-gas installation is operated by means of gas pressure and is located in the base of the marine lantern. This mechanism releases the gas which is lit by a constant burning pilot jet in the lantern, thus causing a flash. The gas is then cut off by means of an automatic valve in the mechanism until the operation is repeated. The flasher may be single, multiple, or complex type.

Automatic Lamp Changers. Automatic lamp changers are generally used for electric installations. The lamp changer has from two to a multiple number of lamps set on a rocking or rotating mechanism, and is operated by a motor. When a lamp burns out, the motor relay is closed, and the motor is set in operation thus actuating the lamp mechanism until a new lamp is brought to the focal center of the lens. As soon as the new lamp is in position, the current again flows into this lamp, and the motor relay is made inoperative thus shutting off the motor. The operation is repeated as each successive lamp burns out.

10.12 Moorings

Moorings are important items for floating navigational aids since the safety and correct station maintenance of buoys and lightships are dependent upon them. They are usually moored by steel or wrought iron chains with concrete, cast iron, or steel anchors.

The chain assemblies are designed to properly take care of all mooring forces caused by tidal, wave, and wind forces, weight of chain, etc.

Anchors may be cast-concrete or cast-iron sinkers, or cast-concrete or steel mushroom types. They are of sufficient size and weight to properly anchor the buoys or lightships. Mushroom anchors are generally used in mud bottoms, and usually sink by their own weight through the soft mud to firm material.

Buoy Moorings. A mooring for all buoys except nun, can, and spherical buoys, consists of a chain bridle, which is attached to the underside of the buoy at two points and fastened to a ring to which the chain is also attached, and an anchor. Moorings for nun, can, and spherical buoys are similar to the above, except that the bridle is omitted, and the chain is attached directly to the underside of the buoy at one point. The length of chain must be sufficient to take care of the combination of depth of water, tidal range, current velocity, and position with regard to weather exposure.

Lightship Moorings. A lightship is usually moored by a single anchor, and the ship is allowed to swing freely. However, if the space is limited such as in narrow passages where the ship cannot swing and in tidal waters, the ship is usually moored by bow and stern anchors.

The United States Coast Guard lightship *Nantucket,* which is 150 ft long with a beam of 31 ft, has an 11-ft draft and a projected wind area of 1,000 sq ft, and is moored by a single 7,000-lb mushroom anchor in a sand bottom.

INDEX

Aerial ropeways, 442, 444
Aguadilla, Puerto Rico, 460, 463
Airy, G. B., 37
Algiers breakwater, Morocco, 209–211
Ambrose Light, 471
American Association of State Highway Officials, 323
American Concrete Institute (ACI) Building Code, 251, 252, 261, 269, 279
American Society of Civil Engineers (ASCE), 32, 38, 44, 46, 53, 56, 58, 222, 299, 331
American Society for Testing Materials (ASTM), 106, 278
Anchorages (*see* Harbors; Moorings)
Anchors, 359–360, 364–366
  chain, 364, 366
Anode, 381
Antwerp, port of, 30, 412, 413
Atlantic Ocean, 2, 38

Banana handling, 414, 417
Bauxite loading, 460
Beach Erosion Board, 43, 44, 56, 223, 224
Beebe, K. E., 56, 58
Belmont, California, 475, 476
Benezit, Victor, 50
Bitts, mooring, 371
Black Sea, 38
Blancato, Virgil, 297, 299
Bollards, 370
Borings (*see* Site investigation)
Brasher, Philip, 217
Breakwaters, concrete block, 174–177
  concrete block and rock-mound, 174–177
    examples, Coco Solo Naval Air Station, 177–182
      Safi, Morocco, 182, 183
      Zonguldak, Turkey, 182–186
Breakwaters, definition, 147
  floating, 223–225
  foundation conditions, 162–165
    stability analysis, 164, 165
  harbor protection, 91
  height, 153, 154
  hydraulic, definition, 217
    experimental studies, 220, 222
  model tests, 152, 153, 156, 196–205
    experimental design studies, 196, 197
    examples of models, Taconite Harbor, Lake Superior, 197–200
      Zonguldak, Turkey, 200–205
  planning, 91
  pneumatic, definition, 217
    experimental studies, 217–221
  rock-mound, 148, 149
    design section, 150–153
    examples, La Guaira, Venezuela, 165–169
      Matarani, Peru, 171–174
      Taconite Harbor, Lake Superior, 167–172
    quarrying rock, 168–171
    stability, 154
      by Iribarren, 154–159
      by Waterways Experiment Station formula, 155–159
    wave run-up, 160, 161
  submerged reef type, 222
  tetrapod and tribar armor, 186–193
    examples, Crescent City, California, 194
      Nawiliwili Harbor, Kauai, 196
      Rota, Spain, 194, 195
      Safi, Morocco, 195, 196
      Sousse, Tunisia, 193
  types, 147
  vertical-wall, advantages over sloping type, 208
    European practice, 149

Breakwaters, vertical-wall, examples, Algiers, Morocco, 209–211
Buffalo, N.Y., 215, 216
Calumet, Lake Michigan, 214, 215
Granili, Port of Naples, 208, 209
Helsingborg Harbor, Sweden, 212, 213
Milwaukee, 211, 212
foundation analysis, 206, 207
types, 208–217
Bretschneider, C. L., 32, 40–46, 56, 59–63
Buffalo, N.Y., 73, 216
Bulk cargo terminals, 11, 12, 73, 438–464
(*See also* Terminals)
Bulkheads, definition, 226
lines for, 82
sheet-pile, 238, 239
anchor-wall support, 239
batter-pile support, 239
Buoys, mooring, 360–364
Lamgar eccentric, 362
navigation, 508–511
moorings for, 520, 521

Caissons, concrete, for breakwaters, 211–213
for wharves, 239–241
California Institute of Technology, 219, 223
Callao, Peru, port of, 132–135
Calumet, Lake Michigan, 214, 215
Capstans, 371
Cargo, bulk, definition, 423
general, definition, 423
tonnage, 75
Cargo-handling equipment, bulk, 439–444
oil, 448–452
general, 423–437
containers, 432–437
in hold, 431
on land, 427–431
loading and unloading, 424–427
in transit sheds, 390, 393, 395
Cargo terminal, definition, 73
(*See also* Terminals)
Carr, A. W., 219
Cathode, 381
Cathodic protection, 381–387
anode, definition, 381
cathode, definition, 381
cost, 385
galvanic-cell battery, 382
provision for future, 385–387
for steel H piles, 385–387
Cathodic protection, types, external impressed current, 382–385
galvanic anode, 382, 383
Catwalks, definition, 357
design conditions, 357
examples, 358, 359
Channels, approach, 94
depth, 94
lines for, 75, 83
markers for, 512
Chaguaramas Bay, Trinidad, 460–462
Chain for rubber fenders, 287
Chicksan loading arms, 450, 452
Chocks, 371
Clapotis, 50, 51
Cleats, 371
Cleveland, port of, 73, 141, 143, 144
Coco Solo Naval Air Station, Canal Zone, 177–182
Cold storage, buildings for, 417, 418
at Southampton Docks, England, 418–420
temperatures for various foods, 418
Conference on Coastal Engineering (Proceedings), Fourth, 61
Sixth, 40–42
Containers, general cargo, 432–437
customs regulations, 434
handling equipment, 435–437
size, 433
standardization, 433, 434
van, 435–437
Containerships, 435–437
Conveyors, aerial ropeways, 442, 444
belt and slat, 427, 430–431, 439–441
bucket, 441–442
bulk cargo, 439–444
Corrosion, in Lake Maracaibo, 214
protection against, 15, 381–387
of steel H piles, 235, 236
Council on Wave Research, 39, 40, 42, 64
Cranes, floating, 426–427
level-luffing, 425
mobile, 427, 430
overhead, 431
wharfside, 425, 426
Cribs, timber, 238, 240
Current, force on ship, 248, 368
observations, 111

Delaware City, Delaware, 450, 464
Delaware River, dredged depth, 94, 447
De Long jack, gripper type, 469, 470
hydraulic type, 494–496
De Long mobile drilling platforms, 493–495
De Long wharf, 467, 468, 471

Docks, definition, 226
design loads, 248
docking impact, 248, 249
earthquake, 249
lateral, 248
vertical, 249
examples of construction, 335–341
materials of construction, 231–235
prestressed-concrete decks, 232, 233
pile and cylinder supports (*see* Piles)
types, selection of, 96, 228, 229
(*See also* Bulkheads; Piers; Wharves)
Dolphins, breasting, 227
definition, 227
design, 341
fixed-berth, 229
mooring, 227
types, 341
cellular sheet pile, 349
steel cylinder, flexible, 345
steel H pile and concrete, 351
example, 350–354
steel pipe, flexible, 346, 347
wood pile, flexible, 343, 344
rigid platform, 348
Dover pneumatic breakwater, 221
Drilling platforms (*see* Offshore drilling structures)
Drydocks, 226

Electric power, marine terminals, 372–375
Embeco, 340
Engineering News formula, modified form, 276
regular form, 276, 282
Equipment (*see* Cargo-handling equipment; Containers; Cranes; Trucks)
Evans, J. T., 219
Exports, United States, 8

Fairway, 83
Fenders, dock, design assumptions, 297, 300, 301
design curves for rubber, 290, 292, 293
examples, rubber, draped, 303
steel-spring, 306–309
steel-wale and rubber, 303–307
wood springing, 301–303
types, camel, floating, 282
gravity, bell dolphin, 297
suspended weight, 298, 299
hung, 283
Raykin buffers, 291, 294, 295
rubber, draped, 286
chain for, 287
Fenders, dock, types, rubber, in end compression, 291
tires, 285
steel piles, 289
with rubber, 289
springs, 291, 296
wood piles, 283–285
with rubber, 288
springing, 284
Fetch, definition, 40
(*See also* Waves)
Fire protection, marine terminals, 377
Franzuis Institute, Hanover, Germany, 219, 220
Frost, Rikord V., 213
Froude's law for model testing, 113, 197, 219, 220, 222

Gaillard, D. D., 38, 51, 52
Galvanic action, 381, 382
General cargo (*see* Cargo-handling equipment; Terminals)
Georges Bank, 470
Gerstner, F. V., 36
Gourret, M., 50
Grand Isle, Gulf of Mexico, 487
Granili breakwater, Port of Naples, 208, 209
Great Lakes, 2, 29, 38, 51, 52, 72, 149, 211, 213–215, 442, 443, 453
Greenheart piles, 281
Gulf of Mexico, 38, 466, 467, 472, 476, 480, 485–490, 492
Gunite, 236

Hamburg, Germany, port of, 30, 137, 138, 425
Hamilton, Ontario, 442
Harbors, anchorage area, 74
breakwaters (*see* Breakwaters)
commercial, 72
definition, 71
depth of, 94
docking facilities, how determined, 95, 96
entrance to, 92
layouts for artificial, 86–89, 91
location, determining, 85, 86
military, 72
model investigations, 113–120
Taconite Harbor, 113–116
Zonguldak, Turkey, 115–120
natural, 90
of refuge, 71
size and shape, 87

Harbors, turning basin, 74
  wave height within, 92, 93
Hartley, Clifford, 448
Hartley hoister, 448, 449
Hasskarl, Joseph F., 148, 216
Havana, Cuba, 30, 451
Hensen, Walter, 219
Hook, releasing, for mooring line, 371
Hose for oil loading, 448–451
Houston, Texas, port of, 73
Hudson, R. Y., 53, 156, 159
Hydraulic model investigations (*see* Breakwaters; Harbors)
Hydrographic surveys, 98, 99

Ilo, Peru, 335–337
Imports, United States, 8
Inglese, I., 209
International Congress of Navigation, Sixteenth, 121, 213, 215
  Twelfth, 148, 209, 216
Interstate Commerce Commission, 23
Iribarren, 49, 154–159, 177, 196, 200
Iron-ore terminals, 452–457

Jetty, definition of, 226
Johnson, J. W., 56, 61

Kuwait, Persian Gulf, 448
Kyushu University, Japan, 220

Lagos, Nigeria, port of, 413–415
La Guaira, Venezuela, port of, 30, 72, 83, 121–123, 165–169, 356, 357, 379, 380, 398–400
Lake Maracaibo, Venezuela, 38, 214, 236, 466, 467, 478–481, 484, 485, 501
Lake Okeechobee, 160
Lamgar eccentric mooring buoy, 365
Lange, Alban, 213
Le Tourneau drilling platforms, 496–501
  rack and pinion drive, 498
Lighthouses, 465, 513, 514
  offshore platforms for, 465, 474, 475
Lighting, marine terminals, 371, 372
Lightships, 474, 514, 515
  moorings for, 521
Long Beach, California, port of, 409, 410
Longshoremen's shelter, 409

Marine Sonoprobe, 85, 104, 105
Marine structures (*see* Lighthouses; Offshore drilling structures; Radar platforms)
Matarani, Peru, port of, 86, 130–132, 171–174
Mediterranean Sea, 1, 29, 38
Milwaukee, Wisconsin, 212
Miragoane, Haiti, 285, 346
Mississippi River Commission, 106, 110
Mobile floating crane, 499, 501
Mobile wharf, 465, 467, 468
Model investigations (*see* Breakwaters; Harbors)
Moles, definition, 354, 355
Molitor, D. A., 38, 51–55
Monsoons, 27
Moon, J., 56, 58
Mooring ship to dock, 370
  accessories on dock, 37, 370, 371
  tying up ship, 370
Moorings, offshore, 73, 359
    anchors for, 364, 366
      concrete, precast, 364, 366
      holding power, 364
    arrangements of, 360–362
    buoys, types, 362–365
    chain, 364, 366
    components, 362
    definition, 227
    example of design, 367–370
    for lightships, 521
    multiple-buoy, 367
    for ships, 227, 228
Morison, J. R., 56, 61
Munk, W. H., 40, 41, 46

Nantucket, 471
Naples, Italy, port of, 208, 209
Navigation, regulation of, 21
Navigation aids, beacon lights, 512, 513
  buoys, can, 510
    characteristics of, 510
    lighted, 511
    nun, 510
    sound warning, 511
    spar, 508
    spherical, 510
  channel markers, fixed, 512
  lanterns, marine beacon, 518
      automatic lamp changers, 520
      flasher mechanisms, 520
      lenses, 519
      sun switches, 519
      types, 518
  lights on piers and wharves, 512
  moorings, 520, 521
  radar reflectors, 518
  range lights, coefficient of sensitivity, 517
    formulas for, 517
    installations for, 515, 516

New York City, Department of Marine and Aviation, 14, 17, 232, 342, 404, 406, 407, 422
NEYRPIC Hydraulic Laboratory, Grenoble, France, 113, 115, 117–119, 182, 186, 189–191, 195, 196, 200–205
Nitrate loading, 457–459

O'Brien, M. P., 56, 61
Offshore drilling structures, 465–506
  fixed platforms, 478–489
    aluminum templates, 481
    concrete construction, 481–483
    prestressed piles, 484, 485
    steel templates, 480, 486–489
    for sulfur mining, 487, 489
    wave pressure on, example of, 63–70
  mobile units, 489–505
    types of, 490, 491
      drill barge or ship, 491, 492
      mobile platforms, 493–501
      submersible, 502–504
  permanent islands, 475–477
  self-contained units, 505, 506
  trends of types of, 466
Oil, crude, world consumption, 10
  world production, 9
Oil tankers (*see* Tankers)
Oil terminals, 11, 12, 446–452
  Chiksan loading arms, 450, 452
  hose, 448–451
  offshore moorings, 359–360, 367–370
  Tidewater refinery, Delaware City, 464
Oil wells (*see* Offshore drilling structures)
Orinoco River, Venezuela, 467, 468

Pacific Ocean, 2, 38, 467, 475, 476, 488
Palletization, at port, 432
  at source, 431
Pallets, 431
Palmer, Robert Q., 186, 187
Panama Canal, dredged depth, 94, 447
Pan-Atlantic Steamship Corp., 435, 436
Passenger terminals, La Guaira, Venezuela, 398–401
  New York City, 405–408
  Southampton, England, 401–404
Persian Gulf, 1, 448, 466, 499
Petroleum industry, growth of, 9
  (*See also* Oil terminals)
Philippines, 30, 448
Pierhead lines, 82
Piers, breakwater, 226
  construction, Ilo, Peru, 335–337
    new Pier 57, New York City, 340–342
Piers, definition, 226
  finger, 228
    example of design, 322–329
  L-shaped, 227–229
  T-head, 227–229
  type of design, 246, 247
    rigid-frame, 246, 247
Piles, connections to deck, 236, 237
  effective length, 250
  end conditions, 250
  precast-concrete, 251–261
    design, 251, 252
      batter pile, 259, 261
    design loads, tables, 254–257
    details, 258, 260
    driving, 252, 253
    H-pile point, 261, 263
    handling, 253
      maximum lengths, 259
    pickup arrangements, 253
    sheet piles, 261, 262
  prestressed-concrete and cylinders, 261, 264–273
    casting yard layout, 272
    design, 264, 265, 269, 270
    design loads, tables, 266–268
    details, 271
    handling, 270
      maximum lengths, 270
  steel H, advantages, 273
    concrete encasement, 235
    design loads, table, 276
    driving, 275–277
    lagging, 273, 274
    protection, against corrosion, 273–275
      against erosion, 277
    splices, 277, 278
  steel-pipe and cylinders, design, 279
    design loads, table, 280
    driving, 278, 279
    specification, 278
    splices, 279
  wood, creosoted, 233, 281
    design loads, 282
    driving, 282
    encasement, 281
    Greenheart, 281, 282
    gunite protection, 236
    marine borer attack, 280
Pilotage, 24
Point Comfort, Texas, 441
Population, world, growth, 3–5
Port administration buildings, 420–422
Port authorities, 16–20
  American Association of, 20

Port of New York Authority, 12–14, 17–20, 24, 232, 234, 281, 407–409, 422
Ports, definition, 72
  design and construction, advancement in, 15
  of entry, 7
  expenditures for, United States, 14
  financing, 24
  free zone, 73
  growth, 1–16
  modernization and rehabilitation, 12
    expenditures, 13, 14
  planning, 83–85
    information sources, 84
    ship characteristics related to, 74, 75
  regulatory bodies, 21–23
    security associations, 23
    waterfront commissions, 23, 24
  site investigation, 97–113
  specialized, 11
  world, 120–146
    Callao, Peru, 132–135
    Cleveland, Ohio, 141, 143, 144
    Hamburg, Germany, 137, 138
    La Guaira, Venezuela, 121–123
    Matarani, Peru, 130–132
    Quebec, Canada, 140–142
    Rio de Janeiro, Brazil, 143, 145, 146
    Rota, Spain, 127–129
    Southampton, England, 136, 137
    Sydney, Australia, 138–140
    Taconite Harbor, Lake Superior, 123–127
    Zonguldak, Turkey, 129, 130
Praeger, Emil H., 340
Princeton University, 368
Puerto Miranda, Venezuela, 345

Quarantine, 23, 74
Quarrying, 168–171
Quay walls, definition, 226
  gravity type, 240, 241
Quebec, Canada, port of, 30, 140–142

Radar platforms, 465, 470–474
  location of, 471
Range lights, 517
Red Sea, 1
Redtenbacher pile-driving formula, 252, 253
Reid, R. O., 43, 44, 56, 59–63
Reynolds number, 57–59
Rincon, California, 476, 477
Rio de Janeiro, Brazil, port of, 30, 143, 145, 146
Roark, R. J., 308
Roebling cable-type jacking equipment, 473
Roll-on roll-off service, 437
Roosevelt Roads, Puerto Rico, 152, 156
Rota, Spain, port of, 127–129, 194, 195
Rouen, France, port of, 414, 416, 417
Russell, J. Scott, 37

Safi, Morocco, port of 182, 183, 195, 196
Sainflou, George, 50, 53–55
Saint Anthony Falls Hydraulic Laboratory, 196, 197, 201, 220
Saint Lawrence Seaway, 2, 72
Saint-Venant and Flamant wave theory, 37, 50
San Diego, California, port of, 381, 410–412
San Juan Bay, Peru, 375, 455–457
Santiago, Cuba, 386, 387
Schaaf, S. A., 56
Seiche, 49
Sheet-pile cells, 238
Shipping, growth of, 6, 7
Ships, ballast, 75
  cargo handling in hold, 431
  characteristics of, bulk carriers, 77
    general cargo, 78
    passenger, 79
    tankers, 76
    United States Navy, 80, 81
  containerships, 435–437
  draft, 75
  growth, in number, 5
    in tonnage, 3–5
  loading and unloading, 424–427, 435–437
    roll-on roll-off service, 437
  self-unloading, 444, 445
  tankers (*see* Tankers)
  tonnage classifications, 74, 75
  wind areas, 82
Site investigation, borings, 101–106
  current observations, 111, 112
  hydrographic surveys, 98, 99
  soil analyses, 106–110
  soundings, 98, 99
  tidal observations, 112, 113
  topographic surveys, 100
Snyder, C. M., 222
Soil analyses, classification, 106, 108–110
  consolidation tests, 111
  routine tests, 106, 107
  triaxial shear tests, 110
  unconfined compressive strength, 107
Soil investigations, 100–111
  borings, 101–106
    drill barges, 102

Soil investigations, borings, drilling equipment, 101–104
dry-sample wash, 103, 104
report form, 105
undisturbed sampling, 103, 104
Shelby tube sampler, 103, 104
by Marine Sonoprobe, 104, 105
Soundings, 98, 99
by fathometer, 99
Southampton, England, port of, 29, 30, 136, 137, 239, 401–403, 418, 419
Specific gravity of soils, 107
Stevenson, Thomas, 38, 49, 92
Stokes, G. G., 37
Storage, in bulk cargo terminals, 438–439
cold, 417–420
Straub, Lorenz, G., 197, 198, 201, 220
Sugar terminal, Aguadilla, Puerto Rico, 460–463
Sverdrup, H. U., 40, 41, 46
Sydney, Australia, port of, 30, 138–140

Taconite Harbor, Lake Superior, 87, 113–116, 123–127, 167–172, 196–200, 214, 337–340, 452–455
Tankers, 11, 76
loading and unloading, 446–447
Chiksan arms, 450, 452
hose, 448–451
offshore moorings, 359–360, 367–370
Taylor, F. M. Du-Plat, 1
Terminals (marine), bulk cargo, 11, 12, 73, 438–464
equipment for material handling, 439
bridge, reclaiming, 442
buckets, clamshell, 441
drag scraper, 442, 443
elevators, 440
car dumpers, 444
conveyors, 439–444
traveling stackers, 440
traveling towers, 441
Hulett-type unloader, 442, 443
marine legs, 440
oil handling, Chiksan arms, 440, 452
Hartley hoister, 448, 449
hose-handling frames, 450, 451
ropeways, 442, 444
self-unloading ships, 444, 445
examples, bauxite, Chaguaramas Bay, Trinidad, 460–462
iron ore, Taconite Harbor, Minnesota, 453–455
San Juan Bay, Peru, 455–457
Terminals (marine), bulk cargo, examples, nitrate, Tocopilla, Chile, 457–459
oil, 446–452
Delaware City, Delaware, 464
sugar, Aguadilla, Puerto Rico, 460, 463
definition, 73
facilities, on-shore, 96, 97
general cargo, design considerations, 244–246
dimensions, 242, 243
layout, 244–246
(*See also* Cargo-handling equipment; Transit sheds)
passenger and cargo, La Guaira, Venezuela, 398–401
New York City, 405–408
Southampton, England, 401–404
utilities, air, compressed, 381
bunkering ships, 381
communications, 373
fire protection, 377–380
lighting, electric, 371, 372
power, electric, 372–376
distribution, 374–376
supply, 373, 374
sanitary waste, 381
steam, 379
water supply, 376, 377, 380
Terzaghi, K., 331
Tetrapods (*see* Breakwaters)
Texas A & M Research Foundation, 56, 59–63
Texas Towers, 465, 470–474
Tidal bores, 31, 49
observations, 112, 113
Tide gauge, 112, 113
Tides, definition, 28
diurnal, 29
levels, definitions, 29, 31
semidiurnal, 29
spring, 28
ranges at major ports, 30, 95
tables, sources, 29
Tocopilla, Chile, 457–459
Topographic surveys, 100
Tractor trains, 430
Transit sheds, area per berth, 390
for banana handling, Rouen, France, 414, 416, 417
cargo, Antwerp, Belgium, 412, 413
Brooklyn, N.Y., Pier 1, 408, 409
Lagos, Nigeria, 413–415
Long Beach, California, 409, 410
San Diego, California, 410–412
doors, location, 392
types, 393, 394

Transit sheds, floor loads, from equipment, 397
uniform live load, 396, 398
floors, construction, 393
function, 388, 389
height, 392
length, 390
lock-up room, 396
for marine terminals, 96
passenger and cargo, La Guaira, Venezuela, 398–400
Pier 40, New York City, 406–408
Pier 57, New York City, 404–407
Southampton, England, 401–403
platforms for truck loading, 395
stevedore's gear room, 396
two-story, 390, 391
compared with one-story, 391, 392
method of operation, 391
Trestles, design conditions, 355
types, center pier, 356, 357
precast-concrete deck, 355, 356
wood pile, timber deck, 357
Tribars (*see* Breakwaters)
Trucks, fork-lift, 427, 428, 434
loading in transit sheds, 393, 395
pallets, 431, 432
straddle, 429, 434
tractor trains, 430
Turning basin, definition, 74
Tyler, H. C., 212, 215

Unconfined compressive strength of soil, 107
United Nations, 3, 6, 10
United States, Army Engineers (Corps of Engineers), 21, 75, 84, 106, 110, 186, 187
Bureau of Reclamation, 106
Coast and Geodetic Survey, 29, 30, 84, 98, 112
Department of Agriculture, 23
Department of Commerce, 3, 21, 22, 84
Bureau of Foreign Commerce, 22
Maritime Administration of, 3, 21, 22
Department of Health, Education and Welfare, 22, 23
Food and Drug Administration, 22
Public Health Service, 23
Department of Justice, 22
Immigration and Naturalization Service, 22
Interstate Commerce Commission, 23
Navy, Bureau of Yards and Docks, 152, 156, 223
United States, Navy, Hydrographic Office, 40, 41, 43, 46–48, 84
ships, characteristics, 80, 81
Treasury Department, 21, 22
Bureau of Customs, 22
Bureau of Narcotics, 22
Coast Guard, 21, 465, 475, 507
Waterways Experiment Station (Vicksburg), 53, 108, 109, 113–116, 152, 155–161, 188, 189, 196, 197, 199
Weather Bureau, 84
University of California, 56, 58
University of Minnesota, 196
Utilities, marine terminals, 371–381

Voids ratio of soils, 107

Warehouses for marine terminals, 97, 388, 389, 393
(*See also* Transit sheds)
Waves, breaking index curve, 32
characteristics, 32, 33
clopotis, 50
decay, 45, 46
diffraction, 45, 47
dimensional relationships, 33
drag coefficient, 56–59
drag force, 56–58, 61
fetch, 38, 40
forecasting height and length, 37
form, 31–36
generation, 31
height, related to fetch and wind velocity, 38
related to wind duration, 41
significant, 39, 40, 42
inertial force, 57, 58, 61
length, 33
mass coefficient, 57–59
orbital motion, 34–36
of oscillation, 31, 32
period, 33
pressure, by Molitor theory, 51–55
on piles, 56–70
example of, 63–70
by Sainflou theory, 50, 51, 53–55
on vertical walls, 49–55
example of, 54–56
reflection, 48
refraction, 47
seiche, 49
shoaling factor, 43
solitary, 31, 37, 59, 60
swells, 49
synoptic weather maps, 40

Waves, theories, 36, 37
  tidal, 31, 49
  of translation, 31, 32
  velocity, 32, 34, 36
Wharves, caissons of concrete, 239–241
  cribs of timber, 238, 240
  definition, 226
  high-level, 231
  mobile, 465, 467, 468
  relieving-platform type, 230, 231
    example of design, 309–322
  sheet-pile cells, 238
    example of design, 329–335
Wharves, at Taconite Harbor, Minnesota, 337–340
Wiegel, R. L., 39, 56, 58, 64
Wilson, B. W., 368
Wind, Beaufort scale, 27
  effect on waves, 40, 41
  monsoons, 27
  pressure, 28
    on ships at anchor, 367, 368
Wind rose, 26, 27

Zonguldak Harbor, Turkey, 115, 118–120, 129, 130, 182–186, 196, 200–205, 241